Marketing
Essentials

Marketing Essentials

Lois Schneider Farese
Marketing Education Teacher-Coordinator
Northern Highlands Regional High School
Allendale, New Jersey

Grady Kimbrell
Educational Consultant
Santa Barbara, California

Carl A. Woloszyk
Associate Professor
Department of Consumer Resources and Technology
Western Michigan University

GLENCOE

Macmillan/McGraw-Hill

New York, New York
Columbus, Ohio
Mission Hills, California
Peoria, Illinois

Photography

After Image xxi; Arco 392; Arnold & Brown 55; AT&T 233; Ralph Barrera/TexaStock 287, 358; Ken Biggs/After Image xxii; Paul Buddle, 495; Bob Daemmrich 156; Mary Kate Denny Photo Edit xvii, 460; Daniel DeWilde 169, 357; Eastman Kodak Company 230; Famous Amos Cookie Company 434; Terry Farmer/Uniphoto Picture Agency 125; Federal Express 230; John Feingersh/Uniphoto 125; Fruitgrowers 263; Gene Fitzer xixx, 12, 14, 41, 44, 49, 51, 52, 55, 61, 75, 79, 88, 104, 122, 142, 145, 147, 151, 163, 202, 205, 211(3), 219, 227, 234, 243, 254, 263, 275, 292, 320, 332, 337, 390, 469 left; Ford Motor Co. 420; Four By Five xii, vii, viii, ix, 2, 24, 33, 36, 40, 86, 105, 113, 132, 168, 185, 209, 258, 267(2), 279; David R. Frazier 396; Tony Freeman/Photo Edit 473(2); Susan Friedman 4, 13, 39, 41, 50, 53, 108A, 115, 117, 135, 137, 138, 154, 160, 169(left), 186, 191, 192, 193, 198, 204, 207, 214, 243, 254, 260, 266, 273, 275, 283, 290, 327(2), 339, 343, 374, 413, 469 right; Richard Fukuhara/Westlight 318; xii; Ben Garacci/Uniphoto cover, ii; Gear, Inc. 246; Jeff Greenberg xxix, 82, 489; Charles Gupton/Uniphoto 73; Christopher Harris/Uniphoto 20; Hertz Corporation 396; Hills Brothers Coffee, Inc. 30; Kellogg xxvi; David E. Kennedy/TexaStock 138; Valerie Krein 83, 3(153), 290, 401; Carol Lee/Uniphoto xiv, 370; Lufthansa German Airlines 230; Rosin Malecki/Photo Edit 396; Stephen McBrady 5; McDonalds Corporation 7, 121; Bob McElwee xvi, 418; Peugeot Motors 67; Dario Perle xix; Photo Edit xxvi; Stacy Pick/Uniphoto 104; Carl Purcell 129; Will and Angie Rumpf 443; The Stouffer Corporation 54; Michael D. Sullivan/TexaStock 114, 134; Tiffany & Company 66; Tom Tracy/Westlight xx; TV Guide 219; Uniphoto 38; Vivitar Corporation, 148; Walker Research & Analysis 373; Westlight xxv, 17, 117; Wide World Photos 46, 251; Dana White Productions xxiii, 5, 17, 125, 216, 218, 381, 396, 406, 410, 430, 439, 462, 466, 470, 477, 478, 480, 484, 493, 507; Duane Zehr 172, 239.

Illustrations by Randy Miyake

Send all inquiries to:
GLENCOE DIVISION
Macmillan/McGraw-Hill
15319 Chatsworth Street
P.O. Box 9609
Mission Hills, CA 91346-9609

ISBN 0-02-820009-8 (Post Secondary Student Edition)
ISBN 0-02-820000-4 (Secondary Student Edition)
ISBN 0-02-820001-2 (Teacher's Annotated Edition)

5 6 7 8 9   95 94 93

About the Authors

A nationally recognized educator in marketing education, **Lois Schneider Farese** has been teacher-coordinator and DECA advisor at Northern Highlands Regional High School in Allendale, New Jersey, for more than 20 years. She has been director of the Northern New Jersey Regional DECA Conference for more than 15 years and has also participated as series director and event manager at state and national DECA conferences.

As a result of her outstanding teaching methods and involvement in numerous marketing-related activities, Farese was named "Teacher of the Year" in 1981 by the New Jersey Association of Marketing Education Teacher-Coordinators. In 1982 she was recognized by the New Jersey Division of the American Vocational Education Association. In 1986, she became the first recipient from her high school of the prestigious New Jersey Governor's Teacher Recognition Program.

Farese has a B.A. in Business and Distributive Education and two Masters degrees (one in Business and one in Psychology) from Montclair State College in New Jersey, along with numerous additional credits in education, administration, and supervision.

Grady Kimbrell, nationally recognized author and consultant on career education, began his career in education teaching high school business in Kansas. After moving to California, Kimbrell taught business courses and coordinated students' in-class activities with their on-the-job experience. He later directed the work experience programs in three high schools in Santa Barbara, California.

Kimbrell has assisted school districts with a wide variety of research and evaluation activities. His research into on-the-job work activities led to the development of a career interest inventory now used in career guidance. In addition, he has served on numerous state instructional program committees and writing teams, designed educational computer programs, and produced educational films.

Kimbrell has degrees in business administration, educational psychology, and business education.

Carl A. Woloszyk has had an extensive and successful career in education and marketing management. He currently teaches retail management and vocational teacher education at Western Michigan University and is Delta Epsilon Chi advisor. He has been a state consultant for marketing and cooperative education, Michigan state DECA advisor, Director of Career and Vocational Education, and a secondary marketing teacher-coordinator and DECA chapter advisor.

Woloszyk has served on the Board of Directors for National DECA and was the State of Michigan representative to MarkED, a national curriculum and research consortium in Columbus, Ohio. He is a charter and executive board member of the Michigan Marketing Educator's Association.

Woloszyk's undergraduate degree in Business Administration and his doctorate in Business and Distributive Education are from Michigan State University. He has a master's degree in Business Education from Eastern Michigan University and an Educational Specialist Degree in Occupational Education from the University of Michigan.

Teacher Reviewers

Paula J. Baker
Marketing Education Teacher
Jenks High School
Jenks Public Schools
Jenks, Oklahoma

Gerald L. Beebe
Marketing Education Teacher
Hartland High School
Hartland Consolidated Schools
Hartland, Michigan

James M. Burrell
Marketing Education Teacher
Central High School
Memphis City Schools
Memphis, Tennessee

Ronald B. Chapman
Marketing Coordinator
Hillsboro Comprehensive High
   School
Metropolitan Nashville Public
   School System
Nashville, Tennessee

Brenda S. Clark
Marketing Education Teacher
Jenison High School
Jenison Public Schools
Jenison, Michigan

Bill G. Cleland
Marketing Education Teacher
Rock Springs High School
Sweetwater County School
   District #1
Rock Springs, Wyoming

Dr. Ann Erikson
Supervisor of Curriculum
   Instruction for Business and
   Marketing
Pittsburgh Public Schools, OVT
Pittsburgh, Pennsylvania

Myrna Craig Evans
Fashion Merchandising/Marketing
   Education Teacher
East San Gabriel Valley Regional
   Occupational Program
West Covina, California

Barbara Zbiegniewicz Foerch
Marketing Education Coordinator
Bryan Adams High School
Dallas Independent School
   District
Dallas, Texas

Nancy Pierce Griffis
Fashion Merchandising/Business
   Management and Ownership
   Teacher
Moore-Norman Area Vocational
   Technical School
Norman, Oklahoma

Cass Haecker
Marketing Education Coordinator
Crockett High School
Austin Independent School
   District
Austin, Texas

Johnnie R. Hamilton
Marketing Education Teacher
University High School
Morgantown, West Virginia

Jayne W. James
Marketing Education Teacher,
   ROP
Temecula Valley High School
Temecula Valley Unified School
   District
Riverside County Office of
   Education
Temecula, California

Tony King
Marketing Coordinator
Appling Comprehensive High
   School
Baxley, Georgia

A.E. Mozisek
Marketing Education
   Teacher-Coordinator
Winston Churchill High School
North East Independent School
   District
San Antonio, Texas

Ann Cunningham O'Conor
Teacher-Coordinator, Fashion
   Merchandising
Roy C. Start High School
Toledo Public School District
Toledo, Ohio

M. Michelina Olmstead
Marketing Education Teacher
Indiana County Area Vocational
   Technical School
Indiana, Pennsylvania

David L. Phillips
Marketing Education
   Teacher-Coordinator
Ashe County Career Center
West Jefferson, North Carolina

Charlane Price Pralle
Marketing Education
   Teacher-Coordinator
Iowa Falls High School
Iowa Falls, Iowa

Fred A. Reed
Marketing Education
   Teacher-Coordinator
Edgewater High School
Orange County School District
Orlando, Florida

Robert A. Ristau
Professor of Business Education
Eastern Michigan University
Ypsilanti, Michigan

Robert M. Rubin
Assistant Principal, Supervision/
   Marketing Education
Norman Thomas High School
New York City School District
New York, New York

Julius Kantor
Business and Marketing
   Education Instructor
Bauder College
Ft. Lauderdale, Florida

Contents

BUSINESS AND MARKETING ESSENTIALS

PART

3

HUMAN RESOURCE ESSENTIALS

BUSINESS AND DISTRIBUTION OPERATIONS

BUYING AND PRICING MERCHANDISE

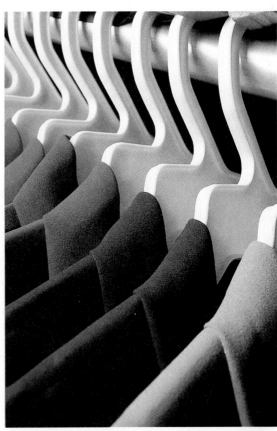

MARKETING INFORMATION MANAGEMENT

PART 9

PRODUCT PLANNING

The World of Marketing

Welcome to the world of marketing—and what an exciting world it is! This text, entitled *Marketing Essentials,* introduces you to one of the most vital career areas you could ever explore—an area that involves determining customers' needs and then deciding how best to satisfy those needs.

Marketing offers you a vast spectrum of interest areas from which to choose. Perhaps selling interests you. Perhaps product promotion looks intriguing.

Perhaps you want to distribute goods . . . or buy them . . . or price them . . . or package them. Maybe you have even dreamed of starting your own business.

In marketing, all of these possibilities are open to you. You could stick to one specific area—selling, for example—and still investigate the many other functions of marketing in the course of doing your daily work. The career opportunities are fascinating and rewarding. Let's take a closer look at them.

Marketing Is Selling

Selling is providing customers with the goods and services they want to buy. This includes selling to the retail market (the final user of the product) or the industrial market (those who make goods for resale).

Marketing Is Promotion

Promotion is any form of communication used to inform, persuade, or remind people about a business's products and improve its public image. This includes advertising, publicity, sales promotion, and personal selling.

Marketing Is Distribution

Distribution is transporting, storing, and handling goods on their way from seller to customer.

Marketing Is Risk Management

Marketing Is Pricing

Pricing means making decisions on how much to charge for goods and services by looking at price in relation to value.

◀ **Risk management** is preventing business loss or failure. This means dealing with economic risk occurring from changes in business conditions, such natural risks as floods or fires, and human risks caused by human mistakes or the unpredictability of employees or customers.

Marketing Is Purchasing

Purchasing is buying goods and services used in the operation of a business or buying goods for resale.

Marketing Is Marketing Information Management

Marketing information management is the process of getting the marketing information needed to make sound business decisions.

Marketing Is Product/ Service Planning

Product/service planning involves all of the decisions a business makes in the production and sale of its product. This includes decisions about packaging, labeling, extended product features, brands, and product mix.

Marketing Is Financing

Financing is getting the money needed to finance the operation of a business.

Using Marketing Essentials

Have you ever seen a blueprint for a house or office building? A blueprint is a plan of action drawn by an architect. It shows where each room will be, how big it will be, and the overall design of the structure.

How well the architect's "vision" is carried out, however, is really up to the builder. Two builders could look at the same blueprint for a house, but each could build a structure with its own unique character by using different bricks or paint or wood for the floors. The basic design of the two houses would be the same, but the two builders could put their own imprint on each.

Think of this book as your blueprint to marketing. It tells you what you need to know to start your career exploration and get a basic understanding of the principles and practices of marketing. It's up to you to put your own unique imprint on your career path.

Part Opening Pages

Marketing Essentials is divided into 11 parts, each of which begins with a part opening presentation. These two pages list the chapters included in the part and present a graphic illustration of a "marketing wheel." The wheel is shown and explained on page 1.

The three inner circles of the wheel show the three foundations of marketing: *Economic Foundations of Marketing, Marketing and Business Foundations,* and *Human Resource Foundations.* The nine functions of marketing are shown on the outer wheel: selling, promotion, distribution, risk management, pricing, purchasing, marketing information management, product/service planning, and financing. The foundations and/or functions that you will be studying in the part are highlighted in color.

Chapter Organization

The fundamental chapters at the beginning of the text will help you understand the foundations of marketing necessary for further study and entry-level employment. They cover the essentials of economics, business, marketing, and human resource development. The remaining parts of the text focus on the more specific areas of marketing. They will help you begin building your own unique marketing career.

Chapter Openers

The chapter opener pages lay out the new information and applications of marketing principles the chapter holds. Each chapter begins with a **photo** that depicts a major concept discussed in the chapter. The **objectives** tell you the skills and knowledge you can expect to master once you have completed the chapter. An **introduction** briefly outlines what you will learn and often gives a brief anecdote that relates the chapter concepts to your own life. The **words to know** are the terms that are printed in bold face and defined in italics throughout the chapter.

Illustrations with Teaching Captions

You'll enjoy looking at the thought-provoking color photos and graphics throughout the text that illustrate major concepts. The captions will help you remember chapter material and relate it to your own life. They'll ask you to answer questions that help you bridge the information in the text to the illustration.

Case Challenges

Case challenges give you real-life applications of the chapter content. You'll recognize many of the companies and brand names in the case challenges. These features include case histories of familiar businesses and products, current marketing practices that address issues relevant to the chapter content and, in the case of the sales unit, applications dealing with selling techniques.

The case challenges end with two to several questions to help you see how the chapter's principles apply to the real-life marketing situation in the case challenge. Some questions even challenge those principles.

Real World Marketing Applications

Each chapter contains one or two of these short features on fun facts about such marketing-related topics as product and brand development, costs of advertising, and successful entrepreneurs. Many will give you that "I didn't know that!" thrill of discovery.

For example, do you know how the Apple Computer was invented? how Life Savers made a mint for ad sales rep Edward Noble? how the Greyhound Bus Company came into being? The answers to these questions are all found in the Real World Marketing Applications.

End-of-Chapter Activities

The end-of-chapter activities help you review and remember the chapter material. Each page is color-screened, which makes it easy to find. The end-of-chapter activities contain several elements. In the **vocabulary review** you are asked to perform a range of activities from simply recalling information to writing the vocabulary words into one or several paragraphs on chapter content. The **fact and idea review** questions require simple recall of material found in the text. **Critical thinking** questions require you to do more advanced decision-making such as interpretation, analysis, comparison, making judgments, or applying concepts.

The exercises entitled **using basic skills** give you realistic, creative applications of chapter concepts to mathematics, communication, and human relations so you can master these three areas and see how they relate to your life.

The **application projects** require you to apply chapter concepts to a real-life situation or develop new ideas from chapter concepts. Many projects are similar to the cases you will encounter in DECA competition. So, you can use them as pre-competition practice.

Glossary and Index

Both the glossary and index are easy to understand and use. The glossary contains more than 350 marketing-related terms. The index lists not only key terms and concepts but also important graphs, charts, and other illustrations relating to the chapter content.

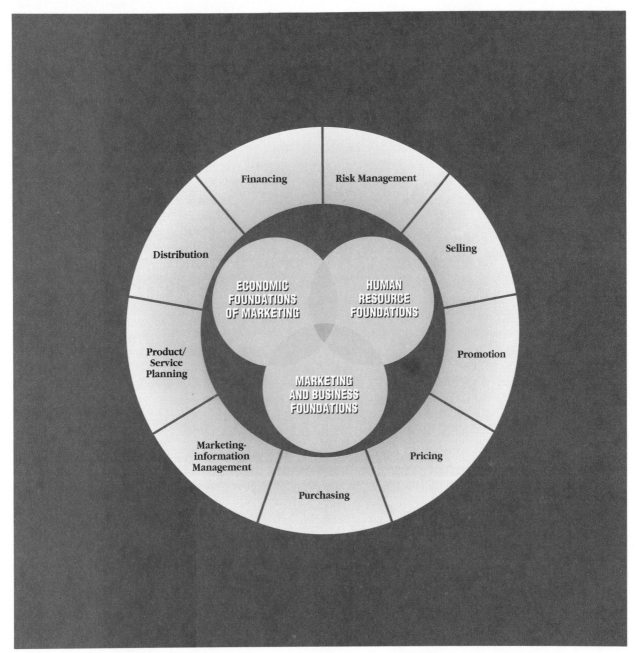

The three inner circles of the wheel show the three foundations of marketing: Economic Foundations of Marketing, Marketing and Business Foundations, *and* Human Resource Foundations. *The nine functions of marketing are shown on the outer wheel: selling, promotion, distribution, risk management, pricing, purchasing, marketing information management, product/service planning, and financing. The foundations and/or functions that you will be studying in the part are highlighted in color.*

PART

1

ECONOMIC ESSENTIALS

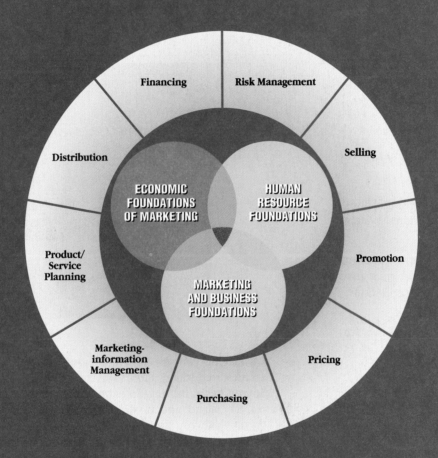

Financing

Risk Management

Distribution

Selling

ECONOMIC FOUNDATIONS OF MARKETING

HUMAN RESOURCE FOUNDATIONS

Product/ Service Planning

Promotion

MARKETING AND BUSINESS FOUNDATIONS

Marketing-information Management

Pricing

Purchasing

CHAPTERS
▼ ▼ ▼ ▼ ▼ ▼ ▼ ▼ ▼

1 Introduction to Economics
2 The Free Enterprise System
3 National and International Economics

After completing this chapter, you will be able to:

1. identify economic goods and economic services,

2. identify the factors of production necessary to create goods and services,

3. explain the concept of scarcity,

4. define an economy,

5. recognize the three basic questions that all economic systems must answer,

6. compare how market economies and command economies answer the basic economic questions, and

7. explain why all economies are mixed.

goods
services
resources
scarcity
economy
market economy
democracy
command economy
communism
democratic socialism
profit

Introduction to Economics

Imagine yourself and nine other people shipwrecked on a deserted island. Survival is an important goal for all of you. So you begin making decisions about how to use the resources on the island and how to share those resources among the group. Like you and your shipwrecked friends, all nations are faced with the same basic problems of how to use and share resources. In this chapter, you will learn how and why nations make economic decisions, and how you are involved in the study of economics.

The Study of Economics

Economics is a field of study about things that touch your daily life. Because you encounter these things so often, there is much that you already know about economics.

For example, you know there are things you want that you have to pay money for. These things are *goods* and *services*, and they are an important concern of economics.

You also know that goods and services do not just happen. They must be produced in some way. And certain things called *resources* are necessary to produce them.

Finally, you know that you always seem to want more goods and services than you can afford to buy or make on your own. This is called the concept of *scarcity*.

Goods and Services

Did you buy your lunch at school today, buy food at the grocery store, or buy a magazine, record, or book? Did you ride the bus to school, pay someone to cut your hair, fix your car, or clean your teeth? If you did any of these things, then you were making use of goods and services. *Goods and services are products of our economic system that satisfy our needs and wants and have monetary value.*

Goods are *tangible* products. This means they can be physically touched. Hammers, automobiles, soda pop, clothing, computers, and bicycles are examples of goods.

Services are *intangible* products. This means they *cannot* be physically touched. For example, services are provided by restaurants, dry cleaning businesses, amusement parks, income tax preparation services, accounting services, and movie theaters.

Identify the goods and services in the photographs below. What characteristics do goods and services have in common?

Resources

Resources are all the things used in producing goods and services. They are also called *factors of production.* They include three basic types of resources: *land, labor,* and *capital.*

Land. To an economist, land means everything on the earth that is in its natural state (another term for this is *natural resources*). It includes everything contained in the land or found in the seas. Coal and oil are natural resources. So are fish in a lake, and the lake itself; and so are trees and plants, and the soil in which they grow.

Labor. Labor includes all the people who work in the economy. This includes full-time and part-time laborers, managers, professional people, and public employees.

Capital. Capital includes the money needed to start and operate a business, as well as the goods needed to produce other goods. Factories, buildings, and tools, for example, are all considered to be capital.

The Concept of Scarcity

Scarcity is what forces everyone to make economic choices. *The concept of scarcity recognizes that people have unlimited wants and needs, but only limited resources.* It means that there is only so much land available, only so much labor, and only so much capital. Because these things are limited, individuals (as well as businesses and nations) must make economic choices.

What Is an Economy?

The way a nation goes about making economic choices is called its *economy* (or *economic system*). *That is, an* **economy** *is how a nation makes decisions for using its resources to produce and distribute goods and services.*

In deciding how to use their resources, people must answer three basic questions through their economic system. They are:

1. *What* goods and services should be produced?
2. *How* should the goods and services be produced?
3. *Who* should share in what is produced?

Figure 1-1 **Economic Resources**

Land, labor, and capital are the three basic types of economic resources used in goods and services. How are underdeveloped nations usually different from highly industrialized nations with regard to the factors of production?

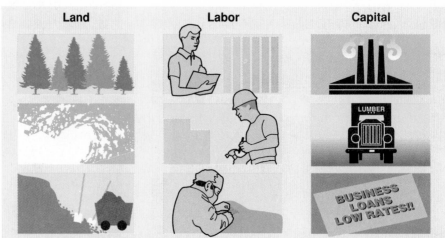

Land   Labor   Capital

The Types of Economic Systems

Economists have studied the way nations answer the three basic economic questions and have classified the systems into two broad categories: *market economies* (sometimes called *capitalism*) and *command* (or *planned*) *economies*. As you will see, no economy can be called a purely market economy or purely command economy. Components of both systems can be found in all economies. For now, however, let's look at these systems in their purest theoretical forms.

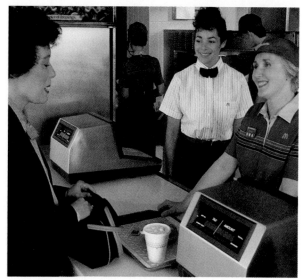

How does this transaction answer the three basic economic questions: what, how, and who?

Market Economies

In a market economy, the government lets the market answer the three basic economic questions.

What, How, and Who in a Market Economy. Consumers in a market system decide for themselves which products they will buy. Businesses respond by producing more of those products. As a result, when consumers decide which products they will buy, they are also determining *what* products will be made.

Businesses in a market economy must keep their prices competitive with other businesses. To do this, they must try to find the most efficient way to produce their goods and services. When they do this, the businesses are determining for themselves *how* the product will be made.

In a market economy, the people who have more money are able to buy more goods and services. To obtain money, people work and invest in business. The pure market economy answers the question *who* by rewarding people according to how much they contribute to the economy.

Democracy in a Market Economy. Generally speaking, market economies follow a democratic form of government. *In a democracy there is usually more than one political party from which to choose representatives to run the government.* People in a democracy are free to elect those candidates who agree with their philosophies on how the government should be run. The United States and Japan are two examples of countries that have a democratic form of government and that follow the market economy for their economic system.

Command Economies

In a command economy, the government makes all three of the basic economic decisions. A central planning committee decides what should be produced, how it should be produced, and who should get what is produced.

The theory behind such an economy is that a government controlling all of these decisions should be able to allocate the nation's resources efficiently and make sure that everyone shares in what is produced.

Two basic types of political systems associated with command economies are *communism* and *democratic socialism*. The differences between the two types of systems are partly economic and partly political.

Communism. *Communism, according to socialistic theory, is socialism in its perfect form.* One political party runs the government to ensure that all people share common economic and political goals.

In a communist country, the government exercises nearly complete control over what people can do in the economy. The government makes all three economic decisions—what will be made, how it will be made, and who will benefit from what is made. This means that the government determines what goods and services will be available and who will be able to buy them.

Democratic Socialism. *Democratic socialism is a combination of capitalism and socialism in economic theory and democracy in political theory.* Countries that follow democratic socialism have more than one political party from which to choose elected officials.

Economically, the government in a democratic socialist country makes the three economic decisions for the country's major industries, such as banking, mining, utilities, medical care, and transportation. Other businesses, however, follow the market economy, and consumers are free to make their own decisions in the marketplace. Sweden, England, and Australia are countries that follow democratic socialism.

For the most part, consumers in a democratic socialistic country can control what will be produced by voting for government officials who share their views, and by making their spending choices in the economy. Broadly speaking, in democratic socialism the government exercises less control over economic decisions than in communism, but more control than in a market economy.

Differences Between Economic Systems

Communism, democratic socialism, and capitalism use different philosophies to deal with many economic issues. Some of these important issues include business ownership, consumer products, employment, ownership of private property, competition, profit and risk, and social services.

Business Ownership. In communistic countries, all industries and resources are owned and operated by the government. In democratic socialist countries, some of the major industries are owned and operated by the government, but private enterprise is encouraged. In capitalism, most businesses are owned and operated by private entrepreneurs, but with some government intervention.

Consumer Products. In democratic socialist and capitalistic countries, there are a variety of goods and services from which to choose. However, in communistic countries, the variety of consumer goods and services is dependent on the government's priorities. Historically, citizens of the Soviet Union and China have had very few food and consumer products from which to select.

Prices in communistic countries are often subsidized so that all people can afford the goods and services that are considered necessities. In socialistic countries, the major industries run by the government also control prices for this reason. In capitalistic countries and in privately run businesses in democratic socialist countries, prices are determined in the marketplace.

Employment. In both socialistic and capitalistic countries, people are free to decide where they want to work. They also have the opportunity to form unions, bargain for wages, and compete for jobs and wages in the workplace. In communistic countries, workers are assigned jobs based on government decisions. In theory, collective bargaining serves no purpose in such countries. However, unions do exist and strikes have occurred in some communistic countries.

Ownership of Private Property. Capitalism and democratic socialism to a large extent both encourage ownership of private property. Citizens are free to own land, homes, factories, tools, toys, and businesses, and to use them as they wish. They may choose to sell their private property, store it, rent it, or put it to a variety of different uses. Under communism, the government owns all land and private property.

Competition. In capitalism and democratic socialism, independent businesses are constantly competing with one another to get more customers. In a purely communistic country, competition would have no place because all businesses are owned and run by the government.

Profit and Risk. In capitalism and democratic socialism, people who go into business for themselves risk failure, but they also have the chance to make a *profit. Profit is the money a business has brought in (its income) after the costs and expenses of running the business are subtracted.* In all industries in communistic countries and in government-controlled industries in democratic socialism, profit is not used to measure success, and risk is not apparent because the government controls those industries. Government-controlled industries produce goods and services needed by the state and the people, as dictated by the central planning committee. Many industries are subsidized by the government. Consequently, these businesses take few risks and have little incentive to improve quality or increase efficiency of production.

Social Services. According to socialistic and communistic philosophies, the government should directly take care of its people's basic needs, such as food, shelter, and medical care. In a pure market economy, the government does not take direct responsibility for these things. However, in the United States and in other capitalistic systems, some programs have been created to directly care for the basic needs of people who are not able to care for themselves.

Education is free in all three systems for the elementary grades. However, in communistic countries the government decides who will be permitted to continue their education. In democratic socialism, the government pays for even the college education of those who qualify and want further schooling. In a capitalistic country such as the United States, a college education must be paid for by the individual. The government may provide some assistance to those who cannot afford it, but that type of support is limited.

Figure 1-2 **Scale of Government Control Over Economic Choice**

This scale shows the range of government control over economic choice. In which countries shown on the scale do the governments have the most control in the economy? In which countries do the governments have the least control? In which countries do the governments have some control?

Medical services in socialistic and communistic countries are provided by the government through socialized medicine. In the United States, two examples of programs that help supply medical services to people who qualify for them are Medicare and Medicaid. Certain states may also provide specialized medical services for qualified people. However, most of the medical expenses incurred by United States citizens must be paid for by the individual. To cover these high costs, many people buy medical insurance.

Mixed Economies

You have seen that the political and economic systems of different nations answer the basic economic questions differently when trying to meet the needs of their people. However, there are also some similarities. No country has an economic system that is purely market or purely command. All countries have *mixed economies.*

Although the United States has a capitalistic economic system, it also uses certain concepts that are borrowed from socialism. For example, the United States provides welfare for low-income people and government subsidies for certain farm industries.

The Soviet Union and China are the two largest and most powerful communist countries. Both countries have had problems with shortages of food and consumer goods, due to low productivity, inefficient use of capital resources, and lack of incentive to improve. In an attempt to solve these problems, the Soviet Union and China have both experimented in recent years with economic ideas borrowed from market economies. (See the Case Challenge on page 10.)

Although all economies are mixed, the differences between market and command economies are significant. It is useful to think of economic systems as being on a scale (see Figure 1-2), ranging from countries where the government makes nearly all of

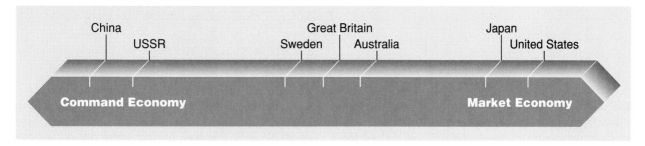

China   USSR   Sweden   Great Britain   Australia   Japan   United States

Command Economy   **Market Economy**

Capitalism in China

China, a communistic country well known for its planned economic policies, began experimenting with capitalistic ideas in the late 1970s. The first reform gave peasant farmers the right to farm some of the land owned by the government for their own profit. The government was very pleased with the results of that experiment because farm production increased.

In the 1980s, China expanded the reforms to certain other industries. The reforms included less government control in the managing and running of factories; reduction of government subsidies to keep prices low for products, thus allowing the marketplace to dictate price; increased wages for workers who were more highly educated and more diligent on the job; and reduction of guaranteed supplies of materials for factories and industries.

The Chinese government took these steps because the country was economically depressed. Workers were paid whether or not they showed up for work, factories were run inefficiently, and there was a lot of waste and overstaffing.

The reforms of the late 1980s created many successful businesses. The coastal regions of China were positively affected by this economic boom. Many companies began producing goods for the world market, importing the necessary raw materials, and exporting finished products.

Thus, one of the benefits of loosening government controls in China was the increase of small businesses owned and operated by individuals. Foreign investment also helped, thus providing the necessary capital to get certain businesses off the ground. Joint ventures and experiments with United States companies took place. (Two of the first Western style fast-food restaurants that opened in China were Kentucky Fried Chicken and Pizza Hut, both subsidiaries of Pepsico, Inc.)

But with any change comes problems. As some economists predicted, high inflation resulted from the new policies. So, in October of 1988, the Chinese government placed limits on price and wage increases in order to control inflation.

By March of 1989, China's leaders decided to retreat from their experiments in capitalism and began to revert back to increased reliance on governmental central planning. In addition, the Chinese people were expected to cut back on consumer purchases and to go back to the simple life.

1. Why did China try to incorporate capitalistic practices into its command economy?
2. Write two major benefits that resulted from the capitalistic reforms implemented in China.
3. Do you think the economic reforms in China led to political reform there? Why or why not?
4. Explain how the economic reforms in China classify it as a mixed economy.

the economic decisions, to countries where the government makes very few of the economic decisions. Communist countries would be on one end of the scale, with more government involvement. Capitalist countries, such as the United States, would be at the other end of the scale with less government involvement. Democratic socialist countries would appear somewhere between the two.

VOCABULARY REVIEW

Write a brief definition of each term, based on your reading of the chapter.

goods
services
resources
scarcity
economy
market economy

democracy
command economy
communism
democratic socialism
profit

FACT AND IDEA REVIEW

1. Look at the items listed below, and classify each as a land, labor, or capital resource.

   a river   steel
   an auto   money used to buy tools
   iron ore deposits a teacher

2. How are economic goods different from economic services?

3. According to the concept of scarcity, why is it impossible for people to have all the products they want?

4. List the three basic economic questions nations must face because of the fact of scarcity.

5. What is an economy?

6. Who answers the basic economic questions in a market economy?

7. How are the basic economic questions answered in a command economy?

8. Name one example each of a country that follows a market system, a country that follows democratic socialism, and a country that follows communism.

CRITICAL THINKING

1. How do countries that follow capitalism differ from countries that follow communism and democratic socialism with regard to answering the three basic economic questions?

2. Tell the political differences between democracy, communism, and democratic socialism. Give examples of countries that follow each type of political structure.

3. Compare and contrast countries that follow capitalism, communism, and democratic socialism with regard to:

   a. ownership of private property

   b. business ownership

   c. consumer products

   d. employment

4. Why are all economies mixed economies? Specifically tell why the United States is a mixed economy.

5. How do countries following capitalism, communism, and democratic socialism view competition, profit, and the government's role in supplying social services to the people?

USING BASIC SKILLS

Math

1. Prepare a budget for a family with a household income of $80,000 a year. Use the following percentages to calculate the budget: 17 percent for food; 28 percent for housing; 13 percent for clothing; 10 percent for transportation; 2 percent for insurance; 25 percent for savings; and 5 percent for miscellaneous expenses.

2. If there were 8,000 farms in the Soviet Union and private farms accounted for 1.5 percent of the farms, how many privately-run farms would that be? If the private plots produced 25 percent of all agricultural products and the total production amounted to $4 billion, what is the dollar amount of the agricultural products that could be attributed to the privately-run farms?

Communication

3. Write a paragraph on the chapter content that incorporates all of the following terms: scarcity, economy, economic goods and services, resources.

Human Relations

4. You work for a grocery store in which the owner prohibits employees from eating food sold in the store. A co-worker on your shift has been eating fresh produce and bakery items. You are worried you may be accused of employee pilferage. What will you do?

APPLICATION PROJECTS

1. Make a chart with three columns at the top: *Capitalism, Democratic Socialism,* and *Communism.* List these categories along the left-hand side of the chart: *business ownership, consumer products, employment choices and wages, ownership of private property, competition, profit and risk,* and *social services.* Then write brief descriptions in each category that show the differences between the three economic systems.

2. Prepare a three- to five-minute oral presentation or a two- to three-page written presentation that illustrates the importance of free public education in order to make better use of a nation's resources, especially its labor.

3. Imagine that you are a student in a country with a command economy, either communism or social democracy. Write a letter to your pen pal in the United States and explain your country's economy. Include at least two examples that will help your pen pal understand the differences between the economy in your country and the economy in the United States.

4. Choose a specific country with a communistic or a socialistic philosophy. Read about the social services the government of that country provides its citizens. Compare those services with the services offered by the United States government. Present your comparison in a five-minute oral report.

5. Select an article from the business section of a local newspaper or from a business magazine. First, write a 150-word summary of the article. Next, identify the specific goods and services mentioned in the article. Finally, list all the resources mentioned in the article and identify each resource as land, labor, or capital.

6. Think about what is happening in the picture below. Imagine that you are a reporter for a local neighborhood newspaper, and write a short news story about the event. Then imagine that you are a reporter for a neighborhood newspaper in a communistic country, and write a news story about the same event. Discuss your two news stories with your classmates. How are the stories different? Why are they different?

The Free Enterprise System

After completing this chapter, you will be able to:

1. identify the freedoms of a free enterprise system,

2. explain the role profit plays in a market economy,

3. explain the function of supply and demand in determining prices in a market economy,

4. explain the role competition plays in a market economy, and

5. explain how the United States government is involved in our modified market economy.

competition
price competition
nonprice competition
monopoly
demand
elastic demand
inelastic demand
supply
modified free enterprise system

In Chapter 1 you learned about the differences between command economic systems and market economic systems in their purest forms. Now it is time to look at how the market economy of the United States operates.

Basic Economic Freedoms

A market economy can be described as capitalism or as a free enterprise system. In a pure market system, all economic decisions take place in the marketplace with no government interference.

Certain freedoms are basic to the free enterprise system:

- The freedom to own private property
- The freedom to open a business
- The freedom to compete
- The freedom to make a profit
- The freedom of choice

The Freedom to Own Private Property. People are free to own private property and, for the most part, to do with it as they wish. They can sell it, rent it, or do nothing with it, as they choose.

The Freedom to Open a Business. People are free to open and operate their own businesses.

The Freedom to Compete. People are free to compete with other businesses in order to be successful. They can raise or lower their prices. They can try different methods to increase efficiency. They can introduce new and different products to attract customers. Competition is an essential part of a free enterprise system. It forces businesses to produce better quality goods and services at lower prices.

The Freedom to Make a Profit. The *profit motive* is a driving force in a market economy. It encourages businesses to be *efficient* and to *cater* to the consumer, since only businesses that supply the goods and services needed and desired by consumers will stay in business. The freedom to make a profit is not a *guarantee* of profit. Along with the freedom to make a profit, there is the risk of failure.

As a matter of fact, one business in three in the United States fails after one year of operation. And risk continues, even if a business survives past the first few years. When an industry develops and profits are great, more people enter that industry, thus increasing competition and the risk of failure for individual businesses. Therefore, risk is ongoing in a free enterprise system.

Profitable businesses are able to acquire resources more easily than businesses that are not profitable. This is because the profits create the capital necessary to expand the business, conduct research, and acquire more equipment and supplies. In addition, profitable businesses are granted higher credit limits and better deals than businesses that may be classified as credit risks.

The Freedom of Choice. People have many choices in a free enterprise system. They may choose the products and services they want to buy, the careers they want to pursue, and the people they want to represent them in government.

Competition

The struggle between companies for customers is called competition. Businesses try to attract new customers and maintain old customers, while others try to take those very same customers away.

Competition is healthy and vital to a market economy. The effects of competition are reasonable prices and better quality products. Let's look at how businesses compete.

These gas stations are competing for customers. What things can they do to try to win customers from each other? In what type of economy would you find this competition?

Price and Nonprice Competition

Businesses are given a fair chance to compete through both *price competition* and *nonprice competition*. *Price competition, as the name implies, focuses on the sale price of a product.* The assumption is that all other things being equal, consumers will buy the products that are lowest in price.

In nonprice competition, businesses choose to compete on the basis of other factors that are not related to price. Some nonprice competition factors are quality of the products, service offered, location of the business, financing offered, reputation of the firm, and the qualifications or expertise of the personnel. In businesses that use nonprice competition, prices may be higher than those of their competitors.

Monopolies

Competition exists when no single seller has control of the market. But when one firm controls the market for a given product, a *monopoly* is established. *A **monopoly** is exclusive control over a product or the means of production.*

Monopolies are prohibited because there is no competition when there is a monopoly. Without competition, a company can charge whatever it wants and can control who gets the products and the quality of the products. Without competition, there is no counterforce to balance product selection, quality, and price.

In the United States, the government permits a few monopolies to exist, mainly in industries where it would be extremely wasteful to have more than one firm. These monopolies, however, are regulated by

REAL WORLD MARKETING

Big Brother Is Watching (TV)

Sometimes advertisers overstep their bounds to sell a product. When they do, the Federal Trade Commission (FTC) usually steps in. Such was the case in a famous incident in 1964 when Lever Brothers, makers of Lifebuoy soap, had an actor in a TV spot shower with Dove because its own product wouldn't make enough lather. The FTC forced Lever Brothers to cancel the ad.

the government. Utility companies are an example of this type of government-regulated monopoly. The gas and electric companies must apply to government agencies for rate increases, and they must provide the government with financial information to warrant the increase.

The telephone company was a government-related monopoly until the breakup of American Telephone & Telegraph (AT&T). At that time, the government decided that telephone service could be deregulated and competition would be beneficial to the consumers. Now many different telephone companies compete for our long distance telephone business.

Benefits of Competition

Competition benefits consumers by forcing businesses to lower prices and offer better quality merchandise and services. Through the struggle to attract customers, businesses constantly look for ways to develop new products or improve old ones. Competition results in a wider selection of products from which to choose. It also provides an incentive for businesses to operate in the most efficient manner possible. The results of these efforts help to increase the nation's productivity and standard of living.

Supply and Demand

In a market economy, supply and demand determine price. Supply and demand interact to determine the price customers are willing to pay for the number of products producers are willing to make. To see the effects of demand and supply on price, let's look at each one separately and then see how they interact to set prices in a market economy.

The Law of Demand

*The consumers' willingness and ability to buy products is defined as **demand**.* According to the law of demand, if the price is low enough, the demand for a product usually increases. For example, a CD player selling for $500 may generate some demand. But the same CD player selling for $100 should generate much more demand because more people would be able to afford it. Thus, lower prices often create demand, while high prices tend to lower demand.

To study demand, businesspeople prepare graphs called *demand curves*. Business owners conduct research and study consumers' reactions to high and low prices for products. The information is organized in a table called a *demand schedule*, which is then used to prepare the *demand curve*.

For example, a clothing store owner might want to know how many sweaters could be sold at prices ranging from $25 to $35. After conducting some research, the retailer might prepare a demand schedule, as shown in Table 2-1. The demand schedule would be used to prepare a demand curve, like the one in Figure 2-1.

A factor that may limit demand is called the principle of *diminishing marginal utility*. In essence, the principle of diminishing marginal utility means that consumers will buy just so much of a given product, even though the price is low.

Table 2-1 Demand Schedule for Sweaters in a Retail Store

Price Per Sweater	Number of Sweaters Demanded by Customers
$35	600
34	800
33	1,100
32	1,500
31	2,000
30	2,600
29	3,400
28	4,600
27	6,200

Demand generally increases as the price decreases. What is the difference between the demand at $30 and the demand at $27?

Figure 2-1 **Demand Curve for Sweaters in a Retail Store**

This demand curve shows how price affects demand for sweaters. Approximately how many consumers will demand sweaters that cost $30 each?

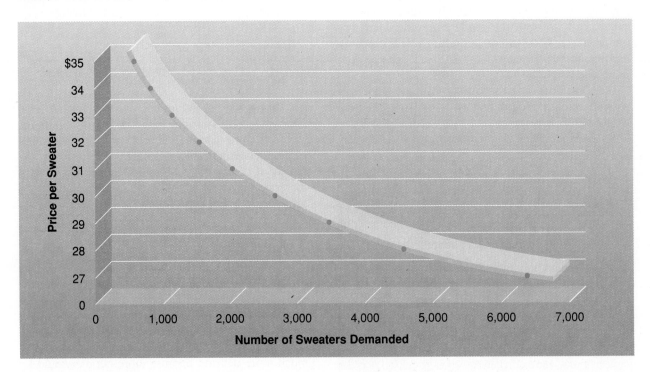

For example, let's say that detergent went on sale, and you bought two cases of it because the price was low. If three weeks later a new sale is announced for the same detergent, you may decide that you already have enough to last you for four months. So, you will not take advantage of the new sale.

Elasticity of Demand. The law of demand says that demand goes up when price goes down, and that demand goes down when price goes up. This principle is accurate as a general rule, but not all products respond easily to changes in price. The degree to which demand for a product is affected by its price is called *demand elasticity*. In terms of demand elasticity, products are said to have either *elastic demand* or *inelastic demand*.

Elastic demand refers to situations when a slight change in price creates a large change in demand. As price decreases, significant changes in demand are noted. Changes in the price of steak will serve as a good example. If the price for steak was $8 per pound, few people would buy the steak. However, if the price dropped to $5, $3, and $2 per pound, demand would increase at each price level, until the law of diminishing marginal utility set in.

Inelastic demand exists when the change in price has very little effect on the demand for a product. Certain food products that are considered necessities, such as milk and bread, would fall under this category. If the price increases, most of us would not buy much less. If the price decreases, there is just so much bread and milk we need.

Medical care is another necessity that demonstrates inelastic demand. An increase in office visit rates from $50 to $55 would probably not cause you to drop a physician who was giving you good health care.

There are four basic factors that indicate whether a product is likely to have elastic or inelastic demand. They include *availability of substitutes, price relative to income, classification of the product as a luxury or necessity,* and the *immediacy of purchase.*

When substitutes are available, demand becomes more elastic. For example, if your favorite detergent raises its price but other brands do not, you may decide to try a new detergent because all detergents will clean your clothes.

When there is no substitute for a product, demand is inelastic. For example, when new prescription medicines first come on the market, their demand is likely to be inelastic because they have no substitutes.

Most people consider dining out in expensive restaurants a luxury, so it is price elastic. Are the foods pictured on the right price elastic or price inelastic?

People may begin to look for a substitute for a product if the product's price goes up. But changes in price are relative to the income of the customer. For example, if your salary increases 30 percent and the price of your favorite brand of mayonnaise increases 10 percent, you may decide to keep buying your favorite brand anyway because the price increase relative to your income was not significant enough to warrant a change. When the price of a product is a large portion of a person's income, demand tends to be elastic. However, when price is a small portion of a person's income, demand tends to be inelastic.

The third factor in determining elasticity of demand is whether a person regards a product as a luxury or a necessity. Here again the classification is relative. What is a luxury for one person may be considered a necessity by another person.

The fourth factor that influences demand elasticity is the urgency with which a purchase must be made. If you are running out of gas and the next gas station charges $.15 more per gallon than you usually pay, you will probably still stop and buy gas so you can finish your trip. If a purchase must be made immediately, demand tends to be inelastic.

The Law of Supply

Supply is the amount of goods producers are willing to make and sell. The law of supply states that at a higher price, producers will offer a larger quantity of products for sale; at a lower price, producers offer fewer products for sale. In other words, as the price for shirts increases, a store is willing to supply more shirts.

Business owners prepare supply schedules (see Table 2-2) to determine how much they may want to supply of a certain product at various prices. Using the information from the supply schedule, a supply curve can be drawn (see Figure 2-2).

Surpluses, Shortages, and Equilibrium

The laws of supply and demand are constantly interacting in the marketplace, creating conditions of *surplus, shortage,* or *equilibrium*. These conditions often determine whether prices will go down, or up, or stay the same.

Surpluses of goods occur when supply exceeds demand. When this happens, businesses respond by

Table 2-2 Supply Schedule for Sweaters in a Retail Store	
Price Per Sweater	Number Supplied
$35	6,000
34	5,800
33	5,600
32	5,400
31	5,000
30	4,400
29	3,400
28	2,000
27	1,000

A supply schedule helps a business owner determine how much to supply of a certain product at various prices. Why do business owners want to increase their supply when price increases?

lowering their prices in order to encourage people to buy more of the product.

When demand exceeds supply, *shortages* of products occur. When shortages occur, businesses can raise prices and still sell the products. For example, when Cabbage Patch Dolls were introduced in the early 1980s and the demand for them exceeded the supply, the prices of the dolls rose significantly.

When the amount of the product being supplied is equal to the amount of product in demand, *equilibrium* is said to exist. On a graph, this is the point where the supply curve and the demand curve meet. (Figure 2-3 shows where this occurs for the demand and supply curves for sweaters.) At this point, the producer is pleased with the price and so is the consumer. The equilibrium price, therefore, is the price at which customers are willing to buy and producers are willing to sell.

The Role of Government

The United States is considered a *modified free enterprise system* because there is some government involvement and intervention in our lives. The government provides services, supports businesses when needed, and enforces rules and regulations to encourage competition and protect our safety.

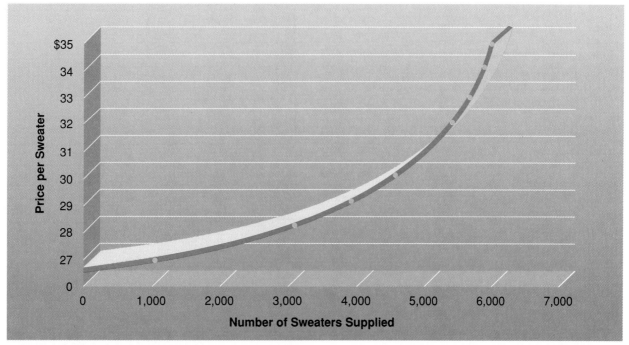

Figure 2-2 .**Supply Curve for Sweaters in a Retail Store**

A supply curve is drawn up from the information in a supply schedule. Approximately how many sweaters will be supplied at $33 each?

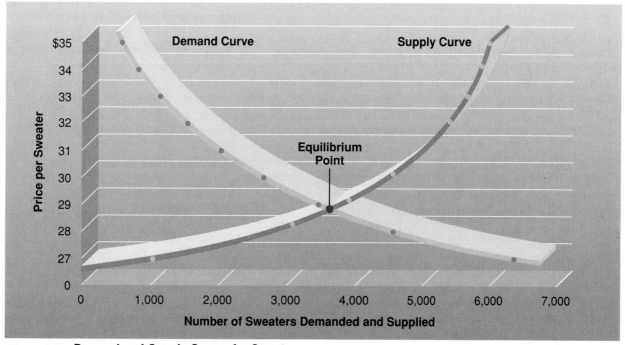

Figure 2-3 **Demand and Supply Curves for Sweaters**

This graph shows the point where the supply curve and the demand curve meet, and thus where equilibrium exists. What is the equilibrium price?

Provider of Services

The services provided by the government include military, police, and fire protection, public education, road and bridge construction, postal services, public libraries, and special programs for the needy. To pay for these services, the government levies taxes on its citizens.

Elected government officials make most of the decisions about what kinds of taxes to use, and how much to collect. They also make most of the decisions about how the money will be spent and what services to provide. By participating in the electoral process, and by making our wishes known to government officials, we as citizens of the United States have control over these decisions.

Enforcer of Rules and Regulations

In addition to providing services, the government also enforces rules and regulations set by the constitution and the government of the United States. These regulations were developed to protect citizens and to encourage and maintain competition. Let's take a closer look at some of these regulations.

Antimonopoly Regulations. Antimonopoly laws have been passed to regulate how businesses operate. Some of the more important laws enacted to prevent monopolies include the Sherman Antitrust Act of 1890, which outlawed all contracts and agreements that would restrain trade or limit competition in interstate commerce. (*Interstate commerce* involves trading between different states in the United States.)

A second law, called the Clayton Antitrust Law, was passed in 1914 to reduce loopholes found in the Sherman Antitrust Act. To help enforce these laws, the Federal Trade Commission Act of 1914 was passed. Since that time, the Federal Trade Commission's powers have been expanded to include investigations of deceptive and misleading business practices, including advertising claims made by business.

In 1950 the government closed a loophole in the Clayton Antitrust Act by enacting the Celler-Kefauver Antimerger Act. The purpose of this act was to prevent companies from buying their competitors' assets, such as factories, equipment, and machinery, if the effect of that sale would result in reduced competition.

Education is one of the services government provides. Give two or three reasons you think the government takes on the responsibility of this service.

Consumer and Worker Protection. The federal government has created many regulatory agencies to protect workers and consumers. Some of those agencies include the Federal Food and Drug Administration, the Equal Employment Opportunity Commission, the Occupational Safety and Health Review Commission, and the Consumer Product Safety Commission. At the state and local levels, government agencies require licensing of people who perform certain services, such as hairdressers and barbers. Also, health departments inspect restaurants and other food handling businesses to protect consumers.

Other Regulations. To protect our environment, the Environmental Protection Agency was established in 1970. Locally, zoning ordinances help to maintain the value of residential real estate and provide for uses that are consistent with the public good.

The Securities and Exchange Commission regulates the sale of stocks and bonds, and is responsible for licensing brokerage firms and investment advisers.

To regulate our rights to private property, the government provides laws and regulations regarding patents, copyrights, and trademarks.

Breakup of a Monopoly

AT&T was recognized as the nation's telephone monopoly in 1919, and remained so for many years. As such, it was subject to federal regulation, but it had no competition.

In 1974, MCI and the Justice Department sued AT&T on antitrust grounds. In 1981, the Justice Department, in conjunction with AT&T, negotiated the breakup of the Bell System. In 1982 AT&T was then allowed to enter the computer business, while local operating telephone companies were separated from the parent company. These local companies were responsible for supplying local telephone service and were commonly referred to as Baby Bells. The Baby Bells were given permission to sell telephone equipment and to publish *Yellow Pages*. The actual breakup of the Bell System occurred in 1984.

Has the breakup of AT&T saved consumers money on their phone bills and resulted in better service? The theory behind the breakup is that competition would improve products and services and would lower rates for the telephone customer. This would occur because other companies would be permitted to enter the long-distance phone market.

Other companies quickly entered the long-distance phone market. The cost of long-distance calls was significantly reduced (by 35 percent), and services such as call-waiting and call-forwarding were made readily available to the average customer. Phone designs were improved, with memory and redial buttons, as well as special options for the business customers such as voice, data, and video networks. There were also more toll-free numbers, and direct dialing to foreign countries was easy and quick. Thus, the breakup certainly did hurry competition along, which resulted in technological improvements and increased service. To take advantage of the breakup, many new telecommunications companies sprang up.

For the average consumer, though, the breakup of AT&T caused confusion. Consumers did not know who to call about problems or to request service. They had to decide to lease or buy their phones, and they had to select a long-distance carrier. In the final analysis, private consumers actually ended up paying higher rates, because local rates went up even though long-distance rates went down. Since the divestiture, the overall price of phone service kept up with inflation, whereas before it was only about a third of inflation, thus keeping rates very low.

In 1989 AT&T still dominated the $50 billion-a-year long-distance industry, so it was still subject to federal regulation. Its competitors, such as MCI, Sprint, and 400 other smaller companies, were not subject to any regulation. They were free to set their own rates.

1. Competition is supposed to decrease costs and improve service and quality to customers. Did the breakup of AT&T accomplish those two goals? Explain fully.
2. If AT&T is no longer a monopoly, why would the government still regulate it? Do you think it is fair? Why or why not?

Supporting the Economy. To help monitor our economy, the government controls the monetary supply and our banking system. To control inflation, for example, our government may increase the prime lending rate to discourage borrowing.

To provide for the welfare of our people, the government has the power to set a minimum wage and may initiate government sponsored training programs to help reduce unemployment.

The government also helps to encourage business enterprise through the Small Business Administration. To help farmers, the government provides assistance in the form of subsidies and purchases of surpluses.

VOCABULARY REVIEW

Write a brief definition of each word, based on your reading of the chapter.

modified free enterprise system
competition
price competition
nonprice competition

monopoly
demand
elastic demand
inelastic demand
supply

FACT AND IDEA REVIEW

1. List the basic economic freedoms of our free enterprise system.

2. Explain why profitable businesses are able to acquire resources more easily than businesses that are not profitable.

3. According to the economic theory of supply and demand, what happens to demand for a product when its price (a) goes down, and (b) goes up?

4. Provide an example of each of the four factors that affects demand elasticity.

5. What is the equilibrium price?

6. Explain price and nonprice competition.

7. Why are monopolies prohibited in a market economy?

8. How does competition benefit the consumer?

9. Why is the United States said to have a *modified* free enterprise system?

CRITICAL THINKING

1. Are new businesses guaranteed success in a free enterprise system? Explain your answer and give examples to make your point.

2. Many diabetics depend on insulin to stay alive. If the price of insulin went up $5, would the demand for insulin go down, as is suggested by the theory of supply and demand? Explain your answer in terms of price elasticity.

3. When the Chrysler Corporation was on the verge of bankruptcy, the United States government intervened by backing loans to get the auto manufacturer back on its feet. In theory, a pure market economy would not help a bankrupt business. Why do you think the United States government decided to help the Chrysler Corporation?

4. If three of the large automobile manufacturers wanted to merge into one large corporation, do you think the United States government would stop them from doing so? Why or why not?

5. Explain the role our government plays in our modified free enterprise system. Do you think the government should be given more or less economic control?

USING BASIC SKILLS

Math

1. Determine the net profit before taxes for a company that generated $1,000,000 in sales, paid $600,000 for the goods that were sold, and had expenses that totaled $300,000.

2. If the expenses of a business amount to 30 percent of sales, and sales are $750,000, what are the business's expenses?

Communication

3. Using a small business in your community, prepare an oral presentation to share with your classmates that presents all the ways the business competes. Does the business compete using price or nonprice competition, or both? Supply examples to make your presentation effective.

Human Relations

4. A customer enters the video store in which you work and rents a video that he could not find at the other video store in town. He then complains that the prices you charge for rentals are higher than those of the other video store.

Your store's rental fees are indeed $.50 per rental higher than your competitor's fees. But the reason for the higher price is that you spend more money to make your store better. To respond to the customer, think of at least one way in which your store is better for the customer, and explain why providing that customer benefit requires you to charge a higher price.

APPLICATION PROJECTS

1. Lakeview Drug Store has been catering to the residents of a town with a population of 30,000 for more than 25 years. Recently a new discount drug store opened a mile from the store. The discount drug store's prices are lower than the Lakeview Drug Store's prices. The owners of the Lakeview Drug Store have come to you for advice. What should they do to compete with this new discount drug store?

2. An alien from outer space, called Lally, arrives in your high school and wants to learn about the free enterprise system. Prepare a three- to five-minute oral or written presentation for the alien. Be sure to explain the main components of the free enterprise system, including freedom to own your own business, as well as private property; freedom to compete; freedom to make a profit; and freedom of choice. The alien will want to know why those features work so well in providing goods and services to the citizens of the United States.

3. Choose one of the five basic economic freedoms. Think about what that freedom means to you now and how you expect to benefit from it in the future. Make a five-minute oral presentation to your class, explaining the importance of that basic economic freedom.

4. Research the history of the United States Postal Service. Find out how and why the Postal Service has functioned as a monopoly. Also find out what specific changes have introduced competition to certain kinds of mail service. Present your findings in a 200- to 300-word written report.

5. Read about the development of the petroleum industry during the past 25 years. How have petroleum shortages affected the industry? What efforts have been made to increase the supply of petroleum and to reduce the demand for it? Explain your answers to these questions in a five-minute oral report.

6. Choose a specific antitrust law: the Sherman Antitrust Act of 1890, the Clayton Antitrust Law of 1914, or the Celler-Kefauver Antimerger Act of 1950. Read about the background and the effects of that law. Then write a 150- to 200-word report about it. Explain the situation that led to enactment of the law, and describe how businesses responded to the passage of the law.

7. Study the demand curve and the supply curve shown below. Write a brief explanation of the information presented in each curve. Then write a paragraph explaining what the B-G Bike Company might conclude from that information.

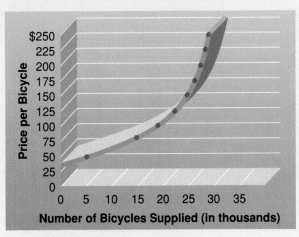

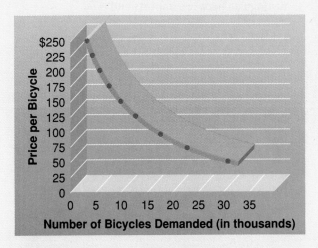

3

After completing this chapter, you will be able to:

1. describe the four phases in a business cycle,

2. explain the methods used for measuring the success of an economy,

3. distinguish between imports and exports,

4. explain why countries trade, in terms of absolute advantage and comparative advantage,

5. describe two important effects of having a negative balance of trade, and

6. identify ways that governments, organizations, and businesses influence international trade.

WORDS TO KNOW

business cycle
Gross National Product (GNP)
standard of living
Consumer Price Index (CPI)
imports
exports
balance of trade
tariff
quota

National and International Economics

Nations measure their economic growth from year to year, just as you measure your personal growth. In this chapter you will look at the measuring devices economists use to report changes in the economy. You will discover how those changes play a part in business cycles that categorize the effects of economic change.

You will also explore international economics. Did you drink Lipton tea or Nescafé coffee this morning, munch a Keebler cookie or a Nestlé chocolate bar at lunch, fill your Toyota with Shell gasoline after school, or watch your Sanyo television? If you did, you may be surprised to discover that you were using products made by foreign-owned companies. In this chapter, you will look at some of the reasons for and the effects of such international trade.

Business Cycles

Because businesses are part of our overall economy, the success of any individual business is strongly affected by events in the economy as a whole. And the economy as a whole is affected by the actions of the individual members within it.

History shows us that sometimes the economy keeps growing, and at other times it slows down. *These changes in the economy are called* **business cycles.** Economists have identified four phases in a business cycle as shown in Figure 3-1: *prosperity, recession, depression,* and *recovery.*

In a period of *prosperity,* the economy is said to be growing—meaning that there is low unemployment, an increase in the output of goods and services produced in the nation, and high consumer spending.

In a *recession,* economic growth slows down—unemployment begins to rise, fewer goods and services are produced, and consumer spending decreases. Sometimes the recession ends relatively quickly, and the economy moves into a recovery period. But sometimes the economy does not quickly begin to recover, and instead the recession deepens into a depression.

A *depression* is a prolonged recession. During a depression, consumer spending is very low, unemployment is very high, and production of goods and services is significantly down. Poverty results because so many people are out of work and cannot afford to buy food, clothing, or shelter. The Great Depression in the early 1930s, which occurred after the stock market crash of 1929, best illustrates this phase of the business cycle.

In the fourth phase of the business cycle—*recovery*—the economy starts to grow again after a depression or a recession.

Factors That Affect Business Cycles

Business cycles are affected by the actions of businesses, consumers, and the government. And, in turn, businesses, consumers, and the government are affected by business cycles.

Figure 3-1 **Four Phases of the Business Cycle**
Prosperity, recession, depression, and recovery are the four phases of the business cycle. The line in the graph represents the national GNP. During which phases of the business cycle are businesses most likely to invest in equipment and increase inventory?

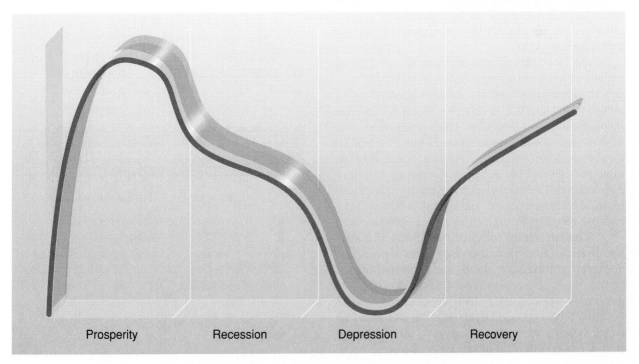

| Prosperity | Recession | Depression | Recovery |

Actions of Businesses. The decisions that individual businesses make have a great impact on business cycles. The interaction between businesses and the business cycles is a two-way street. Businesses make many of their decisions based on forecasts regarding the business cycles. And those decisions tend to prolong or change the business cycles. For example, during periods of prosperity and recovery, businesses are more likely to expand and invest in new properties, equipment, and inventories. That action tends to improve the economy. When businesses sense an economic recession, they refrain from expanding their operations. Businesses generally cut back their inventories to match the lowered demand for goods and services in a recession or depression.

Actions of Consumers. Consumers have an effect on the economy when they increase or decrease their saving and their spending for goods and services. When they decide to increase saving and spending, these actions have a positive effect on the economy. Increased savings allow lending institutions to grant loans to consumers who want to spend money. Businesses react to consumer spending by producing more goods and services. If consumers spend less or save less, the economy is affected through a reduction in demand for consumer products and services.

Actions of Government. Government spending, like consumer spending, can affect business cycles. The government, in fact, sometimes tries to influence business cycles by how much and in what way it spends money.

The government also attempts to control the highs and lows of the business cycle by setting policies designed to influence consumer spending. One method of doing this is taxation. When the government increases or decreases taxes, consumers may have more or less money to spend or save.

In addition to taxes, the government may set other policies that encourage or discourage spending. For example, the Federal Reserve Banking System may increase interest rates for loans. This policy will discourage spending by both consumers and businesses.

When necessary, the government may also institute federally funded programs to spark a depressed economy. For example, during the Great Depression of the 1930s, the government sponsored projects to get people working again, such as building roads. An outgrowth of the Great Depression was our social security system, which was designed to protect people from the effects of another serious depression.

Measurement of an Economy

The goals of a healthy economy are *low inflation, full employment, high productivity,* and *stable prices.*

Inflation is when prices rise. Mild inflation (1 to 5 percent) is good for an economy because it shows the economy is stable. Double digit inflation, which is 10 percent or higher, devastates the economy. When inflation gets that high, people have less money to spend in proportion to the money they earn, because a dollar does not buy as much as it did before. High inflation is especially difficult for people on fixed incomes.

Full employment is established when 96 percent of the total civilian work force is employed, with only 4 percent unemployed. The total civilian work force is defined as all people able to work who are 16 years of age or older.

Productivity is measured by dividing output of production by input of resources and capital. For example, if it takes an untrained person ten hours to build a table, you could increase productivity by training that person. If that person makes the table in seven hours after training, you have increased productivity. You'll produce more tables with fewer work hours. High productivity is a goal of an economy—that is, increasing output in relation to input of labor hours and capital invested.

Stable prices may be defined as prices that do not increase dramatically in a short period of time.

REAL WORLD MARKETING

Launching a Thousand Chips

Famous Amos Chocolate Chip Cookies were the first upscale cookies to come on the market. Started on a dream and borrowed capital, Famous Amos Chocolate Chip Cookie Corporation is now a multimillion-dollar business. The smiling face of Wally Amos is known all over the world. (See page 434 of Chapter 39 for more information on Famous Amos.)

From the mid-1960s to the early 1980s, prices went up threefold in the United States. These high inflationary prices had an impact on all Americans.

Four major indicators help measure whether the economy is achieving its goals. They are *Gross National Product (GNP), standard of living, Consumer Price Index (CPI),* and *unemployment figures.*

Gross National Product

The Gross National Product (GNP) measures the total value of a nation's goods and services produced in a given period of time—generally one year. GNP calculations typically measure four kinds of economic activity.

- Goods and services purchased by individuals (this is the largest portion of the GNP). They include *durable* goods (things that do not wear out quickly, such as refrigerators and automobiles) and *nondurable* goods (things that are used up quickly, such as food and clothing);
- Private investment, which includes money spent on capital goods and business inventories;

- Government purchase of goods and services;
- Goods and services sold to foreign countries, minus what they sold to us.

Changes in the GNP provide information for economic forecasts used by businesses and by the government. These forecasts also help identify where the economy is in the business cycle at that time. Figure 3-2 shows the GNP from 1970 to 1986.

Standard of Living

*The **standard of living** is a measurement of the amount of goods and services that people have in a nation.* This determines their quality of life. To calculate the standard of living, you divide the Gross National Product of a nation by its population. The United States enjoys one of the highest standards of living in the world.

Figure 3-2 **Gross National Product: 1970 to 1986 (In Billions of Dollars)**
The U.S. GNP has increased steadily over the years. What was the percentage increase in the GNP from 1970 to 1986? What does this figure mean?

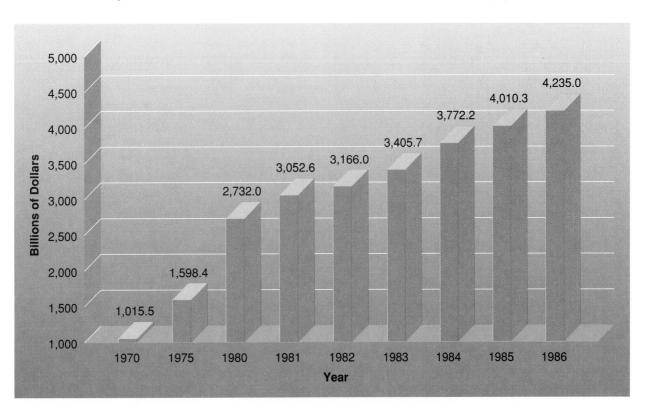

Consumer Price Index

The Consumer Price Index (CPI) measures the change in price over a period time of some 400 specific goods and services used by the average urban household—food, housing, and transportation, for example. It is also called the "cost-of-living" index, because it charts the cost of necessities and inflation.

Prepared monthly by the Bureau of Labor Statistics, the CPI is constructed using a base year valued at 100 as a source of comparison for other years. The percentages of increase or decrease in current prices are then calculated against the base year.

The price of each of the 400 items is averaged. The influence each has on the CPI is weighed against the fraction of the total spending devoted to it. In 1980, for example, about 19 percent of all the urban households' total income was spent on transportation. Thus, transportation that year made up some 19 percent of the total CPI.

Figure 3-3 shows a comparison of the CPIs from 1970 to 1986 for medical care, fuel and other utilities, and food and beverages.

Unemployment Figures

Both the state and federal governments make unemployment figures available. The higher the unemployment rate, the greater the chance of economic recession or depression. Conversely, the lower the unemployment rate, the greater the chance of economic recovery or prosperity. The more people working, the more people are spending and being taxed, and the less social services must be provided. Figure 3-4 shows the unemployment rate from 1983 to 1988.

Other Indicators

Some additional indicators can be classified as *lead* or *lag* indicators. *Lead indicators*, those that occur before business forecasts are made, include the number of business failures, average number of hours worked, residential building contracts, and orders for

Figure 3-3 **Consumer Price Index: 1970 to 1986**
The CPI measures the change in prices over a period of time. Which major group in the Consumer Price Index increased the least from 1970 to 1986? Which group increased the most?

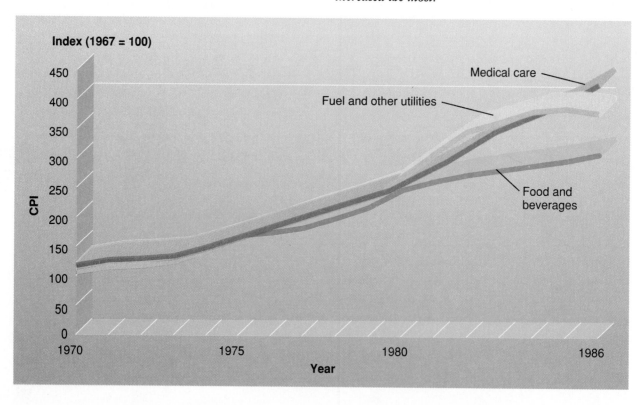

durable goods. *Lag indicators* are those that can occur after a change in the economy has been noticed. They include consumer spending, consumer installment credit, retail store sales, personal income, manufacturer's inventories, and bank rates on business loans.

International Trade

International trade involves the exchange of goods and services between nations. *Goods purchased from other countries are called* **imports**. *Goods sold to other countries are called* **exports**.

Let's look at some reasons why countries trade with one another.

Reasons for International Trade

Most countries are not completely self-sufficient. They need to obtain some of their goods and services from other nations. This is called *economic interdependence,* and it occurs because different countries possess unique resources and specific capabilities.

Unique resources may include a country's weather, raw materials, labor force, capital resources, and location. Some countries have favorable climates for agriculture, such as for growing wheat in the

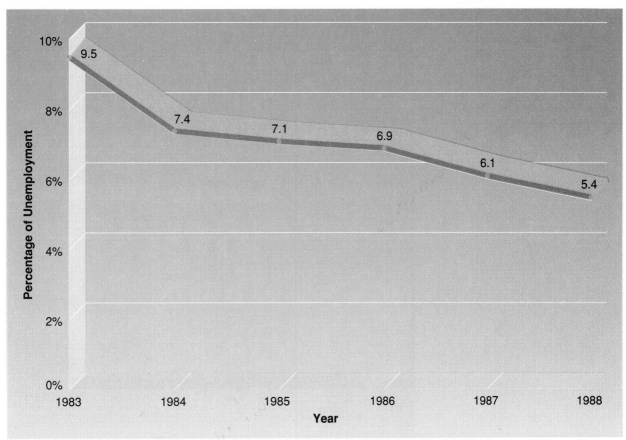

Figure 3-4 **Unemployment Rate: 1983 to 1988**
The graph traces national unemployment as reflected in federal government statistics. What was the trend in unemployment from 1983 to 1988? What does that trend tell you about the U.S. economy during that five-year period?

United States and Canada. The Near East, Africa, and Mexico have crude oil. Other countries have raw materials such as coal or lumber. Some countries have a large labor force, and others have capital and technology necessary for manufacturing.

Because nations need things from each other, they find it advantageous to trade with each other. There are two types of advantages in international trade—*absolute advantage* and *comparative advantage*.

Absolute advantage occurs when a country can produce a product more efficiently than other countries can, and it trades this product for the things that the *other* countries can produce more efficiently.

For example, Colombia grows coffee beans much more efficiently than the United States. But the United States makes machinery more efficiently than Colombia. The theory of *absolute advantage* says that if the United States trades machinery to Colombia for coffee, both nations will benefit.

Even when an absolute advantage does not exist, it can still be valuable for nations to conduct trade. This is because of comparative advantage. *Comparative advantage* refers to the value that a nation gains by selling the goods that it produces more efficiently than other goods. Comparative advantage may be gained in international trade when countries specialize in products well suited for their capabilities. Sup-

The United States could grow coffee beans by using indoor facilities that duplicate the temperature and climate in Colombia. Why does the U.S. instead choose to import coffee beans from Colombia?

pose, for example, that a country is much more efficient than other nations at producing radios, but only slightly more efficient at producing shoes. It would still be to that nation's advantage to sell radios to other nations and buy shoes from them, because it creates more value by using its resources to produce radios.

The Balance of Trade

The difference in value between exports and imports of a nation is called its **balance of trade.** *A positive balance of trade occurs when a nation exports more than it imports.* At the present, the United States has a *negative balance of trade* because it imports more than it exports. (Table 3-1 shows the value of U.S. exports and imports in 1986 and the resulting balance of trade.) This negative trade balance is surprising because the United States is the world's largest exporter. Some people believe the reason for this extraordinary situation is because Americans like to buy more goods and services than people of other nations. Others believe the reason for this negative balance of trade is because the United States has

switched its emphasis from manufacturing and farming to providing services. Therefore, as a nation we import a lot of goods we once manufactured but now find it more economical to purchase abroad. Radios are a good example of this. Although the United States pioneered in the production of radios, most radios now sold in the United States are made in foreign countries, especially Japan.

An unfavorable balance of trade is bad for an economy because it reduces revenue for the country. When more money leaves the country than comes in, the nation becomes a debtor nation. Thus, a negative balance of trade (a trade deficit) increases the national debt of a nation and reduces the nation's GNP.

Some other possible effects of a negative balance of trade are that the citizens of the nation may become unemployed as foreign competitors take business away from the nation's businesses. If this happens, the nation's businesses must improve their products (as U.S. automakers had to do when foreign automakers started producing more gas-efficient, economical automobiles for American consumers). Or, they must switch their manufacturing to products that are more profitable (as many U.S. stereo equipment manufacturers did in the 1980s).

U.S. Exports and Imports for 1986 (In millions of dollars)			
	Exports	**Imports**	**Balance Trade**
*Merchandise, excluding military	224,361	368,700	-144,339
Food, feeds, and beverages	22,580	23,987	- 1,407
Industrial supplies and materials	64,021	102,776	- 38,755
Capital goods, except automotive	79,824	75,446	+ 4,378
Automotive vehicles and parts	25,431	78,084	- 52,653
Consumer goods (nonfood)	14,490	77,802	- 63,312

Note:
* Excludes export of goods under U.S. military agency sales contracts. Includes other end-use items, not shown separately in the itemized listing.

Source: U.S. Bureau of Economic Analysis, *Survey of Current Business*, June, 1987.

Table 3-1
In recent years, the United States has had mainly negative trade balances. What is the only type of merchandise that reflected a positive balance of trade in 1986? How do you explain the positive balance of trade in that category of merchandise?

International Business Concerns

To do business in a foreign country, businesspeople must keep in mind a number of special considerations. Some of these concerns are basic, such as differences in language and customs. Other concerns are political and legal.

A perfect example of the importance of understanding the language occurred when Chevrolet attempted to sell its Nova in South America. Sales did not meet expectations. The reason? The words "No va" in Spanish mean "No go!"

Knowing a country's customs and traditions is also important when conducting business in a foreign country. For example, in certain Asian countries, the customary greeting is a nod of the head instead of a handshake. Public gift giving is expected in some Middle East countries, but gifts must be given privately in some Asian countries.

Colors have meanings that differ in various countries. For example, in the United States, black symbolizes death, but in Japan, the symbol is white.

Legal concerns all firms must address when conducting business abroad may include restrictions on food additives, the use of pesticides, auto emission controls required by law, and patent protection. For example, much U.S. beef cannot be sold in Europe because of the antibiotics we feed our cattle. Foreign-made automobiles sold in the U.S. must be equipped with special emission control equipment. With regard to patent protection, in 1970 Coca-Cola had to stop operations in India when India's government demanded Coca-Cola's secret formula. Thus, each firm must operate under the laws of the country in which it wants to conduct business.

Finally, differences in political ideology can block trade. The United States and China did not trade with each other for almost 20 years for this reason. Once political relations improved between the two countries, the Chinese welcomed the investments of U.S. firms.

1. Identify specific barriers to doing business in foreign countries.
2. If the Soviet Union and the United States experienced improved political relations, how might U.S. businesses react?
3. Why do some foreign-owned companies build factories in the U.S.?

Government Influence on International Trade

Governments may decide to exercise control over their nation's international trade for a variety of reasons.

A government might be concerned with its balance of trade. Or it might wish to protect domestic industries that are just starting out, or it might want to protect domestic jobs.

Also, a government might want to avoid relying on foreign companies for products used for national defense, and it might avoid selling potential military technology to certain other nations. It might want to trade more with nations that share its political ideology.

Some countries, such as the United States, are concerned with controlling both imports and exports. But for most countries, the primary concern is controlling imports. The two most significant trade barriers used for this are *tariffs* and *quotas*.

Tariffs. *A tariff (sometimes called a duty) is a tax on imports.* Tariffs may be used to produce revenue for a country. In the United States, *revenue-producing tariffs* were used as a primary source of income before income taxes were established in 1913. Today, these tariffs are generally low. They may be as little as 25 cents or less per item or pound.

Another type of tariff is protective in nature. A *protective tariff* is generally high to increase the price of imported goods so that domestically made products can compete with imports.

Quotas.

Quotas. An *import quota limits either the quantity or the value of a product that may be imported.* For example, the United States government might place a quota on foreign automobiles that limits the *number* that may be imported. Or, a limit may be put on the *dollar value* of a product that is imported. For example, the government may say that only $1 million worth of Irish crystal may be imported.

Other Factors That Influence Trade

In addition to national governments, there are other organizations that influence international trade. These include *trade alliances, international organizations,* and *multinational companies.*

Trade Alliances. Many countries have formed economic unions or alliances with the goal of reducing tariffs and quotas between member nations. This practice allows each nation to specialize and to trade freely with one another. The most well-known alliance is the *European Economic Community (EEC),* also called the *Common Market.*

The alliances have been important to all nations, but especially to developing nations. By trading with one another, they have been able to secure needed raw materials and enlarge the market for the goods they produced.

International Organizations. There have been several international organizations and trade agreements that influence international trade. Three of the most common are the *Export-Import Bank,* the *International Monetary Fund (IMF),* and the *Organization of Petroleum Exporting Countries (OPEC).*

The *Export-Import Bank,* founded in 1934 by the U.S. government, helps to promote international trade. By providing loans to foreign buyers of U.S. exports, it encourages trade between the United States and other countries. In some cases, it also lends money to foreign governments to promote international trade.

The *International Monetary Fund* is like an international bank. Its objective is to balance exchange rates between countries. Recently it has also been involved in balance of trade problems by helping to stabilize the currencies of countries and by making loans to countries so they can pay their trade debts.

Formed in 1960, the *Organization of Petroleum Exporting Countries (OPEC)* is an organization of oil-producing nations. Its goal for organizing was to con-

trol oil prices by limiting production and exports to other countries. In Figure 3-5 you will see the annual averages of OPEC crude oil prices in dollars per barrel.

Multinational Corporations. Much of America's foreign trade is conducted in the activities of *multinational corporations.* A multinational corporation has headquarters in one country and does business in several countries. Multinational corporations sell their goods and services to many nations and make decisions based on world-wide economic factors. The United States has many multinational corporations, including IBM, General Motors, Exxon, Mobil, Sears, General Electric, and Ford Motor Company.

Multinational corporations enjoy the best of many nations. When they want to obtain raw materials, they build plants in countries where those materials are plentiful and inexpensive. By doing business in several countries, they often increase their ability to sell their products as well.

Figure 3-5 **OPEC Crude Oil Prices Annual Average in Dollars Per Barrel**

OPEC was created to control oil prices. According to this graph, what happened in 1978 to the price of oil sold by OPEC countries?

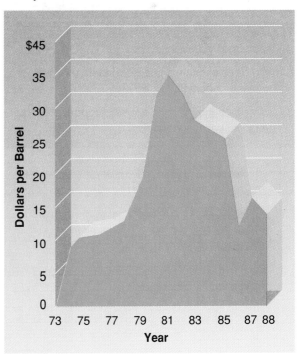

CHAPTER 3 REVIEW

VOCABULARY REVIEW

Write one or two paragraphs incorporating these nine vocabulary words.

business cycle

Gross National Product
  (GNP)

standard of living

Consumer Price Index (CPI)

imports

exports

balance of trade

tariff

quota

FACT AND IDEA REVIEW

1. What are the four phases of a business cycle?

2. How can consumers and the government have an effect on the economy?

3. What are the goals of a healthy economy?

4. Name four major indicators used to measure the economy.

5. How does double-digit inflation devastate the economy?

6. When does a positive balance of trade occur?

7. Describe two possible effects of a *negative* balance of trade.

8. Why does economic interdependence occur between nations?

9. Why do countries often exercise control over their nation's international trade?

CRITICAL THINKING

1. Explain how businesses react to periods of prosperity and recovery, as well as to a recession.

2. What is full employment? Why is full employment the goal of all economies?

3. Why is the GNP such a good indicator of the economic health of a nation?

4. In what way is the Consumer Price Index an indicator of inflation?

5. How can the United States be the world's largest exporter yet still suffer from a negative balance of trade? How do you think this problem could be solved?

6. Hong Kong has very few natural resources. Yet, it is one of the most successful industrialized nations in the world. How do you explain that success?

7. Imagine two trading partners: Nation A and Nation B. Nation A is good at producing apples, but bad at producing VCRs. Nation B is good at producing VCRs, but bad at producing apples. Is it wise for these two countries to trade with each other? Why? Is this an example of absolute advantage or of comparative advantage?

   Now imagine Nation R and Nation S. Nation R is much better than Nation S at producing shoes; it is only slightly better than Nation S at producing bananas. Will it benefit both countries for Nation R to trade shoes to Nation S for bananas? Why? Is this an example of absolute advantage or comparative advantage?

8. All states in the United States trade freely with each other and follow guidelines established by the government for interstate commerce. Since that is the case, would you consider the United States to be an economic alliance like the Common Market? Explain your position.

9. How can political differences in ideology affect international trade?

10. Why would a country impose tariffs or quotas if it wanted to be active in international trade?

11. How do trade alliances and international organizations influence international trade? Give an example of each.

USING BASIC SKILLS

Math

1. Read Figure 3-2 on page 27 and indicate in which year the GNP first reached $3,000 billion.

Communication

2. As a lobbyist in Washington, D.C., write two paragraphs to prepare for an important meeting on the issue of recession. Your business group wants you to explain why the Federal Reserve banking system should not increase interest rates on loans. Your main point must involve how that policy will negatively affect American businesses.

Human Relations

3. A person from another country enters your store and wants to buy something but does not speak any English. What would you do?

4. A customer demands to know where the blouse she wants to buy was made. If it wasn't made in the United States, she will not buy it. You find the label that indicates the cotton blouse was made in a small developing nation. What will you say to the customer?

APPLICATION PROJECT

Read the following excerpts from an article that appeared in the April 17, 1978, issue of *Time* magazine. Write a 100-word summary of the article. Then write a brief explanation of how each strategy mentioned might be expected to fight inflation.

This week, barring a last-minute change of plans, President Jimmy Carter was to make his first substantive statement about an issue that suddenly has become the nation's No. 1 worry: inflation. In a speech to the American Society of Newspaper Editors in Washington, Carter was also to discuss some of the nation's other pressing economic problems: energy and the fall in value of the dollar overseas. But the stress was to be on combatting the rise in prices that threatens to undermine all the achievements of the Administration in promoting economic growth and reducing unemployment . . . .

Rather than outline a comprehensive, drastic policy, Carter was expected to announce a series of small but symbolic, and concrete, steps that the Government would take in order to set an example of anti-inflationary restraint for the rest of the nation. Some probable highlights of the talk:

- A pledge to hold the federal budget for fiscal 1979 within the targeted $60 billion range. That would at least imply a threat to veto any spending bill that seems likely to push the deficit higher . . . .

- An announcement that the 6% pay increase scheduled this fall for 1.4 million federal civilian employees and 2 million military personnel will be trimmed to 5.5%. . . . All Carter's advisers agree that the President must scale down the federal pay raise if he is to have any hope of getting unions in the private sector to take his pleas for wage-price restraint seriously. . . .

- A confession that many well-intentioned federal regulatory efforts contribute to inflation by raising industries' costs, and a pledge to change.

- A renewed plea to unions and industry to hold down wage-price boosts. . . .

Carter's plans could scarcely be called either a drastic or a comprehensive program. . . . But the outlines of Carter's plan, if they hold, do at least constitute a useful recognition that the Government must begin any attack on inflation by getting its own house in order. . . .

Copyright 1978 *Time* Inc. Reprinted by permission.

PART

2

BUSINESS AND MARKETING ESSENTIALS

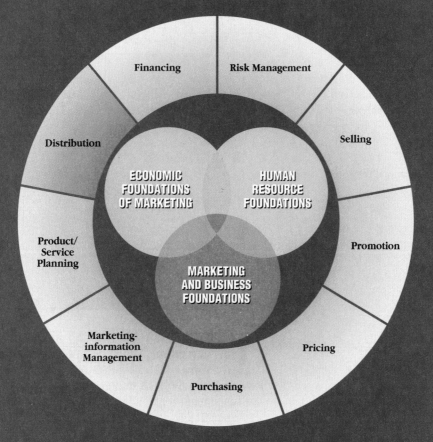

Financing

Risk Management

Distribution

Selling

ECONOMIC FOUNDATIONS OF MARKETING

HUMAN RESOURCE FOUNDATIONS

Product/ Service Planning

Promotion

MARKETING AND BUSINESS FOUNDATIONS

Marketing- information Management

Pricing

Purchasing

CHAPTERS

OBJECTIVES

After completing this chapter, you will be able to:

1. describe the role of business in the United States,

2. describe the roles of production, marketing, and management,

3. define each of the five types of utilities, and

4. discuss aspects of social responsibility in marketing.

WORDS TO KNOW

business
production
marketplace
marketing
management
finance
utility
ethics
consumerism

What Is Business?

You learned in Chapter 1 about the needs that people have for things we call goods and services. Now you will discover how individuals and groups work to satisfy these needs as well as to make a profit by going into business.

Specifically, you will look at the wide range of businesses producing goods and services in the United States, and how these products are sold in the marketplace. So get ready for a fascinating look at the issues of setting up and running a business in our free enterprise economy.

The Scope of U.S. Business

*A **business** is an activity that satisfies economic needs by planning, organizing, and controlling resources to produce and market goods or services.*

In a free market economy, such as the United States, people in business may earn a profit for efficiently satisfying the needs and wants of consumers.

For more than 100 years, the free enterprise system of the United States has nourished some of the most successful businesses in the world.

For example, in 1871, George Huntington Hartford created The Great Atlantic and Pacific Tea Company (called A & P). The world's first giant chain-store system, A & P has survived more than 100 years. In 1988 it had a market value of $1.8 billion and sales of $9.8 billion.

Today there are many successful U.S. companies even larger than A & P. According to *Business Week* magazine, in 1989, a thousand U.S. companies were valued at $332 million or more each—topped by IBM at $66.3 billion!

Thousands of new businesses are started in the U.S. each year, many by people who want the chance to work for themselves in the hope of making at least a moderate profit. And some people are very successful at it. Microsoft, the computer software company started in 1980 by Bill Gates when he was just 18 years old, had profits of $151 million in 1988.

The economic policies of the U.S. government encourage people to start new businesses. Because start-up costs for a manufacturing business are beyond the financial reach of most people, retail and service industries are popular options for new businesses. In fact, the cost of starting up any type of business makes it wise to start small.

A small business is one that is operated by only one or a few individuals. While some new businesses, such as Microsoft, grow rapidly, many continue to operate successfully as small businesses.

There are thousands of these "Mom and Pop" businesses, including neighborhood grocery markets, florists, gift shops, photocopy and print shops, and secretarial services. About 95 percent of all U.S. businesses are classified as small businesses, and they employ over half of the private-sector work force (those who are not employed by government agencies).

About 95 percent of all U.S. businesses are "small businesses," and they employ more than half of the private-sector work force. Name two successful small businesses in your neighborhood.

Nonprofit Organizations

Profit is the motivating factor in starting a business. Most people want to earn as much profit from their business efforts as possible.

But there are many service organizations operated with no intention of earning a profit for those who initiate or manage the organization. Examples of such nonprofit organizations are Boys/Girls Clubs of America, the YMCA and YWCA. Like any business, nonprofit organizations must hire employees and pay the costs and expenses of running the organization. To pay for those things, the nonprofit organization must generate income. But all the income remaining after expenses are paid goes for the charitable cause outlined in the organization's charter.

In addition to charitable institutions, there are other organizations that operate with many of the characteristics of businesses, but they are not intended to earn a profit. Many government agencies and services, such as public schools, fall into this category. These organizations are said to be part of the *public sector*. Businesses not associated with government agencies are part of the *private sector*.

Types of Businesses

There is a wide range of types of businesses in the United States, and there are different ways of classifying them. One way is by looking at the type of product a business provides. There are businesses that provide goods, such as the bread sold in a supermarket, or the flour sold to a bakery to make the bread. There are businesses that provide services, such as the dry cleaners that clean your clothing, or the industrial maintenance company that cleans your school or office after hours. There are also businesses, such as newspapers and magazines, that provide information and ideas. You will learn more about different types of businesses in Chapters 6 and 7.

An airline is a business providing a service. What else can a business do besides provide a service of its own?

The two primary functions of business are *production* of ideas, goods, and services, and *marketing* of ideas, goods, and services. These primary functions depend on an important support activity—*management*—which plans, organizes, and controls all available resources to reach company goals.

Production

Production is creating, growing, manufacturing, or improving on something produced by someone else. A song writer *creates* a song. A farmer *grows* wheat. Ford Motor Company *manufactures* cars. Weyerhauser Lumber Company of Tacoma, Washington, *produces* lumber by cutting down tall trees and slicing them up in saw mills. The raw goods, freshly-cut trees, are thus processed into usable lumber and shipped all over the country. Mobile home manufacturing companies buy the processed lumber, which serves as one of the main materials in the manufacture of mobile homes. Others buy lumber, too, including building contractors who use it to build everything from playhouses to skyscrapers. Harvesting the trees, cutting them into lumber, and making the lumber into buildings are all production activities.

Marketing

When goods or services are created, grown, or manufactured, they must be sold in the marketplace. *The marketplace is wherever a product is sold to a buyer.* It may be in a store, an outdoor market, or simply wherever two or more people agree to buy and sell a product.

The lumber processed by Weyerhauser earns no profit for the company and cannot be used for building anything until the *exchange process* has taken place.

The *exchange process* occurs when customers exchange their money, or their promise to pay, for the goods and services offered. The exchange process is the focus of a broad range of activities that we call *marketing*. *Marketing is determining and satisfying the needs and wants of consumers through the exchange process.*

Production involves creating, growing, manufacturing, or improving on something produced by someone else. What raw good is being used here in the production of a product?

Management

Businesses use natural resources, labor, and capital to produce and market goods or services. These resources must be brought together through good management.

Management is the process of achieving company goals by effective use of resources. Management functions include *planning*, *organizing*, and *controlling*. Because resources must be managed very carefully for a company to earn a profit, good financial planning and accurate records must also be kept. Of course, federal and state tax laws require proper accounting procedures. Large businesses have finance and accounting departments to provide financial planning and accounting support for management.

The word *finance* has several meanings in business. It can mean money or anything that can be sold very quickly to get money. Or, it can mean borrowing money. You may have heard someone talk about *financing* a car. This means borrowing money to buy the car.

As a supporting function for management, finance means money management. Proper accounting procedures provide information needed for controlling financial resources. In small companies, financial planning and accounting are often combined into one department. In larger companies, the finance department is responsible for planning the use of money to reach company goals. Using accounting department records to show what has occurred in the past, the finance department prepares financial forecasts for the company's future.

The exchange process occurs when customers exchange their money, or their promise to pay, for goods or services offered for sale. The exchange process is the focus of what broad range of activities?

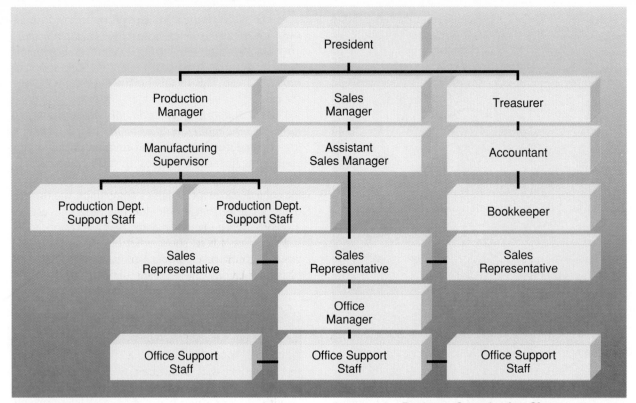

Figure 4-1 **Business Organization Chart**
An organization chart helps define worker relationships in larger companies. How might this chart change if it reflected the structure of a small business?

Who are the people who manage a business's resources? The chief executive officer of a large company is a manager. So is the owner of a small business. Heads of departments, such as personnel, purchasing, and sales are managers, too, but at a lower level. Their titles will vary, depending on the type of business and the individual company. In some businesses, top-level managers are called administrators.

The Business Utilities

You have learned that there are two basic business functions: the *production* of ideas, goods, and services, and the *marketing* of ideas, goods, and services. One way of looking at the different roles that marketing and production have in a business operation is to look at the different *utilities* they create. *Utility is an economic term that means value added.*

To sell products, businesspeople must do something to make the products have value and use. The types of value that are added can be demonstrated with one of the simplest businesses imaginable—the lemonade stand.

The lemons are raw materials. When you mix them with sugar and water to make lemonade, you are creating a product. When you create the product, you are adding value to the raw materials. This is the value of *form*. Economists call it *form utility*.

You set up a stand on the sidewalk where it's convenient and useful for people driving or walking past to buy your product. This adds value to the product. Economists call it *place utility*.

People like to buy lemonade on warm summer afternoons, so you make a point of setting up your stand at those times. Making the product available when people need it also adds value to the product. Economists call this *time utility*.

You put up a sign on the corner that tells people about your lemonade. This informs them about something they might like to have, and that also adds value to a product. This is *information utility*.

Finally, not all of your neighbors have change when they pass by your lemonade stand. Many of them have just been out jogging, and they don't carry money when they do that. So you allow them to pay you just once, on Friday, for all the lemonade they have consumed in the previous five days. This also adds value to the product. This is *possession utility*.

The Production Utility

In the preceding example, the first utility to be created was *form utility*. This is the utility created by production. The manufacturer adds value to each raw material used in making a product by putting those materials together to form a final product that is more useful than its individual parts are by themselves. For example, the parts of a pen, such as the plastic outer shell, the inner tube that holds the ink, the ink itself, the point of the pen, and the top of the pen are useless by themselves. However, once all the parts are put together to make the pen, those parts have increased value or utility as a final product.

The Marketing Utilities

Other utilities that add value to a product are those that help to get the product into the hands of the consumer. These are called *marketing utilities*. The marketing utilities are *place*, *time*, *possession*, and *information*.

Place utility includes all activities involved in getting the product from the producer to the place *where* the consumer can buy it. These activities include transportation, refrigeration for perishable items, storage by the producer and the wholesaler, and storage and display by the retailer.

Time utility involves the movement and planning necessary to get products to consumers *when* they want to buy them. This means, for example, that producers, wholesalers, and retailers must make the necessary plans to get products to consumers at the right time of year. It also means that retailers must stay open to make the goods available when consumers want to buy them.

Possession utility is the actual exchange of a product for money. Every time a product is sold to someone else in the channel of distribution, possession utility is involved. The manufacturer may add value to a product by permitting the wholesaler to buy products and pay for them 30 days later. The retailer may add possession utility to a product by accepting credit or checks for payment. Retailers may also offer layaway plans or installment credit. Possession utility is involved every time legal ownership of a product changes hands.

Information utility involves communication with the consumer. Salespeople provide information to customers by explaining the features and benefits of products. Displays communicate information, too. Packaging and advertising inform consumers about qualities of a product, ingredients, and safety precautions, as well as care and use of the product. Advertising also lets consumers know where to buy the item and how much it costs. Many manufacturers provide owners' manuals to explain how to use their products. (We will talk more about communication with customers in Part Four, Selling, and Part Five, Promotion.)

Benefits of Marketing

There are two important benefits of marketing: *lowering prices* and *developing new and improved products*.

Lowering Prices

Marketing activities can help keep prices down. Advertising, for example, can do this by increasing demand and thus making it more profitable to manufacture and sell items in larger quantities. When a manufacturer makes a product in larger quantities, it can reduce the unit cost of each product. This is because there are *fixed costs*—such as the rent on a building—that remain the same whether the company produces 10 units or 10,000 units. (See Chapter 41 for more details on *fixed costs* and *variable costs*.) When a company produces a larger quantity of a product, it spends less per unit on fixed costs. Thus, it can charge a lower price to consumers.

Marketing activities, such as advertising and promotion, can also help lower prices by increasing competition. Increased competition forces businesses to improve their efficiency so they can lower prices to attract customers.

Hand-held calculators are an example of how competition and marketing activities combined to lower consumer prices. When these calculators were first put on the market, they ranged in price from $50 to $100. As increased consumer demand encouraged more businesses to enter the market and produce more calculators, the quality and selection of calculators increased, while their prices decreased.

Today, you can buy an inexpensive solar-powered calculator for as low as $5. Other products, such as microwave ovens, computers, large screen television sets, and compact disc players, fall into this category of goods that has decreased in price due to the effect of marketing activities.

Competition and market activities helped produce better, lower-priced hand-held calculators to meet consumer demand. Think of two other products that vastly improved in design and price after the original models were first introduced in the market.

Developing New and Improved Products

Marketing activities also guide producers in their search to develop new and improved products that better satisfy consumers' needs. Through research, companies strive to develop new products and improve old ones.

Disposable diapers, for example, went through many years of research and development before they were finally ready to market. Procter and Gamble spent years developing Pampers disposable diapers, then learned through research that its original prototype was not acceptable and that the price was more than consumers wanted to spend. The company redesigned the product several times, and conducted research in several parts of the country, before the final product was sold to consumers. Further market research has led to more improvements in the product over the years.

Not all new products are successful. Companies can spend huge sums of money on research and still produce a loser. The Ford Edsel, sold in the late 1950s, was researched for ten years before it was put on the market. But Ford did not realize that consumers' tastes in car design had changed significantly during that time period. As a result, the Edsel was a failure.

To be successful, businesses must spend money to learn about customers' needs and wants. They also must make enough profit to allow for failures and still remain in business.

Marketing and Social Responsibility

In a free enterprise system, anyone can choose to go into business. But there are state and federal laws that encourage fair business practices and protect consumers, workers, and investors, as well as our environment. Apart from following the law, should business have any further social responsibility? Some businesses feel they should.

For example, Ben & Jerry's Homemade, Inc., an ice cream manufacturer in Vermont, donates 7.5 percent of its pre-tax earnings to the disadvantaged and the needy, as well as to groups that strive for social change and environmental protection.

McDonald's Corporation sponsors the Ronald McDonald House, a facility where children with cancer can live with their parents while the children receive medical treatment.

The Body Shop, a firm that manufactures cosmetics and personal care items, uses in its products all natural ingredients that are not under any environmental threat. It will not sell aerosols, and it keeps its packaging to a minimum to reduce waste.

Let's look at some of the concerns that companies must consider to be socially responsible.

Ethical and Legal Concerns

Ethics are guidelines for good behavior. Ethical behavior is based on knowing the difference between right and wrong—and doing what is right. It considers the well-being of everyone in the society.

In most situations, ethical concerns involving products or marketing are governed by laws. Such things as bait-and-switch advertising, price fixing, and selling unsafe products are prohibited.

Ethical questions that involve debate between our guaranteed freedom of speech and our guaranteed freedom to compete are not as easily answered. For example, if it is ethical to make such products as tobacco and liquor, should the manufacturers be allowed to market them as glamorous, feminine, romantic, manly?

To make the right ethical choices, marketers must answer these three basic questions:

1. Is the practice right? fair? honest?
2. What would happen if the product was marketed differently?
3. What practice will result in the greatest good for the greatest number of people?

In making ethical choices, businesses sometimes look at the legal issues involved in addition to their perceived social responsibility.

For example, sometimes firms face government recall of a product. To reduce losses that could arise from future lawsuits, a socially responsible business will recall an unsafe product before the government forces it to do so. Those irresponsible businesses who will not recall a product on their own will be forced to do so by the Consumer Protection Agency.

In some cases, businesses may recall products even if they are not responsible for its faulty design or the problems it could potentially cause. For example, Tylenol capsules were recalled when a person died after taking a capsule poisoned by someone outside the company. The company immediately alerted all Tylenol users to return the capsules to their stores. All stores took the product off their shelves. The manufacture of Tylenol was temporarily discontinued. The manufacturer then worked with other drug manufacturers to develop tamper-proof packaging. Thanks to this, most over-the-counter drugs today are packaged with a seal around the bottle top or around the entire package to prevent tampering.

Consumption of Natural Resources

The concern for consumption of our natural resources became crucial during the oil crisis of the 1970s. In this particular case, car manufacturers responded by producing smaller, more fuel-efficient autos. Consumers responded by car pooling.

In the 1990s, conservation of our natural resources will depend heavily on cooperation of business, government, and consumers. Some local governments now require consumers to participate in recycling of glass, plastic, and aluminum through the local garbage collection service. Many companies are now making a significant effort to conserve. Alcoa, for example, recycles 15 billion cans a year, a savings of about 60 percent of the aluminum the company uses for cans.

Recycling is important in the United States, which has been called a "throw away" society. We have only 5 percent of the world's population but produce 50 percent of its trash. Each year we throw away 10 million tons of appliances, 200,000 tons of copper, and 1 million tons of aluminum. We also toss out 40 billion glass bottles, 85 billion cans, and 200 million tires. Much of this garbage could be recycled.

Environmental Issues

Almost all environmental issues that affect us are governed by laws. For example, improper disposal of medical, chemical, and other hazardous wastes is prohibited by law. Socially responsible businesses follow the laws and understand their role in helping to preserve our natural resources.

The federal government established the Environmental Protection Agency (EPA) to protect the environment from further pollution. The EPA is probably best known for its efforts to reduce the smog caused

The gasoline shortages of the 1970s made Americans very much aware of the fact that our natural resources are limited. Oil and gas are known as what type of resources?

from automobile emissions. All automobile manufacturers have had to modify their engines to meet EPA standards. Lead in gasoline is a dangerous pollutant, so the EPA has required that all cars built since 1975 must use unleaded gasoline.

Fluorocarbon propellants were used in most hairspray, insecticide, and paint cans until the late 1970s. But fluorocarbons drift into the upper atmosphere where they can decompose and destroy the ozone layer that has protected the earth from the sun's ultraviolet radiation for millions of years. Some socially responsible companies voluntarily quit using fluorocarbon propellants, substituting other propellants or using pump sprays. Ultimately, the EPA banned the use of fluorocarbon propellants, but not before a portion of the ozone layer was destroyed. As a result, scientists say that when we expose our skin to the sun, we receive as much cancer-causing radiation in a few minutes as our parents did in six hours in the 1950s.

Agricultural pesticides have been used for years to grow bigger crops and more attractive fruits and vegetables. Some pesticides, though, have had harmful effects on fish, animals, and ultimately on people. The EPA is constantly checking pesticides, some of which have already polluted our land, streams, lakes, and underground water supplies. When it is determined that a pesticide causes cancer or has other harmful effects in humans or animals, the EPA prohibits its further use.

Industrial waste poses another problem for the environment. Industrial waste often finds its way through porous soil into the underground water supplies used by cities. According to the EPA, the greatest amounts of hazardous waste are generated by such heavy industries as the chemical, electroplating, refining, rubber, textile, and plastics industries. Many states have passed laws controlling disposal of industrial wastes. But in some areas the most dangerous wastes are still not being disposed of safely. The EPA has increased its efforts to enforce proper waste disposal. And some manufacturing companies' executives have even been sentenced to prison for violation of safe disposal standards.

Consumerism

While social responsibility involves the relationship of marketing with all of society, *consumerism* involves only the relationship of marketing with those who buy the company's products and services. *Consumerism is the societal effort to protect consumer rights by putting legal, moral, and economic pressure on business.* This effort is shared by individual consumers, consumer groups, government, and socially responsible business leaders.

Consumerism had its beginning in the early 1900s and focused on product purity, product shortages, antitrust, postal rates, and banking. From the 1930s to the 1950s, consumerism concentrated on product safety, labeling, misrepresentation, deceptive advertising, consumer refunds, and bank failures.

The greatest growth in consumerism took place from the early 1960s until about 1980. It involved all areas of marketing. The beginning of this consumer period was dominated by President Kennedy's *Consumer Bill of Rights* which stated that consumers have four basic rights:

1. To be informed and protected against fraud, deceit, and misleading statements, and to be educated in the wise use of financial resources.
2. To be protected from unsafe products.
3. To have a choice of goods and services.
4. To have a voice in product and marketing decisions made by government and business.

From Garbage to Goods

Americans throw out 160 million tons of solid waste every year, and three-quarters of it is hauled to landfills. By 1995, half of the nation's 5,499 landfills will be full.

Picturing a future with mountains of garbage piling up caused cities across the land to require massive recycling programs for glass, paper, and plastic.

Some of the recycled materials are easily marketed. The nation's largest plastic recycler, Wellman, Inc., accepted most of the 1.5 billion two-liter soda bottles turned in for recycling. Wellman recycled the plastic bottles into a variety of new products, including carpeting, tennis balls, and plastic moldings for new cars.

But the supply is greater than the demand for some recycled materials. Pioneer Paper Company of Minneapolis-St. Paul recycles 40,000 tons of paper every year. In 1989, the growing supply of collected newspapers had depressed the price of newsprint paper so much that Pioneer was considering getting out of that business.

Concerned about the lack of demand for recycled materials, state officials from New York, Rhode Island, and other Northeast states met with publishers and paper industry representatives to encourage use of recycled paper. As a result, inquiries about recycled newsprint increased 100 percent in six months. Garden State Paper Co. of New Jersey is looking for a site to build a new recycling plant.

Some companies have decided that using recycled materials is a marketing necessity. Procter and Gamble now markets Tide, Cheer, and Downy in bottles made from recycled plastic. The company has also begun a pilot project in Seattle for recycling disposable diapers. The plastic, pulp, and absorbent gel are separated and sanitized. The pulp is made into cardboard boxes and the plastic is turned into flowerpots.

When New York began a city-wide recycling program in 1989, a 16-person marketing group was established to create markets for recycled goods. Worried about what to do with ceramics and junk glass, New York began mixing crushed glass with asphalt. "Glassphalt" is now used to pave the streets of New York.

1. Why would a company be eager to advertise to the public that it uses recycled materials?
2. How are consumers who use recycled products showing social responsibility?

Several widely-read books gave impetus to consumerism during the 1960s and 1970s. Ralph Nader's *Unsafe at Any Speed* focused public attention on what the automobile industry could do to make cars safer. Rachel Carson's *Silent Spring* detailed how marketing contributed to a decaying environment. Vance Packard's *Hidden Persuaders* revealed marketing's influence on people.

Consumers were increasingly dissatisfied with poor quality products, deceptive business practices, and the lack of concern for consumer complaints. They got angry and demanded action. The Federal Trade Commission responded by expanding its role in consumer issues.

In the 1980s, consumerism became less active than in the two previous decades. It has now achieved many of its goals. The quality of products and services has improved, and more businesses listen to customer complaints and try to satisfy their concerns. Some companies now maintain 24-hour customer telephone service.

In the 1990s, companies are much more responsive to customer complaints and environmental concerns than they have been in the past 30 years. Many more companies now consider consumer concerns when developing their marketing plans. Product containers that can be recycled, for example, are a direct response to consumers' environmental concerns.

CHAPTER 4 REVIEW

VOCABULARY REVIEW

Write a brief definition of each word, based on your reading of the chapter.

business
production
marketplace
marketing
management

finance
utility
ethics
consumerism

FACT AND IDEA REVIEW

1. What does a business do and why?

2. Provide an example of both a private-sector and a public-sector organization. How are they different?

3. Name the two primary functions of business.

4. What are the three major functions of management in business?

5. Tell what is meant by form utility, place utility, time utility, possession utility, and information utility.

6. What are the two important benefits of marketing?

7. What are the concerns that socially-responsible businesses consider?

8. How has consumerism affected the way businesses conduct themselves?

CRITICAL THINKING

1. What does living in a free enterprise economy mean to you?

2. Why would someone want to start a small business? Describe the success of a small business with which you are familiar.

3. Do you think that products which are potentially harmful to consumers (like cigarettes and alcohol) should be advertised?

4. How should industries that pollute the environment be handled by local governments and by the federal government?

5. As a consumer, what could you do to combat poor quality products and unethical business practices?

USING BASIC SKILLS

Math

1. If the local recycling center pays $.06 per pound for aluminum cans, how many pounds of cans would it take to get back $10?

2. The sales in your electrical parts store have been increasing at a rate of 10 percent per month. Sales for this month were $3,500. If sales continue to increase at the same rate, what do you project the sales to be two months from now?

Communication

3. You are the manager of a book store, and you have just hired a new salesclerk. Ask a classmate to play the part of the new employee. Then inform the new employee of his or her responsibilities. Also describe the standards you expect the new employee to meet.

4. Write a letter to a local government official describing the importance and benefits of recycling.

Human Relations

5. You work for a company that produces textiles, and you have just discovered that the company has been disposing of its wastes in a manner that is unsafe for the environment. How will you handle your concern?

6. You are the manager of a retail office supply store. You have set a high standard for customer service, yet you've noticed one of your employees interacting rudely with the customers. Have a classmate play the part of the employee. Then talk with him or her about the situation.

APPLICATION PROJECTS

1. With a group of other students, research the recycling centers in your community. Make a chart with information about the centers, including their locations, their hours of operation, the materials they accept, and the rates they pay for those materials. Then make copies of your chart. Distribute the copies to families in your neighborhood.

2. Find a local "Mom and Pop" business and interview the owners. Ask them to give you a brief history of the business. Also find out what they like and dislike about having their own business. Then give a five-minute oral report, telling the rest of your class what you learned.

3. Think of a project that would help your school conserve resources and protect the environment. Then write an editorial for the school newspaper. Explain your idea, and try to persuade other students to participate in your project.

4. Read one of the following books:
   - *Unsafe at Any Speed* by Ralph Nader
   - *Silent Spring* by Rachel Carson
   - *Hidden Persuaders* by Vance Packard

   Plan and present a five-minute oral report on the book you read. Give a 200-word written summary of the book. Tell what you think makes the book important.

5. Read about a specific nonprofit organization, such as the Boys Club of America, the YWCA, or United Way. Find out about the history of the organization and the services it provides. Learn as much as you can about how the organization is run, and think about the advantages of working for that nonprofit organization. Present your findings and ideas in a five-minute report.

6. Study the scene in the picture below. Then write an explanation of what is happening with respect to products, marketplace, the exchange process, and marketing.

7. Many companies in the United States take a special interest in social responsibility. Among the large companies known for such interests are McDonald's, Johnson & Johnson, John Deere & Company, Dayton-Hudson, Control Data, Motorola, and NCR. Choose one of these companies, or select another company—small or large—with a particular interest in social responsibility. Research that company's policies and practices, and then write a 150- to 200-word report about the company's social responsibility.

5

After completing this chapter, you will be able to:

1. identify the two goals (objectives) of the marketing concept,

2. distinguish between a sales oriented and a market oriented business,

3. define market and market segmentation,

4. explain how a market can be segmented,

5. identify the four *P*'s of the marketing mix and explain how they should relate to a target market, and

6. explain the concept of market share.

market
mass marketing
market segmentation
geographics
demographics
lifestyle
marketing mix
market share
market position

Marketing Concepts

Businesses constantly try to improve their products to remain competitive and increase their profits. To do so, they study their potential customers. Once they have a good idea of who their customers are, they attempt to reach them through marketing efforts.

This chapter will introduce you to marketing concepts used to direct marketing strategies. These concepts help businesses compete and succeed in reaching potential customers. They also lay the foundation for further study of marketing functions you will explore in future chapters.

The Marketing Philosophy

Profitable businesses generally follow a plan for success called the *marketing concept*. The marketing concept recognizes two main objectives for a business: to satisfy customers' needs and wants, and to make a profit.

To achieve these two goals, businesses spend money on research to learn what consumers need and want. They coordinate their activities so that the personnel in all the various departments, such as shipping, receiving, marketing, financing, and production, are committed to reaching the two goals. Businesses also choose short- and long-range objectives that will guide them as they seek success in both consumer satisfaction and in increasing profits.

Sales vs. Marketing Orientation

At one time, most companies were *sales oriented*. That is, their goods and services were produced and sold without regard for consumer preferences. Little attempt was made to research consumers' needs or desires. Goals were limited to short-term profits. If customers were reluctant to buy a product, a stronger or different sales pitch was used. Some companies may still practice this approach, but it is not likely to bring long-term success today.

In contrast, a *marketing oriented* company focuses on consumer satisfaction and directs company resources to produce the goods and services customers want. The successful marketing oriented company sets long-range goals that are achieved by responding to changing and emerging consumer preferences.

Recognizing Opportunities

Maintaining a consumer orientation helps a company recognize important opportunities for success. The needs of consumers can change, and a consumer orientation will help a company anticipate and respond to those changes.

In the 1980s, Black & Decker spotted marketing opportunities by focusing on how consumers were changing. Through its marketing research, the company learned that the size of the average U.S. household was getting smaller, and that there was an increase in the number of single-person households. It also recognized that consumers wanted appliances that were easy-to-use and small enough to fit in smaller apartments and their equally small kitchens and cabinets.

Black & Decker's response to consumer preferences was to develop space-saver appliances that could be mounted under kitchen cabinets. They developed other convenient appliances, too—the Dustbuster, the Spotlighter flashlight, the cordless screwdriver, the cordless knife, the cordless blender, and a mini food processor. In response to people's fears about forgetting to turn off the iron or coffee maker before leaving the house, the company developed auto-shutoff models for both appliances.

Black & Decker's decision to develop convenient and safe home appliances was based largely on its analysis of the needs and wants of American consumers. In the following sections of this chapter, you will learn more about how assessing consumer needs and wants is a major part of marketing.

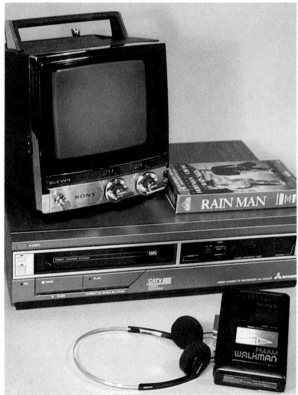

Many firms spot marketing opportunities by studying consumer preferences and lifestyles. What consumer preferences and lifestyle changes are reflected in these products?

What is a Market

To be successful, a business must identify the group of potential customers it wants to reach. These customers must be able and willing to buy enough products for the business to make a profit. This grouping is called a *market*.

A **market** *is defined as all the potential customers that share common needs and wants, and who have the ability and willingness to buy the product.*

There are two basic types of markets for products: the *consumer market* and the *industrial market*. The *consumer market* is all potential customers who will buy the product for *personal* use. The *industrial market* is all potential customers who will buy the product for *business* use. (These two markets are discussed in detail in Chapter 6.)

Marketing Approaches

There are two approaches that firms can use to sell their products in the marketplace: *mass marketing* and *market segmentation*.

Mass Marketing

Mass marketing is using a single marketing plan for one product to reach all consumers. Products that are mass marketed generally have universal appeal and few basic features to differentiate them from competitors.

To mass market a product, businesses select a single, general advertising theme that appeals to most people who use the product. The theme is designed to keep the name of the product before the general public.

Chewing gum is often mass marketed because it has general appeal and few features to distinguish it from its competitors. So each chewing gum manufacturer tries to carve a niche in the market with the one basic benefit of buying its gum. Some companies stress that their gum has good taste or long-lasting flavor. Trident chewing gum, for example, is billed as helping to prevent cavities. Doublemint is advertised as fun to chew ("double your pleasure, double your fun").

Products that are mass marketed have universal appeal and few features to differentiate them from competitors. What slogans have the manufacturers of each of these products used to carve a niche for them in the market?

Household cleaners also have universal appeal and can be mass marketed because they promise one specific benefit—the ability to clean well. Each cleaner has few features to distinguish it from other household cleaners. So manufacturers of household cleaners use imagery such as a trade character (Mr. Clean) or such unique characteristics as a specific scent (Pinesol) to sell their products.

Market Segmentation

Most companies develop products and marketing plans to reach a specific group *within* a market called a *target market*. *Identifying target markets and developing products that appeal to them is called market segmentation.*

Target markets can be classified (or "segmented") according to specific characteristics such as *geographics, demographics, lifestyle*, or *product benefits*. (In Chapter 6 you'll learn more about the field of *demographics* and how it is used to look at these characteristics.)

Geographics. The term *geographics refers to studies about the characteristics of where potential customers live.* One geographic characteristic is population density. Some retail stores, for example, will locate only in areas that have a certain minimum number of people per square mile.

Climate is another important geographic characteristic. Ski apparel and accessories, for example, are best marketed in parts of the country where it snows. In-ground swimming pools, on the other hand, would be segmented geographically into parts of the country that have a warm climate much of the year.

Research into the buying habits of customers may also help marketers segment their markets geographically. For example, a recent study found that 91 percent more consumers in Atlanta have videocassette recorders (VCRs) than consumers in Buffalo. VCR manufacturers may take advantage of this information by advertising more heavily in Buffalo. Or they may concentrate their marketing efforts in Atlanta to sell even more VCRs to a market segment that appears to want them.

Some markets are dominated by the products made by large companies. So one way for smaller companies to enter that market is to adapt the product for sale in a small, specific geographic area. Soho Natural Sodas did just that.

Soho Natural Soda was developed in New York City by Sophia Collier in 1977. Its market originally encompassed only the New York area. Once the soda was successful, other geographic areas were targeted. The company expanded its market to New England, Raleigh-Durham, and San Francisco—areas where it was felt that all-natural sodas and flavored sparkling waters would be well received by discriminating metropolitan consumers. By carving out a small, geographic niche in the soda market, Soho Natural Soda has become profitable and successful. It was so profitable, in fact, that a larger company, Joseph E. Seagram & Sons Inc., acquired it in 1988.

Demographics. *The term demographics refers to statistics about the personal characteristics of a population, such as age, gender, income, ethnic background, education, and occupation.* Demographics help marketers segment the market so products can be categorized and developed based on these characteristics.

Markets are easily segmented by age. For example, a clothing manufacturer can produce a line of clothing for children and another for adults. Toy manufacturers segment the market by age when designing and marketing toys. They often identify on the packaging the recommended age group for each toy or game.

Certain products are segmented by gender. Many cosmetic companies have found they can produce products for both sexes. The original Mennen Speed Stick deodorant was segmented for males. When the company entered the female market, it introduced Lady Speed Stick for women. Traditional women's makeup lines, such as Lancôme and Clinique, now carry men's skin care lines, too.

Many products are targeted for people at specific income levels. For example, American Express offers a Platinum card for affluent people. With this card the holder is granted special services and a higher credit limit. However, the annual fee is much higher than the fee charged for regular American Express cards, and the requirements for its use are more demanding.

Automobiles are often segmented by both income and age. A Ford Mustang is targeted to young adults who want a fashionable yet inexpensive car. The Lincoln Town Car, on the other hand, is targeted to middle-aged people in a higher income bracket.

Many products, such as the American Express card, are targeted for people at specific income levels. What three income levels do these cards represent? What does the color of each card say about the income level?

Ethnic background is also used to develop a market niche. Restaurants, for example, may consider ethnic characteristics of the local population and gear their menus to local tastes.

Lifestyle. *Consumer lifestyles are the patterns of behavior people follow in their daily lives, including how they spend their time and money.* Much of a person's lifestyle is determined by his or her attitudes and values. Marketers call such studies of social and psychological characteristics *psychographics.*

Companies watch for changes in lifestyle to develop new products and segment markets. Microwave food and fast-food restaurants, for example, reflect the value that people today place on doing things quickly and easily.

Lean Cuisine was developed in response to people's concern about weight control. To what specific market segment do you think Lean Cuisine appeals? How does the brand name of this product reinforce its appeal to that market segment?

Food manufacturers have responded to people's great concern for weight control. Weight Watchers, an organization for people who want to lose weight, now markets its own frozen foods. Lean Cuisine is another brand of frozen food that caters to dieters.

Along with the concern for weight, people are now greatly concerned with overall physical fitness. So, many companies have capitalized on this change in lifestyle. Health clubs and gyms are much more prevalent and fashionable today than they were 20 years ago. Fitness machines and exercise video tapes are marketed to a growing segment of the physical fitness market that wants to exercise at home. The apparel industry is profiting from the concern for physical fitness by marketing special work-out clothing.

Yuppies (Young Urban Professionals) represent a market segment with an upwardly mobile lifestyle and attitudes toward spending that include buying for prestige. Perrier, for example, markets its sparkling water to this market segment. BMW and Porsche also target this segment of the market in their advertising.

More women are entering and successfully staying in the work force. So such publications as *Working Woman* magazine carved a niche in the magazine market by catering to career women who are achievement-oriented and have a success mentality.

Product Benefits. Segmenting a market by *product benefits* involves studying consumers' needs and wants. For example, sports shoe manufacturers identify separate market segments for people

Years ago, shoe companies manufactured only a limited line of all-purpose sports shoes, which people wore for exercise and sports. Today shoe manufacturers have identified separate markets for people who want different product benefits in sports shoes. Apart from product benefits, how else do athletic shoe manufacturers segment the total market for their products?

who jog, walk, play tennis, or do aerobics. Each activity requires a shoe that has a particular design. Thus, manufacturers market different shoes for each segment.

A shampoo manufacturer may segment the market according to people with different types of hair (oily, dry, etc.), people who have dandruff, or to people who wash their hair frequently.

Even soda manufacturers that use mass marketing have used segmentation by product benefits to cater to specific segments by developing non-cola, diet, and caffeine-free soft drinks.

Industrial Market Segmentation

The industrial market may be segmented in ways similar to those used for the consumer market.

For example, a wholesaler may study a geographic area to determine if there are enough businesses there to service profitably. Thus, a restaurant supply wholesaler will market its products in an area where there are a large number of restaurants.

The age of the business, its sales volume, area of specialization, and order size may also be studied. For example, a computer company may produce and market computers of varying capabilities for small, medium, and large businesses. A bank may concentrate its marketing efforts on businesses that produce $1 million to $25 million in sales annually.

Product benefits are also used to segment the industrial market by producing and marketing products geared for specific industries. For example, a paper company may make rolls of paper for use on examination tables in doctors' offices and waxed paper for use in restaurants. Packaging may be changed for facial tissues so a supermarket can use the product as a generic brand or as a company brand.

Marketing Mix

Once a company has identified a target market and learned about its characteristics, the next step is to develop a marketing plan. This includes decisions regarding the marketing mix. *A marketing mix is a combination of decisions about product, place, price, and promotion—the four P's of marketing used to reach a target market and make a profit.* The most important aspect of the marketing mix is a company's ability to direct all four *P*'s of marketing to one select target market. If this is not done, the message will confuse the consumer.

Product Decisions

Product decisions involve what product to make, when to make it, its level of quality, how many to produce and sell, its packaging, brand name, and warranties or guarantees. For example, many outerwear clothing manufacturers decided to change the insulation materials used in ski jackets and other outer-wear items when Thinsulate was introduced on the market. A thin insulation material, Thinsulate produces warmth without the bulk of thick polyester fiberfill or down.

Some manufacturers have added liquid detergent to their powdered clothing detergent line. Many have redesigned their packaging for liquid detergent so that the cap of the bottle measures enough detergent for one load of wash.

Place Decisions

Place decisions are based on how the product is to be distributed. Should it be sold directly to the consumer, for example, or should it be sold through wholesalers or retailers?

The product image, the price of the product, and the potential market all have a bearing on place decisions. For example, Estée Lauder chooses to market its Clinique line of cosmetics in department stores rather than in discount stores because it wants to project an exclusive image for the merchandise. Also, people in the target market for Clinique products are discriminating customers who generally shop in department stores rather than in discount stores and are willing to pay higher prices for their cosmetics. (You will learn more about place decisions in Chapter 7.)

The Clinique line of cosmetics is marketed in a department store to project an exclusive image. Think about the brand name of this product. Then look carefully at this display, the merchandise, and how the salesperson is dressed. What product, place, price, and promotion decisions have been made to develop the marketing mix for Clinique?

Pet Rocks: Rock Solid and Market Wise

Almost everyone loves pets. But even the animal lovers among us would sometimes rather have a pet that doesn't bark at night, claw the furniture, or need to be walked, brushed, or bathed.

Advertising copywriter Gary Dahl was joking about his ideal pet with his friends one day, when he thought up the perfect pet: the pet rock.

Dahl borrowed $10,000 from a friend and started Rock Bottom Productions. One of his friends designed a cardboard pet carrier with air holes on the side. Dahl bought several tons of egg-sized beach pebbles from Mexico and packed each one in shredded newspaper in the cartons. He then wrote a 32-page "care and feeding" booklet to be included with each rock. The instructions told new owners how to paper-train their pets, and how to teach them to do tricks like roll over, sit, heel, and play dead. Each pet rock was priced at $4.

When Dahl introduced his pet rocks at fall gift shows in San Francisco and New York, he received 4,800 orders. Within 7 weeks, he had sold 10,000. A month later, he had more than 100 employees and was shipping 15,000 pet rocks a day to department stores and gift shops all over the country. Lots of folks got pet rocks for holiday gifts that year.

Dahl did not formally advertise his pet rocks, but he did receive substantial free publicity. Word-of-mouth advertising soon boosted the demand so much he could hardly keep up with the orders. When asked why the pet rock was so successful, Dahl replied "The country was ready for a giggle."

1. What product, place, price, and promotion decisions did Gary Dahl make about the marketing mix for his pet rocks?
2. Describe the kinds of people (age, background, income, shopping habits) you think would buy a pet rock.

Price Decisions

Price decisions are extremely important for all businesses along the channel of distribution. Producers must know what price people in their target market are able and willing to pay. Other factors that affect price decisions are the quality of the item, the pricing strategy of competitors, and the billing methods and terms of payment appropriate for the target market.

Different pricing strategies are used, depending on the target market and competition. If the target market is in a high income socio-economic group that buys for quality and prestige, then a product will be priced high to give it a quality, prestigious image. (Chapters 29 and 30 will further explore price decisions.)

Promotion Decisions

Promotion decisions include all decisions on educating potential customers about the product and how to develop a good public image with promotional activities. Which media—newspapers, radio, television, or magazines, for example—are best for reaching a target market?

For example, if a cologne manufacturer wants to reach a highly affluent male target market, it makes its promotion decisions with that group in mind. It will be advertised in better men's magazines, such as *Esquire* and *GQ*, and during television shows that men in the target market are likely to watch.

When to advertise is also important. For example, you will see more ads for perfume and cologne during December than during any other month. Perfume companies have found that consumers looking for gifts are most receptive to commercials about perfume and cologne during the holiday season.

Market Share

Another important concept related to the market is *market share*. *A market share is a firm's share of the total sales volume generated by all competitors in a given market.* This is reported as a percentage. Businesses constantly study their market share to see how well they are doing with a given product in relation to their competitors.

Figure 5-1 **Long-Distance Companies' Market Shares After the 1984 AT&T Divestiture**
What was AT&T's market share in 1985? in 1988? What was MCI's market position in 1985? in 1988? What would happen to the market share of AT&T, MCI, and others if Sprint increased its market share to 10 percent in 1990?

Visualize the total market as a pizza. Each slice of the pizza represents each competitor's share of the market. The biggest slice of pizza represents the firm that has the largest percentage of the total sales volume. See Figure 5-1 which depicts the market share for long-distance phone companies.

In addition to market share, each business carefully watches its *market position*. *A market position is a firm's standing in the market compared to its competitors.* To monitor market position, a business keeps track of the changing size of the market and the growth of its competitors.

In its quest for an increased market share, all four P's of marketing are reviewed and revised as necessary to reach that goal. To get a bigger share of the market, a new sales promotion campaign may be launched. Or new distribution outlets may be sought. Getting people in the target market to buy the product may require adjustment to one of the four P's. That is, changing the product, the place where it can be bought, the price, or the way it is promoted.

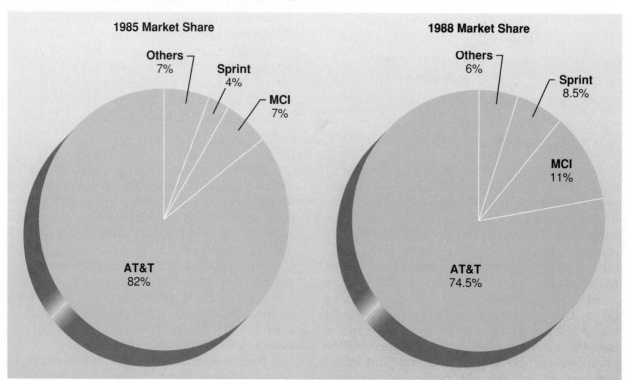

Source: The Yankee Group and Federal Communications Commission

VOCABULARY REVIEW

Write a brief definition of each word, based on your reading of the chapter.

market
mass marketing
market segmentation
geographics
demographics

lifestyle
marketing mix
market share
market position

FACT AND IDEA REVIEW

1. What are the two main objectives recognized in the marketing concept?

2. What is a target market?

3. How can target markets be classified or segmented?

4. Provide an example of how a market can be segmented by age.

5. Provide an example of how a market can be segmented by gender.

6. Provide an example of how a market can be segmented by specific income levels.

7. What are psychographics?

8. What does segmenting a market by product benefits involve?

9. What are product decisions, place decisions, price decisions, and promotion decisions?

10. What is the most important aspect of the marketing mix?

CRITICAL THINKING

1. What is the difference between a mass marketing approach and a market segmentation approach to marketing products?

2. Give one example not mentioned in the chapter of how geographic considerations can help marketers segment a market.

3. Identify two changes in consumer lifestyles that are not mentioned in the chapter, and give two examples of how marketers have responded to meet those changes.

4. How would marketers vary their advertising message when marketing Ben-Gay to college students and senior citizens?

5. Give three examples of how industrial markets may be segmented.

6. How would a business market toilet tissue to both the consumer market and the industrial market?

7. What factors would you use to segment the market for cross-country skis, a new board game, a new hair spray, a new sports car, and a new home exercise video?

8. Give two techniques businesses may use in an attempt to increase their market share.

USING BASIC SKILLS

Math

1. A manufacturer's total costs for running the business equal $5,000 per week. In week one, the factory produced 2,500 widgets. In week two, the factory produced 7,500 widgets. What was the cost per widget the first week? What was the cost per widget the second week? What was the difference in the cost per unit between the two weeks?

2. It has been said that marketing costs plus profit account for 50 percent of the final price of a product. If a consumer pays $19.90 for a product, what is the cost of making the product?

Communication

3. A manufacturer of heavy-duty work jeans has decided to expand production and enter three new markets. All employees have been asked to identify three other market segments for jeans and to explain any product changes needed to enter those markets. You have a meeting in ten minutes with the manufacturer. Identify three new markets

for the jeans and all the changes needed in the marketing of the product to reach the potential customers in each new target you identify.

Human Relations

4. An angry customer approaches you to complain that the calculator advertised for $4.99 is not in the store. The customer is right: the shipment never arrived in time for the promotion. How would you handle this situation and still maintain the customer's confidence and goodwill?

APPLICATION PROJECTS

1. Mike and Nancy live in Kansas where they invented a new recipe for ice cream. They have started a business and have hired you to advise them on how to market their new product. You know the competition is keen and there are many large ice cream manufacturers that Mike and Nancy cannot compete against at the present time. What could you suggest to segment the total market of ice cream lovers and thus carve out a niche for Mike and Nancy's new product so they don't have to initially compete with the large ice cream manufacturers? What advice could you give Mike and Nancy to help them decide on the proper marketing strategy to use with respect to the four *P*'s of the marketing mix?

2. Look at the photo below. What product benefits would you stress if you were trying to mass market this product? What product benefits would you stress if you were trying to sell this to a market segment composed of people with dry skin?

3. Do library research about the work demographers do. Find out what kind of training they need and what kinds of job opportunities are available to them. Present your findings to the class in a five-minute oral report.

4. Select at least three different magazine ads for the same kind of product. For example, you might choose ads for three different automobiles, three different credit cards, or three different banks. Analyze the ads to determine the demographics of the target market. Write a 100-word paragraph describing the target market for each ad.

Identifying Markets

6

After completing this chapter, you will be able to:

1. identify demographic and psychographic trends in the consumer market,

2. explain the external and internal influences that make consumers different,

3. explain the types of organizations included in the industrial market, and

4. explain how the industrial market derives demand from the consumer market.

disposable income
discretionary income
culture
social class
reference groups
family life cycle
industrial marketing
derived demand

To be a successful marketer, you must learn all you can about potential customers. Only then can you achieve the goals of the marketing concept—to satisfy customers' needs and wants and make a profit. Successful businesspeople are always alert to changes in their markets. Changes may present opportunities for new products or new ways to market an existing product.

In this chapter you will review some of the current demographic and psychographic trends in the consumer market, and you will learn how marketers capitalize on those trends. You will also investigate the organizations that comprise the industrial market.

Understanding the Consumer Market

In Chapter 5, you learned that the consumer market is all potential customers who buy goods or services for personal use. There are some 240 million people in the United States, and all of them are considered part of the consumer market.

To be successful in the consumer market, businesspeople need to understand the consumers they want to serve. They need to know where consumers live, how old they are, and whether there are enough of them to support the market for a particular product. They also need to understand how customers make their buying decisions, and what social and psychological factors might influence their needs and wants.

Let's look at the first of these areas—a type of information called *demographics*.

Consumer Demographics

As you discovered in Chapter 5, *demographics* are statistics about the personal characteristics of a population. They are most often obtained for characteristics that can be easily measured and numbered, such as how old the consumers are, or where they live, or how much money they earn. Demographics can help a businessperson identify a market segment. And they can help match products to the needs and wants of a changing population.

Seven of the most important demographic categories are *age, ethnic background, family structure and gender, income, occupation, education,* and *location.*

Age. The way in which the population is distributed into age groups is important to marketers, because people of different ages have markedly different needs and levels of buying power. Figure 6-1 shows the more significant age groups of concern to marketers.

The smallest population group is teenagers. The estimated number of teenagers between the ages of 14 and 17 declined between 1980 and 1987 to less than 15 million. There was also a drop in the number of 18- to 24-year-olds—there were almost 3 million fewer young adults in 1987 than in 1980.

Despite the relatively small size of these two groups, marketers still gear products and marketing efforts to teenagers and young adults. This helps establish brand loyalty early in life. It also helps to sell such goods and services as stereo equipment, records and tapes, clothing, and sporting equipment.

Baby boomers—people born after World War II until 1965—make up the largest percentage of the to-

Figure 6-1 **Selected Age Groups in the U.S. Population, 1980 and 1987**
Shown here are some of the significant age groups of concern to marketers. Which groups are increasing, and which are decreasing?

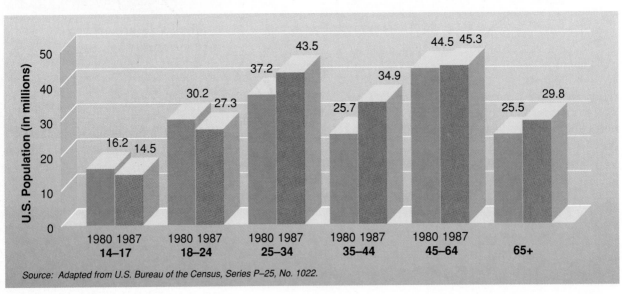

Source: Adapted from U.S. Bureau of the Census, Series P–25, No. 1022.

tal population. Baby boomers range in age from about 25 to 45. Within this age range, the 35- to 44-year-olds are the largest and most significant group. In addition to its large size, marketers particularly like this baby boomer segment because people in this age group are more likely to have high incomes and spend more income than average on luxury and recreational items.

The over-65 age group continues to increase. It grew by more than 4 million between 1980 and 1987. It will probably continue to increase moderately for years to come, and more dramatically when the baby boomers reach their mid-sixties.

Marketers have responded by providing senior citizen discounts and products and services specifically for older adults. Retirement villages offer special services and entertainment. New products have been developed to cater to the special needs of people in this group—"Depends" adult diapers, aspirin for arthritis sufferers, and foods rich in calcium to help ward off diseases that afflict the elderly such as osteoporosis.

The number of newborns, which hit a low in the 1970s, increased in the 1980s. Marketers of baby products are thrilled with this trend, especially since firstborns represented a large percent of this increase. Research indicates that some 25 percent more money is spent on firstborns than on succeeding children born in a family.

Ethnic Background. Marketers sometimes segment the market by ethnic background and create products and advertisements targeted for different ethnic populations.

For example, billboards in Hispanic or Asian neighborhoods are usually written in the native language of the local population. And Hispanic or Asian foods and recognized brands are likely to be heavily marketed there. In a predominantly Black neighborhood, you are more likely to see such publications as *Ebony* and *Jet*, both of which appeal to Black readership.

Family Structure and Gender. The traditional family structure of the 1950s, in which the father worked and the mother stayed home to take care of the house and children, has changed considerably.

This change in family structure greatly affects consumer needs. Marketers have responded to these changes in their advertisements, products, and services. Today, for example, both women and men are pictured in television commercials and print ads preparing meals and taking care of the home and chil-

dren. Some supermarkets have introduced home shopping and delivery services for busy couples unable to get to the grocery store.

The number of women in the workforce is increasing at a greater rate than the number of men. As Figure 6-2 shows, there are still more men in the workforce than women, but the gap between the two is narrowing. As a result, some businesses market business-related products and services, such as credit cards, insurance, briefcases, professional clothing, air travel, and banking, directly to women.

More mothers are working. In 1987, 60.2 percent of working mothers had children under age 18, compared to 54.9 percent in 1982, and 47.7 percent in 1977. So, take-out food services, child-care centers, and housecleaning services are just a few of the products that have been developed to meet working mothers' needs.

Figure 6-2 **Number of People in the Labor Force, by Gender**
Although there are still more men in the workforce than women, the gap is narrowing. In which year was the number of men and women in the workforce most nearly equal? Give two reasons why you think more women have entered the workforce since 1970.

Today, there are many single households because people are marrying later in life, divorcing, or outliving their spouses. According to the U.S. Bureau of the Census, the number of one-person households increased by 20 percent between 1980 and 1988.

Recognizing the fact that so many people are living alone in apartments or small homes, General Electric developed space saver appliances. Many furniture manufacturers also capitalized on this market segment by designing smaller-scaled furniture for smaller living quarters. Food companies began offering their products in single serving sizes.

Income. When analyzing comparisons of income from different years, it is important to keep in mind the differences between *constant* and *current* dollars. *Constant* dollars are dollar amounts that have been adjusted to compensate for increases due to inflation. (Economists call the adjusted amounts *real* values.) *Current* dollars are simply the amounts as they were stated in the different years, *without* adjustment for inflation. (Economists call these *nominal* values.)

This distinction is important, because during periods of high inflation, income levels expressed in current dollars can seem higher than they really are in terms of buying power.

Table 6-1 shows that the median family income in 1987 was $30,853 (in constant dollars), compared to $28,880 (in constant dollars) in 1970. More than half of all families had incomes over $25,000 in 1987.

The table shows that income has gone up since 1970, although not at a consistent rate. It is projected that family income will continue to rise in the 1990s, with more and more family incomes reaching $50,000 or more.

In addition to levels of income, marketers want to know how much money is available for spending on different kinds of products. For this reason, they look at two types of income measurement: *disposable income* and *discretionary income*.

Disposable income is the money left after taking out taxes. Marketers who produce and distribute products that are necessities are interested in changes in consumers' disposable income. *Discretionary income is the money left after paying for basic living necessities such as food, shelter, and clothing.* Marketers that sell luxury products are interested in changes in consumers' discretionary income. Both disposable and discretionary income are expected to increase if real income (income adjusted for inflation) increases.

Occupation. In the United States, employment in white collar and service industries has increased, while blue collar and farm employment has decreased. So, many marketers have responded to this trend toward upward mobility. Airlines, for example,

Family income is an important consumer demographic category. What is the difference, in constant dollars, between the median family income in 1970 and the median family income in 1987?

		Percent Distribution of Families, By Income Level								Median income (1987 constant dollars)
Year	Number of families (1,000)	Under $5,000	$5,000– $9,999	$10,000– $14,999	$15,000– $19,999	$20,000– $24,999	$25,000– $34,999	$35,000– $49,999	$50,000 and over	
1970	52,227	3.5	7.6	9.1	9.9	11.3	22.0	21.2	15.4	28,880
1975	56,245	2.9	8.1	10.0	10.2	10.4	20.9	21.0	16.4	28,970
1980	60,309	3.7	8.2	9.8	10.2	10.2	20.0	20.5	17.5	28,996
1983	62,015	4.8	8.4	10.3	10.1	10.2	19.0	19.2	17.9	28,147
1984	62,706	4.5	8.3	9.7	10.0	9.7	18.4	19.7	19.6	28,923
1985	63,558	4.4	8.0	9.7	9.9	9.9	18.3	19.2	20.6	29,302
1986	64,491	4.5	7.5	9.2	9.6	9.5	17.7	19.8	22.2	30,534
1987	65,133	4.4	7.3	9.1	9.5	9.2	17.5	20.2	22.9	30,853

Table 6-1 Median Family Income, 1970 to 1987 (in constant dollars)

Source: Adapted from *Statistical Abstracts of the United States, 1989.*

offer business-class seating. Hotels offer special rates to attract the business traveler. Television commercials for all types of products from clothing to stereo equipment to cars to food often picture successful young male and female executives enjoying a prosperous life.

Education. The minimum level of education for Americans has continued to rise. In 1970, only 52.3 percent of all adults 25 years and older had completed high school. But that figure rose to 75.6 percent in 1987.[1] The percentage of college graduates also increased during that time from 10.7 percent to 19.9 percent.

Again, marketers responded to an emerging market. Financial planners, such as banks and stock brokers, now have products geared to parents of young children to help them plan for college tuition costs. Independent schools now offer classes that prepare teenagers to take college entrance exams.

Location. Most of the United States population is concentrated in urban areas and surrounding suburbs. Thus, the U.S. Bureau of the Census classifies urban areas into three categories: *Metropolitan Statistical Area*, *Primary Metropolitan Statistical Area*, and *Consolidated Metropolitan Area*.

A *Metropolitan Statistical Area* is a city with a minimum of 50,000 residents, or an urbanized area of at least 50,000 residents, with a total metropolitan population of at least 100,000.

A *Primary Metropolitan Statistical Area* is larger. It has at least 1 million residents and a large urbanized county or cluster of counties that reflect similar economic and social ties to each other.

A *Consolidated Metropolitan Area* is a group of two or more adjacent Primary Metropolitan Areas. In these consolidated metropolitan areas, the population density is high. Some of the most densely populated consolidated metropolitan areas in the United States are found around New York, Los Angeles, Chicago, Philadelphia, and Detroit.

Marketers who want to test market their new products sometimes select areas in these metropolitan statistical areas because they can get feedback quickly from a large concentration of people.

The movement to the suburbs has stabilized since the mass exodus from the cities in the early 1950s. However, much of the economic and social life in America still takes place in suburbia, as shown by the trend of locating shopping malls and industrial parks in suburban areas.

The move away from urban areas continues. But some cities, such as Boston, Philadelphia, Washington, D.C., and Los Angeles are still experiencing increased population.

Marketers also watch for *regional* changes in population. The Sunbelt, which ranges from southern California to South Carolina, has experienced an increase in population. The population in the northern United States has stabilized. Retail chain stores and shopping mall developers follow these trends closely to take advantage of new markets and opportunities to expand.

Lifestyle and Psychographics

Demographic information is descriptive. But by itself it does not give marketers enough information about consumers. Marketers must also know about people's *lifestyles*—that is, how they spend their time and money. As you learned in Chapter 5, attitudes and values help determine a person's lifestyle. Information about attitudes and values is called *psychographics*, and it includes both *external* and *internal* influences.

External Influences. External influences are the social characteristics in life, such as culture, social class, reference groups, family life cycle, and activities.

Culture is the sum total of a people's learned behavior as it relates to heritage. It's important for marketers to study cultural differences because people from different countries often have different values and buying habits. (As you discovered in Chapter 3, businesses involved in international marketing must be ever alert to these cultural differences.) Americans, for example, idealize youth, health, and vitality, and an active lifestyle. So products marketed to Americans, whether for the teen, young adult, or mature adult market, are often portrayed as having the ability to make people more youthful and vibrant.

Social class refers to a way of grouping consumers from upper to lower levels, according to several significant factors that tend to coincide, such as income, education, and occupation. As a general rule, consumers with high incomes tend to have more education than average. Also, certain occupations are associated with certain levels of income and education.

[1]Source: *Statistical Abstracts of the United States, USA Statistics in Brief, 1989.*

Each social class provides marketers with opportunities. Automobiles best illustrate the attention given to social class in advertising. The Hyundai, for example, appeals to people on a dollar-stretcher budget who need a low-priced, economical car. The Mercedes, on the other hand, is obviously targeted to people in the upper social class with enough discretionary income to pay a great deal of money for a car.

Reference groups are the people who influence a person's values, morals, and decisions. In many cases, the family is a primary reference group, as are friends and co-workers. Reference groups can also be people that the consumer does not know but wants to imitate. Marketers design strategies to associate their products with the reference groups that the targeted consumer wants to be part of.

The family life cycle refers to the evolution of a family, from a young single adult to retirement. In general, the traditional stages are *single*, *newly married*, *full nest* (when children live at home), *empty nest* (when children leave home), and *sole survivor* (widowed). Each stage in a family cycle represents opportunities for marketers and makes market segmentation easy.

Marketers associate their products with reference groups the targeted consumer wants to be a part of. What is the implied reference group in this ad?

A precious weave of emeralds and diamonds
in eighteen karat gold. From the Tiffany Vannerie Collection.
Also with rubies, sapphires or all diamonds.

TIFFANY & CO.

NEW YORK LONDON MUNICH ZURICH HONG KONG
SAN FRANCISCO BEVERLY HILLS COSTA MESA DALLAS HOUSTON CHICAGO ATLANTA BOSTON 800-526-0649 ©T&CO. 1989

Price for SW8 as shown $19,995.¹ Also available as SW8 Turbo $25,695.¹

Some Children Lead A Very Sheltered Life.

When you're driving your kids around, there's no such thing as being overly cautious. Which is why you should drive the highly responsive Peugeot 505 SW8.

Unlike other station wagons which force their third seat passengers to sit backwards, staring danger in the face, the Peugeot SW8's third seat faces forward. And it's separated from the rear end by a "crumple zone" that is designed to collapse on impact thereby absorbing the force of a collision. What's more, you can feel secure no matter where you're sitting in an SW8, because the entire passenger compartment is surrounded by a protective cage of cold-rolled steel.

But Peugeot hasn't forgotten the reason you buy a station wagon. So we've designed ours to accommodate eight full-size adults. And you can fold down all or part of the rear seats to create the most spacious European wagon sold in the U.S.

When you buy a Peugeot 505 SW8, you'll also be protected by the most comprehensive roadside assistance plan available: ⓐⓐⓐ.* As well as a 3-year/ 36,000-mile Bumper-to-Bumper limited warranty and a 5-year/50,000-mile limited powertrain warranty.**

So why not call 1-800-447-2882 for the Peugeot dealer nearest you and arrange to test drive the 1989 SW8 or SW8 Turbo. It's one of the few things you can do to protect your kids from the outside world.

¹MSRP. Excludes dest. charge, tax, title, options and registration. *Membership subject to the rules and regulations of ⓐⓐⓐ. **See your dealer for details of these warranties.

The Peugeot 505 SW8 seats eight passengers in the kind of comfort usually reserved for luxury sedans.

PEUGEOT

NOTHING ELSE FEELS LIKE IT™

©1989 Peugeot Motors of America, Inc.

To which family life cycle is this Peugeot ad targeted?

In addition, marketers must be alert to nontraditional family life cycles that are shaping our culture. For example, there are an increasing number of families headed by single parents, a growing number of married couples without children, and a growing number of people who are divorced.

Activities are important to marketers, too, because where people spend their time provides insight into marketing opportunities and strategies. For some people, the average work week is now 35 hours instead of the traditional 40 hours. This means that Americans now have more time to spend on leisure activities.

Internal Influences.

Internal influences are the psychological characteristics that influence your personality, attitudes, and motivation.

Personality includes all the distinct characteristics that make you unique. We generally categorize people as having inner-directed or outer-directed personalities. Inner-directed people make decisions without noting the opinions of others or involving them in the decision-making process. They are less likely to buy products simply because they are prestigious. So, practical and efficient products, such as economically priced wash-and-wear clothing, are targeted to inner-directed consumers.

Outer-directed people depend on others to help them make decisions. They try to please others and often look for their approval. Products that are unique, prestigious, and well-known appeal to them. For example, outer-directed people are likely to enjoy wearing clothes with visible, prestigious company logos (such as the Izod Lacoste alligator) and with designer names (such as Calvin Klein or Gucci).

Attitudes are feelings that a person already has about products, companies, or institutions. An attitude may be based on a previous experience with an item, or on an experience with something the person associates with the item. They can be positive, negative, or neutral, and are molded by a person's social environment and personality.

When marketers plan strategies for new or existing products, they need to be aware of existing customer attitudes toward the product and its attributes. Advertisers will often design campaigns to either reinforce a positive customer attitude or counter a negative one.

Analyzing Lifestyle Factors.

The exact effect of lifestyle influences—especially internal ones—on consumer behavior is difficult to predict. This is partly because consumers keep changing. It is also because the results of human research methodology are sometimes flawed.

Unlike demographics, which are statistical, research into lifestyle factors relies largely on response to personal surveys. But for various reasons, the people surveyed may not always tell the truth about their consuming and purchasing habits. They may want to protect their privacy, for example. Or they may simply give answers they think the researcher wants. Thus, consumers' responses may differ greatly from actual behavior.

In addition, it is difficult to design research that takes into account all the roles an individual consumer may play in the same day. A person may be a parent, spouse, and a corporate executive with important decision-making responsibilities, or a competitive golfer, football fan, and a little league coach. In each role, different personality aspects may emerge.

REAL WORLD MARKETING

Targeting the Black Consumer

When filmmaker Spike Lee and hoopster Michael Jordan joined forces in 1989 for a fast-paced TV spot, first-time viewers may have thought they had tuned in a rock video. In fact, the ad for Nike sneakers was one of a new breed of commercials targeted at the Black consumer. The basis for the trend is an upsurge in Black spending power, which is expected to top the $400 billion mark by the year 2000.

The Industrial Market

When we think of goods and services, most of us think of the consumer products that satisfy our own needs and wants. But another side of marketing, which is even larger than the consumer market, is the industrial market. Many people are not directly involved with it because it consists of business transactions between organizations and does not involve the final consumer.

Industrial marketing is marketing of goods and services to organizations or businesses for their operations or for resale to others. Let's look at the types of organizations that make up the industrial market.

Organizations in the Industrial Market

Six major groups or organizations are included in the industrial market.

1. Extractors
2. Construction and Manufacturing Businesses
3. Wholesale and Retail Businesses
4. Business and Professional Services
5. Institutions and Nonprofit Organizations
6. Local, State, and Federal Governments

Extractors. *Extractors* are businesses that take something from the earth or sea. They include agricultural, forestry, fishing, and mining businesses. Extractors buy equipment and supplies to conduct their business operations.

For example, agriculture in the United States today is big business, largely due to the number of *agribusinesses*—large scale businesses that manage all aspects of food production, processing, and distribution. Agribusinesses buy such sophisticated products as computers to keep track of their operations and costly computerized farming equipment for planting and harvesting.

Construction and Manufacturing. Construction companies, which build such structures as houses, office buildings, shopping malls, and manufacturing plants, buy construction equipment and building supplies. They may also subcontract for the services of such specialists as electricians, engineers, and architects.

Manufacturing involves producing goods to sell to other manufacturers or to wholesalers and retailers. Manufacturers buy the raw materials that go into their products, as well as machinery, computers, and supplies for their operations. They buy office supplies and protective equipment for their workers. And they also buy business services, such as insurance, accounting, advertising, and delivery.

Wholesalers and Retailers. *Wholesalers* (also called *distributors*) obtain goods from manufacturers and resell them to industrial users, other wholesalers, and retailers.

Wholesalers are common in certain industries, such as in the food and automotive industries. As consumers, wholesalers buy the products they resell, as well as trucks, forklifts, warehouses, and business services such as insurance, accounting, and delivery.

Retailers buy goods from wholesalers (or directly from manufacturers) and resell them to the consumer. As consumers themselves, retailers must buy the products they resell, as well as the supplies they need for providing services. In addition, retailers spend money on interior design elements, such as display fixtures and carpeting, to provide attractive, comfortable environments for customers.

Business and Professional Services. Business services include such things as financial planning, insurance, real estate, transportation, communications, utilities, sanitation, data processing, and advertising. Businesses buy other services for their operation, as well as office supplies, cars, trucks, vans, and computers.

Professional services include those of doctors, dentists, and lawyers. They buy office supplies specific to their businesses (syringes for a doctor's office, for example). And they use such services as those of accountants, insurance agents, and cleaning companies.

Institutions and Nonprofit Organizations. Institutions, such as private schools, universities, hospitals, and nonprofit organizations, buy such goods and services as office supplies and advertising and accounting services. To generate money to maintain their organizations, they also buy products for resale.

Governments. The federal, state, and local governments comprise the largest consumer category in the United States. They spend about $2 trillion annually (the federal government spends about $1 trillion by itself). They buy a vast array of products—everything from the complex computers used in space exploration to pens and pencils for schools.

To market goods and services to the government, special guidelines must be followed. For example, the government usually is required to buy the least expensive goods and services that meet its written minimum specifications. So, to be considered by the government, a business must submit a bid quoting

Reynolds Metals: Reaching the Consumer and Industrial Markets

Many manufacturers look for ways to produce products for the consumer *and* the industrial markets. In recent years, Reynolds Metals Company has followed suit. The largest percentage of its revenue comes from the sale of aluminum used industrially in cans and construction. But it also manufacturers aluminum foil, cooking bags, wax paper, plastic wrap, and plastic re-sealable storage bags for the consumer market. In addition, it is considering introducing brand-name trash bags, plastic cups, and utensils.

A major reason for these aggressive moves into the consumer market is to smooth out peaks and valleys in annual sales. The demand for industrial metals fluctuates greatly. So this diversification should help the company balance its earnings between industrial and consumer goods.

1. In what industrial market could Reynolds aluminum foil, plastic wrap, trash bags, and plastic utensils be sold?
2. What changes would Reynolds have to make to the packaging of these products if it sold them in an industrial market?
3. Who are Reynolds' competitors in the consumer market's re-sealable plastic bags?

---

its prices for the particular product or service needed.

When the bid system is not feasible, as in the case of a newly designed piece of military equipment, the government may negotiate a contract with a supplier. All government transactions are controlled by legal and budgetary regulations to help insure the proper use of public funds.

How the Industrial Market Derives Demand from the Consumer Market

The market for industrial goods and services is based on the demand for consumer goods and services. *For this reason, the demand for industrial goods is called derived demand.*

Marketers of industrial goods need to be aware of how their markets will change in response to changes in the consumer market. For example, if consumers decide to buy fewer automobiles, the derived demand for each component of the car, such as steel, tires, radios, batteries, and electrical parts, is reduced.

Demand in the industrial market is generally inelastic, which means that price does not play a big role. This is because price increases can be passed on to the final consumer. As long as the final consumer can and will pay the higher price, industrial businesses will buy the supplies they need to continue production of a product. In a competitive industry, however, prices can reach a point where the producer will look for alternative sources of supply.

Industrial Buying Practices

Because industrial goods are generally bought in bulk, they usually require very high dollar expenditures. To reduce the risk of making such purchases, industrial consumers may require specialized services, such as credit and extended warranties.

Industrial goods are often highly technical. As a result, industrial buyers usually become well versed in the technology and highly trained in assessing the goods and services they buy.

Sellers of industrial goods must become equally knowledgeable and must sometimes give technical assistance in selling their product. The need for technical expertise is usually greater than that required to sell to the final consumer.

VOCABULARY REVIEW

Write one or two paragraphs incorporating these eight vocabulary terms.

disposable income
discretionary income
culture
social class

reference groups
family life cycle
industrial marketing
derived demand

FACT AND IDEA REVIEW

1. List seven important demographic categories.

2. Why do marketers particularly like the baby boom generation?

3. Name three trends that reflect changes in households and families.

4. What is the general trend in education in the United States?

5. Why do marketers sometimes test market their new products in large metropolitan statistical areas?

6. How do marketers use reference groups to reach their targeted consumers?

7. What is the difference between an inner-directed person and an outer-directed person?

8. Why is consumer behavior difficult to predict?

9. What is industrial marketing? Name six major groups or organizations included in the industrial market.

10. What has contributed to agriculture in the U.S. being classified as big business? What kinds of industrial products do these businesses buy?

CRITICAL THINKING

1. Even though the teenage and young adult populations are small, why do marketers continue to target products and advertising to these two groups? Give two examples each of ads and products targeted to these two groups.

2. Discuss how marketers have responded to the growing number of working women and working mothers.

3. Discuss how marketers have responded to the decrease in the size of households and the growing number of single households.

4. Of what significance are changes in disposable income and discretionary income to marketers of necessity products and luxury products? What is the difference between disposable income and discretionary income?

5. How do marketers use trends in consumer lifestyle to their advantage? Give three examples to make your point.

6. Use the concept of derived demand to explain what might happen to sales of cotton in the industrial market if people in the consumer market decided to buy only clothes made of wool or synthetics.

USING BASIC SKILLS

Math

1. Look at Figure 6-1 and answer these two questions. Which age group experienced the largest increase in population from 1980 to 1987? Which two age groups experienced a decrease in population from 1980 to 1987?

2. In 1980, the median family income in the United States was $21,023 in current dollars. In 1981, the median was $22,388 in current dollars. Between 1980 and 1981, inflation caused the prices of consumer goods to go up by 10 percent. In which year—1980 or 1981—did the average family have greater buying power?

Communication

3. Look through magazines and select four advertisements that identify one trend taking place in the changing U.S. consumer market. In a two- to three-minute speech, show the advertisements to the class, and explain how they reflect the trend you have identified.

Human Relations

4. Assume you are working as a salesperson in the cosmetics department of a retail department store. You notice a group of foreign students approach one of your co-workers for help. Since these customers do not speak English, your co-worker ignores them. What would you do?

5. A man and woman dressed in shabby clothes enter an automobile showroom. None of the salespeople is eager to help them because each thinks it would be a waste of time. One salesperson finally waits on the customers and sells them three cars for their business. What is the moral of this story? Does it say anything about how using lifestyle characteristics to identify markets can sometimes be misleading? Have you ever let appearances dictate which customers you will help?

APPLICATION PROJECTS

1. Select one age group, either teenagers and young adults, baby boomers, or the over-65 age group. List five goods and services specifically marketed to that age group.

2. With more mothers working full-time, teenagers and fathers have been sharing the responsibilities for food shopping and cooking. Cut out two magazine advertisements and summarize two television commercials that reflect how marketers have reacted to this growing trend.

3. Bring to class one magazine that targets consumers according to their lifestyle. State what lifestyle you think is being targeted, and show the class at least two examples of advertisements in the magazine that prove your point.

4. Identify five businesses or organizations in your community that are included in the industrial market. List five products you think they would buy to help run their operations.

5. Interview five different people about their reference groups. Find out who most influences the values and decisions of these people. How would your findings affect you as a marketer in marketing to the group you interviewed? In a five-minute oral report, tell the class what you found out and what you concluded from it.

6. Imagine you are a marketer who is about to launch a new line of vitamins. List three ways in which you might reach outer-directed buyers. List three ways to reach inner-directed buyers. How would campaigns for the two kinds of buyers differ? Could you successfully appeal to both markets at once?

7. Think how the trend toward microwave cooking has affected marketers. What new goods and services have come into being because of microwave ovens? What other goods and services suddenly lost business because of them? How did marketers for the latter respond to the challenge? Do some research on this topic at your local market and department store. Look at products and talk with managers. Present your findings as a 150-word news story.

8. List five to ten products that have been traditionally marketed to women. Make another list including five to ten products traditionally marketed to men. Study your lists and determine which of these products are now marketed to both sexes. Provide examples of advertisements that show the change in gender identification of the products now marketed to both sexes.

9. Many goods and services are marketed by appealing to consumers' needs for belonging and love. Find at least five examples of this and share your findings with the class.

Channels of Distribution

After completing this chapter, you will be able to:

1. define a channel of distribution and identify channel members,

2. explain why intermediaries are important,

3. understand the different channels of distribution for consumer and industrial products, as well as for services, and

4. discuss four factors or considerations used in distribution planning.

channel of distribution
intermediary
wholesalers
retailers
direct distribution
indirect distribution
intensive distribution
selective distribution
exclusive distribution

A s you learned in Chapter 5, successful businesses identify their customers and call them their target markets. This identification is then used to create the marketing mix for a product, including decisions about the product, price, place, and promotion. In this chapter you will explore the "place decision"—that is, where the product will be distributed.

Distribution and the "Place" Utility

Marketers need to ask themselves, "How and where will my target market buy my products and services?" This is the *place decision* (one of the four *P*'s discussed in Chapter 5). To make a place decision, marketers must decide on their *channel of distribution*. *A channel of distribution is the path a product takes from the producer or manufacturer to the final user.*

Toothpaste manufacturers, for example, know that customers like to buy such common personal convenience items in supermarkets and drugstores. A toothpaste manufacturer would therefore include such stores in its channel of distribution to the final consumer.

Beginnings and Ends

A channel begins and ends with one product. If a product changes in form, a new channel begins. For example, when oranges are sold to makers of orange juice, a new channel begins. Two separate and distinct channels are involved—one for the oranges and one for the juice. (See Figure 7-1).

Figure 7-1 **Two Separate Distribution Channels**
A channel of distribution begins with a producer/ manufacturer and ends with the final consumer. Why are there two separate distribution channels for oranges and orange juice?

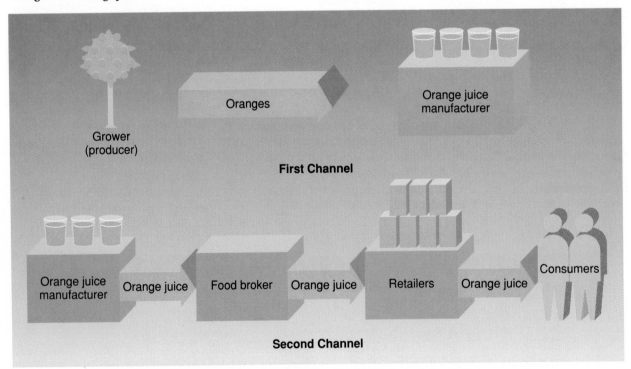

Channel Members

A channel of distribution always begins with the producer or manufacturer and ends with the final user of that product. Producers supply raw materials, and manufacturers make parts and finished goods for use by other manufacturers or ultimate consumers.

When the product is purchased for use in a *business*, the final user is classified as an *industrial user*. When the product is purchased for *personal use*, the final user is classified as a *consumer*—the person who ultimately uses the product.

Apart from producers and final users, there are other channel members called *intermediaries* or *middlemen*. **Intermediaries are channel members that help move products from the producer to the final user.** They are a primary factor in providing place utility.

Intermediaries are classified on the basis of whether they take ownership (or title) to the goods and services. *Merchant intermediaries* take title; *agent intermediaries* do not. Agent intermediaries, usually called *agents*, are paid a commission to help buyers and sellers get together.

Merchant Intermediaries.

The two major types of merchant intermediaries are *wholesalers* and *retailers*.

Wholesalers buy large quantities of goods from manufacturers, store the goods, and resell them to retailers. In the industrial market, wholesalers are called *distributors*. Their customers may include professional or commercial users, manufacturers, governments, institutions, or other wholesalers.

Retailers sell goods to the ultimate consumer. Large retail chain stores, such as Sears, are sometimes so big they are able to take on the wholesaling functions of buying in large quantities, storing, and distributing in smaller quantities to their chain store branches. Smaller retailers generally use the services of wholesalers.

Agents.

Agents are a part of the channel of distribution because they negotiate title of the goods. They do not take title to the goods themselves but instead arrange agreements between channel members. Agents usually work strictly on commission. They receive a certain percentage of the sales by their *principals*, the manufacturers they represent.

There are two basic types of agents—*independent manufacturer's agents* and *brokers*. *Independent manufacturer's agents* represent several related, noncompeting manufacturers in a specific in-

Merchant intermediaries help move products from producer to final user. Why are retailers classified as merchant intermediaries?

dustry. They are not on any manufacturer's payroll. They work independently, running their own businesses.

For example, an independent manufacturer's agent may carry a line of fishing rods from one manufacturer, lures from another, insulated clothing for hunters from a different manufacturer, and outdoor shirts from still another manufacturer. This manufacturer's agent sells the merchandise to sporting goods wholesalers and retailers who specialize in hunting and fishing.

A *broker* also acts as a sales agent for different manufacturers. The broker's roles and responsibilities can be exactly the same as those for a manufacturer's agent, or they can be a little more involved. Most brokers sign agreements with their principals that outline their responsibilities. The broker may be responsible for merchandising and for selling the goods. For example, Pezrow, a food and nonfood broker in the Northeast, follows plans from its principals regarding shelf position and other merchandising requirements when displaying and stocking the products in supermarkets.

Nonchannel Members

Transportation companies and independent storage warehouses are not considered part of the channel of distribution because they are not involved in negotiating title of the goods. They are simply hired to facilitate physical movement of the goods.

Direct and Indirect Channels

In general, channels of distribution are classified as *direct* or *indirect*. ***Direct distribution*** *occurs when the goods or services are sold from the producer directly to the final user; no intermediaries are involved.* ***Indirect distribution*** *involves one or more intermediaries.*

Direct and indirect distribution are both common in marketing goods. But for services, the channel of distribution is more often direct than indirect because most services are performed by the service business itself. For example, employees in a hair salon actually perform such services as cutting customers' hair. (In some instances, however, the channel for services can be indirect, as is the case when an independent insurance agent sells insurance to consumers or businesses.)

Channels in the Consumer and Industrial Markets

As you learned in Chapters 5 and 6, there are two distinct markets: the *consumer market* and the *industrial market*. For each market, different channels are generally used to reach the final consumer.

For example, a manufacturer of paper products may sell toilet tissue and napkins to both the consumer and industrial markets by using two different, distinct channels.

When selling to the industrial market, the company would sell napkins to industrial distributors who, in turn, would sell the napkins to restaurants.

When selling napkins in the consumer market, the paper manufacturer would sell them to a wholesaler or use brokers to sell them to retailers. The retailers would then sell the napkins to consumers for personal use.

The Consumer Market

Both direct and indirect distribution are used to sell consumer goods. Figure 7-2 shows the typical paths followed in distribution of consumer goods.

Direct Distribution. Most consumer goods are not marketed using direct distribution (see channel *A* in Figure 7-2) because consumers are accustomed to shopping in retail stores. However, there are four key ways in which direct distribution is used for consumer goods.

1. Selling products at the site of production, such as a farmer's roadside stand or a factory outlet.
2. Employing a sales force to call on consumers in their homes. The sales forces for Avon, Mary Kay Cosmetics, and Tupperware operate this way.
3. Using mail order to reach the ultimate consumer by advertising in magazines, catalogs, on television and radio, or through direct mail. Frequently, a toll-free number or an order form is provided for convenient ordering.
4. Using telephone solicitation to encourage customers to order over the phone. Magazine subscriptions are often sold this way.

Indirect Distribution. With indirect distribution, a number of different paths are used to get a consumer product to the ultimate user. *Producer or manufacturer to retailer to consumer* (channel *B* in Figure 7-2) is the most commonly used channel of distribution for merchandise that is timely or needs servicing, or for large retailers.

Timely merchandise goes out of fashion quickly, such as fashion apparel and accessories, and certain toys. Products that need servicing may involve contractual agreements among channel members. Such are the agreements between auto manufacturers and their franchised retail dealerships for selling and servicing their autos. Larger retailers, especially chain stores, use this channel because they are financially and physically equipped to buy in large quantities. And they can store and distribute the goods they buy from manufacturers.

The most common distribution method for staple goods is *manufacturer to wholesaler to retailer to consumer* (channel *C* in Figure 7-2). (Staple goods are items that are always carried in stock; their styles do not change frequently.) In this channel, the manufac-

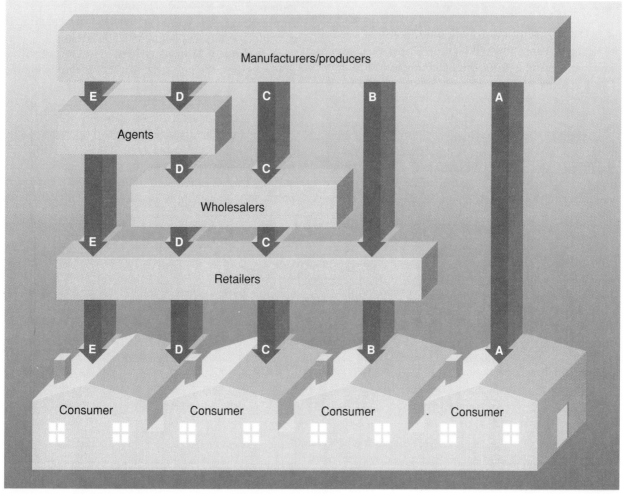

Figure 7-2   **Distribution Channels for Consumer Products**
A channel of distribution is the path a product takes from the producer or manufacturer to the final user. Which channels are classified as direct distribution? as indirect distribution?

turer sells the product to wholesalers. The wholesalers then handle the sales, warehousing, and distribution of the goods to retailers. Some consumer goods sold through wholesalers are supermarket items, fishing tackle, flowers, candy, and stationery supplies.

Manufacturer to agent to retailer to consumer (channel *E* in Figure 7-2) is the channel chosen by manufacturers who do not want to handle their own sales to the retailer. In this case, the agent does not take possession or title to the goods but simply brings the buyer and seller together. Expensive cookware, meat, hosiery, and some apparel and accessories are

sold through agents. In addition, many items in supermarkets are sold through brokers who represent food and nonfood manufacturers. Cosmetics and health and beauty aids also are sold through brokers to retailers.

Sometimes the manufacturer may wish to concentrate on production and leave sales and distribution to agents, wholesalers, and retailers. In this channel, the path is *manufacturer to agent to wholesaler to retailer to consumer* (channel *D* in Figure 7-2). The agent sells to wholesalers who are involved in storage, sale, and transportation to retailers. Then the retailer sells the product to consumers.

The Industrial Market

The channels of distribution for industrial goods (typical paths are shown in Figure 7-3) are usually different and distinct from the channels for consumer goods. This is primarily because industrial users and ultimate consumers shop differently and have different needs.

Direct Distribution. The most common method of distribution for major equipment used in manufacturing and other businesses is direct distribution: *manufacturer to industrial user* (channel *A* in Figure 7-3). The manufacturer's sales force calls on the industrial user to sell the product or service. For example, Xerox sales representatives sell copiers directly to manufacturers and commercial businesses.

Indirect Distribution. Indirect distribution is used in the industrial market by employing the services of agents or industrial distributors.

Manufacturer to industrial distributor to industrial user (channel *B* in Figure 7-3) is used most often for small standardized parts and operational supplies needed to run a business. These industrial distributors take ownership of the products, stock them, and sell them as needed to industrial users. For example, a restaurant supply distributor buys pots, pans,

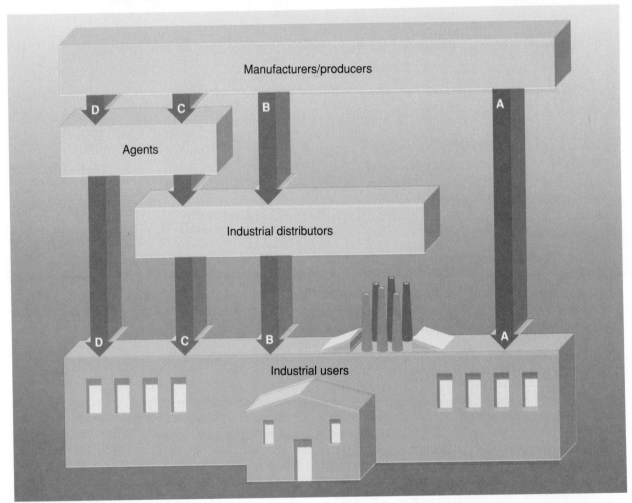

Figure 7-3 **Distribution Channels for Industrial Products**

Direct distribution is more common in the sale of industrial products than consumer products. Why?

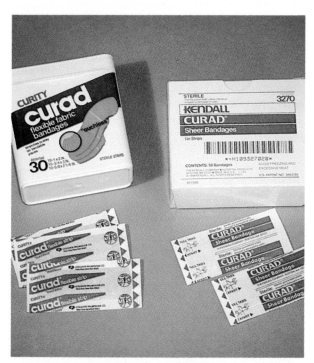

Some firms make products for both the consumer and the industrial markets. What differences do you see here in the packaging for the industrial products and in the packaging for the consumer products? What types of businesses might buy the industrial products?

utensils, serving pieces, and paper products from various manufacturers to sell to restaurant owners.

Manufacturer to agent to industrial user (channel *D* in Figure 7-3) is used when a manufacturer does not want to hire its own sales force. The agent represents the manufacturer for sale of the goods but does not take possession or title. The merchandise is shipped directly from the manufacturer to the industrial user. Construction equipment, farm products, and dry goods are often marketed this way.

Manufacturers that do not want to handle distribution of their product may choose the channel *manufacturer to agent to industrial distributor to industrial user* (channel *C* in Figure 7-3). This allows manufacturers to concentrate on what they do best—production. Some small manufacturers like this channel of distribution because they do not have the time or money to invest in a direct sales force. The agent sells the goods to the industrial distributor who stores, resells, and ships the items to the industrial user. The advantage of using an agent and an industrial distributor is that both are experts and should be

well known in the industry. Their reputation and services may be impossible for a small manufacturer's direct sales force to duplicate.

Considerations in Distribution Planning

Distribution planning involves decisions regarding a product's physical movement and transfer of ownership from producer to consumer. Distribution decisions involve and affect a firm's marketing program. Some of the major considerations are the use of nontraditional and multiple channels, selection of intermediaries, costs, and intensity of distribution desired.

Nontraditional and Multiple Channels

Businesses do not always follow traditional channels. One example of a nontraditional channel of distribution was created by L'Eggs panty hose, a division of Hanes. L'Eggs revolutionized the industry when it began selling panty hose in supermarkets. Before that time, panty hose were sold primarily through department stores and specialty shops. But L'Eggs knew it could reach more women by placing its product where they shopped most often—in supermarkets.

Multiple channels are used when a product fits the needs of industrial and ultimate consumers. (The manufacturers' packaging of products sold to both the industrial and consumer markets—toilet tissue, trash bags, paper towels, and bandages, for example, is often changed.)

Retailers also use multiple channels. A retail stationery store, for example, generally carries stationery supplies, greeting cards, and some convenience items for consumers. But some of its business may involve selling office supplies to businesses in the local area. To cater to this industrial market, the stationery store might offer credit, trade discounts, and delivery services.

Some manufacturers use multiple channels to reach as many consumers as possible. For example, Patagonia, a manufacturer of outdoor clothing and accessories, sells its products in its own retail stores, through catalogs, and through independent retail dealers. This approach to distribution planning can cause problems if the retail dealers feel they are competing with their supplier (Patagonia, in this case) for consumer sales. But if the manufacturer can prove there is no direct competition, retailers will accept this multiple channel of distribution policy.

Some retailers have experimented successfully with catalog sales. Ramsey Outdoor Stores, a New Jersey sporting goods retailer, and L.L. Bean of Freeport, Maine have sold their goods through national catalogs quite successfully for several years.

Intermediaries

Intermediaries simplify the distribution for manufacturers (see Figure 7-4). Wholesalers and industrial distributors make it possible for manufacturers to mass produce their goods and sell in large quantities. This reduces the number of transactions needed to reach the final users of the manufacturers' products.

Figure 7-4 **Intermediaries Simplify the Distribution for Manufacturers**

Without the use of an intermediary, the number of transactions needed for these five manufacturers to reach these five customers is considerably greater than when the channel of distribution includes an intermediary. How many transactions would a manufacturer need to reach each of its customers without an intermediary?

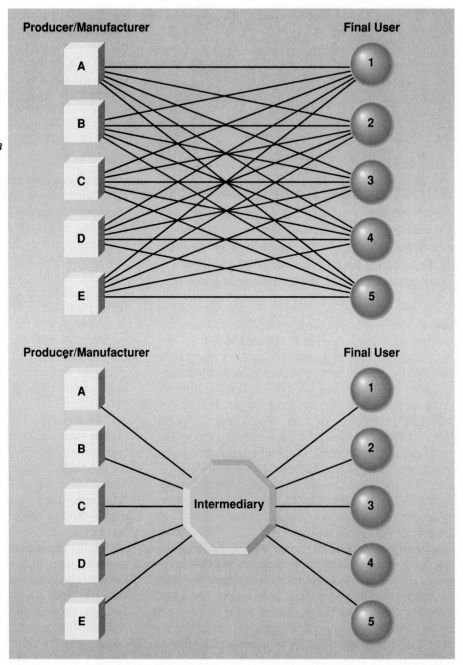

Cooperation in the Channel of Distribution

One major problem retailers face is keeping the quantity of stock high enough so they don't run out, yet low enough to prevent the major markdowns and overstocking that reduce their profits.

A new device called Quick Response, along with cooperation among retail stores, their suppliers, and their suppliers' suppliers, is shortening the ordering cycle by which merchandise makes its way from producer to consumer.

Quick Response is an integrated electronic computer system that uses bar coding to keep an inventory of merchandise in the correct size, color, style, and material. When more merchandise is needed, it is electronically reordered from domestic manufacturers who, in turn, electronically order the raw materials from their suppliers. Thus, each link in the production and distribution chain stocks only as much inventory as needed. This system has been used with apparel merchandise.

This is how the system works. Merchandise is bar coded at the department store. When a customer buys a product, laser scanners at the cash register decode the 12-digit Universal Product Code and enter the key elements of the sale. This information is simultaneously relayed to the store's central computer, which maintains a running inventory of goods.

As soon as the number of items of a particular style, size, and color drops to a certain level, a purchase order for a set number of additional items is automatically written and sent to the manufacturer.

To make this system work, the channel of distribution for the industrial products must also be involved. Thus, the producer of the goods must be linked to the producer of the raw materials needed to make the item. For example, the garment manufacturers must be linked with their fabric suppliers. The fabric suppliers must be linked with their fiber suppliers. This keeps inventories in balance with demand and reduces the time it takes for the goods to arrive at the retail store for sale to the ultimate consumer.

If this system works well, a retailer will seldom have to say to a customer, "Sorry, we are out of that item." And the inventories of all channel members will be matched to their customers' needs.

1. Diagram each separate channel of distribution and indicate the following for each: (a) each member of the channel of distribution and the order of the channel (for example, manufacturer to retailer to consumer); (b) type of product involved as consumer or industrial; and (c) method of distribution as direct or indirect.
2. Do you think the use of Quick Response will change the channels of distribution for other consumer products, such as automobiles, jewelry, or canned fruits and vegetables? Explain.

Retailers are a manufacturer's link to the consumer market. Since most people shop in retail stores to buy the products they need, manufacturers need retailers to sell their products to the final consumer. Retailers also provide customer service, credit, and the merchandising know-how needed to sell to final consumers.

Agents take on the selling responsibilities for manufacturers in both markets so manufacturers can concentrate on what they do best—manufacturing.

Another advantage of using wholesalers or agents is the knowledge and influence that both carry in certain markets. Agents and wholesalers are so entrenched in certain markets, for example, that a new manufacturer would find it difficult to break into that market without their help. For example, Rhino Records, a small record producer, pays a record broker between 15 and 20 percent of the wholesale price to distribute the Rhino label to retail stores.

Control and Costs

A manufacturer has certain advantages in maintaining control in the channel of distribution. But there are costs involved in doing so.

For example, a manufacturer can use its own direct sales force, or it can hire agents to do the selling. A direct sales force is more costly because the in-house sales representatives are on the company payroll, receive employee benefits, and are reimbursed for expenses. The manufacturer, though, has complete control over them. It can establish sales quotas and easily monitor each sales representative.

With an agent, the manufacturer loses some of its control over how sales are made. But the cost of using agents is lower than hiring an in-house sales staff. No employee benefits or expenses are paid because agents are independent businesses. In addition, agents are paid a set percentage of sales, so the cost of sales is always the same in relation to the sales generated.

Thus, manufacturers must make decisions regarding which intermediaries they will use, based on the company's distribution needs, costs, and services intermediaries can offer.

Intensity

When deciding on the strategy to use in the width of distribution, there are three levels of distribution intensity: *intensive*, *selective*, and *exclusive* distribution.

Intensive distribution means use of all suitable outlets for the product. The objectives are intensive market coverage, acceptance by channel members, high sales volume, and high profits. The ultimate goal is to sell to as many customers as possible. For example, STP sells its oil and gasoline additives to service stations, mass merchandisers, and supermarkets.

Intensive distribution is the distribution method selected for products that are highly competitive, frequently purchased, and generally classified as convenience items. Milk, newspapers, candy, light bulbs, hardware, batteries, toothpaste, shampoo, and food products are some consumer goods that fall into this category. Industrial supplies and office supplies fall into this category in the industrial market.

Selective distribution means that a limited number of outlets in a given geographic area are used to sell the product. The objective is to select channel members that are good credit risks, aggressive marketers, and good inventory planners. With this type of distribution strategy, the manufacturer may exert some pressure on intermediaries to move the product. Frequent local advertising may be required of the intermediaries, as well as maintenance of a well-stocked and well-balanced inventory.

When retailers carry goods that are selectively distributed, they face less competition than with products that are distributed intensively. As a result, they are more willing to promote the manufacturer's products. The intermediaries chosen to sell these products are generally the best equipped to maintain the image of the product. They are also selected for their ability to cater to the final users that the manufacturer wants to attract. For example, Ralph Lauren selects only top department and specialty stores to appeal to the affluent target market that will buy its clothing and dry goods.

Most shopping malls contain specialty stores that use selective distribution. Think of two specialty stores in a local shopping center or mall, tell the goods and/or services they offer, and tell the target market for those products.

The Million Dollar Floating Mistake

The bad news was that someone at the Procter soap and candle works in Cincinnati mixed a batch of soap compound too long, allowing it to fill with air. The good news was that the defective soap floated in water—a marketing angle that seemed made in heaven. The name Ivory, as the soap came to be known, seemed made in heaven, too. It came to Harley Procter during a church sermon mentioning "ivory palaces."

Exclusive distribution involves a limited number of intermediaries, so that only one intermediary is assigned to each geographic territory. Prestige, image, channel control, and a high profit margin for both the manufacturer and intermediaries are characteristic of this distribution strategy. When there is an exclusive distribution agreement, the retailer is usually

Sherwin-Williams uses an integrated distribution system to reach its ultimate customers. In what sense is its operation "integrated"?

tied by contract to the manufacturer. Franchised operations are examples of exclusive distribution planning.

In addition to manufacturer-sponsored franchise agreements, wholesalers may sponsor voluntary groups in which a retailer agrees to buy and maintain a minimum inventory of the wholesaler's products. The wholesaler services the account regularly by checking inventory, telling the retailer what needs to be reordered, and by sponsoring special promotions to help sell those products to final consumers. An example of a voluntary group sponsored by a wholesaler is NAPA (National Auto Parts Association). Retail auto parts stores affiliated with NAPA buy most of their stock from that wholesaler and participate in its promotions.

Guidelines set forth by the manufacturer, franchisor, or the wholesaler cooperative ensure exclusivity of the product line to the retailer. The retailers will have limited competition in the sale of the product. And the product's image is maintained through the exclusivity of distribution. It is assumed that buyers will seek the outlets that carry these products.

A variation on exclusive distribution is found in manufacturers that own and run their own retail operations. This is called *integrated distribution*. The manufacturer acts as wholesaler and retailer for its own products. For example, Sherwin-Williams sells its paint in company-owned retail stores.

VOCABULARY REVIEW

Write a brief definition of each word, based on your reading of the chapter.

channel of distribution
intermediaries
wholesalers
retailers
direct distribution
indirect distribution
intensive distribution
selective distribution
exclusive distribution

FACT AND IDEA REVIEW

1. A dairy sells milk to a supermarket and the supermarket sells the milk to a final consumer. Where did the channel of distribution begin? Where did it end?

2. The dairy in question #1 sells the milk to a bakery, and the bakery uses the milk in making bread that it sells to final consumers. How many channels of distribution are involved?

3. How are intermediaries classified? Provide two examples of each classification.

4. Are transportation companies and independent warehouses part of the channel of distribution? Explain your answer.

5. What is the difference between direct and indirect distribution?

6. What channel of distribution is used when the manufacturer only wants to concentrate on production and leave sales and distribution to the distribution experts in the consumer market? in the industrial market?

7. When small standardized parts and operational supplies are distributed to industrial users, what channel of distribution is generally used?

8. What channel of distribution is generally used for services?

9. When are multiple channels used?

10. To develop an effective distribution plan, what four factors must be considered?

CRITICAL THINKING

1. In what ways are independent manufacturer's agents and brokers similar? In what ways are they different?

2. True or False. "Most consumer goods are marketed using a direct channel of distribution." Explain your answer.

3. Assume you are a manufacturer of replacement windows used in homes, and you want to use a direct channel of distribution to reach your potential customer. What options do you have?

4. A fresh produce business bought produce from farmers and sold most of its goods to restaurants, then decided to open a small retail operation to sell its extra produce to the ultimate consumer. How would you classify this business? Diagram the two channels of distribution the business is using to reach the two markets.

5. Compare the advantages and disadvantages of hiring a direct sales force versus using agents to sell goods or services.

6. If you were to make a decision regarding the intensity of the width of distribution for these products, which level of intensity (intensive, selective, or exclusive) would you select and why? (a) IBM personal computers; (b) expensive imported sweaters; (c) new shampoo; and (d) an automobile.

USING BASIC SKILLS

Math

1. A newspaper ad offers hedge trimmers for sale at $5.99 each plus $1.25 for postage and handling, or two trimmers for $9.99 plus $1.85 for postage and handling. What will two hedge trimmers cost?

2. Another newspaper ad is offering a home hairstyler at $19.95 each plus $1.55 for postage and handling, and a box of 3 replacement blades

at $2.50 per box plus $.50 for postage and handling. What is the total cost of the hairstyler? What is the total cost of a box of replacement blades? What is the total charge for 4 hairstylers and 4 boxes of replacement blades?

Communication

3. As secretary for the local association of retail florists, you have been directed by the association president to write to the local wholesale florist who has been selling to the final consumer. Give at least two reasons in your letter telling why the retail florists are upset about this. Tell the wholesale florist that the retail florists will boycott the business if the practice continues.

4. A new sporting goods apparel manufacturer wants to sell its products through catalogs to compete with Lands' End, Cabela's, Patagonia, and L. L. Bean. As the new marketing manager, you just spent a lot of money buying a specialized mailing list of prospective customers. You don't want to send catalogs to all of them until you know they want one. Write a catchy letter to get prospective customers interested in receiving your catalog.

Human Relations

5. You work for a broker as a merchandising specialist in charge of following supermarket planograms for your company's principals. (Planograms are diagrams of shelf positions and other merchandising requirements for stocking products.) During your visit to one of the supermarkets for which you are responsible, you begin to rearrange and stock the shelves, following the planogram. A new assistant store manager approaches you and says, "Who gave you the authority to rearrange these shelves?" What would you do and say?

6. You are a salesperson for Fanny Farmer candies. A customer complains that the selection is small and that she would like to see candy made by other manufacturers sold in the store. Fanny Farmer stores are run by the manufacturer. What would you say to the customer?

APPLICATION PROJECTS

1. More and more consumers are shopping through catalogs. Here are some of the ways businesses obtain merchandise found in these catalogs:
   a. The manufacturer makes the goods found in the catalog.
   b. The manufacturer contracts with other manufacturers to make the goods found in the catalog under the private label of the catalog house.
   c. A catalog house, acting as an independent retailer, buys goods from different manufacturers and places those goods in their catalogs.
   d. A retailer prepares a catalog of goods sold in the store.
   Diagram the channel of distribution for each of the four ways goods are sold through catalogs. Bring one catalog to class and identify the channel of distribution used for the goods in the catalog.

2. Assume you are a small manufacturer of specially designed clothing for people who spend a lot of time outside in cold weather. You currently sell this clothing yourself to retailers near your factory in Pennsylvania. You would like to expand your distribution to retailers in other northern states, but your budget does not permit you to hire the large sales force necessary to reach all the retailers in those states. What options are available to you? Explain the advantages and disadvantages of your options.

PART

3

HUMAN RESOURCE ESSENTIALS

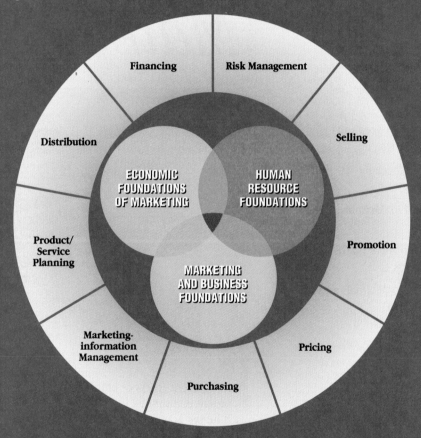

8

After completing this chapter, you will be able to:

1. write numbers in words, using commas and hyphens correctly,

2. understand the meaning of fractional amounts,

3. perform basic math operations with decimal numbers,

4. round answers, especially amounts of money,

5. convert fractions to decimal equivalents,

6. use a calculator to solve math problems, and

7. convert percents to decimals and decimals to percents.

WORDS TO KNOW

digit
fractions
decimal number
reverse-entry system
percent

Fundamentals of Mathematics

In a recent survey, employers in marketing careers were nearly unanimous in saying that entry-level workers need a much better grasp of the fundamentals of math. So in this chapter, you will have a brief review of the numbering system and a more extensive review of fractions, decimal numbers, and percentages. You will also improve your skill in using a calculator.

Writing Whole Numbers

The numbering system we use is composed of ten basic symbols: 0, 1, 2, 3, 4, 5, 6, 7, 8, and 9. These symbols are called *digits*. *Each **digit** represents a number and can be combined to represent larger numbers, such as 14; 215; 4, 237; and 36,852.*

The numbers above are all whole numbers because they can be written without fractions or decimals. Each digit in a whole number represents *how many* of something. The digit on the right represents the number of *ones*. The next digit represents the number of *tens*. So in the number 25, there are five *ones* and two *tens*.

Knowing the placement name for each digit and for groups of digits is necessary when reading numbers and when writing numbers in words. You will use this skill, for example, when you write a check, since you must write the number of dollars in words in one section. Follow these five steps when you read whole numbers or write them in words.

1. Separate the number into groups of three digits: units, thousands, and millions. Very large numbers may include groups of digits for billions, trillions, and so on.

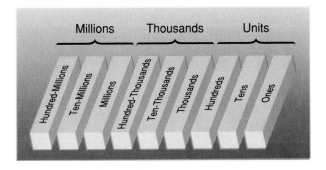

2. Separate the groups with commas.

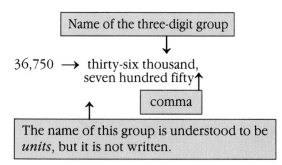

3. When writing whole numbers, never use the word ***and***.

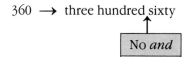

4. Use hyphens in numbers less than 100 that are written as two words.

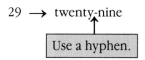

5. When a three-digit group is made up of only zeros, do not write the name of the group.

3,000,375 → three million, three hundred seventy-five

No words are written for the thousands group.

Fractions

You learned about fractions when you were still in grade school, but you may not have had a lot of practice using them. Many jobs in business, especially in marketing, require a good understanding of fractions. *Fractions are numbers used to describe a part of some standard amount.* The top number, the *numerator*, represents the number of parts being considered. The bottom number, the *denominator*, represents how many parts in a whole or how many total parts are being considered. For example, the shaded area in the following rectangle is ⅗ (three-fifths) of the total rectangle.

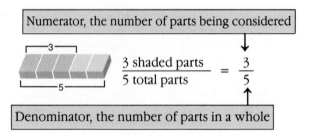

Numerator, the number of parts being considered

$$\frac{3 \text{ shaded parts}}{5 \text{ total parts}} = \frac{3}{5}$$

Denominator, the number of parts in a whole

In the example below, the number of circles is 2/7 (two-sevenths) of the total number of shapes.

$$\frac{2 \text{ circles}}{7 \text{ shapes}} = \frac{2}{7}$$

Examples

$$\frac{\text{Number of shaded parts}}{\text{Total number of parts}} = \frac{3}{8}$$

$$\frac{3 \text{ shaded parts}}{\text{Total number of parts}} = \frac{3}{3} = 1$$

One whole circle is shaded.

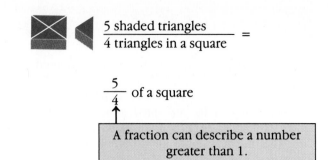

$$\frac{5 \text{ shaded triangles}}{4 \text{ triangles in a square}} =$$

$$\frac{5}{4} \text{ of a square}$$

A fraction can describe a number greater than 1.

When the numerator is greater than the denominator, the fraction describes a number greater than 1 and can be written as a *mixed number*, a whole number and fraction together.

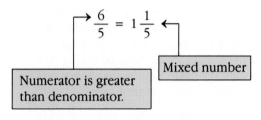

$$\frac{6}{5} = 1\frac{1}{5}$$

Numerator is greater than denominator.

Mixed number

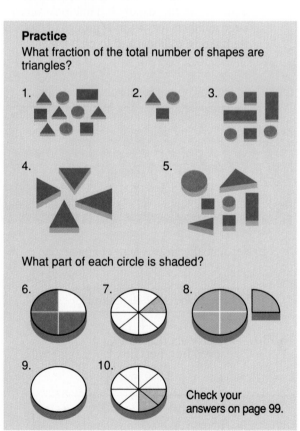

Practice
What fraction of the total number of shapes are triangles?

1. 2. 3.

4. 5.

What part of each circle is shaded?

6. 7. 8.

9. 10.

Check your answers on page 99.

Decimal Numbers

A decimal number is a fraction or mixed number whose demoninator is a multiple of 10. The decimal number 5.3 means 5 + 0.3, or 5 + ³⁄₁₀ or 5 ³⁄₁₀. The decimal number 935.47 can be broken down as 900 + 30 + 5 + ⁴⁄₁₀ + ⁷⁄₁₀₀.

As with whole numbers, knowing the placement names is necessary when reading decimals and when writing them in words. Decimal placement names are used for digits to the right of the decimal point.

Hundreds | Tens | Ones | Tenths | Hundredths | Thousandths | Ten-Thousandths

Decimal point

Decimal placement names

To read a decimal number or write it in words, follow the steps below. Use 15.083 as an example.

Step 1 Begin with the whole number to the left of the decimal point (*fifteen*).

Step 2 Read or write *and* for the decimal point.

Step 3 Read or write the number to the right of the decimal point as a whole number (*eighty-three*).

Step 4 Use the name of the decimal place of the final digit (*thousandths*).

The result is *fifteen and eighty-three thousandths*.

You may also hear decimal numbers read using the whole number and only the names of the digits in the decimal places and *point* for the decimal point. For example, 15.083 might be read as *fifteen point zero eight three*.

Understanding the relationship between decimal numbers and fractions is important when you are writing a check. After writing the amount in decimal form, you must write it again, using words for the dollars and a fraction for the cents.

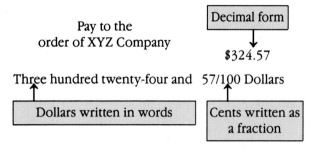

Pay to the order of XYZ Company

Decimal form
$324.57

Three hundred twenty-four and 57/100 Dollars

Dollars written in words

Cents written as a fraction

Practice:

Write the decimal numbers in words. Write the amounts of money (as indicated by $) as you would on a check. Check your answers on page 99.

1. 5.6   2. 0.7   3. 14.5   4. 0.09   5. 3.12

6. 9.05   7. 10.33   8. 25.48   9. $155.87   10. $545.67

Adding and Subtracting Decimal Numbers

To add or subtract decimal numbers, first line up the numbers vertically, keeping the decimal points in the same vertical column. Then add or subtract as you would with whole numbers. Sometimes you may need to write zeros to fill the column.

$$1.45 + 3.4 = ?$$

```
  1.45
+ 3.40
------
  4.85
```

Keep the decimal point in the same vertical column.

Write 0s as needed.

Add as with whole numbers.

$$13.4 - 7.56 = ?$$

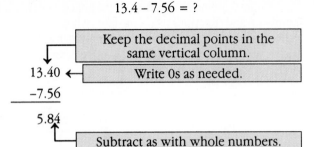

Keep the decimal points in the same vertical column.

13.40 ← Write 0s as needed.

$$\begin{array}{r} 13.40 \\ -7.56 \\ \hline 5.84 \end{array}$$

Subtract as with whole numbers.

Practice:

Complete the following addition and subtraction problems with decimal numbers. Check your answers on page 99.

1. 5.4 + 8.6 =   2. 7.5 + 9.6 =

3. 9.8 + 7.5 =   4. 18 + 7.7 =

5. 17.5 + 4.75 =   6. 7.04 + 71.5 =

7. 6.7 + 0.6 + 2.67 + 7 =   8. 4.6 – 3.3 =

9. 45.9 – 7.76 =   10. $8 – $3.76 =

11. 5.7 – 1.11 + 14.23 + 0.078 =   12. 23.6 – 8.431 =

13. Bob's Bicycle Shop paid the following bills in September: $86.45 for gas, $114.86 for electricity, $187.58 for telephone, $98.36 for insurance, and $875 for rent. What is the total?

14. From a 40-yard bolt of fabric, Carol sold the following pieces: 3.33 yards, 4.5 yards, 2.25 yards, 2.125 yards, and 3. 875 yards. How many yards are left?

Multiplying Decimal Numbers

To multiply decimal numbers, use the following two-step process.

Step 1   Multiply the two numbers as if they were whole numbers. Pay no attention to the decimal points yet.

Step 2   Add the number of decimal places in the two numbers being multiplied. In the product, count from the right the total number

---

of decimal places. Then place the decimal point in the product so the number of decimal places is equal to the sum of the decimal places in the two numbers being multiplied. Sometimes you may need to write zeros in the product in order to place the decimal point.

$$9.05 \times 4.31 = ?$$

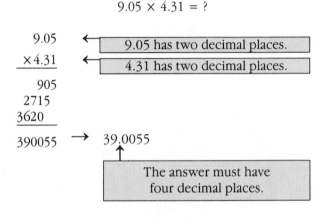

9.05 ← 9.05 has two decimal places.

× 4.31 ← 4.31 has two decimal places.

$$\begin{array}{r} 9.05 \\ \times 4.31 \\ \hline 905 \\ 2715 \\ 3620 \\ \hline 390055 \end{array} \rightarrow 39.0055$$

The answer must have four decimal places.

$$0.25 \times 0.3 =$$

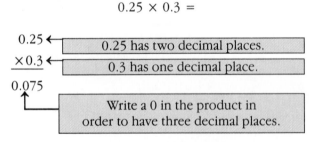

0.25 ← 0.25 has two decimal places.

× 0.3 ← 0.3 has one decimal place.

0.075

Write a 0 in the product in order to have three decimal places.

Multiply amounts of money as you would other decimal numbers. Remember to include the dollar sign in your answer.

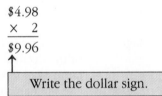

$$\begin{array}{r} \$4.98 \\ \times \quad 2 \\ \hline \$9.96 \end{array}$$

Write the dollar sign.

Rounding with Decimal Numbers.
Sometimes you may need to round a decimal number. This is especially common when multiplying with amounts of money, as when figuring tax amounts, discounts, and so on. Use the following steps to round decimal amounts. Round 16.842, 16.852, and 16.892 to the nearest tenth.

Step 1 Find the decimal place you are rounding to.

16.842   16.852   16.892

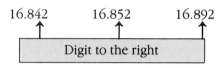

Tenths place

Step 2 Look at the digit to the *right* of that place.

16.842   16.852   16.892

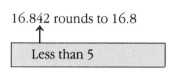

Digit to the right

Step 3 If the digit to the right is less than 5, leave the first digit as is. If the digit is 5 or greater, round up.

16.842 rounds to 16.8

Less than 5

16.852 rounds to 16.9

5

16.892 rounds to 16.9

Greater than 5

When you are working with amounts of money, use these steps to round your answer to the nearest cent (the nearest hundredth).

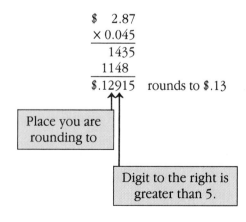

$$\begin{array}{r} \$\ \ 2.87 \\ \times\,0.045 \\ \hline 1435 \\ 1148\ \ \\ \hline \$.12915 \end{array}$$ rounds to $.13

Place you are rounding to

Digit to the right is greater than 5.

Practice:

Complete the following multiplication problems with decimal numbers. Round answers with money amounts to the nearest cent. Check your answers on page 99.

1.   5.2   2.   6.1   3. 31.4   4. 31.6
   × 7   × 4.6   × 7.8   × 6.3

5. 5.08   6. 7.75   7. 0.687
  ×0.68   × 3.2   × 8.02

8. 8.5 × 7.2 =   9. 0.83 × 0.04 =

10. If you earn $8.75 an hour, how much pay should you receive for 39.5 hours of work?

11. At Big Al's Pizza, the cost of delivering orders is $.41 per mile. If the delivery van averaged 458.7 miles per day last week, what is the average daily cost of making deliveries?

Dividing Decimal Numbers

Division of decimal numbers is similar to division of whole numbers. Follow the steps below to divide decimal numbers.

Step 1 Set up the division problem as you would with whole numbers.

69.7 divided by 1.7 = $1.7\,\overline{)69.7}$

69.7 divided by 1.724 = $1.724\,\overline{)69.7}$

Step 2 Shift the decimal point in the divisor so that the divisor becomes a whole number. Then shift the decimal point in the dividend the same number of decimal places. Write zeros in the dividend, if necessary, in order to place the decimal point.

$1.7\,\overline{)69.7}$ $17.\,\overline{)697.}$

Shift the decimal point one place to the right.

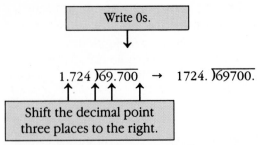

$1.724 \overline{)69.700} \rightarrow 1724. \overline{)69700.}$

Shift the decimal point three places to the right.

Step 3 Place a decimal point in the answer space directly above its new position in the dividend. Then divide as with whole numbers.

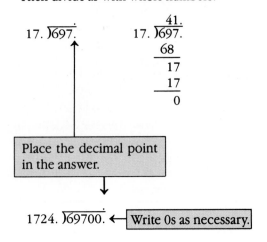

$17. \overline{)697.}$

$$
\begin{array}{r}
41. \\
17. \overline{)697.} \\
68 \\
\hline
17 \\
17 \\
\hline
0
\end{array}
$$

Place the decimal point in the answer.

$1724. \overline{)69700.}$ ← **Write 0s as necessary.**

Sometimes you may need to write extra zeros after the decimal point in order to have a remainder of zero.

$$16.38 \div 6.5 = ?$$

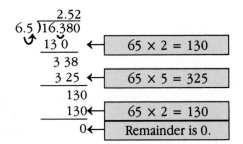

$$
\begin{array}{r}
2.52 \\
6.5 \overline{)16.380} \\
13\,0 \\
\hline
3\,38 \\
3\,25 \\
\hline
130 \\
130 \\
\hline
0
\end{array}
$$

$65 \times 2 = 130$

$65 \times 5 = 325$

$65 \times 2 = 130$

Remainder is 0.

Some decimal answers will continue indefinitely as you write zeros to the right of the decimal point. Some, called *repeating decimals*, will repeat a number or pattern of numbers.

These digits repeat.

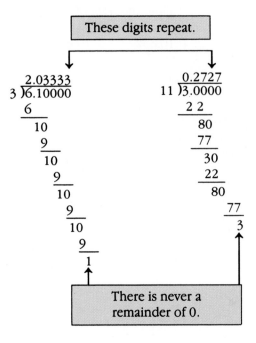

$$
\begin{array}{r}
2.03333 \\
3 \overline{)6.10000} \\
6 \\
\hline
10 \\
9 \\
\hline
10 \\
9 \\
\hline
10 \\
9 \\
\hline
10 \\
9 \\
\hline
1
\end{array}
\qquad
\begin{array}{r}
0.2727 \\
11 \overline{)3.0000} \\
2\,2 \\
\hline
80 \\
77 \\
\hline
30 \\
22 \\
\hline
80 \\
77 \\
\hline
3
\end{array}
$$

There is never a remainder of 0.

Practice:

Complete the following division problems with decimal numbers. Round answers to the nearest hundredth. Check your answers on page 99.

1. $0.75 \div 1.8 =$ 2. $4.76 \div 3.8 =$

3. $1.758 \div 4.64 =$ 4. $8.4 \div 0.015 =$

5. $0.063 \div 2.1 =$ 6. $6.002 \div 0.3 =$

7. Software Corporation paid $2,366.05 for computer paper. If the paper costs $29.95 per box, how many boxes did the corporation buy?

8. Edward averages 80 questions per hour when typing test questions into a computer testbank. How long will it take him to enter 1,800 questions?

Converting Fractions to Decimals.

As you read in the section on fractions, decimal equivalents of fractions are important in many jobs in marketing. To convert any fraction to a decimal, simply divide the numerator by the denominator.

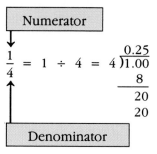

$$\frac{1}{4} = 1 \div 4 = 4\overline{)1.00}$$

$$\frac{1}{4} = 0.25$$

$$\frac{2}{3} = 2 \div 3 = 3\overline{)2.0}$$

There is never a remainder of 0.

In its decimal form, ⅔ is a repeating decimal. When working with repeating decimals, you may round to the nearest hundredth for most applications.

⅔ rounds to 0.67.

Using a Calculator

Nearly everyone in marketing and business uses calculators. There are two types of calculators commonly used today. The most widely used type uses algebraic entry system. This is the type of calculator used in the problems that follow. The other type uses RPN, a reverse-entry system. *The basic difference is that with the reverse-entry system, you enter the first amount, then the second amount, and then enter the operation (added to, subtracted from, multiplied by, or divided into the first amount).* If you have a calculator that uses the reverse-entry system, read the instruction book that accompanies your calculator very carefully.

If you expect to be hired in sales or any other marketing job, you will almost certainly use a calculator. Besides simply knowing which buttons to press, you will be expected to work with accuracy, know how to work with fractions and amounts of money, and have an understanding of how the calculator computes with multiple operations.

When using a calculator, many people follow the *guess-and-check method*: they estimate first, then enter the problem in the calculator, and finally, check the displayed answer against the estimate.

You may wonder why it is important to estimate your answers when you use a calculator. Surely the calculator is more accurate than your estimate. Sometimes, though, you may make errors when entering numbers or even press the wrong operations key. So it's important to have an estimate of the answer in mind. For example, if you're expecting an answer of about 300, you'll know something is wrong if the displayed answer on your calculator is 3,300.

$$388 + 995 = ?$$
Estimate: 400 + 1,000 = 1,400

Displayed answer

Enter the problem:
[3] [8] [8] [+] [9] [9] [5] [=] 1383
Check: 1,383 is reasonably close to the estimate of 1,400.

$$480 \times 112 = ?$$
Estimate: 500 × 100 = 50,000

Displayed answer

Enter the problem:
[4] [8] [0] [×] [1] [1] [2] [=] 53760
Check: 53,760 is reasonably close to the estimate of 50,000.

Another way to ensure accuracy when using a calculator is to check the display after you enter each number and before you press the operation key. If you have made an error, press the *clear entry* key [CE] to remove the last entry. Suppose you want to multiply 5.8 × 7.2, but you enter [5] [.] [8] [×] [7] [2]. Press [CE] to delete the last two keystrokes.

Then you can re-enter the second number correctly. The first number will remain in the calculator. Press the equals key ⊟, and the answer will be displayed: 41.76.

Keep in mind as you enter digits that you can disregard leading zeros to the left of the decimal point (as in 0.6 or 0.375) and final zeros after the decimal point (as in 9.250 or 41.500). You don't need to enter these zeros; the calculator will display all the digits needed.

Number	Keystrokes Entered	Display
0.785	⊡ ⑦ ⑧ ⑤	0.785
5.10	⑤ ⊡ ①	5.1

When dealing with mixed numbers or fractions, you must first convert the fractions to decimal form. Do this by dividing the numerator by the denominator. For example, to enter $5\frac{1}{4}$, first enter ① ÷ ④. Then add the whole number by entering + ⑤.

When solving problems dealing with money, remember to write the dollar sign in the answer. You may also have to round the displayed answer to the nearest cent. To review rounding, see page 92.

Display ↓	Answer written as money amount
5.25	$5.25
25.368216	$25.37 (Round to the nearest cent.)
46.0194	$46.02 (Round to the nearest cent.)
76514.1	$76,514.10 (No commas are shown in large numbers on most calculators.)

A calculator can operate on only two numbers at a time. However, you can perform a string of involved calculations on more than two numbers if you are very careful. When only addition and subtraction are involved, the calculator will perform these operations as they are entered.

⑧ ⊡ ⑥ + ⊡ ② ⑤ + ① ① ⊡ ⑨
⊟ ③ ⊡ ⑥ ② ⊟ 17.13

When only multiplication and division are involved, the calculator will also perform these operations as they are entered.

⑦ ⑦ ⑤ × ⊡ ⑨ ⑥ ÷ ⑤
× ① ⊡ ⑨ ⑥ ⊟ 291.648

However, when a calculation involves a combination of addition or subtraction with multiplication or division, not all calculators work the same way. You will need to check how your calculator performs the operations in this type of problem. Most calculators will do the operations as they are entered.

6 + 4 × 6 will be calculated as

| 6 + 4 | × 6 =
   ↓
   10   × 6 = 60.

6 × 4 + 6 will be calculated as

| 6 × 4 | + 6 =
   ↓
   24   + 6 = 30.

9 – 5 × 2 + 6 ÷ 7 will be calculated as

| 9 – 5 | × 2 + 6 ÷ 7 =
   ↓
   | 4   × 2 |
        ↓
     | 8 + 6 |
        ↓
     14   ÷ 7 = 2

Percentages

Percent means parts per hundred; a number expressed as a percent represents the number of parts per hundred. To write a whole number or a decimal number as a percent, multiply it by 100. A simple way to do this is to move the decimal point two places *to the right.*

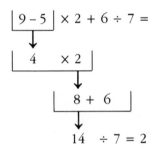

0.70 = 0.70 × 100 = 70%   or 0.70 = 70%
0.05 = 0.05 × 100 = 5%   or 0.05 = 5%
  2.5 = 2.5 × 100 = 250%   or 2.50 = 250%

Move the decimal point two places to the right.

Write 0s as needed.

You can use a calculator to do this operation.

$.70 \times 100 = $ 70 = 70%

$2.5 \times 100 = $ 250 = 250%

To write a fraction or mixed number as a percent, first convert the fraction to decimal form. Do this by dividing the numerator by the denominator. If there is a whole number, add it to the converted fraction. Then multiply by 100. You can use a calculator to do this operation.

½ = $1 \div 2 \times 100 = $ 50 = 50%

⅜ = $3 \div 8 \times 100 = $ 37.5 = 37.5%

4⅖ = $2 \div 5 + 4 \times 100$
$= $ 440 = 440%

You can change a percent to a decimal number by dividing by 100. A simple way to do this is to move the decimal point two places *to the left*.

Move the decimal point two places to the left.

24.8% = 24.8 ÷ 100 = 0.248 or 24.8% = 0.248
0.5% = 0.5 ÷ 100 = 0.005 or 00.5% = 0.005

Write 0s as needed.

You can use a calculator to do this operation.

12.6% = $12.6 \div 100 = $ 0.126
1.4% = $1.4 \div 100 = $ 0.014

You can also convert a percent with a fraction or mixed number to a decimal by using a calculator.

7¼% = $1 \div 4 + 7 \div 100$
$= $ 0.0725

Percent Problems

Percent problems are often encountered on a job. For example, you may be asked to figure a discount amount or the amount of sales tax. Or you may have to figure the total selling price, including the tax. Maybe you will be asked to figure the percent commission on your total sales.

Most percent problems will involve finding a percent of a number. To do that, multiply the decimal equivalent of the percent by the number.

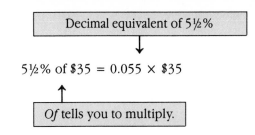

Decimal equivalent of 5½%

5½% of $35 = 0.055 × $35

Of tells you to multiply.

Use these steps to help you solve percent problems.

1. Estimate the answer.
2. Translate the problem into a math statement.
3. Do the calculations.
4. If necessary, round money amounts to the nearest cent.
5. Check your answer.

Many calculators have a percent key $\boxed{\%}$ that can simplify the calculations. Read the instructions for your calculator to find out how to use the percent key.

Two types of percent problems are explained below. The problems can be solved with a calculator without the use of a percent key.

1. Suppose you have sold a set of skis listed at $395.99 to someone eligible for a 15% discount. How much, in dollars and cents, will you allow as a discount on these skis?

   First: Estimate the answer. Round the list price to $400. Figure that 10% of $400 is $40. Since 15% is one and a half times 10%, estimate the discount at about $60 (one and a half times $40).

   Second: Translate the problem into a math statement.
   15% of $395.99 = 0.15 × 395.99

   Third: Do the calculations.
   0.15 × $395.99 = $59.3985

   Fourth: Round the answer to the nearest cent, if necessary.
   $59.3985 rounds to $59.40.

   Finally: Check the answer against your estimate. $59.40 is reasonably close to the estimate of $60. The discount amount is $59.40.

2. If sales tax is 6½%, how much tax should you collect on the sale of these skis? You

Currency Exchange

Every day customer service representatives at Deak International currency exchange house work with everyone's favorite thing: money.

At Deak International, counter tellers are as familiar with Japanese yen, Botswanan pula, and Yugoslavian dinar as they are with American dollars. Deak's 78 branches in the U.S and Canada convert hundreds of millions of dollars from one currency to another every year.

As more companies become international, you, too, may someday have to convert currencies.

Currencies are not equal. For example, one dollar may equal 140 yen, or 2.1 South African rand but only .48 English pounds. The amount of one currency it takes to buy an amount of another currency of equal value is called the exchange rate. The exchange rate often changes daily.

The exchange rate is given as a ratio. For example, the yen to dollar value is said to be 140 to 1, ($^{140}/_1$). (In exchange ratios, the *one* represents the local currency, in this case, dollars.) One dollar buys 140 yen.

How many dollars (or parts of a dollar) does one yen buy? All you need is a pencil and simple fractions to figure it out.

Write down the reciprocal of the ratio of 140 to 1 (or $^1/_{140}$). Now divide 1 by 140. This gives you a figure in dollars: $.00714. One yen equals about seven-one-thousandths of a dollar or seven-tenths of one cent. (Check your answer by multiplying .00714 by 140.)

If you have basic math skills, you'll never have to worry if you misplace your calculator.

1. In what situations might you have to figure costs in terms of another currency?
2. You have 150 French francs. Estimate how many American dollars they buy if the exchange rate is 4.97 francs to 1 dollar. Check your answer with a calculator.

have to find out the net selling price before you can figure the tax amount.

List price – discount = net price
$395.99 - $59.40 = $336.59

Now you can proceed, following these guidelines.
Estimate:
Round 6½% to 7% and $336.59 to $300. A 7% sales tax means that $7 tax is collected on every $100 in sales. So you can estimate the tax to be $21 (3 × $7).

Translate:
6½% of $336.59 = 0.065 × $336.59

Calculate:
0.065 × $336.59 = $21.8784

Round:
$21.8784 rounds to $21.88.

Check:
$21.88 is reasonably close to the estimate of $21. The sales tax to be collected is $21.88.

Answers to Practice Problems

Page 90:

1. $^4/_{10}$ (or $^2/_5$)   5. $^2/_7$ 8. $^5/_4$ (or $1^1/_4$)
2. $^1/_3$ 6. $^3/_4$ 9. no parts shaded
3. 0   7. $^1/_8$ 10. $^2/_8$ (or $^1/_4$)
4. $^4/_4$ (or 1)

Page 91:

1. five and six tenths
2. seven tenths
3. fourteen and five tenths
4. nine hundredths
5. three and twelve hundredths
6. nine and five hundredths
7. ten and thirty-three hundredths
8. twenty-five and forty-eight hundredths
9. One hundred fifty-five and————————87/100
10. Five hundred forty-five and——————67/100

Page 92:

1. 14   2. 17.1   3. 17.3   4. 25.7
5. 22.25   6. 78.54   7. 16.97   8. 1.3
9. 38.14   10. $4.24   11. 18.898   12. 15.169
13. $1362.25   14. 23.92 yards

Page 93:

1. 36.4   2. 28.06   3. 244.92   4. 199.08
5. 3.4544   6. 24.8   7. 5.50974   8. 61.2
9. 0.0332   10. $345.63   11. $188.07

Page 94:

1. 0.41666667   5. 0.03
2. 1.25263158   6. 20.00666667
3. 0.37887931   7. 79 boxes
4. 560   8. 22.5 hours

VOCABULARY REVIEW

Write a brief definition of each word, based on your reading of the chapter.

digit   reverse-entry system
fractions   percent
decimal number

FACT AND IDEA REVIEW

1. You should separate whole numbers into groups when you write them in words. What are these groups?

2. What punctuation should you use between the thousands and the units when writing out a whole number?

3. What is a fraction?

4. What is a numerator? What is a denominator?

5. What is a decimal number? Give some examples.

6. When you multiply two decimal numbers, how do you decide the number of decimal places in the answer?

7. Describe how you would convert a fraction to a decimal number.

8. What can you do to increase your accuracy when using a calculator?

9. What does a percentage express?

10. Why is it important to estimate your answers, even when using a calculator?

CRITICAL THINKING

1. Discuss with other students your particular areas of interest in the marketing field. How are mathematics skills important in each area?

2. A real estate agent sold an exclusive home for $4,000,000. Her commission was 2 percent. How much did she make on this sale? What do you think are the advantages/disadvantages of doing sales on a commission-only basis? Would you be willing to do sales on that basis?

USING BASIC SKILLS

Math

1. Suppose you are a sales representative for a local jewelry maker. You have received a total of $4,567 in orders for the jeweler this month. Your commission is 15 percent. First, estimate your commission for this month. Then, translate the problem into a math statement. Finally, use your calculator to do the arithmetic.

2. Suppose you want to start a word-processing business. The equipment you want to purchase costs $6,700. If your charges to the customer average $22 per hour, how may hours will it take to pay for the equipment?

3. Four of your friends take you out to dinner to celebrate your birthday. The bill comes to $82.45. You decide to leave a 15 percent tip. If your four friends divide the bill evenly, how much will each person pay?

Communication

4. Each of these numbers can be expressed in three ways. Fill in the blanks:

Fraction		Decimal		Percentage
3/5	=		=	
2/70	=		=	
1/1,000	=		=	

5. Write a memo announcing a plan to reduce operating expenses in your office. You plan to reduce office supplies by 1/3, telephone costs by

2/5, and travel expenses by 1/4. Write each of the values in the memo as both a number and a word.

Human Relations

6. Suppose you have a summer job selling fruit at an outdoor stand. You and the other salespeople are expected to weigh and calculate each sale yourselves, either in your heads or with a calculator. You notice that one of the other clerks is make frequent errors in calculation, and mischarging the customers. What would you do?

7. You are the supervisor of a telemarketing team. Your records show that the success rate of your workers varies from 10 percent to 70 percent. Do you think it would be helpful to display these percentages in a chart for everyone to see? Why or why not? Could such a chart be used to motivate workers? What incentives might you offer the higher producing workers to help the lower producing workers?

APPLICATION PROJECTS

1. Get some blank checks from a bank and practice writing them out. For example, write checks to:

General Telephone Co. $15.86
Ford $2,010.05
Great Food $47.55
Radical Clothes $132.00

2. Make a list of 15 to 20 numbers representing dollar and cent amounts (i.e., $23.56, $142.55, $3.09, etc.). Have everyone in the class use a calculator to add the numbers together. What percentage of the class arrived at the same total?

3. Suppose you are a salesperson for electrical parts. In February, you were able to increase your sales by 15 percent over the previous month. On a separate sheet of paper, fill in the table below to represent a continued 15 percent monthly increase, and the projection if you were able to increase 25 percent for March and April.

Sales	Jan.	Feb.	Mar.	Apr.
15% incr:	23,000	26,450		
25% incr:	23,000	26,450		

4. Go to a local store that is having a sale. If you don't know which store to go to, look in newspapers for advertised sales. When you get to the store, carefully inspect the price tags on several items. Write down the regular price and the sale price. Calculate the percentage of savings. Figuring markdowns is a useful skill for you to have. If you worked in the store, it might be your job to determine the markdowns and write the amounts on the price tags.

5. At the library, do some research on sales tax in the United States. Do all states have this tax? If not, which states do not have sales tax? What is the highest percentage of sales tax and the lowest percentage? Are all purchased items subject to sales tax? If not, which items are nontaxable? Organize your material into a five-minute oral report to the class.

6. Talk to someone in your community who owns or manages a retail business. It might be a small store, a restaurant, or a gasoline station. Find out how much it costs that business every time a customer pays with a credit card. Does the percentage the credit card company gets vary from credit card to credit card? How would this influence some businesses about the credit cards they accept?

7. At the library, do some research on the history of the modern calculator. Trace the major changes in the calculator from the first one to modern models. What could the early calculators do? What size were they? How much did they cost? Were they designed to be used in business, at home, or both? Write your findings in a 250-word report.

8. Imagine that you have a terrific idea for some kind of new business. If you're like most people, you'll need a loan to get your business started. Go to a bank and inquire about the cost of business loans. If you borrowed $10,000 to start your business, how much would you have to pay each month? What percentage of the monthly amount would be interest on the loan? What amount would you pay in all if you paid month-by-month until the end of the term? Would it make a difference if the term of the loan was either longer or shorter?

Communication Skills

Studies show that, throughout your life, you will be involved in the communication process about 70 percent of your waking hours. Many of those hours will be spent on the job, where good communication skills are essential.

You will have to speak well to present your thoughts and ideas to your employer, and to be persuasive with customers. You will have to listen well to get feedback from both. You will have to present your ideas in written form, so you must write well. And, you must read well to understand everything from care labels on products, to office memos, to employee manuals.

This chapter explores all of these communication skills—speaking, listening, writing, and reading. Mastering them puts you well on the way to success in the business world.

The Communication Process

Communication is the process of exchanging information, ideas, and feelings. This process is made up of the following primary elements:

- senders and receivers
- messages
- channels
- feedback
- blocks
- setting

Senders and Receivers

Simply sending a message is not communicating. Every message must be sent, received, and understood. Both verbal and nonverbal means are used to send and receive messages. Speaking and writing are verbal means. Nonverbal means include facial expressions and *body language*—your physical actions that communicate your thoughts. (We will talk more about this in Chapter 10.)

In face-to-face conversations, you are often a sender and a receiver at the same time. Suppose that you have asked your employer, Mr. Simms, how he wants you to arrange a window display. As he explains the arrangement, he sends a message by talking. You receive the message by listening. As you listen, though, you may be sending a message at the same time—even if you don't say a word. The expression on your face may be saying, "I don't understand." Mr. Simms may receive this message and start over. Or he may rephrase the message.

Messages

The substance of any communication is the message—the information, ideas, or feelings the sender wants to share. Messages can be shared only if they are represented by symbols. Symbols can be anything that stands for something else. All communication is made up of verbal and nonverbal symbols.

Every word is a verbal symbol with a meaning that can be understood by others who know the same language. Avoiding nonstandard language, such as slang expressions and highly technical terms, will increase the probability that your message will be understood.

Channels

Channels are the avenues by which the message is delivered. In face-to-face conversations, the channels are sound and sight; the participants listen to and look at one another. In telephone conversations, the channel is the sound that is transmitted and received over the telephone lines. The participants speak to and listen to one another.

Another channel of communication is the written word. On the job, many messages are delivered in the form of letters, memoranda, and reports. The participants write and read each other's messages.

Feedback

Feedback is the receiver's response to the message. For example, when your employer explains your part in a new advertising program, you will probably ask some questions. This is feedback. You may restate some of the things your employer has told you. This assures both you and your employer that you understand the message. Feedback is important in communication because it allows participants to clarify the message and know that it was understood by both (or all) parties.

When reading reports, you have little opportunity for feedback. Of course you can respond to a letter or memorandum, but it takes more time than giving feedback in a conversation. The greatest opportunity for feedback is in a face-to-face conversation with another person.

Blocks

Blocks interfere with understanding the message. The three primary blocks to understanding are *distractions*, *emotional blocks*, and *planning a response*. These will be discussed further under "Blocks to Listening with Understanding."

Setting

*The **setting** is where the communication takes place.* Outdoor settings are varied and often hard to control. Indoor settings in a job situation may vary from a large hall to a small office. But you may have control over choosing the room, arranging the furniture, and so on.

When you choose the setting for a group meeting, think first of a room large enough to accommodate those expected to attend. Be sure there will be enough chairs and that they are arranged so everyone can see the main speaker. Check for adequate lighting. If you are giving an audiovisual presentation, arrange for and check the equipment, electrical outlet, and extension cord. You may also want to bring in coffee, soft drinks, and snacks.

When discussing something with one other person in a face-to-face conversation, a small room is more comfortable than a large one. You will also be more comfortable in your own workplace than in someone else's. If you want to make a person feel comfortable in a conversation, go to his or her workplace.

Listening

Earlier, you learned that about 70 percent of your waking hours are spent communicating. Of that 70 percent, studies show that some 45 percent is spent listening. So nearly as much time is spent in listening as in speaking, reading, and writing combined.

Why has this manager chosen to do this employee's quarterly performance review in a comfortable office rather than in a conference room?

Some people never learn the difference between hearing and listening. Hearing is mostly a physical process that takes place in the ears. Listening is a mental process that requires using the brain. Learning to use listening skills is a vital part of being an effective communicator.

Listening Skills

Listening skills help you better understand the messages you receive. These skills involve what to listen for and what to think about as you listen. These same skills help you understand written messages, too.

Identify the Purpose. If a meeting has been scheduled to discuss a particular topic, then you know the purpose of the message before the speaker begins to talk. At other times, you don't have advance notice of the purpose of the message. Then you have to identify the purpose from the content of the message. The sooner you can do this, the easier it will be for you to understand the whole message.

Look for a Plan. When you listen to a structured speech, try to identify a plan of presentation. Knowing the plan makes it easier to see how different components of the message fit together to convey the whole message. For example, sometimes a speaker makes generalizations and then supports them with specific evidence. Or the speaker may use contrasts and comparisons or show cause-and-effect relationships. When you know the plan, you can often anticipate what the speaker will say next. You will also be able to sort out relevant and irrelevant information.

Face-to-face conversations between two (or even several) people are usually not as well planned as a formal speech. In these informal conversations, as long as you know the purpose of the message, it is not important to know the plan.

Give Feedback. If you are in a conversation with one other person, or even in a small group, give feedback to show whether you understand the message. Without interrupting, you can nod your head, raise an eyebrow, or frown. You may have an opportunity to ask questions when the speaker pauses. When the speaker has completed the message, summarize your understanding of it. If your understanding of the message is different from that intended by the sender, ask the speaker to clarify it for you.

Search for an Interest. On the job, many of the messages you receive from your employer or from co-workers relate to your job performance. Because you want to succeed at your job, show an interest in anything that will improve your performance.

You may attend meetings or conferences where you will hear messages that are so uninteresting you want to tune them out. This can become a habit that will cause you to miss important information. Remember, you can learn valuable information from even the most uninteresting message. Listen carefully to find something that interests you.

Evaluate the Message. There are times for listening with empathy and times for listening and making judgments. You will need to be able to distinguish which type of listening is appropriate.

Sometimes a friend will express a need to share his or her innermost feelings. This is a time to listen with sympathy and understanding. To make any judgment would be inappropriate and cause your friend to feel that you do not care or understand.

In most other conversations and when listening to messages, making judgments can help you listen with understanding. Your mind becomes more actively involved in the listening process when you make logical judgments. However, if you let your emotions get in the way, you will not understand messages you do not like. Always keep an open mind.

As you listen, evaluate the validity of the message. Try to distinguish between fact and opinion, and evaluate whether the information presented is relevant to the purpose of the message.

Listen for More Than Verbal Content. You know that there is more to the speaker's message than the meaning of the words. The rate of speech, pitch, volume, and voice quality can add and change meaning. Some experts estimate that 39 percent of the meaning of oral communication is due to vocal cues—not the actual words spoken but the way they are said.

Listen for a Conclusion. You may want or need to take action based on the speaker's conclusion, so listen for it. If the speaker doesn't reach a conclusion, summarize the main points and then draw your own. Don't jump to a conclusion before the speaker has presented the facts or opinions to support it.

Take Notes. If you are in a business discussion or meeting with one or several people, take notes on the main points presented. Employers appreciate employees who care enough to write down what the employer says.

Blocks to Listening with Understanding

Some things interfere with or *block* effective listening. Avoid these blocks, and you will be able to concentrate on the message.

Distractions. *Distractions include noises and other environmental factors, interruptions by other people, and competing thoughts that creep into your mind.*

Have you tried to listen to a person speak while someone is operating a power lawnmower outside your window? Other environmental factors, such as rooms that are too cold or too hot, can distract you, too. To avoid the distraction, you may decide to postpone a meeting or move to a different area.

Have you ever been listening intently to a message only to have a ringing telephone or a knock at

The action of taking notes seems to help people remember better, even if they don't review the notes later. Why do you think this is true?

the door interrupt you at a critical moment? When a message doesn't interest you much, has your mind ever wandered? On the job, most messages will be important. So exercise the discipline necessary to keep your mind on the message, despite distractions or occasional boredom.

Emotional Blocks. *Emotional blocks are biases against the opinions expressed by the sender that block your understanding.* If you don't agree with the sender's ideas, it is especially important to listen and understand. Otherwise, you will not be able to give a meaningful response.

Planning a Response. Planning your response blocks understanding because you can't concentrate on the message and your response at the same time. When the speaker says something that you want to respond to, it's tempting to think about your response and tune out the speaker. But in doing this, you will probably miss some key points in the message and thus respond inappropriately. So, listen to the entire message before you plan your response.

Blocks to understanding can cloud even the clearest message. Being aware of these blocks will help you avoid them and allow you to concentrate solely on the message.

Reading

Reading, like listening, is a process of trying to understand a message. In all careers, reading with understanding is a necessity. For example, to find and apply for most jobs, you have to read help-wanted ads and job applications.

REAL WORLD MARKETING

If U Cn Rd Ths Mssg Bckwrds...

In 1884, the ad manager for Enoch Morgan's Sons, a New York soap manufacturer, put out word that the formula for the firm's Sapolio soap dated to ancient Egypt. He claimed the message "Oilopas Esu," meaning "Sapolio scours the world," had been found in an Egyptian tomb. The claim seemed believable—as long as the consumer didn't read the mysterious Egyptian phrase backward.

Know the Purpose of Your Reading

You will be a more efficient reader if you determine why you are reading before you begin. For example, when you read a novel or magazine, you are reading for pleasure. So you can read as fast or as slowly as you want, to get whatever information you want. When you read a job application form or a company memo, you have to read every word to be certain you understand all the appropriate information.

Read for Meaning

One of the many things required to succeed on the job is reading and understanding written messages. These three skills will help you do both:

- focus your mind
- form pictures
- improve your vocabulary

Focus Your Mind. No one's mind focuses on a subject automatically, without effort. Your mind will focus only through constant concentration. When you don't concentrate, the message will be unclear. As you read, monitor your thoughts. If your mind wanders when you are reading, refocus on the subject.

Form Pictures. Try to form pictures of the people, places, things, and situations described. When you see elements of the message in your mind, the message is easier to understand.

Improve Your Vocabulary. When you read, don't simply skip over unfamiliar words without giving them any thought. If you do, you may miss key points in the message. Try to figure out the meaning by the way the word is used in the sentence or paragraph and then look up the word in a dictionary. This will broaden your vocabulary and improve your understanding of written communication.

In your job-related reading, you will come across some technical terms called *jargon*. *Jargon is made up of words that have meaning only in a particular career field.* Many of these words aren't even listed in most dictionaries. At first, you may be embarrassed to ask their meaning. But it is better to ask and learn than to guess at the meaning and make a serious mistake in your work responsibilities. Most marketing jobs have their own jargon. You will learn many of these words as you study this book.

Speaking

Many jobs in marketing require better than average speaking skills. But whatever your job in any career field, you will need to express yourself clearly so your employer and co-workers can understand the messages you are sending.

Know the Purpose

Before you formulate what you will say, know the purpose of the message you will send. In most cases, you will speak to inform, persuade, or entertain.

Speaking to Inform. In most informal conversations and in many business meetings, the main purpose is to inform. The participants exchange information, frequently changing roles from sender to receiver and back again. When you are speaking to inform, get right to the point. Say what you want to say clearly and succinctly.

Speaking to Persuade. On any job there will be times when you will need to persuade others to see or do things your way. Perhaps the most important skill in persuading others is determining the listener's needs, then showing how you can satisfy at least some of those needs. You will look at this more closely in Part 4, Selling.

Speaking to Entertain. Sometimes the purpose of speaking is to entertain others. If you are a salesperson, for example, you may need to entertain clients. You don't have to be a comedian to enjoy joking and telling stories. This kind of speaking is usually quite informal.

CASE CHALLENGE

Tickling the Business Funny Bone

We all love to laugh. We enjoy remembering and sharing funny lines from movies or good jokes. But business is serious business. There is no room for funny stuff.

Or is there?

Advertisers know you will remember their products better if they can make you laugh. And now humor consultants are beginning to teach managers the value of laughter in office communication.

Humor bonds people together, says Robert Orben, who has written numerous books on humor in business. "If you can laugh together, you can work together," he adds.

Humor relaxes people and makes them more open to your ideas. Laughter (even a smile) reduces tension and hostility. And it can motivate people. (Which teachers do you work the hardest for?)

But this doesn't mean your business conversation should be an endless stream of one-liners. Humor must be used sparingly and thoughtfully. Getting the message across—not getting a laugh—is the most important thing.

Malcolm Kushner (who has taught humor classes to the Internal Revenue Service) says humor should be brief and relevant to the point you want to make. And you should not be afraid to poke fun at yourself.

So even in the business world, don't leave home without your sense of humor.

1. Why does humor improve communication with others? Give some examples of business situations in which you might use humor successfully.
2. When can humor hurt your ability to communicate with others? What kinds of humor might keep you from getting your point across?

Speaking Formally

Many jobs in marketing and other careers will require you to deliver structured messages usually sent to inform or persuade. There are four basic patterns you may use to organize a structured message.

Enumeration. *Enumeration* is listing several items in order. For example, when instructing a new worker on how to perform a certain task, you may begin by saying, "There are four steps in performing this task." The new worker will listen for four separate but related things to do. The steps will be easier to understand because the listener is expecting them. Use *signal words*, such as *first, second, third,* or *next,* to help the listener. (*Signal words* show the relationship between what you have already said and what you will say next.)

Generalization with Example. Many speakers use *generalizations*—statements that are accepted as true by most people—to make a point. Then they support the generalizations with examples and evidence to show that the statement is true. For instance, don't make a general statement such as, "Automobiles are the leading cause of accidental deaths in the United States." You could say, "Of all accidental deaths in 1989, almost half were due to auto accidents." Using evidence to support your generalization clarifies your message and helps your listeners remember the main points. Use signal words such as *for instance* and *for example.*

Cause and Effect. When you discuss an issue in terms of cause and effect, you lead the listener from the cause of something to the effect. This is an effective way to explain many topics. You can reverse this method by first presenting the effect and then considering possible causes. Use signal words such as *therefore, consequently,* and *as a result.*

Comparison and Contrast. Another good method of explaining something is to use comparison and contrast. You can explain new concepts by showing how they are similar to or unlike those your listeners already know. Use signal words such as *similarly, however, nevertheless,* and *on the other hand.*

Using Your Voice. You will need to use your voice effectively to be a good communicator. With practice, you can develop a pleasant voice that is neither too high nor too low. Your voice will sound relaxed if you speak in a medium, even tone. When you are tense, your voice will sound shaky and high.

One good way to explain something is to use comparison and contrast. What could this salesperson compare and contrast about these two bicycles?

Speak loudly enough to be heard without blasting your listeners. Also, vary your inflections by stressing certain words and syllables. Variations of speed and loudness, along with inflections, will make you sound interesting and help you communicate your message.

Telephone Skills

If you take a job in marketing, you will probably speak to many people on the telephone. A pleasant voice is even more important on the telephone than in face-to-face conversations. Your listener can't see you, so you can't rely on facial expressions and body language to help get your message across.

Use your most pleasant tone, enunciate clearly, and speak directly into the mouthpiece. Speak loudly enough for the other person to hear, but don't shout. Listen as well on the telephone as you do in a face-to-face conversation—and never interrupt when the other person is speaking.

Writing

Writing a message takes more time and thought than simply having a conversation. However, there are times when it is more appropriate to write your message so you can organize your thoughts, review, and revise your message before it is sent.

Many people forget most of the message in a conversation within the first 24 hours. But a written message is a permanent record. A written message can be read and reread until it is clearly understood, then filed for future reference and review.

It's hard to ignore a written message. The person receiving it is more likely to take appropriate action than if the same message were delivered in a conversation.

Basic Considerations in Writing

In every type of writing, there are three basic considerations:

- know your reader
- know your purpose
- know your subject

Know Your Reader. Before you begin writing even your first draft, think about the people who will receive your message. Who are they? Why will they read your message? What do they know about the subject? Answer these questions and any others that will help you know your reader. You can write a more meaningful message when you understand your reader's needs.

Know Your Purpose. The second consideration before you begin writing is the purpose of your message. Most of your writing will be done to inform, request, confirm, persuade, inquire, or complain. Some messages, of course, combine two or more of these purposes.

Know Your Subject. You will need to know your subject well to write a clear message about it. You may learn enough on the job so that you won't

have to do further research on many of the subjects you will write about. While you are still new on the job, though, you will probably improve your written messages by researching the topic first.

Develop a Writing Style

Executives usually set the style and tone of writing for their companies. You will probably have opportunities to read company letters, memos, and reports before writing any yourself. This will help you determine the style used by the company.

The trend in business writing is toward a direct, conversational style. Remember, you are writing to communicate a message to one or more receivers. Use a crisp, clear style that is easy to read. Don't use your business writing to impress others with your extensive vocabulary.

Using the name of the person who will receive your message will personalize it. The receiver will have a warmer feeling toward you because of it.

You will probably need to use some jargon in your messages to people in your career field. However, avoid jargon or explain any jargon you must use when writing to those outside your field.

Letters, Memos, and Reports

There are many types of written communications. In business, most written messages are in the form of letters, memos, or reports.

Business Letters. The main form of written communication with people outside your own company will be business letters. Figure 9-1 shows a standard business letter. Most business letters include eight standard parts.

1. **Return address**—the address of the letter writer. Most companies have their address printed on stationery called *letterhead*. When you type a business letter on blank paper, type the return address at the top of the page.
2. **Date**—shows the reader when the letter was written. In business, it is important to document when you write a letter. Having the date on the letter is security against a faulty memory.
3. **Inside address**—the name and address of the person who will receive the letter. The same address is typed on the envelope.

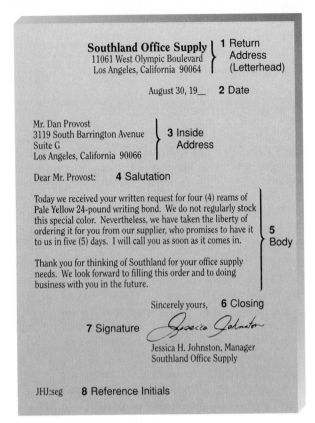

Figure 9-1   Standard Business Letter
Letterhead stationery simplifies letter preparation by eliminating the first major element to be typed—the return address. What does the last element to be typed, the letters at the lower left, stand for?

name unless you are on a first-name basis with the reader.

8. **Reference initials**—the initials of the writer, and the initials of the typist. They are typed two spaces below your typed signature, beginning at the left margin. The writer's initials are always typed first.

Memos.   *Memo* is an abbreviated form of the word *memorandum*. Memos are written messages to someone in your company. They are usually brief and cover only one subject. Look at the sample memo on this page, Figure 9-2.

Reports.   Business reports cover such topics as yearly sales, survey results, or problems that need attention. Some are called *in-house reports* because they are to be read only by company employees. Others, such as reports to stockholders, are written for a wider audience.

4. **Salutation**—the greeting. The most commonly used salutation is "Dear (Mr., Mrs., Miss, Ms.) _____." If you usually call the person by his or her first name, you can use it in the salutation: "Dear Adam." A colon always follows the salutation in a business letter.
5. **Body**—the message of the letter.
6. **Closing**—a respectful goodbye. Formal closings for business letters are "Yours very truly" and "Yours truly." Less formal, more friendly closings are "Sincerely" and "Cordially." A comma should follow the closing.
7. **Signature**—the handwritten name of the writer. Sign your name in ink above your typed name. Write both your first and last

Southland Office Supply

Memorandum

To:	All Office Employees
From:	Jessica Johnston
Subject:	Filling Special Stationery Requests
Date:	August 30, 19 – –

Over the last three weeks, we have received three (3) customer requests for 24-pound writing bond in unusual colors that we do not regularly stock. Please fill any such orders from South Bay Suppliers in Santa Monica at 391-4300.

Let me know if you have any questions.

JHJ

Figure 9-2   Standard Business Memo
Business memos are intended for internal company use rather than outside correspondence. How does the format of a business memo differ from the format of a business letter?

VOCABULARY REVIEW

Write a brief definition of each word, based on your reading of the chapter.

communication
channels
feedback
blocks

setting
distractions
emotional blocks
jargon

FACT AND IDEA REVIEW

1. What is communication?

2. What are the primary elements of the communication process?

3. Describe how the communication of a message is a two-way process.

4. What constitutes the message in the communication process?

5. What variables make up the setting of a communication?

6. Name the eight listening skills that will help you understand messages.

7. Discuss when and how making judgments as a listener can be helpful.

8. Discuss why taking notes is part of being an effective listener.

9. List some of the potential blocks to listening effectively.

10. What guidelines can you use to become a more efficient reader?

11. What should you do if you encounter a word you don't know while you are reading? Why?

12. What are the main purposes of speaking?

13. List the basic patterns that are usually used in organizing a structured message.

14. What are some of the advantages of a written rather than a verbal message?

15. What style of writing do most companies prefer?

CRITICAL THINKING

1. Why is it important to be a good listener? Which listening skills could help you most in school? How?

2. Describe a situation in which it would be appropriate and helpful to make judgments as a listener. Describe another situation in which it would not be helpful.

3. Choose a career that interests you. Describe how being a good reader could help you in that job.

4. What key elements must a speaker keep in mind in order to be an effective communicator?

5. Why is it important to know your reader before you begin writing a message?

6. Describe an appropriate setting for an in-home cosmetics presentation and for a stockbroker's meeting. How and why should the two settings be different?

USING BASIC SKILLS

Math

1. Communication via the telephone can be expensive. If the rate from 8 a.m. to 5 p.m. for a call from Chicago to Dallas is $.25 for the first minute and $.022 for each additional minute, how much would a ten-minute call cost? If the rate were 35 percent less between 5 p.m. and 11 p.m., how much would you save by waiting until after 5 p.m. to make the call?

2. To FAX a document anywhere in the United States, a local business charges $5 for the first page and $2 for subsequent pages (plus the cost of the long-distance telephone call). If a FAX machine costs $1,200 to purchase, how many single-page documents could you send commercially for the same price?

Communication

3. Watch the television or a video with the sound turned off. What nonverbal messages do you observe? What can you interpret from them?

4. Using the words *peanut butter*, experiment with changing the pitch, volume, and intensity of your voice to communicate various messages, such as disbelief, awe, confusion, and uncertainty.

5. Review yesterday's activities in your mind. What blocks to listening (distractions, emotional blocks, planning a response) did you experience during those activities? How did these blocks interfere with effective communication?

Human Relations

6. You are a manager of a home electronics store. You observe a new salesman who is obviously trying to impress a customer with his technical expertise and terminology. You can see that his overuse of jargon is offensive to the customer. What should you do?

APPLICATION PROJECTS

1. Observe a conversation among friends. What examples of feedback do you notice?

2. Listen to a structured speech or read a short essay. What was the purpose of the communication? How do you know that? What pattern or structure was used? Make a brief outline of how the speech or essay was organized.

3. Research a career field of interest to discover some of the jargon used in that field. List the terms.

4. Pretend you are telephoning classmates to enlist them to work at a car wash to raise money for your school. Prepare your telephone speech, and act out your phone call in front of the class.

5. Using the eight standard parts discussed in the text, write a formal business letter from your company, Jack's Construction, to Acme Hardware. The hardware store has delivered some faulty pipe to you, and you are writing to correct the situation.

6. TV news makes use of visual images to help convey its stories. By contrast, radio news relies on the newscaster's words and his or her vocal cues. Listen to three radio news stories and, as you do, take notes on each story. Use your notes to summarize the important points of each story for your class.

7. In a local paper, read the help wanted ads for a career that interests you. Become aware of the special reading task involved in reading classified ads: decoding abbreviations. List the abbreviations you found in ads for jobs in your field. Write what each of these abbreviations means.

8. You are the director of a youth program in which youngsters sell candy door-to-door. You must tell your sales force the steps involved in the selling process. Present your speech to the class, keeping your audience in mind and using signal words.

9. Imagine you received Jessica Johnston's memo (see Figure 9-2 on page 110). As a conscientious employee, write a memo to give her some feedback. First confirm that you received her memo and are carrying out her request. Then inform her of four more orders for the special paper. Ask whether this trend might call for Southland to begin stocking the special paper in the near future.

Interpersonal Skills

OBJECTIVES

After completing this chapter, you will be able to:

1. identify nine things you can do to influence others,

2. list six things you can do to sell an idea, and

3. describe ten personal traits and skills that are important in all relationships.

WORDS TO KNOW

body language
empathize
assertive

The alarm signals the start of another day. At breakfast, you greet your family and talk to your brother about trading weekend chores so you can attend a soccer game on Saturday. At school, you chat with your friends and make plans for carpooling to the game. In classes, you and your teachers discuss new ideas. After school, you greet the bus driver as you head to your part-time job in a sporting goods store. Once there, you and a co-worker divide responsibilities for pricing new merchandise and checking stock.

Every day, a major portion of your time is spent relating to other people. Developing *interpersonal skills*, the skills you use in relating to others, helps you get along well with the many people you encounter. Using these skills is especially important on the job. Studies show that between 80 and 85 percent of a person's success in the world of work is due to having good interpersonal skills.

Understanding Others

The first step in getting along with others is getting to know them. Finding out others' interests helps you understand them better. Interests often reflect values, and understanding people's values is helpful in most relationships.

Trying to understand the reasons for others' behavior also facilitates good relationships, both on and off the job. You won't have time for an in-depth study of every person you deal with. But you can learn to be sensitive to certain aspects of everyone's behavior. Observe the way a person deals with others. Does the person relate differently to different people in the same situations? Can you figure out why? Which of the person's personality traits might affect your relationship with him or her?

Observing *body language* is another key way to learn about a person. ***Body language is the physical movements and positions of the body that communicate thoughts.*** For example, the person who leans slightly forward and occasionally nods in agreement with you is obviously paying attention. The person with an expressionless stare is looking but not listening.

Body language communicates our thoughts and feelings. What do you think each person pictured here is thinking or feeling?

Facial expressions are often good indicators of emotions and feelings. A pleasant, smiling expression, for instance, usually indicates a positive outlook.

Your eyes tell a lot about you, too. When you are happy, for example, your pupils get larger. When you are unhappy, the pupils constrict. In most people, this is an automatic response. So, if you are close enough to see a person's eyes clearly, you can learn more about him or her. Suppose you are interviewing a candidate to help you with an advertising campaign. As you explain the job responsibilities, look into the person's eyes for an indication of his or her feelings.

One study of body language found that people sometimes say one thing verbally and another through body language. Body language is often the more accurate indicator of the person's thoughts and feelings. By observing people in many different situations, you can learn to read body language with considerable accuracy.

Influencing Others

Sometimes, to achieve your goals, it's necessary to influence others. This is particularly true on the job where there will be many situations in which you will want to persuade others to see things your way. Here are some interpersonal skills to help you do this.

Show an Interest in Others

In *How to Win Friends and Influence People*, Dale Carnegie said, "You can win more friends in two months by becoming interested in other people than you can in two years by trying to get other people interested in you."[1] The most effective way to influence others is to become genuinely interested in them. Asking about others' interests, family, or activities will encourage good feelings and make them more receptive to your ideas.

Smile

Others react to you more favorably when you smile. A smile says, "I like you." It attracts others. If you don't feel like smiling, force yourself. *Acting* like you are happy tends to make you *feel* happy. Many successful people say their smiles were responsible for their earning millions. And it's yours for free!

[1] Carnegie, Dale. *How to Win Friends and Influence People.* New York: Simon and Schuster, 1936.

A sincere smile will do much to attract and influence others. What was your immediate reaction to the person in this picture?

Make Others Feel Important

Many people satisfy their basic needs for food, safety, and a sense of belonging. But they lack esteem because they don't feel important. Everyone, even a person with good self-esteem, wants and needs to feel important. Think about your own feelings. When someone says something that makes you feel important, it makes you feel good, too. As a result, you have warm feelings toward that person.

One way to make a person feel important is to know and use his or her name correctly. Another way is to give the person your undivided attention. If a co-worker wants to explain a new idea for keeping inventory records, for example, meet at a time when you will not be interrupted. Ask questions to show your interest in the idea. If you think the idea is good, say so. You can make your co-worker feel good by giving your sincere attention.

Empathize

You can earn a person's trust and respect faster by empathizing. *To empathize means to understand a person's situation or frame of mind.* Learn to respect the other person's point of view, even when you don't agree with it. This technique is especially important in dealing with customers.

Let Others "Save Face"

When people realize they have made a mistake, they have a temporary loss of self-esteem. After a while, they may admit the mistake and even take pride in admitting it. If you tell a person "You were wrong" or "I told you so," you will alienate him or her.

If you are in a position in which you must discuss someone's mistake (perhaps if you are reviewing an employee's performance), give the person the opportunity to admit the mistake. Encourage him or her to offer suggestions on how to avoid making the same mistake in the future. Make sure that your criticism is positive and shows your concern for the other person's welfare.

Admit Your Own Mistakes

Although it is bad to point out the mistakes of others, it's good to admit your own. Mature people quickly admit their own errors and work just as quickly to correct them. They also gain the respect of others—which makes it easier to deal with and influence people.

Praise Lavishly

Everyone wants to please a person who gives sincere praise. So, when you want to influence someone, or cause a change in behavior, never begin with negative criticism. This approach puts people on the defensive. Instead, begin by talking about things that you feel are worthy of praise.

Accentuate the Positive

People with a negative outlook have a hard time influencing others. Happy, upbeat people, on the other hand, are much more persuasive. If you want to influence someone, be optimistic. Get in the habit of always being positive.

Be Assertive

*Being **assertive** means standing up for your rights, beliefs, and ideas.* People will respect you if you can be assertive without being pushy or aggressive. Show confidence and speak with authority. This does not mean that you should sound like a know-it-all, but you do have to know what you are talking about.

Winning Friends

Most of us are nervous about speaking to a group, even if that "group" is only two or three people. But in the business world it is important to be an effective public speaker.

In 1912, Dale Carnegie started teaching public speaking. Almost immediately he realized people needed more help in "the fine art of getting along and dealing with people." So he started studying and interviewing famous people. He learned the secrets of their success and wrote a book called *How to Win Friends and Influence People*. And he started the Dale Carnegie Training program, which focuses on helping people develop self-confidence in public speaking. Students give one- to two-minute speeches on assigned topics. They are also asked to speak off-the-cuff in class.

In the field of human relations, students learn to remember people's names, to appreciate and encourage others, to avoid criticizing and complaining, to be interested in others, and to smile. More than 3 million graduates (including Chrysler Corporation's energetic Lee Iacocca) have found that these simple techniques pay astonishing dividends.

Many of the ideas taught in Dale Carnegie Training sessions have become standard in today's self-help books. Most modern sales training courses depend on them. A lot of big companies, such as IBM, Quaker Oats, Du Pont, TRW, and Mattel, believe strongly in Carnegie classes. They even pay for their employees to attend the courses.

Today, Dale Carnegie Training is known and respected for creating the positive attitude that helps so many businesspeople succeed.

1. Why is public speaking important? When will you have to use public speaking skills?
2. Why do large companies pay for their employees to take Dale Carnegie Training?

As a new employee, it will probably be difficult to be assertive on the job until you have improved your knowledge and skills through experience. But as you gain more experience, you will gain confidence. Then you will be in a better position to influence others.

Selling an Idea

A good idea represents value and power. So some of your co-workers may resent you for having an idea when they don't have one. To lessen the probability of others' resentment, sell *yourself* first. Here are some suggestions directed toward selling an idea. Follow them, and you will usually get the support you need.

REAL WORLD MARKETING

The Note with a Peel

Arthur Fry, an engineer at 3M Company, liked singing in his church choir. However, he didn't like losing his place in his hymnal every time his bookmark slipped out. Fry needed a page marker that would stay put. So, he invented one. Using glue left over from an unsuccessful experiment, Fry came up with Post-It Notes, little paper squares that can be pressed onto a page and easily peeled off again. Post-Its have given Fry peace of mind—and they have given 3M $50 million a year in sales.

Writing your thoughts on paper is an important technique for selling an idea. How does writing down your thoughts help you prior to discussing ideas with others?

People tend to be more agreeable when they're in a good mood. Why do you think it is so much better to talk business and discuss ideas during a good meal?

Know Precisely What You Want

Most ideas for changing things need the cooperation of one or more other people. Outline your idea on paper before you tell anyone about it. This will help you clarify and improve it. Make revisions and rewrite your outline, specifying numbers, people, budgets, and deadlines. When you begin to discuss your idea with others, show your outline as a focus point. This proves that you have thought your ideas through.

Catch the Mood

People tend to be agreeable to new ideas when they are already in a good mood. So, try to present them when people are happy and relaxed. To get a better gauge of anyone's mood, listen for enthusiasm, tone of voice—any clues to tell you how they feel.

You can enhance your chances of selling an idea by taking people to lunch or dinner. The best time to talk people into anything is during a good meal when they are happy, relaxed, and receptive.

Solve Someone's Problem

People are far more willing to listen to a new idea when they clearly see how they will benefit. Before presenting your idea, write across the top of a sheet of paper, "What's in it for them?" Then list the benefits. You may want to review your list, type it up, and show it to the people to whom you are trying to sell your idea. If not, at least keep those benefits foremost in your mind and in their minds during your presentation. Phrase your idea in terms of *their* interests.

Share Credit for Your Ideas

You can work for months, even years, trying to sell others on the value of your own idea. But if you get others involved by accepting their suggestions for improvement, you may be able to sell an idea quickly.

Sometimes, of course, you don't *want* to share the credit for a good idea. After all, ideas carry value and power—and often lead to promotions. If you want to retain full credit for an idea, follow your presentation with a memo outlining the action steps to be taken and thanking everyone for their support.

Answer Objections with Benefits

Even when you have a great idea, others will probably come up with a reason why it won't work. Often, of course, these objections are based only on the fact that your idea wasn't *their* idea. Don't try to overcome objections by arguing or pointing out errors in their logic. Just keep emphasizing what's in it for them.

If you can anticipate potential objections, consider raising and resolving them yourself. An opponent is not likely to object to an idea based on a problem that you have already brought up and solved.

Show Gratitude

Getting people to support you on one idea increases the chance that they will support you on others. You can increase the likelihood of further support with a sincere thank-you. A few moments of time spent in thanking someone will help ensure a good working relationship. A written thank-you is even more effective than a verbal one. And it will be remembered longer.

Personal Traits and Skills

Certain personal traits can serve you well in your interpersonal relationships both on and off the job. Work on the following ten traits to improve your effectiveness in dealing with others.

1. *Attitude.* Keep a positive attitude by always looking for and talking about the good in situations and in other people. Don't complain.
2. *Common Sense.* Use past experiences to guide you in making decisions. Good judgment usually means doing what is reasonable and avoiding making a decision based on your emotions.
3. *Courtesy.* Always be courteous to others. Courtesy is worth a great deal in making others like you. Make politeness and good manners habits.
4. *Enthusiasm.* Be happy and energetic. To be successful in any career, you will have to sell

something. In most cases, you will make the sale because of your commitment to the product, service, or idea. In your work relationships, show your enthusiasm in everything you say and do.
5. *Friendliness.* Be friendly. If you are friendly toward others, most will be friendly toward you.
6. *Open-Mindedness.* Always keep an open mind. Consider both sides of every discussion. The moment you close your mind to what someone is saying, you are incapable of learning. By keeping an open mind, you will learn many new, fresh ideas.
7. *Self-Control.* Control your emotions. Your effectiveness in interpersonal relationships will depend on controlling negative feelings, such as anger. Learn to express these feelings in nondestructive ways.
8. *Sense of Humor.* Don't take life too seriously *all the time*. Learn to enjoy the funny side of life, and people will feel more comfortable around you.
9. *Tact.* Say and do things that make others comfortable. Learn to point out problems in ways that do not offend people.
10. *Voice Control.* Use your voice effectively. The tone and quality of your voice affect others as much as what you say.

REAL WORLD MARKETING

We Try Harder

"**G**ive us 90 days," said Bill Bernbach to Robert Townsend. Bernbach, head of the New York ad agency Doyle Dane Bernbach, assured Townsend, chairman of the board of Avis Rent A Car, that his firm only needed 90 days to come up with a winning ad campaign to better compete with Hertz. Ninety days later, however, Bernbach came back with discouraging news. The "only honest thing" his agency could say about Avis was that the company was second largest, and people were trying harder. The slogan "We try harder" increased Avis's sales growth rate by 25 percent in the next two years. (See page 441 of Chapter 40 for more information on Avis.)

CHAPTER 10 REVIEW

VOCABULARY REVIEW

Write one paragraph incorporating these three vocabulary words.

body language   assertive
empathize

FACT AND IDEA REVIEW

1. Why does finding out other people's interests help you understand them better?

2. Describe at least five behaviors that can help you influence others.

3. How should you inform co-workers about their mistakes?

4. What does it mean to be assertive?

5. Tell how you would successfully sell an idea.

6. Tell when and why you might want to share the credit for an idea.

7. Describe eight personality traits that contribute to successful interpersonal relationships.

CRITICAL THINKING

1. Describe at least three interpersonal skills important to success in each of these careers: marketing manager, retail salesperson, cashier, buyer.

2. Tell how people might behave at work in order to satisfy their need for esteem.

3. Describe the body language you would expect to see in a shy person, a defensive person, and a self-confident person.

4. In helping a young couple buy a new car, a salesperson asked the couple many questions about their family, their driving habits, their previous automobile, etc. Why did the salesperson do this? What effect do you think it had on the couple?

5. Describe some ways in which you can make other people feel important.

6. When presenting a new idea, why should you want to address its problems before anyone else brings them up?

USING BASIC SKILLS

Math

1. You have calculated that your idea to use plastic instead of metal for Part A in the manufacturing of your company's Gadget would save $.13 per Gadget. If your company can produce 600 Gadgets per day, and there are 250 production days in the year, how much will your idea save the company in a year?

Communication

2. During your presentation of a new idea to your company sales force, one person is full of objections. What would be an effective strategy to win this person over?

3. As an insurance agent, you have just met with a prospective buyer and discussed a particular health insurance plan. A brief written note would be an effective follow-up. What would you include in that note?

Human Relations

4. Go to a store and buy something. Do not smile at the salesclerk. Go to another store; this time, make eye contact with the clerk and smile. Describe the two experiences and the reactions of each salesclerk.

5. You have an idea that you think will benefit your company, and you have an appointment to discuss it with your manager. At the beginning of the meeting, you discover that she has just read a report which shows the company's profits have dropped substantially this quarter. She is frowning and seems agitated. What would you do?

APPLICATION PROJECTS

1. Seeing and respecting another person's point of view is an important part of effective human relations. Suppose that you are involved in a company that is suffering financially. As a result, a number of jobs need to be terminated. Put yourself in the position of a manager who needs to do the job terminations. Describe how you might feel, your concerns, and your needs. Now put yourself in the position of a secretary who may lose his job. Describe how you might feel in his position.

2. Imagine that you are a parent of two small children and that you are trying to convince the company you work for to provide on-site childcare. What steps would you take to sell your idea?

3. As manager of a retail gift shop, you find yourself in the following situations. Tell the class which interpersonal skills you would use and exactly how you would use them.

   a. You ordered 15 items from a particular supplier. Ten of these items arrived broken. The other five arrived in one piece, but they were the wrong color.

   b. One employee has been doing an especially good job of gift wrapping. Her work is quick and attractive, and customers are pleased.

   c. A different employee has failed to follow part of your shop's procedure all week. His error makes your sales records incomplete.

   d. A regular customer brings his child with him, and the child starts playing with expensive items. The customer's business is important to you, but the child's behavior can't go on.

   e. A different customer has picked out several items and brought them to the register. When you ring up the sale, you discover that the customer's credit card has expired. She gets very angry and insists that her credit is fine.

   f. A delivery service calls to inquire about nonpayment of your bill. You evidently made a mistake. You want to rectify the error as quickly as possible.

4. Interview someone who works for an employment agency about the importance of interpersonal skills in the business of marketing people. Find out which skills come into play most often in that business and which one skill your interviewee considers the most important. From the notes you take during the interview, report your findings in a five-minute speech to the class.

5. At the library, do some research on training in assertiveness or self-esteem. Find out what kinds of classes are available and how they relate to success in business.

6. Think of an idea that you would like to sell to your family or school. Outline your idea to help you clarify it. Then revise and improve your outline until you are satisfied with it. List the benefits of your idea to your family or school. If possible, go ahead and present your idea. See where your presentation is strongest and weakest.

Management Skills

A position in management is one of the greatest challenges any employee can face. Management involves the communication skills and interpersonal skills we have looked at so far, plus the ability to plan, organize, supervise, and solve problems. As you will see, management has its pluses and minuses. Managers usually earn more money and have positions most consider prestigious. But they are also expected to set standards and constantly be responsible. And they are often targets of criticism.

Does management appeal to you? You will more than likely have a chance to take a management job at some point in your marketing career. This chapter will help you explore the management process and the skills managers at all levels in a company need to function effectively and reach specific goals.

Levels of Management

Management is the process of reaching goals through the use of human resources, technology, and material resources. There are three basic levels of management: *top management, middle management,* and *supervisory-level management.* Managers at all levels perform the same functions. But their responsibilities differ according to their management level.

Top Management

*The men and women with the greatest responsibility to plan, organize, and control the use of the company's human, technical, and material resources are usually called **top management**.* In large companies, top management consists of the chief executive officer (CEO) or president, and other key executives who may have the title of vice president. These key executives make many company decisions and meet regularly with the CEO or president.

Smaller companies, of course, don't need a lot of top-management personnel. In fact, most small, locally-owned businesses have only one top-level manager—the owner/manager. In a small business, the *manager* is top management, middle management, and supervisory-level management all rolled into one. This may sound like a lot of responsibility for one person. However, the manager of a small business doesn't have problems of communicating with and motivating lower levels of management.

Middle Management

*Those who carry out top management's decisions are known as **middle management**.* If you accept a job in middle management, you will provide the link between top management and supervisory-level management. You will be responsible for motivating those at the supervisory level so the company can reach the goals set by top management.

Figure 11-1 **Basic Levels of Management**

The responsibilities of managers differ according to their management level. Give at least two specific responsibilties for each management level shown here.

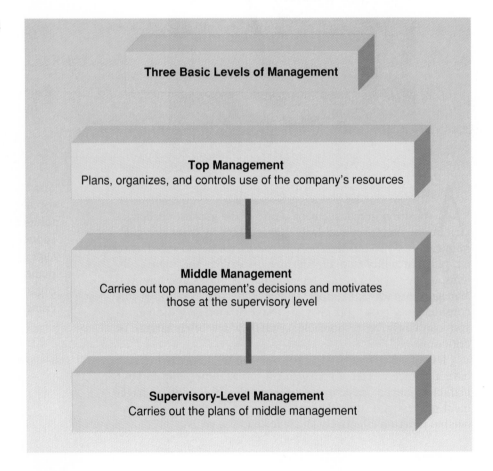

Three Basic Levels of Management

Top Management
Plans, organizes, and controls use of the company's resources

Middle Management
Carries out top management's decisions and motivates those at the supervisory level

Supervisory-Level Management
Carries out the plans of middle management

Supervisory-Level Management

*Those who directly assign work duties and supervise workers on the job make up **supervisory-level management**.* If you accept a job in supervisory-level management, you will probably be called a *supervisor*. *A **supervisor** is responsible for carrying out the plans of middle management.*

The supervisory level is sometimes called *first-level management* since it is the first, or lowest, of the three levels of management. It is also the first management experience for most people.

Management Functions

Managers at all three levels perform the functions of *planning*, *organizing*, and *controlling*. They *plan* when they set goals and determine how to reach them. They *organize* when they decide who will do what and how they will do it. They *control* when they set standards and evaluate performance.

All three of these management functions involve making decisions. Some decisions will be fairly simple or routine. Other decisions will be difficult and complicated. In these cases, following the formal, step-by-step procedure listed below can be beneficial.

1. Define the problem.
2. Identify the options available.
3. Gather information and determine the consequences of each option.
4. Choose the best option.
5. Take action.
6. Evaluate the results.

Planning

The first step in the management process is planning. *Planning involves deciding what will be done and how it will be accomplished.*

Good management planning at any level is realistic, usually written out, comprehensive, communicated, flexible, and revised regularly. It includes plans for the short- and long-range uses of people, technology, and material resources.

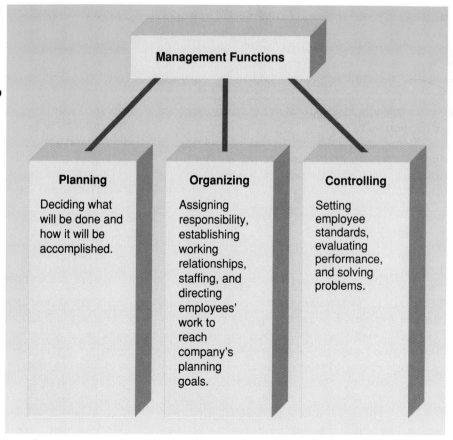

Figure 11-2 **Management Functions**
Managers at all three levels plan, organize, and control. Assume your company, an auto manufacturer, is going to produce a new model—an off-road vehicle. Give one decision of each type that would have to be made.

Management Functions

Planning
Deciding what will be done and how it will be accomplished.

Organizing
Assigning responsibility, establishing working relationships, staffing, and directing employees' work to reach company's planning goals.

Controlling
Setting employee standards, evaluating performance, and solving problems.

When writing out a management plan, managers should include most details without trying to anticipate every possibility. A long document with too many details can be misinterpreted. The plan is distributed to and discussed with everyone who needs to know. Managers keep their management plans flexible so they can easily revise for clarity or respond to change. They also review and revise their plans often.

Organizing

Organizing, a coordinated effort to reach the company's planning goals, involves assigning responsibility, establishing working relationships, staffing, and directing the work of employees.

Assigning responsibility and establishing working relationships are functions usually carried out by top and middle management. Staffing, which includes selecting and training new employees, is often shared by middle management and supervisors. Supervisors usually direct employees' work.

The organizing function in a large company is complex. In the largest companies, there may be hundreds of middle-level managers, thousands of supervisors, and tens of thousands of employees. The work is divided among many people, so middle-level managers and supervisors in large companies are usually given a relatively narrow range of responsibilities. Because of the large number of people on the company "team," organizing for a coordinated effort in a large company requires exceptional interpersonal and communication skills.

The organizing function in smaller companies is simpler, but just as important. In smaller companies, managers are usually given a wider range of responsibilities.

Controlling

When managers assign responsibilities as part of the *organizing* function, they do so based on a general idea of what can be accomplished with their resources. In the *controlling* function, managers must be more precise about expected productivity. *Controlling involves setting employee standards, evaluating performance, and solving problems.*

When setting employee standards, management must decide on the relative importance of *quality* versus *quantity* in the product or service it will provide. If management believes the market will demand very high quality and will be willing to pay a fairly high price, then standards will be based primarily on quality. Employees will be directed to spend enough time to produce high-quality products or services. But if the market is expected to make purchases based mainly on low price, then standards will be based primarily on quantity. Employees will be directed to provide more products or services, spending less time in the process.

After deciding on the balance between quality and quantity, specific standards can be established. These standards may include promptness of deliveries, customer satisfaction, frequency of returns, and sales quotas. Management may also require employees to adhere to a dress code or to follow specific guidelines about behavior on the job.

After employee standards have been established, managers continue the controlling function by evaluating both company and individual performance. Comparing performance against the standards helps identify problems that need to be solved.

There are a number of indicators of performance. For the company as a whole, these include an analysis of delivery times, customer satisfaction surveys, the number of sales returns, and total sales. For individuals, employee performance is often measured by productivity, such as total dollar volume in sales. Employees' on-the-job activities are usually observed, too, and written evaluations are prepared on overall job performance.

When employee performance does not meet established standards, managers must identify and solve the problem. Sometimes employees are not capable of performing up to standards. More often, they are capable but need further direction from management, such as suggesting changes in work activities, additional training, or placement in another job.

Handling Responsibility

Some people look on the responsibilities of management as an opportunity for increased power and prestige, and they are eager to join the management team. Others are frightened by the prospect of such responsibilities and consider a management position something to be avoided. The responsibilities of planning, organizing, and controlling people, technology, and material resources may, indeed, seem overwhelming.

In the controlling function, management often sets specific standards for employees to follow. In each case shown here, what dress code are the employees following? What do you think are their specific guidelines about behavior on the job?

Most managers begin their careers as company employees. They are promoted to managers when they have gained experience and shown certain leadership qualities. If you are offered a promotion to a position with management responsibilities, should you accept it? To help you decide, let's consider some of the advantages and disadvantages of being a manager.

Advantages of Being a Manager

Managers usually earn more money than non-management employees. Supervisors may earn only a little more than other employees, but middle-level managers earn considerably more. Many top-level managers earn well over $100,000 a year. Some top-level managers in large companies earn millions.

Employees recognize managers as leaders, and good leaders are respected. So, management-level jobs are usually considered prestigious positions.

Because managers are leaders, they have more influence than other employees on how the company is run. They have more power than other employees do in planning, organizing, and controlling company resources.

Managers' duties are usually quite varied; thus, they make decisions about many things. They have greater control over their own time and how they will use it than other employees do.

Disadvantages of Being a Manager

Managers usually have a different type of relationship with other employees than the employees have among themselves. Employees are often guarded about what they say when their managers are around. After all, they don't want to jeopardize their standing in the company. Some managers consider this changed relationship a disadvantage.

Managers are often targets for criticism and are often blamed by employees when things go wrong (even if the problem is caused by another employee).

When managers do make mistakes, they are often more costly to the company than other employees' mistakes because managers' decisions affect the actions of many employees. So there is more pressure on managers to do everything right. This is often a source of job-related emotional stress.

Effective Management Skills

Your first management position will probably be at the supervisory level. You may be called a supervisor, an assistant manager, or something similar. The management skills discussed in this section apply to all levels of management, but they are described in terms of being a supervisor.

Management responsibilities, even at the supervisory level, may seem difficult at first. But they become easier as you gain experience and make thoughtful decisions. The following suggestions will help you become an effective supervisor:

- give clear directions,
- train new employees well,
- be consistent,
- treat employees fairly,
- be firm when necessary,
- consider employees' welfare,
- set a good example, and
- delegate responsibility.

Give Clear Directions

Directing others requires good communication skills. Good communication is necessary at every level of management. Even the best employees won't be productive if they don't know what they are expected to do.

As a supervisor, give all the direction required for each job. Ask for feedback to determine whether your directions are fully understood. Usually, you will need to repeat some of your directions, perhaps using a different approach. Encourage employees to ask questions about your directions. Communication will improve dramatically when they feel comfortable asking questions.

Train New Employees Well

All new employees need some on-the-job training. As a supervisor, you may train new employees yourself or you may delegate training to another experienced employee. If you delegate the training to someone else, choose someone who knows the job well and is a good teacher. Then supervise the training. Make sure that all tasks of the job are explained and that the new employee understands how to complete them.

Treating People Right

One of the best ways to help employees become more productive is to listen to their concerns. Federal Express does just that. While some corporations treat employees like replaceable parts, Federal Express founder Frederick W. Smith treats them like the valuable human resources they are.

Employees are encouraged to make suggestions that are evaluated by a special department. If the idea saves time or money, the employee receives an award of up to $25,000.

When employees have concerns or see problems that need solving, quality action teams of managers and employees go to work to come up with solutions. In addition, Smith has an "open door" policy—any employee can come to his office to talk over problems or concerns.

If employees have complaints they feel their supervisors have not handled fairly, they may ask their supervisors' managers for a hearing. If they still are not satisfied with the solution, they may continue to appeal—all the way up to the senior vice-president level. Final decisions are not always in management's favor. One year, out of five employees who asked for review, two were decided in the employees' favor.

In its struggling early years, Federal Express occasionally asked employees to delay cashing their paychecks until the money was in the bank to cover them. Today the multi-million dollar company not only pays on time, but also distributes some of its profits among employees twice a year.

Smith also remembers that employees have family lives. To honor that symbolically, each Federal Express cargo plane is named for an employee's child.

1. Tell five or six personal rewards you think Federal Express employees get from working there.
2. Give five or six benefits Federal Express receives from treating its employees so well.

Be Consistent

When you say that a job must be done in a certain way, make certain that it is *always* done that way by every employee. Don't make exceptions unless there is a good reason to do so. Always follow through on what you say. If you say that you will deduct part of an employee's salary for being late to work, do it. If you don't follow through on your decisions, employees will not respect what you say.

Treat Employees Fairly

Employees will be more productive under your supervision if you treat them fairly. Expect the same standards of performance from *every* employee. Don't give special privileges to a few favorites. But do set reasonable standards of performance that your employees can achieve.

Listen and consider acting on suggestions from employees. If someone thinks you are being unfair, look at the situation from the employee's point of view as well as your own. The employee may be right. If so, be honest enough to admit it and make changes. If you believe the employee is wrong, take the time to explain your reasoning. The person may understand your position and agree with you. If not, he or she will appreciate your effort to be fair.

Be Firm When Necessary

Sometimes supervising others requires a firm hand. Never let an employee take unfair advantage of you, the company, or another employee. Learn to be firm without losing your temper.

Each situation requiring disciplinary action is different. A friendly suggestion is all that is necessary to get most employees on the right track. Some people, though, don't respond to friendly suggestions. In these cases, you have to be direct and firm. Give whatever directions are appropriate, and be certain the employee understands what you expect. But again, don't lose your temper.

Some employee problems are caused by the inappropriate behavior of one employee toward another. In such cases, it may be difficult to reason with one or both of them. Listen to what they have to say, and be reasonable but firm. In severe cases, you may have to move an employee to another department.

Consider Employees' Welfare

Whenever possible, do what is best for your employees. Of course, you cannot and should not do everything they ask you to do. But consider their welfare, and show your willingness to treat them fairly. Do whatever you can to help them without sacrificing the amount or quality of work done. If appropriate, talk with your immediate supervisor about changes that will benefit your employees.

Set a Good Example

Set a good example in everything you do on the job. Doing this one simple thing will make your supervisory job a lot easier.

For example, Frank, a department manager in a large retail store, wrote computer programs at night to earn extra money. He seldom went to sleep before 2 a.m., and he found it very difficult to arrive at the store on time. Other employees in his department noticed that Frank was usually half an hour late, so they decided they could sleep 20 minutes longer and still arrive at the store ahead of him. By following Frank's example, the whole department began arriving late for work. After several weeks of this, Frank was replaced.

Karen, the new department manager, always arrived at the store a few minutes early. When the other employees realized this, they reset their alarm clocks and began arriving early, too. Karen didn't have to say a word to anyone; she simply set a good example.

Delegate Responsibility

Some supervisors and many middle-level managers simply do too much work themselves. Some take work home almost every night. This may be necessary at times, but it usually means resources are not being managed well. Those who take work home are probably not delegating many tasks and responsibilities to others. Yet they often have capable employees with light work schedules who are willing to do more.

As a supervisor, don't try to do everything yourself. Organize your work responsibilities, then decide which ones you can delegate to others. Decide which employee can best handle each task. If necessary, take time to teach some employees how to do new tasks.

By turning over selected responsibilities to others, you will do a better job with your own responsibilities. Your employees will appreciate the chance to show they can handle greater responsibility, and they will become more productive. Of course, don't give away so many responsibilities that you have little left to do.

Managing Through a System of Rewards

The things that get rewarded get done. Keep this in mind when you become a manager by following these simple yet effective principles.

1. *Reward real solutions, not quick fixes.* Provide frequent feedback to employees and formally evaluate them yearly. Identify goals to be achieved over three to five years. Then reward employees who contribute to these goals.

REAL WORLD MARKETING

Taking It Personally

"It's the personal touch that counts" is Mary Kay Ash's credo. It's also a major factor in the success of Mary Kay Cosmetics, which realizes sales each year in the hundreds of millions. The lively Ms. Ash, who started her Dallas-based beauty empire in 1963, makes a point of never getting a name wrong. She also sends each of her 185,000 beauty consultants a personally designed card every Christmas. (See page 197 in Chapter 18 for more information on Mary Kay Cosmetics.)

2. *Reward smart work, not busy work.* In many companies, people are rewarded for working long hours and looking busy. Thus, they invent all sorts of ways to look busy. But if results are rewarded, you will get results.

   Begin by getting the right people in the right jobs. Give them the tools they need, and fully explain what is expected of them. Tell everyone they will be rewarded for results. Encourage employees to spend a few minutes each morning organizing their day, including setting goals for the day.

3. *Reward simplification, not complication.* In some companies, everything is complicated because complicators have been rewarded. Ordering a $2.79 pen from the supplies department at Intel Corporation, for example, used to take 95 steps and 12 pieces of paper. Intel recognized the problem and simplified the procedure. Now it takes 8 steps and 1 piece of paper.

4. *Reward quietly effective people, not squeaky wheels.* Many managers reward complainers and ignore those who actually do the work. Seek out those who quietly do a good job, and tell them what you like about their work. Take a sincere interest in them, and they will perform even better. When you learn who the chronic complainers are, ignore them. They will quiet down when they realize no one is listening.

5. *Reward quality work, not just fast work.* Doing the job right the first time lowers costs, increases productivity, and increases worker pride. Identify those workers who value quality, not speed. Ask them to suggest ways to improve job performance; they probably know more about the job than anyone else. Reward employees who suggest improvements.

6. *Reward creativity, not mindless conformity.* A reasonable amount of conformity is necessary in every company. But some managers let conformity stifle creativity. The most important asset in any business is ideas. Encourage employees to be creative. Then reward them when they come up with good ideas.

   A young engineer named Steve Wozniak was bored with his job working on computer chips. He asked on three occasions if he could work on designing a personal computer. His manager said no each time. So he built the first Apple computer—in his garage—and became one of the most successful entrepreneurs in history.

7. *Reward loyalty.* Enthusiastic long-term employees are the key to success in most companies. Reward loyalty by investing in continuing education for employees and promoting from within. If the company is in a difficult financial position, avoid layoffs by cutting pay across the board, if necessary.

Many companies recognize outstanding employee contributions or performance with awards. What are some other ways of rewarding employees?

VOCABULARY REVIEW

Write one or two paragraphs incorporating these eight vocabulary words.

management
top management
middle management
supervisory-level
  management

supervisor
planning
organizing
controlling

FACT AND IDEA REVIEW

1. What is management?

2. List the three levels of management. What is the difference between these levels?

3. At what level will your first management position probably be?

4. What is the responsibility of a middle manager?

5. What main functions do managers perform?

6. What are the characteristics of good management planning at any level?

7. What is usually involved in the *organizing* function of management?

8. *Controlling* includes what three activities?

9. Tell two advantages and disadvantages of being a manager.

10. Why is it important to ask for feedback after giving directions to an employee?

11. How does being consistent contribute to effective management?

12. Why is *delegating responsibility* such an important management skill?

13. List eight effective management skills.

14. What is the basic principle underlying the use of a system of rewards?

15. List seven work activities and attitudes that should be rewarded.

CRITICAL THINKING

1. Compare top-level management in a large company to that of a small company.

2. Discuss the disadvantages of being a manager. Do these disadvantages turn you against becoming a manager?

3. Why is it important for both manager and employees that a manager delegate responsibility?

4. Describe how being fair is an effective management skill. Discuss experiences you have had or heard about in which managers were not fair. What were the results of the unfair treatment?

5. Discuss why it is sometimes necessary to use a firm hand when supervising others.

6. Why do you think rewards get better results than punishments?

USING BASIC SKILLS

Math

1. The vice-president of a company makes an annual salary of $65,000 and works an average of 40 hours per week. The president of the company makes an annual salary of $100,000 and works an average of 60 hours per week. On a per-hour basis, who earns more money?

2. In a mail order clothing company, 3 percent of the orders were being shipped incorrectly. Each incorrect shipment cost the company $10 to re-ship plus an untold loss in future business due to customer dissatisfaction with the service. By offering a cash incentive to improve accuracy in the shipping department, the rate of incorrect shipments dropped to 1 percent. How much money did this save the company for every 100 orders?

Communication

3. Practice giving clear verbal directions. Ask another student to play the part of a new employee. Assume you are training the new employee, whose job is to bag groceries in a supermarket. Make sure all the tasks of the job are covered and that the employee understands *exactly* what to do.

4. Imagine that you are the manager of a large bookstore. One of your salesclerks makes a suggestion about rearranging the children's section to include a few small tables and chairs. You like the idea and intend to carry it out. Write a thank-you note to the salesclerk for the suggested improvement.

Human Relations

5. Although Susan is proud of her promotion to supervisor, the other workers are making it hard for her. Before her promotion, they were her friends, and now they give her the cold shoulder. Susan wants to keep her new position, but is unhappy with the new relationship with her former co-workers. What should she do?

6. Abe works as a travel agent for a small firm. The manager of the travel agency has just hired a new agent who happens to be the manager's personal friend. The manager is showing her friend obvious favoritism. Abe likes his job, but he feels increasingly uncomfortable with the manager's unfair and inconsistent behavior. What should Abe do?

APPLICATION PROJECTS

1. Describe what would go into the *planning*, *organizing*, and *controlling* of a school club car wash.

2. One of the disadvantages of accepting responsibility is the increase in pressure and stress. Find out what two managers in local businesses do to reduce job-related stress.

3. What might someone at a *supervisory* level do when working at a shoe store, a warehouse, a women's apparel store, and a family restaurant.

4. Ask the work experience coordinator or co-op coordinator at your school to help get names of people in the community who work in managerial positions. Invite one of them to come to your class to discuss the roles and responsibilities of their job positions.

5. Rewarding good work not only gets things done but also contributes to the morale and enthusiasm of the employees. This, in turn, provides further benefit to the company. Brainstorm some creative ways that companies could reward their outstanding employees.

6. Discuss the different ways in which a supervisor might handle the employees in the situation shown here.

PART

4

SELLING

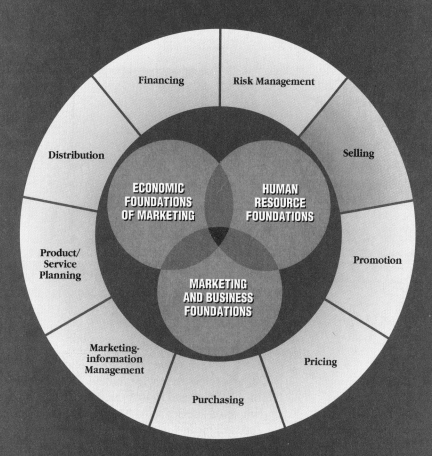

Financing

Risk Management

Distribution

Selling

ECONOMIC
FOUNDATIONS
OF MARKETING

HUMAN
RESOURCE
FOUNDATIONS

Product/
Service
Planning

Promotion

MARKETING
AND BUSINESS
FOUNDATIONS

Marketing-
information
Management

Pricing

Purchasing

CHAPTERS

12

After completing this chapter, you will be able to:

1. define selling,

2. explain the goals of selling,

3. explain how selling skills can be helpful in careers other than professional sales,

4. identify the different classifications of selling according to method used and kind of product sold, and

5. name eleven traits or skills of a successful salesperson.

selling
inside sales
outside sales
telemarketing

What Is Selling?

Selling involves providing customers with the goods and services they wish to buy. The sales profession itself is one of the oldest and most valued—particularly in the United States, where businesses must compete for their share of the market to realize a profit.

In this chapter, you will learn about different types of selling situations and the traits and skills you need to become a professional salesperson. Even if a sales career is not for you, the information in this chapter and in this entire unit will help prepare you for success in whatever you do.

Why Study Selling and Selling Skills?

When most people think of selling, they think of products sold in a store. But selling takes place in many different situations. A waiter or waitress who suggests that you order the special of the day is selling you on a certain dish. A friend trying to convince you to go to a ball game is selling you on the idea of attending a particular event.

All successful business people use selling skills, especially when trying to get new ideas accepted and put into effect. Even the chief executive officer of a major corporation uses selling techniques to get approval on new policies from the company's board of directors.

You can see that selling, in its broadest sense, occurs whenever one person tries to convince another to do something or act in a certain way. You probably use selling skills every day. When you apply for a job, ask classmates to vote for you in a school election, or ask your parents to let you drive the family car, you are trying to get someone to act based on information you present. Thus, selling skills are useful to you now and will be in the future, regardless of whether you pursue a career in sales.

Definition of Selling

Selling is helping customers make satisfying buying decisions by communicating how products and their features match customers' needs and wants. Let's look at each part of this definition.

Helping Customers Make Satisfying Buying Decisions. Because many customers find it difficult to decide on purchases, one of a salesperson's primary goals is to help people make satisfying buying decisions—those decisions the customer will be happy with after the sale. (In Chapter 15 you will learn many techniques for doing this.) Why is customer satisfaction so important? Businesses want repeat business. But they will only get it if customers are happy enough with their purchases to return again and again.

Communicating How Product Features Match Customer Needs and Wants. Customers have different priorities when considering a purchase. For example, one customer in a shoe store might need a comfortable pair of shoes

Customers have different priorities when considering a purchase, so matching product features to their needs and wants is essential. What product features of this food processor would you point out to this customer if he told you he lived in an apartment with a small kitchen?

because she stands most of the day at her job. Another customer might want a pair of dress shoes for a party. An alert salesperson will select one or several pairs of shoes appropriate to each customer's needs and wants. In Chapter 13 you will learn more about how to use product knowledge to satisfy customers' needs and wants.

Thus, the goals of selling are to help customers decide on purchases and to ensure customer satisfaction so the firm can count on repeat business. To accomplish these goals, the salesperson needs to match features of each product to the customer's needs and wants. This concept is called *feature-benefit selling*. We will look at it more closely in Chapter 13.

Basic Classifications of Selling

Because selling is such a broad concept, we need to look at it from two points of view: where the selling takes place (*inside* or *outside* the firm) and the *type of product sold*. We will also look at a specialized selling technique called *telemarketing*.

Inside Sales vs. Outside Sales

Inside sales are selling efforts that take place at the salesperson's place of business. Most salespeople who work for retailers, for example, meet their customers in the retail store.

Outside sales are selling efforts that take place outside the salesperson's firm. People who work in outside sales travel to meet their customers at each customer's place of business or home. (Remember that the distinction is whether the selling is inside or outside the seller's *place of business*. It does not matter whether the selling is indoors or outdoors.) A door-to-door salesperson who comes to your home and a Xerox salesperson who services accounts at her clients' places of business are both in outside sales.

CASE CHALLENGE

Commission Pay in Retailing

Just a few years ago, most department stores offered straight commission only to salespeople in high-ticket departments, such as large appliances. But more and more major department stores are switching from an hourly wage to straight commission on sales in all departments.

Nordstrom Inc., a Seattle-based department store known for its skilled salespeople and good service, has always paid all of its salespeople on commission. Now many other retailers are following suit. By July of 1989, all 113 department stores in Carter Hawley's five divisions were fully on commission. Federated and Allied stores had all sales associates on some form of commission by the end of 1990.

Employers get many benefits from incorporating straight commission into their pay structure. First, overhead is controlled. Salaries increase in direct proportion to increases in sales and vice versa. In addition, some retailers have found that they can increase the number of hours sales personnel work by 10 percent without increasing the cost of labor because salespeople are only paid for sales, not for the hours spent on the job.

One of the biggest problems for stores that use straight commission is getting and keeping qualified sales personnel. Because of the sink-or-swim challenge of working on commission, the personnel turnover rate is usually very high. Nordstrom, for example, reports an average annual turnover rate of 30 percent.

For sales personnel, the straight commission system can mean an increase in personal income. Those who generate high sales will see immediate financial rewards for their efforts. Nordstrom reported in 1989 that some of its salespeople earned upwards of $25,000 a year.

Some analysts believe the move to paying salespeople straight commission makes retail sales more professional.

1. Would Nordstrom's sales personnel be classified as inside or outside salespeople?
2. What are the advantages and disadvantages to employers and to the salespeople of paying retail sales personnel straight commission?
3. Why do you think that paying sales personnel straight commission will make retail sales more professional?

Why is a door-to-door salesperson considered to be in outside sales?

Type of Product

Another way to classify selling is according to the type of product sold. As you learned in Chapter 5, there are two types of goods and services in our economy: *consumer* and *industrial*. The two types are distinguished by who uses them. Consumer goods and services are purchased by people for personal use. Industrial goods and services, on the other hand, are purchased for use in a business.

For example, when you buy a quart of milk to pour on cereal at home, the milk is a consumer product because you are a consumer using the milk yourself. But when a bakery buys a thousand gallons of milk for its doughnut batter, the milk is an industrial product because it is used by the business to create another product.

The distinction between consumer and industrial products is useful because the selling methods for the two types of products are usually different.

Most consumer goods and services are sold in retail stores—such as the grocery store where you buy milk, the department store where you buy clothing and other tangible goods, and the dry cleaners where you take your clothing. The sales positions for these products are usually *inside* sales positions.

On the other hand, most industrial goods and services are sold through *outside* sales efforts. Industrial sales representatives generally call on prospective buyers or purchasing agents at their places of business. A sales representative for a milk wholesaler, for example, will call on a bakery to sell large orders of milk. A sales representative for a local newspaper will call on retailers (sometimes by telephone) to discuss the benefits of advertising in the newspaper.

There are a number of exceptions, however. Some consumer products and services are sold through outside sales efforts. Avon sales representatives, for example, sell their consumer products by visiting potential customers in their homes. A *route salesperson* travels a given geographic area called a *territory* and makes home deliveries of such consumer products as snack foods or bottled water. Insurance agents and real estate agents may sell their consumer services through inside *or* outside sales efforts. Some industrial products may be sold through inside sales. Many manufacturers and wholesalers have product showrooms that may be located in their manufacturing or wholesaling facility. The buyers and purchasing agents come to the showroom in the salesperson's place of business to buy.

Telemarketing

A specialized type of selling is *telemarketing*. *Telemarketing is the process of selling over the telephone*. It is a form of inside selling. Both consumer and industrial products may be sold through telemarketing. For example, service contracts for

Telemarketing is a popular method of selling both industrial and consumer goods and services. How do you think the sales approach differs when buyers and sellers meet on the phone rather than in person?

newly purchased televisions and computers, lawn care services, magazine subscriptions, and business stationery supplies are all sold through telemarketing.

Traits and Skills of Successful Salespeople

You may wonder whether you have the qualities to be successful in a sales position. Don't be disillusioned by the old cliché that a salesperson is born and not made. You can succeed at selling if you are willing to develop the basic communication and business skills needed for the job.

Successful salespeople are problem solvers. They are people-oriented, enjoy dealing with the general public, and are courteous, caring, tactful, and diplomatic. They also realize that they represent their firm, whether the firm is Burger King, The Limited, or IBM. Thus, they always try to reflect a positive image of their employer. To see how one person became suc-

cessful in sales because of her concern for her customers and her solid sales skills, read "Janice's Story" on page 139.

Janice's story will show you why she was successful. She developed the good communication skills of listening and speaking that you learned in Chapter 9. She demonstrated the essential human relation skills you explored in Chapter 10.

In addition to these human resource skills, effective salespeople have the skills in mathematics that are essential in selling, because every sales transaction requires calculation and negotiation in terms of the sale.

Customers expect salespeople to be experts in their field. So, good salespeople have thorough product knowledge. This may require the salesperson to make an extensive study of both the product and the industry. In an automotive supply center, for example, customers expect the salespeople to know exactly which parts are needed to repair a certain model car. In industrial selling, customers expect the salespeople to thoroughly understand their methods of manufacturing, wholesaling, or retailing.

Product knowledge is essential to success in selling. What specific types of product knowledge should this salesperson have in order to work in an automotive supply center?

Janice's Story

When Janice Fielding was 16, she took a job with Burger King as a counter person. In that same year, she also took a marketing course where she learned that many of the techniques she was using at work, such as asking customers if they would like french fries with their order, helped create more sales. But Janice did not see herself as someone with a sales personality. She believed that a salesperson had to be fast-talking and manipulative.

In her senior year, Janice's marketing teacher suggested that she apply for a sales position with The Limited, a popular women's clothing store, as part of her cooperative work experience. Janice had some reservations about this because she was definitely more reserved than she thought a salesperson should be. However, she often shopped at The Limited and liked its merchandise. So, she applied for the job and was hired. Janice was surprised at how much she liked helping customers make decisions about their purchases and how successful she was in doing so.

After graduation from high school, Janice continued to work for The Limited while she attended a local four-year college, majoring in marketing. When researching careers in marketing, Janice learned that one of the best ways to advance into marketing management is to begin in a sales position with a major firm that has a policy of promoting from within the firm. She also learned that most industrial firms offer higher starting salaries and better benefits than retail stores. So Janice applied for a position as an IBM service representative and was hired.

While participating in IBM's extensive product and sales training, Janice found out just how much she already knew about the basics of selling. She also realized that her first priority in retail sales—always trying to satisfy her customers' needs and wants—applied directly to industrial sales, too.

Beyond these skills, most successful salespeople have or develop common personal traits, such as sincerity, attitude, enthusiasm, empathy, poise, and perception.

Sincerity means having a genuine interest in your customers and being honest with them. In Janice's story, you learned that she was successful because she cared about satisfying her customers' needs and wants. If you think back to salespeople you liked and bought from, you will probably remember them as being very sincere.

In sales, maintaining a positive attitude is essential to success. A positive attitude includes working hard, getting along well with others, and bouncing back quickly from the feeling of rejection when a sale is lost. It also means analyzing and learning from your mistakes.

All successful salespeople have enthusiasm about the products they sell. Janice shopped at The Limited and liked the clothes sold in that store. She probably found it easy to be enthusiastic about the store's merchandise because she liked it herself.

Empathy is the essence of customer-oriented selling. To be a successful salesperson, you must always be able to see things from the customer's point of view. So you must constantly ask yourself these two questions: "What are my customer's buying motives? What are the qualities of the product that will make my customer satisfied with the purchase?"

Having poise means remaining calm under pressure. Poised people are generally self-confident and have self-control and tact.

Being perceptive means understanding something about a person or situation that may not be immediately obvious. The tone of voice people use and the way they sit or stand give a salesperson clues about their emotions and state of mind. Being perceptive helps a salesperson determine how and when to proceed in certain selling situations and with different types of customers.

C H A P T E R   1 2   R E V I E W

VOCABULARY REVIEW

Use each of the following vocabulary terms in a sentence.

selling   outside sales
inside sales   telemarketing

FACT AND IDEA REVIEW

1. Describe two situations in which a person not directly involved in the sale of a product nevertheless uses selling strategies.

2. Define selling and explain the goals of selling.

3. Why is it so important for customers to be pleased with their purchases?

4. What is the difference between inside and outside sales? Give an example of each type.

5. What are consumer products? Are most consumer products sold through inside or outside sales? Give two exceptions to your answer.

6. What are industrial products? Are most industrial products sold through inside or outside sales? Give two exceptions to your answer.

7. What is telemarketing? Explain two ways in which salespeople use telemarketing.

8. Identify at least six personal traits of an effective salesperson.

CRITICAL THINKING

1. In what ways are industrial sales different from consumer sales? In what ways are they the same?

2. Think of a time when a telemarketer called your home. Was this person's selling effort successful or unsuccessful? Why?

3. After reading this chapter, do you think you could be a successful salesperson? Give at least three reasons for your answer.

USING BASIC SKILLS

Math

1. Calculate the commission a sales representative will earn for selling $500,000 worth of machinery to a new account if the commission rate is 4 percent of sales.

Communication

2. Write a classified advertisement for a sales position in the school store. Include a brief description of the job responsibilities, as well as the characteristics and skills required for the position.

Human Relations

3. One of the benefits of working as a salesperson for a retail store is employee discounts. Jeff works in sales for Herman's Sporting Goods and receives a 20 percent employee discount on purchases. He and his friend Craig are planning a skiing weekend. Jeff knows that Craig needs a new pair of skis but does not have enough money to buy the pair he really wants. When they discuss this issue, Craig asks Jeff to use his employee discount to buy the skis for him. In order to do that, Jeff would have to pretend that he was buying the skis for himself. What should Jeff do?

4. An industrial sales representative is speaking with a customer and is about to close a $50,000 sale when the customer tells her that the only way he will buy the goods is if they can be delivered in two weeks. The sales representative will make $2,500 on this one sale. She knows, however, that she can only have the goods delivered in three weeks. Should the sales representative tell the truth? Why or why not?

APPLICATION PROJECTS

1. Using the classified section of a newspaper, cut out one advertisement for each of the following types of sales positions: retail sales, outside sales, inside sales, route sales, and telemarketing sales. Paste the ads on a sheet of paper. In your search for these ads, read other classified ads for sales positions, and identify eight traits or skills required for those positions. How do those skills and traits match the ones included in this chapter?

2. Many different terms are used to identify sales positions. These include sales representative, sales associate, route sales representative, sales engineer, sales agent, sales trainee, sales/technical representative, sales consultant, direct marketing representative, and sales coordinator.

   a. Look through the classified section of a Sunday newspaper for ads that use these terms to identify sales positions and cut them out.

   b. Find three other ads that use different terms to identify the sales positions and cut them out.

   c. Identify which terms are used for retail sales positions and which for industrial sales positions.

   d. Analyze the requirements for each sales position with regard to need for previous experience and educational background, as well as the starting salary.

   e. On a piece of paper, paste up the help wanted ads in order, starting with the ads for jobs that require little knowledge or experience, and work your way up to ads for jobs that demand the most expertise and offer the highest salaries.

   f. Write two or three paragraphs revealing what you learned from this activity in terms of the types of sales positions currently available in your area.

3. As you have learned, any time we try to convince someone to do something we are selling. Think of three of your unsuccessful "selling" attempts, whether it was asking for permission to go away for a weekend or trying to convince a community businessperson to donate something to your club. Analyze why you were unsuccessful. Work in small groups with your classmates to brainstorm ideas that might have helped you succeed.

4. Contact someone in your community who does outside sales (such as insurance, cosmetics, or household products) and someone who does inside sales (such as in a department store, jewelry store, or automotive store). Ask the person to speak to your class. Prepare several questions to ask him or her, such as how he or she prepares for selling and handles difficult selling situations.

5. It takes special traits and skills to become a successful salesperson.

   a. First, list all of the traits you think you have that will help to make you successful in sales. Then list all your traits and skills you think you need to improve.

   b. Next, have a classmate make the same lists of your strong and weak points. You may be surprised at the difference in the lists.

   c. Then, working with your classmate, brainstorm ways to turn your weaknesses into strengths.

13

After completing this chapter, you will be able to:

1. list nine types of information salespeople need to obtain about their products and company,

2. identify and give examples of four general sources of product and company information,

3. define a product feature,

4. define a customer benefit,

5. define and give examples of rational and emotional buying motives,

6. list and explain the six stages of the consumer's decision-making process, and

7. explain the three levels of decision making used in buying products.

WORDS TO KNOW

product feature
customer benefit
rational motive
emotional motive
stimulus
cognitive dissonance
extensive decision making
limited decision making
routine decision making

Understanding Customers

How much confidence would you have in a camera salesperson who could not tell you the type of film a particular camera uses? What would you think of a salesperson who said, "I've sold this gown to several other young ladies from your school who are also attending the senior prom, so I'm sure you'll want it, too"?

In each of these examples, the salesperson's lack of product knowledge or lack of understanding regarding the customer would probably prevent him or her from making a sale.

Successful salespeople learn all they can about the products they sell so they can help their customers make wise buying decisions. They also learn what motivates customers to buy and how they make buying decisions. In this chapter, we'll look at the things salespeople can do to better understand their products and customers.

Developing Product Knowledge

Regardless of whether salespeople are selling inside or outside a firm, they must learn the following information about their company and its products to be successful.

1. *Company Background.* A company's history is often a strong selling point. A company that has been in business a long time has probably been successful in satisfying customers' needs.
2. *Company Policies and Services.* Successful salespeople need to know and follow company policy and services. Know company return policies, product guarantees, financing terms, and when orders will be shipped.
3. *Product Composition and Manufacturing Process.* Knowing a product's composition and manufacturing process helps you explain why your products are better than competitor's products. This wins customer confidence.
4. *Product Appearance.* Appearance is highly regarded in most consumer and industrial products. You will be more effective when you point out the elements that make your products look more attractive than your competitors' products.
5. *Product Use.* An effective salesperson explains a product's use and emphasizes when it has more than one use. This helps educate customers and presents products that fit their needs.
6. *Care of the Product.* This includes knowing how to clean, service, and store the product to ensure its safety and reliability.
7. *Product Price and Comparison.* Product pricing and comparison are related. Customers expect salespeople to explain why one product is more expensive or less expensive than a competitor's, or than another product carried by the salesperson's own company. To do this, it's often necessary to explain varying degrees of quality or specific product features.
8. *Stock Condition.* Successful salespeople always know how much stock is available, where it is located, and how quickly delivery

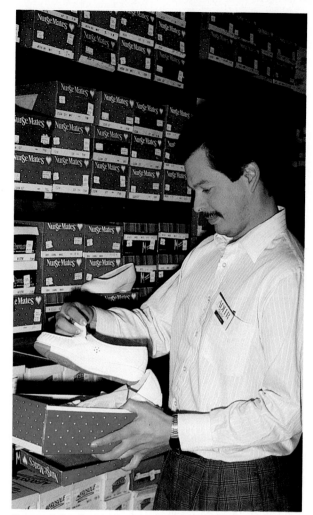

Successful salespeople always know the availability and location of stock, and how quickly it can be delivered. Why are these factors so crucial in closing a sale?

can be made. These factors are often crucial in closing a sale. For example, if you tell a customer that an item is out of stock or cannot be delivered in a particular time frame, the customer may do business elsewhere.

9. *Items Related to the Product.* The successful salesperson knows whether a product has accessories and how they should be used. For example, when selling a copier, the salesperson should explain what paper, dry ink, and other chemicals are necessary for its operation, and suggest that the customer buy these at the time of purchase.

Sources of Product Information

Salespeople can find all the information they need through four main sources: *direct experience with the product, printed material, other people,* and *formal training provided by the employer.* Let's take a closer look at each.

Direct Experience

Using a product is probably the best source of direct experience with it. So, some businesses offer their salespeople discounts to encourage them to buy and use the company's merchandise.

You also get direct experience with a product by studying products on display, and comparing the prices, styles, and special features of different models. Or you can visit the manufacturers' and wholesalers' showrooms and tour the facilities where the product is made.

Printed Materials

Printed materials come from several reliable sources. For example, product ingredients are usually printed on bottle, can, and box labels. Seals of approval indicating quality or safety are often attached to the product.

User's manuals on product care and operation, manufacturers' warranties or guarantees found in the packaging or in the user's manual, and retailers' prod-

---

C A S E   C H A L L E N G E

Selling an Idea

Diana Troup, senior vice president of preliminary design for Mattel Toys, uses product knowledge and knowledge of her market to get her ideas accepted by top management.

For example, when Troup designed the California Dream Barbie as an addition to Mattel's existing Barbie doll line, she questioned colleagues to anticipate potential problems with her idea.

A major problem colleagues were concerned with was the company's ability to sell the doll throughout the United States and abroad. To prepare for her presentation, Troup researched the print media and found marketing studies, and magazine and newspaper articles that indicated the California look had universal appeal. She even clipped ads from French fashion magazines of shirts with "Malibu" printed on them. Her research convinced Mattel that national and international familiarity with California would assure the success of California Dream Barbie.

In addition to thoroughly researching her ideas, Troup makes sure her presentations to top management are enthusiastic. She believes that when you are selling an idea, you are also selling your conviction about the idea. To make her presentations come alive, she uses visual aids and actual products. She has also used videotapes of children happily playing with a prototype toy.

Most of all, she concentrates her presentation on the basic question she knows her idea must answer—"How will this new idea benefit the consumer and, in turn, the company?"

1. What sources did Troup use in developing her ideas for the California Dream Barbie? How are those sources similar to the sources salespeople use to develop product knowledge?
2. What does Troup know about the company's decision makers which is similar to what all salespeople should know about their customers?
3. Identify an idea you want to sell and explain what you would do to prepare for your sales presentation to a company's decision maker(s).

uct fact sheets are also good sources of product information. Employee handbooks and company reports sometimes give product information, too.

Promotional materials, such as newspaper and magazine advertisements, along with radio and television commercials, give insight on product features and customer benefits. Advertisements in trade journals and in catalogs usually include the most important selling features.

The library is an excellent source of product information. Look for *Consumer Reports*, which tells the materials used in the manufacture of a product and gives the results of product testing done by independent laboratories. Also, look for trade and technical publications that give useful information on the uses of products, sales trends, and merchandising techniques.

Other People

Friends, relatives, and customers who use the products can share their thoughts about them and tell which brands and styles they prefer. They may also

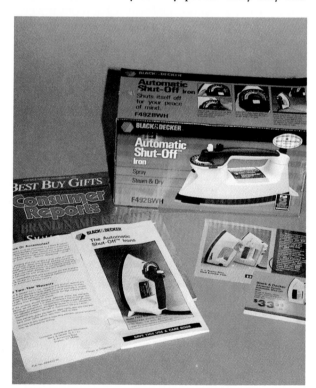

Printed materials are ready sources of product information. What types of product information would a customer get from these items?

reveal new uses for a product—or ways to save time when using it.

Co-workers and supervisors can give helpful tips on product presentation. They may also be able to explain the styles and features of different models and how the product compares with competitors' products.

Because they deal with many businesses, vendors' sales representatives can usually predict trends. They are also often the people with the most in-depth knowledge of how a product will perform.

Finally, technical experts are a rich source of information about a product's capabilities. Industrial salespeople in particular must often talk with their firm's technicians and specialists to get technical information for a customer or client.

Formal Training

Most industrial sales representatives receive much of their product knowledge through formal training sessions. Some sales representatives spend several months attending classes and observing experienced sales representatives before being assigned their own territories.

At the retail level, the training is likely to be less intense and less formal. As new merchandise is received or as items are selected for promotional campaigns, the sales staff may be trained through weekly meetings with management.

How to Use Product Information

It is often said that customers do not buy products, they buy what the products will do for them. Here are some products and the possible reasons people buy them.

- Leather shoes are purchased for their appearance, easy care, comfort, and long life.
- A computer is purchased for increased productivity.
- Insurance is purchased for emotional and financial security.

A salesperson needs to learn how a product's qualities or features will benefit the customer. *A product feature is a physical characteristic or quality of the good or service that explains what it is.* The illustration on page 148 depicts product features of the Vivitar TL125 camera.

In general, product features are physical things a person can see, touch, hear, taste, or smell. Some features are not this obvious, however. An important feature of a running shoe might be the air pockets in the heel.

Customer Benefits

When the features of a product are developed into *customer benefits,* they become selling points. *Customer benefits are the advantages or personal satisfaction a customer will get from a good or service.* It is a salesperson's job to analyze the product features from the customer's point of view to determine the benefits. As a salesperson, you will need to answer two questions about each product feature.

1. *How does the feature help the performance of the product?*

The answer to this question represents the first step in developing a customer benefit. For example, the air pockets in the heel of the running shoe cushion the blow of a foot pounding on the pavement.

2. *How does the information about the feature help the customer and thus give the customer reasons for wanting to buy the product?*

In terms of our running shoe, the cushioning effect of the air pockets gives the wearer more comfort

when running or walking and helps protect the foot from injury.

After identifying the features of a product and their benefits, it is often helpful to put together a *feature-benefit chart.* This is a two-column chart in which each product feature is listed in the left column, and corresponding customer benefits are noted in the right column. See page 149 for a feature-benefit chart on the Reebok ERS Trainer Running Shoe.

Always remember in selling that the more useful a feature is, the more valuable the product is to the customer.

Learning About the Customer

Salespeople determine the customer benefits of a product's features from their knowledge of customers. They are concerned with what motivates customers to buy and what decisions customers make before finally purchasing a product.

Customers may have rational or emotional motives for making their purchases. *A rational motive is a conscious, factual reason for a purchase.* Rational motives include product dependability, time or money savings, convenience, comfort, health, safety, recreation, service, and quality. *An emotional motive is a feeling of satisfaction a customer desires in a product, such as social approval, curiosity, recognition, power, love, affection, or prestige.* Both rational and emotional motives may be present in the same decision to make a purchase.

Successful salespeople determine customers' rational and emotional motives in a potential buying situation. Then they suggest the features and benefits of the product that best match those motives.

Each customer is an individual with different needs and wants that are constantly changing and becoming more or less important. For example, a teenager may be motivated by economy when he purchases his first automobile. As a single, career-oriented adult, he may be motivated by recognition and social approval when he buys his second car. Later, as a father of two, he may be motivated by safety and convenience in selecting a car. Effective salespeople are sensitive to these changing needs and wishes.

A rational motive is a factual reason for a purchase. An emotional motive relates to the satisfaction a customer is looking for in a product. What rational and emotional motives might a customer have for buying each of these products?

How Consumers Make Buying Decisions

There are six stages in the consumer's decision-making process: *stimulus, problem awareness, information search, evaluation of alternatives*, and the *purchase* and *postpurchase behavior* stages. People do not always go through all these stages when making a purchase, however. Generally, they will only do so when the purchase is important or the product is expensive. For example, the purchase of a pair of socks requires much less thought and effort than the purchase of a business computer system.

The consumer may decide *not* to buy at any stage in the process. For instance, a person may decide not to buy a new bicycle after learning the prices of the latest models.

Stimulus. *A stimulus is a cue that motivates a person to act.* In the decision-making process,

the stimulus is the cause of the person's need or desire for a product. Some cues that motivate people to buy are internal, such as hunger or thirst. But most cues come from external sources, such as advertisements for new products, discussions with other people, or positive experiences with products. If the stimulus is simply not strong enough, the decision-making process will stop here. However, if it is strong enough, the person will go on to the next stage.

Problem Awareness. Recognizing an unfulfilled need or desire as a result of a stimulus occurs in the problem awareness stage. For example, if your car breaks down (a stimulus), you recognize that there is a problem. You know that you need more information (problem awareness).

If the stimulus is sufficient but the problem is not worth solving, the person may decide not to continue the decision-making process. For example, a

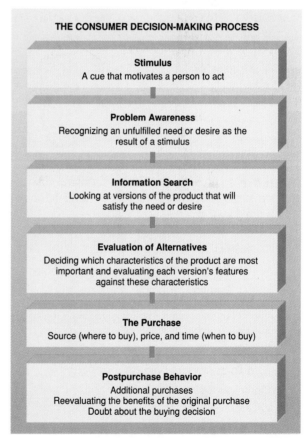

THE CONSUMER DECISION-MAKING PROCESS

Stimulus
A cue that motivates a person to act

Problem Awareness
Recognizing an unfulfilled need or desire as the result of a stimulus

Information Search
Looking at versions of the product that will satisfy the need or desire

Evaluation of Alternatives
Deciding which characteristics of the product are most important and evaluating each version's features against these characteristics

The Purchase
Source (where to buy), price, and time (when to buy)

Postpurchase Behavior
Additional purchases
Reevaluating the benefits of the original purchase
Doubt about the buying decision

Figure 13-1 **Consumer Decision-Making Process**
There are six stages in the consumer's decision-making process. Describe possible stimulus and problem awareness stages for someone buying a new car.

FEATURES OF THE VIVITAR TL125 CAMERA

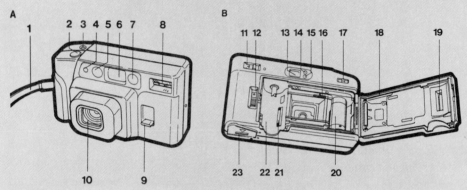

Description of Controls and Features

Front View (Illustration A)	Rear View (Illustration B)
1 Wrist Strap	11 Flash On/Off Switch
2 Shutter Release Button	12 Film Door Latch
3 Frame Counter	13 Viewfinder Eyepiece
4 Exposure Sensor	14 Red Low Light Warning
5 Auto Focus System Window	15 Green Flash Ready Light
6 Viewfinder Window	16 Film Sprocket
7 Auto Focus System Window	17 Rewind Button
8 Electronic Flash	18 Film Door
9 Lens Switch	19 Film Cartridge View Window
10 Wide Angle and Telephoto Lenses	20 Automatic Film Take-Up Spool
	21 DX Coding Contacts
	22 Film Chamber
Source: Vivitar Corporation.	23 Battery Compartment Cover

FEATURE-BENEFIT CHART FOR
REEBOK ERS TRAINER RUNNING SHOE

FEATURE	BENEFIT
Upper—perforated nylon with synthetic suede	Both fabrics breathe and are lightweight and durable, providing comfort and long wear.
Outsole—patterned with solid Duratech rubber	Duratech rubber is a high-abrasion compound that provides excellent durability. Patterned design, which provides excellent traction on any surface, makes the shoe versatile.
Removable molded anatomical PEEVA sockliner	Provides cushioning and full-length arch support.
ERS—(Energy Return System) design with DuPont Hytrel tubes under the ball of the foot and under heel that compress and return to original shape. Molded EVA and polyurethane midsole, which incorporates ERS in rear foot.	ERS design absorbs shock for comfort and stores energy to propel the foot. Shock absorption dispersion provides cushioning for comfort and stability when running; midsole is also lightweight for ease in running.
Sizes for men and women Men: 6½ to 15 Women: 5 to 12	Available for both men and women runners Fits most men Fits most women

Colors
Men: silver/black/gray
      silver/blue/gray
Women: stone/navy/silver
       silver/fuchsia/gray
	Two color combinations for men and two for women; the first matches everything; the second provides a choice in color combination.

Suggested retail price (1989) $59.95	Reasonable price for all the features and benefits included in this shoe.
Reebok brand	Company is known for quality and innovative product design, which promotes wearer confidence.
Ed Eyestone and Mike Conover, USA Olympic runners, ran in Reebok shoes in the 1988 Summer Olympic Games in Seoul, Korea.	If Olympic runners wear Reebok running shoes, they must be good for all runners.

Used with permission of Reebok International Ltd.

businesswoman sees computer-generated graphics in a competitor's annual report (stimulus) and realizes that the graphics in her company's annual report are not as well done as the competitor's (problem awareness). However, she decides that, for now, she cannot afford to buy a new computer program. She will be content to use the old program with basic graphics.

She has determined that her problem is not worth solving, so her decision-making process stops here. Or perhaps it is delayed for a while.

Information Search. When the consumer thinks the problem is worth solving, he or she begins an information search by looking at products that will satisfy the need or desire. The consumer considers different products or different product features and benefits, such as type, model, style, color, size, brand, and quality.

The person can start this information search simply by recalling previous experiences with various products. He or she can use such sources as printed materials or discussions with other people to gather information about potential products. The consumer will probably check several sources to compare several types, models, or styles of the same product.

If the person decides there is simply not enough information about the products to make a buying decision, the information search may end here—along with the decision-making process. However, if the consumer feels that several versions of a given product may help fill the need or desire, the person goes on to the next stage.

Evaluation of Alternatives. In evaluating alternatives, the person decides which characteristics of the product are most important and then evaluates each version's features against these characteristics. For example, a man in the market for a motor scooter may decide that price and overall safety are the most important characteristics figuring into his purchase. He will therefore first evaluate any scooters he looks at on the basis of their price and overall safety.

If the person cannot find any version that matches the characteristics desired in a particular product, the decision-making process ends here or will at least be delayed. However, if the consumer does find a version of the product that satisfactorily matches all the criteria, the person will go on to the next stage—the purchase.

The Purchase. Up to this point in the decision-making process, the customer has decided on his or her need and the product that will satisfy that need. The only remaining factors that must be considered before a purchase is made are *source*, *price*, and *time*.

The consumer evaluates where to buy the product (the *source*) just as he or she evaluates the product. *Patronage motives*—reasons for choosing to do business with one firm over another—may help the person make this decision. Patronage motives may include the firm's convenient location and fine reputation, helpful attitude of the firm's personnel, and services offered, such as credit and a liberal return policy. In the customer's mind, the value of a product must equal or exceed the *price*—or the customer

doesn't buy it. So, the customer must be familiar with a product's features, benefits, and value.

When to buy (*time*) is an important consideration. The time period a person has in which to make the buying decision (when to buy) may have a great impact on the decision-making process. For example, if a motorist's car is almost out of gasoline, he or she will undoubtedly stop at the next gas station for gasoline. But when the need or desire is not this urgent, the person may choose to shop around and research the possibilities before making a purchase.

Postpurchase Behavior. Postpurchase behavior may involve additional purchases, a reevaluation about the benefits of the original purchase, or doubt about the buying decision.

Additional purchases often occur immediately after the original sale. For example, after buying a new computer, a person may buy software for it so that he or she can use it immediately.

Customers may continue to evaluate the benefits of a product after purchasing it. If the product performs well and the customer is satisfied, he or she will consider buying the same product again when the original needs to be replaced.

When customers are unsure about a purchase, *cognitive dissonance* occurs. *Cognitive dissonance is doubt about the buying decision.* For example, after buying a new car, a person may continue to look at other models to be assured that her purchase decision was correct and that she paid a fair market price.

To avoid cognitive dissonance, salespeople often suggest related merchandise to make the original purchase more satisfying. They often reassure customers that their buying decision was a good one by reviewing product benefits during the sales presentation. They may even follow up with a customer by calling a week after the sale to ensure his or her satisfaction. In addition, businesspeople provide warranties and guarantees on their products and provide service to their customers after a purchase. Many offer free training for new equipment or assistance in assembly of an item.

Types of Decision Making

As we said earlier, people do not go through all six stages in the decision-making process every time they make a buying decision. Depending on the situation, some stages are omitted or the decision is made quickly and easily. In other situations, much time and effort is devoted to each stage of the process.

We therefore speak of three levels of decision making: *extensive*, *limited*, and *routine*. Which type of decision making a person uses depends on these factors:

- the amount of previous experience the person has had with the product and company,
- how often the product is purchased,
- the amount of information necessary to make a wise buying decision,
- the importance of the purchase to the consumer,
- the *perceived risk* involved in the purchase (the sense of fear that the product will cause financial loss, physical or emotional harm, or that it won't function properly),
- the time available to make the decision, and
- the person's degree of ego involvement in the product.

Extensive Decision Making. *Extensive decision making is used when there has been little or no previous experience because the item is infrequently purchased.* Goods and services that have a high degree of perceived risk and are very expensive or very important to the potential customer fall into this category. Such products include expensive machinery used in manufacturing, land for a new building site, or daily limousine service to and from the office.

Limited Decision Making. *Limited decision making is used when a person buys goods and services that he or she has purchased before, but not on a regular basis.* There is a moderate degree of perceived risk involved in the purchase, so the person often needs at least some information to buy the product.

Consumer goods and services in this category might include a second car, certain types of clothing and accessories, a vacation, household appliances, and furniture. Goods and services a firm might buy using limited decision making include accounting services, ad agency services, computer programs, office equipment, and certain products used in manufacturing or bought for resale.

Routine Decision Making. *Routine decision making is used when a person needs little information because of a high degree of prior experience with the product or the low perceived risk.* The perceived risk may be low because the price is low, the product is bought frequently, or satisfaction with the product is high. Some consumer goods and services in this category are grocery items, newspapers, dry cleaning services, hairdressing services, and certain brand name clothing and cosmetics. Customers who have developed brand loyalty for a product will use routine decision making. Even more expensive items, such as automobiles, may be purchased routinely if the customer has strong brand loyalty.

Businesses that simply reorder goods and services without much thought are using routine decision making. Products that businesses often buy routinely are raw materials, office supplies, maintenance services, and staple goods bought for resale. These products will continue to be routine purchases until a problem occurs with them or with the supplier. If this happens, limited decision making is required to change suppliers or products.

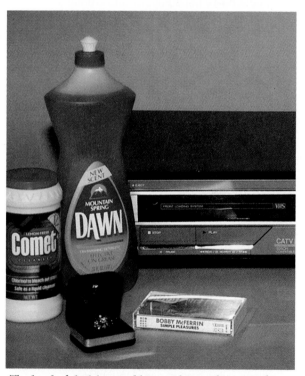

The level of decision making used to make a purchase depends on previous experience with the product, frequency of purchase, amount of information needed to make the decision, importance of the purchase, risk involved, time availability, and ego involvement in the product. What level of decision making would a customer use when buying each of these products and why?

VOCABULARY REVIEW

Write a brief definition of each word, based on your reading of the chapter.

product feature
customer benefit
rational motive
emotional motive
stimulus

cognitive dissonance
extensive decision
 making
limited decision making
routine decision making

FACT AND IDEA REVIEW

1. List nine facts that a salesperson should learn about his or her company and products.

2. Name four sources of product information.

3. What is a product feature? Name one product feature of a running shoe.

4. When do features of a product become selling points?

5. What two questions about a product feature does a person need to answer to determine a customer benefit of that feature?

6. What are the six stages in the consumer's decision-making process?

7. Once a consumer has decided to buy a product, what are the three remaining factors he or she must consider before actually making the purchase?

8. What are the three levels of decision making?

9. When do consumers usually use extensive decision making?

10. Name three goods or services a firm might buy when using limited decision making.

CRITICAL THINKING

1. Why are direct experiences with a product helpful in developing product knowledge? Describe direct experiences you have had with products that would help you if you were asked to sell those products.

2. Think of a purchase you or your family recently made and explain the meaning of the following statement: "Customers do not buy products, they buy what the products will do for them."

3. Determine a customer benefit for each of the following product features:

 a. running shoe with a built-in arch

 b. ski jacket with a storm flap over the zipper

 c. a beige sweater

 d. a camera with automatic focus

4. Explain your reasons for agreeing or disagreeing with the following statement: "Customers love to buy but hate to be sold."

5. Explain the difference between a rational motive and an emotional motive. Give an example of how each may be present in a buying situation.

6. Select one of the following products and develop specific ways a firm and its sales representatives can reduce cognitive dissonance: computer, bicycle, pair of skis, automobile, and microwave oven.

7. How much sales assistance do consumers need when using extensive, limited, and routine decision making? Explain your answers with examples.

USING BASIC SKILLS

Math

1. In your research for a sales presentation of an all-purpose cleaner, you made the following comparisons:

Cleaner	Fluid Ounces	Price
A	22	$2.79
B	28	$3.29
C	40	$9.89

Calculate the price per ounce for each cleaner and then identify which all-purpose cleaner is the best buy for the money.

2. If a customer wants to buy two cans of soda and the price of a six pack is $2.99, how much will you charge the customer?

Communication

3. Share an incident with classmates that recounts the decision-making process, beginning with the stimulus that started it. How far did the decision-making process go? If the decision-making process ended before the last stage, explain why it stopped at that point.

4. Write a letter to the manufacturer of a product in which you are interested, requesting specific information on the product. Mail the letter. When you receive an answer, share it with classmates.

Human Relations

5. You are a salesperson in a camera store and a customer asks you the price of a camera on display. As soon as you tell her the camera is priced at $150, the customer exclaims, "That's outrageously expensive!" What would you say next?

6. You are working in a clothing store. You sell a suit to a customer, but he returns it two days later and says he doesn't need it. However, you notice that the suit has been worn. What do you say?

APPLICATION PROJECTS

1. Prepare a report on a local company of your choice. Include a brief history of the company and its methods of product delivery, return policies, product guarantees, and financing terms.

2. Select a product of your choice and prepare a feature-benefit chart for it. This product should be one that would require limited decision-making, that is, study and comparison before purchasing it. You will be using this project to develop a sales training manual in later chapters.

3. Choose four products you use regularly. Using the nine categories of product knowledge as a guide, evaluate what you know about the products as if you were going to sell them. Include all the

information you can by referring to printed material, guarantees, and by asking your classmates and family about the products.

4. Below are photos of three cars with very different images. List the different features and benefits of each car that a salesperson would emphasize when showing each car to a working mother, an attorney, a building contractor, a retail store owner, and a graphic designer.

14

After completing this chapter, you will be able to:

1. list the eight steps professional salespeople go through in helping a customer make a purchase,

2. explain the prospecting step of a sale,

3. list seven sources or methods salespeople use for prospecting,

4. describe how the preapproach is used in retail sales and in industrial sales,

5. explain the importance and purposes of the initial approach in the sales process,

6. explain three approach methods retail salespeople use and when it is appropriate to use each method, and

7. describe how industrial sales representatives conduct the initial approach.

prospect
endless chain method
cold canvassing
service approach method
greeting approach method
merchandise approach method

The Sales Process

Now that you have an understanding of product knowledge and the consumer's decision-making process, you are ready to begin your study of the sales process.

This chapter gives you a general overview of the steps of a sale. Then you will learn how salespeople find potential customers, how they get ready to sell, and how they approach customers in both retail and industrial sales situations.

The Steps of a Sale

Professional salespeople go through eight steps in helping a customer make a purchase. (Experts sometimes use different names for the same steps, but the principle behind each is the same.)

1. *Prospecting.* Looking for potential customers.
2. *Approaching the customer.* First, getting ready for the sale by checking one's appearance, preparing the product and work area, and gathering background information on the customer (*preapproach*). Second, actually approaching the customer in the face-to-face selling situation (*initial approach*).
3. *Determining needs.* Learning what the customer is looking for in a good or service in order to decide what products to show the customer, and which product features to present first in the next step of the sale.
4. *Presenting the product.* Educating the customer about the product's features and benefits.
5. *Handling questions and objections.* Learning why the customer is uncertain about buying or is reluctant to buy. Then providing information to remove the uncertainty or objection and helping the customer make a satisfying buying decision.
6. *Closing the sale.* Getting the customer's positive agreement to buy.
7. *Suggestion selling.* Suggesting the customer buy additional merchandise or services to help him or her better enjoy the original purchase.
8. *Reassuring and following up.* Helping a customer feel confident that he or she made a wise purchase. Getting in touch with the customer after the sale to ensure his or her satisfaction with the purchase.

In the rest of this chapter, we will concentrate on the first two steps: *prospecting* and *approaching customers.* In later chapters, we will examine the other six steps.

Prospecting

*A **prospect** (also called a lead) is a potential customer.* Prospecting is looking for customers. Successful industrial salespeople are always prospecting, using a variety of methods and sources to suit the products they sell.

Most retail salespeople don't do prospecting because customers come to their stores. But prospecting is essential in most industrial sales situations, for several reasons:

- Certain large-ticket items are sold to businesses only once in ten or more years. Thus, industrial salespeople need new customers.
- Many industrial sales representatives are evaluated on how many new accounts they open each year.
- Many industrial sales representatives are paid on commission. The more they sell, the more they get paid.

Once they have prospects, salespeople *qualify* their potential customers before continuing the sales process by asking themselves these questions:

- Does the prospect need this product or service?
- Does the prospect have the financial resources to pay?
- Does the prospect have the authority to buy?
- Will the prospect see me?

Sources and Methods of Prospecting

A rich supply of prospect sources is available to enterprising salespeople. Among them are *employer leads, telephone directories, trade and professional directories, newspapers,* and *commercial lists.* In addition, *customer referrals* and *cold canvassing* are used to solicit leads.

Employer Leads. Employers get leads from their involvement in trade shows and from advertising in trade journals and consumer magazines. Prospective customers often respond to this promotion by requesting further information. Once received, leads are passed on to the sales representative responsible for the territory in which each prospec-

Employers often get customer leads from their involvement in trade shows where they show new products to current and potential distributors and wholesalers. Give at least two other ways to generate prospects.

tive customer is located. Some firms also use telemarketing services to get leads.

Many firms send direct mail pieces to people in a given geographic area or to businesses in a given industry. The main thrust of their message is, "Call us if you're interested."

Telephone Directories. The white pages of telephone directories provide names, addresses, and telephone numbers of potential customers in given geographic areas. The yellow pages list businesses that may be potential customers for certain industrial goods and services.

Trade and Professional Directories. Industrial sales representatives can use trade and professional directories to locate potential customers by type of business. A well-known directory is *Thomas' Register of American Manufacturers*.

Newspapers. Newspapers provide good leads for some salespeople. For example, birth announcements are good leads for insurance salespeo-

The Yellow Pages list businesses that may be potential customers for certain industrial goods and services. Choose two businesses on this page and tell three goods and/or services each business might buy.

ple. Engagement announcements provide bridal shops, caterers, florists, and printers with prospects. Reports of business mergers and announcements of new personnel in business firms also provide leads.

Commercial Lists. Salespeople may buy lists of potential customers from companies that specialize in categorizing people by such criteria as education, age, income, credit card purchases, and location. Lists of businesses categorized according to net sales, profits, products, and geographic locations are also available for sale.

Customer Referrals. Satisfied customers often give salespeople *referrals*—the names of other people who might buy the product. Thus, referrals give you the chance to talk to potential customers you might not have reached if they hadn't been recommended.

When salespeople ask previous customers for names of potential customers, they are said to be using the endless chain method. Some companies offer discounts or gifts to customers who give referrals.

Cold Canvassing. *In cold canvassing, a salesperson tries to locate potential customers with little or no direct help other than that, perhaps, from a telephone directory.* This is sometimes called *blind prospecting.* Here are some examples of cold canvassing:

- A real estate agent goes door to door in a neighborhood, asking people if they would like to sell their homes.
- A stockbroker selects peoples' names from a telephone book and calls them.
- A salesperson for a clothing manufacturer visits a new store in his or her sales territory.

Approaching the Customer

As you learned earlier, the second step in a sale is approaching the customer. This two-part step involves the *preapproach* and the *initial approach* in the selling situation.

The Preapproach

The *preapproach* is getting ready to sell. In all selling situations, salespeople can prepare for the sale by studying their products and keeping abreast of industry trends. Reading periodicals related to their industry is helpful. In addition, they should also pay attention to their personal appearance. Beyond this basic preparation, retail and industrial salespeople get involved in specific activities.

The Preapproach in Retail Sales

The preapproach in retail sales centers around preparing the merchandise and the work area. This involves stockkeeping and housekeeping activities:

- straightening, rearranging, and replenishing the stock,
- adjusting price tickets before and after special sales,
- learning where stock is located and how much is available,
- taking inventory,
- arranging displays, and
- vacuuming the floor, dusting the shelves, and keeping the selling area neat and clean.

The Preapproach in Industrial Sales

In industrial sales preapproach activities vary, depending on whether the sales call is with a previous customer or a new prospect.

When dealing with previous customers, industrial salespeople analyze past sales records. Knowing what and how much customers purchased in the past helps salespeople with new orders.

Knowledgeable salespeople also review their notes about the previous buyer's personality, family, interests, and hobbies. In general, people are pleased when others take the time to remember them as individuals and not just as another potential sale.

In addition to the information a salesperson gathers on a new prospect in the prospecting step, he or she also seeks other information in the preapproach stage. Specifically, the salesperson wants answers to the following questions:

- How well are the prospect's goods or services received in the market?
- How can my goods and services help this prospect's business improve?
- If the new prospect is using my competitor's goods or services, how satisfied is the prospect with them?

To find answers to these questions, you may make inquiries by calling other sales representatives who sell noncompeting lines. You may also read the company's annual reports. Or you may visit the retail store or the manufacturing facility in question to get answers.

Making the appointment to see a prospect or the previous customer is the final step of the preapproach.

The Initial Approach

The initial approach is the first face-to-face contact with the customer. Although different selling situations require the use of different methods in the initial approach, its importance and general purposes are the same in all selling situations.

Because salespeople can make or break a sale during their first few minutes with a customer, the initial approach is a critical part of the sales process. At this time, customers often pass judgment on salespeople. Customers who are turned off by the initial approach will be difficult to win over. Thus, the initial approach sets the mood or atmosphere for the other steps of the sale.

Use the initial approach for three purposes: to begin conversation, to establish rapport with the customer, and to focus on the merchandise. Let's look at how these purposes are accomplished.

To begin conversation, you need to be alert to what interests the customer. This is usually easier in industrial sales because you have time to conduct re-

The initial approach is extremely important in setting the mood for the rest of the sale. If this same salesperson approached you in a retail setting, what kind of impression would you get based on her clothing, facial expressions, and overall manner?

search prior to the initial meeting. In retail sales, you must be observant and perceptive from the moment the customer enters the store or department.

To establish rapport, treat the customer as an individual. There should be no stereotyping of a person because of age, sex, race, religion, or appearance. Moreover, you must be perceptive of the customer's buying style. Some customers like to do business quickly. Others prefer a more methodical, slower pace. In any case, a customer likes to feel important.

Just Looking

Lee works for Herman's World of Sporting Goods in the athletic shoe department. A couple enters the department, begins looking at running shoes, and soon focuses on the Reebok ERS Trainer. Lee eagerly approaches the couple with "Can I help you?" The man responds, "No, thank you. Just looking."

The approach appeared to be correct to Lee because the timing was right, and the message was sincere. The only thing Lee can do now is walk away and wait for the couple to ask for help.

1. What was wrong with Lee's approach?
2. What could Lee have said instead?

To put a customer at ease and to establish a positive atmosphere for the rest of the sale, do the following:

- be courteous and respectful,
- establish good eye contact,
- be enthusiastic,
- show a sincere interest in the customer,
- be friendly and genuine,
- use the customer's name (if known), and
- time the approach appropriately.

The Initial Approach in Retail Sales.

When and how you approach a customer in a retail setting are important considerations.

When the customer is in an obvious hurry, approach the customer quickly. When a customer is undecided, it is better to let him or her look around before making the approach. When a customer is comparison shopping, encourage the customer to look around and ask questions. Many customers shop around before buying and appreciate helpful salespeople who take an interest in their buying problems.

There are three methods you can use in the initial approach to retail customers: the *service, greeting,* and *merchandise approach methods.* The selling situation and the type of customer determine which method is best.

In the service approach method, the salesperson asks the customer if he or she needs assistance. For example: "May I help you with something?" This method is acceptable when the customer is obviously in a hurry or if you are an order-taker for routine purchases.

In all other sales situations, this method is ineffective because it usually elicits a negative response such as "No, I'm just looking." In this case, you lose control of the sales situation. In addition, the customer may feel awkward asking for help later after initially rejecting it.

In the greeting approach method, the salesperson simply welcomes the customer to the store. The greeting can be formal or informal. Formal greetings are "Good morning," "Good afternoon," or "Good evening, Mrs. Gonzales" (if you know the customer's name). Using the customer's name makes the customer feel important.

When you know the customer, an informal greeting is appropriate, with a personal comment specifically related to the customer. For example, "Congratulations on winning last week's tennis tournament, Alice." Small talk helps establish rapport.

After greeting the customer, pause for a few seconds. Out of courtesy, most customers will feel obligated to respond. Many customers will say why they are shopping. If they need help, they will tell you how you can help them. If they are just looking, they will let you know. In any case, this approach method begins conversation, and it establishes a positive rapport. But it does not focus on the merchandise.

In the merchandise approach method, the salesperson makes a comment or asks questions about a product that the customer is looking at. The only time you can use this method, of course, is when a customer stops to look at a specific item. Then you can open with a statement about the product's features and benefits.

Select the appropriate thing to say by noticing what interests the customer. For example, if a customer is looking at a label, you might say, "That shirt is made of a cotton and polyester blend, so it's machine washable." If a customer is simply looking at the item and you have no indication of the exact interest, you can talk about the popularity of the item, its unusual features, or its special values. Or you can ask a question about the item, such as "Is that the size you need?"

The merchandise approach method is usually the most effective initial approach in retail sales because it immediately focuses attention on the merchandise. It also gives you an opportunity to tell the customer something about the features and benefits of the merchandise. This helps arouse customer interest.

The Initial Approach in Industrial Sales. In industrial sales the salesperson generally calls on the customer at his or her place of business, after having set up an appointment in the preapproach stage.

Arriving early for your appointment will show your interest in the customer and give you time to organize your thoughts before walking into the customer's office. Introduce yourself and your company with a firm handshake and a smile. Use the customer's name. Some salespeople also give the customer a business card.

If you are an industrial salesperson, the initial approach depends on your prior dealings with the customer or the work you did in the preapproach. When meeting with customers you visit frequently, you can be more personal (but within bounds). Some sales representatives keep records of their customers and also read trade news. Comments on recent happenings in the customer's industry or personal recollections about the customer's family, interests, or hobbies can help make the initial approach a smooth one. Learning what is appropriate to say regarding personal matters, however, is the key to using this information properly. When used correctly, it immediately puts the customer at ease and helps open lines of communication. Small talk is sometimes expected. It is good for establishing rapport and for building a relationship with the customer.

When meeting a new customer, choose your words carefully. Comment on something important to the customer so the person will continue to listen. Reducing costs, making money, and being better than competitors are general concepts that many industrial salespeople use as a basis for their opening statements. Prior research on the prospect conducted in the preapproach will suggest other possible opening comments.

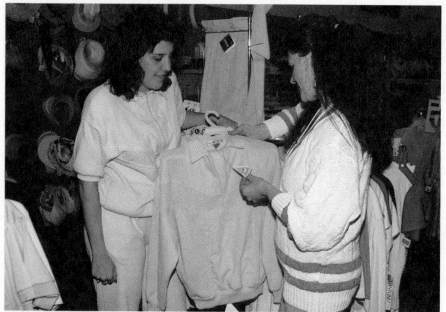

Customers often read labels and hangtags for product information. What method could this salesperson use to approach this customer?

VOCABULARY REVIEW

Define the term *prospect*. Then give one example of each of the following methods of prospecting for or initially approaching a prospect.

endless chain method
cold canvassing
service approach
 method

greeting approach
 method
merchandise approach
 method

FACT AND IDEA REVIEW

1. Name the eight steps of a sale.

2. What is prospecting?

3. List seven sources or methods salespeople use for prospecting.

4. Define and give two examples of cold canvassing.

5. In all selling situations, what can salespeople do to prepare for the sale?

6. What does preapproach in retail sales center around and what does it involve?

7. What is the final step of the preapproach in industrial sales?

8. What are the three purposes of the initial approach?

9. Tell at least five things a salesperson should do in the initial approach to put the customer at ease and to establish a positive atmosphere for the rest of the sale.

10. "May I help you?" is an example of which type of retail approach method?

11. When is it acceptable to use the service approach method with a retail customer?

12. What should a salesperson do after using the greeting approach method with a retail customer?

13. When can a retail salesperson use the merchandise approach method?

14. Name five general things industrial salespeople should do in their initial approach.

15. What general concepts do many industrial salespeople use as a basis for their opening statement when meeting a new customer?

CRITICAL THINKING

1. Why would a salesperson prefer using the endless chain method of prospecting rather than cold canvassing?

2. Discuss the relative importance of prospecting in retail sales and in industrial sales.

3. If you were an industrial salesperson and had an appointment with a previous customer, what would you do to prepare for that meeting (preapproach)? How would that differ if the appointment was with a new customer?

4. Explain how a salesperson can decide when to approach a customer in a retail sales situation.

5. If you were an industrial buyer and a salesperson with no appointment tried to call on you, how would you react? Why?

6. How can learning about a customer's family, interests, hobbies, and personality traits help a salesperson? Why is it important for the salesperson to learn what is appropriate and inappropriate to say in regard to such personal matters?

USING BASIC SKILLS

Math

1. Your customer is located 100 miles from your office. You can travel an average of 45 miles in one hour. If you have a 10:30 a.m. appointment and you want to arrive 15 minutes early, what time do you have to leave your office?

Communication

2. Introduce yourself to a teacher or classmate as a sales representative of Lane Manufacturing. Imagine this is the first time you are approaching this customer in an industrial sales situation. Be sure to use the prospect's name. Introduce yourself and your company while using a firm, business-like handshake. Smile! Was this easy or difficult for you? Why?

3. Write merchandise approaches that can be used in a retail sales situation for a camera, a pair of jeans, and a pair of work boots.

4. Write a catchy opening statement to be used in an industrial sales approach for an advanced copier that can reproduce, collate, and staple 20 copies in one minute.

Human Relations

5. You are stuck in traffic and know you are going to be late for a very important appointment with a highly qualified prospect. What should you do? How could you prevent this situation from happening again?

6. You are the assistant buyer of your firm. A new sales representative from Gantor Manufacturing arrives and is rude to you. Then you observe her behaving in a very cordial manner with your boss. If you had the opportunity, what would you say to this sales representative about her behavior and its possible effect on sales in this firm? What advice could you give her?

APPLICATION PROJECTS

1. You are beginning a continuing project for this part—a sales training manual. For all aspects of this manual, you will use the product for which you prepared a feature-benefit chart in Chapter 13. Write the approach section of your sales training manual. Explain how to properly approach a customer and provide a sample approach in dialogue form. Be sure to include how a salesperson should prepare to sell the product.

2. Pretending to be a customer, conduct your own informal survey of the professionalism of three retail salespeople. After your encounter with each, note what he or she did or failed to do to put you at ease and establish a positive atmosphere in the initial approach. Ask yourself these questions. Was the person courteous, respectful, and enthusiastic? Did the person show sincere interest in you? Was the person friendly and genuine? Did he or she use your name (if known)? Finally, did the salesperson use a timely approach? Also tell which of the three retail approach methods each salesperson used. Write a one-paragraph conclusion on your findings.

3. List all the types of businesses that might use the product for which you have prepared your feature-benefit list. Then go to the library and, using the appropriate references, prospect for clients. Locate two or three local businesses in each category that might use or sell your product. Think about the different ways you would approach the businesses in each category.

4. Your teacher will ask another teacher or member of the business community to come into your class and act as a buyer. Acting as if you are selling the product for which you have prepared your feature-benefit chart, approach the buyer and attempt to sell your product. Be sure you dress and act appropriately. Afterward, have your classmates point out your strengths and/or suggest ways you can improve.

Determining Needs and Product Presentation

After completing this chapter, you will be able to:

1. determine your customer's needs in various industrial and retail sales situations,

2. understand why determining needs is essential in the sales process,

3. recall three methods used for determining needs,

4. listen effectively during the sales process,

5. explain how questioning is used in the sales process,

6. list two things that should be avoided when questioning a customer,

7. conduct an effective presentation of a product or service, and

8. explain how to make a product presentation effective.

WORDS TO KNOW

nonverbal communication
open-ended question
layman's terms

I n many ways, selling is like putting together a jigsaw puzzle. You analyze various parts of the puzzle by shape and size. Then you select the straight-edged pieces to use for the frame. In selling, you likewise analyze your customer's needs and buying motives. Then you use these to begin framing your product presentation.

In this chapter you will be introduced to techniques that can help you with these steps (*determining needs* and *product presentation*), both of which are critical to the sales process.

Determining Needs

Customer needs are directly related to buying motives. As you may recall from Chapter 13, these motives can be rational, emotional, or a combination of the two. In this step of the sale, your job is to uncover the customer's reasons for wanting to buy. In some instances, these motives or needs will be quite obvious; in other cases, they will not.

In either situation, taking a sincere interest in the customer is essential to this important step in the sales process. When the customer's needs are satisfied, everyone benefits. The business makes a sale. The satisfied customer often becomes a repeat customer. You, as a salesperson, experience that welcome feeling of success.

When to Determine Needs

So you can focus everything you do and say on your customer, it is important to determine his or her needs as soon as possible in the sales process.

Here is an example of what can happen when a salesperson does not determine needs early on:

Salesperson: This is one of our most popular tennis racquets. (initial approach) It's perfect for you. The grip is the correct size. The large sweet spot should help you improve your game.

Customer: That's very interesting, but I'm not buying the racquet for myself. I don't play tennis. I play golf.

In the above example, the salesperson went right into the product presentation before determining the customer's needs. After the initial approach, the salesperson could have asked, "Are you interested in a racquet for yourself?"

The answer to that simple question could have guided the salesperson into additional questions about the person for whom the racquet was being purchased. It also could have helped the salesperson decide which racquet to show the customer and which features to emphasize.

In retail sales, you should begin to determine needs immediately after the approach. This is the earliest you can start because you usually cannot research a customer before he or she comes to your store. In industrial sales, needs can be determined in the preapproach. In both situations, you will continue determining needs throughout the sales process.

Three methods will help you in the process of determining customer needs: *observing, listening* for clues, and *questioning.*

Figure 15-1   **Three Methods to Help Determine Customer Needs**
Observing, listening, and questioning help salespeople determine customer needs. Why is it so important to begin determining customer needs as early as possible in the sales process?

Determining Customer Needs

Observe
- For nonverbal communication
- How long a customer looks at a product
- A buyer's office to determine person's interests
- A buyer's product lines, price levels, and type of customer

Listen
- Maintain good eye contact
- Give feedback
- Give your undivided attention
- Listen with empathy and an open mind
- Never interrupt

Question
- To confirm selling points
- To encourage customers to communicate
- To clarify the customer's point of view
- To regain customer's attention

Observing

When you observe a customer, you look for buying motives that are often reflected through their *nonverbal communication*. **Nonverbal communication is expressing yourself through body language.** Facial expressions, hand motions, eye movement, and other forms of nonverbal communication can give you clues about interest in the product and/or the customer's mood.

In addition, there are other details you can observe in retail and industrial sales situations that may provide even more clues about customers.

When you observe how long a customer in a retail store looks at a product, you get an initial idea about his or her interest in it. Also, how long the customer holds the product during a sales presentation (if he or she holds it at all) can indicate personal feelings for it.

In an industrial sales situation, you can generally get ideas about a buyer's interests by looking around his or her office. Trophies for winning company-sponsored tennis tournaments or paintings of horses, for example, probably indicate personal interests.

When calling on a retail buyer, walk through the store before visiting the buyer. This will give you interesting information about the types of customers the retailer serves, the price levels of lines carried, complementary and competing products offered, and opportunities for additional sales.

The key to observing in both retail and industrial situations is proper selection of facts that are important to the sales process. Avoid stereotyping people and/or drawing conclusions from your observations before getting additional facts.

Listening

Listening helps you pick up clues to the customer's needs for use in the product presentation. Here is an example:

Customer: I want to get a camera so I can take pictures of my daughter while she is performing gymnastics. I am not a very good photographer.

From these statements, you learned that the customer is not an experienced photographer and therefore needs an easy-to-use camera. He or she also needs a camera that has a fast shutter because it will be used in taking action shots.

To develop good listening skills, you must learn how to listen and understand. In Chapter 9 we explored listening skills and blocks to listening with understanding. So, if you need to brush up, read the appropriate sections in that chapter again. Remember, however, these five important listening skills when talking to your customers:

- maintain good eye contact,
- provide verbal and nonverbal feedback,
- give customers your undivided attention,
- listen with empathy and an open mind, and
- do not interrupt.

Questioning

Questioning is an important skill that must be done carefully. When questioning is done effectively, it not only helps determine needs, but can also help *confirm selling points, encourage customers to communicate, clarify the customer's point of view,* and *regain the customer's attention.*

Always bear in mind that some customers will be protective of their privacy. They may resent even general, nonpersonal questions. So, watch for nonverbal communication from the customer that may indicate the person's general discomfort with being questioned. In any case, remember these simple rules of careful questioning.

- Don't ask too many questions in a row. This will make the customers feel as though you're cross-examining them.
- Don't ask questions that may put a customer on the defensive or make the person feel em-

---

REAL WORLD MARKETING

In the (Chocolate) Chips

The name Mrs. Fields summons up images of a sweet granny. Nevertheless, the queen of the chocolate chip cookie, Debbi Fields, is a trim, attractive young woman. A Palo Alto, California, newly-wed in search of a career, Debbi thought that if she offered the public freshly baked cookies, people just might bite. They did—to the tune of $30 million in the first six years.

CASE CHALLENGE

Good Listening is the Key to Success

A salesperson approached a young man in the shoe department of Herman's Sporting Goods.

Salesperson: Hi. I noticed that you've been looking at the Reebok ERS Trainer. That's a fine running shoe.

Customer: I've been wearing my high-top basketball shoes for running.

Salesperson: Do you run competitively?

Customer: No. I just run to keep in shape.

Salesperson: What do you like and dislike about running in your basketball shoes?

Customer: They're comfortable. But I think they're too heavy for running. I'm also wearing them out quickly.

Salesperson: Let me show you how the Reebok ERS Trainer is constructed. The outsole is made of Duratech rubber, a high-abrasion compound that is extremely durable. Where do you do most of your running?

Customer: Primarily on the track in the park near my home. But I also run on the street and on the track in a gym.

Salesperson: Notice the pattern design on the sole of the shoe. It gives you excellent traction on any surface. This is good for you because you run on various surfaces. ERS stands for Energy Return System. Look at this diagram of the shoe's construction. The whole shoe is designed to absorb shock and store energy, making it very comfortable. You mentioned that your basketball shoes were too heavy for running. The ERS Trainer is lightweight. The upper shoe is made of perforated nylon and synthetic suede—both lightweight, comfortable fabrics that allow the foot to breathe. The ERS Trainer gives you the features you're looking for in a running shoe, doesn't it?

Customer: Yes. It has all the benefits I need from a running shoe.

Salesperson: What size running shoe do you wear?

Customer: Usually, a size 10.

Salesperson: Let me see if we have that size. Would you prefer silver/black/gray or silver/blue/gray?

Customer: I prefer the silver/black/gray.

Salesperson: Great! Let me get you a pair to try on.

1. Identify the questions used to determine this customer's needs and the product presentation techniques used.
2. How did the salesperson's good listening skills make for a smooth product presentation?

---

barrassed. For example, never ask, "How much do you want to spend?"

- Ask questions about intended use and previous experience. The answers should give you enough information to direct you to the correct price range.

Determining Needs. When it comes to making a purchase, not every customer can clearly express needs and motives. This sometimes occurs because of basic uncertainty and/or some difficulty in self-expression. In such a situation, your well-chosen questions can help uncover needs and buying motives.

When you begin determining needs, first ask general questions about intended use and previous experience with the product. Use *who, what, when, where, how,* and *why* to develop these basic questions. Once you get an idea about general needs, you can ask specific questions relating to color, size, model, and quantity.

Confirming Selling Points. Throughout the sales process, you should see if you have correctly determined your customer's needs by confirming selling points. For example: "The automatic focus is useful because it helps create perfect pictures every time. How do you like that feature?"

Encouraging Customers to Communicate. One way to encourage your customers to communicate is to ask *open-ended questions. Open-ended questions require more than yes or no answers.* For example: "How much experience have you had with 35mm cameras?"

Clarifying the Customer's Point of View. To do this, use opening lines, such as "Let me see if I understand you. . . ." or "Am I correct in assuming you are looking for a product that can. . . ?" This way, you know that you and the customer are thinking along the same lines.

Regaining the Customer's Attention. If you lose your customer's attention, you cannot get feedback or continue determining needs. To regain the customer's attention, ask a simple question directly related to the product. For example: "Now that you have seen the features of this camera, what do you think about this model?"

Product Presentation

During the product presentation phase of the sale, you show the product and tell about it. As you are determining the customer's buying motives, you will be displaying products that match the uncovered needs. The goal of the product presentation, of course, is to match the customer's needs with appropriate product features and benefits.

You can reach this goal by following certain guidelines that can make your product presentation smooth. These include careful selection of the product to show the customer, limiting the number of products to show, and knowing what to say and do during the presentation.

Selecting Products

After you have learned the intended use of the product, you should be able to select a few items that match those needs. For example, if you learned that a customer wants a camera for professional use, you would select a technically advanced camera.

When you don't know the customer's price range and your knowledge of the intended use is insufficient to determine a price range, begin by showing a medium-priced product. That way, you can move up or down in price once you get the customer's feedback.

Number of Products

To avoid overwhelming your customer, show no more than three products at a time. It is difficult for most people to remember all the features of more than three items during one presentation. When a customer wants to see more than three, remove the products that have been displayed and are no longer of any interest to the customer.

To avoid overwhelming the customer and to make the buying decision easier, this salesperson has the product selection narrowed down to two items. What has the salesperson done so far to find out which products matched this customer's needs?

What to Say During the Presentation

In this step of the sales process, you talk about the product's features and benefits. Here is a good place to use the information from your feature-benefit chart to inform your customer of the product features that match his or her buying motives and needs.

When describing product features, use descriptive adjectives and action verbs. Avoid nondescriptive words, such as *nice*, *pretty*, and *fine*. Instead, use action and emotion words. For example, "This full-cut sleeve allows *complete rotation* of the arm, making it *extremely comfortable* when skiing."

Choose your words carefully; avoid slang and double-meanings. For example, when selling an expensive suit to an executive, you would not say, "You're going to blow them away in that suit."

When selling industrial products, use the appropriate jargon so you communicate with industrial buyers at their level of expertise. When selling products to retail customers, however, use *layman's terms*.

Layman's terms are words the average customer can understand. Remember, show enthusiasm through your level and tone of voice and your facial expressions.

What to Do During the Presentation

To make a product presentation come alive, display and handle the merchandise effectively. Demonstrate the product in use, and use dramatic actions and sales aids to point out special features. Also involve the customer in your presentation.

Displaying and Handling the Product. Creatively displaying the product is the first step in an eye-catching presentation. Some products, of course, lend themselves more naturally to visual display. Others will challenge your creativity. Diamond rings, for example, look best on a black velvet display pad. An attractive display of vacuum cleaners, on the other hand, takes more thoughtful planning.

All products should be handled carefully during the product presentation to convey respect for it and show its quality. What adjective would you use in describing this particular product to a customer?

This salesperson is using an outline of a diamond to explain how a diamond's cut affects its brilliance and sparkle. What other sales aid could this salesperson use to explain diamond cut? How would this person best display an actual diamond?

As a part of product presentation, this customer has been encouraged to try on a coat. In what other ways can a salesperson involve his or her customer in the sales process?

The way you handle a product presents an image of its quality. Handle it with respect, and use hand gestures to show the significance of certain features. Expensive crystal goblets, for instance, should carefully be held up to the light.

Demonstrating. Demonstrating the product in use helps to build customer confidence. This is especially true if you are showing an item that requires manipulation or operation, such as a television, camera, radio, food processor, clock, typewriter, or computer.

To prove selling points or claims made by the manufacturer, you may need to demonstrate a product in a more dramatic way. For example, you could drop an unbreakable dish on the floor to prove that it is durable.

Sales Aids. When it is impractical to demonstrate the actual product or when you want to emphasize certain selling points further, you can use sales aids in your sales presentations. Sales aids include samples, reprints of magazine and newspaper articles, audio-visual aids, models, photographs, drawings, graphs, charts, specification sheets, customer testimonials, and warranty information.

Be creative when determining which sales aids will help you in your particular product presentation. For example, a manufacturer of industrial machinery may show a videotape of how quickly a machine performs. An insurance salesperson may use graphs and charts to show how dividends will accumulate or to compare the benefits of one policy with another.

Involve the Customer. You can involve your customer in the sale by continuing to request agreement of selling points and by encouraging the use of one or more of the five senses. For example, you could have your customers hold and swing golf clubs, type on a typewriter or computer keyboard, test drive an automobile, or taste and smell food products.

When you involve a customer in the sale, you help the person make intelligent buying decisions. You also help yourself because a customer is generally more attentive when doing more than just listening to what you say.

VOCABULARY REVIEW

Write a paragraph incorporating these three vocabulary terms.

nonverbal communication   layman's terms
open-ended question

FACT AND IDEA REVIEW

1. In general, when do you determine customer needs in the sales process?

2. Specifically, when should you begin determining needs in retail sales? in industrial sales?

3. Name three methods that will help in the process of determining customer needs.

4. What can you look for when you observe a customer in retail situations? in industrial situations?

5. What does effective listening help you do in the product presentation?

6. List five things you should do to be a good listener.

7. What two things should you avoid doing when questioning a customer?

8. In addition to determining needs, how else can effective questioning help a salesperson?

9. What is one of the best ways to engage a customer in two-way communication?

10. What is the goal of the product presentation step of the sale?

11. When you are having a difficult time determining the customer's intended price range, what priced product should you show the customer? Why?

12. How many products should you show your customer at one time during the product presentation? Why?

13. Name four techniques you can use to make the product presentation come alive.

14. Name five sales aids you can use in the product presentation.

15. How could you involve the customer in the product presentation?

CRITICAL THINKING

1. Why is determining customer needs an essential step in the sales process?

2. How is a feature-benefit chart used in the product presentation step of the sale?

3. What is wrong with these two selling statements?
"You look great in that suit."
"This fabric is made of 420/420 denier nylon."

4. Explain why you should never ask a customer, "How much did you want to spend?" How can you avoid this situation?

5. How would you effectively display a set of china during a sales presentation?

6. Identify three features of a typewriter and explain how you would demonstrate them.

7. Selling service is sometimes more difficult than selling goods that can easily be seen. Explain what a landscape designer can do to sell landscape designs and maintenance services to a prospective customer.

8. What would you do to involve your customer if you were selling a bicycle, a pair of boots, a camera, a typewriter, and a clock radio?

USING BASIC SKILLS

Math

1. What is the total amount due from a customer who purchases three shirts at $25 each, two pairs of pants at $50 each, and four ties at $15 each? The sales tax on the clothing is five percent.

2. If a customer wants to buy 6¾ yards of fabric and the price per yard is $12.50, how much would you charge the customer?

Communication

3. Role play the *determining needs* and *product presentation* steps of the sale by using a product in the classroom, such as a jacket, a calculator, or a purse. Choose a partner. One of you should portray the customer. The other should portray the salesperson. The rest of the class should observe and take notes on all the steps taken (both correctly and incorrectly) by the salesperson. Before the enactment begins, students in the audience should make a list of guidelines for listening, observing, asking questions, and presenting a product. During the role-playing, they should place a check mark next to each guideline observed, take notes on other procedures being used (particularly if they are incorrect), and then share their evaluations.

Human Relations

4. For each of the following situations, indicate what you would say next to gather information to determine a customer's needs tactfully.

   a. A customer enters the men's area of a large department store and says, "I need to get some clothes."

   b. A woman begins looking at the size 7 dresses and says, "I used to wear size 7 in dresses, but I have gained a few pounds." In reality, the customer is probably a size 12.

5. You notice that your customer is taking longer than most people take in the dressing room. You are concerned that he may be shoplifting. What do you say or do to prevent shoplifting and still maintain a congenial rapport? Remember, your suspicion of shoplifting may be unfounded.

APPLICATION PROJECTS

1. Continuing with your sales project, prepare the determining needs step of a sale for your training manual. Include a brief description of the importance and techniques used in this step of the sale. Finally, prepare a list of ten questions that may be used to determine your customer's needs. Begin with general questions regarding the intended use and previous experience. End the list with specific questions about the particular features of the product or service, such as color, size, design, and quantity desired. Base your questions on the product for which you prepared a feature-benefit chart.

   Note: If you have not completed a feature-benefit chart, select a product that would require a customer to spend time shopping for and comparing features. Some product ideas include a camera, computer, pair of running shoes, microwave oven, and bicycle.

2. Using the product for which you prepared a feature-benefit chart, or the one you used to complete the Application Project #1 above, prepare a detailed plan for the product presentation step of the sale. Use this plan as the next chapter in your sales training manual. For each product feature, include what you will say, how you will demonstrate that feature, what sales aids you will use, how you will use them, and how you will involve your customer with each feature. When appropriate, incorporate sample dialogue.

After completing this chapter, you should be able to:

1. handle objections in a sales situation,

2. distinguish between an objection and an excuse,

3. explain why objections should be welcomed in the sales process,

4. give examples of common objections based on the five buying decisions of *need*, *product*, *source*, *price*, and *time*,

5. identify the four-step process of handling objections, and

6. demonstrate seven specific methods of handling objections.

objection
excuse
objections analysis sheet
paraphrase
yes, but method
boomerang method
question method
superior point method
direct denial method
demonstration method
third party method

Handling Customer Questions and Objections

I n studying the sales process so far, you have learned how to prepare for the sale, approach a customer, determine customer needs, and present your product or service. Now it is time to look at handling customer questions and objections.

For example, a customer may like everything about a product except its color. Simply showing the same item in another color may solve the problem. Learning how to handle customer objections is an important part of your sales training because such objections are extremely useful in the sales process.

Objections vs. Excuses

Objections are concerns, hesitations, doubts, or other honest reasons a customer has for not making a purchase. Objections should be viewed as positive because they give you an opportunity to present more information to the customer.

Objections can be presented as either questions or statements:

Customer: Do you carry any other brands?
Salesperson: Yes. We have an extensive number of brands available.
Customer: These shoes don't fit me properly.
Salesperson: Perhaps you would be more comfortable in a different style.

Excuses are insincere reasons for not buying or not seeing the salesperson. A customer may use excuses when not in the mood to buy or when concealing real objections. Some general excuses are:

- "I'm too busy to see you today."
- "I'm just shopping around."
- "I didn't plan to buy anything today."

It is often hard to distinguish between objections and excuses. In some cases, a statement or question that seems to be an objection really means "I don't want to buy today." This is an excuse.

When you are faced with this in a retail sales situation, be polite and courteous. Encourage the customer to look around and ask you any questions he or she may have.

In industrial sales, the procedure is different. If a potential customer refuses to see you when you make a call, leave a business card and ask if it is possible to see the person at a more convenient time.

There are cases when seeming excuses are actually attempts to hide real objections. "I didn't plan to buy today" may really mean, "I don't like the styles you have available."

Welcome Objections

Objections can occur at any time during the sales process and should be answered promptly. A customer who must wait to hear responses to questions or concerns tends to become preoccupied with the

Objections and Excuses	
Objections	**Excuses**
"I don't really need another coat."	"I'm in a real hurry so I really can't shop today."
"I can't wear this dress to work."	"I didn't bring any money with me today."
"The last time I ordered something from your store, I didn't get it for four weeks."	"I'm just browsing."
"This is much too expensive."	"I'll have to talk to my wife about purchasing it."
"My budget won't allow me to buy anything this expensive until next month."	"I'll stop back in next week."

Figure 16-1   **Objections and Excuses**
Some objections are really excuses in disguise and vice versa. What could you say to a customer in answer to each of these objections and excuses?

objection. When that happens, you may lose your purchaser's attention and confidence. So, answer objections when they occur.

As we said earlier, you should welcome objections. They can guide you in the sales process by helping you redefine the customer's needs and determine when the customer wants more information.

For example, a customer may say, "This item is very expensive." What the person may really mean is, "Tell me why this product should warrant such a high price." In addition to letting you know why the customer is reluctant to buy, this objection gives you an opportunity to bring out additional selling points.

Plan Ahead for Objections

You can be prepared for most objections that may occur in a sales situation by preparing an *objection analysis sheet. An objections analysis sheet is a list that enumerates common objections and possible responses to those objections.* The actual objections, of course, may be slightly different from those you anticipated. But the exercise of thinking through the responses gives you some idea of how to answer in actual sales situations.

Sometimes you can incorporate anticipated objections into your product presentation so they do not become objections at all. You must be cautious about this, however. You don't want to include so many objections in your product presentation that you prevent your customer from talking. Remember, you still want your customer to be involved in the sale.

If you do include objections in the product presentation, always avoid introducing doubt—especially if none existed before. If you say, for example, "I guess you are worried about the safety of this snowmobile," you may introduce a fear that was not even a concern to the customer before you mentioned it.

A better way to handle the same situation would be to emphasize the safety features of the vehicle. For example, "The suspension on this snowmobile is specially designed to prevent it from tipping over; thus, it is safe to operate."

Common Objections

To prepare an objections analysis sheet, think about common objections. Most of them are based on the five buying decisions of *need*, *product*, *source*, *price*, and *time*.

Need. Objections related to need usually occur when the customer has a conflict between wanting something but not truly needing it. A comment such as, "I really like that sweater, but it doesn't match anything I have" is an objection based on a conflict between a need and a want.

Figure 16-2 **Ojection Analysis Sheet**
An objection analysis sheet enumerates common objections and possible responses to those objections. Why should you be cautious about incorporating anticipated objections into your product presentations?

**Objection Analysis Sheet
for
Compact Disks and Disk Players**

Objection	Possible Response
Disks cost too much.	They cost more than records, but they are virtually indestructible and last a lifetime.
Will compact disks replace records?	They have already begun to replace records. Major retailers are now devoting more floor space to compact disks than they are to records.
I'm afraid to buy a disk player now because the manufacturers will come out with a new model soon.	I can see your concern. However, you could be enjoying the quality of sound a disk player produces right now. Most improvements won't change the quality of sound. They will only improve such things as size.
I can't record on a compact disk as I can on a cassette player.	The technical and audio advances of the compact disk player far surpass this minor limitation. Besides, there is no consumer source of music that is higher in quality of sound than the compact disk. Why would you want to listen to anything else?

Product. Objections based on the product itself are more common. They include concerns about such things as the quality, size, appearance, brand name, or style. For example: "I am not sure this dress style is appropriate for work."

Source. Objections based on the source often occur from negative past experiences with that firm. A buyer may say, "The last time I dealt with your store, my order was three weeks late. How can I be sure this one will arrive on time?"

Price. Objections based on price are more common with high quality, expensive merchandise. You might hear such objections as "That's more than I wanted to spend."

Time. Objections based on time reveal a hesitation to buy immediately. These objections are sometimes excuses. But at other times, customers have a real reason for not wanting to make a purchase on the spot. A customer may say, "I'm not in a position to make that type of purchase now. I won't be ready for at least two months."

You can develop common objections for all types of goods and services by using the five buying decisions as the basis for them. Once you begin selling, you will probably hear more objections. Note them for future reference.

Four-Step Process for Handling Objections

To handle objections, you can follow four basic steps: *listen carefully, acknowledge the objection, restate the objection*, and *answer the objection*.

Listen Carefully. To demonstrate sincere concern for your customer's objections, follow these key rules for effective listening: *be attentive, maintain eye contact*, and *let the customer talk*. Chapters 9 and 15 discuss listening skills further.

Acknowledge the Customer's Objections. Acknowledging objections demonstrates that you understand and care about the customer's concerns. Some common statements used to acknowledge objections are "I can see your point" or "I've had other customers ask the same thing."

These acknowledgements make a customer feel that the objections are understandable, valid, and worthy of further discussion.

In some situations you may feel like saying to the customer, "You are wrong." But this will probably put the customer on the defensive; you then risk los-

Four Steps
for
Handling Objections

Listen carefully.

Acknowledge the customer's objections.

Restate the objections.

Answer the objections.

Figure 16-3 **Four-Step Process for Handling Objections**
These four basic steps help salespeople successfully handle objections. Why is each step in this process so important?

ing the rapport you have established up to this point. So, remember to acknowledge a customer's objections in a positive way.

Restate the Objections. To be sure you understand the customer, you can restate his or her objections in a number of ways:

- "I can understand your concerns. You feel that. . . . Am I correct?"
- "In other words, you feel that. . . ."
- "Let me see if I understand. You want to know more about. . . ."

Don't repeat the customer's concerns word for word. Instead, you should paraphrase the objections. *To paraphrase is to restate the meaning in different words.*

For example, a customer might say, "The style is nice, but I don't like the color." You can paraphrase the objection by asking, "Am I correct to assume that you might be interested in the jacket if we can find your size in another color?"

The Price is Too Low!

A salesperson has covered the major selling points for a pair of Reebok ERS Trainer running shoes when the customer asks his first question.

Customer: I have flat feet and need a shoe with arch supports. Do these shoes have them?

Salesperson: Yes, as a matter of fact, the ERS has a removable molded anatomical PEEVA sockliner that provides full length arch support and cushioning.

Customer: How much do these running shoes cost?

Salesperson: The retail price for Reebok's ERS Trainer running shoe is $59.95.

Customer: Is that all they cost? My friend paid almost double that for a pair of New Balance running shoes. How can these Reeboks be any good? New Balance running shoes must be much better than Reebok.

Salesperson: I am glad you are so honest about your concern with the quality of these shoes because it gives me a chance to tell you a little bit about Reebok. The company is known for its quality and innovative product designs. It spends a lot of money on research and product development, as you can tell by the ERS design that improves shock absorption, and the Duratech rubber outsole that improves traction and durability.

Two U.S. Olympic runners, Ed Eyestone and Mike Conover, wore Reebok running shoes in the 1988 Summer Olympics. So you can see that Reebok is a good product endorsed by people who do much more running than you or I do.

1. Identify steps two, three, and four of the four-step process for handling objections. Did the salesperson perform the first step, too? Explain.
2. In most sales situations, customers object that the price is too high. If this was the case in the above situation, how would you have answered the objection, "That is more than I wanted to spend for a pair of running shoes."

When paraphrasing, don't change the meaning or content of what your customer says. Accurate paraphrasing shows the customer you understand his or her objections. It also helps you open the lines of effective communication when a customer has difficulty expressing concerns.

Answer the Objections.   Try to find a point of agreement with the customer before answering each objection. Then answer each objection tactfully, keeping in mind the customer's feelings. Never answer with an air of superiority or with indifference to the person's concern.

Think of yourself as a consultant, using the objections to further define or redefine the customer's needs. For example, if price is the objection, go back to determining the customer's needs. If a higher priced item is warranted based on these needs, explain the features and benefits of the more expensive model and why that item is best suited for the customer.

Specialized Methods of Handling Objections

There are seven specialized methods for handling objections: *yes, but*; *boomerang*; *question*; *superior point*; *direct denial*; *demonstration*; and *third party*. Some of these techniques are effective only in specific situations. Others are more commonly used.

Yes, but. *The yes, but method first acknowledges the customer's objections and then reveals another point of view.* You don't want your customer to feel as though you are accusing him or her of being wrong. So, you should acknowledge the customer's point of view with a statement such as, "Yes, I understand your reaction. I used to feel the same way. But I have since learned that. . . ."

While this method can be quite effective, it should not be used exclusively because it can put the customer on the defensive. Selecting the most appropriate time to use the *yes, but* method will depend on the rapport you have with your customer and the nature of the objection.

Boomerang. Just as a boomerang returns to the thrower, you can return an objection to the customer by using the *boomerang method. With the boomerang method, the objection comes back to the customer as a selling point.* Here is an example.

Customer: This ski jacket is so lightweight. It can't possibly keep me warm.
Salesperson: Actually, the lightness of the jacket is due to a new insulation called Thinsulate, which is lightweight and warm. The manufacturer guarantees that Thinsulate will keep you warmer, without the bulk, than comparable fiberfill insulation.

When using the boomerang method, you must be careful not to sound as if you are trying to outwit the customer. Instead, use a friendly, helpful tone when explaining how the objection is really a selling point.

Question Method. *The question method is a technique in which the customer is questioned in an effort to learn more about the objections raised.* As a salesperson, your questions may reveal hidden objections and/or may help you learn more about the customer's needs and wants. While answering your

Figure 16-4 **Seven Specialized Methods for Handling Objections**
Some of these techniques are more commonly used than others. Think of one objection and one answer for each objection.

Seven Specialized Methods for Handling Objections

Yes, but	Acknowledges customer's objections and then reveals another point of view
Boomerang	Objection comes back to the customer as a selling point
Question	Customer is questioned to learn more about objection raised
Superior Point	Permits salesperson to acknowledge objections as being valid and to offset those objections with other features and benefits
Direct Denial	Provides proof and accurate information in answer to objections
Demonstration	Answers objections by illustrating one or more features of a good or service
Third Party	Using a previous customer or other neutral person to give a testimonial about the good or service

inquiries, the shopper may even come to realize that the objections are not serious or valid.

Sometimes the question method can put the customer on the defensive. To avoid such a negative situation, never ask questions in an abrupt manner that may appear to show rudeness on your part.

For example, if a customer comments, "I don't think my sister will like this purse," never respond with a simple, "Why not?". Instead, show courtesy and respect by asking a more complete question such as, "Why don't you think she'll like it?"

Superior Point. *The superior point method is a technique that permits the salesperson to acknowledge objections as being valid and to offset those objections with other features and benefits.* Because products and services are not perfect, there are often trade-offs that take place when making a selection. The superior point method allows you to admit disadvantages in certain products but then to present superior points to offset or compensate for the disadvantages. The customer is then put in a position to decide between the different features and thus see additional reasons for buying. Here is an example:

Customer: Your prices are higher than your competitors' prices.
Salesperson: You are correct. Our prices are slightly higher, but with good reason. We use better quality nylon in our garments. These garments will last five to ten years longer than our competitors'. Plus, we guarantee the quality for life. If you have a problem with this item, you can return it. We will repair it free of charge.

Direct Denial. *The direct denial method provides proof and accurate information in answer to objections.* It is best used when the customer has misinformation or when the objections are in the form of a question. For example:

Customer: I think this shirt will shrink.
Salesperson: This shirt will not shrink because its fabric is made of 50 percent cotton and 50 percent polyester. The polyester will prevent it from shrinking.

When using the direct denial method, the negative reply must be backed up with proof and accurate facts.

Demonstration. *The demonstration method is a technique that answers objections by illustrating one or more features of a product or service.* It exemplifies the adage, "Seeing is believing."

Customer: I can't believe that food will not stick to the bottom of the pan if you don't use oil or butter.
Salesperson: I'm glad you brought up that point. Let me demonstrate how this Teflon-coated pan permits you to cook without oil or butter.

The demonstration method can be quite convincing and should be used when appropriate. But only conduct demonstrations you have tested. Make sure they work before using them on a customer in a sales situation.

Third Party. *The third party method involves using a previous customer or another neutral person who can give a testimonial about the product.* Some salespeople keep letters from satisfied customers to use as testimonials when handling objections. Others get permission from previous customers to permit a prospective customer to call and verify the salesperson's claims. For example:

Customer: I can't see how this machine can save me a thousand dollars in operating costs the first year.
Salesperson: Mr. Frank Smith, one of my customers, questioned the same point when he bought his machine a year ago. Now he praises its efficiency and says that his costs have gone down by $1,200. Here's a letter I recently received from him.

While these seven methods of handling objections give you ideas on how to handle specific objections, do not use all methods in each sales situation. As you practice using these methods, you will probably create combinations that can be effective in specific situations.

VOCABULARY REVIEW

Write one to three paragraphs about how to handle customer questions and objections, incorporating these 11 vocabulary words.

objection
excuse
objections analysis sheet
paraphrase
yes, but method
boomerang method

question method
superior point method
direct denial method
demonstration method
third party method

FACT AND IDEA REVIEW

1. In a sales situation, what are objections?

2. When can objections occur in the sales process?

3. How can you plan for objections?

4. On what are most objections based?

5. What are the four basic steps to follow when handling any type of objection?

6. What happens to the customer's objection when you use the boomerang method?

7. In which specialized method of handling objections do you ask the customer questions to learn more about the objections raised?

8. Which specialized method of handling objections allows you to offset the objections with other features and benefits?

9. When is direct denial best used in handling objections?

10. Which specialized method of handling objections involves using a previous customer or another neutral person who can supply a testimonial about the product?

CRITICAL THINKING

1. Distinguish between an objection and an excuse. Give an example of each.

2. Why should you welcome objections in the sales process?

3. What precautions must you take if you want to include anticipated objections in your product presentation?

4. Acknowledge and then paraphrase the following objection: "I worry about radiation leaking from the door of a microwave oven. I believe that radiation can be dangerous."

5. How and when should the following methods of handling objections be used?
   - yes, but
   - boomerang
   - question
   - superior point
   - direct denial
   - demonstration
   - third party

6. Do you think it's possible to go through the entire sales process without one customer objection? Explain your answer.

USING BASIC SKILLS

Math

1. How much does a customer save on an item marked down 15 percent from the original selling price of $69.95?

2. What is the final sales price of an item marked down 25 percent from $128.75?

Communication

3. Role play the parts of salesperson and customer and answer each of the following objections in a presentation to the class.
    - "This coat is too expensive."
    - "This Walkman is extremely lightweight. How can it produce quality sound?"
    - "No shoes ever fit me properly. I doubt whether this pair will be any different."
    - "I had no idea ten-speed bicycles were this expensive."

4. Write a dialogue that illustrates the four-step process of handling objections. You may select the product and objection to use. Share the dialogue with your classmates by assuming the role of salesperson and having another student role play the part of the customer.

Human Relations

5. An argumentative customer questions the price of a $125 tennis racquet. He or she tells you that retailers are greedy people who buy less expensive goods and sell them for outrageously high prices. How would you respond?

6. An industrial customer who had a negative experience with your firm before you were hired indicates that he or she does not wish to see you or anyone from your company. How would you handle this problem?

APPLICATION PROJECTS

1. For each of the following objections, identify the buying decision on which the concern is based. The common buying decisions from which to choose are *need*, *product*, *source*, *price*, and *time*.
    - "I don't like the assortment of rakes I received."
    - "I'm really not sure I want to spend that amount of money on an automobile."
    - "I just love those shoes, but I'm not sure I'll have much use for them after the wedding."
    - "I really don't know if I want to spend my money in this store. The last time I charged something and returned it, you didn't credit my charge account."
    - "I want to think about it. I don't usually buy the first thing I see that I like."

2. As part of your continuing project, write the introduction for the handling objections section of your sales training manual. Explain the importance of this step to the entire sales process. Then complete Application Projects #3 and #4 below, and make them part of the handling objections section of your manual.

3. Write one objection for each of the five buying decisions using the product for which you prepared a feature-benefit chart. If you did not prepare a feature-benefit chart, use a pair of sneakers, a desk lamp, a computer, or a typewriter.

4. Using the objections from the preceding question and a few new ones, prepare an objections analysis sheet. Answer one objection following the four-step process and answer the remaining objections by using each of the seven specialized methods of handling objections. Identify the method or methods used to answer each objection. Write your response as though the customer were standing in front of you.

Closing the Sale and Follow-up

A t a certain point in the sales process, your customer will be ready to make a purchase. When this becomes apparent, it is up to you to close the sale.

Sometimes the decision to buy is quick and easy. At other times, it's more difficult. In this chapter you will learn how to detect buying signals and how to close the sale. You will also learn how to suggest additional merchandise to the customer.

Finally, this chapter will also give you information on the proper follow-up sales procedures essential for customer satisfaction and repeat business.

Closing the Sale

Closing the sale is obtaining positive agreement from the customer to buy. All your efforts up to this step of the sale have been involved with helping your customer make buying decisions. So, closing the sale should be a natural part of the sales process. In fact, it is sometimes so natural that your customer closes the sale for you by saying, "I'll take it." In many sales situations, however, a customer waits for you to initiate the close. That's why it is important for you to learn when and how to close the sale.

Timing the Close

You close the sale when your customer is ready to buy. Since some customers are ready to buy sooner than others, you must be flexible. You may show a customer one product and almost immediately detect an opportunity to close the sale. At other times, you may spend an hour with a customer and still find that he or she is having difficulty making a decision.

In either case, do not feel obligated to complete an entire sales presentation just because you have planned it that way. Remember, the key to closing the sale is customer readiness.

Buying Signals

To detect an opportunity to close the sale, look for *buying signals*. *Buying signals are things a customer does or says to indicate a readiness to buy.* These buying signals include facial expressions, actions, and comments. For example, a customer who is holding the merchandise and smiling is usually sending you buying signals. Comments that imply ownership are also buying signals. You know a customer is ready to buy when you hear comments such as, "This is exactly what I was looking for."

Trial Close

To test the readiness of the customer and your interpretation of a positive buying signal, you can attempt a *trial close*. *A trial close is an initial effort to close a sale.* Trial closes are beneficial for two reasons. First, if the close does not work, you have still learned from the attempt because a customer will probably tell you why he or she is not ready to buy. Second, if

the trial close works, you will have reached your goal of closing the sale.

Thus, in both situations you retain control of the sale and are in an excellent position to continue with the sales process. The rule, then, is always be ready to close.

General Rules for Closing the Sale

You will find it easier to attempt trial closes and to close more sales if you follow a few general rules.

Rule 1. If you think the customer is ready to make a buying decision, stop talking about the product. Continuing to sell to a customer who is ready to make a purchase may have a negative effect or even cause you to lose the sale.

Eight Rules for Closing the Sale

Rule 1   When the customer is ready to buy, stop talking about the product.

Rule 2   When a customer is having difficulty making a buying decision, stop showing additional merchandise.

Rule 3   Summarize the product's major features and benefits.

Rule 4   Don't rush a customer into making a buying decision.

Rule 5   Use words that indicate ownership.

Rule 6   Use major objections.

Rule 7   Use effective product presentations.

Rule 8   Look for minor agreements on selling points.

Figure 17-1   **General Rules for Closing the Sale**
There are eight basic rules for closing the sale. What could happen if a salesperson disregards Rules 1, 2, and 4? Why?

Rule 2. When a customer is having difficulty making a buying decision, stop showing additional merchandise. You should also narrow the selection of items by removing those things that are no longer of interest to the customer. You can do this by asking "Which of these items do you like the least?" Once you get the selection down to two, you can concentrate on helping the customer make a decision.

Rule 3. Help a customer decide by summarizing the major features and benefits of a product. You can also tell the advantages and disadvantages of the item being considered. Both methods help you to focus the decision making on important considerations.

Rule 4. Don't rush a customer into making a buying decision. Be patient, courteous, polite, and helpful. Always remember that your primary interest is in customer satisfaction.

Rule 5. Use words that indicate ownership, such as you *and* your. When presenting selling points, say such things as, "You will enjoy using this camera on your vacation."

Rule 6. Use major objections to close the sale. The effect of having a major obstacle removed usually makes a customer receptive to buying the product or service.

Rule 7. Use effective product presentations to close the sale. Dramatic product presentations often prove important selling points and get a customer excited about owning the product. Take advantage of high customer interest at these times and attempt to close the sale.

Rule 8. Look for minor agreements from the customer on selling points that lead up to the close. Ask questions such as, "Those walking shoes are comfortable, aren't they?" In general, if you get positive reactions from your customer throughout the sales process, that same positive frame of mind will help make the closing natural.

Specialized Methods for Closing the Sale

Once you recognize a buying signal, you will attempt to close the sale. How you go about this depends on the selling situation. Certain selling situations warrant the use of specialized methods, such as the *which close, standing room only, assumption close, direct close,* and the *service close.*

Which Close. *The which close encourages a customer to make a decision between two items.* You should remove unwanted items to bring the selection to two. Review the benefits of each item and then ask the customer, "Which one do you prefer?" This method makes it easy for a customer because only one decision must be made.

Standing Room Only Close. *The standing room only close is used when a product is in short supply or when the price will be going up in the near future.* Because it can be perceived as a high pressure tactic to close a sale, it should be used infrequently and *only* when the situation honestly calls for it. For example, "This is the last pair of shoes I have in your size."

Assumption Close. *In the assumption close, you assume the close when you think the customer is ready to buy.* If you followed the rules for closing the sale, you have already obtained agreement from the customer on some selling points. So, it should seem natural to get confirmation on one more point. This additional agreement can be based on delivery terms, the clerical aspects of the order, payment methods, or quantity needed. For example, "Would Monday, October 10th, be a good day to deliver this bedroom furniture?"

A variation of the assumption close used in industrial sales involves asking for information to fill out the purchase order. A simple question such as, "May I have your address?" lets a customer know the salesperson is ready to take the order.

Positive customer responses to this type of question mean you were correct in assuming that your customer was ready to buy. If a customer is not ready, simply continue with the sales presentation.

Direct Close. *The direct close is a method in which you ask for the sale.* To be effective, the asking should be done subtly, with a conversational approach. For example,

Salesperson: How do you like this camera?
Customer: It's terrific.
Salesperson: I think you've made an excellent choice.

Another direct close is to say, "That should wrap it up." You can use this statement when you have covered all the selling points, your customer has shown you only positive reactions, and the customer is eager to buy.

Service Close. Sometimes you run into obstacles or instances that require special services in order to close the sale. *The service close explains services that overcome obstacles or problems.* Such services include gift wrapping, a return policy, special sales arrangements, warranties and guarantees, services, and bonuses or premiums.

You could, for instance, offer gift wrapping when you know the purchase is a gift. You can explain the store's return policy when a customer is hesitant about a purchase, especially when the item is being purchased for someone else.

Special sales arrangements are used to close the sale when the customer needs help in paying for the item or the order. In such a case, an industrial sales representative talks about terms of the sale, discussing such points as when payment is expected (which may be 30 to 60 days after the date of the invoice). A customer may also need information about credit terms to help him or her decide to buy. In retail sales, acceptance of credit and checks as well as special buying plans such as installment or layaway agreements can be suggested. These make it easier for a customer to buy. When a customer questions the quality of the merchandise, you can explain that the warranty or guarantee is offered on the product.

Specialized Methods for Closing the Sale	
Which Close	Encourages customer to make a decision between two items.
Standing Room Only Close	Used when a product is in short supply or when the price will be going up in the near future.
Assumption Close	Salesperson assumes the close when he/she thinks the customer is ready to buy.
Direct Close	Salesperson asks for the sale.
Service Close	Explains service that overcomes obstacles or problems.

Figure 17-2 **Specialized Methods for Closing the Sale**

Certain selling situations warrant the use of specialized closing methods. Give one example of a selling situation where you would use each closing method described here.

Offering something special can also be an effective closing technique, particularly if the customer will save money and/or time as a result. Some enticements might include a free roll of film with the purchase of a camera or free alterations on a dress.

When your business offers the same quality merchandise at the same price as your competitors, your service may be the *only* factor that affects the buying decision. In such a case, promising better service than the customer is presently getting may help close the sale.

Failure to Close the Sale

Don't despair if your initial attempts to close a sale are unsuccessful. You will have many more opportunities to close the sale, particularly if you treat your customer with courtesy and respect.

In a retail setting, invite the customer to shop in your store again. In industrial sales, ask if you may call again. In both situations, remember that every sales contact has the potential to become a sale in the future.

Suggestion Selling

Suggestion selling is selling additional goods or services to the customer. This does not mean loading customers with unneeded or unwanted goods and services. When used properly, suggestion selling is an important customer service. It means saving the customer time and money by suggesting additional purchases that will make the original purchase more enjoyable.

For example, consider the customer who buys a camera, takes it home, and realizes there is no film in it. Another trip to the store is necessary before the camera can be used. The salesperson would have had a sure sale by suggesting film for the camera.

Benefits of Suggestion Selling

Suggestion selling benefits the salesperson, the customer, and the company. You benefit because customers will want to do business with you again. Your customer benefits because he or she is more pleased with the original purchase. The firm benefits because the time and cost involved in suggestion selling is less than the cost of making the original sale.

The extra time spent on suggestion selling significantly increases a firm's net profit. Note on the example below that the expenses increased, but not in proportion to the sales volume. This is because less time and effort are needed for suggestion selling (than in the original sale) and certain business expenses remain the same.

Pair of pants		$75	Pair of pants		$75
—			Shirt		$35
Cost of Goods		−$37	Cost of Goods		−$55
Expenses		−$12	Expenses		−$15
Net Profit	=	$26	Net Profit	=	$40

Rules for Suggestion Selling

There are five basic rules for suggestion selling.

Rule 1. Do suggestion selling after the customer has made a commitment to buy and before payment is made or the order is written. Introducing additional merchandise before the sale has been closed can create undue pressure on the customer.

There is, however, an exception to this rule. Salespeople who sell products whose accessories are one of the major selling benefits often introduce these additional items during the sales process to help close the sale. For example, a toy manufacturer may show a retail store owner the accessories for a new doll to encourage the buyer to purchase the doll.

Rule 2. Make your recommendation from the customer's point of view and give at least one reason for your suggestion. For example, "If you want to use your camera immediately, you will need film for it."

A customer is usually willing to listen to your suggestion when it sounds as though you have his or her best interest at heart.

Rule 3. Make the suggestion definite. Don't ask, "Will that be all?" Instead say, "This oil is recommended by the manufacturer for the engine."

Rule 4. Show the item you are suggesting. Merely talking about it is not enough. In some cases, the item will sell itself if you let the customer see it and handle it. For example, putting a matching purse next to the shoes a customer just decided to buy can be quite effective, particularly with some commentary. You might say, "This purse matches your shoes perfectly, doesn't it?"

Rule 5. Make the suggestion positive. For example, you could say, "This scarf will complement your coat beautifully. Look how perfectly it matches the color and how fashionable it looks on."

Rules for Suggestion Selling

Rule 1 Do the suggestion selling after the customer has made a commitment to buy and before payment is made or the order written.

Rule 2 Make your recommendation from the customer's point of view and give at least one reason for your suggestion.

Rule 3 Make the suggestion definite.

Rule 4 Show the item you are suggesting.

Rule 5 Make the suggestion positive.

Figure 17-3 **Rules for Suggestion Selling**
There are five basic rules for suggestion selling. Demonstrate these rules by framing a statement you could use to suggest a customer buy extra ribbons for a newly purchased typewriter.

Items Used in Suggestion Selling

There are five types of merchandise or services used in suggestion selling: *merchandise or services related to the original purchase, larger quantities of the original item, new merchandise, sale merchandise,* or *holiday merchandise.*

Related Merchandise. *Related merchandise can be a product or service that a customer should have to increase the use or enjoyment of the original purchase.* Introducing related merchandise is probably the easiest and most effective suggestion selling method. For most purchases, there are accessory items that can be sold with the original purchase, such as a scarf to match a blouse or special service contracts for new appliances.

Larger Quantity. In retail sales, suggesting a larger quantity usually works with inexpensive items and when a savings of money, time, and/or convenience will be realized. For example, you may tell a customer who wants to buy one pair of pantyhose, "One pair costs $4. You can buy three pairs for $10, a

Suggestion selling serves a customer by calling attention to his or her actual needs. Give five types of merchandise and/or services you could suggest to the customer buying these golf clubs.

Advertised or Sale Merchandise. Most shoppers appreciate the opportunity to take advantage of a bargain. Salespeople are obligated to both the store and the customer to present information about such bargains. For instance, you could comment on a special sale by explaining, "We are having a one-day sale on household appliances today. Take a look around while I write up your purchase."

Special Occasion Merchandise. Special occasions and holidays present an opportunity to sell more merchandise. You can suggest gift items to customers around such occasions as Christmas, Hanukkah, Valentine's Day, Father's Day and Mother's Day.

savings of $2. Buying three pairs will also save you a trip to the store next time you need a pair."

Industrial salespeople may suggest a larger quantity so the customer can take advantage of lower prices or special considerations. In addition to offering a better price per item, some manufacturers also include special services. Buying a certain quantity, for instance, may allow a retailer to take advantage of free freight and/or free advertising.

New Stock. In retail sales, routinely inform your customer of the arrival of new merchandise. Regular customers appreciate this special service because they like having the opportunity to see the new merchandise before others see it.

Some industrial sales representatives save new items to show their customers until after they have completed the sale of merchandise requested. Thus, the salesperson has an opportunity to establish a rapport with the customer before introducing new merchandise.

After-sale Activities

After-sale activities include *taking payment* or *taking the order*, *departure*, *follow-up*, and *evaluation* of your sales effort. Think of these as preparation for future sales.

Taking Payment or Taking the Order

Take payment or take the order with courtesy. Work quickly to complete the paperwork. Avoid saying or doing anything to irritate your customer at this stage of the sale. You have probably seen an annoyed customer saying, "Forget the order. I don't want it anymore." If you are courteous and efficient, you can usually avoid this type of negative experience.

Departure

Before the customer departs or before you leave your client's office, reassure the person of the wise buying choices which have been made.

If an item needs special care or specific instructions, take the time to educate your customer about it. You may want to remind the customer, for example, that a silk blouse should be dry cleaned instead of hand laundered. Helpful, well intended comments will make your customer feel you are interested and concerned. It also helps insure customer satisfaction.

Always thank your customers. Even when a customer does not buy, express your gratitude for the time and attention given to you. Invite him or her back to the store or ask for permission to call again in the near future.

Follow-up

The follow-up includes making arrangements to follow through on all promises made during the sales process and checking on customer satisfaction with the purchase. If you promised a certain delivery date, call the shipping department to confirm the date. Then check to make sure delivery occurs as promised. If there is a problem, call the customer and explain the delay. If you promised to call back in one week, make that notation on your calendar. To check on customer satisfaction, phone the customer a week or two

---

C A S E   C H A L L E N G E

The Power of Suggestion

A sales associate has been speaking with a customer for 15 minutes and has answered all her questions and objections about a pair of Reebok ERS Trainer running shoes. After walking around the department to make sure they fit properly, the customer takes off the shoes.

Customer: I can't wait to see if the ERS design makes a difference in the way my legs feel after I run.

Salesperson: You have made an excellent choice. I know you will enjoy running in these shoes. Will you be paying by cash or credit card?

Customer: Do you take MasterCard?

Salesperson: Yes we do. Earlier in our discussion you mentioned how important shock absorption and comfort were to you. Let me show you these specially designed socks that have extra cushioning in the ball of the foot and heel. They are also extra absorbent. You could say these socks make great running shoes even better.

Customer: How much are they?

Salesperson: They are only $7.99 a pair. How many would you like?

Customer: I'll take two pairs.

Salesperson: Wait here while I write up your sales slip. May I please have your credit card?

The salesperson rings up the sale and asks the customer to fill out the credit card slip. He hands the bag to the customer and says, "Thank you for shopping at Herman's. Enjoy your new running shoes."

1. Was the closing technique the salesperson used appropriate for the situation? Explain.
2. Identify the effective suggestion selling techniques used by the salesperson in the above dialogue.
3. What other related merchandise could have been suggested in conjunction with the sale of running shoes?
4. What principles of departure did the salesperson follow when completing the sales transaction with the customer?
5. What could the sales associate do to be sure the customer liked the running shoes and returned to the store?

after the purchase to see if he or she is happy with it. You can also send a thank-you note with your business card attached.

In addition, you can use the time immediately after the sale to plan for your next visit with the customer. Take notes on your conversation with the customer. Keep this in a file for future reference. In retail sales, note a customer's preference in color and styles, as well as sizes, address, and telephone number.

In industrial sales, record personal information on the buyer's marital status, children, and/or hobbies to assist with future sales visits. Record changes in buying patterns which may lead to future sales.

Evaluation

After the sales process is completed (even if you closed the sale), evaluate yourself. Consider everything you did in the sale. What were the strong points of your sales presentation? What did you do wrong? How could you have improved your performance? What would you do differently next time?

Objective evaluations of your sales techniques helps you improve your selling skills. Through honest evaluation of your selling technique, you will learn to look forward to your next sales opportunity. And with each new sales contact, you should become more effective and thus more successful.

Hopkins, Beth Ann
4325 Grantwood Avenue
Los Angeles, CA 90064

Age: *About 35*

Phone: *213-591-4200*

Occupation: *Attorney*

Prefers business suits and dresses in neutral colors — navy, gray, brown. Will not wear plaids or prints.

Blouse: *Size 7*

Skirt: *Size 7*

Dress: *Sizes 7 & 9*

Record of purchases:

June 8, 1990	*Evan Picone suit and silk blouse*
September 22, 1990	*Cashmere sweater*
December 22, 1990	*Cocktail dress*
March 3, 1991	*Two silk blouses with matching scarves*
April 21, 1991	*One leather belt*

Keeping records of your customer's purchases, likes, and dislikes can help you establish a long-standing relationship with them. How can the information recorded on this file card be helpful to the salesperson in the future?

VOCABULARY REVIEW

Write a brief definition of each term based on your reading of the chapter.

closing the sale
buying signals
trial close
which close
standing room only close

assumption close
direct close
service close
suggestion selling
related merchandise

FACT AND IDEA REVIEW

1. When should you close the sale?

2. Give an example of a buying signal.

3. What can you do to test the readiness of the customer and your interpretation of a positive buying signal?

4. List eight general rules for closing the sale.

5. When should the standing room only closing method be used?

6. Name six services that can help close a sale in certain situations.

7. What should you do if you did not close the sale in a retail situation? in an industrial situation?

8. When should you use suggestion selling?

9. Tell the five rules for suggestion selling.

10. List five types of merchandise that can be used effectively in suggestion selling.

11. What should be included in after-sales activities?

12. Excluding taking payment and writing the order, identify three things you should do before you or your customer depart.

13. What does follow-up include?

14. Why should you evaluate yourself after the sales process is finished?

CRITICAL THINKING

1. Why are trial closes beneficial to the sales process?

2. If a customer has five items in view and you are not sure which ones are of interest to him or her, what can you do to narrow the selection to two?

3. What can you do in the close to help focus the buying decision on important considerations?

4. Which close would you use if a customer said, "I can't wait until my friends see me in this outfit." Why?

5. Tell how suggestion selling benefits the salesperson, the customer, and the firm. Give examples.

6. For each of the following items, list at least three related items that can be used for suggestion selling: typewriter, suit, microwave, bicycle.

7. Explain how after-sale activities are a preparation for future sales.

USING BASIC SKILLS

Math

1. For the following sales transaction, calculate the total amount due. A customer wants to purchase 2 shirts at $35 each, 3 pairs of pants at $90 each, and 2 ties at $25 each. Sales tax is 6 percent.

2. Credit card customers are granted a 10 percent discount on all purchases, except sale merchandise, from November 5 through November 15. Calculate the total amount due by a credit card customer who wants to buy the following items during the discount period: 2 blouses at $50 each, 4 pairs of pantyhose at $4.00 each, and 1 sale item at $78.99. The 6 percent sales tax is applied after the discount is taken.

Communication

3. Role play with a classmate to demonstrate how to close the sale when the customer says, "I'm not sure my mother will like this dress, and I'm not even sure it's her size. I'll have to come back tomorrow."

4. Prepare a memo instructing all new sales employees about the importance of suggesting related merchandise. Give the new employees a few recommendations and guidelines so they are encouraged to attempt suggestion selling.

Human Relations

5. A customer wants to return a clock radio because he was not able to set the time or the alarm. The customer is probably not aware of a memory key that must be depressed at the same time you set the time and alarm. How could this merchandise return have been avoided? How will you handle this return?

6. You promised your customer delivery two weeks from the day the order was placed. It is one week later, and you call the shipping department to check the order. You are told the department has no record of the order and cannot possibly have the goods ready for shipment next week. That means your customer will receive the merchandise one week late. What should you do?

APPLICATION PROJECTS

1. For your continuing project, write an introduction for the closing a sale step. Include a discussion of its importance and its timing. Then write five different dialogues to demonstrate when and how to close the sale for your product. Each dialogue must demonstrate a different specialized closing method.

2. For your continuing project, write an introduction for the suggestion selling step of the sale. Include a discussion of its importance and the proper timing of this step. Finally, do the following:
   - List all the related merchandise you can use for suggestion selling.
   - Write exactly what you would do and say to suggest one of the related items of merchandise. Remember to follow all the rules for suggestion selling.

3. Prepare an evaluation sheet to use in judging a sales demonstration. Include all the steps of the sale in the evaluation sheet, including *approach*, *needs determined*, *product presentation*, *handling objections*, *closing the sale*, and *suggestion selling*, as well as *departure* and *communicative ability*. Under each step of the sale, indicate exactly what should be evaluated and give total points to each criteria. The evaluation sheet should total 100 points.

4. Plan a complete sales presentation for your product. Have your teacher select a classmate to role play the part of the customer while you role play the part of the salesperson. Make your presentation in class, and ask your classmates to evaluate your sales skills.

5. Customers' body language often tells you they are ready to buy. It also tells you when they are not interested. With a partner, prepare a skit on closing a sale with one of you acting as the salesperson, the other as the customer. Using a variety of body language, present the skit to the class. (For example, have the customer respond to the salesperson with only non-verbal signals.) Have your classmates write down all the non-verbal signals they see, and tell what those signals say about the customer's willingness to buy and the salesperson's attitude.

Recording Sales

Your customer's decision to buy does not conclude the sales process. After you close the sale, you must record the transaction and present the customer with proof of your agreement and payment.

The methods of recording sales transactions vary from company to company, especially between retail and industrial firms. This chapter will briefly address those differences. Then we will concentrate on such essential retail procedures as operating a cash register, safeguarding against theft, writing out sales slips, and handling sales transactions.

Recording Sales in Different Sales Situations

In industrial sales, the salesperson and the buyer agree on the terms of the sale and record the information in a legal contract. The most common type of contract is the *purchase order*. This lists the quantity, price, and description of the products ordered, along with the terms of payment and delivery.

In other situations, especially those related to the sale of services and to construction work, the cost of materials and the payment schedule are both written in a contract. Usually, the buyer makes a down payment on the goods or services when the contract is signed. When the goods are shipped or the services completed, the seller sends an invoice for final payment.

To further explore purchase orders and invoices, see Chapters 25 and 32. In the remainder of this chapter, we will concentrate on retail sales transactions.

Cash Registers

*The **sales transaction** is the process of recording the sale and presenting the customer with proof of payment.* Most retailers today use cash registers to record sales and provide customers with receipts. Cash registers fill three important functions of sales transactions.

First, they provide a convenient way to enter information about the sale. This usually includes the department, the type of transaction, the salesperson, and the amount of the sale. On most cash registers used today, you will also enter the amount tendered by the customer. The register responds with the amount of change due.

Second, cash registers provide a convenient, organized way to keep cash, checks, charge slips, and refund slips. Coupons and other sales-related documents may also be kept in the cash register drawer.

Third, cash registers automatically provide a receipt for customers.

Electronic Cash Registers

The electronic cash registers now in common use automatically perform many functions of a sales transaction. These include totaling quantity purchases, figuring sales tax, calculating and subtracting discounts, subtracting refunds and returns, and calculating the change due the customer.

Some electronic cash registers are linked to a mainframe computer as part of an electronic *point of sale* (POS) computer system. Using this equipment,

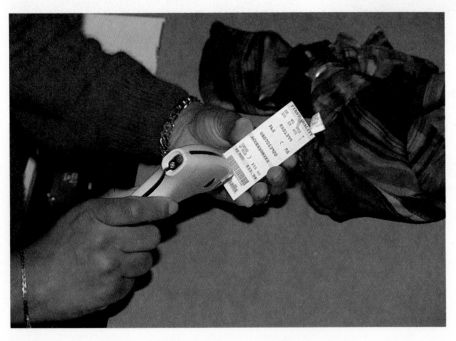

The universal product code is scanned by an electronic wand to enter sales transactions. On what types of products have you seen universal product codes?

THE DRESS SHOP
STORE NO. 26

MFG.		DEPT.
29000		01603

PRICE	SIZE	STYLE
$14.99	12	07503

29000 07503

Figure 18-1   **Universal Vendor Marketing Code**
The numbers on a UVM code provide such data as stock size and color that the salesperson enters into the cash register with an electronic wand. Give one advantage of having such stock information immediately on hand.

you can check a customer's credit electronically. The computer can update inventory records with each sales transaction and automatically reorder items in short supply. It can also print out financial statements, sales trends, and reports of sales personnel productivity.

Information on sales transactions can be entered into an electronic cash register in several different ways. The most common are *manual key entry, electronic wand entry*, and *optical scanning*.

Manual Key Entry

Even with electronic cash registers, many businesses have their salespeople enter all sales transactions manually by using the register keys. All registers provide a numeric keyboard for entry in case other input devices do not function correctly.

Electronic Wand Entry

More and more retailers (especially department and clothing stores) are using electronic wands to enter sales transactions. The salesperson simply moves the point of the wand across the data printed on a tag attached to the article sold.

Two types of codes are widely used for electronic entry. *The Universal Product Code (UPC) is a symbol which is read by an electronic wand and which appears as a series of bars and a row of numerals on the item to be scanned.* The UPC is used in most large grocery stores on most items offered—even candy bars.

The Universal Vendor Marketing (UVM) is a type of code read by an electronic wand and which appears as numbers across the top of a price tag.

With each of these codes, the wand reads the data and enters it into the electronic cash register. Then the information is transferred to a mainframe computer for further processing. In some cases the wand is not able to read the data, and the salesperson must enter the information manually.

Optical Scanning

Many supermarkets have improved their efficiency in recording sales transactions at the checkout counter by installing optical scanners. With optical scanners you do not have to enter prices manually for most items. You simply drag the item across the scanner so it can read the UPC (bar code). If the scanner cannot read the UPC, you have to key the information manually.

Both speed and accuracy of recording transactions have been improved with the optical scanners used in many supermarkets. How would this person enter the sales transaction if the scanner cannot read the code?

Cash Register Operations

Most salespeople operate a cash register. In some retail stores, including many department stores and all supermarkets, cash register operations are the responsibility of a cashier or checkout clerk.

Before you assume the responsibility of using a cash register and handling money, you will need to become familiar with all aspects of cash register operations.

Cash Drawer Arrangement

Checks and currency collected in sales transactions are generally deposited in the *till*. *The till is the cash drawer of the cash register.* There are usually five compartments in the back half of the till and five compartments in the front half. Although some companies vary the arrangement, bills are usually kept in the back half of the drawer and coins in the front.

In the section for bills, the first compartment on the left often remains empty. Sometimes it is reserved

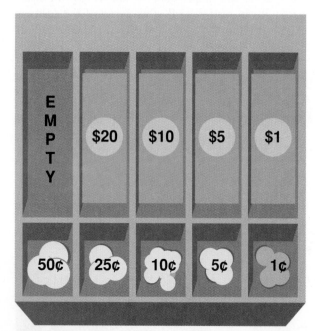

Figure 18-2 **Cash Drawer Arrangement**
Most companies arrange their cash drawers as shown here, with bills in the back and coins in the front. How does this arrangement facilitate change making?

for checks or for some special purpose. The second compartment contains $20 bills, the next one $10 bills, then $5 bills; and the last one on the right is used for $1 bills. When a customer tenders a $2 bill, it is placed under the $1 bills.

In the section for coins, the first compartment on the left is used for silver dollars and half-dollars. The next compartment is for quarters. The next one is for dimes, then nickels. The last compartment on the right is for pennies.

This arrangement facilitates change making because the $20 bills are behind the quarters, the $10 bills are behind the dimes, the $5 bills are behind the nickels, and the $1 bills are behind the pennies.

Verify Opening Change Fund

At the beginning of each business day, the manager or someone designated to do so will provide change for each cash register. *The opening change fund is the coins and currency designated for a cash register for a given day's business.* To verify the opening change fund, the designated employee first counts the coins and places them, one denomination at a time, in the correct compartment. He or she then does the same with the currency.

As the coins and currency are counted, the amount is written down to make sure the total matches the amount planned for the register. If it matches exactly, the change fund is even. If there is more than planned, the fund is over. If there is less than planned, the fund is short. If the change fund is short or over, it should be reported to the manager or person who supplied the fund.

Check for Adequate Change

If you are a salesperson who handles a large number of transactions during a business day, you may run short of change in certain denominations. Check your cash drawer during any slack time you have to see if you need any bills and/or coins. If you do, request the change you need. This preventive procedure can help you avoid delays when customers are waiting for service.

Making Change

A customer who has made a decision to buy usually wants to pay quickly and then move on. That's why accuracy and speed are of primary concern in recording sales. If you work as efficiently as possible, taking great care to make the proper change, you will usually be able to keep your customer happy. Each step of the transaction should show the customer that you have control of the situation.

As soon as you have entered the transaction in the cash register, announce to the customer the total amount of the sale, such as "$17.65." When the customer offers payment in cash, announce the amount tendered, such as, "Out of $20." Then place the money on the shelf above the cash drawer. Leave it there until you have given change to the customer. This eliminates most disputes over the amount tendered.

Use as few coins as possible in making change. Count all change silently as you remove coins and currency from the cash drawer. The most common method is to count up from the purchase price, taking out the smallest denominations of coins and currency first. Then repeat the same procedure as you count aloud and hand the customer change. For example, if a customer hands you $20 in payment for a purchase totaling $17.65, count and return change by saying "17.65 out of $20, $17.75 (giving the customer a dime), $18 (giving a quarter), $19 and $20 (giving two one-dollar bills, one at a time).

Many customers try to avoid getting a lot of small change by tendering an odd amount of change to pay for their purchases. For example, if a sale totals

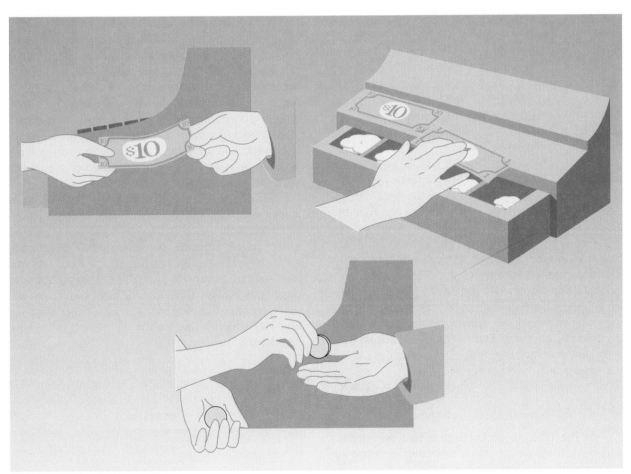

Figure 18-3 **Making Change**
When making change, name the amount of money received from the customer. Leave the money on the shelf above the cash drawer until you have given the change to the customer. Count up from the purchase price to the amount of payment. Why is it essential to work as quickly and efficiently as possible when making change?

$18.39, the customer may give you a $20 bill and 39 cents. The amount tendered is $20.39. Use the 39 cents to cancel the "odd cents" of the sale, and give change for the $20 bill. If the customer tenders $20 and two quarters for the $18.39 sales, count the odd cents first. Say, "18.39 out of $20.50." Then count, "That's 40 cents (giving a penny), 50 cents (giving a dime)." Finally, count the bills, $19 and $20 (giving two one-dollar bills, one at a time).

If you are not sure how to handle an odd-cent transaction, write down the amount tendered ($20.50) and subtract the amount of the sale ($18.39). Then both you and the customer can see that the change is correct.

On newer cash registers that calculate and display the amount of change, it is easier to begin with the largest denomination. For a $17.65 purchase, for example, the register will display $2.35 due the customer. Select the change from the cash drawer by taking out two one-dollar bills, a quarter and a dime. Because the customer knows (from the display) exactly how much change is due, you can count it out the same way.

Balancing Cash

At the close of each business day, salespeople and cashiers who use a cash register must account for the day's sales and money. Newer registers automatically keep a sales *tally* (a summary of the day's sales). This makes the job much simpler. The person responsible for each register counts the money, fills out a brief closing balance report, removes the tape from the cash register, and sends the money, report, and tape to a central office.

Some cash registers do not keep an automatic sales tally. If your company uses one of these registers, then sales slips may be written for each sale and the information recorded on a tally sheet after each transaction. At the end of the day, sales must be reviewed.

Safeguards Against Theft

Every employee who uses a cash register should be familiar with some safeguards against the theft of money. The number one rule is *always close the cash drawer between transactions*. Even while you are counting change to a customer, you should partially close the register drawer. After giving change, remove the money tendered by the customer from the register itself, place it in the drawer, and close it. Rule number two is *if you leave the register, lock it*.

You may occasionally encounter a customer who interrupts you while you are counting change. In a rare case, the person might be trying to distract you in the hope that you will make incorrect change in his or her favor. More often, however, the customer may make a sincere request or ask a question that breaks your concentration. In any case, ignore the interruption while you are making change. You can politely address the customer's request or answer a question once the transaction has been completed.

From time to time, counterfeit bills show up in almost every city. Every company has, or should have, printed information on how to identify counterfeit money. There are some common tip-offs. Legal bills, for example, have crisp portraits on the front side and tiny colored threads in the paper. The portraits on counterfeit bills are often not as crisp looking, and the paper usually does not have threads. Other information varies, depending on the counterfeit bills being circulated.

Sales Slips

More businesses are using electronic cash registers and point of sale computer systems, so fewer are using sales slips. Writing out sales slips takes more time than scanning or keying in a sales transaction on a register. Still, there are times when they prove beneficial.

Sales slips, for instance, provide the company with information that is not otherwise available, such as address, phone number, date, and time of purchase. They also give the customer an itemized receipt. If you use sales slips, at the time of the sale you should fill in all the information requested by the company. It is very difficult to accurately reconstruct a sales transaction sometime later.

Companies that use sales slips often have a metal or plastic register that contains a supply of continuous sales slips in duplicate or triplicate form. When a slip is completed, you simply pull a handle and eject one or two copies. A second or third copy is kept inside the sales register, and a new sales slip moves into place for the next transaction.

Some businesses use a sales slip book that contains two or three copies of each form. You can use it in the same way as a sales slip register.

Types of Sales Transactions

As a salesperson or cashier, you will handle several types of sales transactions. Most will be cash or charge sales. Variations include *discount sales*, *layaway*, or *will-call sales*, *on-approval sales*, and *COD sales*. You will also be dealing with *returns*, *exchanges*, and *allowances*.

C A S E   C H A L L E N G E

Selling Beauty the Mary Kay Way

Mary Kay Ash worked for 25 years in direct sales. But she had a dream of founding a company that would give women unlimited opportunity for growth and advancement. So, she founded Mary Kay Cosmetics in 1963 with only $5,000 from her savings account and a lot of determination.

Today there are 185,000 independent Mary Kay beauty consultants. Each one works for herself, buying products from Mary Kay. Their commission is 40 to 60 percent of the retail price of the products.

To sell her products, each consultant arranges skin care classes in the home of a hostess, who invites no more than five friends. The consultant gives the guests a two-hour demonstration of Mary Kay cosmetics. The women get to try the products in a relaxed atmosphere among friends. The consultant usually sells some of her products.

She also tries to interest others in becoming Mary Kay consultants. A consultant gets a bonus for each new beauty consultant she recruits, as well as a percentage of the newcomer's sales.

There are other bonuses, too. For example,

to receive a new Pontiac Grand Am, a consultant must sell $600 (wholesale) worth of cosmetics every month for 4 months. During that time, she must also recruit at least 8 active consultants. Her recruits must sell a total of $3,000 a month for those 4 months.

Women who sell and recruit well often become Sales Directors, managing and training the consultants they recruit. When their unit (consultants they have recruited) sells $90,000 (wholesale) worth of Mary Kay products for two consecutive quarters, the Sales Director is awarded a pink Cadillac.

Mary Kay Sales Directors can make up to $100,000 a year. A third of them have made more than a million dollars in commissions during their careers.

1. Why is it important for a Mary Kay consultant to keep a careful record of her recruit's sales?
2. What method of recording sales would you expect Mary Kay consultants to use? Why?
3. How do you think Mary Kay customers will probably pay for their purchases?

Cash Sales

A cash sale is a transaction during which the customer pays for his or her purchase(s) by cash or check. The simplest cash sale occurs when the customer tenders cash. In this case, you simply record the transaction on the register, give the customer change and a cash register receipt, and wrap up the package.

Each business has its own rules about accepting checks, and you will have to follow the check policy of the company or store where you work. When your customer writes a check, you will probably need to verify one or two forms of identification. Most businesses request a driver's license and a major credit card.

In most establishments, you will give the portion of the cash register tape showing the transaction to the customer. In other businesses, you will write a sales slip to provide the accounting department with more information than the cash register records. A customer, too, may request a sales slip—especially if the cash register tape does not provide an itemized list of purchases.

Charge Sales

Most businesses today accept one or more of the major credit cards, such as Visa, MasterCard, and American Express. Many large oil companies and department stores issue their own credit cards in addition to accepting the major credit cards. The goal is to make it easier for the general public to shop. This, of course, increases sales.

Credit cards have become an efficient, popular alternative to more traditional forms of payment. Some people, however, abuse the privilege of using a credit card by charging more than they can pay. So,

Credit cards have become efficient, popular alternatives to more traditional forms of payment. Why do you think stores have a floor limit on credit card charges?

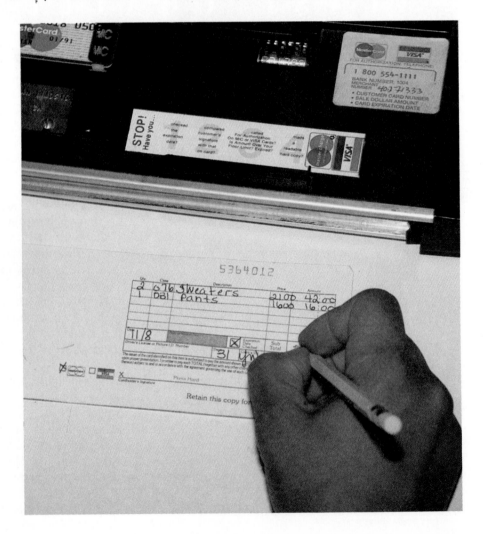

many businesses, especially retail stores, have a set limit on credit card charges. *The floor limit is the maximum amount a salesperson may allow a customer to charge without special authorization.* Usually, the manager or credit department must approve charges that exceed the floor limit.

To confirm that a customer has been approved to charge the amount of a sale, more and more businesses are using electronic credit authorizers. Many point-of-sale electronic cash register systems, in fact, include an integrated credit authorizer. Some electronic credit authorizers are separate pieces of equipment, smaller than a telephone, that read data encoded on credit cards. The data is transmitted to a computer, and approval or disapproval is usually received in less than a minute.

Companies that do not use electronic credit authorizers check for approval of charges in other ways. With a major credit card, for example, you may wait while a salesperson calls a central authorization telephone number for approval of charges. Or the salesperson may look for your credit card number on a list of delinquent account numbers. The electronic credit authorizers are the most efficient, and they don't keep the customer waiting long.

Discount Sales

Some customers do not pay full price for their purchases. *A discount sale is a reduced price for customers who qualify.* Many businesses, for example, extend discounts on company products to all their employees. These usually range from 10 to 30 percent off the retail price, depending on the type of product and company policy. A business may also grant price breaks to non-employees, including senior citizens and long-standing customers.

Discounts also play a significant role in industrial sales. A large corporation, for instance, may offer quantity discounts to suppliers who buy in bulk. Or it may offer service discounts for buyers who call for or send trucks for their orders, thus saving the company freight charges. The amount of such price savings depends on a number of factors, including the product, size of the order, and time of year the order is placed.

Layaway or Will-Call Sales

With layaway (also known as will-call), the merchandise is removed from stock and kept in a separate storage area until the customer pays for it. Many department stores sell clothing on layaway. This ap-

peals to many shoppers, so it often increases sales. Usually, the customer makes a deposit on the merchandise. He or she must agree to pay for the purchase within a certain time period. The customer may have the merchandise when it is fully paid for. If it is not paid for within the agreed-upon time, the goods are returned to stock.

On-approval Sales

Some department stores and specialty stores extend a special privilege—*on-approval sale*—to their regular customers. *An on-approval sale is an agreement that permits a customer to take merchandise, usually clothing, home for further consideration.* If the goods are not returned within an agreed-upon time, the sale is final. The customer must then send a check or pay for the merchandise at the store.

COD Sales

A COD (cash on delivery) sale is a transaction that occurs when a customer pays for merchandise at the time of delivery. Before credit cards gained widespread use, many mail-order catalog sales were shipped COD. Some department stores and other businesses still ship merchandise COD. But because the customer must be on hand when the merchandise is delivered, COD sales are not as efficient as other types of sales transactions.

Returns, Exchanges, and Allowances

A return is merchandise brought back for a cash refund or credit. Customers return merchandise for various reasons. Perhaps they received a gift they don't particularly need. Perhaps they do not have an immediate use for a product they initially thought they needed.

An exchange is merchandise brought back to be replaced by other merchandise. Items of clothing that are the wrong size or color are commonly exchanged.

An allowance is a partial return of the sale price for merchandise that the customer has kept. These are usually given when there is a defect in the merchandise.

Each of these will require you to do a different type of sales transaction. We will talk more about returns, exchanges, and allowances in Chapter 28.

VOCABULARY REVIEW

Write one to three paragraphs incorporating these fourteen vocabulary terms.

sales transaction	discount sale
UPC	layaway
UVM	on-approval sale
till	COD
opening change fund	return
cash sale	exchange
floor limit	allowance

FACT AND IDEA REVIEW

1. Once a customer has decided to buy an item, what steps are involved in the sales transaction?

2. What information does a cash register provide about a sale?

3. What does a point of sale computer system do?

4. List the three methods of entering information into electronic cash registers.

5. What is a UPC?

6. Describe the typical arrangement of cash in a cash register drawer.

7. What is the first thing you should do when you receive the opening change fund?

8. What two factors are most important to the customer about the way you make change?

9. What information does a tally provide?

10. With a cash register that calculates total sales for the day, what does the person responsible for that register need to do at the end of the day?

11. To protect against theft, what are the two cardinal rules about using a cash register?

12. What is the disadvantage of using sales slips to record sales?

13. What is usually required when making a purchase by check?

14. What is an electronic credit authorizer?

15. What happens to an item purchased on layaway?

CRITICAL THINKING

1. Why is the money in a cash drawer always arranged the same way?

2. In what stores have you noticed that salesclerks use electronic wands to record sales?

3. When is a good time during the day to check that the cash register has enough change?

4. What is the end-of-day tally? How is it calculated?

5. What happens at the end of the day if the amount of cash in the register does not match the calculated sales total? If there is less cash than the sales total, should the difference be taken out of the salesclerk's or cashier's paycheck?

6. When the bank allows a business to accept credit card payment from its customers, the bank customarily charges the business a fee. As a business owner, would you consider it worth the extra expense?

7. What types of goods are you still likely to purchase COD?

USING BASIC SKILLS

Math

1. Obtain or make a set of "play" money. Using the old-fashioned method in which the cash register does not calculate the amount of change due the customer, count the change aloud for:
   - a $15 payment for a $13.22 purchase
   - a $70 payment for a $67.43 purchase
   - a $40.50 payment for a $39.40 purchase
   - a $10.27 payment for an $8.27 purchase
   - a $25.75 payment for a $23.64 purchase

2. A department store offers a 20 percent discount for senior citizens. If your grandmother purchased items at $17.99, $15.95, and $3.59, what is her total bill?

Communication

3. Practice writing out a sales slip. What information should you include?
4. Imagine you work as an order taker for a mail order business called Endless Gadgets. List the information you need from your customers to take their orders. Then choose one other person in class. Practice a dialogue between you and a customer calling in an order.

Human Relations

5. You work as a cashier, and today has been exceptionally busy. You give change to a woman for a $10 bill. She claims she gave you a $20 bill. Unfortunately, you neglected to leave the bill out while making change. Do you assume the error? Do you take her word for it? Do you call the manager?
6. A children's clothing store uses an old-fashioned cash register that requires entering the amount of each sale by hand. One of the salespeople often enters the amount incorrectly. This means you have to take extra time at the end of the day to reconcile the difference between the amount of money taken in and the amount of recorded sales. What would you do to improve the salesperson's accuracy?

APPLICATION PROJECTS

1. Get information at the library about the grocery store conversion to optical scanners. How does the increased speed and accuracy of these systems affect a grocery store's profits?
2. Ask class members to visit the school office, the school bookstore, the school cafeteria, and any other place in the school where there is a cash register. Under the supervision of a school staff member, observe the arrangement of the cash in the drawer. Does it match the description in your text? Report back to the class.
3. Using information from the library or from the computer instructor in your school, find out what the bars and numbers in the UPC represent.
4. Call your local police department for advice about identifying counterfeit money and what to do if you suspect it.
5. Credit cards can be stolen and used fraudulently. What steps would you take to prevent someone from using a card fraudulently? What do you think you should do if someone tries to use a stolen credit card?
6. Have someone in the police department's fraud division come out to your school and talk to your class about the different ways con artists can switch money, distract salespeople, and pass bad checks.
7. Discuss the ways that a store manager might train employees to prevent loss through credit card fraud, bad checks, and counterfeit currency.

PART

5

PROMOTION

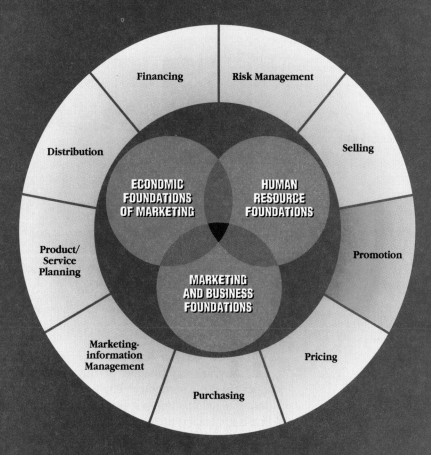

Financing

Risk Management

Distribution

Selling

ECONOMIC
FOUNDATIONS
OF MARKETING

HUMAN
RESOURCE
FOUNDATIONS

Product/
Service
Planning

Promotion

MARKETING
AND BUSINESS
FOUNDATIONS

Marketing-
information
Management

Pricing

Purchasing

CHAPTERS

19

After completing this chapter, you will be able to:

1. explain the role of promotion in selling,

2. identify the various types of promotion,

3. tell why promotional mix is important, and

4. explain the use of brands.

promotion
advertising
publicity
image
sales promotion
premiums
contests
sweepstakes
rebate
product sample
promotional mix
brand
generic products

What Is Promotion?

How do you find out about new breakfast cereals, this year's car models, or the good things an organization does for the community? The first thing that probably comes to mind is advertising—television, radio, and newspaper. Advertising is a special type of communication that we call promotion.

In this chapter you will learn about the role of promotion in selling. You will be introduced to the various forms of promotion that businesses use and explore the concept of promotional mix. Finally, you will see how the use of brand names and trademarks helps promote products.

The Role of Promotion

***Promotion** is any form of communication a business or organization uses to inform, persuade, or remind people about its products and improve its public image.* Typically, a business uses promotion to convince potential customers to buy from it instead of from a competitor. In doing this, the business also

- explains the major features and benefits of its products,
- tells where those products are sold,
- advertises sales on those products,
- answers customer queries,
- introduces new products, and
- creates a favorable image for itself (especially in relation to competitors).

Promotion is an important part of our economy. Every year, U.S. automakers spend $2 billion on promotion. U.S. retailers spend $1.5 billion. Nationwide almost 8 million people are employed in sales or sales support. Some 200 billion coupons are issued annually, and more than $200 million in sweepstakes prizes are awarded.

Types of Promotion

There are four basic types of promotion: *advertising*, *publicity*, *sales promotion*, and *personal selling*.

Advertising

***Advertising** is the nonpersonal presentation and promotion of ideas, goods, and services by an identified sponsor.* Advertising is distinguished from other forms of promotion by three features:

1. The time or space devoted to it is paid for.
2. It uses a set format to carry the message rather than personal, one-on-one selling.
3. It identifies the sponsor of the message.

More than $3.6 billion was spent by the 100 leading advertisers in 1987. This figure does not in-clude the millions of dollars spent by smaller companies and independent businesses throughout the United States.

Businesses spend so much on advertising because it offers these six advantages:

1. A large number of people usually see the advertiser's message.
2. Advertising costs per potential customer (whether that customer is a viewer, reader, or listener) are usually low.
3. Businesses can choose the most appropriate media to reach their target market, since there are many different ways to advertise (billboards, newspapers, radio, and television, to name a few).
4. A business can control the content of an advertisement and adapt it to the medium and method of presentation.
5. Advertisements integrated into television shows, magazines, or newspapers are subject to repeat viewing. This fixes the advertiser's message in people's minds.
6. Advertisements can "presell" products—that is, they can influence people to make up their minds about a purchase before they shop.

Businesses favor advertising as a promotional device because it allows them to reach large numbers of potential customers. What is the target market for this ad? What advantages does this form of advertising have over word-of-mouth?

As overwhelming as its advantages might seem, advertising has four principal drawbacks.

1. Advertising cannot focus on individual needs because the message is the same for all customers.
2. Some forms of advertising, such as television, can be too expensive for many businesses.
3. In certain respects, advertising is wasteful and inefficient. Newspaper ads, for example, are seen only by people who read newspapers; television ads, only by viewers of specific shows.
4. Because of the cost and the need to attract and hold the attention of potential customers, advertisements must be brief—too brief to inform in depth. Other forms of promotion—personal sales presentations, for example—can be far more complete.

A more detailed explanation of advertising, its purposes, and the various forms available is given in Chapter 20.

Publicity

Publicity involves creating demand for a business or product by placing news about it in publications or on radio, television, or stage. A business can use publicity to promote particular events, such as the ground-breaking ceremonies for a new store, or particular products, such as a new line of computers. The principal function of publicity, however, is building an *image. Image is the way a business or organization is defined in people's minds.* It is an impression based on a combination of factors—physical surroundings, personal experiences, and things written or said in the media.

The right kind of publicity can create a positive image for a company and maintain or improve that image within the community. Examples of business activities that are pure image builders include sponsoring cultural events, such as concerts and art exhibits, awarding scholarships and prizes, and donating land or equipment for public use.

How does publicity differ from advertising? Publicity is free—at least in terms of its placement; advertising is not. A one-minute story about a company or one of its products on the evening news costs nothing. Fifteen seconds of advertising time on the same broadcast would cost a great deal.

Publicity has other advantages as well. The audience for news is huge, and the sources that produce it are held in high esteem by the public. (Newspapers, news programs, and news reporters are usually viewed as more objective than advertisers.) This means that people are more likely to pay attention to news stories than to advertisements. They are also more likely to believe news stories.

It would be inaccurate, however, to say that businesses using publicity get something for nothing. Sometimes they get just what they pay for because they give up much of their control over their message—not only the content but when and how it is presented.

Consider the case of a business owner who wants to promote the opening of a new store. She might send a *news release*—an article containing all the information about the event—to the local newspaper. What happens to the article from that point on is totally out of her hands. The newspaper could decide that the story is not newsworthy and ignore it. The paper could run the story but bury it in the back of a section where few will see it. Finally, the paper could run the story in a prominent place, but only as a two-sentence announcement omitting most of the details that the business owner considers essential.

Why risk any of these outcomes? The price is right. If the story runs in any form, the business owner gets the benefits of promoting her enterprise without having to pay for advertising space in the paper.

There is at least one other key risk associated with the use of publicity. Not all publicity is positive. Negative stories can hurt a company's image. Consider the following actual case.

In 1988, ARA Mesa Verde Company published a visitors' brochure listing all of its hotels, restaurants, and campgrounds near Mesa Verde National Park in Colorado. The brochure became an instant source of controversy among local residents. What caught their attention were three words on the back panel: *Printed in Japan.* Why, residents wondered, was the printing done abroad? As it turned out, ARA had ordered the printing to be done by a California company, but that firm had subcontracted the work to a Japanese supplier. As a result, ARA had to answer some tough questions about why it was not doing business with local firms. To make matters worse, the story was picked up by Associated Press and run in newspapers throughout the country. ARA's image suffered locally and nationally.

To avoid such problems (or to repair the damage when they do occur), larger companies have *public relations* departments. The people in these departments write news releases and plan events designed to present a favorable image of the company. Maintaining a staff to do this kind of work represents one of the costs associated with publicity.

Sales Promotion

Sales promotion is the use of marketing devices, such as displays, premiums, and contests, to stimulate purchases. It includes such special events as fashion shows and vendor demonstrations. It does *not* include personal or face-to-face selling (you will look at this further on page 209), advertising, or publicity. The objectives of sales promotion are to increase customer traffic (and thus sales), to inform customers about new products and policies, and to create a positive store image.

Displays. Window, floor, and counter displays are all forms of visual merchandising. By exposing potential customers firsthand to a company's products, displays stimulate sales and serve as in-store advertisements. A complete discussion of visual merchandising and display can be found in Chapter 22.

Premiums. The most popular and frequently used sales promotion devices at the consumer level are premiums. *Premiums are prizes or rewards offered to a customer as an added inducement to make a purchase.* They are designed to increase sales by building product loyalty, attracting new customers, and increasing store traffic.

There are three main types of premiums.

1. *Trading Stamps* are printed stamps, each of which represents a certain amount of money. S&H green stamps and Blue Chip stamps are two familiar types of trading stamps. The stamps are given to customers based on the total amount of their purchases. The customers save the stamps and later redeem them for merchandise such as towels, dinnerware, or encyclopedias.
2. *Coupons* are certificates given to customers, entitling them to cash discounts or merchandise. Manufacturers use coupons to introduce new products, to enhance the sales of existing products, and to encourage retailers to stock and display both. Retailers and service businesses use coupons to introduce a grand

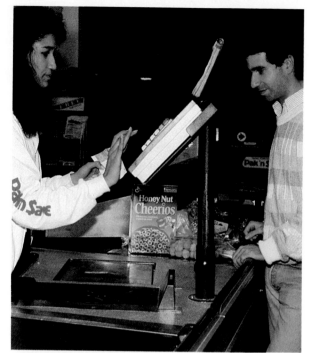

Manufacturers pay retailers a handling charge for redeeming coupons. What costs do you think this charge is designed to cover?

opening, to invite new customers to visit or call, and to encourage repeat business by current customers. Coupons reach potential customers through a variety of routes. They are placed on or inside product packages, printed in newspapers and magazines, and sent through the mail. Most retailers use the mail; manufacturers use all three methods.
3. *Factory packs* are free gifts placed in product packages. This form of premium is especially popular with cereal manufacturers, who use it to increase their products' appeal to children. A variation on this is having the customer return one or several proof-of-purchase seals from a product in exchange for a gift or rebate.

Of these three promotional devices, coupons are probably the most popular. For example, according to the Manufacturers' Coupon Center in Clinton, Iowa, manufacturers issued more than 200 billion coupons in the United States in 1986. Consumers redeemed 7.32 billion of these coupons and in so doing saved themselves nearly $3 billion.

CASE CHALLENGE

Using Your Potato Head

What makes a successful promotion? Consider one of the most successful—the campaign by Wendy's International to promote its Kids' Meals by giving away six different Potato Head Kids playmates.

Made by Playskool, the toys came free with the purchase of a Kid's Meal—a two-ounce hamburger, "small-fry" fries, and a small soft drink. In each Kid's Meal box there was one synthetic potato head with arms attached plus a removable hat and feet.

The target market for the premium was kids. However, as one Wendy's vice-president put it, "With every child comes a parent." Obviously, the parents were impressed as well. More than 50 percent of parents surveyed in a Wendy's poll said the premiums influenced their decision to dine at Wendy's—an extraordinarily high percentage. Wendy's has four to eight such Kid's Meals promotions each year—a pace matched by its competitors in the fast food industry.

1. As a premium, into which category would Wendy's Potato Head Kids fall?
2. What other groups besides young children and their parents do you think might have been attracted to this particular promotion? Why?
3. If you were a Wendy's vice-president and you wanted to design a promotion to appeal to teens, what sorts of things would you suggest? In each case, explain your reasoning.
4. List any potential problems you see in running eight such promotions a year.

Of course, there are costs involved in using premiums. These costs are ultimately paid by the businesses offering them. With coupons, for example, the stores accepting manufacturers' coupons send them to their company headquarters or to a clearinghouse to be sorted and passed along to redemption centers. The centers, in turn, reimburse the stores for the face value of each coupon plus a handling charge of about 8 cents per coupon. They then bill the manufacturers.

Contests, Sweepstakes, and Rebates. Many products are promoted through contests and sweepstakes. These are used by businesses to create excitement and interest and thereby generate sales.

Contests are games or activities that require the participant to demonstrate a skill. This can include writing a short story or essay about a product, naming a new product, or creating a new advertising slogan. Contest winners are awarded such prizes as all-expense paid trips and money.

A sweepstakes is a game of chance. It requires no skill. For example, customers at fast-food restaurants may be given a game card with or without a purchase. They must then scrape away a section of the card to win a free product or collect a number of cards to qualify for a prize. By law in most states, customers cannot be required to make a purchase in order to enter a contest or sweepstakes.

Rebates are discounts offered by manufacturers for purchasing an item during a given time period. Auto and household appliance manufacturers frequently make use of rebates to encourage customers to buy their products.

Product Samples. Another form of sales promotion is the product sample. *A product sample is a free trial size of a product that is sent through the mail, distributed door-to-door, or through retail stores and trade shows.* Detergents, toothpastes, shampoos, deodorants, and colognes are frequently promoted this way.

Samples are especially important in promoting new products. Drug manufacturers frequently give samples to doctors and dentists to try with their patients. Teachers sometimes receive sample textbooks to encourage them to buy classroom sets.

Sales promotions such as premiums, contests, and sweepstakes have several advantages in common. Each device is unique and has eye appeal for the potential customer. Each gives the customer something of value and thereby helps promote store traffic and maintain product loyalty. As a result, buying often increases. In certain cases, as with a contest or sweepstakes, the customer has fun in the process.

There are some disadvantages to sales promotions, however. They are often difficult to end without the customers becoming dissatisfied (or at least disappointed that the promotion is finished). If the promotion is not properly planned and managed, store image and sales can suffer. Finally, sales promotions are only designed to supplement other promotional efforts and cannot make up for poor products.

Personal Selling

Advertising, publicity, and sales promotion are forms of *nonpersonal selling*—communicating with customers in ways other than through direct contact. The remaining way for a business to communicate with its customers is through *personal selling*—making an oral sales presentation to one or more potential buyers. It is the principal responsibility of sales personnel.

There are two types of sales personnel—*order-taking* and *order-getting*.

Order-taking personnel, such as cashiers, counter clerks, and sales associates, perform routine tasks. At the retail level, they set up displays, stock shelves, answer customer inquiries, and operate cash registers. Industrial order takers usually work with customers over the telephone.

Order-getting personnel, such as professional salespeople, are more involved in informing customers and helping them to buy. Generally, order-getting sales personnel sell big-ticket consumer items, such as real estate, automobiles, home appliances, and industrial goods and services. They usually receive more intensive training than their order-taking counterparts.

Personal selling, whether order-taking or order-getting, is designed to complete a sale once a customer is attracted to a business by advertising, publicity, or sales promotion. If the sales presentation is done well, personal selling improves customer satisfaction. This is because the salesperson can use information gained from the personal contact to address the customer's unique concerns and problems.

Personal selling is one of the key ways a business communicates with its customers. Give one advantage and one disadvantage to personal selling.

Personal selling, then, is the most flexible and individualized of the promotion devices available to business. However, it has some obvious disadvantages. First, a salesperson can help only one person at a time. This may mean a larger sales staff is needed. Second, businesses that rely on personal selling must make sure their employees completely understand the selling process to ensure continued sales and goodwill. This may mean additional training. As a result, the cost of personal selling is likely to be higher than, say, the cost of *self-service selling* (selling in which no salesperson assists you).

The Concept of Promotional Mix

After a business establishes a promotional budget, it must determine its promotional mix. *Promotional mix is the combination of different types of promotion a business uses to persuade customers to buy its products.*

Most businesses use more than one type of promotion. For example, McDonald's uses a combination of local and national advertising; public relations and publicity efforts; sales promotions; and courteous, well-groomed sales personnel.

Each type of promotion is designed to complement the other. For example, advertising creates awareness of a business's product while publicity creates a favorable image for the business itself. Sales promotion efforts stimulate sales and reinforce advertising and selling efforts. Finally, personal selling builds on all of these previous efforts by helping the individual customer and completing the sale.

All types of promotion must be coordinated. For example, national advertising should be accompanied by local advertising so local businesses can take advantage of the national campaign. Decorations and in-store displays should be coordinated to back up the promotion. To ensure a smooth promotion, sales personnel should be made aware of premiums, trading stamps, coupons, discounts, rebates, and other promotional tools that will be used. (Sales are lost and customer dissatisfaction created when products mentioned in ads are not available or the sales staff is uninformed about the promotion.)

In large companies, the marketing department usually establishes a promotion budget, allocates resources, coordinates the campaign, and determines the right promotional mix for the company. Large companies have separate managers for advertising, personal selling, sales promotion, and public relations. In smaller businesses, these responsibilities often rest with the owner-operator or are shared with one or two people responsible for all the promotional activities.

Brands

An important part of promotion is the use of brands. *A brand is a name, design, or symbol that identifies the products of a company or group of companies.* Brands are good promotional devices because they help customers identify with a company and its products.

Products that do not carry a brand name are called generic products. These are often found in supermarkets. In general, such products are lower in price. They receive little or no advertising.

In marketing, there are four brand categories:

1. A *brand name* is a word or group of words that identifies a product and indicates a standard of quality and price. Some examples are Kleenex, Pepsi, Arby's, Imperial, Miracle Whip, and Cup-a-Soup. Since brand-named products are advertised extensively, they usually cost more than similar unbranded merchandise.
2. A *brand mark* is a symbol or design with distinctive coloring or lettering. Some examples of brand marks are the United States Postal Service's eagle, Ford's blue oval, Cadillac's crown and crest, and Greyhound Bus Line's greyhound.
3. A *trade character* is a personified brand mark (that is, one given human form or characteristics). Some examples include McGruff the Crime Dog, the Pillsbury Doughboy, Bird's Eye's Jolly Green Giant, and the Keebler elves.
4. A *trademark* is a brand name, brand mark, trade character, or a combination of these that is given legal protection. When used, it is followed by a registered trademark symbol. Examples include Johnson's Wax®, Raid®, VISA®, and Jif®. When brand names, brand marks, and trade characters are registered, they cannot be used by competitors.

REAL WORLD MARKETING

Brand X

Listen carefully the next time you hear a commercial for Sanka decaffeinated coffee. You will notice it is always referred to as "Sanka brand." Sanka is one of several products (like Band-Aid and Q-Tips) whose names have become synonymous with the product itself. By adding the word brand, Sanka's promoters are hoping consumers will insist on Sanka, rather than settling for "Brand X." This also protects their exclusive right to use this as a trademark.

Here are seven national brands that you will probably recognize. Which include brand names? brand marks? trade characters? Which are registered trademarks?

In creating an image for a brand, manufacturers usually employ slogans in their advertising. What images do these well-known slogans bring to mind?

"Pepsi—the choice of a new generation"
"You're in good hands with Allstate"

To compete with brand-named merchandise, some retailers establish brand names of their own called private labels. *Private labels* are merchandise lines manufactured exclusively for retailers. Many large department stores and retail chains now have their own private brand names. Examples include Dayton Hudson's "Boundary Waters," Macy's "Morgan Taylor," The Limited's "Forenza," and Saks Fifth Avenue's "Real Clothes."

Prices on private label clothing are often 30 to 50 percent lower than for name brands because stores contract with manufacturers to make their goods. The idea behind private branding is for the customer to see comparable merchandise at great savings next to brand names that are priced significantly higher. At some major department stores, private labels will soon amount to some 40 percent of all stock.

The use of branding is important in promotion for several reasons.

1. The product is well-known and easily identified by the customer. Brands sell themselves.
2. The quality of products carrying the same brand is consistent. This reduces the risk that the customer will be dissatisfied with his or her purchase.
3. The firm that manufactured the product is identified, unlike those firms manufacturing generic products. When an identified company advertises a product, the customer already knows its general characteristics.
4. Branding helps address target markets. By simply adding new brands, different markets can be reached.
5. Brand names help introduce new product lines and categories. Customers are more willing to try new products if they carry a familiar brand.

We will talk more about branding, packaging, and labeling in Chapter 36.

VOCABULARY REVIEW

Write a brief definition of each term, based on your reading of the chapter.

promotion
advertising
publicity
image
sales promotion
premiums
contests

sweepstakes
rebate
product sample
promotional mix
brand
generic products

FACT AND IDEA REVIEW

1. For what specific purposes do businesses typically employ promotion?

2. List the four basic types of promotion.

3. What features distinguish advertising from other forms of promotion?

4. What are the principal advantages and disadvantages of using publicity as a promotional device?

5. List the most common premiums offered to customers by businesses.

6. Explain the difference between a contest and a sweepstakes.

7. How do the duties of order-taking and order-getting sales personnel differ from each other?

8. "McDonald's has a good promotional mix." What does this statement mean?

9. Why is branding an important part of promotion?

10. What is the difference between a brand mark and a trademark?

CRITICAL THINKING

1. Some people think advertising is a waste of money that raises the prices of goods and services needlessly. What do you think—is the money spent on advertising justified? Provide at least two arguments to support your position.

2. Identify a situation, incident, or event that brought a local or national business negative publicity. Could the business have avoided the unfavorable outcome? Could it have limited the damage to its image? If so, how?

3. Why don't manufacturers who issue coupons simply lower the prices of their products to attract customers? What is the value of coupons to such businesses?

4. Why do many department stores carry both their own private label clothing lines and nationally recognized brands? Why not carry just one or the other?

USING BASIC SKILLS

Math

1. Promotional discounts are given to stores by manufacturers to place products in preferred locations or to pay for ads, displays, or in-store demonstrations. Calculate the store's cost to stock the following items and the percentage of the discount given.

Item	Purchase Amount	Discount Amount	Net Cost to Store	Percent of Discount
Bicycles	$4,570	$95	_____	_____
Snowmobiles	$15,995	$480	_____	_____

Communication

2. Skim an issue of a newspaper to find stories dealing with local or national companies. Identify each company and then categorize the publicity received as either positive or negative. Support your conclusions in each case with a paragraph or two explaining what the facts are and how their publication helps or harms the business.

Human Relations

3. Assume a regular customer of Trendy Department Store visited the store's sportswear department three successive Friday nights. On each occasion, the customer found the salesclerks using the department phone for personal calls. This has inconvenienced her only once (the other two times she was just browsing). Nonetheless, she brought this situation to the store's attention. As manager of the sportswear department, how would you handle the complaint?

APPLICATION PROJECTS

1. Make a list of ten companies and their advertising slogans. Try to include firms that have related products. Do the slogans have anything in common? Identify any similarities or differences you see in the approaches the various companies take.

2. Identify three businesses in your community that use order-getting sales personnel and three that use order-taking sales personnel. Interview someone in each kind of position. Ask them what they like most (and least) about their work. Have them describe the nature and duration of any training they received. Finally, ask them what things they have found most impress (or disturb) the buying public.

3. Plan a promotion for a product of your choice.

   a. As thoroughly as possible, describe the market you want to reach. Include information on people's ages, occupations, income, education, hobbies, etc.

   b. Describe what public image you would like your product to have.

   c. Choose a name, brand mark, and trade character for your product, explaining why you think each will appeal to your market audience.

   d. Consider the most important benefit or aspect of your product. Create a slogan, bearing in mind the image you want to project.

   e. Describe where you will sell your product (catalog, retail store, discount store, industry). Tell why this is the best outlet to reach your chosen market.

   f. Decide whether you will depend on order-taking personnel (cashiers and clerks) or order-getting personnel (salespeople) to sell your product. Explain your choice.

   g. What kind of premiums might you offer to promote your product? What kind of premiums would not be suitable?

20

After completing this chapter, you will be able to:

1. define advertising and explain its purposes,

2. identify the various types of advertising media (along with their advantages and disadvantages),

3. calculate media costs, and

4. suggest some standards for selecting promotional media.

WORDS TO KNOW

promotional advertising
institutional advertising
media
print media
broadcast media
specialty media
milline rate
network radio advertising
national spot radio advertising
local radio advertising

Advertising Media

In the United States alone, advertising is a multibillion dollar business. Take a look at your own daily life. Advertising is everywhere—on television and radio, in magazines and newspapers, on billboards and buses.

Why do businesses spend so much money on advertising? (What, in fact, does it cost to advertise?) How do businesses select the right media to advertise their products? In this chapter, you will learn the answers to these questions.

Advertising and Its Purpose

Recall from the previous chapter that advertising is the paid, nonpersonal promotion of ideas and products by an identified sponsor. To reach customers, advertising uses a set format that is defined in terms of time (a 30-second television commercial) or space (a half-page newspaper ad). In addition to product information, advertising always identifies the name of the business that paid for it.

The main purpose of advertising is to present its message so well that the customer will buy the product or accept the idea presented. In doing so, advertising also gives people the essential information they need to decide whether or not to buy. It identifies the product and its special features, gives its price, and tells where it can be found. It may also tell when the business selling the product is open.

There are two main types of advertising—*promotional* and *institutional*. *Advertising designed to increase sales is known as promotional advertising.* It helps businesses by

- creating an interest in products,
- introducing new products,
- presenting product information,
- supporting personal selling efforts,
- introducing new businesses, and
- creating new markets.

Promotional advertising does have limitations, however. It cannot improve a bad product, and it is unlikely to change the mind of any customer who has already decided to purchase another product.

Institutional advertising creates a favorable impression and goodwill for a business or an organization. It does this by presenting information about a company's role in the community, important public issues, and topics of general interest, such as public health and education.

Types of Media

Advertising messages are presented to the public through *media.* *Media are the agencies, means, or instruments used to convey messages.* There are three general categories of advertising media: *print media*, *broadcast media*, and *specialty media*.

Print Media

Print media include everything from newspapers and magazines to direct mail pieces, signs, and billboards. Print media advertisements are done in written form. They are among the oldest types of advertising and are still among the most effective.

Newspaper Advertising. Newspapers are the main form of print media for many businesses. Most newspapers are local or national dailies or weeklies. Local newspapers are distributed to local subscribers or sold through local vendors. National newspapers, such as *USA Today* and the *Christian Science Monitor*, are also sold to subscribers or through vendors but are distributed to larger regional markets throughout the country. Newspapers called *shoppers* contain little or no editorial content and are delivered free to all households in a certain area. (Grocery stores often use shoppers to advertise weekly specials and sales.)

Newspaper advertising is popular because it offers a business four advantages.

1. Newspapers have a large readership and a high level of reader involvement. These characteristics are an outgrowth of content. Newspapers carry daily news items and manufacturers' coupons—both of which attract readers.
2. Newspaper circulation is known, so businesses using them can target their advertising to people living in certain geographical areas.
3. The cost of newspaper advertising is relatively low because the quality of paper and print is less expensive than, say, the quality of paper and print used in magazines and direct mail pieces. Also, some of the publishing costs are paid by the subscribers.
4. Ads can be timely because deadlines are as short as 24 to 48 hours before the paper goes to print.

Newspaper advertising has three limitations.

1. There is sometimes wasted circulation (as when papers are sent to a wider area than the target market).
2. The life of an advertisement is limited because in most households newspapers are thrown away daily.

3. The quality of reproduction is poor in relation to other media. The black-and-white format of most newspaper advertisements makes them generally less appealing than other print media. However, color is becoming more common in such ads, despite its increased cost.

Magazine Advertising. Magazines are classified into local, regional, and national weeklies, monthlies, and quarterlies. Local and regional magazines are often developed for cities or metropolitan areas. They usually promote local entertainment, restaurants, and businesses in their immediate geographical area. Many national magazines have regional editions and rates. *Field and Stream*, for example, has seven regional editions.

Examples of national weeklies include such news magazines as *Business Week*, *Time*, and *News-*

Publication in a magazine extends the life of an ad by exposing readers to it again and again for as long as they own the periodical. For what kinds of products is this long-term exposure helpful? For what kinds is it less advantageous?

week. Special interest magazines include *Sports Illustrated*, *Good Housekeeping*, *Better Homes and Gardens*, *Reader's Digest*, and trade journals such as *Women's Wear Daily*.

Magazine advertising closely follows newspaper advertising in popularity because of the four major advantages it offers.

1. You can select your audience because the circulation and characteristics of regular readers are known.
2. Magazines are often read more slowly and thoroughly than newspapers, so the information in an ad is more likely to be grasped and retained.
3. The print quality in magazines is higher than that in newspapers.
4. Magazines have a long life because they are generally kept for an extended period of time, during which they (and the ads in them) may be reread.

Despite these advantages, there are three drawbacks to magazine advertising.

1. Compared to newspapers, magazines have less mass appeal within a geographical area.
2. Compared to newspaper advertising, magazine advertising is more expensive.
3. The ads in magazines usually are not as timely as those in daily newspapers because the deadline for inserting ads is often many months before publication. Also, the immediate impact of a magazine advertisement on a product's sales is harder to measure than that of newspaper advertising.

Direct Mail Advertising. Direct mail advertising, as its name suggests, is sent by businesses directly to prospective customers. According to the Direct Mail Advertising Association, direct mail sells more than $80 billion in goods and services annually for local and national advertisers.

Types of direct mail advertising include newsletters, credit card solicitation mailings, catalogs, coupons, samplers, price lists, circulars, invitations to special sales or events, and postage-paid reply cards and letters. Local businesses often enclose direct mail pieces with their monthly bills and statements. Nationally, large retailers and manufacturers often send direct mail catalogs and price lists to prospective customers.

One of the most important considerations in direct mail advertising is the mailing list used. It can be assembled by the advertiser from current customer records or purchased from a direct mail specialty firm that sells lists of potential customers. Whatever its source, however, the list must be accurate. Otherwise, a large part of the expense incurred for the mailing will be wasted.

Here are four advantages of direct mail advertising.

1. The advertiser can be highly selective about who will receive the mailing.
2. The advertiser can be flexible about the timing of the mailing.
3. The advertiser has a wide choice of advertisement forms (letters, coupons, etc).
4. The advertiser can keep competitors from seeing the advertisement.

Direct mail advertising has three major limitations.

1. Customer lists can become dated, in which case the advertiser will not reach the maximum number of potential customers in the target market.
2. Mailing costs are high and getting higher.
3. Many people think of direct mail advertising as "junk mail," to be discarded without opening (or at least without careful reading).

Outdoor Advertising.   Both local and national businesses use outdoor signs, or billboards, for advertising. There are two types of outdoor signs—*nonstandardized* and *standardized*.

Nonstandardized outdoor signs are used by local firms at their place of business or in other locations throughout the community. For the off-site signs, businesses usually pay rent to the owners on whose property the signs are displayed.

Standardized outdoor signs are available to local, regional, or national advertisers. Such signs are purchased from outdoor advertising companies, come in standard sizes, and are placed near highly traveled roads and freeways.

Three types of outdoor advertising are *posters*, *painted bulletins*, and *spectaculars*. Posters are pre-printed sheets put up like wallpaper on outdoor billboards. They are changed three to four times each year. Painted bulletins are painted billboards that are changed about every six months to a year. Spectacu-lars are outdoor advertising signs constructed for advertisers and contracted for a three- to five-year period. Most spectaculars use lights or moving parts and are situated in heavy pedestrian traffic areas, such as in densely populated metropolitan cities.

Outdoor advertising is popular with some advertisers. However, its use is declining in rural areas and on less traveled highways because of environmental and safety concerns. The signs are said to mar scenic views and distract drivers. As a result, most outdoor billboards today are confined to urban areas zoned for commercial and industrial uses.

The four advantages of outdoor advertising are that it:

1. appeals to many people at the same time,
2. is relatively inexpensive,
3. permits easy repetition of a message that works 24 hours a day, and
4. is geographically selected so it can be tailored to reach people in a given area.

The three disadvantages of outdoor advertising are:

1. the message has to be short,
2. the makeup of the audience is unknown, and
3. many people consider such advertising to be both a form of blight and a traffic hazard.

Directory Advertising.   Directory advertising is placed in alphabetical listings of households and businesses called *directories*. The best-known of these listings are telephone directories. They are commonly divided into the White Pages and a classified section known as the Yellow Pages.

In the White Pages, businesses receive a free alphabetical listing along with other commercial and non-commercial telephone customers. In the Yellow Pages, businesses pay for an alphabetical listing and, if desired, a larger ad. These appear under general headings, such as florists, physicians, recreational vehicles, or travel agencies.

Advertising in the Yellow Pages has several advantages.

1. Yellow Pages advertising is inexpensive.
2. Telephone directories are found in just about every home, so the potential audience for directory advertising is huge.
3. Telephone directories are usually kept for at least a year and are seldom thrown away until another is provided.

The Yellow Pages can place a business's ad on a virtually permanent basis in the homes of huge numbers of potential customers. Can you think of any disadvantages to advertising in the Yellow Pages?

The biggest disadvantage to Yellow Pages advertising is that directories are usually printed yearly. So, advertisers cannot change their message easily. Just like any other medium, advertisers must make sure that the entire market is covered by the directory to avoid advertising waste.

Service businesses like to use directory advertising. If you check your local Yellow Pages, you will see ads for such service providers as lawyers, electricians, plumbers, and physicians. Note that these are all people you are likely to call only when you have a problem. Because people use them infrequently, such businesses often combine directory advertising with other forms of advertising to attract customers *before* an emergency or service problem occurs.

Transit Advertising. Transit advertising uses public transportation facilities to bring advertising messages to people. It includes

- printed posters found inside buses and commuter trains,
- exterior posters on the outside of taxis and buses, and
- station posters located near or in subways and in railroad, bus, and airline terminals.

Nationwide, $100 million is spent annually on transit advertising. It has three key advantages.

1. It reaches a wide and (in the case of bus and train passengers) captive audience.
2. It is economical.
3. It has a defined market (usually an urban area).

There are three major disadvantages to transit advertising.

1. It is often unavailable in smaller towns and cities.
2. It is subject to defacement.
3. It is restricted to certain travel destinations.

Broadcast Media

Radio and television together compose the broadcast media. The average person over a lifetime of 70 years will spend nearly 10 years watching television and almost 6 years listening to the radio. So, you can see why advertising through the broadcast media is effective.

People listen to radio and watch television not only for entertainment but also to get information. In fact, people are more likely to believe the information they get from television than the information they get from the print media. Because they can both see and hear the television message, it comes alive for them.

In the United States, there are approximately 8,000 AM and FM radio stations. Most of the 800 commercial television stations are affiliated with one of three major networks—ABC, CBS, or NBC. In addition, there are some 5,000 cable television stations. Given this tremendous availability and the popularity of broadcast media, it is no surprise that many businesses use them to sell their products, despite the higher advertising costs involved. Let's take a closer look at advertising on each type of broadcast media.

CASE CHALLENGE

TV Guide

In late 1952, a newspaper publisher proposed the creation of a local television-listing magazine for Philadelphia and a number of other cities. The magazine was to feature a color section with articles of national interest along with local television listings. Many other publishers thought the idea would not work.

The first issue of *TV Guide*, as the magazine was called, appeared April 3, 1953, at a price of 15 cents. It had a circulation of 1.56 million for ten different city editions. By 1963, circulation was up to 8.5 million for 70 editions. Twenty years later, in 1988, its circulation was 17 million at 75 cents a copy for 107 editions. *TV Guide* had become one of the most popular magazines in the United States.

Businesses spend more than $33 million annually to advertise in *TV Guide*—more advertising dollars than they spend on any other magazine. Advertisers like *TV Guide* because it reaches a large audience. Unlike some magazines targeted to certain markets, *TV Guide* is read by people at every income level with every type of life-style.

1. Television listings are found in national and often in local newspapers. Give one reason why you think people would buy *TV Guide* when they already have television listings in their newspapers.

2. List three products you might find advertised in *TV Guide*. In each case, tell why you think the advertiser chose *TV Guide* as the proper advertising medium.

3. *TV Guide* itself is a product that must be advertised. On which advertising medium do you think the publication relies most heavily? Why?

Radio Advertising. It is estimated that radio reaches 96 percent of all people age 12 and over in any given week. This ability to reach a wide audience makes radio an extremely effective advertising medium.

The best times for radio advertising are in the morning, when people are driving to work, and during the afternoon or early evening, when they are coming home. These are called *prime times* for radio advertising because advertisers are guaranteed a more concentrated audience.

Radio advertisements are presented in 15-, 30-, or 60-second time slots. The messages are effective in encouraging people to buy because the announcer or actors (along with background music, jingles, and/or sound effects) add excitement, drama, or humor.

There are three key advantages to radio advertising.

1. With radio, the advertiser can select an audience (such as teenagers, various ethnic groups, farmers, etc.) by advertising on stations targeting that particular market.
2. Radio is more flexible than print advertising because messages can be changed easily. For example, an advertiser can make changes in the script for an advertising message a few days or even just a few minutes before the message is recorded.
3. Radio is a mobile medium that can be taken just about anywhere—shopping, jogging, hiking, driving, or attending sporting events.

Although there are numerous advantages to radio advertising, there are some disadvantages as well.

1. Radio advertising has a short life span. When the message is broadcast, it is gone—unless the business pays to have it rebroadcast later. (In fact, radio advertisers usually buy several time slots instead of just one.)
2. In markets where there are many stations competing for listeners, audience fragmentation is a problem. In these areas, several stations often compete for the same audience. So, potential advertisers must decide on which radio station to advertise—or advertise on several.
3. Due to the lack of visual involvement, listeners might become distracted during radio advertisements and miss some or all of the message.

Television Advertising. For many businesses, television is the ultimate advertising medium because it can communicate a message with sound, action, and color. Prime time for network television is between 7 p.m. and 11 p.m., when millions of viewers are watching.

Television has several advantages for advertisers.

1. Perhaps more than any other medium, television can pull together all the elements necessary to produce a creative advertising message. (Think of the catch-phrases and jingles you know by heart simply from hearing them on TV commercials.)
2. People are more inclined to believe what they see happen rather than what they merely read about.
3. Because it comes directly into the viewer's home, television is like door-to-door selling. It somehow seems more personal and is therefore more effective.
4. Television can reach a mass audience—millions of people nationwide.
5. A televised advertising message can be adapted to take advantage of holidays, seasonal changes, and special-events programming (such as the Super Bowl or an awards show).

There are three major disadvantages to using television as an advertising medium.

1. Television has the highest production costs of any type of media and a high dollar cost for the time used. Prime-time costs, in particular, are sometimes prohibitive. They keep many

smaller companies from using television advertising or force them to buy time in less desirable periods when fewer people are watching.

2. The audience size is not assured.
3. Many viewers consider television commercials a nuisance. Such viewers may switch channels or leave the room during commercial breaks. As a result, advertising dollars are wasted.

Specialty Media

Specialty media are relatively inexpensive novelty items with an advertiser's name printed on them. In addition to businesses, churches, schools, and charitable organizations often use specialty media to promote their services and philosophy. The items are usually given away, with no obligation attached to receiving and keeping them.

To be successful as advertising tools, specialty items must be practical, subject to frequent use, and likely to be placed in locations where they will be seen often. Common items, such as calendars, pens, pencils, memo pads, potholders, bottle openers, key chains, and luggage tags, fit this description and are

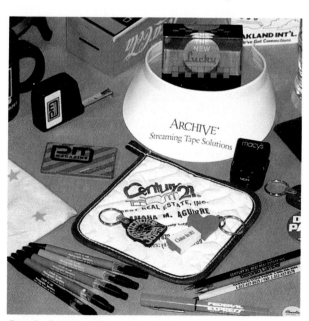

Genuinely attractive and useful specialty items do more than advertise a firm—they build goodwill. Suggest three similar items not shown or listed here that a business might use in this fashion.

popular specialty items. When designed well, specialty items carry the name and address of the business sponsoring them and an advertising message urging the reader to action. Sometimes, however, the size of the item prevents the use of a message, and only the name and address of the business appear.

Specialty advertising has two serious limitations. First, the distribution of the items is usually somewhat limited. Second, the items might be given to people who would never consider buying the product or patronizing the sponsoring business.

Other Advertising Media

Businesses are constantly creating exciting, innovative means of transmitting their messages to potential customers. Other media not easily classified are sports arena billboards, commercials run in movie theaters and in home videos, skywriting, faxed messages to businesses, and prerecorded ads run on television monitors above checkout counters in retail stores. You can probably add to this list as new media are designed to help advertisers get their messages out to potential customers.

Media Costs

Media costs vary greatly, not just with type of media but with geographical location as well. For example, a quarter-page newspaper ad in a large-city daily could cost four to eight times more than the same size ad in a small-town weekly. Given such variation, it is virtually impossible to quote exact rates for each type of media advertising. It is possible, however, to generalize about how those rates are set.

When businesses want to access rates for the various media, they look up the rates in the publications of Standard Rates and Data Service. It publishes rate cards for most major media according to general categories, such as print media or broadcast media.

Another advertising industry service important to both advertisers and print media is the Audit Bureau of Circulation (ABC). Print media publishers subscribe to the ABC to have it verify their circulation figures. This is important in print media because advertising rates are based on circulation. Circulation figures are important selling points for the media to use when trying to attract advertisers to the publication.

Newspaper Rates

Newspaper advertising rates are classified into two categories depending on whether the ad is a *classified ad* or a *display ad*. Classified ads are placed in a section of the newspaper that has specific categories, such as help wanted, real estate, and auto sales. Display ads are found throughout the newspaper and advertise products or services. This section will focus on newspaper display advertising.

Newspapers traditionally quoted their rates based on *agate lines*, which is 14 lines to a column inch. Recently, more and more newspapers have been changing their method of quoting display advertising rates to column inches. If a newspaper quotes the column inch rate, you simply multiply the number of inches by the number of columns that represent the total space of an ad. For example, if the rate for a column inch is $4.90, then an ad that measures 4 inches long by 3 columns will cost $58.80

$4.90 × 4 inches × 3 columns = $58.80

If that same newspaper quoted its rates by agate lines, the line rate would be $.35 per agate line. The calculations for the cost of the ad are:

$.35 × 14 agate lines × 4 inches × 3 columns = $58.80

A number of factors can change the *regular rate* (called *run-of-paper* because it can run anywhere in the paper). Preferred positions that specify a location, advertising on the last page of a section, and use of color all raise the rate. The frequency of advertising lowers the rate. The more you advertise, the less you pay per insertion.

Businesses that advertise in the newspaper on a *transient basis (infrequently)* usually must pay the *open* or *flat rate*. Businesses that advertise frequently often contract with the newspaper to guarantee they will use a certain number of agate lines or column inches for the year. Thus, they are granted *contract rates*, which are discounted from the open rate. The line rate or column inch rate decreases as the total contracted lines or column inches increase.

Newspapers that grant advertising agency commissions generally charge them the open rate. When national advertisers buy advertising space in newspapers, they are often charged a different rate from local advertisers.

Another rate from an advertiser's viewpoint that is useful for comparison is the *milline rate*. The *mil-line rate compares the cost of advertising per person reached in one newspaper to the cost per person reached in another newspaper.* The comparison is made by using the formula

$$\frac{R \times 1{,}000{,}000}{C} = MR$$

Where R is the rate per agate line, C is the newspaper's circulation, and MR is the milline rate.

Consider an example. If the *Times* has a line rate of $1 per agate line and a circulation of 500,000, its milline rate would be calculated as follows:

$$\frac{\$1 \times 1{,}000{,}000}{500{,}000} = \frac{\$1{,}000{,}000}{500{,}000} = \$2$$

If the *Tribune*, a competing paper, has a line rate of $.90 per agate line and a circulation of 300,000, its milline rate would be as follows:

$$\frac{\$.90 \times 1{,}000{,}000}{300{,}000} = \frac{\$900{,}000}{300{,}000} = \$3$$

All things being equal, an advertiser would probably choose the *Times* over the *Tribune* because it would cost less per person reached.

Of course, all other things might not be equal. The *Tribune's* circulation could include more of the advertiser's target market, or the paper could offer a special placement for the ad. The point is that the milline rate is a convenient measure, one that puts all newspapers on the same footing. It is a factor to be considered in the placement of advertising.

Magazine Rates

Magazine rates are based on circulation and quality of readership. To calculate the actual cost of magazine advertising, you need to become familiar with some terms found on magazine advertising rate cards, including *bleed*, *black-and-white rates*, *color rates*, *discounts*, and *cost-per-thousand rate* (CPM).

Bleed means that half-page or full-page ads are printed to the very edge of the page, leaving no white border. Magazines generally charge between 10 to 20 percent extra for bleeds.

The lowest rates magazines offer for display ads are black-and-white rates for black-and-white advertisements. *Color rates* are offered for color ads. Each time the magazine adds color to the ad, the rates increase. Four-color advertisements, called *full-color*, are the most expensive magazine ads.

Frequency discounts are offered to advertisers who want to run the same ad several times during the year. A special discount rate may be offered. Or the magazine may publish an entire schedule of rates for the number of times during the year an advertiser contracts to advertise. The rate per issue decreases as the frequency increases.

Another discount is a 15 percent commission granted to the advertising agency for placing the ad for the advertiser.

Finally, a cash discount may be offered for paying the bill earlier than its due date (this may be written 2/10, net 30). This cash discount would permit the advertiser or ad agency to take a 2 percent discount if the bill is paid 10 days from the date of the invoice. The payment, if the discount is not taken, is due 30 days from the date of the invoice.

Take at look at the rate card in Figure 20-1. You would calculate the cost of a full page, four-color advertisement with bleed as follows:

1 page, four-color rate	$23,300
	× .15 bleed
	$ 3,495 extra for bleed

$23,300
+ 3,495 bleed
$26,795 for 1 page, four color, with bleed

If an ad agency placed the ad and it took the cash discount, the total cost of the above ad to the agency would be:

$26,795
× .15 Ad agency's commission
$4,019.25

$26,795.00
– 4,019.25 agency's commission
$22,775.75 net cost of ad to agency after commission
× .02 cash discount percentage if paid within 10 days of invoice
$ 455.52 cash discount

$22,775.75
– 455.52 cash discount
$22,320.23 net cost to advertising agency for one full-page, 4-color ad, with bleed.

GENERAL RATES

RATE BASE: Rates based on a yearly average of 1,100,000 net paid A.B.C.
A member of the Audit Bureau of Circulation

SPACE UNITS	BLACK & WHITE	BLACK & ONE COLOR	FOUR COLOR
1 page	$16,000	$19,630	$23,300
2 columns	11,620	14,560	18,170
1/2 page	10,130	13,550	17,200
1 column	5,920	9,530	12,180
1/2 column	3,020		

COVERS			
Second Cover			$25,520
Third Cover			23,300
Fourth Cover			27,020

BLEED CHARGE: 15%
AGENCY COMMISSION: 15%
CASH DISCOUNT: 2% 10 days, net 30 days

BLEED accepted in color, black & white, and on covers, at an additional charge of 15%. No charge for gutter bleed in double-page spread.
Premium Positions: A 10% premium applies to advertising units positioned on pages 1, 2, and 3. A surcharge of 5% applies to bleed units in premium positions.
Rate Change Announcements will be made at least two months in advance of the black & white closing date for the issue affected. Orders for issues thereafter at rates then prevailing.

ISSUANCE AND CLOSING DATES

A. On sale date approximately the 15th of month preceding date of issue.
B. Black & white, black & one-color, and four-color closing date, 20th of the 3rd month preceding date of issue. Example: Forms for August issue close May 20th.
C. *Orders for cover pages non-cancellable. Orders for all inside advertising units are non-cancellable 15 days prior to their respective closing dates.* Supplied inserts are non-cancellable the 1st of the 4th month preceding month of issue. Options on cover positions must be exercised at least 30 days prior to four-color closing date. If order is not received by such date, cover option automatically lapses.

Figure 20-1 **A Magazine Rate Card**
Based on the rates shown here, what is the cost of a black-and-white half-page ad paid in ten days from issuance of the invoice?

In order to compare the cost of advertising in several magazines with regard to cost and circulation, the *cost-per-thousand* (CPM) formula is used:

$$\frac{\text{cost of ad}}{\text{thousands of circulation}}$$

If a magazine had a circulation of 2 million and its full-page black-and-white ad rate was $35,000, the cost-per-thousand rate would be $17.50.

$$\frac{\$35,000 \text{ cost of a black-and-white full page ad}}{2,000 \text{ thousands of circulation}} = \$17.50$$
(2 million ÷ 1,000 = 2,000)

Radio Rates

After a business decides to buy radio time, it needs to decide what kind of radio advertising to use. There are three options—*network radio advertising*, *national spot radio advertising*, and *local radio advertising*.

If a business is national in scope, it usually chooses network radio advertising or national spot radio advertising. *Network radio advertising is a broadcast from a studio to all affiliated radio stations throughout the country.* Network radio advertising allows an advertiser to broadcast an ad simultaneously to several markets through sponsorship of a special program, activity, or radio personality.

National spot radio advertising is also used by national firms to advertise on a local station-by-station basis for selected target markets in the country.

Local radio advertising is done by a local business for its target market and is limited to a specific geographical area.

When selecting advertising it is important to know the difference between *spot radio* and *spot commercials*. *Spot radio* refers to the geographical area an advertiser wants to reach with its advertising. So, when selecting spot radio, businesses need to identify their target market and their potential customers. *Spot commercials* are advertising messages of one minute or less. It is important to realize that spot commercials can be carried on network or spot radio.

Each radio station determines actual advertising rates by time of day. Rates are generally higher during peak listening times, such as early mornings and late afternoons. Because target audiences, audience size, and discounts vary from station to station, a business should carefully review and compare the rates of the radio stations on which it might advertise.

Television Rates

Advertising rates for television also vary with time of day. It is more expensive, for example, to advertise during the prime-time hours of 7 to 11 p.m. (known as Class AA time) than during other hours. The rates charged for other time slots, such as Class A, Class B, Class C, and Class D, are less because of diminishing viewership. Businesses try to place their advertisements in time slots during which potential customers will most likely see them.

A business considering the purchase of television time contacts a television media representative. The representative helps the business determine coverage times available and arranges package deals that can be developed to give the advertiser more advertising spots, or volume or seasonal discounts.

Selection of Promotional Media

The choice of an advertising medium depends on the product to be advertised, the habits and lifestyles of the target audience, and the types of media available in the area. These questions can help determine what type of media to use.

1. Does the medium reach the greatest number of customers at the lowest cost per customer?
2. Does the medium provide opportunity for illustrating the product?
3. Does the medium provide an opportunity to present an adequate selling message?
4. Does advertising in this medium pose any special problems?
5. What is the medium's flexibility in terms of making last-minute changes in the message?
6. Does the medium provide an opportunity to sell the product or just announce its availability?
7. Does the medium provide enough excitement for special promotions?
8. Does the medium fit the image of the business and offer enough prestige and distinction?
9. Does the medium cover the targeted geographical area?

VOCABULARY REVIEW

Write one or two paragraphs using the following ten vocabulary terms.

promotional advertising
institutional advertising
media
print media
broadcast media
specialty media

milline rate
network radio advertising
local radio advertising
national spot radio
 advertising

FACT AND IDEA REVIEW

1. Explain the differences between promotional and institutional advertising.

2. Identify three general categories of advertising media.

3. What are the principal advantages and disadvantages of using newspaper advertising?

4. In what respects is magazine advertising superior to newspaper advertising?

5. What is direct mail advertising? Give five examples of direct mail advertising.

6. Why is outdoor advertising losing popularity in some areas of the country?

7. What is the major reason that so many businesses use the broadcast media for advertising?

8. Why is a knowledge of milline rates and cost-per-thousand rates helpful to newspaper and magazine advertisers, respectively?

9. How do network radio advertising, national spot radio advertising, and local radio advertising differ from each other?

10. What determines the rates charged for television advertising?

CRITICAL THINKING

1. How would consumer buying habits be different if advertising in all of the forms discussed in this chapter did not exist?

2. Why is institutional advertising necessary? (*Hint:* Think of at least three situations in which promotional advertising would be either inappropriate or inadequate.)

3. Assume you are a member of a legislative committee considering a ban on "junk mail" advertising. What information would you like to have from people on both sides of the issue before making your decision?

4. Will a prime-time television slot always guarantee an advertiser the best results in selling a product? Why or why not?

USING BASIC SKILLS

Math

1. Prepare a table or graph comparing the milline rates for each of the newspapers below.
   - *Chronicle:* Circulation 1,400,000; line rate $1.10
   - *News:* Circulation 750,000; line rate $.90
   - *Post:* Circulation 575,000; line rate $1.25
2. Calculate the cost-per-thousand rate for a magazine that has a circulation of 1.5 million and charges $25,000 for a full-page black-and-white ad.

Communication

3. Gather information about a single product from five different advertising sources (for example, the Yellow Pages, a magazine, a newspaper, television, and a billboard). Write a two-page analysis of how these sources differ from each other in their presentation of the product and approach to the consumer.

Human Relations

4. Your company has a hard choice to make—to stick with your current radio ads or switch to a new approach. The current ads feature a humorous character popular with the public. The ads win awards, but they don't sell the product. The new approach features mind-numbing repetition of the product name in an irritating voice. Your market research shows that people hate the voice—and remember the ad (kids in particular like to imitate it). Make your best case for the approach you favor.

5. You are in the same situation as in the human relations problem above. You want the company to switch from radio to television advertising. Again, make your best case.

APPLICATION PROJECTS

1. Look through newspapers and magazines to find examples of promotional and institutional advertising. Clip four appropriate ads and contribute them to a classroom display contrasting the two types of advertising.

2. Prepare an advertising log for one hour of your television viewing. List the products advertised, characterize the advertising approach taken, identify the sponsor as either a national or local advertiser, and describe what you believe to be the target market. Note any trends you see in terms of these factors.

3. Make a directory of local radio stations. Include the call letters, dial location, and programming type (hard rock, classical, country and western, news/talk, etc.) for each entry. Then characterize the station's audience by age, education, ethnic background—whatever standards seem appropriate. Which markets are most and least fragmented in your community?

4. For a product of your choice, make some decisions about how to advertise it. Assume that money is no problem.

a. Bearing your target audience in mind, select the media through which you will advertise. Consider the times at which you would want television and radio ads to run and the size of ads in print media. Choose the publications you think are best suited to reaching your audience.

b. Decide whether you will use institutional or promotional advertising or a combination of both. Describe your promotional advertising—such as humorous, informational, serious—and your institutional advertising. Explain why they are appropriate for the product and the audience.

c. If your product will sell better during different seasons, decide when and in which media you will increase your advertising.

d. At the library, research television and radio costs and the newspaper and magazine rates for the publications you have chosen. If you have chosen direct marketing or specialty advertising, research the costs of those. Estimate your advertising budget per month and per year.

5. Direct mail advertising comes to most homes every week. Start looking at the direct mail your family receives. Take five pieces that interest you. Analyze them in terms of artwork and description of the good or service, and try to determine why they appeal to you.

6. Using the examples you have collected in Application Project #5 as models, write a direct mail marketing letter for the following:

a. a new condominium development,

b. a book club that sends a different book each month,

c. a hiking magazine, and

d. a charity or special interest group of your choice.

As you write each letter, think about the market you would target. Decide what other pieces should go into the package with each letter, such as reply cards or testimonial letters from famous people.

Preparing Written Advertisements

OBJECTIVES

After completing this chapter, you will be able to:

1. understand how ads are developed,

2. explain the parts of a print advertisement,

3. develop advertising headlines,

4. prepare advertising copy,

5. select advertising illustrations,

6. develop advertising layouts,

7. explain the use of color in advertising,

8. select type styles for print advertisements, and

9. check advertising proofs.

WORDS TO KNOW

advertising agencies
cooperative advertising
headline
copy
illustration
signature
clip art
ad layout
advertising proof

Successful advertising campaigns help sell products. Think of all the ads you've seen in newspapers and magazines that made you want to buy such things as sporting equipment or clothes.

How are such ads developed? Who writes them? How do they know which approach to take, what will work, and what won't? How do they think of those catchy slogans and choose the illustrations to go with them?

In this chapter you'll explore all of these questions. You'll get answers specific enough to allow you to try your own hand at ad writing, from headline to final layout.

The Advertising Agency

After a company decides which product to promote, which media to use, and how much to spend, the next step is to develop the advertisement. The size and the financial resources of a business usually determine who will create its ads.

Large businesses often use professional *advertising agencies*. *Advertising agencies are companies that exist solely to help clients sell their products.* There are about 10,000 such agencies in the United States, employing only about 100,000 people. So, you can see that advertising agencies represent a fairly small group of specialists—especially when you consider that General Motors, by comparison, employs about 700,000 people.

Most of the major U.S. advertising agencies (the ones that employ the most people and make the most money) are in New York City, Chicago, and Los Angeles. In 1987, one of the largest agencies, Leo Burnett in Chicago, employed approximately 4,700 people, had offices in 43 countries, and had $2.5 billion in advertising billings.

Advertising agencies are usually organized into four departments.

1. *Client service* works with agency groups and individual businesses to identify opportunities for advertising. (Many of these employees are called *account executives*.) This department prepares marketing plans, forecasts, and budgets, and coordinates promotion and marketing activities.
2. *Creative service* creates the advertising messages and produces the ads. Artists, copywriters, and other creative people work in this department.
3. *Research service* studies target markets, the attitudes of potential customers, and their buying behavior. This department helps determine what type of message will have the greatest appeal for a particular market segment.
4. *Media service* makes decisions on how much of the client's advertising budget will be spent on television, radio, and print advertising. This department also decides on the timing and frequency of the advertisements. The media plans developed by this department for a company's products are based on the region, city, number of men and women, income, education, and the reading and television viewing habits of people in the target market.

Cooperative Advertising

Smaller firms use cooperative advertisements prepared by national advertisers. *Cooperative advertising is advertising of manufacturers' or suppliers' products that are placed by local merchants in local media with the merchant's name.* The manufacturer or supplier pays all or part of the cost of placing the advertisements.

Depending on the size of the manufacturer and the cooperative advertising program, a variety of advertising and promotional materials are supplied to the retailer. These might include newspaper ads with space for the retailer's name and address, television and radio ads with time allotted to insert the retailer's name and location, window and counter displays, and posters.

To participate in cooperative advertising, a retailer must sign a contract with the manufacturer. The contract gives the specific conditions for advertising the manufacturer's products in newspapers, on radio or television, and in other media. After the advertising is completed, the manufacturer reimburses the retailer for the agreed-upon costs of the campaign.

Parts of a Print Advertisement

Print advertisements, whether they are prepared by a professional advertising agency, through a cooperative advertising arrangement, or even by the sponsoring business itself, must contain certain essential elements. These include a *headline*, *copy*, *illustrations*, and a *signature*.

To communicate successfully, an ad must attract attention, arouse interest, create desire, and finally produce action. To accomplish all of this, each of an ad's key parts must be coordinated with the others.

Headline

*The **headline** is the lettering, slogan, or saying that gets the readers' attention, arouses their interest, and leads them to read the rest of the ad.* Headlines are responsible for 70 to 80 percent of the sales effectiveness of most advertisements, so many experts consider them the most important part of a print ad. Here are some innovative and attention-getting examples from retail store advertising.

> With Prices Like These, Who Needs a Headline?
> This Weekend, Watch a Pleasant, Sophisticated
> Store Go Berserk
> Each Time We Punch This Coupon, You'll
> Get 20% Off

In a recent study, creative directors from major advertising agencies analyzed award-winning print ads to determine what their headlines had in common. They discovered that some 32 percent of the headlines used familiar sayings with a twist. For example, a headline used by a boot manufacturer stated,

> Most Boots Have a Hard Time Coping with the
> Realities of Life.

About 23 percent of the headlines made use of opposites, such as "up/down" and "lie/truth." For example, a ski lodge ran this headline on its print ad:

> After a Day of Downhill Skiing, Getting a Fine Meal
> Shouldn't Be an Uphill Battle.

Other headlines reviewed by the creative directors used these techniques to attract attention:

- news and information to announce a new product or service,
- shock or surprise treatment of a subject to arouse attention or emotion,
- questioning to get the reader involved, and
- arousing curiosity by using such phrases as "how to" or "you should know."

Headlines give advertisements more selling power when they are attention getters. They should be directed to the reader and appeal to the self-interest of the potential customer. They should be short, light, and informational. They should tell readers just enough to entice them into reading the rest of the ad.

Copy

*The **copy** is the selling message in a written advertisement.* It should directly expand on the information in the headline. It should specifically stress the benefit of the product in a brief, effective statement. The last line of copy should ask for positive action.

Copy can be written in the form of a conversation, or it can be written as an educational tool. It can be a testimonial to the benefits of using the product, or it can describe how an institution can help you. It can make its point with humor.

In all of these cases, however, the copy should appeal to the senses. Through the words used, the customer should be able to see, hear, touch, taste, and/or even smell a product.

Copy can be dramatic, emotional, and direct. For example, Northwest Airlines ran a dramatic ad showing a close-up photo of a wide-eyed child. The headline read, "There's always someone waiting for you at home." The copy went on to explain that Northwest Airlines strives to get travelers to their business connections and back home again to their loved ones quickly, safely, and comfortably.

Humor and entertainment themes are also effective. In an ad that the Lotus Development Corporation used to sell its Jazz integrated software, the illustration showed a man and a woman jumping for joy. The copy read, "You know you make me wanna shout."

Illustration

*The **illustration** is the photograph or drawing used in a print advertisement.* Its primary function is to attract attention. It should also create interest, arouse a desire to buy, and encourage a purchase deci-

REAL WORLD MARKETING

The Sweet Smell of Success

If you thought perfumed ads were a new idea, think again. The first one appeared March 25, 1937, in the *Daily News* of Washington, D.C. The ad was for a flower sale at Peoples Drug Stores.

Now Flying Tigers Delivers 40 Years Of Worldwide Experience To Federal Express. Overnight.

STAND OUT IN A CROWD. CALL KODAK

The four main parts of an ad are the headline, the copy, the illustration, and the signature. Find these elements in each of the ads shown here.

sion for the advertised product. The illustration, together with the headline, should lead the potential customer to read at least the first sentence of the copy.

The illustration is usually the first thing a reader sees in the ad. So, it should transmit a total message that would be hard to communicate with words alone. Illustrations should show:

- the features of the product,
- how the product works,
- the advantages of owning the product,
- the safety features of the product,
- the possible uses for the product,
- the need for the product, and
- an image associated with the product, such as prestige, status, or leisure.

Signature

No advertisement is complete without its sponsor. *The signature, or logotype (logo), is the distinctive identification symbol for a business.*

In national ads, the logo is the name of the firm and possibly its trademark and slogan. The signature in a retail ad usually includes the business's name, address, telephone number, business hours, and slogan (if there is one).

A well-designed signature gets instant recognition for a business. Even though readers may not be interested in the particular product advertised at the moment, the signature should be so easy to remember that they will identify with it at a later time.

As noted earlier, a successful advertisement results from the careful coordination of headline, copy, illustration, and signature. Let's take a look at how each of these elements is developed. As we go along, try to put yourself in the position of an advertising copywriter. Read the technique hints, study the example, and then try your own hand at creating some ads.

Developing Advertising Headlines

A headline stresses one primary benefit of a product. So, it should be brief, easy to understand, and powerful. It should tell a benefit, convey surprise, or give the reader a very good reason to read the copy. Most headlines are brief because most people cannot take in more than seven words at one time.

Here are some examples of well-written headlines that use seven or fewer words.

Kodak Film . . . Because Time Goes By (Kodak)
The Rewards of Money (*Money* magazine)
We Do It Like You'd Do It (Burger King)

Every headline should have a single focus, or main idea. Before writing a headline, try to sum up the main idea in a single sentence. This technique will help you remain focused on the subject and thus produce a headline with impact.

Here are some other techniques you can use when writing headlines.

1. *Alliteration* (repeating initial consonant sounds)—Ruffles Have Ridges
2. *Paradox* (a seeming contradiction that could be true)—You're Not Getting Older, You're Getting Better
3. *Rhyme*—Bounty . . . The Quicker Picker-Upper
4. *Pun* (a humorous use of a word that suggests two or more of its meanings or the meaning of another word similar in sound)—Every Litter Bit Hurts
5. *Play on Words*—For Soft Babies and Baby Soft Hands

More than 80 percent of the people who look at a print advertisement just read the headline. Thus, you want your headlines to be powerful enough to draw potential customers into reading the copy. Here are three suggestions that will help you write powerful headlines.

1. Attract readers with one or more of the three most powerful words in advertising—*new*, *now*, and *free*.
2. Make your headline long enough to feature one product benefit, but short enough (seven words or less) to encourage people to read the rest of the advertisement.
3. Arouse reader curiosity by promising something—a free offer, more miles per gallon, better service, fewer cavities, etc.

The key point to remember is that headlines for an ad must use simple language. Readers will mistrust or misunderstand ads with complex headlines. By using simple language in headlines, you can ensure that nearly everyone will understand your message and no one will resent it.

Preparing Advertising Copy

Copy is the selling message. While the headline stresses the primary benefit of the product, the copy stresses its secondary benefits. Thus, good copy, like a good headline, is simple and direct.

Your copy will be competing with hundreds of other advertisers for the reader's attention. So, the first sentence of the copy must be dramatic. It should:

- establish contact with the reader,
- create awareness,
- arouse interest, and
- build preference for the product.

Key words used in copy, such as *compare*, *introduce*, *now*, *price*, *save*, *easy*, and *new*, establish immediate contact with the reader by arousing interest and creating awareness and desire.

In addition to using key words, your copy should explain the benefits and features of the product in short sentences that repeat key ideas and use many adjectives. Give your copy news value by providing specific information. Tell the who, what, when, why, where, and how of your product. Remember, too, that facts about your product are more powerful than claims. If possible, use case histories, statistics, performance figures, dates, and quotes from experts.

Advertising copy should be written in the active voice to make it more immediate. In other words, you would write, "This item will help you," rather than "You will be helped by this item." Try to use warm, personal language and expressions familiar to your target audience.

Finally, the last line should ask for action. It helps to include a penalty for not acting now. Words such as *today*, *now*, *before it's too late*, and *without delay* help create action.

Selecting Advertising Illustrations

There are two types of advertising illustrations—photographs and drawings.

Photographs should be used in advertisements when a sense of reality is necessary. Sometimes it's important for the customer to know exactly what the product looks like or how it's used. For example, consumer products such as food, clothing, cosmetics, jewelry, furniture, or stereos should be illustrated with photographs.

Drawings are often used to show a part of a product that the reader would normally not see. For example, cut-away drawings of such products as cars and tools help show important features not visible in a photo.

Businesses often get photographs from suppliers, manufacturers, or trade associations. In addition, professional photographers are often hired to photograph situations or products.

The photos used in advertisements should be sharp and clear with good contrast between light and dark areas. Good photographs draw attention to the subject, show the main benefits of the product, and tie into the headline and copy.

Although original photos and artwork are ideal for illustrations, businesses often use *clip art* in their print advertisements. ***Clip art consists of stock drawings, photographs, and headlines clipped from a printed sheet and pasted into an advertisement.*** Because clip art is ready for reproduction and printing, it is inexpensive, quick, and easy to use.

When designing advertisements, pay careful attention to where the reader's eyes will be directed. The best ads contain *lines of force* that guide the reader to the copy through the illustrations. For example, the models in photos or drawings should be facing or looking at the copy. A model in an illustration that looks out of the ad space moves the reader's eyes away from the copy.

Whether photographs or drawings, illustrations determine the image a business projects to the public. After a business selects an illustration style, it normally does not change that style for a period of time. Thus, to maintain its image, a business should not only select its illustrations carefully but periodically evaluate them for consistency as well.

A few suggestions for those who decide to go with another international long distance company.

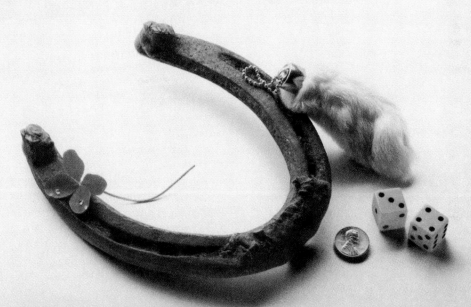

Feeling lucky?

Then you probably don't need the long distance company with over 60 years' international experience.

The company with faster connections to more countries than any other.

The company whose Worldwide Intelligent Network

©1989 AT&T

ensures that your calls will go through with unsurpassed clarity.

In other words, you probably don't need to call **1 800 222-0400 ext. 1277.**

After all, that's a number you should only call if you need more than luck on your side.

AT&T
The right choice.

The best ads quickly catch your attention, make you want to read them, and convey a lasting image of both product and company. How do the ads shown here and on page 230 do these things? Which do you feel are most effective? Why?

Developing Advertising Layouts

*An **ad layout** is a rough draft that shows the general arrangement and appearance of a finished ad.* It clearly indicates the position of the headline, illustration, copy, and signature.

Whether you are dealing with a newspaper salesperson, a magazine representative, or a printer, each will probably need only a rough draft to complete a print advertisement. So, you do not have to be an artist to develop an ad layout. You do need to make sure, however, that the information is correct.

Ad layouts should be developed with the following general ideas in mind.

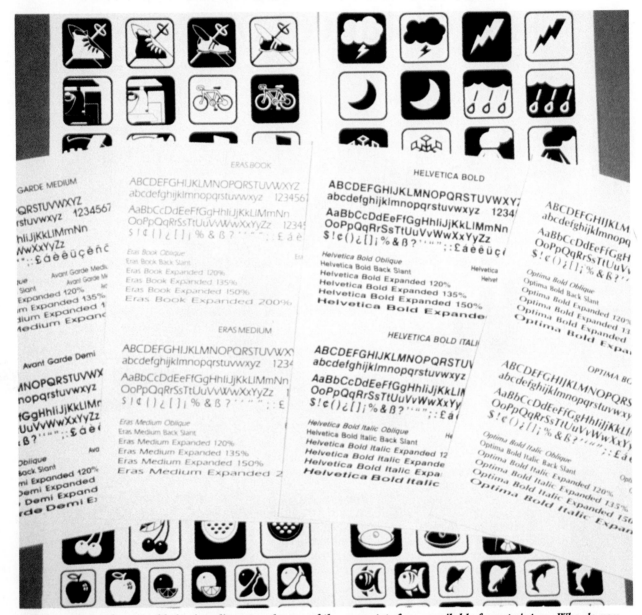

Effective ads can be assembled using clip art and some of the many typefaces available from printers. Who do you think might use this alternative and why?

1. They should be prepared in exactly the same size as the final advertisement.
2. Illustrations should be large enough to show all product features.
3. The ad should make generous use of white space for an uncluttered look.
4. The image projected in the layout should be appropriate for the target audience.
5. The *typeface* (style of printing type) and size should be easy to read and appropriate for the target audience.

Using Color in Print Advertisements

A little color makes an advertisement stand out on the printed page. Also, color ads draw higher response rates than black-and-white ads because they are more realistic. In fact, research has proven that color newspaper ads can increase the reading of copy by as much as 80 percent over black-and-white ads. Studies have also shown that full-color ads are more cost effective than two-color ads (black plus a color).

Although color adds excitement and realism, each added color raises the cost of the advertisement. Adding a second color alone can increase costs by as much as 35 percent. Therefore, when businesses use color in advertisements, the added cost must be continually measured against the desired results.

Selecting Typefaces and Type Sizes for Print Advertisements

There are a variety of typefaces and type sizes available for use in print ads. Different typefaces and type sizes can affect the way a reader feels about an advertisement. For example, a typeface that is too small or difficult to read will lower the readership of an ad. A study done by the Newspaper Advertising Bureau found that nearly one-third of readers over 65 had trouble reading newspaper type. This means that some one-third of newspaper readers over 65 may not be reading ads at all unless they have larger, simple type and a good, uncluttered design.

The size of the type and the typefaces themselves must be appropriate for the business and for the target audience, yet distinctive, too. In general, print advertisers should use one typeface for head-

lines and prices and another typeface for copy. You can add variety and emphasis by using different sizes, italics, and boldface versions of the two basic typefaces selected for the advertisement.

Checking Advertising Proofs

When advertisements are given to a newspaper or magazine staff for preparation, an advertising proof is developed. *The **advertising proof** shows exactly how an ad will appear when printed.*

The advertising proof is sent to the advertiser for review and approval. The advertiser carefully checks the proof to make sure that the ad was done exactly as planned. It is particularly important to make sure that all prices are accurate and all brand names correctly spelled. If errors are found in the proof, the errors are marked and returned to the newspaper or magazine publisher for correction.

Before giving final approval to a written advertisement, the advertiser should do one final evaluation on it by answering these questions.

1. Is the ad bold enough to stand out on a page, even if it is placed next to other ads?
2. Does the headline arouse interest and attract attention?
3. Is the illustration large enough and done well enough to highlight the product?
4. Is the signature plate apparent and distinctive?
5. Is the copy simple, direct, and understandable?
6. Does the layout guide the reader to and through the copy?
7. Are the typefaces and type sizes easy to read?

Car Ads—Images That Last for Years

In recent years, foreign competition has forced U.S. carmakers to improve their products' fuel economy, performance, design, handling, and safety. Today, most new cars are equal in terms of their technology. As a result, new-car customers have been forced to look for other factors on which to base their purchase decisions. Automakers have obliged them with carefully crafted images, developed and cultivated over long periods of time.

Chevrolet's "Heartbeat of America" campaign, for example, has run since 1986. In all the Heartbeat ads, Chevrolet's cars take a back seat to the people around them. The image portrays Chevrolet as *the* car at the center of American life, the car everyone should have.

Chrysler's ads with company chairman Lee Iacocca as spokesperson have also run for years. The ads stress longer, better warranties and customer satisfaction. The emphasis is on quality, and the image is that of a reliable car that can be counted on to perform well.

Ford Motor Company, by contrast, took a hard-sell approach for years. Ford cast its cars as its stars. When people appeared in ads, they were usually part of the background. The campaign and the products it sold were winners, and Ford (following conventional wisdom) didn't tamper with success. The company used the same singer, the same music, and the same theme ("Have you driven a Ford lately?") for more than seven years!

Today, however, that campaign is used mainly for Ford's trucks. For its other product lines, the company appears to be making a gradual shift in its image. Ford automobiles now share the advertising stage with a new spokesperson, television's Bionic Woman, Lindsay Wagner. The ads are low key and traditional in content but spare and futuristic in their look. With the new look has come a new theme—Ford as a leader in auto design and research, the company most likely to bring you the cars of the future first.

Car advertising campaigns like these last longer because it takes longer for people to identify with cars. Under these circumstances, it would be not only risky but also wasteful to invest in a brand new advertising approach every year.

1. Identify one other car company not mentioned here. What image of its products does it project in its advertisements?
2. Assume you are a marketing executive with a major car company. You must devise a print ad for a new vehicle, a four-wheel drive truck. What kind of image would you try to create for the product? What specific things would you include in the ad to project this image?
3. What elements of print media ads are found in broadcast media ads?

VOCABULARY REVIEW

Write a paragraph incorporating all of the following vocabulary terms.

advertising agencies   signature
cooperative advertising   clip art
headline   ad layout
copy   advertising proof
illustration

FACT AND IDEA REVIEW

1. Identify the four major departments found in most advertising agencies and tell what each does.

2. What is "cooperative" about cooperative advertising?

3. What are the four essential elements of a written advertisement?

4. Why should headlines consist of no more than seven words?

5. Identify three techniques you can use to develop attention-getting headlines.

6. What are the two types of illustrations used in print ads and when should each be used?

7. In an ad, what is a signature and what does it include?

8. List four principles that should be followed in developing layouts for print advertisements.

9. Give three reasons for using color in print advertisements.

10. What are the major considerations in selecting type for print advertisements?

CRITICAL THINKING

1. Discuss the advantages and disadvantages for both manufacturer and retailer in a cooperative advertising arrangement.

2. Why do you think supermarkets, local banks, and travel agencies frequently use print advertising?

3. Why would a business develop different print ads for the same product if it advertised that product in both newspapers and magazines?

4. What special concerns would you have in designing a print ad for a product used by senior citizens?

USING BASIC SKILLS

Math

1. You are checking proofs for the advertising flyer your sporting goods store puts out monthly, a portion of which appears below. Do you have any corrections?

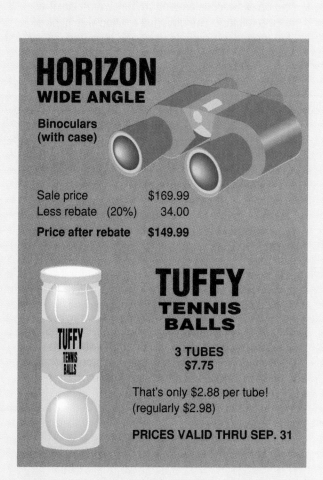

HORIZON
WIDE ANGLE

Binoculars
(with case)

Sale price $169.99
Less rebate (20%)   34.00
Price after rebate $149.99

TUFFY
TENNIS
BALLS

3 TUBES
$7.75

That's only $2.88 per tube!
(regularly $2.98)

PRICES VALID THRU SEP. 31

Communication

2. From your local newspaper or a magazine, select three ads that use illustration primarily to establish mood. Clip the ads and mount them on individual sheets of paper. Then, for each, write a paragraph describing the tone you think the ad's sponsor was trying to set.

3. Identify five household or consumer products you are familiar with and develop advertising headlines for each. Base your headlines on opposite words such as *up/down*, *hot/cold*, or *inside/outside*.

Human Relations

4. Your local restaurant chain is in the midst of one of its most successful advertising campaigns. The ads feature a pair of elderly spinsters who bumble their way through the restaurant's menu, treating the daily specials as though they were classified by the military. The dialogue is filled with slips of the tongue, memory lapses, and muddled thinking—all of which the general public apparently finds both amusing and persuasive (purchase of the specials is up by 30 percent). However, members of a local senior citizens group are not amused. They have arranged a meeting with you, the head of the restaurant's public relations staff. What will you say to the senior citizens? How would you suggest changing the ads to satisfy their complaints?

APPLICATION PROJECTS

1. Select a product. Then develop an ad for it (original headline and copy) using the techniques and suggestions identified in this chapter.

2. Collect corporate slogans or advertising headlines for use in an unofficial class quiz. Write each slogan or headline on a note card, along with the name of the sponsoring company. Read each slogan aloud and have your classmates identify the business using it. Examples:

   You Deserve a Break Today. (McDonald's)
   Don't Leave Home Without It. (American Express)

3. Do the same activity as above, substituting corporate logos for corporate slogans. Wherever possible, omit the company name. See if your classmates can still identify the firm and its main product (food, automobiles, clothing, etc.).

4. Prepare a layout for an ad announcing the grand opening of a new clothing store in your community. Be sure to include the following information:

   a. the actual headline,

   b. the location of any illustrations,

   c. the location of copy,

   d. any introductory offers and special pricing that will be featured, and

   e. a signature plate including the store location and hours.

5. There are five techniques that can help you write memorable headlines: alliteration, paradox, rhyme, puns, and play on words. Develop two headlines using each of these techniques.

6. A jewelry store has received a special selection of estate jewelry set with emeralds, sapphires, and rubies. Although the ad should be in color, the jeweler can only afford black and white. Discuss some of the ways the jeweler could increase the effectiveness of the ad without increasing the expense.

7. Go through magazines and newspapers you usually read. Pick out ads that do and do not appeal to you and separate them into two piles. Analyze the ads and write short paragraphs explaining why they did or did not capture your interest. Then explain how you would change the ads you didn't like in order to appeal to the market you represent.

Visual Merchandising and Display

After completing this chapter, you will be able to:

1. define visual merchandising and distinguish it from display,

2. explain how exterior and interior features contribute to a store's image,

3. list the various kinds of displays,

4. describe the choice of merchandise, fixtures, and settings available for displays,

5. describe the various artistic considerations involved in display preparation, and

6. summarize the proper procedures for maintaining and dismantling displays.

visual merchandising
display
storefront
marquee
store layout
fixtures
complementary colors
adjacent colors
proportion
formal balance
informal balance

Y ou enter a new store for the first time. You're looking for a sweat top to knock around in on weekends—something oversized and soft and *cheap*. Your eye immediately fastens on the very item—right size, right color, right texture. Everything is right, until the salesclerk rings up the price—$122!

It could never happen to you, right? You could never be that wrong about a store. Why? To start, you'd probably look at the price first. But the fact is you probably wouldn't have to. Before you even got to the counter, dozens of signals—most of them visual—would be telling you that you weren't in a discount store. There would be the width of the aisles, the sophistication of the displays, the amount and look of the merchandise.

In this chapter, however, you will learn about them from a retailer's viewpoint.

What Is Visual Merchandising?

Visual merchandising refers to the coordination of all physical elements in a place of business so that it projects the right image to its customers. The "right" image is one that invites interest in the merchandise or services being offered, encourages their purchase, and makes the customer feel good about where he or she is doing business.

Successful businesses create distinct, clear, and consistent images for their customers. A good image helps separate a business from others that offer similar products, making it appear unique. Such an image is a blend of customer characteristics, store location, products, prices, advertising, publicity, and personal selling. However, its most important component is sales promotion, of which visual merchandising is a form.

This chapter primarily focuses on retail visual merchandising. But it is important for you to know that manufacturers and wholesalers also use visual merchandising to sell their products. Visual merchandising is used extensively, for example, at industrial trade shows.

The term *visual merchandising* is sometimes used interchangeably with the term *display*. The two are not the same, however. Display is a much narrower concept. It is only one part of visual merchandising. *Display refers to the visual and artistic aspects of presenting a product to a target group of customers.* Visual merchandising, by contrast, involves the visual and artistic aspects of the entire business environment.

With the growth of self-service retailing, visual merchandising has increased tremendously in importance. Consider the example of the supermarket. In such a retail environment, there is no personal selling. Products must sell themselves if they are to move. This fact has spurred manufacturers of food and grocery items to develop innovative product designs, packaging, and displays. These have had a strong influence on the promotional activities of many full-service retailers.

People involved with visual merchandising, then, are responsible for the total merchandise or service presentation, the overall business image, and even the building and placement of design elements.

Today's visual merchandiser is an active member of the decision-making team that promotes a business.

Elements of Visual Merchandising

Visual merchandising is used to make a store and its merchandise so attractive that the customer will enjoy the shopping experience and want to return. To achieve this end, stores manipulate four key elements: *storefront*, *store layout*, *store interior*, and *interior displays*.

Storefront

The total exterior of a business is known as the storefront. The storefront includes the entranceways, display windows, marquee, and the building itself (its design and setting).

The importance of an effective storefront cannot be overestimated. Well designed, it can project an appropriate image—discount or expensive, conservative or trendy. It can also attract potential customers by making the business stand out from its competition.

Marquee. One of the first things customers see after they take in the general outlines of the building and any landscaping is the marquee. *The marquee is a sign that is used to display the store's name.* Such a sign can be painted or lighted. It can be used alone or with a recognized trademark. Marquees are designed primarily to attract attention and advertise a business's location. Like any form of typeface, they can also be used to project image. A discount appliance store, for example, might use bold, blocklike capitals in its marquee; an upscale department store, an elegant script.

Entrances. Entrances are usually designed with customer convenience and store security in mind. Normally, smaller stores have only one entrance, while larger stores (such as department stores) have several. The average midsize business probably needs at least two entrances—one leading in off the street for pedestrians and another adjacent to the parking lot for patrons who drive.

There are several types of entrances. There are revolving, push-pull, electronic, or climate-controlled entrances. (The latter are found in enclosed shopping malls.) Each of these projects a certain image. Electronically controlled sliding doors, for example, suggest a practical, self-service business. Push-pull doors, which often have fancy metal or wooden push plates or bars, suggest a full-service establishment.

Window Displays. Display windows, when available on a building's exterior, are especially useful for visual merchandising. Displays placed in these windows can begin the selling process even before the potential customer enters the store.

Window displays are designed to attract the customer by suggesting both the type of merchandise and the type of atmosphere that lie within. There are three basic kinds of window displays.

Promotional displays promote the sale of one or more of the store's items. They do so by presenting the item with special lighting, signs, and/or props. An arrangement of Halloween candy accented with pumpkins, skeletons, and black and orange trim is an example.

Institutional displays promote store image rather than specific products. Such displays are designed to support sales indirectly by building customer goodwill. Examples include displays featuring store employees and their achievements, tributes to organizations that the business officially sponsors (such as Little League teams), and seasonal decorations presented for their own sake.

Public service displays focus on public causes, worthy ideas, or community organizations. Such displays might feature the activities of the International Red Cross or local volunteer efforts on behalf of the "Reading Is Fundamental" program. The purpose of such displays is to enhance store image by showing that the business is interested in the welfare of the community.

Store Layout

Store layout refers to the way floor space is allocated to facilitate sales and serve the customer. A typical layout divides a store into four different kinds of space.

1. *Selling space* is assigned for interior displays, sales demonstrations, and sales transactions.
2. *Merchandise space* is allocated to items that are kept in inventory.
3. *Personnel space* is assigned to store employees for lockers, lunch breaks, and restrooms.

4. *Customer space* is assigned for the comfort and convenience of the customer. Such space may include a restaurant, dressing rooms, and lounges.

Once selling space has been allocated, visual merchandising personnel work closely with management to decide the best locations for particular kinds of merchandise. Typical questions that must be answered at this point include the following:

1. Where will the general product categories be located in the store?
2. Which products will be located closest to doors, elevators, parking lots, and other exits?
3. Where should impulse and convenience goods be placed?
4. How should related items, such as shirts, ties, and belts, be displayed?
5. Where should seasonal and off-season products be located?
6. Where should bulky items be located?
7. How close should interior and window displays be to the related department or inventory?
8. What traffic patterns should be designed to encourage customer shopping?
9. How can merchandise be placed to encourage shopping and eliminate crowding?

Store Interior

Once the general placement of merchandise has been determined, store personnel can begin developing the visual merchandising approaches that they will use on the building's interior. The selection of such diverse elements as floor and wall coverings, lighting, colors, and store fixtures can powerfully affect store image.

Take flooring, for example. Discount stores use linoleum or tile floors to project an inexpensive, practical image. Jewelry stores use thick carpeting to send just the opposite message to their customers.

Colors and lighting can be used in a similar fashion. Bright colors and light pastels (or plain white) appeal to different types of customers. Stores catering to teens might favor bright colors and bright lighting. Stores catering to adults would probably choose pastels and soft, subtle lighting effects. Discount stores would choose simple fluorescent lighting, while prestige retailers might install expensive chandeliers.

The principal installations in a store, however, are the fixtures. *Fixtures are store furnishings, such as display cases, counters, shelving, racks, and benches.* These can be permanent or movable.

A business seeking an upscale image might enhance its fixtures by painting them or covering them with textured materials of various kinds (carpeting, fabric, cork, or reed, for example). A business catering to discount buyers would most likely leave its fixtures plain and exposed.

Walls are another interior feature that can be covered to reinforce store image. For example, small or subtly patterned paper is often used by women's specialty stores, while department stores tend to favor plain white.

The width of a store's aisles probably influences behavior more directly than any other element of visual merchandising. Wide, uncluttered aisles create a more positive impression than narrow, cramped ones. Customers shop longer and are more relaxed when they are not pressed by crowds or delayed by long lines.

Finally, the size, variety, and quality of the merchandise assortment carried by a store affects its clientele. High-end, brand-named merchandise conveys an entirely different image from low-end, generic (nonbrand) goods. Each will attract (or put off) a different kind of customer.

Interior Displays

Strictly speaking, the displays in a store are part of the general store interior. However, as elements of visual merchandising, they are so significant that they are commonly considered in a category by themselves. This is because such displays generate one out of every four sales. They do so by showing merchandise, providing customers with product information, getting customers to stop and shop the store, reinforcing print and other forms of advertising, and promoting the store's image.

Interior displays are usually promotional. They use counters, cases, ledges, columns, platforms, islands, and floor fixtures to showcase merchandise. If they are done exceptionally well, they enable customers to make a selection without personal assis-

CASE CHALLENGE

From Supermarket to Supermercado

In 1987, the Kroger Company became the largest nationwide supermarket operator to target a specific ethnic group. Kroger remodeled a seven-year-old food and drugstore combination unit in San Antonio, Texas, and targeted the store to the city's large Mexican-American population.

The store was given a face-lift to create an open and bright atmosphere. The walls were painted blue. Tasteful murals were placed above the dairy, meat, and produce departments. Oversized piñatas were hung from the ceiling and bunches of balloons tied to the checkstands.

The result has been a resounding success. Customers say the decor reminds them of Mexico, where grocery shopping is often an hours-long affair in which the whole family participates.

1. Why do you think Kroger made such a major investment in visual merchandising in its San Antonio store?
2. What image is Kroger trying to project with the newly renovated store?
3. How should the store's merchandise selection be changed to reinforce the new image? What kinds of new services might be offered?
4. What other circumstances might cause a business to remodel or renovate its facilities?

Retailers use the store interior—including displays—to project the kind of image and reach the kind of customer they want. What do these displays say about their respective stores? What kinds of customers is each trying to attract?

tance. Thus, they occupy an especially important place in today's selling environment where many stores are self-service.

There are five types of interior displays.

Closed displays allow customers to see but not handle merchandise. They are found in catalog showrooms or businesses such as jewelry stores where security or breakage is a concern.

Open displays allow customers to handle and examine merchandise without the help of a salesperson. Hanging racks for suits and dresses or countertop and shelf displays for cosmetics are examples.

Architectural displays consist of model rooms that allow customers to see how merchandise might

look in their homes. Such "rooms" need not be defined by walls or partitions. Area rugs or the arrangement of the furniture itself can be used to suggest the setting.

Point-of-purchase displays are open displays designed primarily to promote impulse purchases. They are usually supplied by a product manufacturer for use at or near the point of sale (checkstand, cash register, etc.). Frito Lay potato chips, Bulova watches, Hanes panty hose, and Mars candy products are examples of merchandise often sold through point-of-purchase displays.

Store decorations are displays that coincide with specific seasons or holidays. Banners, signs, props, and similar items used to invoke the spirit of Christmas, Valentine's Day, summer, or fall are examples.

Display Design and Preparation

In the ordinary retail environment, a display has about three to eight seconds to attract a customer's attention, create a desire, and sell a product. This restricted time frame means that a business must target its displays carefully to appeal to its core customer. If it fails to do so, it not only risks losing sales but ruining its image as well. For example, the traditional clothing store that suddenly begins showing abstract displays of trendy merchandise is likely to attract some new style-conscious customers. It is also likely to alienate many of its regular customers.

Thus, before displays are built, promotional and visual merchandising staffs should agree on the answers to these questions:

1. What is the image of our business?
2. Who are our customers?
3. What kind of merchandise concept is being promoted (trendy, conservative, formal, casual, etc.)?
4. Where will the display be built and located?
5. What merchandise will be displayed?
6. How will the selection of merchandise affect the display's design? How will it affect our business's image?

Selecting Merchandise for Display

The merchandise selected for a display determines its scope. There are four possibilities.

A *one-item display* shows a single item. An example would be Swatch watches displayed on a counter with the Swatch logo or a promotional sign. One-item displays are usually constructed for a single product promotion or an advertised special.

A *line-of-goods display* shows one kind of product but features several brands, sizes, or models. An example would be a display of running shoes put out by various manufacturers or a display of all the different running shoes put out by a single manufacturer.

A *related-merchandise display* features items that are meant to be used together. In a sporting goods store, for example, such a display might feature camping gear—tents, cooking equipment, backpacks, and sleeping bags. Related-merchandise displays are designed primarily to entice the customers to buy more than one item.

A *variety display* (also called an *assortment display*) features a collection of unrelated items. Such displays usually emphasize price and tell customers that a wide variety of merchandise is available for sale. They are typically used by variety stores, discounters, and supermarkets to make a special appeal to bargain hunters.

Choosing a Setting Type

Displays can be presented in a number of different types of settings. Which type a business favors will be determined largely by the image it is trying to project.

A *realistic setting* depicts a room, area, or recognizable locale. The scene could be a restaurant, a park, or a party. The details are provided by props, such as tables, chairs, plants, risers, books, dishes, and mannequins. In a realistic setting, make sure the merchandise being featured is not overshadowed by the setting itself or by the props.

A *semirealistic setting* suggests a room or locale but leaves the details to the imagination of the viewer. For example, a cardboard sun, beach towel, surfing poster, and a sprinkling of sand would be enough to invoke the rest of the scene—an oceanfront beach—in the viewer's mind. Semirealistic settings are used when either space or budget do not permit the construction of realistic settings.

An *abstract setting* does not imitate (or even try to imitate) reality. Its artistic values are form and color rather than faithful reproduction of actual objects. For example, wide bands of torn colored paper used as an accent behind or around merchandise can create an attractive visual image that has nothing to do with reality.

Abstract settings are gaining popularity, mainly because they are inexpensive and do not require large amounts of storage space for accumulated props. Display specialists are increasingly accenting products with such items as cardboard, paper, string, yarn, ribbon, and paint in preference to more traditional and realistic items.

Using Fixtures

Display specialists work with a great variety of fixtures. Counters, closed cases, shelves, ledges, tables, risers, and platforms increase designers' options and provide the latitude they need to do both effective and creative work. In this section, we will discuss some of the more important fixtures on which display specialists rely.

Counter units are display fixtures designed to hold small merchandise, such as jewelry and cosmetics. They can be constructed of metal, wood, plastic, or any combination of these. Counter units are considered part of the store's decor as well as part of its fixturing. Therefore, stores place much importance on selecting the proper bases, finishes, and decorative details.

Demonstration cubes are also widely used. They come in a variety of sizes and can be upholstered, painted, laminated, or wood-finished. Cubes are used as stands for mannequins, display surfaces for merchandise, and props in product demonstrations. They are especially effective for island displays placed right in or immediately off aisles. Such placements are used to get special attention for merchandise.

Ledges are areas above the storage units that are customarily placed behind selling counters. Ledge displays tend to be higher than eye level and often take advantage of the architecture of the store. They make powerful presentations because of their elevation above the merchandise and the customer traffic. Ledges are good locations to place signs, present merchandise, and identify product sections.

Shadow boxes are miniature display windows, usually at eye-level, that can be placed either inside or outside a selling area. Shadow boxes are used to display small, expensive items, such as rings and necklaces. Because of the small size of most shadow boxes, they are effective for highlighting one piece of merchandise.

Enclosed displays are fully glassed-in island platforms that can hold one or several mannequins. Enclosed displays are used at the entrance to a department or aisle or as part of a perimeter wall. Enclosed displays show merchandise and also protect it from soiling, customer handling, and possible theft.

Walls and *columns* are also used to display merchandise. For example, clothing can be pinned to both surfaces. This technique has the advantage of both saving space and attracting customers with higher-than-eye-level displays.

Display Props

Props used in displays are generally classified as *decorative* or *functional*. Decorative props include such things as background scenery used to indicate a season or simply to create an interesting setting. Functional props include such functional items for holding merchandise as mannequins and shirt forms.

Obviously, the types of props used will vary with the merchandise displayed. Display designers often look for unusual props or unusual ways to use common items as props. Imaginative jewelry display designers, for example, have used such things as open candy boxes to display colored stone rings in the candy papers.

Manipulating Artistic Elements

The artistic elements of a display include *line*, *color*, *shape*, *direction*, *texture*, *proportion*, *motion*, and *lighting*. These elements influence your perception of a display in ways that you are probably not aware of.

Line. Since people read books from left to right, they also tend to read displays the same way. Therefore, visual merchandisers try to create lines within displays that travel from left to right over all the products featured.

Various types of lines create different impressions. Straight lines suggest stiffness and control; curving lines, freedom and movement; diagonal lines, action; vertical lines, height and dignity; and horizontal lines, width and confidence.

REAL WORLD MARKETING

What Color Is Your Label?

In a blind coffee tasting test, coffee from a yellow can impressed consumers as too weak. Coffee from a brown can struck them as too strong. Nevertheless, the coffee in the two cans was identical. This supports the theory, now common among market researchers, that the color of a product's packaging affects its sales. When Canada Dry switched its sugar-free ginger ale cans from red to green and white, sales shot up by 27 percent.

Color. Color can make or break a display. Displays whose colors match their surroundings too closely may not catch the customer's eye. Displays whose colors are too bright or contrasting may overwhelm the merchandise being presented. In either case, the displays will fail.

The colors selected for a display should contrast with those used on the walls, floors, and fixtures around them. For example, a store done in pastels should have displays featuring darker, stronger colors.

Which colors make the most effective contrasts? The answers can be found in the standard color wheel (Fig. 22-1), which illustrates the relationships among colors. *Complementary colors are found opposite each other in the color wheel and create the greatest contrasts.* Red and green, blue and orange, and violet and yellow are examples of complementary colors.

Adjacent colors (also called analogous colors) are located next to each other in the color wheel and contrast only slightly. Successive adjacent colors (such as blue-green, blue, and blue-violet) form families, or groups of colors that blend well with each other.

Effective displays use these color groupings to advantage to create visual calm or excitement. For example, colors from the warm side of the color wheel, such as red and yellow, convey a festive, party mood

that works well with lower-priced merchandise. Such colors must be used cautiously, however. Their contrast is so great that it can detract from the merchandise and even irritate customers. This problem can usually be avoided by varying the shades of the colors somewhat to lessen their contrast yet still retain their warmth and friendliness. Colors from the cool side of the color wheel, such as blue and green, connote calm and refinement. They are often associated with higher-priced merchandise.

Customers' expectations about color are also important in planning displays. People have come to expect certain color schemes at certain times of the year or for certain kinds of merchandise—for example, green for St. Patrick's Day, orange and brown for fall, and pastels for infant's clothing.

Finally, customers' reactions to color also figure into planning displays. Red, for example, evokes excitement. So, you would not use it in a display designed to convey tranquility.

The best way to learn about color use in displays is to visit stores with regularity and observe what color combinations are being used. Another way is to read visual merchandising, trade, and fashion magazines, such as *Visual Merchandising*, *Interior Design*, and *Vogue*.

Shape. *Shape* refers to the physical appearance, or outline, of a display. It is important to con-

Color can excite, soothe, shout, or showcase. Which does it do in this display? How well does the use of color conform to color-wheel theory?

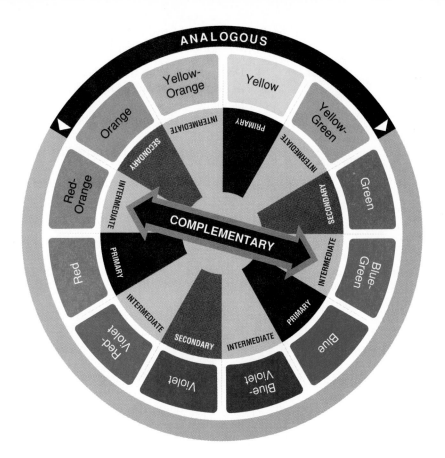

Figure 22-1 **The Color Wheel**

The color wheel is structured to show both similarities and differences in colors. Which colors are most like each other? Which show the greatest contrast?

sider shape when selecting display units and the merchandise used in a display.

Shape is determined by the props, fixtures, and merchandise used in the display. However, the shape of a display is not limited by the merchandise itself. Squares, cubes, circles, and triangles are some of the shapes that display units may resemble. Displays that have little or no distinct shape—called *mass displays*—are also possible. Mass displays are often used to display large quantities of merchandise and to convey a message of low price.

Direction. A good display guides the viewer's eye over all the merchandise, moving smoothly from one part of the display to another. It does not skip around. This smooth visual flow is called *direction*.

Good displays create direction by using color, repetition, lighting patterns, ribbons, and by arranging merchandise in a pattern to guide the customer's eye.

Displays should have a *focal point*. A good method of creating a focal point is to build a display around an imaginary triangle (having more merchan-

dise at the bottom of the display than at the top, for example). This arrangement helps keep the eyes moving up and center.

Displays that lack direction are said to be *unfocused*. Typically, they contain too many unrelated items, too many colors, or too many lines that both confuse the customer and detract from the merchandise.

Texture. Texture refers to the way the surfaces in a display look together. These surfaces can be either smooth or rough. The contrast between them creates visual interest.

Products that are smooth, such as flatware, should be placed against backgrounds or props that are rough. Items that are rough, such as jewelry, should be displayed against smooth surfaces (a dark velvet cloth is traditional).

Proportion. *Proportion is the relationship between and among objects in a display.* The merchandise should always be the primary focus of a display. Props and signs should be in proportion to the merchandise—they should never overshadow it in importance. Poor use of proportion creates a display that is either too crowded or too empty.

Balance. *Placing large items with large items and small items with small items in a display is called formal balance.* For example, if a large item is placed on one side of a display, an equally large item should be placed on the other side to balance the arrangement.

The opposite technique can also be exciting in a display. *Balancing a large item with several small ones is called informal balance.* An example would be a display in which an adult mannequin is juxtaposed with several short baskets of flowers raised to the mannequin's height.

Motion. Motion can be made part of a display through the use of motorized fixtures and props. For example, animated figures, such as mechanical mannequins, have been used for years in holiday displays.

Motion should be used sparingly to accentuate merchandise. Like color, it can become distracting if it is overdone.

Lighting. Proper lighting makes merchandise appear more attractive in displays. As a general rule, it is recommended that display lighting be two to five times stronger than a store's general lighting. The actual strength will depend on whether the display is interior or exterior.

Display lighting should follow three basic rules.

1. It should match the image of the business.
2. It should not cast shadows over the merchandise being displayed.
3. It should not create a glare.

Colored lighting can be used in displays to create dramatic effects. For example, tinted lamps can cast sharp black or grey shadows against a background. When using such lamps, however, you should keep in mind that the customer must always be able to see the merchandise in its true colors.

Display Maintenance

Once a display has been constructed, it needs to be maintained. The merchandise especially must be kept clean and attractive during its presentation life.

Individual businesses have different policies, procedures, and practices regarding the duration of displays. Most businesses, however, observe the same general rules for display maintenance.

1. Displays should be checked daily for damage or displacement caused by customer handling.
2. Missing merchandise should be replaced immediately.
3. Lights should be checked periodically and replaced as necessary.
4. Display units and props should be cleaned and merchandise dusted on a regular basis.

Proper display maintenance can keep the merchandise fresh and attractive in the eyes of customers. Poor maintenance, on the other hand, can create a negative image not only of the merchandise but of the store as well.

Dismantling Procedures for Displays

Specific procedures for dismantling displays also vary with each business. Some general procedures that should be followed are suggested by the questions below. All should be answered yes to ensure that materials, merchandise, fixtures, backgrounds, and props remain in good condition after display use.

1. Were the proper tools gathered before the display was dismantled?
2. Was the display dismantled safely?
3. Was the merchandise removed without damage?
4. Was the merchandise checked for problems before it was returned to stock?
5. Was any damaged merchandise properly recorded?
6. Was the merchandise returned to stock or to the selling area?
7. Was the background removed without damage?
8. Were the mirrors, if any, polished?
9. Was the display area cleaned?
10. Was the floor vacuumed or cleaned?
11. Were the props cleaned or polished?
12. Were the fixtures and props returned to display storage?
13. Were the lights checked for possible replacement?

VOCABULARY REVIEW

Write a brief definition of each term, based on your reading of the chapter.

visual merchandising
display
storefront
marquee
store layout
fixtures

complementary colors
adjacent colors
proportion
formal balance
informal balance

FACT AND IDEA REVIEW

1. Explain the relationship between visual merchandising and display.

2. What is the difference between a storefront and a marquee?

3. List the three different types of window displays and give an example of each.

4. Identify the four types of space found in most store layouts.

5. Describe the five different types of interior displays and provide an example of each.

6. What questions must every business address before constructing displays? Why?

7. Identify the four different merchandise assortments used in constructing displays.

8. What kinds of settings are used in displays?

9. Give three examples of common display fixtures.

10. Distinguish between complementary and adjacent colors.

11. Explain the difference between formal and informal balance.

12. What does display maintenance entail?

CRITICAL THINKING

1. Assume you are the display manager for a large department store. What basic skills would you require in any visual merchandiser you hired?

2. Explain why it is important to know your community and your customers when designing store displays.

3. Is it necessary for a visual merchandiser to know basic selling techniques? Justify your response.

4. Entrances should be designed for customer convenience. However, retailers in some locations are limiting the number of functioning entrances because of concern over shoplifting and pilferage. Discuss some other strategies you think might be used in stores to reduce theft risks around or near entrances.

5. Manufacturers often provide point-of-purchase displays to retailers. If you were a retailer, what criteria would you use in deciding whether or not to accept such a display?

6. The newest colors in ready-to-wear—hot pink, lime green, and irridescent orange—clash with your store's conservative, beige-on-brown decor. You must display the merchandise. How do you do so without creating jarring or irritating effects?

7. A new store is opening in your community. From the parking lot, flower beds, shrubbery, potted trees, and benches bracket the main entrance. There's even a two-storey sculpture attached to the front wall below the store's marquee. What image is this business trying to project?

USING BASIC SKILLS

Math

1. Assume the following are your costs for an interior display: staple gun ($18.95), two rolls of double-stick tape ($14.00 each), box of hot glue ($6.75), glue gun ($12.50), and a dozen chrome hangers ($.75 each). What would be your total bill in each of these cases?

   a. The prices remain as indicated.

   b. Your supplier gives you a 5 percent discount on all items.

   c. All tools are discounted 20 percent.

2. You must install vinyl wall covering in a display area. The surface to be covered is 12 feet by 24 feet. If you must pay $1.65 per square foot for vinyl, what amount would you budget for the job?

3. You must recondition a half dozen mannequins (two adult and four youth). If reconditioning a youth mannequin costs $90 and reconditioning an adult mannequin costs 50 percent more, what amount should you budget for the entire job?

Communication

4. You work as a visual merchandiser for the largest department store in your community. You would like the store to devote one of its main display windows to a public service that you strongly support. Write a formal proposal detailing your views. Be sure to name the public service, describe the nature of the display, and indicate how you believe the store will benefit. Also be prepared to counter the argument that window space is too valuable to devote to public causes, that less visible space will suffice and can be found inside the building.

Human Relations

5. Your store recently installed lock racks for all ready-to-wear items costing more than $100. In some departments this means that all the merchandise is secured with locks, keys, and metal cords that must be removed by store personnel before an item can be tried on. The fixtures have cut theft losses by half but are extremely unpopular with customers. Salespeople, who must deal firsthand with the public, are taking the brunt of the criticism. "Well, *I* don't steal," they're told, and "I don't have time for this. It's only a jacket—I mean, it's not worth

the trouble. I *can* shop somewhere else, you know." If you were one of these salespeople, how would you respond to these customers?

APPLICATION PROJECTS

1. Draw a floor plan showing the layout of a local business. (If you choose a department store, diagram only one floor.) Color code those areas provided for merchandise, selling, customers, and personnel. Then critique the layout in terms of ease of entry, traffic flow, utilization of display space, and availability of customer conveniences.

2. Select a holiday or season as a theme. Then describe an effective window display based on that theme and suitable for use by one of the businesses listed below. Be sure to specify the kinds of merchandise you would feature.
   a. Toy store
   b. Pet store
   c. Travel agency
   d. Lawn and garden supply store

3. Visit your cooperative education training station or a local retailer. Identify at least eight different types of interior displays and specify the kinds of merchandise featured. Examples: countertop—stationery; cases—pen-and-pencil sets; point of purchase—key chains.

4. Visit a local department store to observe and rate the displays. For each display considered, do a simple sketch, indicate color, and briefly describe both the merchandise featured and any apparent theme. Evaluate each display in terms of the artistic elements discussed in this chapter.

Publicity and
Public
Relations

OBJECTIVES

After completing this chapter, you will be able to:

1. describe the various elements of public relations,

2. explain the nature of company participation in community affairs,

3. tell why publicity is good for a business,

4. write news releases that benefit a business, and

5. describe the role of public relations and publicity in a company's promotional mix.

WORDS TO KNOW

public relations
customer advisory boards
consumer affairs specialists
community relations
news release

T he largest department store in town sponsors the Thanksgiving Day parade. An electronics firm releases some of its employees to teach math and science classes at a local high school. Throughout the main business district, shops put out donation containers for the United Fund.

None of these activities is likely to bring their sponsors a dime of profit—at least, not directly. Some, in fact, are likely to cost money. So, why do the businesses do it? The answer is simple: it's good public relations.

In this chapter, you will learn what public relations specialists do, and you will develop an understanding of the role that publicity and public relations play in a company's promotional mix.

Elements of Public Relations

A business, like you, has a personality. Your personality is the face you show the world. A business's personality is its image.

Just as your personality is made up of many facets, so is the image of a business. People form an impression of a business based on how well its employees treat the public, how reliable its products are, how well its locations are maintained. They also consider what its policies are, what its advertising and publications say, how it is presented in the media, and what it contributes to the civic and cultural life of the community.

Well-run businesses do not leave these things to chance. They work hard to create a favorable image. How? They engage in public relations.

Public relations refers to any activity designed to create goodwill toward a business. This goodwill benefits a business by

- increasing sales,
- reinforcing the firm's good reputation,
- increasing the receptivity of consumers to the firm's advertising,
- conditioning customers to expect quality products from the firm,
- reducing the impact of problems (complaints, critical news stories, employee disputes) when they do occur, and
- helping to obtain better treatment from government regarding zoning, licenses, and taxes.

The types of activities that qualify as public relations and the audiences to which they are targeted are many and varied. Businesses are concerned with their employees, customers, and the general public.

Employee Relations

To customers, employees are the company. Successful businesses have loyal and well-motivated employees who feel they are important to the company. The public relations staff works with management to design programs that foster such attitudes. These programs include

- job training,
- newsletters for and about the company and its employees (these are commonly called *house organs*),
- open communication between management and employees,
- promotion from within, and
- employee suggestion programs and awards for improvements in performance and efficiency.

The importance of good employee relations cannot be overestimated. Effective and well-run organizations should be able to answer yes to these questions:

1. Are job descriptions and responsibilities clearly identified?
2. Does the organization's structure minimize duplication and maximize the use of each employee's skills?
3. Do employees know how they will be rated for promotion and salary increases?
4. Is the wage and benefit package competitive with other businesses in the field?
5. Are training or advanced study opportunities available to employees?
6. Is there a formal motivation program for employees?
7. Does the company avoid discriminatory employment practices?
8. Are employees informed in advance about events and plans that will affect their work?
9. Are regular staff meetings held?
10. Are rules and regulations explained to employees? Is each employee given a copy of these rules and regulations?
11. Are employees informed of job openings in other departments?
12. Does an open-door management policy exist for suggestions and communication?

Customer Relations

Good communication between employees and customers is vital in promoting a favorable business image. What you say and how you say it can make all the difference between a dissatisfied customer and a loyal patron. Courtesy, helpfulness, interest, tolerance, and friendliness bring customers back. This repeat business is what makes a company successful.

Many retail firms, however, go further than just friendliness and courtesy. They offer shoppers special services and amenities in order to maintain good customer relations. These services and amenities include restaurants, child-care facilities, gift wrapping, and free delivery.

Other public relations efforts are less obvious. *Customer advisory boards are panels of consumers who make suggestions on new products and services.* Customer advisory boards are used by manufacturers and retailers alike to test new products or services. For example, a local retailer might want to learn about customer preferences regarding store hours, billing procedures, or delivery services. By consulting with an advisory board, the retailer can adjust or change policies to meet the needs of customers.

Some larger department stores also hire consultants to assist customers with their purchases. Fashion, makeup, travel, bridal, and interior decorating consultants are examples of employees with specialized training who are hired by some retail firms.

National companies often employ consumer affairs specialists to handle customer complaints and to serve as consumer advocates within the firm. Consumer affairs specialists design programs to reflect customer needs, such as nutrition, health, and product safety.

Many businesses also sponsor special events to foster positive customer relations. Examples include fashion shows, preferred-customer sales, and benefit raffles.

Community Relations

Community relations refers to the activities that a business uses to acquire or maintain the respect of the community. Businesses foster good community relations by participating in and sponsoring activities that benefit the civic, social, and cultural life of a community. Some examples of community relations activities include sponsoring Little League teams, awarding scholarships to deserving students, financing guest speakers for civic organizations, and making matching donations to local charities.

Community relations is an important activity for businesses. Employees, who represent the company in the community, are often encouraged to join and remain active in civic organizations, such as the Jaycees, Rotary Club, Junior Achievement, or the local chamber of commerce. Some companies reward their employees with time off for participating in charitable fund-raising efforts aimed at community improvement or enhancement.

Businesses need to be active members of their communities. Although the primary aim of community relations work is to promote civic pride and help the local residents, these events also help create goodwill for their business participants. Customers and the general public do pay attention to the sponsors of community-wide activities.

Publicity

Recall from Chapter 19 that publicity involves placing newsworthy information about a company in the media. The basic difference between advertising and publicity is that publicity is not paid for by the business, a fact that makes it more credible to many people. For this reason, publicity is an excellent way to spread information about a company and its products.

The disadvantage of publicity, of course, is that it cannot be controlled by the business. The bad stories are as likely to get publicized as the good. Thus, businesses work to generate positive publicity about themselves whenever possible.

Public relations specialists attempt to get good publicity for their companies by creating news events. Here are some examples:

- the opening of a new store,
- an interview with a company official,
- the launching of a new product or product line,
- the announcement of promotions or retirements,

REAL WORLD MARKETING

Tamper Tantrum

After a Chicago woman died late in 1982 from swallowing cyanide-laced Tylenol capsules, leaders at McNeil Laboratory had a fit of despair over the bleak future of their product. However, modern advertising know-how and innovative product design helped them win back the public's trust. The answer to their woes—the tamper-proof package—appeared within weeks of the incident, spurring one of the most dramatic recoveries in consumer merchandising history.

Every time the news media do a story involving a particular company, that firm's name is put before the public. What company is the probable subject of this report? What sort of company events might the media deem newsworthy enough to feature?

- the presentation of an award to the company or one of its employees,
- a community activity, such as a parade or an exhibit sponsored by the business, and
- a charitable activity in which the business participates, such as the U.S. Marines' "Toys for Tots" campaign.

What Public Relations Specialists Do

If you are employed in public relations, you will work with more than just customers, employees, and the media. You will also consult with social and professional groups, legislators and government officials, consumer activists, environmentalists, stockholders, and suppliers. Your principal task in all these encounters is to get out the good news about the company and its products—and to control the damage done by any bad news.

The public relations specialist's principal tool is the news release. *A news release is a prewritten story about a company that is sent to the various media.* It usually contains information about the company's employees, stores, operations, products, or corporate philosophy.

A news release must contain a certain amount of newsworthy information in order to be picked up and carried by the media. To be successful, then, public relations personnel must observe certain guidelines in planning and carrying out publicity projects.

1. Publicity projects should be selected for multiple uses. For example, information gathered for a news release should also be appropriate for use in a new company brochure or ad.
2. Public affairs staff should send only important news releases to the media. (For example, a news release telling of a shopping mall expansion that will result in many new jobs created in a community has a good chance of being run by the media.) If a media source is overwhelmed with submissions, it will tend after a while to disregard them. By sending significant news releases periodically, a business has a better chance of having its material published.
3. News releases should be sent to all media, both print and broadcast, at the same time. The chances that one will use the material are greater when all are contacted.
4. News releases should have a continuity of theme extending over many months or even years. Similar repeat messages will achieve maximum impact on an audience. For example, a consistent message might be that a business is community-minded. Such is the case with Lady Foot Locker, which has been a major sponsor of the largest Women's 5K Run in the Southwest since 1986. Annual proceeds from the race benefit a local foundation in its fight against cancer. As a result, the race has been well publicized in newspapers and on television.

5. Remember that the press, radio, and television are interested in news, not publicity. Therefore, the word *publicity* should never be used when communicating with media personnel.

While news releases are the major corporate documents for which public relations specialists are responsible, they are not the only ones. Public relations staff also prepare annual reports, brochures, flyers, and responses to customer inquiries. Occasionally, they even write short feature articles for trade magazines.

Writing, however, is only half the public relations specialist's job. Public relations personnel frequently meet customers and the public face-to-face. They attend conventions, run trade-show exhibits, and prepare and deliver audiovisual presentations.

Public relations specialists work in the public as well as the private sector. The public sector includes schools, hospitals, universities, government agencies, charitable organizations, and the military. Like private businesses, public agencies also have a need to project a favorable image.

Public Relations in the Promotional Mix

Recall from Chapter 19 that in most businesses publicity is only one part of a promotional mix that also includes advertising, personal selling, and sales promotion.

Unlike other components of this mix, public relations and publicity do not always increase sales. Often their real value lies in the relationship that they build between the business and the general public.

Public relations brings a special set of benefits to the promotional mix itself. Through public relations,

- accurate information (from the business's viewpoint) is shared with the public,
- potential problems can be anticipated and explained before any controversy results, and
- questions that affect the business can be answered before they are asked by the media.

CASE CHALLENGE

Giving Till It Burps

The Gerber Products Company is a leading producer of baby foods in the United States. There are more than 160 Gerber food products that are made in three U.S. plants. Gerber baby foods are sold in the United States and more than 80 foreign countries. Gerber also markets stuffed animals, toys, baby clothes, and car seats.

In 1988, Gerber donated more than $300,000 to three national charities—the March of Dimes, Childhelp USA, and the Special Olym-

pics. In addition, Gerber regularly donates food, toys, and clothing to families with triplets, quadruplets, and quintuplets to help ease the financial impact of the new arrivals.

1. What image is Gerber projecting with its program of giving, particularly to families who have recently experienced multiple births?
2. Defend this statement: "Gerber targets its giving as carefully as it targets its products." Is this a good policy? Why or why not?

CHAPTER 23 REVIEW

VOCABULARY REVIEW

Write a paragraph incorporating all of the following vocabulary terms.

public relations

customer advisory
  boards

consumer affairs
  specialists

community relations

news release

FACT AND IDEA REVIEW

1. What is public relations?

2. List three programs and/or policies that businesses use to improve their image in the eyes of their employees.

3. How do the duties of a customer advisory board differ from those of a consumer affairs specialist?

4. List three community relations activities that businesses commonly participate in or sponsor.

5. Suggest three business occasions that might be newsworthy enough to generate favorable publicity for a company.

6. What is a news release?

7. List three do's and don'ts that public relations specialists observe when submitting news releases to the media and explain the rationale behind each of them.

8. What special contributions do public relations and publicity make to a company's promotional mix?

CRITICAL THINKING

1. What is meant by the statement "To the customer, the employees *are* the company."

2. Explain the difference between public relations and publicity.

3. Marketing specialists concentrate nearly all of their attention on two audiences—customers and prospects. Public relations specialists, however, recognize other audiences who have legitimate interests in what businesses do. Identify five of these "other audiences" and explain why businesses should respond to them.

4. Identify local businesses that have community relations programs. What kinds of activities are they using to enhance their reputations in the community?

USING BASIC SKILLS

Math

1. Assume that you must submit a budget for your marketing program's public relations activities over the next school year (ten months from September to June). You have $500 to spend. Identify the activities that you would schedule and the costs associated with each (by month). *Note:* You can spend on special events, guest speakers, news releases, personal letters, and newsletters—but not advertising.

Communication

2. Write a job description for a public relations specialist, based on what you have learned in this chapter.

3. Write a news release announcing the grand opening of the school store for the upcoming school year. Limit your copy to 250 words.

4. Write a letter inviting a guest speaker to address your class on a topic of interest within the field of publicity and public relations. (Consult your teacher for a list of acceptable speakers and topics.) In your letter, be sure to describe the audience, any areas of special interest, the format to be used, and any scheduling requirements. Have your letter proofread by your teacher before you mail it.

Human Relations

5. As a rule, middle managers in your company participate in a program of corporate giving. Once a month, a certain amount is automatically deducted from each participant's paycheck and transferred to a corporate account from which distributions are regularly made to established charities. The vice-president to whom you report asks you to participate. You are reluctant. You would prefer to pick your own charities and schedule your own donations. How would you explain your position to your superior?

APPLICATION PROJECTS

1. Collect employee newsletters from relatives, friends, or acquaintances, and contribute them to a class display. After you have had a chance to study all the available publications, select the one that you feel projects the most positive image of the company publishing it. Be prepared to defend your choice by listing those features you found most impressive in the publication you selected— and least impressive in those publications you rejected.

2. Watch a local television news program or read a local newspaper for one week. Keep a log of all stories relating to businesses, local or national. Note the gist of each story, try to determine whether it had its origins in a news release, and note whether the publicity was positive or negative.

3. For each of the following businesses, describe the kinds of public events you might sponsor and the public projects in which you might participate. Explain why they would be good for each business.

   a. A small recycling facility that employs a number of immigrants and minorities.

   b. The largest furniture store in a medium-sized city that boasts two colleges.

   c. A music/videotape store near a retirement community.

4. Choose one event sponsored by each of the companies above and write a news release for it.

5. Your company produces a product that is tampered with after it reaches the stores. As a result, 24 people have become ill enough to need medical care. As public relations officer for the company, what steps would you recommend that the company take?

6. Choose an event or project in your city that is sponsored by a business in the community. Contact the public relations department of the company and ask a representative to speak to your class about the planning that goes into such an event.

7. National Geographic, Hallmark, Mobil Oil, and McDonald's often sponsor TV specials. List three programs you have seen that were sponsored exclusively by these or other companies. Think about the program itself and the type and number of commercials for the sponsor. Describe what image you think the company is trying to project and, by explaining how you felt about the program, tell whether or not you think the company succeeded in its goal.

PART

6

BUSINESS AND DISTRIBUTION OPERATIONS

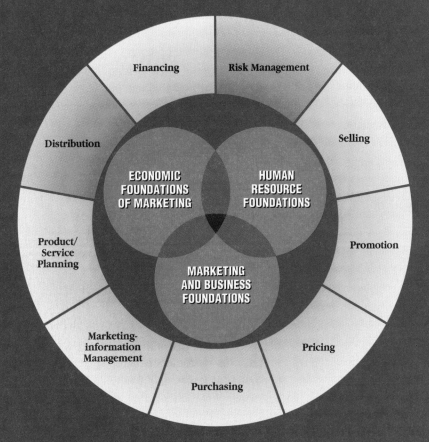

Financing

Risk Management

Distribution

Selling

ECONOMIC FOUNDATIONS OF MARKETING

HUMAN RESOURCE FOUNDATIONS

Product/ Service Planning

Promotion

MARKETING AND BUSINESS FOUNDATIONS

Marketing-information Management

Pricing

Purchasing

CHAPTERS
▼ ▼ ▼ ▼ ▼ ▼ ▼ ▼

24 Physical Distribution

25 Receiving, Checking, and Shipping

26 Stock and Inventory Control

27 Risk Management

28 Marketing Math Applications

24

OBJECTIVES

After completing this chapter, you will be able to:

1. explain the nature and scope of physical distribution,

2. identify transportation systems for the distribution of products,

3. give examples of transportation services,

4. understand storage functions, and

5. identify various types of warehouses.

WORDS TO KNOW

physical distribution
transporting function
common carrier
contract carrier
exempt carrier
private carrier
ton-mile
carload
parcel post
private parcel carrier
express carrier
storage function

Physical Distribution

Physical distribution is the key link between a business and its customers because it delivers the right product at the right time to the right place.

In this chapter you will learn about physical distribution and its relationship to marketing. You will explore transportation systems used by business. You will discover the importance of warehousing to the distribution process. You will also look at the types of warehouses businesses use to store merchandise.

The Scope of Physical Distribution

After a seller makes a purchase, the goods must be moved to the buyer. *Physical distribution is the process of transporting, storing, and handling goods on the way from seller to customer.*

Physical distribution includes freight transportation, warehousing, materials handling, protective packaging, inventory control, warehouse site selection, order processing, market forecasting, and customer service. Given all these activities, you can see that physical distribution is an important link between a business and its customers.

Physical distribution must be coordinated with other business functions, such as purchasing, finance, production, promotion, and advertising. For example, since promotional activities are planned in advance, the distribution system must have the products at the right time and place for the promotion.

As you can imagine, transporting, storing, and handling goods are expensive. In fact, physical distribution is the third largest expense for most businesses. It is surpassed only by the cost of material and labor.

The actual cost of physical distribution differs from business to business. Department stores and speciality stores spend about 2 percent of their total sales on transporting, receiving, storing, and distributing merchandise. Physical distribution costs printers, publishers, and clothing and machinery manufacturers between 4 and 5 percent of total sales. Petroleum refiners spend some 25 percent of their total sales for distribution.

As you learned earlier, physical distribution involves three marketing functions: transporting, storing, and handling merchandise. In this chapter you will look at transportation and storage. In Chapter 25 you will explore merchandise handling.

The Transporting Function

Once something has been sold, it usually needs to be moved from the seller to the consumer. *The transporting function is the marketing function of moving goods from sellers to buyers.* Manufacturers, wholesalers, and retailers all use the transporting function, but the degree of use and the amount each pays for it vary.

Goods are moved by five major transportation forms: *motor carriers, railroads, waterways, pipelines,* and *air carriers.* Most businesses involved in the transportation function are subject to some kind of federal and/or state regulation of the rates they charge and their operating procedures.

Motor Carriers

Motor carriers (trucks) are primarily used for lightweight shipments over moderate distances. They handle nearly 80 percent of those shipments weighing less than 1,000 pounds each. Most businesses use motor carriers for local deliveries.

Motor carriers used for interstate commerce are regulated by a federal agency called the Interstate Commerce Commission (ICC). Prior to the passage of the 1980 Staggers Rail and Motor Carrier Acts, the ICC had a great deal of authority and regulated all rates and routes for interstate mail, train, and truck lines. In today's era of deregulation, the ICC has lost much of its power to set rates and operating procedures for interstate commerce.

Motor carriers that transport goods in one state only are regulated by that state's transportation agency or department.

REAL WORLD MARKETING

Leave the Driving to Him

In 1914, Carl Eric Wickman had a better idea. One of few car owners in the Minnesota mining town where he lived, he offered to drive miners to and from work for a small fee. In order to hide the mud and dust of the road, Wickman painted his car gray—which led one observer to remark that the car looked like a "greyhound dog streaking by." Wickman liked the image so much, he adopted it as an emblem and name for his company: Greyhound Bus Company.

There are four types of motor carriers: *common carriers, contract carriers, exempt carriers,* and *private carriers.*

Common Carriers.

Most motor carriers are *common carriers. Common carriers provide transportation services to any business in its operating area for a fee.* A common carrier receives a "certificate of convenience and necessity" from the state and federal governments.

Common carriers can specialize in handling a single *commodity* (good), such as household items, steel, or petroleum. Or they can handle a number of different commodities.

A common carrier must publish its freight rates. However, it can change its rates or the geographical area it services, as long as it does not discriminate against the shipper of the merchandise with respect to pricing or service. More than one-third of all motor freight is handled by common carriers.

Contract Carriers.

A contract carrier provides transportation services on a selective basis, according to agreements between the carrier and the shipper. A contract carrier can provide services on a one-time-only basis or on a continuing basis.

The transportation fee is negotiated and may differ from agreement to agreement. The contract carrier can haul commodities for more than one business and can charge different rates to each different business.

A contract carrier must file a contract with the appropriate state or federal regulatory agency.

Exempt Carriers.

Exempt carriers are free from direct regulation with respect to rates and operating procedures. They carry agricultural products at rates lower than the common carriers. Exempt carriers exist mainly because strong agricultural *lobbyists* (those who try to influence legislators) convinced Congress that some carriers should be exempt from direct regulation.

Because of the complexity of the short-haul market, exempt carrier status can also be granted to local transportation firms operating within specified trading areas in cities.

Private Carriers

Private carriers are owned and operated by an individual business that is providing its own transportation services for its commodities.

Every business is free to choose carriers from each of these classifications. Starting a private carrier operation involves a large investment in equipment and facilities. But a business that regularly ships a large amount of merchandise may like this alternative.

Advantages and Disadvantages of Motor Carriers.

Motor carriers are convenient. They can pick up products at a factory or warehouse and deliver them to various urban and rural geographical locations through our nation's extensive highway network.

Using motor carriers helps reduce the packaging costs for some products. A truck does not have to be unloaded until it reaches its destination; thus, the goods require less protective packaging.

Trucks can make rapid deliveries and therefore reduce the need to carry large inventories between shipments. This significantly reduces inventory costs.

Among the disadvantages of using motor carriers are their susceptibility to traffic jams, equipment breakdowns, and traffic accidents, all of which cause delays in delivery. In addition, businesses can generally ship products over long distances less expensively by other means.

Railroads

Railroads are a major type of transportation in the United States. Trains move nearly 1½ times more *ton-miles* of freight than motor carriers. *A ton-mile is the movement of one ton of freight one mile.*

Trains are important for moving heavy and bulky freight, such as coal, steel, lumber, chemicals, grain, farm equipment, and automobiles over long distances. To compete with motor carriers, railroads have aggressively advertised the benefits of shipping by rail. They are now also offering several specialized and innovative pricing and delivery services, including *piggyback service, specialized service, package cars, diversion-in-transit,* and *processing-in-transit.*

Piggyback Service.

Piggyback Service is shipping loaded truck trailers on flatcars. When the train reaches its destination, the loaded piggyback trailers are attached to trucks and continue to their destination by highway.

Specialized Service.

Some products need to be hauled in special railroad cars. For example, refrigerated cars keep perishable products from spoiling over long distances. Other specially designed

Our nation's railroads and waterways offer the transportation method of choice for moving bulky freight. What special advantage do both means of transportation offer?

freight cars are used for hauling combustible or hazardous materials, such as chemicals.

Package Cars. Shippers can get lower railroad transportation rates if they can fill an entire boxcar *carload. A **carload** is the minimum number of pounds of freight needed to fill a boxcar.* Carload weights are established for different classifications of goods. Once a shipper's product reaches the minimum weight, the lower rate applies, regardless of the size of the car or whether the shipment fills it.

In *package* (or *pool*) arrangements, goods from several shippers who are sending their items to a common destination are combined to fill an entire carload. If the goods were sent separately, each shipper would have to pay a higher rate since it would be shipping less than a carload.

Diversion-in-Transit. *Diversion-in-transit* service allows the redirection of carloads already en route. For example, a vegetable grower in the South can send the vegetables north and find the best price for them while they are en route. When the grower finds a buyer, the railroad will divert the shipment to the buyer—even if the buyer is not at the originally anticipated destination. Of course, the railroad charges a fee for this service.

Processing-in-Transit. *Processing-in-transit* permits shippers to have products processed while in transit. For example, wheat can be made into flour on its way to its destination.

Advantages and Disadvantages of Railroads. By handling large quantities, railroads can ship at relatively low costs. In addition, trains are seldom slowed by bad weather.

The biggest disadvantage of train transportation is its lack of flexibility. Trains cannot reach as many places as motor carriers. They can pick up and deliver goods only at stations along rail lines.

Waterways

Shipment by waterway is one of the oldest methods of moving merchandise. Today water transportation is regulated by the United States Maritime Commission. Transportation by water is particularly important for international product shipments, especially oil, ore, and grain.

Waterways, such as the St. Lawrence Seaway, the Mississippi and Ohio rivers, and the Great Lakes, are important to waterway transportation. The St. Lawrence Seaway (a combination of rivers, canals, and lakes) as well as the Mississippi and Ohio rivers all give ocean-going vessels access to the heartland of America. Agricultural and industrial products of the Midwest are regularly shipped from the Great Lakes to other parts of the world.

Advantages and Disadvantages of Waterways.
The biggest advantage of waterway transportation is low cost. Ships and barges are the cheapest form of freight transportation. They are also the slowest. This is not a problem when shipping bulky, non-perishable items, such as coal, sand, and cement. However, for perishable goods such as dairy products that need to arrive quickly at their destination, the shippers would want to use another form of transportation.

Water transportation has several disadvantages. If the buyers are located far from the waterway, products must be off-loaded from ships onto railroad cars or motor carriers to reach their destination. This greatly reduces the cost advantages of waterway transportation.

Waterways also suffer during bad weather. Great Lakes shipping, for example, is generally closed for two to three months during the winter.

Pipelines

Pipelines are normally owned by the company using them, so they are usually considered private carriers. In the United States, there are more than 175,000 miles of pipelines.

Pipelines are most frequently used to transport oil and natural gas. For example, they move crude oil from oil field to refinery, where it is processed. The refined products, such as gasoline, are then moved by motor carrier to retail outlets.

Pipelines are more important in the physical distribution process than most people think. They carry some 24 percent of the ton-miles of freight transported in the United States. By comparison, trains ship about 36 percent and motor carriers about 24 percent of the total ton-miles of freight traffic.

Advantages and Disadvantages of Pipelines.
While the construction of pipelines requires a high initial investment, the operation costs are small. They are a dependable mode of transportation not subject to delays due to such things as inclement weather.

Air Carriers

Shipment by air carrier is the most expensive form of distribution. Air shipment rates are usually twice as costly as truck rates. For some shippers, however, the advantage of greater speed of delivery may outweigh the extra costs.

Currently, air transportation is less than one percent of the total ton miles of freight shipped. High-value, low-weight items, such as electronic and computer equipment, are often shipped by air. Certain perishable products, such as live lobsters, fresh cut flowers, and medicine, are also often shipped by air.

Air transportation is regulated by the Federal Aviation Agency. Since 1977, however, the cost of air freight has been deregulated. So, the airlines and air transport companies have become more aggressive in seeking out new markets. They now offer such things as large-bodied jets that can ship more goods, and specialized packaging developed to help prevent damage. Specialized freight planes now under development will allow air carriers to reach and serve more markets in the future.

Advantages and Disadvantages of Air Carriers.
The greatest advantage to air transport is its speed. Many companies, such as Federal Express, advertise overnight delivery. This fast delivery time allows businesses to reduce inventory expenses and storage costs for warehousing.

Some disadvantages of air transportation include mechanical breakdowns and delays in delivery caused by bad weather.

Transportation Service Companies

Transportation service companies handle small and moderate-sized packages. There are three kinds of transportation service companies: *government parcel post, private parcel carrier,* and *express carrier.*

Roadway's Inroads

United Parcel Service (UPS) had virtually all of the national small-package delivery business when the Roadway Package System, based in Pittsburgh, was established in 1985. Today, however, Roadway Package System is making strides against UPS, the current industry leader, in small-package delivery service. (Roadway Package System is a division of Roadway Express, one of the nation's largest transportation companies.)

To compete with UPS, Roadway Package invested $43 million in equipment and began to offer services UPS did not offer, such as itemized computer billings, bar code scanners for package tracing, high-speed material handling, and a toll-free phone number for tracking and claims processing. The Roadway Package System now has more than 130 terminals serving 55,000 communities in 37 states.

The high technology investments allowed Roadway Package to reduce labor costs to about 40 percent less than that of UPS. Roadway's delivery charges were the same as UPS's, but the company began to offer volume discounts of up to 8 percent to larger shippers.

Roadway Package System has only a small share of the existing market for small package delivery service from business to business. It is not yet involved in residential or short-haul delivery. Nevertheless, industry observers are saying that the company has nowhere to go but up. For the first time in years, UPS has some competition.

1. What does this increased competition mean to businesses and consumers shipping goods via UPS?
2. What should UPS do to combat this new competitor?
3. Think of one other example of where a small newcomer has challenged an established giant.

Government Parcel Post

Government parcel post is operated by the U.S. Postal Service. *Parcel post is classified as fourth-class mail.*

Packages weighing more than 16 ounces that are *not* classified as letters or postcards, newspapers and magazines, or printed matter that weighs less than 16 ounces are considered fourth–class mail.

Parcel post can be insured or sent COD. It can also be express-mailed to guarantee next day delivery.

Private Parcel Carriers

Private parcel carriers specialize in transporting packages weighing up to 50 pounds. United Parcel Service (UPS) is currently the largest private parcel carrier. However, competition is growing. See the Case Challenge above which tells how Roadway Package System is now a direct competitor of UPS.

Regular service usually takes from two to three days. More expensive next-day service is also available.

Private parcel carriers have several advantages over parcel post. These advantages include:

- automatic pickup for regular shippers,
- up to three attempts to deliver a parcel on consecutive delivery days,
- computerized tracing networks for lost packages, and
- automatic loss and damage insurance.

Federal Express offers next-day delivery for packages. Why are express carriers most often used for small packages?

Express Carriers

Specialized express carriers, such as Federal Express, guarantee national next-day delivery for items weighing approximately ten pounds or less. Express carriers are generally used for small packages because of the high delivery rates.

The Storage Function

The storage function is the marketing function of holding goods. The amount of goods stored is called an *inventory.* (We will talk more about inventories in Chapter 26.)

Storing goods is an essential activity for marketers. Manufacturers need to store goods until they re-

ceive orders from purchasers. Wholesalers store merchandise before selling it to retailers. Lastly, retailers store merchandise for customers.

Merchandise might also be stored for the following reasons:

- Production has outpaced consumption, and the surplus needs to be stored.
- Some products, such as agricultural commodities, are available only during certain times. Storing helps to stabilize prices.
- Some purchasers buy items stored in quantity to get discounts on their purchases.
- Merchandise is stored at convenient locations to meet customer delivery needs better.

Thus, storing adds time and place utility to products by making them available when and where customers want them.

The costs involved in storing products include space, equipment, and personnel, as well as the cost of tying money up in inventory rather than investing it in an activity that could benefit the business. Businesses try to balance the costs of holding merchandise in inventory against the possibility of not having merchandise available when customers want it.

Products are stored in a number of ways. For example, cars and trucks are stored in an outdoor lot, petroleum products in specialized storage tanks, and grain in grain elevators.

Determining *where* to store goods is an important decision. Efficient, adequate storage reduces the storage costs for a business and helps assure good customer service. Most products are stored in *warehouses*—facilities in which goods are received, identified, sorted, stored, and prepared and dispatched for shipment.

Private Warehouses

A *private warehouse* is a facility owned by a company, manufacturer, wholesaler, or retailer for its own use. A private warehouse is designed to meet the specific needs of its owner. Specialized conditions, such as a temperature-controlled environment, are built into the facility.

In addition to storing merchandise for the firm, private warehouses often house other parts of the business operation, such as offices. Private warehouses are costly to build and maintain. They should

The storage function is an essential part of marketing goods. What forms of storage are shown here? What costs does each involve?

be considered only when a significant amount of merchandise needs to be stored, and their operating costs are lower than those of public warehouses.

Public Warehouses

A *public warehouse* is a facility available to any business that will pay for its use. Public warehouses not only rent space, but also provide services to businesses. For example, many public warehouses perform inventory counts, provide local deliveries, and process customer invoices.

There are five types of public warehouses:

1. *Commodity warehouses* are used primarily for agricultural products, such as tobacco, cotton, or grain.
2. *Bulk storage warehouses* keep products only in bulk form, such as chemicals and oil.
3. *Cold storage warehouses* are used for the storage of perishables, such as fruits, vegetables, and frozen products.

4. *Household goods warehouses* handle personal property storage, household articles, and furniture.
5. *General merchandise warehouses* store any item that does not require specialized handling.

Distribution Centers

A variation of the private and public warehouse is the *distribution center*—a warehouse designed to speed delivery of goods and minimize storing costs. The main focus in a distribution center is on moving products, not on storing them. Distribution centers consolidate large orders from many sources and redistribute them, as separate orders, for individual accounts or stores within a chain.

Normally, products stay no more than a month in a distribution center. Many times they are shipped within two weeks. It is bad business practice to store goods for long periods of time without good reason. Goods in storage cannot make money for a business.

CHAPTER 24 REVIEW

VOCABULARY REVIEW

Write three or four paragraphs on the physical distribution process, incorporating these 12 vocabulary terms.

physical distribution
transporting function
common carrier
contract carrier
exempt carrier
private carrier

ton mile
carload
parcel post
private parcel carrier
express carrier
storage function

FACT AND IDEA REVIEW

1. What is physical distribution? Identify several activities involved in physical distribution.

2. What federal agency regulates interstate commerce for motor carriers?

3. Explain the differences among the four types of motor carriers.

4. Identify the advantages and disadvantages of motor carriers.

5. Identify three specialized services offered by railroads.

6. What are some advantages and disadvantages of railroads?

7. What types of products are typically shipped by waterways?

8. Why are most pipelines classified as private carriers?

9. What is the single most important advantage in using air carriers?

10. What are the three kinds of transportation service carriers?

11. What is a warehouse and what are its key functions?

12. What is the difference between a private and public warehouse?

13. List the five types of public warehouses and tell what they generally store.

14. How does a distribution center differ from a warehouse?

CRITICAL THINKING

1. Some experts believe that marketing costs can be reduced by better physical distribution systems rather than through reduced costs for materials and labor. Do you agree or disagree with this assessment? Why?

2. Explain the difference between the cost of distribution as a percentage of sales for department stores and petroleum refiners. What factors account for these differences?

3. Do you believe carriers of agricultural products should be granted exempt carrier status for agricultural commodities? Why or why not? Should other special interest groups be given the same exempt status?

4. From the following modes of transportation, identify six examples of merchandise that would be shipped by each. Tell whether this mode of transportation would be the only one used, and give reasons to support your answer.
   a. motor carrier
   b. rail carrier
   c. air carrier
   d. water carrier

5. Identify the primary mode of physical transportation for each of these items:
   a. flowers from Holland to be transported to Detroit
   b. iron ore from Duluth, Minnesota, to be shipped to New Jersey
   c. gasoline to be delivered to a local retailer
   d. farm equipment manufactured in Canada and shipped to the Midwest

e. crude oil from the Southwest to be shipped to Boston, Massachusetts

Tell why you think the mode of transportation you chose is best in terms of speed of delivery, dependability, capacity to handle heavy and bulky items, access to delivery location, and cost.

6. Most of the inland waterways were developed with federal funds, while pipelines were built by the oil companies themselves. Why do you think the federal government supports one mode of transportation and not the other?

7. Give two benefits and two disadvantages of a company owning its own warehouse.

USING BASIC SKILLS

Math

1. A train has 35 cars. The average load per car is 104,500 pounds of grain. How many tons of grain is the train carrying?

2. A private carrier's tractor-trailer rig has an empty weight of 24,500 pounds. It is carrying 22 tons of steel. How much more could the truck carry without exceeding an 80,000 pound limit? (Hint: there are 2,000 pounds in one ton.)

3. A large manufacturer can save 28 percent by using a piggyback service. The cost of shipping the manufacturer's products without the piggyback service will total $43,972. How much will the manufacturer save by using the service?

4. There are more than 5.3 million people currently employed in wholesale distribution. According to the National Association of Wholesale Distributors, wholesaling employment is growing at a rate of 4.2 percent per year. Use this data to compute how many more people will be employed next year.

Communication

5. Write a 50-word paragraph telling why you think the use of warehouses increases or decreases the prices charged to customers.

Human Relations

6. You are employed as a traffic manager in a large company. For years, your company has been served by a well-known national package shipper. Recently, you have received promotional materials from a shipper advertising services and rates better than your current shipping company. However, your immediate supervisor is very loyal to your existing shipper. How would you convince your supervisor to employ the new shipping company?

APPLICATION PROJECTS

1. Talk to a local businessperson about why his or her company uses the type of transportation it does for physical distribution. Write a 100-word report on your findings and share it with your class.

2. Use library sources to research the pros and cons of deregulation on the trucking industry.

3. Use library sources to research the pros and cons of deregulation on the railroad industry.

4. Choose a self-storage warehouse business in your area and write a 100-word report on how the business got started, its monthly fees, the type of merchandise stored there, and plans for business expansion.

After completing this chapter, you will be able to:

1. explain the process for receiving and checking merchandise,

2. identify terms and forms used in the routing/shipping process,

3. explain the importance of price marking,

4. describe price-marking techniques and the procedures used to change prices, and

5. list the reasons for routing/shipping merchandise.

WORDS TO KNOW

dock
invoice
receiving record
apron
blind check method
direct check method
dummy invoice check method
spot check method
preretailing marking method
source marking

Receiving, Checking, and Shipping Merchandise

In Chapter 24, you learned about the nature and scope of physical distribution. Now you will learn about the importance and nature of the receiving and checking process.

You will also explore the benefits and procedures used to price mark merchandise. And you will discover the procedures for routing or transferring merchandise within a business.

Shipping Arrangements

As you read in Chapter 24, a variety of carriers are used to deliver goods to buyers. The selection of the carrier depends on these factors:

- type of merchandise,
- quantity of merchandise,
- urgency of delivery,
- availability of transportation carriers,
- cost, and
- extenuating circumstances, such as the need for specialized equipment (for example, refrigerated boxcars).

After the carrier has been selected, the seller and the buyer negotiate payment of the shipping charges. Shipping arrangements vary in each industry. However, all businesses try to save money by making the most economical shipping arrangements. Here are four commonly used arrangements.

1. *F.O.B. (free on board) destination.* The title or ownership of the goods remains with the seller until the goods reach their destination. The seller pays the transportation charges and assumes the responsibility for the condition of the goods until they arrive at the buyer's place of business.
2. *F.O.B. shipping point.* The buyer pays the shipping costs and is responsible for losses or damages that occur in transit.
3. *F.O.B. factory freight prepaid.* The goods become the property of the buyer at the factory. The seller, however, pays the shipping charges.
4. *F.O.B. destination charges reversed.* The merchandise becomes the buyer's only when goods are received. The buyer pays for the transportation charges. If the goods are lost or damaged in transit, the buyer's investment is protected because the goods do not yet belong to the buyer.

Of these four arrangements, buyers generally want F.O.B. destination terms because there is little risk of loss. The goods and the shipping charges are the responsibility of the seller until they reach the buyer.

Sometimes the seller will not give the most favorable shipping terms but will make special buying arrangements. The seller might provide quantity or seasonal discounts or enter into *consignment* and *memorandum* arrangements to help the buyer. You will look at these buying arrangements in more detail in Chapter 32.

Receiving Merchandise

Where merchandise is received depends on the type and size of the business. Smaller businesses may have a back room or even use store aisles for receiving merchandise. Most stores, however, have enough space to devote a part of the basement, upstairs, or first floor to receiving.

Large businesses and chain stores usually have separate warehouses to receive and store merchandise before it is routed within the company. *The specific area where deliveries are made by carriers is called a dock.*

Docks usually have platforms for the merchandise, are covered or enclosed to protect the merchandise from weather damage, and are large enough to accommodate the type and size of shipment the business normally receives.

When merchandise is received, it is unpacked, counted, checked, recorded, ticketed, and stored. In larger businesses, this is done by a number of people. In smaller businesses, it is usually done by a salesperson, manager, or even the owner.

To order the merchandise, the buyer usually prepares a *purchase order*. This begins the merchandise handling process for the purchaser and the seller. (You will learn more about purchase orders in Chapter 28.)

REAL WORLD MARKETING

Filling the Bill

Inflated ad claims are at least as old as the Civil War. It was around that time in our country's history that traveling theater troupes put out word of coming attractions by tacking up posters, or bills, in towns where they would soon be appearing. The shows seldom lived up to the fantastic claims made in these ads. The expression **fill the bill**, meaning **deliver what was promised**, remains with us to this day.

Invoices

After receipt of a purchase order, the seller initiates an invoice. *The invoice is the supplier's statement that the order has been filled and the merchandise is being sent*. The invoice also serves as the bill for the merchandise. The shipment is usually received after the supplier sends the invoice.

The following information is usually found on all invoices.

- The name of the shipper and method of shipment. This entry gives the name of the carrier that delivered the merchandise.
- The kind of merchandise shipped. The purchase is identified by style, description, quantity ordered, unit cost (the cost for each item), and total cost. If an item was ordered but is unavailable, the quantity *back-ordered* is shown. This means that the seller was temporarily out of stock on the item and will send it at a later time. If an item is marked *OS* (out of stock), the product has been discontinued.
- The date the merchandise was shipped. This entry tells the purchaser when the merchandise left the seller's place of business.
- The number of items in the shipment.
- The weight of the shipment. This information shows the basis of the freight charges.
- The merchandise packer's name or identification number.
- Terms of payment. This entry alerts the purchaser as to when payment is due. *Net 30 days*, for example, means the invoice is payable within 30 days of the date the invoice was issued. *Net EOM* tells the buyer the invoice is due by the end of the month.

Sellers frequently offer cash discounts to encourage early payment. These differ according to industry, type of product, and quantity purchased. Often they are adjustable, offering the buyer the option of paying early and receiving a discount or paying later and not receiving a discount. Here are some examples of such discounts as they commonly appear on invoices. You will look at them in more detail in Chapter 32.

- *2/10, 1/30, n/60*. The buyer receives a 2 percent discount if the invoice is paid within 10 days, a 1 percent discount if it is paid within 30 days, or the net amount is due within 60 days with no discount.
- *2/15, n/30*. The buyer receives a 2 percent discount if the invoice is paid within 15 days. The total net amount is due within 30 days.
- *2/10, n/30*. There will be a 2 percent discount for paying within 10 days or the net amount is due in 30 days.
- *3/10, n/60*. There is a 3 percent discount for payment in 10 days. The net amount is due in 60 days.
- *3/10, 1/30, n/60*. The buyer receives a 3 percent discount for payment in 10 days and a 1 percent discount for payment in 30 days. The net amount is due within 60 days.

Invoices are sometimes called by different names. A seller may use the term *sales invoice*; the buyer may use the term *purchase invoice*. There is no difference between the two.

A seller usually prepares four copies of an invoice. One copy goes to the buyer, one to the shipper, and one is enclosed with the merchandise. The fourth copy is retained by the seller for accounting purposes.

Receiving Records

Every business records the goods it receives in a *receiving record* or *log*. *A receiving record is a form that describes the goods received by a business*.

The items on a receiving record depend on the needs of the business using it. They can include:

- person who received the shipment,
- shipper of the merchandise,
- place from which the goods were shipped,
- name of the carrier,
- carrier's number,
- number of items delivered,
- weight of items delivered,
- shipping charges,
- department that ordered the merchandise, and
- date the shipment was received.

Some retail stores use a short form of receiving record called an *apron*. *An apron is a form attached to the invoice before the merchandise moves through checking and marking*.

If a store uses an apron system, the receiving number may be called an apron number. Prepared by a store's buyers, apron forms stay with the merchandise until it reaches the sales floor. They list the steps the merchandise takes to reach the selling floor.

The information found on the apron includes:

- the receiving number,
- the department number,
- the purchase order number,
- any terms on the purchase order and on the invoice,
- routing, and
- the date the shipment was checked.

The apron system helps prevent the payment of duplicate invoices because the apron is made out only when the shipment is received.

Check-in Procedures

Received merchandise must be checked to verify quantity and condition. In larger businesses, checking is usually done in the receiving area. In small retail stores, it may be done in the aisles.

To increase accuracy and efficiency, specially trained employees called *receivers* inspect and record newly arrived merchandise. Merchandise is carefully opened and checked for damage.

Here are the check-in procedures receivers follow.

- All cartons and merchandise are checked for damage.
- All merchandise is sorted and counted.
- Invoice and shipping tickets are verified against counts.
- The count is verified against the purchase orders.
- All incorrect items are identified and reported.
- All damaged merchandise is identified and reported.
- All items ordered but not received are identified and reported.
- Other merchandise check-in procedures are followed, as the business requires.

Returning Merchandise

Careful receiving practices can save a business enormous amounts of money. All inaccuracies on invoices or damaged goods that have been received must be identified and reported according to the policies of the business. When this is done, the business can get proper credit or adjustments from the carrier or the seller.

Receivers carefully check new merchandise for defects or damage before it is put out for sale. What sorts of things might this employee be looking for?

Apart from damage, there are many other reasons a business might return merchandise. Perhaps it received something it did not order or decided to cancel an order after it was shipped. Perhaps the seller sent too many items or the merchandise arrived too late. Perhaps the seller agreed to take back unsold merchandise after a specific time period.

Upon return of the merchandise, the seller issues a *credit memorandum*. This piece of paper is notification that the buyer's account has been credited for the value of the returned merchandise.

Whatever the reason for the return of the merchandise, the buyer always takes these important steps.

- The correct vendor is identified.
- The necessary shipping documents are prepared.
- The merchandise being returned is checked and counted.
- The reason for the return is identified.
- The merchandise is properly packed.
- Shipping labels are prepared.
- All necessary shipper's information—original invoice, invoice number and date, shipping date, name of shipper—is included.
- The shipper is contacted for the return of the merchandise.
- Signatures are obtained to verify that the merchandise was returned to the vendor.

Accounting for Merchandise

There are four methods used to check merchandise: *blind check, direct check, dummy invoice check*, and the *spot check*.

*With the **blind check method**, a list is made from an invoice of only style numbers and descriptions*. This list is then compared to the numbers on the actual invoice or purchase order for discrepancies. The blind check method is accurate but time consuming.

*With the **direct check method**, the merchandise is checked directly against the actual invoice or purchase order*. This procedure is faster than the blind check method, but errors can arise if the invoice is incorrect. Also, some receivers do not completely check the total number of items once they see the amount listed on the invoice. If the amount looks correct, they may not bother to take an actual count.

*With the **dummy invoice check method**, the count is made on a form similar to an invoice, but descriptions, quantities, sizes, and styles are omitted*. The receiver counts the merchandise. Then it is checked against the actual invoice. This variation is similar to the blind check method. Both the blind check and the dummy invoice check are used when merchandise needs to be moved quickly to the sales floor.

*The **spot check method** is a random check of one product only (such as 1 in 20) in a carton*. The carton is checked for quantity. If the contents are as stated on the invoice, the remaining cartons are assumed to be the same. Spot checking is often used for canned goods, paper products, and pharmaceuticals.

Marking Merchandise

After it has been received and checked in, merchandise must be marked with the selling price and other information. There are a variety of marking methods for various kinds of merchandise.

Some businesses use a *preretailing marking method. With the **preretailing marking method**, pricing information is marked in advance by the seller on the retailer's copy of the purchase order*. This information is transferred to the invoice when it arrives. Normally used for staple items unlikely to have price changes between the time of the order and receipt of the merchandise, preretailing marking saves time because merchandise is price marked immediately.

Snack items, such as potato chips, popcorn, and pretzels, are frequently *source marked* by the manufacturers. ***Source marking** means the seller or manufacturer has marked the price on the merchandise before delivering it to the retailer*. Merchandise can be moved directly from the receiving area to the sales floor. This saves the retailer both money and time.

Source-marked merchandise often has a *Universal Product Code (UPC)*. As you learned in Chapter 18, UPC codes consist of a grouping of parallel bars and a row of numerals printed on each package. These bars describe the merchandise. This description, along with price information, is entered into a computer by the retailer.

Merchandise can also be marked with a hand stamper (this is sometimes used in supermarkets), by hand with ink or a grease pencil (commonly done for price reductions), by an electric or hand-operated pricing machine, or simply by placing a sign over the shelf or bin.

Finally, merchandise can be marked with the familiar price tickets. In large stores, price tickets are prepared by hand or by machine in a marking room or in a stock room. *Gum labels* are used on merchandise, such as books, with a flat, hard surface. *Pin tick-

Source-marking merchandise with a UPC is a real timesaver for both businesses and customers. Does the procedure have any disadvantages for either group?

ets are used on merchandise that will not be damaged by the pinholes, such as socks or scarves. *String tags* are used for larger articles, such as dresses, shirts, and suits.

Importance of Price Marking

Obviously, price marking identifies the price of the merchandise. Most businesses also include other important information on price tickets, such as store numbers, model or style numbers, color, sizes, fabrics, manufacturer's number, and lot numbers. They can also include numbers indicating the season the item was placed in stock.

A price ticket can also include a cost code made up of nonrepeating letters, additional digits, or abstract symbols to indicate prices. For example, here is a cost code for $18.57:

Some cost codes use additional digits before or after the cost. So, the cost code for $18.57 might be 271857 or 27185716.

Other cost codes are based on the use of abstract symbols.

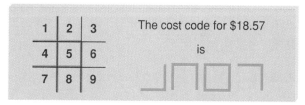

Seasons are frequently coded on price tickets, thus indicating when the merchandise was placed in stock. Seasons can be coded with a letter and a number or with the addition of an arbitrarily selected figure.

For example, a letter might be used to designate a three- or six-month season, a number to designate a month. The letter *A* might represent all the months from August through January. Merchandise placed into stock in October would then be coded as A3.

Figures can also be added to a date to indicate seasonal coding. Under this system, September 15, 1991 (91591), would be written as 791591.

Coding the seasons helps identify merchandise that moves slowly. It also assists sales personnel with markdowns and reductions.

POS Systems Make Data Management Easy

As the need for good data management increases, mass merchandisers are updating their point-of-sale (POS) systems. The new systems include computer-driven devices that speed up customer service, recognize price changes, and access inventory information.

Supermarkets were the first mass merchandisers to use scanners to read manufacturer's Universal Product Codes (UPCs). Scanners minimized cashier errors, increased customer service by speeding up checkouts, and saved the labor needed to price products on shelves.

In addition, when certain merchandise goes on sale or is used in a big promotion, stores do not need to price each particular item separately or manually. The price change is recorded in the main computer. When the scanner reads the UPC, it records the new price.

Naturally, as computer systems become more sophisticated, new functions have been added to meet the specialized needs of each retailer. Some scanning systems even talk to customers. Since 1980, the Grand Union stores have featured Posi-Talkers that speak in a female voice as each item passes through the scanner. Though unnerved at first by a robotic female voice, most Grand Union customers now enjoy the space-age image.

1. Why do you think supermarkets were the first users of computerized POS systems?
2. What are some possible drawbacks to computerized POS systems?
3. What specific benefits do computerized POS systems have for consumers?

Transferring Merchandise

Once merchandise is received, checked, and marked, it is ready to be transferred to the sales area. From there, it is often transferred to different departments within the business.

Stock transfer from a department or store to the warehouse occurs at the beginning of each season when old merchandise must be removed from the department sales area to make room for new merchandise. Old merchandise is put on sale for a short period of time. Merchandise that does not sell is transferred to a warehouse.

Merchandise sent to a warehouse is accompanied by a form describing the items, style numbers, colors, sizes, cost, and retail prices. Duplicate copies of the transfer forms are retained as a record of merchandise on hand.

Stock transfers between departments can occur:

- when merchandise is carried by more than one department,
- when the demand for merchandise in one department creates a need for additional merchandise,
- when the merchandise is used for sales promotions, such as displays, advertising illustrations, or fashion shows, and
- when the merchandise is used for installation or repairs in various departments.

Stock transfers between stores can occur to fill orders or requests by customers due to inadequate stock in a store. Finally, stock transfers from store to distribution outlet can occur when off-season and nonsaleable merchandise is sold to surplus or discount stores.

C H A P T E R   2 5   R E V I E W

VOCABULARY REVIEW

Write two or three paragraphs on receiving, checking, and shipping merchandise, incorporating these vocabulary terms.

dock
invoice
receiving record
apron
blind check method
direct check method

dummy invoice check
  method
spot check method
preretailing marking
  method
source marking

FACT AND IDEA REVIEW

1. Identify five factors that can influence the selection of a shipping carrier.

2. Describe four commonly used shipping arrangements.

3. What items are commonly found on an invoice?

4. What is the difference between Net 30 days and Net EOM?

5. Why are cash discounts frequently given to retailers?

6. What is a receiving record? Identify ten things commonly found on receiving records.

7. Explain the check-in procedures receivers follow.

8. Identify the steps that should be followed when returning merchandise.

9. How do the blind check, direct check, dummy invoice check, and spot check methods differ from each other?

10. What is the preretailing marking method? What is source marking?

11. What types of information are frequently placed on price tickets?

12. Identify four reasons for transferring merchandise once it has been received, checked, and marked.

CRITICAL THINKING

1. Consumer advocates argue that every UPC-coded item should also be individually price marked to assist customers. Retailers, however, say that using only UPC marking ultimately helps consumers by reducing overall merchandise costs. What do you think? Is UPC marking enough, or should all products be marked with the actual price, too?

2. Explain why cash discounts are used on invoices. Should retailers always take advantage of cash discounts? When would it be ill advised?

3. Explain why source marking is important for a small business.

4. Why do you think retailers often code or disguise the actual cost of merchandise on price tickets? Do you think this information should be kept from customers? Why or why not?

USING BASIC SKILLS

Math

1. The cash discount terms on an invoice are 2/10, net 30. The invoice is date January 10 for a net amount of $4,645. Determine the following:
   a. the deadline for taking the discount,
   b. the amount of the discount,
   c. the amount payable if the discount is taken, and
   d. the deadline date for paying the invoice.

2. The cash discount terms on an invoice are 2/10, 1/30, n60. The invoice is dated May 5 for a net amount of $1,575. Determine the following:
   a. the deadline for taking the initial discount,
   b. the amount of the initial discount,
   c. the amount payable if the initial discount is taken,
   d. the deadline for taking the second discount,
   e. the amount of the second discount,

f. the amount payable if the second discount is taken,

g. the amount saved by taking the initial discount, and

h. the final deadline for paying the invoice.

Communication

3. Develop a list of desirable personal attributes and skills to look for in a person who is employed as a receiver in a department store. Tell why you think these attributes and skills are essential.

Human Relations

4. You are working in the receiving room of a large supermarket. You observe a co-worker damaging incoming merchandise through careless behavior. You are concerned that management may suspect you, and you fear you might lose your job over the incident. Explain how you would handle this situation.

APPLICATION PROJECTS

1. Obtain an invoice used by your cooperative education training station or one furnished by your instructor. Review the various types of information detailed on the invoice and explain what each represents.

2. Obtain a receiving record used by your cooperative education training station or one furnished by your instructor. Review the items detailed on the receiving record and explain what each represents.

3. Using a form provided by your instructor, calculate the cash discount and due dates for various invoices.

4. Identify ten consumer products and the type of price ticket used most frequently to price mark the item.

5. Working in small groups or individually, contact a retail business in your community. Ask for permission to visit the store and have someone explain their receiving, marking, and stocking procedures. Be on time for your appointment, dress appropriately, and send a thank-you note to the person responsible for setting up the appointment.

Give a five-minute oral report of your visit. With your classmates, discuss the differences you find between companies.

6. Stores occasionally lose merchandise through employee theft. Which are the most and the least secure methods for accounting for received merchandise? Explain why. Discuss ways a receiving procedure could eliminate pilferage.

7. There is usually a variety of information on a price tag. Discuss why a business might include store numbers, manufacturer's numbers, season codes, and cost codes on a price tag.

8. Using this cost code:

A	B	C	D	E	F	G	H	I	J
1	2	3	4	5	6	7	8	9	0

write codes for these prices:

a. $257.89

b. $6.47

c. $143.08

d. $25.99

9. Devise your own numerical, alphabetical, or abstract cost code. Then give a classmate a list of four coded prices and a copy of the code and have him or her figure out each price.

Stock and Inventory Control

OBJECTIVES

After completing this chapter, you will be able to:

1. explain the importance of merchandise assortments,

2. explain the nature of inventory control systems,

3. describe inventory record-keeping procedures,

4. list the types of unit inventory control systems,

5. identify the causes of inventory shrinkage, and

6. discuss the impact of computers on inventory systems.

WORDS TO KNOW

merchandise assortment
basic stock list
model stock list
never-out list
stock turnover
dollar control
unit control
physical inventory system
stock shortage
shrinkage
perpetual inventory system

K eeping track of merchandise and planning for proper assortment are important elements in the distribution system of any successful business.

In this chapter you will read about the importance of merchandise assortments and accurate stock counts. You will learn about the purpose of inventory control and the various types of inventory control systems. You will also come to understand the importance of accurate inventory records and how computerized management information systems are being used to assist in inventory management.

Merchandise Assortment

Customers who make a special trip to a specific business are very disappointed when they arrive and find the product they wanted is out of stock. Businesses that are continually running out of stock are chasing away potential customers.

One of the key decisions in business is determining the *merchandise assortment*. **Merchandise assortment is the amount of merchandise to stock for customers.** Merchandise assortment refers to both *width* (which products to carry) and *depth* (how many of each product to buy). We will talk more about product width and product depth in Chapter 36.

Several questions need to be answered when deciding on merchandise assortment. Will more product variety result in more sales? How much space will be required? How fast will the merchandise sell? For retail stores, two additional questions must be answered. Where will merchandise be displayed in the store? How should the mix be divided among manufacturer, private label, and generic brands?

A business must be cautious when planning merchandise assortment. Risk increases as its product assortment expands. For example, more merchandise increases the investment in inventory and the potential for loss if the products become obsolete or don't sell. Personnel need to be trained in more product lines and may be ill-prepared to answer customer questions and satisfy customer needs. In addition, a wide and deep product assortment makes inventory procedures more complex.

As you can see, stock control over the merchandise assortment strategy is necessary. Stock control should answer four questions for any business:

- What merchandise is on hand?
- What merchandise is on order?
- What has been sold?
- What needs to be ordered?

The kind and amount of paperwork for effective stock control depends on the type of business. Stock lists must be prepared to keep track of merchandise. There are three types of stock lists used by retailers: a *basic stock list*, a *model stock list*, and a *never-out list*.

A basic stock list is used for staple items, such as groceries, hardware, cosmetics, housewares, china, and stationery. Based on expected sales for a given period, a basic stock list specifies the minimum amount of merchandise that should be on hand for specific products. It shows the quantity of items that should be reordered, as well as the colors, brands, styles, and sizes that should be carried.

A model stock list is a more general list of usually fashionable items subject to changes in demand and style that should always be kept in inventory. It tells the styles, colors, sizes, and numbers of a broad category of merchandise a retailer should carry, such as apparel and furniture.

For example, a women's fashion apparel store might have an extensive model stock list for several sizes and colors of a particular line of merchandise. The store might have a larger quantity of a certain dress in popular sizes and a limited quantity of less popular sizes to round out the assortment.

A discount store, however, might have a less extensive model stock list to attract customers who are willing to buy from a less extensive assortment in one product line in exchange for lower prices.

A basic stock list differs from a model stock list because it identifies items that are standardized, rarely change, and should never be out of stock. A model stock list is used primarily for non-standardized high fashion items. You will look again at basic stock lists and model stock lists in Chapter 32.

A never-out list is used for best-selling products that make up a large percentage of sales volume. Items are added to or taken off the list as their popularity increases or declines. For example, a video rental store will keep a popular movie on the never-out list and keep a large quantity of the video cassettes in the store. After the movie declines in popularity, only regular quantities of it will be maintained. It will be taken off the never-out list and other, more popular titles will be added to it.

Most businesses use a combination of a basic stock list, a model stock list, and a never-out list to maintain a balanced inventory.

The Nature of Inventory Control Systems

Inventory is one of the most visible aspects of a business operation. As you learned in Chapter 24, inventory refers to an amount of goods stored. Examples of a manufacturer's inventory include such things as raw materials, goods in process, and finished goods. Retail inventory includes all goods for resale. Inventory represents a large business investment and must be well-managed to maximize profits for the business.

Inventory Management

Inventory management involves the steps a business goes through to acquire and maintain a proper assortment of merchandise for sale while controlling costs for ordering, shipping, handling, and storage.

If inventories are not properly controlled, they become a drain on the resources of a business. Many businesses lose money because they cannot absorb losses caused by poor inventory management.

Inventory management is difficult because of the conflicting demands placed on a business for various types of merchandise. For example, it is expected that a business must:

- maintain a wide assortment of popular merchandise that never runs out of stock,
- maintain a high amount of merchandise turnover without compromising on customer service,
- keep an adequate amount of merchandise to minimize investment without running out of stock,
- keep volume purchases of new merchandise at the lowest prices but never buy or make merchandise that doesn't sell, and
- have a current inventory without letting the merchandise become old and obsolete.

Good inventory management maintains a balance between the costs of inventory and the benefits of maintaining a large inventory. The costs of inventory include not only the cost of the items in stock, but also storage, insurance, and taxes. Inventory ties up a business's *working capital*—money that could be used for other purposes. Successful inventory management, on the other hand, helps increase the amount of available working capital because the business does not have to borrow money to pay for other expenses.

Stock Turnover

The most effective way to measure how well inventory is being managed is to look at *stock turnover*. *Stock turnover is the number of times the average inventory has been sold and replaced in a given period of time.*

Stock turnover is a good measure of success for buyers to use in evaluating vendors and products from year to year. Buyers also use stock turnover rates to compare a store's entire operation with the operations of similar stores. For example, the stock turnover rate for a supermarket can be compared with rates of other supermarkets but not with the rate of a furniture store.

If a store keeps records of the retail value of its stock, it computes its stock turnover rates by dividing the net retail sales by average inventory on hand (in retail dollars). Thus, the formula looks like this:

$$\frac{\text{Net sales (in retail dollars)}}{\text{Average inventory on hand (in retail dollars)}}$$

For example, if the net sales during a particular time period are $49,500 and the average inventory is $8,250, the stock turnover is 6.

$$\frac{\$49,500}{\$\ 8,250} = 6$$

To arrive at average inventory, buyers use average inventory figures for all the months included in the time period being considered and divide the result by the total number of stock figures. The sales figure equals total net sales for the entire month. For example:

Month	Average Inventory	Net Sales
January	$50,000	$10,000
February	$55,000	$15,000
March	$68,000	$20,000
April	$64,000	$19,000
May	$63,000	$21,000
June	$60,000	$20,000
Totals	$360,000	$105,000

To get the average inventory for the six-month period, divide $360,000 by 6 (number of months) which equals $60,000 (average inventory). To calculate stock turnover, divide $105,000 (total net sales) by $60,000 (average inventory). This equals 1.75 (stock turnover). In essence, the average inventory was sold and replaced 1.75 times during the six-month period.

When information about stock is available only in terms of cost, stock turnover can also be calculated in terms of cost with this formula:

$$\frac{\text{Cost of goods sold}}{\text{Average inventory on hand (at cost)}}$$

If a store wants to look at the number of items carried in relation to the number of items sold, it calculates its stock turnover rates in units with this formula:

$$\frac{\text{Number of units sold}}{\text{Average inventory on hand in units}}$$

Stock turnover rates for selected retailers are available from trade associations and commercial publishers such as Dun and Bradstreet Credit Services, which publishes the reference *Industrial Norms and Key Business Ratios*.

Dollar Control and Unit Control

Inventory management involves both *dollar control* and *unit control* of merchandise held in inventory.

Dollar control represents the planning and monitoring of the total inventory investment that a business makes during a stated period of time. A business's dollar control of inventory involves information about the amount of sales, purchases, dollar value of beginning and ending inventory, amount of markups and markdowns, and stock shortages. With this information, a business can determine the cost of goods sold and the amount of gross profit or loss during a given period of time. By subtracting operating expenses, the business can determine its net profit or loss. Additional information about developing profit and loss statements is found in Chapter 28.

Unit control refers to the quantities of merchandise that a business handles during a stated period of time. Unit control allows the business to keep stock adjusted to sales, and lets the business determine how to spend money available under a planned budget.

Unit control records provide a business with valuable information. They give sales information on the items that are or are not selling. Therefore, better merchandising decisions can be made. Sales promotions can be run, for example, to sell slow-moving items or to spotlight popular ones. Unit control records also allow purchasing personnel to see what brands, sizes, colors, and price lines are selling. By keeping track of this information, buyers can understand customer preferences and order accordingly.

Finally, unit control records specify when items need to be ordered. This ensures that adequate assort-ments are available and helps avoid out-of-stock situations.

Types of Unit Control Systems

Merchandise must be counted to get information for effective inventory management. Stock can be counted periodically with a *physical inventory system*. Or it can be counted by using daily sales with a *perpetual inventory system*.

Physical Inventory Systems

Under the physical inventory system, stock is visually inspected or actually counted on a periodic basis to determine the quantity on hand.

Visual Inspection. Visual inspection is used to monitor inventory levels. For example, hardware stores often place stock cards on pegboards with stock numbers and descriptions for each item displayed. The stock cards specify the number to be kept in stock. The amount to reorder is the difference between those on hand and the specified number to be stocked.

Although a visual inspection system is easy for stock clerks and ordering personnel to use, it does not tell the rate of sales for each item. The number to stock may be an estimate of the quantity to have on hand.

Counting Stock. Businesses take physical inventory at least once a year. In many cases, the business will close so employees can count the entire inventory. Employees usually work in pairs—one counts merchandise while the other records. After the counting is finished, the total retail value of the inventory is determined.

A sales figure is obtained by adding beginning inventory and all purchases made during the period, and then subtracting the ending inventory. Here is an example.

	Number of items for 1/1/-- to 6/30/--
Beginning inventory, 1/1/19--	1,000
Total purchases for the period	300
Total units available for sale	1,300
Ending inventory 6/30/19--	250
Sales and shortages for period	1,050

The sales during the period are based on an actual count of merchandise. Sometimes sales based upon a count of merchandise are lower than the actual recorded sales figures on the cash register/POS terminal. *The difference between the recorded sales and the sales based on the actual count is known as* ***stock shortage*** *or* ***shrinkage***. Stock shortages are caused by theft, incorrect counting when merchandise is received, or errors at the cash register.

The stock counting method requires more paperwork than the visual inspection method. However, sales data can be provided for a given period and a *stock-to-sales ratio* can be calculated at the time of the physical count. The stock-to-sales ratio indicates how much stock is necessary to accommodate sales

Many retailers, large and small, typically close their doors for inventory. Why do you think this is so?

volume. You will explore stock-to-sales ratios further in Chapter 32.

Perpetual Inventory System

The other method of inventory management is the perpetual inventory system. Rather than actually counting stock as in a physical inventory system, a business records the unit sales of items.

A ***perpetual inventory system*** *keeps track of the number of items a business handles by adjusting for sales, returns, allowances, and transfers to other stores and departments*. With a perpetual inventory system, a business keeps track of sales as they occur. This information is collected manually or with a point-of-sale system.

Manual Systems. With a manual system, employees gather information by collecting sales checks, price tickets, merchandise receipts, transfer requests, and other documents for coding and tabulation.

Printed on merchandise tags is information about the vendor, date of receipt, department, product classification, color, sizes, and style. The merchandise tags from items sold are sent in batches to a company-owned tabulating facility or to an independent computer service organization where the coded information is analyzed by a computer.

Point-of-Sale Systems. A point-of-sale system uses light pens, hand-held laser guns, stationary lasers, or slot scanners to feed information directly from merchandise tags or product labels into a computer. Point-of-sale systems are quicker and more accurate than manual systems.

A business does not have to choose between a physical inventory system or a perpetual inventory system. In fact, many businesses use both, comparing one to the other, to determine such things as stock shrinkage.

The Impact of Computers on Inventory Management

Regardless of how data are collected at the point of sale, electronic data processing is a sound way to manage inventory.

Today, sophisticated information-gathering systems can track items from the purchase order to the customer sale. By using computers, buyers can receive weekly updates on sales, inventory, receiving, replenishment, and inventory turnover rates.

Keeping Track of the Parts

Burbank Aircraft Supply, Inc., in Sun Valley, California, supplies parts to every major airline in the world. From tiny fasteners that lock bolts into place to enormous bolts used to hold the tail wheel on a plane, they have it all—400,000 different parts.

You might think the company would have a sophisticated computer to keep track of it all. However, with the number of people who use the inventory system every day, company managers say a computer would be too slow. So, employees keep the inventory by hand.

Each part in the warehouse has its own inventory card. Each card is divided in half. On the right half is purchasing information—where and when the part was purchased, how many were purchased, and how much they cost. On the left half of the card is the sales information—the company the parts were sold to, the date and purchase order number, the number of parts sold, and the selling price.

The cards are kept in hundreds of long drawers that line the walls of a large room. A staff of 15 to 20 people posts purchasing and sales information to the cards. In addition to recording the facts, they also subtract the number of parts sold from the number of parts on hand or add the number of new parts purchased.

Salespeople use the card files constantly to find the price of an item, see if it is in stock, and give a customer an approximate shipping date. Buyers consult the files before making purchases.

The company also uses the system to take inventory continuously. Unlike other businesses, Burbank Aircraft Supply cannot shut down to take inventory. With so many parts in stock, it would take weeks to count them all. So, for this company, the old-fashioned way is still the best way.

1. What skills do you think you would need to keep track of Burbank Aircraft Supply's inventory?
2. Why is keeping an accurate inventory just as important as selling the parts?

Electronic data processing is no longer just for big businesses. Now even the smallest stores can get low-cost, computer-generated reports containing sales figures, inventory, and markdowns—all by product classifications. This type of information reduces markdowns, improves turnover, and increases profits by pinpointing where inventory is too high or too low.

Most computer manufacturers offer free written information on the inventory management systems available for their equipment. Computer service companies also have materials available on such programs.

Good inventory management has become increasingly important for successful businesses. The improvement of inventory management through the use of computers has led to more efficient inventory management and thus to increased business profits.

REAL WORLD MARKETING

An Apple a Day

At the time, building a computer the average person could use might have seemed like mission impossible. Nevertheless, that was the mission California computer whizzes Steve Jobs and Steve Wozniak set for themselves. They worked on the design for their machine in a lab at Hewlett-Packard. They built the prototype in the garage of Steve Jobs' parents. Today, Apple Computers, the company they founded, is a multi-million dollar enterprise.

VOCABULARY REVIEW

Write each of these vocabulary terms in a separate sentence.

merchandise assortment   unit control
basic stock list   physical inventory system
model stock list   stock shortage
never-out list   shrinkage
stock turnover   perpetual inventory system
dollar control

FACT AND IDEA REVIEW

1. What is merchandise assortment? What questions must be answered when deciding a merchandise assortment?

2. Explain the differences among a basic stock list, a model stock list, and a never-out list.

3. What is inventory management and why is it important?

4. What is stock turnover and how is it calculated?

5. What is the difference between dollar control and unit control as they relate to inventory management?

6. What advantages does unit control provide?

7. What methods are used to monitor inventory under a physical inventory system?

8. What is a stock shortage? What are its causes?

9. What are two kinds of perpetual inventory systems?

10. What is a point-of-sale system? What are some of its advantages?

CRITICAL THINKING

1. Explain the difference in merchandise assortment strategies between a men's apparel specialty store and a department store.

2. Why do you think inventory management is so difficult? What expectations are placed on a business that complicate inventory management?

3. Why do stock turnover rates vary by the type of business? Give examples of businesses with high and low turnover rates.

4. Which inventory system requires more paperwork—the physical inventory system or the perpetual inventory system? Explain.

5. How can the use of computers assist in the inventory management procedure?

6. Explain why the use of computers for inventory management is no longer considered inappropriate for small businesses.

USING BASIC SKILLS

Math

1. Calculate stock turnover rates for the following retail institutions using the data provided:

Type of Institution	Net Yearly Sales	Average Inventory (Retail)	Stock Turnover Rate
Department store	14,503,000	3,085,744	_____
Shoe store	875,000	265,150	_____
Jewelry store	245,800	102,400	_____
Grocery store	1,542,875	96,430	_____
Service station	155,900	5,575	_____

2. A woman's apparel shop had a beginning inventory of $45,800 on August 1 and an ending inventory of $32,450 on August 31. What was the average inventory on hand for the month of August?

3. A jewelry store had an average inventory on June 1 of $6,700, on July 1 of $12,300, on August 1 of $8,640, and on September 1 of $10,393. What is the average inventory for the quarter?

4. Given the following information, calculate the stock turnover rates in units for the following situations:
Units sold during the year: 12,000; 2,500; 5,000; 1,580; 3,475
Average inventory on hand in units: 1,500

5. Given the following information, calculate the stock turnover rates in retail dollars for the following situations:
Net yearly sales: $15,560; 17,500; 12,540; 16,000; 11,575
Average inventory on hand at retail: $6,000

6. Calculate the annual stock turnover at cost for the following situations:
Cost of goods sold during the year: $55,700; 36,780; 64,975; 44,560; 48,725
Average inventory at cost: $13,475

Communication

7. Write a 50-word explanation of the importance of stock turnover rates and why they vary by type of retail institution.

8. Consult the most recent edition of *Industry Norms and Key Business Ratios* published by Dun & Bradstreet in your local library or media center. List the annual stock turnover rate for five different retailers.

Human Relations

9. You see a customer whom you suspect has shoplifted an item from your store. Identify the steps and correct procedure you would follow in this situation. You may want to ask your supervisor or consult your employee manual for assistance.

APPLICATION PROJECTS

1. With guidance from your instructor, conduct a physical inventory of items by department in your school store.

2. Make a line graph or bar chart of merchandise sales for your school store for each hour of the business day or for each day of one month. Analyze the chart for slow and peak sales times.

3. Research catalogues of merchandise provided by your instructor to be sold in a school store. Make a list of ten items and describe each by type, brand, style, etc. List the cost, your retail price, and the markup for each. Decide on the quantities to stock for each item chosen. Justify all your selections.

4. Compare and evaluate profit and loss statements from various businesses and select items that are the result of efficient merchandising for comparison.

5. Write a 100-word paper on why stock turnover rates vary for two retailers of your choice (e.g., a grocery store and a jewelry store).

6. Research computer-based inventory systems. Develop a list of five to ten questions you would ask a computer company representative if you were converting a small, family-owned toy manufacturing business from an old inventory system to a computer-based one.

7. Contact a computer company that makes computer-based systems and invite a representative to speak to your class. Ask him or her the questions you developed in Application Project #6.

8. From your discussion with the computer company representative, write a report to the toy manufacturer in Application Project #6. Describe how the computer system would help the business, how the conversion would be made, the length of time it would take, and the initial cost versus the long-term savings of having a computer-based inventory system. Be sure you address all the different types of inventory you might expect to find in a toy manufacturing business.

Risk Management

OBJECTIVES

After completing this chapter, you will be able to:

1. discuss the various types of business risks and

2. identify the ways businesses deal with risks.

WORDS TO KNOW

business risk
economic risks
natural risks
human risks
insurance policy
extended coverage
coinsurance policy
fidelity bonds
performance bonds

For many reasons, businesses are constantly confronted with the possibility of loss or failure. A business can never be certain its products and services will sell. Customer preferences, life-styles, and product and service demands change. Despite the best research and planning, some products simply fail in the marketplace. Or products may be damaged, stolen, destroyed, or lost.

In this chapter, you will learn about these types of business risks and the methods businesspeople use to prevent or at least minimize them.

Kinds of Risks

Business risk is the possibility of business loss or failure. There are three kinds of business risks—*economic, natural,* and *human.*

Economic Risks

Economic risks occur from changes in overall business conditions. These changes can include the amount or type of competition, changing consumer life-styles, population changes, limited usefulness or stylishness of some products, product obsolescence, government regulation, inflation, or recession.

Businesses that fail to change their products or services when competitors offer more features and benefits experience economic risk through lost sales. Also, foreign competition is an economic risk for many U.S. companies. Foreign products often can be produced and sold for less than similar domestic products. However, foreign competition does force U.S. companies to adjust production or marketing efforts to compete successfully.

Consumer life-styles and population changes are other economic risks facing modern businesses. More households headed by women, dual-income families, the aging of the baby boom generation, and the increasing number of singles delaying marriage all present potential risks for businesses that fail to adapt products and services to meet changing needs.

The limited usefulness or stylishness of some products is another potential economic risk. If products are not sold before a new model year or before the new fashion styles or colors are introduced, prices have to be reduced to sell them. This obviously reduces sales volume and profits.

Some products inevitably become obsolete. This is called *product obsolescence.* It represents another type of economic risk for businesses that depend on fashion and the latest trends to market goods and services.

Government regulation can also present economic risks. Product recalls by the U.S. Product Safety Commission can affect sales and profits. Companies that have products recalled face making costly repairs and/or replacements.

State and local laws and regulations requiring businesses to pay for such things as street and sewer improvements or parking and general maintenance also represent economic risks.

Finally, changes in the general business environment caused by inflation or recession present economic risks. For example, all businesses in an area experiencing high unemployment will suffer.

Natural Risks

Natural risks occur because of natural causes, such as floods, tornadoes, fires, lightning, droughts, and earthquakes.

Some products and services depend on predictable weather conditions for success. For example, a hardware store in the Midwest that sells snowblowers depends on a predictable season of heavy snow to sell the product. A mild or light snowfall during the winter represents a natural risk to the business. (Conversely, a dry summer or a drought will affect the sales of lawnmowers.) The sale of recreational products, such as boats, snow skis, motorcycles, swimming pools, snowmobiles, and related clothing items are all affected by weather conditions.

Finally, natural disasters, such as tornadoes, fires, and earthquakes, are natural risks that can spell financial ruin for a business.

Human Risks

Human risks are caused by human mistakes and the unpredictability of employees or customers. Some of the more common human risks are:

- customer or employee dishonesty—taking goods or money;
- employee carelessness—for example, failing to properly store food products which eventually spoil;

The Limited Tests Its Limits

During much of the 1980s, The Limited, Inc., of Columbus, Ohio, set the tone and style for women's apparel retailers with its fashionable clothing at reasonable prices. However, in the late 1980s, The Limited was unable to zero in on the changing needs and wants of its clientele—fashion-conscious women between 18 and 40 years of age.

The company tried introducing many different clothing lines and styles. They sold so slowly, however, they had to be reduced sharply in price just to move them off the racks. Analysts estimated that sales rose only 1 percent to around $985 million; operating earnings fell for two years to about $117 million.

To counter reduced earnings, the company repositioned itself to appeal to the "thirtysomething" crowd that wants fashionable yet practical clothing. For example, it introduced the Out-back Red label—a line of clothing that is attractive, reasonably priced, and versatile enough to wear to the office or for leisure time activities. The company now offers a broader mix of accessories, lingerie, and higher-priced career wear in larger outlets, as well as such special services as making custom coats to order.

Some analysts feel that it's risky to sell higher-priced goods that will compete with high-priced lines sold in department stores. In spite of this, The Limited plans to open more superstores and offer more high-priced apparel in the future.

1. What kind of risks is The Limited facing?
2. What do you think will be the outcome of The Limited Stores' new high-priced product lines?

- employee incompetence—for example, lacking the skills to do the job well;
- customer or employee accidents—a customer falls over merchandise left in the aisle, breaks an arm, and sues the store, or an employee badly cuts a finger while creating a display;
- employee illness—for example, becoming ill as a result of inhaling the toxic fumes from a chemical cleaner used at work.

Handling Business Risks

There are four basic ways that businesses can handle risks: *risk prevention and control, risk transfer, risk retention,* and *risk avoidance.*

Risk Prevention and Control

When you are asked to perform a new job, some form of training or instruction is normally provided. The training may be as brief as a few seconds of verbal instruction or as extensive as months or years of intensive academic work.

Based on the number of workers who sustain job-related injuries and illness, safety and health information is sorely lacking in many of these training programs. This lack of adequate information and training costs businesses millions of dollars annually.

Good training that includes safety and health information is essential in minimizing business risk. Lack of adequate training usually results in costly job-related injuries and illness.

Providing Safe Conditions and Safety Instruction. When employees have received safety instruction and are provided with safe work conditions, the potential for on-the-job accidents is greatly reduced. In marketing jobs, for example, common accidents include falls that occur while moving merchandise or injuries due to improper lifting techniques.

To prevent such risks, businesses can design storerooms and selling areas for efficient foot traffic and merchandise storage. They can also provide

Many businesses provide safety training for their employees. What injury avoidance technique is being demonstrated here?

Businesses can help to deter shoplifting by:

- educating employees about shoplifting prevention guidelines;
- planning effective store layout with adequate lighting and orderly displays;
- keeping expensive items in locked display cases or tagged with electronic sensors that trigger alarms if the merchandise is carried out of the store;
- using security personnel and such security devices as two-way mirrors, closed circuit television, and wall and ceiling mirrors.

Some states have passed legislation to deal with the problem of shoplifting. For example, Michigan enacted several retail fraud laws that do such things as allow store personnel to make "citizen arrests" of those suspected of tag switching or seeking fraudulent refunds. The laws also make the parents of shoplifters, tag switchers, and fraudulent refund seekers who are minors liable in small-claims court.

Retail businesses selling ready-to-wear often tag their merchandise with electronic sensors to reduce theft. What are the advantages of this security device for both salespeople and customers?

safety instruction on proper ways to lift and store merchandise.

Screening and Training Employees. The best way to prevent the human risk of employee carelessness and incompetence is through employee screening and training. Larger businesses have personnel departments to screen, test, and train employees to minimize the risk caused by improperly trained personnel. Smaller businesses often rely on high school job placement and cooperative education programs to provide entry-level employee training. Properly trained personnel are better able to meet customer needs and wants and to prevent the risk of lost sales through human error.

Preventing Shoplifting. One of the largest and most costly forms of human risk is shoplifting. *Shoplifting* is a form of theft done by people who conceal merchandise in purses, shopping bags, clothing, or through other means.

In 1988, an estimated $33.3 billion worth of merchandise was stolen from U.S. retail establishments. Experts believe that shoplifting is one of the fastest growing crimes against property in the country. It probably accounts for one-third of all property stolen in the United States.

It is important to remember that *everybody* is affected by shoplifting. Faced with increased costs of doing business and reduced sales from theft, businesses are forced to raise prices to compensate.

Controlling Employee Theft. Another major problem for businesses is employee theft. Most employee theft occurs at the point-of-sale (POS) terminal, or cash register. To protect themselves from employee theft, many businesses have installed closed circuit television systems and point-of-sale terminals that generate computerized reports.

POS computerized reports monitor void transfers, cash discrepancies, sales reports, refunds by employees, employees' discounts, and cash register transactions. By carefully analyzing these data, businesses improve the chances of apprehending dishonest employees.

Closed-circuit television systems used in conjunction with POS terminals lower the risk of employee theft. Closed-circuit systems include "pinhole" cameras concealed in mannequins, ceilings, or walls. Usually operated by security personnel in a control room, they are backed up with a video recorder.

Other prevention techniques include:

- pre-employment testing to detect attitudes about honesty (some states, however, have banned the use of lie detectors for pre-employment screening);
- incorporating policies to prosecute dishonest employees;
- internally publicizing cases of employee thefts and the consequences;
- setting internal business standards of honest and dishonest behavior; and
- promoting open discussions dealing with employee honesty.

Preventing Robberies. No matter where a business is located, it has a chance of being robbed. Many local police departments provide instruction on how to prevent and handle robberies. Sometimes businesses band together to form business watch programs similar to neighborhood watch programs.

Businesses can lower their risk from robberies by:

- limiting the amount of money kept on hand,
- installing video cameras to help identify robbers,
- hiring extra employees so that no one is alone in a business at any time,
- hiring security guards,
- installing bullet-proof glass in cashier cubicles,
- installing switches near cash registers that allow employees to lock outside doors, and
- increasing lighting inside and outside of the establishment.

Risk Transfer

Some business risks can be reduced, controlled, or eliminated by transferring the risk to another business or to another party. Three of the most common risk transfers are *insurance, guarantees and warranties,* and *transferring risks through business ownership.*

Purchasing Insurance. Businesses can insure property and people against potential loss by purchasing insurance policies. *An insurance policy is a contract between a business and an insurance company to cover a certain business risk.*

Insurance companies estimate the probability of loss due to such risks as fire, theft, and natural disasters. Then the insurance company looks at the business's location, past experience, and type of business and determines an insurance rate.

The insurance rate charged depends on the degree of risk associated with an insurable feature, such as fire or theft. For example, if the risk of robbery is higher in a neighborhood where a business is located, the insurance company will charge higher rates for adequate coverage against theft. The business has a higher likelihood of being robbed and of thus making a claim against the insurance company for coverage of its losses.

Types of Insurance. A business can purchase one of several insurance policies to protect its property or business operations.

One of the most common insurance policies purchased is fire insurance. The coverage in a fire insurance policy is designed specifically to replace buildings, furniture, machinery, supplies, and merchandise lost through fire. Fire insurance policies can be purchased for the full replacement value of the building, merchandise, and other items or for a portion of the replacement value.

Sometimes fire insurance policies are purchased with *extended coverage. Extended coverage is addi-*

Businesses can purchase insurance to protect themselves against many forms of risk. What type of insurance would help in these circumstances?

tional protection on a basic fire protection policy to cover such natural disasters as wind, earthquake, explosion, or smoke damage.

With a **coinsurance** policy, the insured business and the insurance company both share in the risk if there is a loss. For example, a business may be insured for 80 percent of the replacement value. This means that, in case of a loss, the insurance company pays 80 percent of the covered items and the business pays 20 percent.

Business interruption insurance compensates a business for loss of income during the time repairs are being done to a building or property after a natural disaster. Business interruption insurance covers certain expenses that continue during the repair period, such as interest on loans, taxes, rent, advertising, telephone, and salaries.

Vehicle insurance protects against loss in the event of theft of or property damage to cars, trucks, or other vehicles. It also protects against personal injury to the driver or passengers.

Forgery insurance protects against losses caused by forged or altered checks. Businesses accepting checks need to review check-handling procedures carefully with employees to avoid losses through accepting bad checks.

Burglary and robbery insurance protects against losses due to theft of money, merchandise, and other business items identified in the policy. It does not cover employee theft or shoplifting.

***Fidelity bonds** protect a business from employee dishonesty.* Usually, businesses require employees who handle money, such as bank tellers and cashiers, to be bonded. If a bonded employee steals money, the bonding company pays the loss. Individuals who are bonded undergo personal reviews of their character and background before they are bonded.

***Performance bonds** (also called surety bonds) insure against losses that might occur when work or a contract is not finished on time or as agreed.* For example, a building contractor might be required to purchase a performance bond to guarantee completion of the job on time and according to specifications. The company that issues the performance bond is responsible for damages if the contract is not completed.

Personal liability insurance covers claims for damages suffered by customers and employees near or in the business establishment.

Product liability insurance protects against business loss resulting from personal injury from products manufactured or sold by a business. For example, a product may cause skin infections, burns, or even injury or death because of defective parts or poor construction.

Many businesses purchase product liability insurance to guarantee against losses even after products have been tested extensively by private companies and government agencies.

Life insurance is often purchased to protect the owners or managers of a business. For example, a sole proprietor (sole business owner) is usually required to have life insurance in order to borrow money. The policy will guarantee that there will be money to pay off the sole proprietor's debts and obligations if he or she dies.

Life insurance on a deceased partner can provide the money needed for other partners to continue the business (if named as *beneficiaries*—those who will receive the money from the policy).

Credit insurance protects a business from losses on credit extended to customers.

Credit life insurance pays the balance of any loans granted by banks, credit unions, and other financial agencies in the event the borrower dies.

Finally, *guarantees* and *warranties* are promises by the seller or manufacturer concerning the performance and quality of a product. We'll look further at guarantees and warranties in Chapter 37.

Transferring Risks Through Business Ownership

In a sole proprietorship, the individual owner assumes all risks. Partnerships enable the partners to share in the business risks.

Corporations allow the stockholders, as owners, to share the business risks. The corporate form of ownership offers the most protection from losses. We'll explore the advantages and disadvantages of the three forms of business ownership in Chapters 38 and 40.

Risk Retention

In some cases, it is impossible for businesses to prevent or transfer risks, so they *retain* or assume responsibility for them. This is called *risk retention.* For example, if customer trends change and merchandise remains unsold, the business has to assume the loss. That is, it retains the risk.

Businesses and businesspeople retain certain business risks because:

- they are unaware of the risk (for example, they are unaware of employee theft);
- they underestimate the risk, as when merchandise is purchased in anticipation of high sales, but weather, trends, and customers' habits change;
- they anticipate a profit by taking a risk such as purchasing land for development and future profit on its sale for a subdivision.

Risk Avoidance

Certain risks can be avoided by anticipating them in advance. For example, market research can lead businesses to conclude that investment in a product or service is not worth the risk.

As you can see, businesses have several ways of handling risks. Owning and operating a business, however, always involves a degree of risk. The way a business manages its risks determines its success or failure.

REAL WORLD MARKETING

They're Less Bullish on Production Crews

During the classic TV ad for the investment firm Merrill Lynch, a bull carefully maneuvers through a china shop. The firm that created the ad, Ogilvy & Mather, took great pains to ensure that the animal was well trained. However, it should have taken as much care training the production crew. On the day of the filming, a butter-fingered set designer accidentally dropped and smashed a candelabrum valued at $3,500.

VOCABULARY REVIEW

Write a brief definition of each term, based on your reading of the chapter.

business risk
economic risks
natural risks
human risks
insurance policy

extended coverage
coinsurance policy
fidelity bonds
performance bonds

FACT AND IDEA REVIEW

1. What are the three kinds of business risks?

2. Give three examples of economic risks.

3. Give three examples of natural risks.

4. Give three examples of human risks.

5. What are the four basic ways businesses can control or prevent risks?

6. How can businesses reduce the human risk of on-the-job injuries?

7. How can businesses reduce the human risk of carelessness and incompetence?

8. What is shoplifting? How can businesses deter shoplifting?

9. Explain procedures that can be used to control employee theft.

10. Explain procedures that can be used to deter the risk of armed robberies.

11. Identify three types of insurance that can be purchased to protect property. Give examples of items covered by each type of insurance.

12. Explain the difference between a fidelity bond and a performance bond.

13. Explain the difference between personal and product liability insurance.

14. Explain the difference between credit insurance and credit life insurance.

15. How can warranties and guarantees transfer business risks to other parties?

16. How can the type of business ownership affect the risks of the owners of the business?

17. Why must some businesses retain risks?

18. What is risk avoidance?

CRITICAL THINKING

1. Businesses face risks everyday. Why are businesspeople willing to assume risks when it would be much easier to work for someone else?

2. Some people think that shoplifting only affects the retailer's business. Explain the consequences of shoplifting for the individual and for society.

3. Identify some factors that may affect the insurance rates charged to a retailer for fire protection.

4. How does a business determine what kinds of insurance to carry? Do you think it's possible for a business to carry too much insurance?

5. Insurance rates are partially based on past experience. Do you think it appropriate to deny auto insurance to companies with poor driving records, or robbery insurance to businesses in high crime areas? Analyze the two situations, and be prepared to defend your answer.

6. Jury judgments on personal and product liability cases have led to huge cash settlements for injured parties. How do these claims affect businesses and you? Should there be set limits on the cash amounts given for injury or death? If so, how would you determine the settlement amounts?

7. What important factors should a business consider when selecting an insurance company?

8. "It's insured, so don't worry about it." Is there anything wrong with this statement?

USING BASIC SKILLS

Math

1. A business is required by its insurance company to carry 80 percent of the value of property appraised at $400,000. If a loss occurs, the insured business can recover any loss up to the insured amount of $320,000. Determine the amount of money to be paid by the insurance company and the business in the event of a loss in the following situations:

Amount of Loss	Amount Paid by Insurance	Amount Paid by Business
$200,000		
$300,000		
$320,000		
$325,000		
$350,000		
$400,000		

2. Given the following information, calculate the annual amount a small business pays for insurance.

   a. Property insurance of $716.18, paid semiannually
   b. Liability insurance of $76.25, paid quarterly
   c. Business interruption insurance of $205.50, paid annually
   d. Vehicle insurance of $315.00, paid quarterly
   e. Employee group life and medical insurance of $524.15, paid quarterly

Communication

3. Write a 100-word paper on the responsibilities parents have to instill honesty and respect for personal property in their children so they do not shoplift.

Human Relations

4. You are planning to start a small arts and crafts shop with a friend after graduation. Your proposed partner argues that the business should be freed of risks through the purchase of complete insurance coverage on the building, vehicles, merchandise, staff, etc. You believe that there are some aspects of the new business for which you will not need insurance coverage. Identify those risks in the proposed business that you feel do not need insurance coverage. Convince your friend of the logic behind your decisions.

APPLICATION PROJECTS

1. List five products or services whose sales could be affected by seasonal changes. Identify the seasonal factor (for example, snowfall or rain) and explain how this affects the sale of the product.

2. Identify ten products or services that experience increased sales during each of the four seasons.

3. Contact your local Chamber of Commerce, Retail Merchants Association, police department, or state retail trade association for information about your state's legislation on shoplifting. Report your findings.

4. Report on your training station's or employer's policy regarding the apprehension and handling of shoplifters.

5. Report on the accident procedures used at your training station or place of employment.

6. Develop a 200-word report on life insurance. Explain the difference between the various forms of life insurance and how life insurance rates are established.

7. Conduct a survey of retailers in your local community to determine the methods they use to prevent shoplifting.

28

Marketing Math Applications

I n Chapter 8 you brushed up on your basic math skills, especially as they relate to marketing functions. In addition, math instruction and practice are included throughout this book.

There are, of course, many business functions that require an in-depth study of mathematics beyond the scope of this text. This chapter will give you practice in performing certain math applications relating to marketing functions.

Purchase Orders

If you are responsible for ordering goods for resale, one of your duties will be to prepare purchase orders. Notice in Figure 28-1 that the order information includes item, quantity, description, unit, unit cost, and total.

1. The item number, usually taken from a vendor's catalog, identifies the merchandise you are ordering.
2. The quantity or number of units ordered is 10.
3. The description explains precisely what is being ordered.
4. The unit column shows that this item is packaged and priced by the ream (500).

5. The unit cost (in this case, the cost per ream) is $5.16.
6. The total column shows the extension. That is, the number of units multiplied by the cost per unit: 10 reams of photocopy paper at a cost of $5.16 per ream equals $51.60.

You may order several items on the same purchase order. If so, the total of all extensions is typed near the bottom of the total column.

Example:
Look at the purchase order in Figure 28.2.
To find the first extension:
$$15 \times \$37.50 = \$562.50$$
To find the second extension:
$$20 \times \$11.75 = \$235.00$$

Figure 28-1 **Purchase Order**

Purchase orders are used for ordering goods for resale. How much would 15 reams of photocopy paper cost?

Mountain-Air Bicycle Shop
Purchase Order

Invoice and ship to:
Mountain-Air Bicycle Shop
123 State Street
Santa Barbara, CA 93101

Purchase Order Number: **1004**

Date: Oct. 15, 19 – –

Vendor:
Channel Paper Distributors
436 Ocean Avenue
Mission Hills, CA 91345

ITEM NO.	QUANTITY	DESCRIPTION	UNIT	UNIT COST	TOTAL
K2007	10	Photocopy Paper	500	$5.16	$51.60

			TOTAL AMOUNT:	$51.60
			TAX	3.10
			TOTAL DUE:	$54.70

Figure 28-2 **Purchase Order**

What is the total of the first and second extensions on this purchase order?

ITEM NO.	QUANTITY	DESCRIPTION	UNIT	UNIT COST	TOTAL
K94	15	Calculators	ea.	$37.50	$562.50
J411	20	Binders	ea.	$11.75	$235.00

ITEM NO.	QUANTITY	DESCRIPTION	UNIT	UNIT COST	TOTAL
K2007	10	Photocopy Paper	500	$5.16	
J1012	6	Large Paper Clips	100	1.15	
B0017	1	Calculator	1	39.95	
				TOTAL AMOUNT:	

Invoices

When a vendor fills your order, based on your purchase order, you will receive a *purchase invoice* like the one in Figure 28-3 with the delivered merchandise.

Figure 28-3 Purchase Invoice

When a vendor fills your order, you receive a purchase invoice with the delivered merchandise. Why are tick marks used?

Tick marks (simple check marks) are used to verify that numbers or amounts are correct, that they match the numbers or amounts on other documents, or that an extension is correct.

When your company ships merchandise, a *sales invoice* is included with the shipment. Extensions and totals are calculated the same as for purchase orders.

CHANNEL PAPER DISTRIBUTORS
Invoice

SOLD TO: **Mountain-Air Bicycle Shop**
123 State Street
Santa Barbara, CA 93101

Invoice No. : K5005

Date: Nov. 1, 19 – –

YOUR ORDER NO. 1004	DATE SHIPPED 11/01/ – –	SHIPPED VIA UPS	FOB M. HILLS	TERMS 2/10, N30

ITEM NO.	QUANTITY	DESCRIPTION	UNIT	UNIT COST	TOTAL
K2007 ✓	10 ✓	Photocopy Paper ✓	500	$5.16 ✓	$51.60 ✓
J1012 ✓	6 ✓	Large Paper Clips ✓	100	1.15 ✓	6.90 ✓
B0017 ✓	1 ✓	Calculator ✓	1	39.95 ✓	39.95 ✓

TOTAL AMOUNT: $98.45 ✓
TAX 5.91 ✓
UPS 12.18 ✓

TOTAL: $116.54 ✓

ITEM NO.	QUANTITY	DESCRIPTION	UNIT	UNIT COST	TOTAL
J 14687 ✓	20 ✓	Ball Point Pens ✓	ea.	$4.95 ✓	$99.00 ✓
M14027 ✓	50 ✓	Notebook Pads ✓	ea.	1.25 ✓	6.25
M24532 ✓	18 ✓	Computer Diskettes (5 1/4) ✓	10	6.95 ✓	1,251.00

ITEM NO.	QUANTITY	DESCRIPTION	UNIT	UNIT COST	TOTAL
C00118 ✓	5 ✓	Speedex Bicycles ✓	ea.	$318.00 ✓	$1,590.00 ✓
K00238 ✓	10 ✓	Mountain Rider Bicycles ✓	ea.	420.00 ✓	2,100.00
L 0128 ✓	25 ✓	Stay-Tight Pedals ✓	2	22.50 ✓	1.125.00

Sales Checks

Some businesses do not use automated cash registers. If you work for one of these companies, you will have to prepare a handwritten sales check like the one in Figure 28-4 for every sale. Many businesses that do use automated or point-of-sale cash registers require handwritten sales checks, too. The accounting department may use the sales check as the source document for entering data into a computer.

When you prepare handwritten sales checks, you will have to do some math. If a calculator is unavailable, you must know how to perform the necessary

Figure 28-4 **Sales Check**
If your business does not use automated cash registers, you will have to prepare handwritten sales checks. How much would 3 shirts at $18 each cost with 6 percent sales tax?

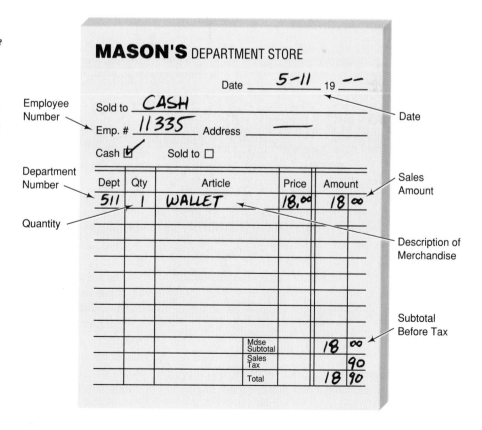

Employee Number

Department Number

Quantity

Date

Sales Amount

Description of Merchandise

Subtotal Before Tax

Figure 28-5 **Sales Check**

Dept	Qty	Article	Price	Amount	
30	5	DISKS	14.98	74	90
33	3	MAGAZINES	2.50	7	50
27	1	BOOK	14.95	14	95
63	1	PRINTER STAND	25.00	25	00

math operations by hand. Customers often buy more than a single unit of each item. So, you will multiply the unit price times the quantity to get the amount you will extend to the last column (see Figure 28-5).

When you multiply the unit price times the quantity, remember that the last two digits on the right are cents. Place a decimal point in front of the last two digits. Most sales checks have a vertical line separating dollars and cents.

Practice:
Use a separate sheet of paper for your answers. Calculate the amount for each item by multiplying the unit price times the quantity of each item.

Sales

Dept.	Quantity	Item	Price
12	10	Vests	$85.00
16	5	Footballs	$15.95
18	11	Clocks	$26.50
21	20	Irons	$39.95

Check page 315 for the answers.

When completing sales checks on the job, you will usually perform at least four math functions:

1. Multiplying the unit price times the quantity for each item and extending the amounts.
2. Adding the amounts for a subtotal.

3. Calculating the amount for tax—or looking it up in a tax table—and writing the amount of tax on the line under the subtotal.
4 Adding the subtotal for merchandise and the amount of tax to get the total.

Many times, you will also need to calculate discounts or shipping costs, too.

Discounts

When you allow a discount on a sale in a retail store, you multiply the amount of the sale times the percentage of the discount. Then you subtract the discount amount to arrive at the net amount of the sale. You must calculate the discount *before* adding sales tax or shipping charges.

For example, suppose you sold items of clothing totaling $350 to a customer who qualified for a 15 percent discount. You multiply the $350 by (.15) to get the amount of the discount, $52.50. Then you subtract the $52.50 discount from the $350 total for clothing to get the net amount of the sale, $297.50. Finally, you calculate and add the amount for tax.

Manufacturers and distributors allow discounts, too, because discounts stimulate additional business and encourage prompt payment. There are many types of discounts. The ones you are most likely to encounter, however, include cash discounts, trade discounts, quantity discounts, seasonal discounts, and promotional discounts. We will briefly discuss each type here. You will look at each in more detail in Chapter 30.

Cash Discounts

Cash discounts encourage payment in a short period of time. This is the most common type of discount. If there are other discounts allowed, a cash discount is subtracted from the amount due *after* all other discounts have been deducted but *before* calculating tax on retail sales.

Some retailers allow cash discounts to charge customers who pay within a specified time, usually 10 days. Manufacturers and distributors allow cash discounts on a variety of terms, such as 2/10 or n/30. (You looked at these in Chapter 25 and will explore them further in Chapter 30.) The discount or credit terms are usually listed specifically at the top of the invoice next to the word *terms*.

Practice:
Use a separate sheet of paper for your answers.
1. The cash discount terms on an invoice are 2/10, n30. The invoice is dated October 15 for a net amount of $950. Find the following:
   a. Last date to take the discount.
   b. Amount of discount.
   c. Amount payable if discount is taken.
   d. Last date to pay the net amount.
Check page 315 for the answers.

Trade Discounts

Trade discounts provide a way of arriving at a wholesale price based on suggested retail prices. Suppose you sell automobile tires. The company you buy tires from will list suggested retail prices for each size and type of tire. In order for you to earn a profit when you resell the tires, you will be given a specified trade discount.

Let's say your trade discount is 40 percent. Calculate your cost by multiplying the suggested retail price by 40 percent (.40), then subtracting the discount from the suggested retail price. When you buy a tire with a suggested retail price of $120, you will get a trade discount of $48—so your net cost will be $72. When you resell the tire for $120, your margin will be $48.

Quantity Discounts

Small orders are not very profitable for manufacturers and distributors, so they encourage larger orders by giving *quantity discounts*. If you buy just one ream of photocopy paper, you may pay $6.50. If you buy 100 reams, you may have to pay only $4.50 a ream.

Sometimes *cumulative quantity discounts* are allowed when your purchases total more than a specified amount in a specified time. Suppose you operate a photocopy business and buy hundreds of reams of paper every month. Your distributor may allow a 2 percent discount on your purchases when they total $2,500 in any three-month period.

Seasonal Discounts

You are probably aware that retail stores reduce prices on summer clothes as fall approaches, and that you can get a lower price on skis in the summer. Manufacturers and distributors often give seasonal discounts to businesses that buy merchandise during the off-season, too.

Seasonal discounts are calculated the same way as cumulative quantity discounts. You simply multiply the price times the percent of discount.

Promotional Discounts

Promotional discounts are often given to businesses that actively promote a product. For example, if you provide widespread advertising on a new style of mountain bike or display a new brand of computer in the front window of your store, you may be given a promotional discount. You may qualify for promotional discounts on even inexpensive items, such as shaving cream and hairspray, if you give them preferred shelf space in your supermarket or drugstore.

Promotional discounts may be stated as a percent or as a dollar amount. If it is stated as a percent, you will calculate it in the same way you do seasonal discounts. If it is stated as a dollar amount, you simply subtract it from the total purchase price.

Sales Tax

Sales tax must be paid by the buyer on all retail sales. It is calculated as a percentage of the sale price. For example, suppose you sell new cars at the dealership in Santa Barbara, California. The sales tax in California is 6 percent. So, you will have to multiply 6 percent times the selling price of each car and add the tax to the selling price. To do this, you must change the 6 percent to its decimal equivalent (.06). So, if you are selling a $14,000 car, you would calculate the sales tax as follows:

$$\begin{array}{r} 14,000 \\ \times\ .06 \\ \hline 840.00 \end{array}$$

On a $14,000 car, you will add $840 sales tax. This tax is collected by the retailer and forwarded to the state. All but five states now collect sales tax. Many cities and counties have sales taxes, too.

Many businesses have tax tables that are helpful in determining the amount of sales tax. These tables have many columns and rows of numbers. The easiest way to calculate sales tax is to change the percent to its decimal equivalent and use a calculator.

Calculating Shipping Charges

Most manufacturers and distributors—and some retailers—use the U.S. Post Office or United Parcel Service to deliver merchandise. Customer charges for delivery are added *after* the tax has been calculated and added.

The cost of shipping merchandise depends on the service used, the weight, and the distance it is sent. If you take your packages to the U.S. Post Office, you will probably send them *parcel post*. The parcel post rates in 1990 are shown in Table 28-1.

Zones 1 and 2 are within 150 miles of the post office where you mail your packages. Zone 3 is between 150 and 300 miles away. The farther away the destination, the higher the zone number. Your local post office has a chart showing the zones according to zip codes. A *local zone*, not shown in the table, gives cheaper rates for packages mailed to addresses in the same city.

When you weigh a package that is over one pound, count any part of a pound as a full pound. That is, if a package weighs 4 pounds and 3 ounces,

Table 28-1
Parcel Post Rates for 1990

Weight Not Exceeding (pounds)	Zones						
	1 & 2	3	4	5	6	7	8
2	$1.69	$1.81	$1.97	$2.24	$2.35	$2.35	$2.35
3	1.78	1.95	2.20	2.59	2.98	3.42	4.25
4	1.86	2.10	2.42	2.94	3.46	4.05	5.25
5	1.95	2.24	2.65	3.29	3.94	4.67	6.25
6	2.04	2.39	2.87	3.64	4.43	5.30	7.34
7	2.12	2.53	3.10	4.00	4.91	5.92	8.30
8	2.21	2.68	3.32	4.35	5.39	6.55	9.26
9	2.30	2.82	3.55	4.70	5.87	7.17	10.22
10	2.38	2.97	3.78	5.05	6.35	7.79	11.18
11	2.47	3.11	4.00	5.40	6.83	8.42	12.14
12	2.56	3.25	4.22	5.75	7.30	9.03	13.09
13	2.64	3.40	4.44	6.10	7.78	9.65	14.03
14	2.69	3.48	4.56	6.27	8.02	9.96	14.50
15	2.75	3.55	4.67	6.44	8.24	10.24	14.94
16	2.79	3.63	4.78	6.60	8.45	10.52	15.35
17	2.84	3.70	4.88	6.75	8.66	10.77	15.74
18	2.89	3.76	4.98	6.90	8.85	11.02	16.11
19	2.93	3.83	5.07	7.03	9.03	11.25	16.45
20	2.98	3.89	5.16	7.16	9.20	11.47	16.79
21	3.02	3.95	5.25	7.29	9.37	11.68	17.10
22	3.06	4.01	5.33	7.41	9.53	11.88	17.41
23	3.10	4.07	5.41	7.53	9.68	12.08	17.70
24	3.14	4.12	5.49	7.64	9.83	12.26	17.97
25	3.18	4.18	5.56	7.75	9.97	12.44	18.24
26	3.22	4.23	5.64	7.85	10.11	12.62	18.50
27	3.26	4.28	5.71	7.96	10.24	12.79	18.75
28	3.29	4.33	5.78	8.05	10.37	12.95	18.99
29	3.33	4.38	5.85	8.15	10.50	13.11	19.23
30	3.37	4.43	5.91	8.25	10.62	13.26	19.45
31	3.40	4.48	5.98	8.34	10.74	13.41	19.67
32	3.44	4.53	6.04	8.43	10.85	13.56	19.89
33	3.47	4.58	6.10	8.51	10.97	13.70	20.10
34	3.51	4.62	6.16	8.60	11.08	13.83	20.30
35	3.54	4.67	6.22	8.68	11.18	13.97	20.50

If you send packages through the U.S. Post Office, you will probably send them parcel post. What is the cost of sending a 6 pound 7 ounce package to Zone 8?

look up 5 pounds in the parcel post rate table. To find the cost of shipping a 4 pound 3 ounce package sent to Zone 6: (a) read down the weight column until you come to 5 pounds, (b) read across to Zone 6 and you will see the cost is $3.94. If your company charges customers for shipping, you will estimate the weight of the package, including the box and packing materials, then look up the cost in a table like this one. Remember, don't charge tax on shipping costs—the tax is calculated on the price of merchandise only. Shipping costs are added last.

Your company may send merchandise COD (collect on delivery). When you ship COD, the postal carrier will collect the amount due and forward it to your company. However, your company must prepay the shipping charges. The amount due may include both the total for merchandise and shipping costs. In addition, the customer must pay a fee for the COD service. The amount varies depending on the amount collected. Up to $500 may be collected on delivery by the postal carrier.

Some businesses prefer using United Parcel Service for COD shipments because the amount collected is not limited to $500, and the shipping charges do not have to be prepaid.

When you need to ship something fast, you may use the express mail service provided by the U.S. Post Office. There are two types of express mail service: (1) post office to addressee and (2) post office to post office.

Post office-to-addressee service is available for most zip codes, and delivery by 3 p.m. on the next day is guaranteed in most areas. Post office-to-post office service is less expensive, but next day delivery is available to only a few zip codes. Express mail rates are shown in Table 28-2.

There are also a number of private companies that provide fast delivery service. These include Federal Express, United Parcel Service, and Emery Worldwide Courier. Look under *air cargo service* in your local telephone directory for other carriers. In many areas, Greyhound Bus Company provides delivery to nearby cities in a matter of hours.

When you want to ship something fast, you can use the next-day express mail service provided by the U.S. Post Office. What is the cost of sending a 10 pound package next day and second day from post office to post office?

Table 28-2
Express Mail Rates

Postage Rate Unit (Lbs.)	Next Day & Second Day PO To Addressee	Next Day & Second Day PO To PO	Postage Rate Unit (Lbs.)	Next Day & Second Day PO To Addressee	Next Day & Second Day PO To PO
½	$ 8.75	$ 8.50	36	$52.00	$49.85
1	12.00	9.85	37	53.10	50.95
2	12.00	9.85	38	54.15	52.00
3	15.25	13.10	39	55.25	53.10
4	15.25	13.10	40	56.35	54.20
5	15.25	13.10	41	57.45	55.30
6	17.75	15.60	42	58.50	56.35
7	18.45	16.30	43	59.60	57.45
8	19.15	17.00	44	60.70	58.55
9	19.85	17.70	45	61.80	59.65
10	20.55	18.40	46	62.85	60.70
11	21.25	19.10	47	63.95	61.80
12	21.95	19.80	48	65.05	62.90
13	22.65	20.50	49	66.15	64.00
14	23.35	21.20	50	67.20	65.05
15	24.05	21.90	51	68.30	66.15
16	25.10	22.95	52	69.40	67.25
17	26.45	24.30	53	70.55	68.40
18	27.80	25.65	54	71.55	69.40
19	29.20	27.05	55	72.65	70.50
20	30.55	28.40	56	73.80	71.65
21	31.90	29.75	57	74.90	72.75
22	33.30	31.15	58	75.90	73.75
23	34.65	32.50	59	77.05	74.90
24	36.00	33.85	60	78.15	76.00
25	37.40	35.25	61	79.25	77.10
26	38.75	36.60	62	80.35	78.20
27	40.10	37.95	63	81.40	79.25
28	41.45	39.30	64	82.50	80.35
29	42.85	40.70	65	83.60	81.45
30	44.20	42.05	66	84.70	82.55
31	45.55	43.40	67	85.75	83.60
32	46.95	44.80	68	86.85	84.70
33	48.30	46.15	69	87.95	85.80
34	49.65	47.50	70	89.05	86.90
35	50.90	48.75			

Credit Card Sales

If you are employed as a salesperson for a retail business, you will probably sell merchandise to customers who want to charge their purchases on a credit card. In this case, you will complete the basic math operations necessary for credit card sales.

Sometimes you will multiply quantity times unit cost to get the amount to be extended, as shown in Figure 28-6. You will add the amounts for several types of items, calculate the tax, and add the tax to the subtotal for merchandise to get the total amount.

If you are a salesperson in a store that accepts credit cards, you must be able to prepare the sales (charge) slips. There are many variations in credit card sales slips. However, there are usually at least three copies: one for the customer, one for the seller, and one for the bank or credit card agency. You may use a mechanical imprinter to transfer the customer's name and account number to the sales slip, or you may write the information on the sales slip. In some businesses, you may not use a credit card sales slip at all. Instead, you will record all of the needed information electronically.

If you do use credit card sales slips for charges to bank cards (VISA, MasterCard, etc.), you (or someone in your company) may deposit them much like you deposit checks in your company account. A special deposit slip must be prepared to accompany the bank copies of the bank card sales slips, and they can be credited to your company bank account as quickly as the checks you deposit.

Copies of sales slips on travel and entertainment credit cards, and oil company credit cards, must be sent to the company that originated the card for credit. So, it takes a little longer to turn these charges into cash in the bank.

If your company accepts credit cards, it will have to pay a fee to the bank or agency that handles the billing and record-keeping. This is a percent of credit sales, based on a sliding scale. For example, if you had VISA sales of $100,000 during the same period that another company only had VISA sales of $2,000, then your company will pay a smaller percentage for handling. The handling fee for travel and entertainment cards is usually slightly higher than for bank cards.

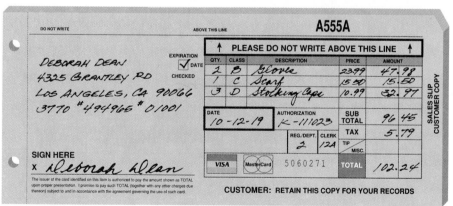

Figure 28-6 **Credit Card Receipt**

There are many variations in credit card slips. You may use a mechanical imprinter to transfer the customer's name and account number to the sales slip. Or you can write in the information. How much would four pairs of gloves, two scarves, and two stocking caps cost?

Returns, Exchanges, and Allowances

If you sell merchandise, some of your customers will return their purchases and ask for a refund or an exchange. As you know, a return is merchandise brought back for a cash refund or credit. State and federal laws prevent returning some types of merchandise, such as mattresses. Some businesses adopt a policy of *no returns*. Most businesses feel, however, that accepting returns (unless illegal) is an important part of good customer relations. Some businesses accept returns but don't give cash refunds. Instead, they issue credit slips that can be used to pay for other merchandise purchased from that business.

With an exchange, merchandise is brought back to be replaced by other merchandise. Most businesses are happy to make the exchange because they want the customer to be satisfied. If the item returned and its replacement are priced the same, it is an *even* exchange. If not, it is an *uneven* exchange. For example, suppose John decides he needs a calculator for his personal use but wants a less expensive one than he was given for his birthday. Say the original calculator was priced at $90, and John wants to exchange it for one priced at $60. You will refund the difference, $30, plus the sales tax on $30. If sales tax where your business is located is 6 percent, you will refund $30 plus $1.80 for a total of $31.80. Sometimes customers want to exchange an item for one that is more expensive, and the procedure is reversed.

When you refund cash to a customer on a return or an exchange, you will probably have to fill out a refund slip similar to the one shown in Figure 28-7.

As you learned in Chapter 18, an allowance is a partial return of the sales price for merchandise kept

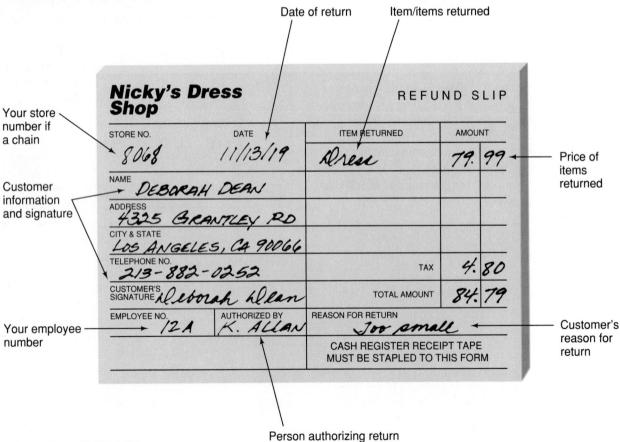

Figure 28-7 **Refund Slip**
When you refund cash to a customer, you will have to fill out a refund slip. How much would two dresses at $79.99 each cost?

by the customer. Allowances are usually given when there is some defect in the merchandise sold, such as clothing with missing buttons or a small snag in the material where it won't show.

Practice:

Use a separate sheet of paper for your answers. How much will you return to the customer in each of the following cases?

1. Mrs. Smith returned a $150 dress that was too large and selected a smaller size in another style priced at $115. How much, including tax at 6 percent, will you return to Mrs. Smith in this uneven exchange?
2. Mr. Jordan returned a $45 radio because it was apparently defective. He selected another model priced at $75. How much, including tax, will you charge Mr. Jordan?

Check page 315 for the answers.

Calculating Gross Sales and Net Sales

The total of all sales for any period of time is called gross sales. If your company sells only on a cash basis, then your gross sales will simply be the total of all cash sales. If your company sells merchandise on account, accepts credit cards, and sells gift certificates, then all of these different types of sales must be totaled to arrive at gross sales.

Because most businesses have some customer returns and allowances, the gross sales figure does not reflect the actual income from sales. *The total of all sales returns and allowances is subtracted from gross sales to get net sales.* The net sales figure is used on the income statement to calculate the amount of profit or loss.

Profit and Loss

Every business strives to earn a profit. If you are an owner or manager, you won't know exactly how profitable your business is until you see the income statement at the end of the year.

The income statement, sometimes called a *profit and loss statement* or *operating statement*, clearly shows how much the business earned or lost during the year. The income statement is used for making many kinds of business decisions, such as whether to expand the business, or to cut back in certain areas that do not appear productive. The income statement is also required to compute state and federal income taxes.

Calculating your company's net profit is much the same whether your company is a service business or a merchandising business. To find the net income for a service business, subtract the operating expenses (all costs incurred in operating the business, such as rent, payroll, and office supplies) from the total revenue.

For example, suppose that you own World-Wide Travel Agency, and had total revenues of $145,540 during the year. Your total operating expenses for the year were $79,630, so your net profit was:

$$\$145,540 - \$79,630 = \$65,910$$

Finding the net profit for a merchandising business requires an additional step. A merchandising business sells goods instead of services. So, you must subtract the *cost of goods sold* from net sales to find the gross profit.

For example, suppose you are employed by Seaside Surfboards—a company that sold $96,785 worth of surfboards last year. The company books show a total of $1,470 in sales returns and allowances. When you subtract the sales returns and allowances from total (gross) sales, you get net sales of $95,315. As the person responsible for preparing the income statement, you must find the gross profit before you can find the net income. If your accounting records show that the cost of goods sold for last year totaled $18,960, your gross profit was:

$$\$95,315 - \$18,960 = \$76,355$$

From this gross profit, you will subtract total operating expenses for the year to find the net income. If operating expenses totaled $39,869, your net profit was:

$$\$76,355 - \$39,869 = \$36,486$$

Practice:
    Use a separate sheet of paper for your answers.
    The income statement for Mountain-Air Bikes is shown below.
1. How much did Mountain-Air pay for the bikes it sold?
2. How much was the gross profit for the year?
3. How much were total operating expenses?
4. Which operating expense was the most costly?
5. How much net income was earned during the year?
    Check page 315 for the answers.

Mountain-Air Bikes
Income Statement
For the Year Ended December 31, 19—

Revenue:		
Sales	$212,015	
Cost of Goods Sold	109,614	
Gross Profit		$102,401
Operating Expenses:		
Salaries	$24,019	
Rent	11,211	
Utilities	4,514	
Advertising	2,422	
Total Operating Expenses		42,166
Net Income		$60,235

The procedures for finding the net income for a merchandising business are simple. Nevertheless, it is necessary to do some preliminary work before you begin work on the income statement. The total for cost of goods sold, which you subtract from net sales, must be calculated. Before you can do that, you must take an inventory. Here is the procedure for finding the cost of goods sold:

a. Find the cost of goods on hand at the beginning of the year (last year's ending inventory).
b. Find the cost of goods purchased for resale during the year.
c. Add the beginning inventory (a) to goods purchased (b) to get the total goods available for sale.
d. Subtract the goods not sold (this year's ending inventory).

Practice:
    Use a separate sheet of paper for your answer.
    Use steps *a, b, c,* and *d* above for finding the cost of goods sold for Tamara's Tennis Toggs. The ending inventory last year was $24,918. During the year, Tamara purchased goods totaling $31,745. This year's ending inventory was $20,416.
    What was the cost of goods sold during the year?
    Check page 315 for the answer.

Interest

When people borrow money, someone must lend or invest the money. Companies often borrow or invest large amounts of money. *The amount borrowed or invested is the* **principal**. *The money paid for the use of that money is called* **interest**.

There are two kinds of interest, simple and compound. *Simple interest is paid only on the amount borrowed or invested (principal). Compound interest is paid on both the principal and the accumulated interest.*

Interest is expressed as a percentage of the principal and is called the **rate of interest**. If you borrow $100 at 11 percent interest, the principal is $100 and the rate of interest is 11 percent. To find the amount of interest for one year, multiply the principal (p) times the rate of interest (r) times the length of time (t). This formula is stated as:

$$i = prt$$

The units in the rate of interest and time must agree. That is, if the rate of interest is expressed in years, then the time must be expressed in years as well. Both may be expressed in months. If the rate is given without reference to a time period, assume that it is for one year.

Suppose you are quoted a yearly rate and need to convert it to a monthly rate. Because there are 12 months in a year, divide the yearly rate by 12, and you will get the monthly rate. If you are quoted a monthly rate and want to convert it to a yearly rate, multiply the monthly rate by 12.

More interest is paid when it is compounded than when it is computed as simple interest. Suppose your company invested $100,000 for two years at nine percent compounded annually (once a year). At the end of the first year, your company would be credited with nine percent interest on $100,000:

$$i = prt = \$100,000 \times .09 \times 1 \text{ year} = \$9,000$$

Your company investment is now worth $109,000. When you apply the $i = prt$ formula at the end of the second year, you will find that your investment is worth $118,810 because the principal, including accumulated interest, has increased to $109,000:

$$i = prt = \$109,000 \times .09 \times 1 \text{ year} = \$118,810$$

Your earned interest at the end of two years is thus $9,000 plus $9,810 for a total of $18,810. By compounding the interest annually, your company would have earned $810 more than it would with simple interest. In fact, the more often interest is compounded, the greater the earnings. If your company's $100,000 had been compounded four times a year (quarterly), total interest for two years would have been $19,483.11—which is $673.11 more than the earnings based on compounding annually. The formula for calculating compound interest is:

$$A = p\left(1 + \frac{r}{x}\right)^{yx}$$

In this formula, A represents the amount (including principal and interest) and p is the principal. The r represents the yearly rate, y is the number of years, and x is the number of times interest is compounded each year.

Calculating compound interest by hand, using a pencil, takes a lot of time. If you have a calculator, use it. Many businesses also have tables that you can use to look up interest compounded at various rates and for various lengths of time. However, many businesses do *not* have compound interest tables, so it is important to be able to solve compound interest problems using a calculator.

Practice:
Use a separate sheet of paper for your answer. Use the formulas shown above to solve these interest problems.

a. Find the interest on $4,000 for two years at 9% per year.
b. Find the interest on $11,000 for one year at 1½ % per month.
c. Find the interest on $65,000 for two years at 10% compounded four times a year.

Check page 315 for the answers.

Payroll

If you are responsible for payroll records, you will have to be especially careful that your records are accurate. Payroll records are very important both to your employees and your company. They are used to prepare income tax returns, so the federal and state governments are interested in their accuracy, too.

Your payroll records may be part of the cash disbursements journal where you keep records of all cash payments. Or you may keep your payroll records in a separate payroll journal. If you use a separate journal for payroll records, you may use a separate page for each employee. Each page will show one employee's pay period, hours worked, earnings, deduc-

Name	Nancy Baker							Wage rate	$ 11.00 / Hr			
Date of Birth	11-19-64							Date employed	8-1-86			
Soc. Sec. No.	514-62-5254							Employee No.	9			
No. of Allowances	1							Department	B			
Address	317 Sycamore											

Pay Period Ending	Hours							Total Regular	Over-time	Earnings	Deductions				Net Pay
	S	M	T	W	TH	F	S				FICA	Federal Income tax	State Income tax	Misc.	
8-14		8	8	8	8	8		40			35.20	36.80	22.00		
8-21		7	8	8	8	8		39			34.32	35.90	21.45		

Figure 28-8 **Payroll Journal**

A payroll journal summarizes each employee's pay period, hours worked, earnings, deductions, and net pay. What is Nancy Baker's net pay for the period ending August 21?

tions, and net pay. Or you may use a payroll journal that summarizes all of this information for many employees (see Figure 28-8).

The amount earned by an employee is called *gross pay. Net pay* is what the employee receives after deductions for taxes, insurance, and voluntary deductions. For example, if Nancy Baker earns $11 an hour and worked 40 hours during the week, her gross pay is $440 ($11 × 40 hours).

If Nancy's deductions total $94, you would calculate her net pay by subtracting the deductions from her gross pay: $440 - $94 = $346 (net pay).

In some companies, each department is responsible for keeping a record of the hours worked by each employee in that department. You may use a payroll statement like the one in Figure 28-9 to summarize payroll information for each employee, then send the payroll statement to your company's payroll department (which usually writes the payroll checks). In many companies, information shown on a payroll statement is entered into a computer, and a computer produces the checks.

Some companies keep a payroll register similar to the one shown in Figure 28-10. It summarizes the payroll information for many employees.

You will need to use a table like Table 28-3 to find the amount to be deducted from each employee's pay for federal income tax. The percentage of gross pay to be deducted for FICA (Social Security) changes almost every year. Get the latest information from your local Social Security Office.

Payroll Statement

Employee __NANCY BAKER__

Employee No. __A8__   Department __Small Appliances__

Payroll Classification: __HOURLY__

Soc. Sec. No. __514-62-5254__

Payroll Period __8-7-89__ To __8-14-89__

Earnings				Deductions		
Salary		440	00	FICA	35	20
Overtime		—		Fed. Income Tax	36	80
				State Income Tax	22	00
Total Earnings		440	00	Total Deductions	94	00
Earnings Due				$ 346	00	

I RECEIVED A COPY OF THIS STATEMENT AND THE AMOUNT OF EARNINGS LISTED ABOVE

__Nancy Baker__   __8-14-89__

Employee Signature   Date

_____   _____

Dept. Supervisior Signature   Date

_____   _____

Payroll Dept. Signature   Date

Figure 28-9 **Payroll Statement**

A payroll statement summarizes payroll information for each employee. It is sent to the company's payroll department which usually writes the payroll checks. List three ways a payroll statement is different from a page in a payroll journal.

PAYROLL REGISTER

WEEK ENDING 8-14-89

| NAME | EARNINGS | | | | DEDUCTIONS | | | | Net Pay |
	Hourly Rate	Reg. Hrs.	O.T. Hrs.	Gross Pay	Federal Inc. Tax	State Inc. Tax	F.I.C.A.	Misc.	
NANCY BAKER	11 00	40 00	—	440 00	36 80	22 00	35 00		346 00
TOTALS									

Figure 28-10 **Payroll Register**
A payroll register summarizes payroll information for employees. If Nancy Baker had worked six hours of overtime, what would her gross salary have been?

Example:
Find the net pay for Joel Hardin, who worked a total of 44 hours during a week at $12/hour. Joel is paid time and a half for overtime (hours worked beyond 40 hours in a week).

Step 1—find the gross pay.
$480.00   ($12 × 40 hours)
+ 72.00   ($12 × 4 hours × 1.5)
$552.00

Step 2—subtract the total deductions.
$552.00   (gross pay)
- 98.40   (total deductions)
$453.60   (net pay)

Practice:
Use a separate sheet of paper for your answers.
Mr. Wilson pays all of the employees at his Pizza Palace $6 an hour. Find the *gross pay, FICA, federal income tax to be withheld, total deductions,* and *net pay* for the following employees. Calculate FICA at 8 percent of gross pay, and use the tax table for single persons shown in Table 28-3 to find withholding tax.

Employee	Tax Information	Hours
Ann Lewis	Single, 1 allow.	40
John Light	Single, 0 allow.	35
Carol Murray	Single, 0 allow.	24
Neil Windsor	Single, 1 allow.	36

Check page 315 for the answers.

Table 28-3
Federal Income Tax Table

SINGLE Persons—WEEKLY Payroll Period   (For Wages Paid After December 1988)

And the wages are—		\multicolumn{11}{c}{And the number of withholding allowances claimed is—}									
At least	But less than	0	1	2	3	4	5	6	7	8	9	10
		\multicolumn{11}{c}{The amount of income tax to be withheld shall be—}									
$120	$125	15	9	4	0	0	0	0	0	0	0	0
125	130	16	10	4	0	0	0	0	0	0	0	0
130	135	17	11	5	0	0	0	0	0	0	0	0
135	140	17	12	6	0	0	0	0	0	0	0	0
140	145	18	12	7	1	0	0	0	0	0	0	0
145	150	19	13	7	2	0	0	0	0	0	0	0
150	155	20	14	8	2	0	0	0	0	0	0	0
155	160	20	15	9	3	0	0	0	0	0	0	0
160	165	21	15	10	4	0	0	0	0	0	0	0
165	170	22	16	10	5	0	0	0	0	0	0	0
170	175	23	17	11	5	0	0	0	0	0	0	0
175	180	23	18	12	6	0	0	0	0	0	0	0
180	185	24	18	13	7	1	0	0	0	0	0	0
185	190	25	19	13	8	2	0	0	0	0	0	0
190	195	26	20	14	8	3	0	0	0	0	0	0
195	200	26	21	15	9	3	0	0	0	0	0	0
200	210	28	22	16	10	5	0	0	0	0	0	0
210	220	29	23	18	12	6	0	0	0	0	0	0
220	230	31	25	19	13	8	2	0	0	0	0	0
230	240	32	26	21	15	9	3	0	0	0	0	0
240	250	34	28	22	16	11	5	0	0	0	0	0
250	260	35	29	24	18	12	6	0	0	0	0	0
260	270	37	31	25	19	14	8	2	0	0	0	0
270	280	38	32	27	21	15	9	3	0	0	0	0
280	290	40	34	28	22	17	11	5	0	0	0	0
290	300	41	35	30	24	18	12	6	1	0	0	0
300	310	43	37	31	25	20	14	8	2	0	0	0
310	320	44	38	33	27	21	15	9	4	0	0	0
320	330	46	40	34	28	23	17	11	5	0	0	0
330	340	47	41	36	30	24	18	12	7	1	0	0
340	350	49	43	37	31	26	20	14	8	2	0	0
350	360	50	44	39	33	27	21	15	10	4	0	0
360	370	52	46	40	34	29	23	17	11	5	0	0
370	380	53	47	42	36	30	24	18	13	7	1	0
380	390	56	49	43	37	32	26	20	14	8	3	0
390	400	58	50	45	39	33	27	21	16	10	4	0
400	410	61	52	46	40	35	29	23	17	11	6	0
410	420	64	53	48	42	36	30	24	19	13	7	1
420	430	67	56	49	43	38	32	26	20	14	9	3
430	440	70	59	51	45	39	33	27	22	16	10	4
440	450	72	62	52	46	41	35	29	23	17	12	6
450	460	75	64	54	48	42	36	30	25	19	13	7
460	470	78	67	56	49	44	38	32	26	20	15	9
470	480	81	70	59	51	45	39	33	28	22	16	10
480	490	84	73	62	52	47	41	35	29	23	18	12

You need a tax table to find the amount of federal income tax that should be deducted from each employee's gross pay. How much would be deducted from the pay of a single person making $425 and claiming no allowances? one allowance?

CASE CHALLENGE

The Hidden Costs of Theft

In 1984, Wherehouse Entertainment, a chain of glitzy, high-tech home entertainment stores in the western United States, was enjoying record sales and profits after two years of extensive reorganization. The chain had closed a number of unprofitable stores while opening new stores in better locations.

The company also began moving into new product lines to supplement its traditional fare of prerecorded audio records and tapes. Most notable of these new product lines was prerecorded video tapes, which were either sold or rented to customers.

Wherehouse and other video rental operations preferred renting movies over selling them. Video movies were rented for an average of $3.50, or sold for about $75 (with an average unit cost of about $59). A movie had to be rented approximately 17 times to pay for itself. Popular titles, which were rented every day, easily produced a monthly gross profit of $46 ($3.50 \times 30 = 105.00 - 59.00 = 46.00$). At the end of the month, the inventory was still producing profits. In a very short time video rental became a big part of the chain's revenue.

In late 1985, however, a major problem developed with Wherehouse's video rental business, causing profits to plunge. The company's marketing strategy with video movies had been to place them on the sales floor so customers could help themselves. Unfortunately, this display arrangement was an open invitation to shoplifters.

Wherehouse immediately took steps to stop this theft. The loss of inventory was so large, however, that, in the first fiscal quarter of 1986, the company's profits declined 28 percent, though sales had climbed 34 percent. Analysts estimated that Wherehouse lost as much as $2 million in stolen videotapes in 1985.

The result of this loss is easily computed using one tape as an example. Say a movie was stolen on its first day on the shelf and was immediately replaced. The company had to spend another $59 for replacement. However, the true loss doesn't stop here.

The replacement tape had to be rented 17 times ($59 \div 3.50$) to cover its unit cost. It had to be rented another 17 times to pay the unit cost of a new tape. If the tape was rented once a day, the store had to wait a total of 34 days (17 + 17) to realize a profit.

Even if sales on other items go up (as was the case with Wherehouse), profits still decline because of the cost of replacing stolen tapes.

1. In your own words, explain how the company lost profits, even though sales increased.
2. How do you think companies such as Wherehouse should deal with losses due to theft?

Answers to Practice Problems

Page 298:

K2007	$51.60
J1012	$ 6.90
B0017	$39.95
Total	$98.45

Page 299:

M14027	$ 62.50
M24532	$ 125.10
K00238	$4,200.00
L0128	$ 562.50

Page 300:

Dept. 12	$850.00
Dept. 16	$ 79.75
Dept. 18	$291.50
Dept. 21	$799.00

Page 301:

1a.	October 25
1b.	$ 19.00
1c.	$931.00
1d.	November 14

Page 302:

	Amount of Discount	Amount to be Paid
1.	$ 772.50	$1,802.50
	$1,102.50	$2,047.50
	$1,460.00	$2,190.00
	$3,231.00	$3,949.00
	$3,217.15	$5,477.85
2.	$ 69.20	$3,390.80
	$ 64.20	$2,075.80
	$ 114.38	$4,460.62
	$ 314.30	$8,665.70
	$ 363.53	$9,330.47
	None	$9,876.00

Page 302:

Item	Tax	Total Amount
Tires	$18.90	$333.90
Ski boots	$11.10	$196.10
Clock	$ 6.30	$111.30
Books	$ 6.63	$117.13
Washer	$25.74	$454.74

Page 304:

Postage

$ 1.69
$ 2.20
$ 3.46
$ 3.76
$ 13.83

Page 307:

1. $37.10
2. $31.80

Page 308:

1. $109,614
2. $102,401
3. $42,166
4. Salaries
5. $60,235

Page 308:

$36,247

Page 309:

a. $720.00
b. $1,980.00
c. $14,196.18

Page 312:

	Ann Lewis	John Light	Carol Murray	Neil Windsor
Gross Pay	$240.00	$210.00	$144.00	$216.00
FICA	$ 19.20	$ 16.80	$ 11.52	$ 17.28
Fed. Tax	$ 28.00	$ 29.00	$ 18.00	$ 23.00
Tot. Ded.	$ 47.20	$ 45.80	$ 29.52	$ 40.28
Net Pay	$192.80	$164.20	$114.48	$175.72

VOCABULARY REVIEW

Write one or two paragraphs using the following seven vocabulary terms.

gross sales
net sales
principal
interest

simple interest
compound interest
rate of interest

FACT AND IDEA REVIEW

1. What is included in the order information on a purchase order?

2. If the business you work for uses an automatic cash register, why might you still be required to write out a sales check?

3. Describe how you calculate an *extension*.

4. Describe how you would calculate the amount of the sale, the tax, and the total due on a $495 item with a 15% discount.

5. What is a *trade discount* and how is it calculated?

6. How is sales tax calculated?

7. The cost of shipping is based on what factors?

8. What does COD stand for, and how does the service work?

9. What are some options for shipping, other than the U.S. Post Office?

10. How do you arrive at the *net sales* amount?

11. What is the purpose of preparing an income statement?

12. If you have a merchandising business, what must you do before you can calculate the cost of goods sold?

CRITICAL THINKING

1. Why is it so important to verify numbers and amounts on invoices?

2. What is the purpose of a *cash discount*?

3. Why do businesses offer *seasonal discounts*?

4. What do you think are the advantages and disadvantages of accepting credit cards?

5. How do you deposit in the bank the "money" you have made from credit card sales?

6. What does a manager or owner do with the information revealed in a profit and loss statement?

7. What is the difference between *simple* and *compound* interest?

8. Why is it so important to have accurate information on a payroll statement?

USING BASIC SKILLS

Mathematics

1. Calculate the extensions for these purchases:
   a. 6 chairs at $59.95 each
   b. 6 place mats at $6.95 each
   c. 6 napkins at $2.95 each

2. Write out the sales check for the purchase of these school supplies (use a 6% sales tax):
   a. 8 spiral notebooks at $1.95 each
   b. 2 dozen lead pencils at 1 dozen for $2.09
   c. 1 dozen ball point pens at $3.50 per dozen
   d. 2 printer ribbons at $3.95 each

3. Write out the sales check for these purchases during a promotional 20% discount on cotton sweaters (6% sales tax):
   a. 2 cotton sweaters at $39.00 each
   b. 1 pair of stockings at $3.95 a pair

4. The cash discount terms on an invoice are 2/10, n30. The invoice is dated August 24 for a net amount of $1,444.

   a. What is the last date to take the discount?

   b. What is the amount of the discount?

   c. What is the amount payable if the discount is taken?

   d. What is the last date to pay the net amount?

5. You buy computer components for resale at a trade discount of 50%. When you buy a monitor with a retail price of $460, what is your discount? What is your net cost? When you resell the monitor for $460, what will your gross profit be?

6. Suppose you buy computer disks in boxes of ten for $5.90. How much does each disk cost? With a 13% discount for buying in lots of 100, how much would each disk cost? (Round off to the nearest cent when necessary.)

7. With a state sales tax of 6% and a city tax of ½%, what would the total tax be on a sale of $15.95?

8. Presume that the bank fee for handling your VISA billing is 3% of the credit sales for amounts between $0.00 and $5,000. Your credit sales for this period are $3,748. What handling fee will you need to pay?

9. If a customer exchanges a $47 auto part for one that costs $35, how much refund (including sales tax at 6%) will you give the customer?

10. What is the interest on $2,000 for five years at 9% compounded annually?

Communication

11. Using the text as a guide, write out an end-of-the-year profit and loss statement for the "Lovely You" beauty supply retail store. Total sales were $698,450. Calculate the cost of goods sold at 37% of the total sales. Salaries include three salespeople at $12,000 each annual salary. Rent is $1,500 per month. Utilities are $615 per month. Advertising costs were $5,030 for the year.

12. Using the text as a guide, write out a purchase order from your store, "Music, Music, Music," to a recording company named "Plastic Pizza." Order a list of your favorite albums/CD's in quantities of 5. Your price for these albums/CD's is 60% of the retail price.

Human Relations

13. You often buy merchandise from a friend's company. Recently, however, you have discovered a source of the same merchandise at a 5% discount. You'd like to save the money, but don't want to risk hurting your friend's feelings (or business!) by buying elsewhere. What do you do?

14. A customer comes into your store to return an item and becomes irate because you won't give him a cash refund. Your store policy provides a credit slip only on returns. Should you stand firm on your policy, or bend the rules to satisfy this irate customer?

APPLICATION PROJECTS

1. What is the sales tax rate for your state? Find out what happens to the sales tax collected by a store.

2. Bring a mail-order catalog to the class. Compare the way each company handles its shipping and handling charges. Are they all based on weight and distance?

3. Take a look at interest rates. Make a few telephone calls to local banks and compare the interest rates they are offering on savings accounts.

BUYING
AND PRICING
MERCHANDISE

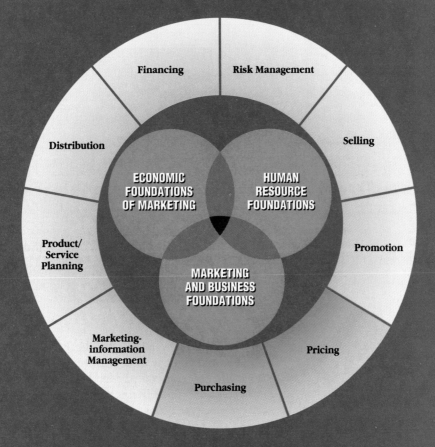

CHAPTERS
▼ ▼ ▼ ▼ ▼ ▼ ▼ ▼
29 Price Planning
30 Pricing Strategies
31 Pricing Math
32 Buying

29

After completing this chapter, you will be able to:

1. define price,

2. explain the importance of price,

3. discuss factors affecting price, and

4. identify goals of pricing.

WORDS TO KNOW

price
price guarantee
break-even point
price fixing
price discrimination
loss leader
unit pricing

Price Planning

Let's play a version of "The Price Is Right." What price would you pay for a one-pound box of candy—$6 or $50? What price would you pay for a used car with 10,000 miles on it—$100 or $7,000? If you picked $6 for the candy and $7,000 for the car, you evaluated the prices in relation to the value you would expect to get from each. You probably felt that $50 was more than you wanted to spend for the candy. You probably assumed that a $100 car was a lemon.

Just as you did in the above two examples, marketers consider price in relation to value when making pricing decisions. They also look at several other factors we'll explore in this chapter. Sometimes a difference in price of a few dollars (or even a few pennies) can make the difference between the success or failure of a product.

What Is Price?

Price *is the value of money (or its equivalent) placed on a good or service.* It is usually expressed in monetary terms, such as $5.50 for a pen. It may also be expressed in nonmonetary terms, such as free goods or services in exchange for the purchase of an item.

The Role of Product Value

The key to pricing is understanding the value buyers place on a product. Value is a matter of anticipated satisfaction. If consumers believe they will get a great deal of satisfaction from a product, they will place a high value on it. They will also be willing to pay a high price for it.

A seller must be able to gauge where a product will rank in the customer's estimation—valued much, valued little, or valued somewhere in between. This information can then be taken into consideration in the pricing decision. The seller's objective is to set a price high enough for the firm to make a profit and yet not so high that it exceeds the value potential customers place on the product.

Various Forms of Price

Price is involved in every marketing exchange, regardless of whether the term *price* is used. The fee you pay a dentist to clean your teeth, the amount you pay for a new pair of shoes, and minor charges such as bridge tolls and bus fares are all prices. Rent is the monthly price of an apartment. Interest is the price of a loan. Dues are the price of membership. Tuition is the price you pay for an education. Wages, salaries, commissions, and bonuses are the various prices that businesses pay workers for their labor. Price, then, comes in many forms and goes by many names.

Importance of Price

Price is an important factor in the success or failure of a business because it helps establish and maintain a firm's image, competitive edge, and profits.

Many customers, for example, use price to make judgments about products and the companies that make them. To some customers, a higher price means better quality from an upscale store or company. To other customers, a lower price means more for their money from a value-oriented retailer or company. In these cases, price is a vital component of store image.

Sometimes price is the main thrust of a firm's advertising strategy. Some retailers stress that they offer the lowest prices in town or promise that they will beat any other store's prices. In such cases, price plays an important role in establishing the edge a firm enjoys over its competition.

Finally, price helps determine profits. Marketers know that sales revenue is created by multiplying the price times the quantity sold. Thus, sales revenue may be increased by selling more items or by increasing the price per item. The only problem with this simple equation is that the number of items sold may not increase or even remain stable if prices are increased. Table 29-1 shows what may happen when the price of an item is changed.

It is also important to remember that an increase in price can only increase profits if costs and expenses can be maintained. You will further explore costs and expenses in relation to price later in this chapter.

Table 29-1 Projected Effects of Different Prices on Sales			
Price per Item	× Quantity Sold	=	Sales Revenue
$30	100		$3,000
27	120		3,240
24	130		3,120
21	140		2,940
18	160		2,880
15	200		3,000

An increase in the price of an item may not produce an increase in sales revenue. Why?

Factors Affecting Price

Many factors affect price, including *supply and demand, consumers, channel members, competition, costs and expenses,* and *government regulations.*

Supply and Demand

The basic theories of supply and demand affect price. In theory, people will buy less of an item when the price is higher and more when the price is lower. Figure 29-1 illustrates this principle using a demand curve for a coffee maker.

Suppliers, however, may not be willing to produce as many items at a lower price as at a higher price. Look at Figure 29-2, which shows the supply curve for the coffee maker. Note that at a price of $20, suppliers are willing to produce only 50,000 coffee makers. At a price of $50, by contrast, they are willing to produce 300,000.

Figure 29-3 illustrates the coffee maker's equilibrium price—the price at which the demand curve and

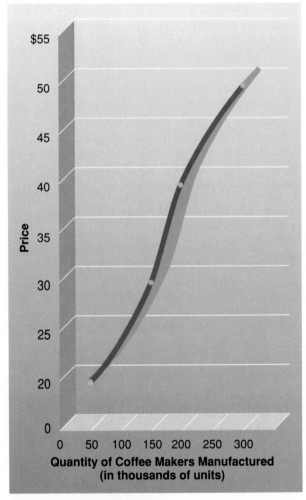

Figure 29-1 **Demand Curve**
Customers are willing to buy more coffee makers as the price declines. How many times more will they buy at $30 than at $50?

Figure 29-2 **Supply Curve**
Suppliers are willing to manufacture more coffee makers as the price rises. How many more will they provide at a price of $50 than at a price of $30?

the supply curve meet—$35. A price close to this figure would likely satisfy both buyers and sellers. (Refer to Chapter 2 for further discussion of supply and demand and how they create surplus, shortage, or equilibrium.)

Consumers

Consumer perceptions about price and consumer purchasing habits also play a role in price planning. As you learned in Chapter 2, when the purchase is dependent on price, we say the demand is *elastic*. In essence, buyers are sensitive to price changes. If a

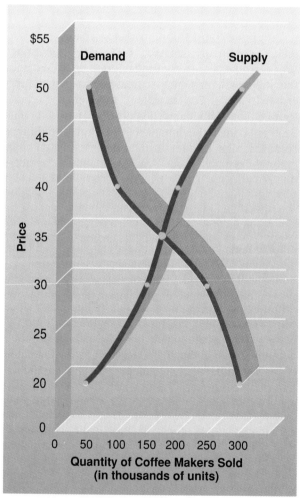

Figure 29-3 **Equilibrium Price**
The intersection of the supply and demand curves locates the equilibrium price. What is the equilibrium price for coffee makers?

price is lowered, consumers will purchase more of the item. If the price is increased, consumers will buy less.

However, consumers will buy some items regardless of price. When that happens, we say the demand is *inelastic*, or not dependent on the price. Items for which a consumer has developed a brand loyalty fall into this category. When brand loyalty is strong, consumers see the product as different from its competitors and therefore will not accept a substitute.

The availability of a product also has a bearing on the price consumers will pay for it. If a person has a flat tire that must be replaced immediately, he or she will be willing to pay more for a new tire than someone who has time to shop around.

Consumers' perceptions about the relationship between price and quality or other values also play a role in price planning. As already noted, some consumers equate quality with price. They believe a high price reflects high quality. A high price may also suggest status, prestige, and exclusiveness. For example, consumers who want to purchase the newest fashions expect to pay high prices because of the exclusiveness of the items. Once a fashion becomes popular and is mass-produced, prices tend to drop.

Not all consumers are equally price conscious, however. Consumers who are interested primarily in bargains will shop for values and will be sensitive to price changes. Others may be less concerned with price because they value personalized service or the image of a particular firm or product. A marketer must be concerned with subjective price—that is, the price the consumer perceives as high or low. The perception of the price is what counts.

Channel Members

All along the channel of distribution, each channel member plays a part in setting the price of an item. All members are concerned with generating sales, making a profit, and maintaining a certain image.

Wholesalers and retailers require a certain profit margin to cover expenses and make a profit. Expenses may include salaries, utilities, rent, and advertising. Therefore, manufacturers must be concerned with the profit margins of these channel members when setting the prices of items sold to them. If a price is so high that the wholesalers and retailers cannot add their customary profit margins to it, they will not carry the item.

Manufacturers strive to create brand loyalty among consumers so people will buy their products—whatever price is charged. When manufacturers succeed in developing such brand loyalty, retailers and wholesalers are guaranteed sales and are therefore less concerned with price increases.

In some cases, powerful manufacturers gain control over price by selecting only a few distributors or by running their own retail stores. In these cases, the manufacturers have complete control over the image of their products, as well as a strong influence on prices.

In most cases, however, cooperation among channel members is important in setting prices. Manufacturers are careful to take wholesalers' and retailers' profit margins into account when deciding on a price. Manufacturers may also offer retailers and wholesalers price guarantees. *A price guarantee is a promise that all discounts given to competitors will be offered to original purchasers as well.* Guarantees are most often offered with new products or by new firms trying to gain entry into a channel. Manufacturers may also offer special deals, such as limited-time discounts and free merchandise, to wholesalers and retailers. This practice is used to encourage wholesalers and retailers to pass the savings on to customers and thus increase sales.

When a price needs to be increased, the effects of the increase on all channel members must be considered. With items that have customary prices, such as candy and newspapers, channel members may absorb the price increase rather than pass it on to consumers. When this happens, the costs should be equitably distributed among channel members.

Competition

Because price is one of the four P's of the marketing mix (the others are product, place, and promotion), it must be evaluated in relation to the target market. When a company knows that the target market is price conscious, a lower price will be effective. When the target market is not price conscious, nonprice competition may be used to influence consumers. As you learned in Chapter 2, nonprice competition minimizes price as a reason for purchase by creating a distinctive product through other means such as availability and customer service. The more unusual a product is perceived to be by consumers, the greater is the marketer's freedom to set prices above those of competitors.

In price competition, marketers change prices to reflect consumer demand, cost, or competition. When products are very similar, price often becomes the sole basis on which customers make their purchase decisions. For example, if shoppers see no difference between Maxwell House coffee and Hills Brothers coffee, they are likely to buy the brand that costs less. For this reason, competitors watch each other closely. When one company changes its prices, others usually react. For example, when AT&T was forced to compete after losing its monopoly status, it cut its long-distance telephone rates. That caused its competitors to do the same. (See the Case Challenge on page 21 in Chapter 2.) The benefit of this competition was lower long-distance prices for consumers.

When competitors engage in a fierce battle to attract customers by lowering prices, a price war is the result. Some airlines, for example, engaged in a price war when People's Express first began offering low-cost, no-frills airfares in the early 1980s. The problem with price wars is that firms reduce their profits while trying to undercut their competitors' prices and attract new customers. This may result in excessive financial losses and, in some cases, actual business failure.

In price competition, then, marketers influence demand through price. In nonprice competition, marketers emphasize marketing factors other than price.

Costs and Expenses

As noted earlier, sales, costs, and expenses determine a firm's profit. As a result, in today's competitive environment, businesses constantly monitor, analyze,

CASE CHALLENGE

Everyday Low Prices at Sears

In 1989, Edward A. Brennan, Chief Executive Officer of Sears, announced plans to introduce "everyday low prices" at Sears. Sears had been reporting a decline in earnings for several years. So, this new pricing strategy was one part of an overall plan to make Sears more profitable in the years to come.

The theory behind discount pricing follows the principles of supply and demand. The lower the price, the higher the demand. Stores are able to sell more of an item because they offer it at a lower price than others and in so doing generate a higher dollar sales volume.

Sears had been losing market share to discounters over the years, even though the store had never been classified as a discounter. With its new pricing policy, some analysts now classify Sears as a discounter.

Under its former pricing policy, Sears regularly ran sales. The effect of that strategy was that customers quickly learned to wait for the sales to make their purchases. In fact, 55 percent of many Sears products were sold at reduced prices under the old system.

Under the new plan, prices have been reduced permanently on many items. For example, an item that normally sold for $20.99 and went on sale three times a year for $14.99 is now priced at $17.99 permanently.

The market tests conducted in Wichita, Kansas, supported the new pricing strategy. Analysis revealed that sales of national brands were high. Sales of Sears brands were steady and slightly higher than with the old plan.

An added benefit of the new pricing policy is reduced expenses in buying, distributing, and marking the advertised specials. With the new system, hundreds of models have been dropped from stock in order to buy more of the most popular brand name items. Savings are also evident in work hours that are not now needed to plan and prepare for special sales events. In the past, each time there was a big sale, sales associates and stock personnel spent hours to move the goods and reprice them.

1. How did consumers' buying habits help to influence Sears to change its pricing strategy?
2. Do you think Sears' new pricing plan now puts it in competition with K-Mart and Wal-Mart?
3. How will Sears be more profitable if it is permanently *reducing* prices on almost all its products?

and project prices and sales in the light of costs and expenses. What do marketers do when costs or expenses increase? Do they increase prices? Some do, and some find other ways to maintain their profit margins.

Some businesses have found that price is so important in the marketing strategy of a product that they have reduced the size of the item or the quality of the materials used in making it rather than change the price. For example, a candy manufacturer may reduce the size of a candy bar from 4 to 3½ ounces rather than increase its price. In such a case, the cost of making the candy bar would be reduced so the manufacturer could still make a profit at the established price (provided, of course, the same quantity of the product was sold).

Other manufacturers may improve a product by adding more features or upgrading the materials used in order to justify a higher price. In this way, the ordinary increase caused by higher costs or expenses may be incorporated into the higher price along with the changes made to the item. The idea here is that because the quality of the item has been improved, the customer should be willing to pay the higher price.

On occasion, prices may actually drop because of decreased costs and expenses. Aggressive firms are constantly looking for ways to increase efficiency and thus decrease costs. Improved technology and less expensive but better-quality materials may help create better-quality products at lower costs. For example, personal computers have gone down in price because of the improved technology of microprocessors that require less wiring and assembly time. Technological advances have also improved the durability and memory capability of computers.

Manufacturers are always concerned with making a profit. They are especially concerned, however, in two situations—when marketing a new product and when trying to establish a new price. In these circumstances, manufacturers carefully analyze their costs and expenses in relation to unit and dollar sales. They do this by calculating their break-even point.

The *break-even point is the point at which sales revenue equals the costs and expenses of making and distributing a product.* After this point is reached, businesses begin to make a profit on the product.

For example, suppose a toy manufacturer plans to make 100,000 dolls that will be sold at $6 each to retailers and wholesalers. The cost of making and marketing the dolls is $4.50 per unit, or $450,000 for the 100,000 dolls. How many dolls must the toy manufacturer sell to cover its costs and expenses? To calculate the break-even point, the manufacturer divides the total amount of costs and expenses by the selling price:

$$\frac{\$450,000}{6} = 75,000$$

To break even, the firm must sell 75,000 dolls. After 75,000 are sold, the firm will begin to make a profit.

Government Regulations

Federal and state governments have enacted laws controlling prices. Therefore, marketers must be aware of their rights and responsibilities regarding *price fixing, price discrimination, resale price maintenance, minimum pricing, unit pricing,* and *price advertising.*

Price Fixing. *Price fixing occurs when competitors agree on certain price ranges within which they set their own prices.* Price fixing can be proved only when there is evidence of *collusion.* This means that there was communication among the competing firms to establish a price range. Price fixing is illegal because it eliminates competition, which is the cornerstone of the free enterprise system.

The federal law concerned with price fixing is the Sherman Antitrust Act of 1890, which outlawed monopolies. Recall that a monopoly prevents competition because one company controls the supply of one type of economic goods.

Price Discrimination. *Price discrimination occurs when a firm charges different prices to similar customers in similar situations.* The Clayton Antitrust Act of 1914 defines price discrimination, stating that it creates unfair competition. In 1936, the Robinson-Patman Act was passed to strengthen the provisions of the Clayton Act. In general, the Robinson-Patman Act prohibits sellers from offering one customer one price and another customer another price if both customers are buying the same product in similar situations.

The Robinson-Patman Act was intended to help smaller retailers compete with the large chain stores. It was presumed that bigger stores would be in a position to demand lower prices because of the volume of goods they could purchase and that smaller retailers would therefore find it difficult to compete.

Thus, the Robinson-Patman Act created restrictions on pricing and other price-related options, such as rebates, credit terms, warehousing, premiums, coupons, guarantees, discounts, and delivery. However, there are a few exceptions. Price discrimination within a channel of distribution is permissible under these circumstances:

- when products purchased are physically different,
- if noncompeting buyers are involved,
- if prices do not hurt competition,
- if costs justify the differences in prices,
- if production costs go up, and
- if prices are changed to meet another supplier's bid.

In addition, discounts are permitted if the sellers can demonstrate that they are available to all channel members on a proportional basis, are graduated to allow small and large buyers to benefit and qualify, or that the discounts are justified by savings incurred. For example, a cumulative quantity discount for purchases made over a period of time, which account for the total amount purchased, may create cost savings for the supplier. Obviously, price discrimination is a complicated matter that must be studied carefully to be sure pricing is in line with the provisions of the Robinson-Patman Act.

Resale Price Maintenance. Resale price maintenance was prevalent prior to the 1970s. Some manufacturers would set the retail price of an item and force retailers to sell the item at that price. If a retailer sold the item at a lower price, the manufacturer could punish the retailer by withholding deliveries or refusing promised discounts or allowances. The manufacturers wanted to control retail prices in order to control the image and prices of their products. That control over prices ended when the price maintenance laws were repealed in the 1970s. Now manufacturers may provide suggested list prices but may not require retailers to follow their suggestions. Retailers are free to price products as they see fit.

Minimum Price Laws. Many states have enacted minimum price laws (also known as unfair sales laws) which supposedly prevent retailers from selling goods below their cost plus a percentage for expenses and profit. Some states have passed such laws that cover all products, while others have included only specific products (such as bread, dairy products, and liquor) in their laws.

An item priced at cost to draw customers into a store is called a loss leader. Retailers select highly popular, well-advertised products to use as loss leaders in the hope of increasing store traffic and sales of other goods carried by the store. Although loss leaders are prohibited under minimum price laws, the laws are rarely enforced because loss leaders benefit the consumer.

Unit Pricing. A number of states have passed laws to make it easier for consumers to compare similar goods that are packaged in different sizes or come in different forms (such as frozen or canned

Supermarket shelf labeling helps shoppers decide which brands and which package sizes represent the best buys. What is the unit price for the item whose label is shown here? How was the figure calculated?

foods). *Unit pricing allows consumers to compare prices in relation to a standard unit or measure, such as an ounce or pound.* Foods stores have been most affected by these laws and have responded with shelf labels and computer records of unit prices.

Price Advertising. The Federal Trade Commission (FTC) has developed guidelines for advertising prices. Some of the more common standards applied to price advertising include the following:

- A company may not advertise a price reduction unless the original price was offered to the public on a regular basis for a reasonable and recent period of time.
- A company may not say that its prices are lower than its competitors' without proof of such comparison based on a large number of items.
- A premarked or list price cannot be used as the reference point for a new sale price unless the item has actually been sold at that price.
- *Bait-and-switch advertising* is illegal. In bait-and-switch advertising, a firm advertises a low price for an item it has no intention of selling. When a customer comes in and asks for the advertised item, salespeople switch the customer to a higher-priced item by saying that the advertised product is out of stock or is of poor quality.

Goals of Pricing

While marketers are concerned primarily with earning a profit, they do have other goals, such as obtaining a *share of the market*, achieving a *return on sales*, and *meeting competition*.

Share of the Market

Recall that a market is composed of all potential customers for a given good or service. As you learned in Chapter 5, when a firm sets out to obtain a specific percentage of the total sales in a given market, it is seeking *market share*.

In addition to market share, which is reported as a percentage, marketers are interested in their relative standing in relation to their competitors, or their *mar-*

ket position. To monitor market position, a firm must keep track of the changing size of the market and the growth of its competitors.

Pricing may play a role in establishing and maintaining a firm's market share and market position. When a company wants to increase its market share, it may engage in price competition in order to take business away from its competitors. Of course, it may also use other competitive tools, such as increasing the frequency of advertising and using new advertising media and messages.

Return on Investment

Marketers who are concerned about accusations of earning unreasonably high profits may set a goal of achieving a specific return on investment based on given sales levels. Government-controlled monopolies, such as utility companies, frequently use this pricing goal to limit their profits, which are scrutinized by the government to protect customers from rate-gouging. These companies are permitted to make a reasonable profit to plan for continued growth of the company and also to pay stockholders' dividends.

Meeting Competition

Some marketers set their pricing goal simply to meet the prices of their competition. In so doing, they either follow the industry leader or calculate the average price and then position their product close to that figure. Two products priced in this manner are automobiles and soft drinks. Competing products in both these categories tend to be very similar and thus may be priced closely to one another.

Some marketers choose to use nonprice competition, mentioned earlier in this chapter. In those cases, marketers price their products higher than the competition's because they believe the quality or service their company offers warrants the higher prices. For example, a company may charge more for a television set if it offers a longer or more comprehensive warranty than its competitors. You will further explore warranties in Chapter 37.

Thus, price competition is not always necessary. Other factors in the marketing mix that may allow different kinds of competition include quality of product, uniqueness of product, convenience of business location or hours, and quality service.

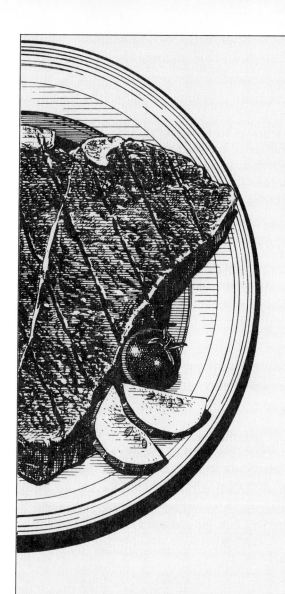

SMART SHOPPERS MEAT PRICE COMPARISON

SURVEY ITEMS		LUCKY	ALBERTSONS	RALPHS	VONS
*Filet Mignon Beef Steak	Lb.	**5.97**	5.99	6.19	6.19
Fresh Cherrystone Clams	Lb.	1.15	**.99**	NA	1.59
Jimmy Dean Mini Hamburgers	9.6 Oz. Pkg.	**2.39**	2.79	2.69	2.69
Hillshire Farm Smoked Polska Sausage	Lb.	2.57	**1.99**	2.09	2.89
Beef Chorizo	1 Lb. Pkg.	**.99**	1.09	1.09	1.09
Lard	1 Lb. Ctn.	.59	.59	**.55**	.69
Turkey Pastrami	Lb.	**2.99**	3.19	**2.99**	3.09
Fresh Pork Shoulder Butt	Lb.	**1.09**	1.69	NA	1.89
Jimmy Dean Link Sausage	12 Oz. Pkg.	**1.89**	2.29	1.98	1.98
Hormel Curemaster Boneless Ham	Lb.	**3.59**	3.88	3.99	NA
Center Cut Ham Slice, Bone-In	Lb.	**2.79**	2.99	3.79	3.79
Ground Turkey, Frozen	1 Lb. Pkg.	1.27	1.89	**1.19**	1.39
Sirloin Cut Pork Loin Chops	Lb.	1.97	2.09	**1.89**	2.39
Smoked Pork Hocks	Lb.	1.49	**1.29**	1.57	NA
Swift Pork Sizzlean	12 Oz. Pkg.	1.44	**1.43**	1.59	1.59
Grade A Turkey, Frozen, 10 to 22 Lb. Avg.	Lb.	**.69**	.98	.98	**.69**
Boneless Pork Loin Roast, Center Cut	Lb.	**3.69**	3.99	4.49	4.49
Fresh Western Oysters	8 Oz. Jar	3.25	3.29	**2.99**	3.69
Fresh Pork Spareribs	Lb.	1.89	**1.79**	1.99	1.98
*Boneless Beef Top Sirloin Steak	Lb.	**1.99**	3.59	3.59	2.69
Louis Rich Turkey Ham	Lb.	**2.19**	2.69	**2.19**	2.59
Hillshire Farm Smoked Sausage	Lb.	2.57	**1.99**	2.09	2.89
Corned Beef Brisket, Flat Cut	Lb.	1.99	2.59	2.29	**1.89**
*Beef Sirloin Tip Roast	Lb.	3.19	2.89	2.89	**2.69**
Lard	4 Lb. Ctn.	2.39	2.35	2.39	**2.29**
*Beef Loin T-Bone Steak	Lb.	4.19	4.29	4.99	**2.99**
Fresh Dover Sole Fillet	Lb.	**4.19**	4.39	4.69	4.79
Fresh Pork Shoulder Roast, Picnic Style	Lb.	1.27	1.29	**1.25**	1.29
Fresh Whole Body Frying Chicken, Grade A, Southern	Lb.	**.69**	.89	**.69**	NA
Halibut Steak, Center Cut, Frozen	Lb.	5.29	**4.99**	6.49	7.98
Boneless Chicken Breasts, California Grown	Lb.	**3.39**	3.89	3.66	3.89
Canadian Bacon, Chunk Style	Lb.	5.99	5.99	**5.69**	**5.69**
Whole Pork Tenderloin	Lb.	4.75	4.79	4.79	**4.69**
Butt Portion Ham, Bone-In	Lb.	**1.49**	1.59	**1.49**	1.59
Chicken Drumsticks, Family Pak	Lb.	.85	**.79**	.97	1.09

MOST OPEN 24 HOURS

Lucky
Still the Low Price Leader.

Companies engaged in price competition keep a close watch on their competitors. Why do you think the firm running this ad went to such lengths in drawing its price comparisons?

VOCABULARY REVIEW

Use all of these vocabulary terms in an original paragraph on price planning.

price
price guarantee
break-even point
price fixing

price discrimination
loss leader
unit pricing

FACT AND IDEA REVIEW

1. Give four examples of pricing in marketing exchanges.

2. Why is price an important factor in the success or failure of a business?

3. Name six factors that affect price.

4. What is a break-even point in marketing?

5. List six types of government regulations about which marketers must be knowledgeable.

6. What were the purposes of resale price maintenance laws and when were they repealed?

7. What are unfair sales laws?

8. What is unit pricing? Why have some states passed laws requiring businesses to post the unit prices of items?

9. Is bait-and-switch advertising legal? Why or why not?

10. Name three goals of pricing in addition to making a profit.

CRITICAL THINKING

1. "Setting prices higher than the competition's will put your business on a fast track to failure"—true or false? Explain the reasons for your answer.

2. A firm expects to sell 10,000 widgets at $10 each. The cost of manufacturing and marketing the widgets is $7.50 each. Calculate the break-even point for the widgets. Of what significance is this analysis to the manufacturer?

3. The Robinson-Patman Act imposes restrictions on pricing but also permits several exceptions, such as bidding and reductions in price when savings can be justified. Considering all the exceptions to this law, how effective do you think the Robinson-Patman Act is in regulating price discrimination? Provide examples to support your opinion.

USING BASIC SKILLS

Math

1. Calculate the break-even point for a notebook that costs a business $1.00 to make and market and that will be sold for $1.50. The total quantity that will be sold at that price is 60,000.

2. Using graph paper and the following information, draw the demand and supply curves for a silver pen. Identify the pen's equilibrium price on your graph.

Price	Demand	Supply
$10	30,000	10,000
$12	25,000	14,000
$13	22,000	16,000
$14	18,000	18,000
$15	15,000	20,000
$16	12,000	23,000

Communication

3. Prepare a two-minute speech on the value of price (or nonprice) competition.

4. Prepare a two-minute talk explaining why all consumers are not equally price conscious and why knowledge of the consumer is so important in pricing decisions.

Human Relations

5. You are working in a snack shop. A steady customer approaches you to ask about a new package of chewing gum that contains ten sticks instead of the customary six. The customer is used to buying the six-stick pack for $.25 and is not happy with the new package, which sells for $.50. What do you say to this customer to maintain her goodwill?

APPLICATION PROJECTS

1. Your firm is thinking of entering the soft drink market. Your boss asks you to prepare a report analyzing Soda Manufacturer E's previous two years' history in terms of market share (increased from 10 to 15 percent) and market position (up from fifth to third).

   Begin your report by drawing a diagram of the change in E's market share. Next, explain how that change affected E's market position.
   Note: The first-year market shares for all companies competing in the soft drink market are as follows:

   Soda Manufacturer A—35 percent
   Soda Manufacturer B—25 percent
   Soda Manufacturer C—15 percent

Soda Manufacturer D—12 percent
Soda Manufacturer E—10 percent
Soda Manufacturer F—3 percent

Conclude your report by explaining how Soda Manufacturer E could have used price to accomplish its goals of a 5 percent increase in market share and a change in market position from fifth place to third.

2. You are the manufacturer of a new 10-ounce bottle of shampoo called Hair Joy and must determine the price you should charge wholesalers and retailers for the product. Hair Joy promises users more manageable hair that is full of body. Market research indicates that consumers want this type of shampoo.

   a. Visit one or two local stores and jot down the prices of at least four comparable shampoos. Then calculate the average price.

   b. Your cost of manufacturing and distributing the shampoo to wholesalers and retailers is $1.85 per bottle. Retailers generally double the price they pay for shampoo from the manufacturer. Considering that fact and your research, what would you suggest as the price retailers should be charged?

   c. Considering that you expect to make 200,000 bottles of shampoo at the price you decided upon, what will be your break-even point?

30

After completing this chapter, you will be able to:

1. apply the three basic pricing strategies (cost-oriented, demand-oriented, and competition-oriented) to pricing a product,

2. describe the effects wholesalers and retailers have on a manufacturer's pricing decisions,

3. explain how prices are determined during a product's life cycle,

4. identify various pricing techniques, and

5. list the steps in setting prices.

WORDS TO KNOW

markup
cost-plus pricing
skimming pricing
penetration pricing
one-price policy
flexible-price policy
price lining

Pricing Strategies

FENDI.
The Latest Roman Masterpiece
Swiss-Made Timepieces From $250 to $750 • Water Resistant to 5 ATM (165ft) • Quartz.

Y ou have just been hired as a product manager for Continental Cookies, Inc. Your first assignment is to review the pricing structure used for all current products and to develop a price for a new cookie called Coconut Surprise that will be introduced shortly.

Continental is a small cookie manufacturer that sells half-pound, one-pound, and two-pound packages of cookies in decorative tins and specially designed paper packages. Some of the firm's more popular varieties are chocolate chip, peanut butter swirl, and oatmeal raisin.

After reviewing all the factors that go into price planning, what strategy will you use to arrive at a price for the new cookies?

Basic Pricing Strategies

As you start your analysis, remember that a major factor in determining the profitability of any product is price. You need to find the right price for your target market. Only then will you have a chance of being successful.

There are three basic strategies that you may want to consider in determining the price for Coconut Surprise cookies: *cost-oriented pricing, demand-oriented pricing,* and *competition-oriented pricing.*

Cost-Oriented Pricing

In *cost-oriented pricing,* marketers first calculate the costs of acquiring or making a product and their expenses of doing business. Then they add their projected profit margin to these figures to arrive at a price. *Markup pricing* and *cost-plus pricing* are two of the most common methods of cost-oriented pricing.

Markup Pricing. *Markup pricing* is used primarily by wholesalers and retailers who are involved in acquiring goods for resale. *A markup is the difference between the price of an item and its cost.* It is generally expressed as a percentage. If a business is to be successful, the markup on its products must be high enough to cover the expenses of running the business and must include the intended profit. Details and calculations related to markup pricing are given in Chapter 31.

Cost-Plus Pricing. *In cost-plus pricing, all costs and expenses are calculated and then the desired profit is added to arrive at a price.* Very similar to markup pricing, cost-plus pricing is used primarily by manufacturers and service companies. The method is more sophisticated than markup pricing, however, because all fixed and variable expenses are calculated separately for different goods and services. For example, when a manufacturer is running at full capacity, the fixed expenses become a smaller percentage of total sales and thus permit the manufacturer to charge a lower unit price for goods. If a company receives a rush order and must pay overtime to employees in order to get out the job, the increased labor costs may be calculated into the price of the goods.

Service businesses, such as market research companies and accounting firms, determine the costs involved in each job and then add on a profit to arrive at a price. Many companies have specialists and use sophisticated computer programs to study all fixed and variable expenses involved in each job. Figure 30-1 illustrates how cost-plus pricing can be used to calculate price.

Demand-Oriented Pricing

Marketers who use *demand-oriented pricing* attempt to determine what present consumers are willing to pay for given goods and services. The key to using this method of pricing is the consumer's perceived value of the item. The price set must be in line with this perception. If it is not or if the perceived value itself is misread, the item will be priced too high or too low for the target market, either of which could cause the product to fail.

Another aspect of demand-oriented pricing involves demand differentials. When there are few substitutes for an item and there is demand inelasticity, demand-oriented pricing is effective. Consumers are

Bradley's Print Shop

Paper (40 reams @ $10/ream)	$400
Labor (10 hours @ $10/hour)	100
Printing materials	60
Artwork	140
Expenses	50
Profit	50
Final price to customer	**$800**

Figure 30-1 **Cost-Plus Pricing**
Cost-plus pricing breaks down into its component parts and expenses. If you wanted to show the similarity between markup pricing and cost-plus pricing, how might you relabel the entries here?

generally willing to pay higher prices because they believe an item is different from its competitors. Companies try to achieve this status by developing brand loyalty.

In other cases, the prices do not reflect major differences in the good or service. They only reflect the *demand* for the good or service. For example, theaters often charge different prices for tickets on the basis of the location of the seats. Some seats will be more expensive than others. Everyone who buys a ticket will see the same performance but from a different vantage point. Telephone companies may charge higher rates for long-distance calls made during peak times. The cost of providing that service may not change, but the demand for the service increases.

Manufacturers may also create prices for different styles on the basis of a demand differential that is not a reflection of the cost of making the item but rather the demand for a given style. For example, white washing machines may be priced at $300, while those that are yellow or beige may be sold for $350. The difference in price is not based on an increase in the cost of producing color machines. Rather, it is based on the demand for fashionable colors.

Competition-Oriented Pricing

Marketers who study their competitors to determine the prices of their products are using *competition-oriented pricing*. These marketers may elect to take one of three actions after learning their competitors' prices: price above the competition, price below the competition, or price in line with the competition. What is different about this method of pricing is that there is no relationship between cost and price or between demand and price. Marketers simply set prices on the basis of what their competitors charge. Two basic types of competition-oriented pricing strategies are *competitive-bid pricing* and *going-rate pricing*.

Competitive Bid Pricing. Determining the price for a product on the basis of bids submitted by competitors to a company or government agency is called *competitive bid pricing*. Most government agencies are required by law to request bids based on certain specifications so they can select the company that offers the lowest price on the desired product. In such cases, some companies will elect to enter a very low bid in order to obtain the contract. They will accept a smaller profit in order to keep their employees working.

Going-Rate Pricing. Almost all firms engage in some form of *going-rate pricing*, which involves studying the competition's prices to be sure one's own prices are in line. Going-rate pricing is especially important in businesses where the competing products are similar. The firm with the leading market share may be the leader in setting prices. How other companies elect to price their products (above, below, or in line with the market leader) depends on their philosophy of doing business and their market position in relation to the leader.

Combined Pricing Strategies

Even though the three basic pricing strategies just described were introduced as separate options, in reality most marketers use all three to determine prices. The cost-oriented pricing strategy is helpful to marketers in determining the price floor for a product—that is, the lowest price for which it can be offered for sale and still earn the company a profit. Demand-oriented pricing may be used to determine a price range for the product, defined on one side by the price floor and on the other by a ceiling price (the highest amount consumers would be willing to pay). Finally, competition-oriented pricing may be used to examine the competition to make sure the final price matches the standing the firm wishes to have in relation to its competitors.

Influences of Wholesalers and Retailers

In addition to using the foregoing strategies to arrive at a price, manufacturers may also consider the prices they will charge wholesalers and retailers for their products. This means working backward from the final retail price or forward from costs and expenses to the final retail price. Figures 30-2 and 30-3 illustrate these two methods.

In Figure 30-2, which describes the steps in working backward, the retail price is set first, on the basis of consumer demand and competition. Next, the markups desired by the wholesalers and retailers are deducted from the suggested retail price. Finally, the price that the manufacturer will charge the wholesaler is determined.

Estimated retail price	$25.00
Retailer's markup (40 percent of retail)	–10.00
Wholesaler's price to retailer	$15.00
Wholesaler's markup (30 percent of wholesale)	–4.50
Manufacturer's price to wholesaler	$10.50

Figure 30-2 **Pricing Backward from Retail Price**

One way a manufacturer can arrive at a wholesale price is by subtracting all markups from the retail price. Suppose in the example shown here the manufacturer's cost was $11. What would the manufacturer have to do?

Cost of producing item	$9.00
Manufacturer's expenses and profit (25 percent of cost)	+2.25
Manufacturer's price to wholesaler	$11.25
Wholesaler's markup (42.9 percent of cost)	+4.83
Wholesaler's price to retailer	$16.08
Retailer's markup (66.67 percent of cost)	+10.72
Retailer's price to consumer	$26.80

Figure 30-3 **Pricing Forward from Manufacturer's Cost**

Adding markups to cost is another way manufacturers can price their goods. Suppose in the example given here market research had shown consumers would pay as much as $30 for the item. What would the manufacturer's options be?

In Figure 30-3, which illustrates the steps in working forward from the manufacturer's cost of the item to the final retail price, the wholesalers' and retailers' markups are added to the cost to arrive at the final selling price. If the price is set at this point, competition and consumer demand are left out of the pricing decision. When the marketer does not consider these two factors, the final retail price may be higher than a competitor's and higher than the price consumers are willing to pay. On the other hand, if the differentials in the product warrant a higher price, the company will enjoy an even higher profit margin than it would if it used the backward method.

Pricing and Product Life Cycle

Products move through four stages: introduction, growth, maturity, and decline. When products are no longer profitable to a company, they may be dropped from the line. Pricing plays an important role in this sequence of events.

New Product Introduction

Depending on the philosophy of the business and market conditions, one of two pricing methods may be used when a new product is introduced—*skimming pricing* or *penetration pricing*.

***Skimming pricing** is a pricing policy that sets a very high price for a new product to capitalize on the high demand for it during its introductory period.* At this time, the high price is geared toward trendsetters, who are generally willing to pay higher prices in order to be the first to own or avail themselves of a new product. Businesses that use this method recognize that once the market for the product changes to more price-conscious customers, the price will have to be lowered. However, while the product is new and "hot," the marketer will enjoy a high profit margin. This margin will help cover the research and development costs incurred in designing the product and create a prestigious image for it. Another advantage of skimming pricing is that the price may be lowered without insulting the target market.

The disadvantage of skimming pricing is that the high initial price generally attracts competition. Once other firms begin to compete successfully, the price will have to be lowered. Another problem occurs if the initial price is far above what consumers (even the trendsetters) are willing to pay. In that case, sales will be lost and profits diminished because the market will not take the item seriously.

Penetration pricing is the opposite of skimming pricing in that the initial price for a new product is set very low. The purpose of penetration pricing is to encourage as many people as possible to buy the product and thus penetrate the market. This type of pricing is most effective in the sale of price-sensitive products, which are items with elastic demand.

Mass production, distribution, and promotion must be incorporated into the marketing plan to penetrate the market quickly. The product should take hold in a short period of time, allowing the marketer to save on fixed expenses (through mass production) and to increase the profit margin (through volume sales).

The biggest advantage of penetration pricing is its ability to capture a large number of customers for a company in a relatively short period of time, thus blocking competition. Another advantage of penetration pricing is its ability to move into a market in which the leaders are offering higher prices and lure large numbers of customers away from other brands.

A major disadvantage of penetration pricing occurs if the product is not in high demand by customers. In that case, the lower price will cause the marketer to suffer a bigger loss than it would have if a higher initial price had been set.

Other Product Stages

Pricing during subsequent periods in a product's life cycle will be determined on the basis of which pricing method was originally used—skimming or penetration. During the growth stage, sales increase rapidly and total costs per unit decrease because volume absorbs fixed costs. The main goal of marketers is to keep products in this stage as long as possible.

If the product was introduced with skimming pricing, sales should be monitored closely. Once sales begin to level off, the price should be lowered to appeal to the next target market, which is slightly price conscious. If the product is considered a fad, the price may be lowered drastically.

C A S E   C H A L L E N G E

No More Ordinary Wastebaskets

In 1989, Mobil Chemical, manufacturer of Hefty trash bags, decided to enter the wastebasket business with a new "Hefty Designs" line. Mobil designed upscale waste containers as an answer to the ordinary wastebasket. The company invested $5 million in ads and promotions to compete in the plastic wastebasket market led by Rubbermaid.

Mobil decided to market wastebaskets to people who were looking for upgraded models. It suggested a retail price of $19.99 for its top-of-the-line product. (By comparison at the time, Rubbermaid's top-of-the-line wastebasket retailed for $17.99.)

Mobil thought customers would pay more for designs that add value. Some of Mobil's models have two pedals—one to open the lid and another to close it. Other models prevent disposable trash bags from slipping by incorporating a specially designed retainer ring to hold the bag in place. An attachment for storage of replacement bags is also included in some designs.

Mobil projected sales in 1989 of $20 to $30 million.

1. Why did Mobil decide to price its new wastebaskets higher than Rubbermaid's? Was that decision more cost-oriented, demand-oriented, or competition-oriented?
2. Would you classify the new product line's introduction as skimming pricing or penetration pricing? Why?
3. What problems might Mobil encounter in persuading retailers to carry these new wastebaskets?

If the product was introduced with penetration pricing, very little price change will be made in the growth stage. Rather, other promotions will be used to keep sales high.

Once the product reaches the maturity stage, when sales begin to level off because demand is cut in half, competition is generally very keen. At this stage, marketers look for new market segments to hold the prices for their products. For example, a baking soda marketer may stress non-cooking uses for baking soda, such as deodorizing or cleaning refrigerators.

The marketer's principal goal during the maturity stage is to stretch the life of a product. Some companies revitalize a product in this stage by adding new features or improvements to it. When successful, such efforts can actually put a product back into its growth stage. When such efforts are not successful, the product moves into its decline.

In the decline stage, sales decrease and profit margins are reduced. To maintain profitability, marketers therefore try to reduce the costs of manufacturing or carrying the product, or they cut back their advertising and other promotional activities. Once a product is no longer profitable, it is phased out.

One-Price vs. Flexible-Price Policy

A one-price policy is one in which all customers are charged the same price for the goods and services offered for sale. Under a one-price policy, prices are quoted to customers by means of signs and price tags, and no deviations are permitted.

A flexible-price policy, on the other hand, permits customers to bargain for merchandise. In this type of situation, a price is quoted by either the buyer or seller and then the bargaining begins. Most retail stores avoid using a flexible-price strategy because it can cause legal problems and because many customers do not like it. However, customers do expect to find a flexible-price strategy in effect with such goods as used cars, antiques, furniture, and selected jewelry.

Pricing Techniques

Now that we have looked at general pricing strategies, it is time to look at specific pricing techniques that marketers use. These techniques include *psychological pricing* and *discount pricing*.

Psychological Pricing

Psychological pricing refers to techniques that create an illusion for customers or that make shopping easier for them. In either case, psychological pricing techniques appeal to particular market segments because of their shared perceptions and buying habits. Among common psychological pricing techniques are *odd-even pricing*, *prestige pricing*, *promotional pricing*, and *price lining*.

Odd-Even Pricing. A technique that involves setting prices that all end in either odd or even numbers is known as *odd-even pricing*. The psychological principle is that odd numbers, such as $.79, $7.95, and $59.99, present a bargain image. Even numbers, such as $1, $10, and $100, present a quality image. Whether or not this is true, you will find that many marketers follow the odd-even technique in an effort to project a certain image.

Odd-numbered prices like those shown here suggest to many customers that they are getting a bargain. Would such prices or advertising be used to promote the merchandise shown in the opening photo of this chapter? Why or why not?

Prestige Pricing. Another psychological technique is *prestige pricing*, the practice of setting higher-than-average prices to suggest status and prestige to the consumer. As noted in Chapter 29, many customers infer that higher prices mean higher quality. Thus, they are willing to pay more for certain goods and services. For example, Rolls Royce automobiles, Perrier bottled water, Waterford crystal, and Lenox china are all prestige-priced. By contrast, when prices are set very low, this target market perceives the products as "cheap" or of little value.

Even customers who are known to prefer higher-priced products, however, have limits on what they will spend for prestige goods and services. To avoid exceeding these limits, marketers must set ceiling prices very carefully.

Promotional Pricing. The psychological technique of *promotional pricing* is generally used in conjunction with sales promotions when prices are lower than average. Two basic types of promotional pricing are loss leader pricing, discussed in Chapter 29, and special-event pricing. As you will recall, loss leader pricing is used to increase store traffic by offering very popular items of merchandise for sale at cost or slightly above. Customers who are familiar with the prices of these items will be attracted by the bargain and will come to the store to shop. Marketers hope that while customers are in the store they will also buy other items at the customary markup and will return on subsequent occasions.

In special-event pricing, items are reduced in price for a short period of time. Some examples of this technique can be found in back-to-school specials, Presidents' Day sales, dollar days, anniversary sales, and the like. At the end of a season, businesses also run clearance sales to get rid of the old merchandise in order to make room for the new.

Price Lining. *Price lining is a special pricing technique that requires a store to offer all merchandise in a given category at certain prices.* For example, a store might price all of its blouses at $25, $35, and $50.

When deciding on price lines, marketers must be careful to make the price differences great enough to represent low, middle, and high prices for the category of goods being offered. Price lines of $25, $26, $28, and $30, for example, would confuse customers because they would have difficulty discerning their basis. (Slight price differences translate into equally slight quality differences.) When price lines are properly drawn (that is, not too closely), customers can easily compare items, both within a single line and between the various lines.

An advantage of price lining is that the target market is fully aware of the price range of products in a given store, and this helps the store maintain its image. In addition, price lining makes merchandising and selling easier for salespeople, who can readily draw comparisons between floor and ceiling prices. The technique also helps salespeople trade up—that is, offer a higher-priced, better quality item to a customer to better satisfy the customer's needs.

Discount Pricing

Discount pricing involves the seller's offering reductions from the usual price. Such reductions are generally granted for the buyer's performance of certain functions. These discounts include *cash, quantity, trade*, and *seasonal discounts*, as well as *promotional discounts* and *allowances*.

Cash Discounts. Cash discounts are offered to buyers to encourage them to pay their bills quickly. Terms are generally written on the invoice. For example, 2/10, net 30 means a 2 percent discount is granted if the bill is paid in 10 days. If the buyer does not take advantage of the discount, the full amount must be paid within 30 days.

Quantity Discounts. Quantity discounts are offered to buyers for placing large orders. Sellers benefit from large orders through the lower selling costs involved in one transaction as opposed to several small transactions. Quantity discounts also encourage buyers to purchase more than they originally intended to purchase.

There are two types of quantity discounts: *noncumulative* and *cumulative*. Noncumulative quantity discounts are offered on one order, while cumulative quantity discounts are offered on all orders over a specified period of time. Cumulative discounts may be granted for purchases made over six months, for example, in which case all purchases for that period are used to determine the quantity discount offered. In other cases, buyers may be required to sign a contract that guarantees a certain level of business. For example, advertisers who agree to use a specified number of display lines in their newspaper ads might be charged contract rates that reflect usage. Generally, the more you advertise, the less you pay per line.

Trade Discounts. Trade discounts are not really discounts at all but rather the way manufacturers quote prices to wholesalers and retailers. Since many manufacturers establish suggested retail prices for their items, they work off those prices, which are called *list prices*. They grant members of the channel of distribution discounts from the list price for performing their respective functions. Thus, a manufacturer might grant wholesalers a 40 percent discount from the list price and retailers a 30 percent discount. Or, the manufacturer might quote the discounts in a series, such as 25 and 10 percent for retailers and wholesalers, respectively. Series discounts such as this are also called chain discounts and are calculated in sequence, as follows:

$50 (list price) $\times$ .25 (25%) = $12.50
$50 – $12.50 = $37.50   Cost to retailer
$37.50 (cost to retailer) $\times$ .10 (10%) = $3.75
$37.50 – $3.75 = $33.75   Cost to wholesaler

In series discounts, note that the wholesaler's discount is based on the retailer's discount, not the original list price.

Seasonal Discounts. Seasonal discounts are offered to buyers who are willing to buy in advance of the customary buying season. Manufacturers offer such discounts to obtain orders for seasonal merchandise early so that production facilities and labor can be utilized throughout the year. Manufacturers sometimes call these discounted purchases "early-bird orders" because they encourage buyers to act before a certain date.

A variation on this device is used by resorts. They offer vacationers lower rates to encourage use of resort facilities during the off-season.

Other businesses use seasonal discounts to cut anticipated costs. Many retailers, for example, drastically reduce prices on Christmas cards and decorations the day after Christmas. Such retailers prefer to sell this merchandise at a lower markup than pay the costs of warehousing it until the following year.

Promotional Discounts and Allowances. Promotional discounts are offered to wholesalers and retailers who are willing to advertise or promote a manufacturer's products. The discount may take the form of a percentage reduction in price or free merchandise. The latter is called an *allowance*. Another alternative, discussed in Chapter 21, is cooperative advertising in which the manufacturer and the retailer share the costs of advertising, with the manufacturer paying the lion's share.

Some kinds of promotional discounts are offered directly to the consumer. As you learned in Chapter 19, a *rebate* is a partial refund on the cost of a

The day after Christmas is traditionally one of the busiest shopping days of the year, mainly because of heavy discounting by retailers. At what other times of the year do stores use this technique to minimize inventory?

particular item from the manufacturer. To receive the rebate, a customer buys the product and then sends in a rebate form along with some proof of purchase.

Trade-in allowances also go directly to the buyer. Customers are offered a price reduction if they sell back an old model of the product they are purchasing. Consumers are generally offered trade-in allowances when purchasing cars or major appliances. Companies are usually granted such allowances when purchasing machinery or equipment.

Steps in Setting Price

Now that you have studied pricing strategies and techniques, it is time to put all that information into six easy steps for determining a price.

Determine Pricing Objectives

What is your purpose in setting a price for your product? Do you want to increase sales volume or sales revenue? Do you want to establish a prestigious image for your product and your company? Do you want to increase your market share and market position? The answers to these questions will help you define your objectives. These, in turn, will allow you to keep prices in line with other marketing decisions.

Study Costs

Since the main reason for being in business is to make a profit, give careful consideration to the costs involved in making or acquiring the goods or services you will offer for sale. Determine whether and how you can reduce costs without affecting the quality or image of your product.

Estimate Demand

Employ market research techniques to estimate consumer demand. The key to pricing goods and services is to set prices at the level consumers expect to pay. In many cases, those prices are directly related to demand.

Study Competition

Investigate your competitors to see what prices they are charging for similar goods and services.

Study the market leader. What is the range of prices from the ceiling price to the price floor? Will you price your goods lower than, equal to, or higher than your competitors'?

Decide on Pricing Strategy

Once you have considered all the above factors, select a pricing strategy that will achieve the objectives you have set. Estimate demand and costs involved and analyze your competition to arrive at a basic plan for pricing. At this point, you may decide to price your product higher than the competition's because you believe your product is superior. On the other hand, you may decide to set a lower price with the understanding that you will raise it once the product is accepted in the marketplace.

Set Price

After you have evaluated all the foregoing factors, apply the pricing techniques that match your strategy and set an initial price. Be prepared to monitor that price and evaluate its effectiveness as conditions in the market change.

By applying all the principles you learned in this and the previous chapter, you should now be able to establish a price for a given product or service. So, go back to page 332 and decide what price you think would be most appropriate for Coconut Surprise cookies.

VOCABULARY REVIEW

Use each of the following vocabulary terms in a sentence that reveals the term's meaning.

markup   one-price policy
cost-plus pricing   flexible-price policy
skimming pricing   price lining
penetration pricing

FACT AND IDEA REVIEW

1. How does a marketer determine prices when using a cost-oriented strategy? Name two common methods of cost-oriented pricing.

2. What do marketers who use demand-oriented pricing attempt to determine? Cite two situations in which demand-oriented pricing is used.

3. How does competition-oriented pricing differ from cost-oriented and demand-oriented pricing? Name two basic types of competition-oriented pricing strategies.

4. Explain how cost-oriented, demand-oriented, and competition-oriented pricing strategies can be coordinated to determine price.

5. Name and explain two pricing methods that may be used when a new product is introduced into the market.

6. What are four common psychological pricing techniques?

7. What are the advantages of price lining to customers and to salespeople?

8. Why are cash discounts offered to buyers?

9. Name and explain two types of quantity discounts.

10. What are seasonal discounts? Why are they offered by manufacturers? by vacation resorts? by retailers?

11. Why do manufacturers offer promotional discounts to wholesalers and retailers? In what form do manufacturers offer such discounts to consumers?

12. List and briefly explain the six steps in setting a price.

CRITICAL THINKING

1. As product manager at Continental Cookies, which method would you use to introduce the new Coconut Surprise cookies—skimming pricing or penetration pricing? Why?

2. If you were marketing a new high-tech computer with capabilities that other computers did not as yet have, which method would you use to introduce it—skimming pricing or penetration pricing? Why?

3. Johnson & Johnson promoted its baby shampoo to adult male athletes by touting the product's gentleness, even when used every day. At what stage in the shampoo's life cycle do you think this promotion took place? What do you think Johnson & Johnson was trying to accomplish by promoting its baby shampoo to adult males?

4. You shop at a local department store and pay the price marked on the price tag. Does the store have a one-price or a flexible-price policy? Explain.

5. In establishing price lines for men's sweaters, which of the following would you select and why?
   a. $50, $52, $53, $55, $65, $67, $69, $72, $74, $77, $80
   b. $50, $65, $80

6. Some marketers contend that trade discounts are not really discounts at all. What do you think? Explain.

USING BASIC SKILLS

Math

1. Determine the price a wholesaler would pay for an item with a list price of $100 if the series trade discounts were 40 percent and 10 percent for retailers and wholesalers, respectively.

2. A retail store is having a sale in which dresses are marked down 20 percent and suits are marked down 30 percent. What is the sale price of a dress priced at $120? What is the sale price of a suit priced at $215?

Communication

3. As a salesperson for a toy company, explain to a retail buyer why you are seeking an order in February for toys that will be sold in the retail store in November and December.

Human Relations

4. You work for a retail jeweler who uses a flexible-price strategy with a few selected customers. You are alone in the store and wait on a steady customer. When you ring up the sale, the customer tells you that you did not deduct the customary 20 percent discount. What would you do?

APPLICATION PROJECTS

1. As product manager for Continental Cookies, you have ascertained the following facts:
   - Cost to make and market a one-pound tin of Coconut Surprise cookies is $1.
   - Market research indicates a strong demand for coconut cookies.
   - Wholesalers and retailers both use a 40 percent markup on cookies.
   - Most similar cookies retail for between $2.50 and $3.25 per pound.

   Write a pricing memo to your boss. In it, answer these questions:

   a. Considering costs, demand, and competition as well as the effects of wholesalers and retailers on price, what should be the retail price of a pound of Continental's new Coconut Surprise cookies?

   b. What should Continental charge wholesalers for the cookies?

   c. What should it charge retailers?

2. At the grocery store, choose four types of products, such as facial tissue. Then choose four product lines within that group (for example, Kleenex, Nice and Soft, or the store generic brand). Compare the prices of the items in each product line. Write a short paragraph, explaining how the prices in each line compare and why you think there is a difference.

3. Shop a discount store, a department store, a grocery store, and a specialty store. At each store, do the following:

   a. Find two products that you would price forward to retail and two that you would price backward from retail. Explain why you would choose that particular method for the product.

   b. Find two products that you would introduce by skimming pricing and two for which you would use penetration pricing. Explain why each strategy would effectively introduce the product to the market you want to reach, and why it would be the best way to realize a profit.

   c. Find two products that use odd/even pricing, two that use prestige pricing, two that use promotional pricing, and two that use price lining. For each example, briefly explain the market you want to reach and why the particular pricing strategy you have chosen would be effective.

Pricing Math

After completing this chapter, you will be able to:

1. explain how a firm's net profit or loss is related to pricing,

2. calculate dollar and percentage markup based on cost or retail,

3. calculate markdown in dollars and determine sale price as well as maintained markup,

4. determine unit selling price,

5. calculate various kinds of discounts, and

6. calculate sales tax.

gross profit
maintained markup

$\mathbf{N}$ow that you understand the principles of pricing, it is time to learn how to calculate prices. This chapter is devoted to the pricing mathematics used by wholesalers and retailers as well as manufacturers and service industries.

As you learned earlier, pricing is related to a company's profitability. Now you will see precisely *how* it is related. In this chapter, try to work through all the Practices before checking your answers on page 354.

Profit vs. Markup

A businessperson makes the following statement: "We made a profit of $50—bought the whatsit for $100 and sold it for $150." The businessperson is only partially correct. The difference between the retail price ($150) and the cost ($100) is the markup, not the profit. Profit is the amount left from revenue after the costs of the merchandise *and expenses* have been paid.

Figure 31-1 makes this clear. It compares a profit and loss statement and the calculations for the retail price of an item. As you can see from the percentages, the markup on an item is similar to *gross profit. Gross profit is the difference between sales revenue and the cost of goods sold.* Expenses must still be deducted in order to get net, or actual, profit. Thus, for a business to be successful, its markup (like its gross profit) must be high enough both to cover expenses and provide the profit sought.

Basic Markup Calculations

Retailers and wholesalers use the same formulas to calculate markup. To make these formulas easy to understand, we will use only retail prices here. Note, however, that wholesale prices can be substituted in any of the formulas discussed.

The most basic pricing formula is the one for calculating retail price. It states in mathematical terms a relationship we have been discussing in the last two chapters: retail price is a combination of cost and markup. If you know these two figures (if, for example, a paperweight costs $10 and a retailer marks it up

PROFIT AND LOSS STATEMENT

Sales revenue	$5,000	(100%)
Less cost of goods sold	2,750	(55%)
Gross profit on sales	2,250	(45%)

Expenses

Salaries	250	
Advertising	150	
Utilities	400	
Rent	500	
Loan interest	100	
Depreciation	200	
Insurance	100	
Miscellaneous	50	
Total expenses	$1,750	(35%)
Net profit before taxes	$500	(10%)

MARKUP PRICING FOR ONE ITEM

Retail Price	$50.00	(100%)
Cost	27.50	(55%)
Markup	22.50	(45%)

Figure 31-1 **Profit and Markup Compared**

Markup is comparable to gross profit in a profit and loss statement: both figures must be sufficient to cover expenses and actual (or net) profit. Assume the share of expenses apportioned to a single item is one one-hundredth of that shown in the profit and loss statement. What amount of expenses would be deducted from the markup? What would be the profit on the item?

$4), you can calculate retail price. Here's how.

$$\text{Cost (C)} + \text{markup (MU)} = \text{retail price (RP)}$$
$$\$10 + \$4 = \$14$$

From this basic formula can be derived two others, those for finding cost and markup, respectively.

$$\text{Retail price (RP)} - \text{markup (MU)} = \text{cost (C)}$$
$$\$14 - \$4 = \$10$$

$$\text{Retail price (RP)} - \text{cost (C)} = \text{markup (MU)}$$
$$\$14 - \$10 = \$4$$

Once again, notice that all three formulas are based on the principle that if you know two related variables, you can find a third. For example, if you know retail price and cost, you can find markup. If you know retail price and markup, you can find cost.

Throughout this chapter, you will rely on these three formulas. From this point on, when they (or their terms) are needed, we will cite them in abbreviated form (as C + MU = RP).

Practice:
Use the retail price formula and its variations to do the following problems.

1. If a calculator costs AB Products $25 and the markup is $12, what is its retail price?
2. If a tennis racket retails for $135 and its markup is $75, what is its cost?
3. Jake's Lawn Shop paid $100 for a lawn mower and is selling it for $225. What is the markup in dollars?

Percentage Markup

In all of the examples and problems above, markup was expressed as a dollar amount. In most business situations, however, the markup figure is expressed as a percentage. From this point on, we shall distinguish between these two forms of markup (dollar and percentage). In calculations, we shall represent dollar markup with the abbreviation *MU($)* and percentage markup with the abbreviation *MU(%)*.

Expressing markup in either dollar or percentage form is not the only choice that wholesalers and retailers face in making markup calculations. If they choose to use the percentage form, they may also elect to compute their markup on either cost or retail price.

Most choose to do the latter for three reasons. First, the markup on the retail price sounds like a smaller amount and thus sounds better to customers. Second, future markdowns and discounts are calculated on a retail basis. Third, profits are generally calculated on sales revenue. Thus, it makes sense to use markup on retail prices when comparing and analyzing data that play a role in a firm's profits.

Here are the steps used to calculate the percentage markup on retail. They will be easier to follow if we have an example to work with. Assume that you want to calculate the percentage markup on a pair of bookends that Frump's Department Store stocks for $49.50 and sells for $82.50.

Step 1 Determine the dollar markup.

$$\text{RP} - \text{C} = \text{MU($)}$$
$$\$82.50 - \$49.50 = \$33.00$$

Step 2 To change the dollar markup to the percentage markup, divide it by the *retail price*. The result will be a decimal.

$$\frac{\text{MU($)}}{\text{RP}} = \text{MU(\%) on retail}$$
$$\$33.00 \div \$82.50 = .4$$

Step 3 Change the decimal to a percentage. This figure is the percentage markup on retail.

$$.40 = 40\%$$

Shift decimal point two places right.

Retailers may occasionally find the percentage markup on cost to be helpful. In such cases, the calculation is the same, except for one step. In Step 2, you divide by cost instead of retail. Using the same facts as in the illustration above, you calculate the percentage markup on cost as follows:

Step 1   Determine the dollar markup.

$$RP - C = MU(\$)$$
$$\$82.50 - \$49.50 = \$33.00$$

Step 2   To change the dollar markup to the percentage markup, divide by *cost*.

$$\frac{MU(\$)}{C} = MU(\%) \text{ on cost}$$
$$\$33.00 \div \$49.50 = .6667$$

Step 3   Change the decimal to a percentage. This figure is the percentage markup on cost.

$$.6667 = 66.67\%$$

Shift decimal point two places right.

Practice:
Calculate the percentage markup in each of these situations.

1. If the retail price of a jar of jam is $2.50 and the cost is $1.25, what is the percentage markup based on cost price? based on retail price?
2. An electric sander costs $95, and its markup is $23.75. Find its percentage markup on cost price. Then calculate its percentage markup on retail price.
3. If a gallery sells a framed print for $100 and its markup is $25, what is its percentage markup on cost price? on retail price?

Markup Equivalents Table

If you calculated enough problems using the formulas for computing percentage markup based on cost and retail, you would begin to notice a correlation between the two figures. This fact led marketers to develop a calculation aid called a Markup Equivalents Table, a portion of which is shown as Table 31-1. The table lists markup percentages based on retail and the equivalent percentages based on cost. To use the table, you locate the percentage markup on retail and read its cost equivalent in the adjacent column or vice versa.

Practice:
Use Table 31-1 (the Markup Equivalents Table) to answer the following questions.

1. If the markup on retail is 25 percent, what is its equivalent markup on cost?
2. If the markup on cost is 60 percent, what is its equivalent markup on retail?

Table 31-1 Markup Equivalents			
Markup On Retail	Markup On Cost	Markup On Retail	Markup On Cost
4.8%	5.0%	25.0%	33.3%
5.0	5.3	26.0	35.0
6.0	6.4	27.0	37.0
7.0	7.5	27.3	37.5
8.0	8.7	28.0	39.0
9.0	10.0	28.5	40.0
10.0	11.1	29.0	40.9
10.7	12.0	30.0	42.9
11.0	12.4	31.0	45.0
11.1	12.5	32.0	47.1
12.0	13.6	33.3	50.0
12.5	14.3	34.0	51.5
13.0	15.0	35.0	53.9
14.0	16.3	35.5	55.0
15.0	17.7	36.0	56.3
16.0	19.1	37.0	58.8
16.7	20.0	37.5	60.0
17.0	20.5	38.0	61.3
17.5	21.2	39.0	64.0
18.0	22.0	39.5	65.5
18.5	22.7	40.0	66.7
19.0	23.5	41.0	70.0
20.0	25.0	42.0	72.4
21.0	26.6	42.8	75.0
22.0	28.2	44.4	80.0
22.5	29.0	46.1	85.0
23.0	29.9	47.5	90.0
23.1	30.0	48.7	95.0
24.0	31.6	50.0	100.0

A Markup Equivalents Table, one page of which is shown here, allows users quickly to convert markups on retail to markups on cost and vice versa. A 50 percent markup on retail is equal to what markup on cost?

Marketing Glacier Water

The United States has already imported upscale bottled water such as Perrier and Evian, so why not upscale domestic water from a glacier? In Alaska, some enterprising entrepreneurs have begun harvesting ice from glaciers to be sold to consumers. In harvesting the ice, the producers select lighter-colored ice that has broken away from the bigger glacier and fallen into the sea. That portion of the glacier has tiny air pockets that produce a popping sound when the ice warms in drinks.

Glacier ice is more dense that its refrigerator-made counterpart because it was formed under great pressure. The benefit of the high density is that the ice lasts longer than other commercially made ice cubes. In addition, glacier ice is pure because it was around thousands of years ago when we had much less pollution.

In an attempt to market the glacier ice, producers found it difficult to establish a feasible and effective means of distributing it to consumers. In order to make the enterprise profitable, the ice would have to be sold in truckload containers to wholesalers and would have to be displayed prominently in upscale food or liquor stores. The investment needed to carry the product made the plan impractical.

So, the glacier-ice entrepreneurs turned to the next best thing—bottled glacier water.

Because of the purity of glacier water, they thought they would be able to compete in this market.

Given the cost of harvesting glacier ice, however, the retail price will have to be much higher than that of other domestic bottled waters. In fact, bottled glacier water will probably sell for $2.50—double the price of liter bottles of domestic water. It will even be priced higher than imported bottled waters such as Evian.

1. Do you think the high suggested retail price for glacier water is necessary to establish an upscale image for the product?
2. Do you think that customers will be willing to pay double the price for glacier water? Explain.
3. The cost of bottled water to retailers is usually 40 percent of the retail price. What do retailers pay for one-liter bottles of domestic water?
4. What would be the dollar markup of the glacier water? of the domestic water?
5. If a retailer sold 100 liter bottles of water, of which 30 percent was glacier water and 70 percent was domestic water, what is the dollar gross markup for each type of bottled water sold and for the total sold?

Cost Method of Pricing

Sometimes marketers only know the cost of an item and its markup on cost. In such a situation, they use the *cost method* of pricing.

As an example, consider a board game that a toy store buys for $8.50 and sells for cost plus a 40 percent markup on cost. To arrive at the retail price, follow these steps:

Step 1   Determine the dollar markup on cost. Multiply the cost by the percentage markup on cost in decimal form.

$$C \times MU(\%) = MU(\$)$$
$$\$8.50 \times .40 = \$3.40$$

Step 2   Add the dollar markup to the cost to get the retail price.

$$C + MU(\$) = RP$$
$$\$8.50 + \$3.40 = \$11.90$$

Often, however, the situation isn't that simple. Suppose, for example, you have the cost, but the only markup figure you know is the markup on *retail*. How do you proceed? The answer is, you can't—at least, not without some adjustment. Markup on cost can only be applied to a cost figure; markup on retail, only to a retail figure. But one kind of markup can be *changed* to the other by using the Markup Equivalents Table.

Consider a sample problem. A marketer knows that the customary markup for a particular cosmetics firm is 33.3 percent on retail and that the cost of its best lipstick is $3.48. To project the lipstick's retail price, follow these steps:

Step 1   Use the equivalents table to get all the information in the same (cost) form. Find the markup on cost equivalent of a 33.3 percent markup on retail.

Markup On Retail	Markup On Cost
32.0	47.1
33.3 $\longrightarrow$	50.0
34.0	51.5

Step 2   Apply the cost method to determine the retail price. First calculate the dollar markup on cost.

$$C \times MU(\%) = MU(\$)$$
$$\$3.48 \times .50 = \$1.74$$

Step 3   Then calculate the retail price.

$$C + MU(\$) = RP$$
$$\$3.48 + \$1.74 = \$5.22$$

Retail Method of Pricing

Another way to compute the retail price when all you know are cost and the markup on retail is to use the *retail method*. This method is based on changing the information you have into retail figures.

Consider this problem. The owner of a sporting goods store wants to know what the markup and retail price should be for a sun visor that costs $6.75. His customary markup on retail is 40 percent. The steps in his calculation are as follows:

Step 1   Determine what percentage of the retail price is equal to cost. This is simply a matter of subtracting the known retail markup figure from 100 percent, which represents the retail price.

$$RP - MU = Cost$$
$$100\% - 40\% = 60\%$$

Step 2   To determine the retail price, divide the cost by the decimal equivalent of the percentage calculated in Step 1.

$$\$6.75 \div .60 = \$11.25$$

Step 3   Calculate the dollar markup.

$$RP - C = MU(\$)$$
$$\$11.25 - \$6.75 = \$4.50$$

Step 4   If you like, check your work by multiplying the retail price you calculated in Step 2 by the percentage markup on retail given originally. If your retail price is correct, the answer will match the dollar markup you calculated in Step 3.

$$RP \times MU(\%) = MU(\$)$$
$$\$11.25 \times .40 = \$4.50$$

You can use a visual device called the retail box (Figure 31-2) to help you remember this sequence of calculations.

Practice:

Calculate retail price and markup in these two problems by using the retail method.

1. Find the retail price and dollar markup for a handmade sweater that costs the Woolens Closet $90 and has a 40 percent markup on retail.
2. A machine-made sweater costs the Woolens Closet $44 and has a 22 percent markup on retail. Calculate this sweater's price and dollar markup.

Markdowns

To reduce the quantity of goods in stock, a business will sometimes mark down merchandise by a certain percentage. This reduction is based on the retail price. Consider as an example a record store that wants to mark down by 25 percent compact disks that originally sold for $16. The steps for calculating the sale price are as follows:

Step 1   Determine the dollar markdown. Multiply the retail price by the percentage markdown.

	$	%
Retail Price	E.	A. 100
Markup	F.	B.
Cost	D.	C.

	$	%
Retail Price	E. 11.25	A. 100
Markup	F. 4.50	B. 40
Cost	D. 6.75	C. 60

Computation: $C = A - B$

$$E = \frac{D}{C}$$

$F = E - D$

Check: $E \times B = F$

$C = 100 - 40 = 60$

$E = 6.75 \div .60 = 11.25$

$F = 11.25 - 6.75 = 4.50$

$11.25 \times .40 = 4.50$

Figure 31-2   Retail Box

To compute retail price using the retail method, fill in the boxes following the letter sequence (B though F). The amounts that go in B and D are usually known (that is, given as part of the problem). The computations you must do are summarized below the diagrams. In the finished box, how do the entries at the top (E and A) related to those below?

$RP \times MD (\%) = MD(\$)$
$\$16 \times .25 = \$4$

Step 2   To determine the sale price, subtract the markdown from the retail price.

$RP - MD(\$) = SP$
$\$16 - \$4 = \$12$

Another way to arrive at the same answer is to consider what percentage of the original price will equal the sale price. The procedure is still two steps long, but the percentage calculation is so easy that you can probably do it in your head and thus save some time. Here are the steps involved.

Step 1   Determine what percentage of the original price will equal the sale price. This is simply a matter of subtracting the markdown percentage from 100 percent.

$RP - MD = SP$
$100\% - 25\% = 75\%$

Step 2   To find the sale price, multiply the retail price by the decimal equivalent of the percentage calculated in Step 1.

$RP \times SP(\%) = SP$
$\$16 \times .75 = \$12$

Practice:
    Calculate the sale prices for the items described below.

1. A suit that sells for $125 is to be marked down 40 percent. What is its new price?
2. During a store-wide sale next week, all women's dresses will be marked down 20 percent. What will a $75 dress sell for during the sale?

Maintained Markup

When a marketer marks down goods, the markup and markup percentage change. *The difference between an item's final sale price and its cost is called the maintained markup.*

Let's consider an example. Assume that a cassette recorder that cost Zap Electronics $25 and originally sold for $50 is marked down 20 percent. The maintained markup (expressed in both dollars and as a percentage) is calculated as follows:

Step 1   Calculate the new sale price.

$$100\% - 20\% = 80\%$$
$$\$50 \times .80 = \$40$$

Step 2   To determine the maintained markup in dollars, subtract the cost from the sale price.

$$\$40 - \$25 = \$15$$

Step 3   To determine the maintained markup percentage, divide the maintained markup by the sale price.

$$\$15 \div \$40 = .375$$
$$.375 = 37.5\%$$

Practice:
Now try the same type of computation on your own.

A computer that costs Compco Industries $150 to stock sells for $350. The firm wants to mark down the computer 30 percent. Determine the sale price and maintained markup in dollars. Then calculate the maintained markup percentage.

Unit Selling Prices

To encourage customers to buy in quantity, marketers will often sell in quantity. For example, they may offer three pairs of stockings for $10.99.

To find the selling price of one item priced in this fashion is a simple matter of dividing the price by the number of units, when the division is even ($12

÷ 4 = 3). However, when the division is not even, any fractional amount is charged to the customer (as shown below).

$$\$10.99 \div 3 = \$3.663 \text{ or } \$3.67$$

Practice:

1. Determine the price for one can of soda when a six-pack sells for $2.17.
2. Determine the price for one roll of film when three rolls sell for $12.25.

Discounts

A *discount* is simply a reduction in the price of goods and services sold to customers. Retailers offer discounts to their employees as a job benefit. Manufacturers and distributors offer discounts to their customers to encourage prompt payment and stimulate business.

The general procedure for calculating discounts involves two steps:

Step 1   Multiply the price (P) by the discount percentage [D(%)] to get the dollar amount of the discount [D($)].

$$P \times D(\%) = D(\$)$$

Step 2   Subtract the discount from the price to get the net price (NP), or the amount that the customer will actually pay.

$$P - D(\$) = NP$$

Employee Discounts

Businesses offer employee discounts to encourage workers to buy the products they sell or manufacture. Employee discounts can range from 10 percent to 30 percent for entry-level employees, and as high as 50 percent or more for top-level executives.

Employee discounts are an employee benefit and, at the same time, a good business practice. Employees who buy and use their company's products project confidence in and enthusiasm about them. These traits are especially important for company sales personnel to demonstrate.

Discounts from Manufacturers and Distributors

Some common types of discounts offered by manufacturers and distributors are *cash discounts, trade discounts, quantity discounts, seasonal discounts*, and *promotional discounts*, all of which were explained in Chapter 30. The remainder of this chapter is devoted to explaining how each of these types of discounts is calculated.

Cash Discounts. Consider the invoice terms 3/15, net 60. Recall that the first number (3) represents the percentage of the discount applicable to the invoice total. If that total is $1,000 and the customer takes advantage of the discount, the calculations are as follows:

Step 1 Determine the dollar discount.

$$P \times D(\%) = D(\$)$$
$$\$1,000 \times .03 = \$30$$

Step 2 Determine the net price.

$$P - D(\$) = NP$$
$$\$1,000 - \$30 = \$970$$

Cash discounts can be calculated on a unit basis as well. For example, if there are 100 items at (@) $10 each listed on the invoice, the net unit cost is figured as follows:

Step 1 Determine the dollar discount.

$$P \times D(\%) = D(\$)$$
$$\$10.00 \times .03 = \$.30$$

Step 2 Determine the net price.

$$P - D(\$) = NP$$
$$\$10.00 - \$.30 = \$9.70$$

The net amount payable by the customer would still be the same, of course—$970 ($9.70 × 100).

Practice:
    Determine the amounts payable by the following customers.

1. Southbend Trucking receives an invoice in the amount of $25,000 showing the terms 2/10, net 30. The invoice lists five trucks at $5,000 each. If Southbend takes advantage of the discount, what will be the net price of the invoice? the net price per truck?
2. The Wilderness Store receives an invoice for seven dozen jackets at $120 per dozen. The terms are 4/15, net 60. If the store takes advantage of the discount, what will be the net price of the invoice? the net price per jacket?

Trade Discounts. Recall that trade discounts are based on manufacturers' list prices. They are calculated in the same way as cash discounts. For example, to figure a 40 percent trade discount for an invoice totalling $5,789, you would do the following:

Step 1 Determine the dollar discount.

$$P \times D(\%) = D(\$)$$
$$\$5,789.00 \times .40 = \$2,315.60$$

Step 2 Determine the net price.

$$P - D(\$) = NP$$
$$\$5,789.00 - \$2,315.60 = \$3,473.40$$

If an invoice contains several items, the trade discount is applied to each item separately to determine its net unit cost to the business.

Practice:
    Now try the same type of computation on your own.
    A manufacturer gives retailers a 25 percent trade discount. If an invoice received by Frump's Department Store totals $7,650, what is the amount of the store's discount? What is the amount payable to the manufacturer?

Quantity Discounts. Quantity discounts may be quoted as either a percentage of price or as part of a price list like Table 31-2. To determine how much you would pay per item, you use a quantity price list. For example, if you purchased 50 pairs of socks, you would pay $.85 per pair. Your total bill would be $42.50 ($.85 × 50 = $42.50).

Sometimes businesses offer cumulative quantity discounts, whereby a certain minimum purchase must be made during a specified period of time for the discount to be activated. For example, a firm may offer a 2 percent cumulative quantity discount to any company that purchases $3,000 worth of products in a six-month period. If a firm's purchases total $2,500 during that period, no discount is permitted. If they total $4,000, however, the discount is allowed. It would be calculated in the following manner:

Step 1   Determine the dollar discount.

$$P \times D(\%) = D(\$)$$
$$\$4,000 \times .02 = \$80$$

Step 2   Determine the net price.

$$P - D(\$) = NP$$
$$\$4,000 - \$80 = \$3,920$$

**Table 31-2
Quantity Price List**

Item	1–24	25–48	49–72	73+
Socks	$.95 ea.	$.90 ea.	$.85 ea.	$.80 ea.

Quantity discounts are often presented in an easy-to-use schedule like the one shown here. If you purchased 25 pairs of socks, how much more would you have to pay per pair than if you purchased 75?

Promotional Discounts. Promotional discounts are given to businesses that agree to advertise or in some other way promote a manufacturer's products. When the promotional discount is quoted as a percentage, it is calculated the same way as a cumulative discount.

Sometimes, however, marketers are granted a dollar amount as a promotional discount. In such cases, they may want to determine the net purchase price or the percentage of the promotional discount for themselves. Consider an example. The Cycle Shop buys Speedo bicycles for $10,000 and is granted a $250 promotional discount for displaying the bikes in its store window during the month of March. To determine the percentage discount, follow these steps:

Step 1   Divide the dollar discount by the original price. The answer will be a decimal.

$$D(\$) \div P = D(\%)$$
$$\$250 \div \$10,000 = .025$$

Step 2   Change the decimal to a percentage. This figure is the percentage discount.

$$.025 = 2.5\%$$

Shift decimal point two places right.

Practice:

Now try these problems involving quantity discounts.

1. Refer to Table 31-2. How much would a buyer pay for 24 pairs of socks? for 100 pairs?
2. Suppose a firm is required to buy $10,000 worth of goods by September 15 in order to qualify for a 10 percent cumulative quantity discount. Would a firm that purchased $5,000 worth of goods by that date get the discount? What about one that purchased $10,005 worth?
3. Based on the terms in problem 2 above, what is the dollar amount of the discount for a firm that purchased $12,000 worth of goods by September 15? What is the amount payable to the sock manufacturer?

Seasonal Discounts. Sellers offer seasonal discounts to encourage buyers to purchase goods long before the actual consumer buying season. For example, purchasing Halloween costumes before July 31 and ski apparel before May 1 might qualify retailers for seasonal discounts.

Seasonal discounts are calculated in the same way as other discounts. Here is an example. Lobo, Inc., offers an 8 percent seasonal discount to all buyers who purchase Christmas decorations before August 1. If an order is placed on July 30 for $1,500 worth of decorations, the net purchase price is calculated as follows:

Step 1   Determine the dollar discount.

$$P \times D(\%) = D(\$)$$
$$\$1,500 \times .08 = \$120$$

Step 2   Determine the net price.

$$P - D(\$) = NP$$
$$\$1,500 - \$120 = \$1,380$$

Sales Tax and Prices

Many states charge a sales tax to consumers for goods and services purchased. A sales tax increases the total purchase price of an item. Some businesspeople prefer to include the sales tax in the price of merchandise to make sale prices even. For example, a vendor selling candy, soda, and hot dogs at a sporting event will often include the sales tax in the quoted price in order to make change quickly and easily. For example:

$$.66 \text{ (soda)} \times .06 \text{ (sales tax)} = .0396$$
$$66\cent + 4\cent = 70\cent$$

In this case, the sales tax is included in the price the customer pays at the time of purchase. Most retailers, however, do not do this.

In most cases, the sales tax is added to the retail price at the time of purchase. Assume, for example, that you purchase a pair of slacks for $55.95. The state sales tax is 6 percent. The total purchase price is calculated as follows:

Step 1   Determine the dollar amount of the tax. Multiply the retail price of the slacks by the sales tax rate.

$$\$55.95 \times .06 = \$3.36$$

Step 2   Determine the total purchase price. Add the tax to the retail price of the slacks.

$$\$55.95 + \$3.36 = \$59.31$$

Answers to Practice Problems

Page 345
1. $37
2. $60
3. $125

Page 346
1. 100% on cost
   50% on retail
2. 25% on cost
   20% on retail
3. 33⅓ % on cost
   25% on retail

Page 346
1. 33⅓ %
2. 37.5%

Page 348
1. $150 retail price
   $ 60 dollar markup
2. $100.41 retail price
   $ 56.41 dollar markup

Page 349
1. $75
2. $60

Page 350
$245 sale price
$95 maintained markup
38.8 maintained markup %

Page 350
1. $ .37
2. $4.09

Page 351
1. Net price of the invoice $24,500
   Net price per truck $4,900
2. Net price of the invoice $806.40
   Net price per jacket $9.60

Page 351
Store discount $1,912.50
Amount payable to the manufacturer $5,737.50

Page 352
1. For 24 pairs of socks = $22.80
   For 100 pairs of socks = $80.00
2. For $5,000 in purchases—no discount
   For $10,005—would get discount
3. The amount payable to the sock manufacturer
   would be $10,800.

Page 353
1. 1%
2. The dollar amount of the discount is $36.75
   The net price of the retailer's invoice would
   be $698.25

Page 353
1. $9,885.90 net amount payable
2. Net unit cost per pair—$98.86 each

Page 353
1. $79.12
2. $11.43

VOCABULARY REVIEW

Explain the meanings of the following terms by giving an example of each.

gross profit   maintained markup

FACT AND IDEA REVIEW

1. What is the most basic formula you need in order to calculate retail price?

2. List three reasons why most wholesalers and retailers elect to compute their markup on the selling price.

3. What is the formula for calculating the percentage markup on retail price? on cost?

4. What steps are used to calculate prices according to the cost method?

5. What steps do marketers follow when using the retail method?

6. On what is a markdown based?

7. What steps do you follow to calculate maintained dollar markup and maintained percentage markup?

8. What do you do to find the selling price of one item when three of the same item are being sold for a dollar?

9. What procedures are used to calculate the dollar amount of a discount and the final selling price?

10. What is the difference between noncumulative and cumulative quantity discounts?

11. What is the formula for determining the percent of a promotional discount?

12. How is a sales tax calculated? How is the total purchase price, including sales tax, determined?

CRITICAL THINKING

1. Explain how a firm's net profit or loss is related to pricing.

2. If a buyer wanted to buy goods that cost $100 and the customary markup on retail was 40 percent, what two methods could the buyer use to calculate the retail price? Explain.

3. Is the initial markup calculated for an item sometimes the same as the maintained markup? Explain.

4. If you were given a trade discount of 30 percent and a seasonal discount of 10 percent and you also took advantage of a cash discount of 2 percent, would you be entitled to a 42 percent discount? Explain.

5. Why do you think some candy store owners and ice cream vendors at stadiums calculate the sales tax and add it to an item's price before quoting the purchase price to customers?

USING BASIC SKILLS

Math

1. If a dress costs a business $72 and the markup is $45, what is the retail price?

2. If a pair of slacks retails for $110 and the cost is $50, what is the markup?

3. If a hammer sells for $16.95 and its markup is $6.75, what is the cost?

4. If a wallet costs a business $27 and sells for $37.80, what is the percentage markup on cost?

5. If a stationery store sells greeting cards for $1.00 and pays $.60 each for them, what is the percentage markup on retail?

6. What is the equivalent markup on cost for the following percentage markups on retail?
   a. 25.0%
   b. 23.1%
   c. 33.3%
   d. 50.0%
   e. 40.0%
   f. 28.5%

7. A pencil sharpener that costs a business $12.50 has a markup of 50 percent on retail price. Use a retail box to calculate the sharpener's retail price and check your answer.

8. If a television set that has been selling for $199.99 is marked down 20 percent, what is its new sale price?

9. Determine the maintained markup in dollars for a bracelet that is to be marked down 25 percent from its original retail price of $35.99. The bracelet costs the business $18.

10. The dating terms on a $3,000 invoice are 3/10, net 30.

   a. If the buyer takes advantage of the cash discount, what will the net price be?

   b. If the same invoice has on it 300 scarves at $10 each, what will be the net unit price of each scarf?

11. Determine the sales tax and final purchase price to the customer for a radio bearing a price tag of $72 in a state where the sales tax is 6 percent.

Communication

12. A customer asks you how to determine the retail prices of shirts on a rack with a sign that reads ''20 percent off ticketed price.'' What answer would you give the customer?

13. As head cashier, you have noticed that the cashiers are making mistakes when calculating the unit price of items that are priced at three, four, and six for a given price. Therefore, you have decided to write a memo to all cashiers, instructing them on how to calculate unit prices. What will you write?

Human Relations

14. Employees are not permitted to let friends use their employee discounts. A co-worker asks you to ring up a sale for her and to apply her employee discount to the purchase. Normally, that would be okay. However, you noticed that your co-worker had been talking to a friend and that the friend had picked out the item that your co-worker is buying. What would you do?

15. A check dated May 15 arrived today from a business that impermissibly deducted a cash discount (the invoice was dated April 30, with terms 2/10, net 30). You must call the business and ask for payment of the full amount. What will you say?

APPLICATION PROJECT

For a one-week period, look through current magazines and newspapers for advertisements and notices of consumer discounts—for example, promotional, introductory, holiday, and end-of-season sales. For each ad or notice, write down the name of the discounter, the item discounted, the amount of the discount, and the original retail price (when included). At the end of the week, share your list with the class.

   What conclusions can you draw from your and other students' lists? For example, are certain types of products—say, electronic items—frequently discounted? Are there more sales on certain days of the week than on others?

Buying

T he buying function is performed in all types of businesses. Manufacturers buy the equipment, machinery, raw materials, and supplies needed in the manufacturing of goods. Wholesalers and retailers buy goods for resale. Service businesses buy the supplies they need to perform their services.

In addition to purchases needed for the daily operation of the business, firms also may buy office equipment and furniture, stationery supplies, cleaning supplies, and services such as advertising, automatic data processing, accounting, and cleaning.

In this chapter you will learn who is responsible for buying these products and what is involved in the buying process.

OBJECTIVES

After completing this chapter, you will be able to:

1. explain the difference between organizational or industrial buying and buying for resale,

2. discuss the buying process and strategies used to make buying decisions,

3. describe two basic buying plans retailers use to decide what to buy,

4. list places where buyers can go for supply source information, and explain the criteria buyers use in selecting supply sources, and

5. compute the mathematics related to a retail merchandise plan.

WORDS TO KNOW

purchasing agent
wholesale buyer
retail buyer
resident buying office
advance dating
extra dating
end-of-month (EOM) dating
receipt-of-goods (ROG) dating
consignment buying
memorandum buying
open-to-buy (OTB)

Types of Buyers

There are two purposes to the buying function. The first purpose is to buy goods and services for use in the operation of a business. *Purchasing agents, also called organizational or industrial buyers, buy products and services that meet certain specifications for the lowest possible price from reliable vendors.*

The second purpose for buying is to purchase goods for resale. *Wholesale and retail buyers, referred to simply as buyers, select goods for resale.* Their main role is to forecast the needs of their firm's customers and to buy products that will meet those needs and thus be profitable for the firm to carry.

Buying Situations

There are three kinds of buying situations: *new-task purchase, modified rebuy*, and *straight rebuy*.

In a *new-task purchase* situation, a purchase is made for the first time. Such purchases may be triggered by a formerly unrecognized need or a desire to change existing operations in a firm. For example, a retail or wholesale operation may be considering a new product line. A manufacturer may be considering a new way to make its product, such as using robots instead of people to handle one phase of the manufacturing process. Obviously, much research into the advantages and disadvantages of a new purchase is needed.

In a *modified-rebuy* situation, the buyer has had experience buying the good or service, but some aspect of the purchase changes. Perhaps the buyer is purchasing from a new vendor because the previous vendor went out of business or increased prices significantly. In a modified-rebuy situation, the buyer usually gets proposals from several vendors before making a buying decision.

In a *straight-rebuy* situation, the buyer routinely orders the goods and services purchased from the same vendor(s) in the past. Staple goods fall into the straight-rebuy category for wholesale and retail buyers. The purchase of routine office supplies may be considered a straight rebuy for most purchasing agents.

Steps in the Buying Process

Some aspects of the buying process are different for purchasing agents and wholesale and retail buyers. Other aspects are quite similar.

There are four steps in the buying process:

1. Determining needs.
2. Identifying and selecting sources.
3. Placing the order.
4. Obtaining feedback and evaluating purchases.

Let's see how these steps are carried out by purchasing agents and/or by wholesale and retail buyers.

Step One: Determining Needs

The most striking differences between industrial and resale buying are the purpose of the purchase and how each type of buyer determines the needs of the firm.

Buyers often get advice and assistance from co-workers in their purchasing decisions. Other than the purchasing agent, what influentials may have been involved in the decision to buy the computer system used in this office?

Industrial Buying. As you learned earlier, purchasing agents buy goods and services that will be used in the operation of the business. For this reason, other members of the organization, often referred to as *influentials*, sometimes determine the firm's needs and identify the sources.

Some influentials may talk to the purchasing agent and others in the business to determine the characteristics and quantity of the good or service needed. For example, if new manufacturing equipment is to be purchased, the people who will use the equipment as well as the top executives in the manufacturing division will be involved in the decision-making process. Depending on the situation, other influentials may dictate the standards to be used in evaluating vendors. They may also make the final buying decision for major purchases. The purchasing agent will then actually order the goods or services.

In routine situations, the purchasing agent will determine the needs of various departments and get requests for goods and services from organization members. The purchasing agent then makes the arrangements with the sources regarding final price, delivery, services expected, and method of payment. Thus, the purchasing agent governs all the steps in the process and establishes a working relationship with the vendors.

Resale Buying. The buying process for wholesale and retail buyers who buy goods for resale is similar to that of industrial buyers except for the three distinct activities involved in determining needs:

- analyzing customers' needs and wants,
- studying industry trends and consumer buying habits, and
- determining goods and quantities of goods to purchase.

In analyzing customers' needs and wants, wholesale buyers must anticipate the needs of their customers—who may be other wholesalers, industrial businesses, service businesses, or retail operations. Wholesale buyers must forecast those needs and buy products that will service all their customers.

Retail buyers must anticipate retail customers' needs and wants. Many retail firms ask their salespeople to prepare *want slips* (customer requests for items not carried in the store) like the one shown in Figure 32-1. Other firms may contact customers directly through professional market research studies, con-

HAMELL'S DEPARTMENT STORE
REQUEST FOR MERCHANDISE

Item requested _____

Brand name _____

Size _____ Size _____ Style _____

Quantity _____

Item requested _____

_____

Your name _____

Address _____
      (Street)   (City)   (State)   (Zip code)

Telephone (   ) _____

EMPLOYEE: PLEASE FORWARD IMMEDIATELY TO YOUR SUPERVISOR.

Employee Signature _____

Store No. _____ Dept. No. _____ Date _____

Figure 32-1 **Want Slip**
Want slips provide valuable information to retail buyers. In a retail situation, who prepares want slips?

sumer panels, or direct questioning by sales personnel. So much time and effort is devoted to determining customers' needs because, as the saying goes in retailing, "goods well bought are half sold." Retail buyers who buy goods that customers want will make the job of selling those goods much easier.

In studying industry trends and consumer buying habits, buyers analyze their previous sales records and gather market information. They do the latter by reading trade journals and other business publications, comparison shopping, talking with sales representatives, hiring the services of resident buying offices, and attending trade shows.

A *trade journal* is a business publication that covers a specific business. *Women's Wear Daily*, for example, covers the women's apparel industry. Other good sources of business information are general business publications, such as *Forbes* and *Business Week*. Business sections of newspapers provide information about current local and national economic conditions.

Comparison shopping of competitive stores involves visiting those stores to see what goods and services they offer. Brands carried, prices, and quantities of items are all noted.

Sales representatives from suppliers are familiar with trends because they see what other businesses order. In some cases, they can predict the success of certain products because they have information about reorders of popular products.

Resident buying offices are retailers' representatives in the central market. A *central market* is a geographic area where many suppliers are located. New York City, for example, is a central market for apparel. A large number of garment manufacturers have showrooms there. The Dallas Apparel Mart (shown in the chapter opening photo) and the Chicago Merchandise Mart are other examples of central markets for apparel where all the showrooms are located under one roof in a large building. High Point, North Carolina, is a central market for furniture; hundreds of furniture manufacturers are located there.

Resident buying offices send to member stores bulletins and notices that report special buys in the market, new merchandise offerings, closeouts, fashion trends, and market conditions. They may also provide information about vendors that can help the stores in choosing them.

Buying offices sometimes provide services, such as allocating space in their offices where buyers may come to meet potential suppliers and conduct business. They may also arrange schedules for a buyer's trip to the market, and place orders when given the authority to do so.

At *trade shows*, suppliers for a given industry present their goods for buyers to see. Trade shows are sponsored by trade associations, which charge suppliers for the space they use on the floor of a show. Suppliers display their goods and services and have sales representatives available to discuss the products with interested buyers.

When buyers are determining the actual goods and quantities to buy for resale, the merchandise image, brand policies, and a firm's pricing policy are important. For example, suppose you are the buyer for a men's clothing store. To evaluate new sweaters for the fall line, you need to determine whether the styles and quality of the garments match the store's present image and price lines. You have to calculate the markup percentages for the suggested sweaters to see if their cost will permit you to sell the sweaters at $35, $50, and $75 (price lines for your store).

Retailers use two basic buying plans to help them make buying decisions about the goods and quantities of goods to purchase. As you learned in Chapter 26, these plans are called *basic stock lists* and *model stock lists*.

Basic stock lists (see Figure 32-2) show the staple items that should always be in stock. The list includes *stockkeeping units (SKUs)* for all the staples. The SKU for each item contains coded information that gives the item's brand, size, color, and other characteristics.

Model stock lists (see Figure 32-3) are used with fashion merchandise. Because fashion items change relatively rapidly, these lists are less specific than basic stock lists. The information contained in model stock lists identifies goods by general styles (blouses, skirts, dresses, slacks) and style categories (short sleeve, long sleeve), sizes, materials, colors, and price lines. Style numbers are not included because each manufacturer's style numbers change each year. Thus, although model stock lists identify how many of each type of item should be purchased, the buyer must actually select specific models at the market.

Step Two: Identifying and Selecting Sources

Even though the purpose for buying is different for purchasing agents and for wholesale and retail buyers, both are involved in selecting sources.

Stock	Description	Size	Packing Units	Cost	Retail	Min. Stock	October Sales This Year	October Sales Last Year	November Sales This Year	November Sales Last Year	December Sales This Year	December Sales Last Year
1381	Skippy Peanut Butter	32 oz.	24			4						
1382	Skippy Peanut Butter	18 oz.	24			8						
1383	Skippy Peanut Butter	12 oz.	24			8						
1384	Jiff Peanut Butter	32 oz.	24			4						
1385	Jiff Peanut Butter	18 oz.	24			8						
1386	Jiff Peanut Butter	12 oz.	24			8						

Figure 32-2 **Basic Stock List**

Basic stock lists tell the staple items that should always be in stock. How do basic stock lists help buyers make buying decisions?

PRODUCT CLASS ___*Misses Sportswear*___ SEASON ___*Spring*___

General Style	Specific Style	Price Range	Color	Total Units	Size 6	Size 8	Size 10	Size 12	Size 14
Blouse	*Sleeveless Tailored*	*$25*	*White*	*12*	*1*	*3*	*3*	*3*	*2*
			Black	*12*	*1*	*3*	*3*	*3*	*2*
			Blue	*12*	*1*	*3*	*3*	*3*	*2*
Blouse	*Short-sleeve Oversize*	*$35*	*Pink*	*24*	*2*	*6*	*6*	*6*	*4*
			Orange	*24*	*2*	*6*	*6*	*6*	*4*

Figure 32-3 **Model Stock List**

Model stock lists are used with fashion merchandise. How do they differ from basic stock lists?

Buyers and Suppliers: Working Together in the 90's

As an outgrowth of the demand for quality products so U.S. companies can better compete in today's marketplace, buyers and suppliers are entering into partnerships.

In buying partnerships, buyers make long-term purchasing commitments with selected suppliers in return for quality products from the supplier. This creates a positive relationship based on mutual problem-solving, with shared goals of increased productivity and reduced costs.

The major risk for firms entering into a buyer/supplier partnership is a reduction in the number of vendors they deal with. For example, when Xerox instituted this new philosophy, it reduced its vendors from some 2,000 to 350. Such a practice can be risky if the selected vendors do not meet the firm's expectations. However, those risks can be lowered through a careful selection process and a good system to check performance.

Many companies have instituted a vendor certification program that provides vendors with training in how to control quality and service. For example, firms expect suppliers to follow their lead in incorporating statistical process control (SPC), which helps eliminate defects *during* the production process instead of at the end of the process when the product is finished.

There are many benefits of buying partnerships: reduced inventory, cost control, dependable supply levels, reduced lead times, reduced paper processing, improved quality control, and more technical support.

Another important benefit is improved relationships with suppliers. In fact, suppliers become involved in solving a firm's problems and in planning product changes and development in the early stages of the planning process.

The result of this new buyer/supplier relationship has changed the role of the buyer. The buyer is no longer just a procurer of goods with the goal of getting the lowest price. The buyer becomes an active member of the management team and is involved in making important business decisions in product design and development.

1. What do buying partnerships involve and how do they change the old adversarial relationship between buyers and suppliers?
2. What is the major risk to a firm that enters into a buying partnership with suppliers?
3. In a buying partnership, suppliers often give price concessions, are required to improve their quality control systems, and must increase services to firms. Why would a supplier be interested in such a partnership?

Where to Find Information on Supply Sources. Purchasing agents rely on manufacturers, catalogs, and distributors for information on supply sources. Because they are buying goods for use in the operation of a business, the products needed may be highly specialized and require direct contact with manufacturers' representatives. When buying inexpensive supplies, a manufacturer's or distributor's catalog may provide all the necessary product information. In other cases, some of the supplies may only be carried by distributors. Thus, distributors' salespeople may call on manufacturers to sell them these items.

Wholesalers and retailers may locate sources of supply by dealing directly with manufacturers' sales representatives and wholesalers or by visiting manufacturers' showrooms in central markets. They may also locate sources by hiring the services of a buying office, attending trade shows, and visiting international markets.

Criteria Used for Selecting Sources.

Some of the criteria for deciding on sources involve previous experiences with a source, services offered, and quality of the goods and services. Other criteria are credit terms, dealer aids, delivery terms, and reputation for shipping the correct goods and meeting delivery deadlines.

When dealing with a source for the first time, buyers may request specific information, such as its production capabilities. They may also visit the facilities to see its operation in person. In addition, buyers may solicit business references to determine the source's reputation in the industry.

Many buyers maintain *resource files* that document past experiences with vendors. All basic information, such as products carried, prices, delivery and dating terms, and the names of the sales representatives, is recorded. Also noted is the ability of each product to live up to expectations, and the supplier's promptness of delivery and ability to service the firm and handle complaints.

To evaluate sources, buyers must know the terminology related to the negotiations. They should be able to compare and contrast deals offered by various suppliers to determine which deal is best for their firm. The variables that they should review are discounts, dating, and delivery terms.

Discounts are reductions from quoted prices. Discounts that should be reviewed include cash, trade, quantity, seasonal, and promotional. All of these were discussed in Chapters 28, 30, and 31.

Dating terms state when the bill must be paid and the discount permitted for paying early.

Ordinary dating occurs when the dating terms are based on the invoice date. For example, ordinary dating of 2/10, net 30, specifies the percent of discount permitted for paying early, the number of days within which you can take advantage of the discount, and the total number of days within which you must pay the invoice in full.

In addition to ordinary dating terms, you should also know several other dating terms, including *advance dating, extra dating, EOM dating,* and *ROG dating*.

Advance dating, which is sometimes offered to businesses that buy before the buying season, occurs when manufacturers indicate a date other than the invoice date from which the dating terms take effect. For example, an invoice may be dated January 15 and include the following advance dating terms: 2/10, net 30—as of March 1. In this situation, the date of the invoice is disregarded, and March 1 is the date from which the billing terms take effect. If the bill is paid by March 11 (10 days from March 1), the buyer can take advantage of the 2 percent cash discount. If the buyer does not take advantage of the discount, the bill must be paid by March 31 (30 days after March 1).

Extra dating grants additional days before the dating terms take effect. In special deals, the manufacturer may offer extra dating to encourage a buyer to purchase new merchandise. Extra dating terms are written 3/10, net 30, 60 extra. Thus, the 3/10, net 30 stipulations apply after the 60 extra days have passed.

One simple way of determining the dates for payment is to add the extra days to the dating terms. For example, an invoice dated July 15 with terms of 3/10, net 30, 30 extra, could be changed to 3/40, net 60 (10 + 30 = 40 and 30 + 30 = 60). Therefore, August 24 is the date on which the discount expires, and September 13 is the last date for full payment of the invoice.

End-of-month (EOM) dating is changing the date from which the billing terms take effect to the end of the month. The exception to this occurs when the date of the invoice is after the 25th day of the month. In that case, the buyer is permitted to go to the *end of the next month* to begin the dating terms.

Here are two examples of end-of-the-month dating. In the first example, an invoice is dated March 2, with terms of 2/10, net 30, EOM. In this case, the dating terms begin on March 31, the last day of the month. Therefore, the date up to which the buyer can take advantage of the discount is April 10 (10 days after March 31), and the last date to pay the bill is April 30 (30 days from March 31). In the second example, an invoice is dated April 27, with terms of 3/10, net 30, EOM. Here the terms begin on May 31 because the date of the invoice is after the 25th of the month. Therefore, to take advantage of the discount, the buyer's firm must pay this invoice by June 10. The final date for payment of the invoice is June 30 (30 days after May 31).

In receipt-of-goods (ROG) dating, the terms begin when the buyer's firm receives the goods. Therefore, you do not consider the invoice date when determining the dates for payment of the invoice. An example of ROG dating is 3/10, net 30, ROG. If the invoice is dated June 1 and the goods are received July 15, the end date for taking advantage of the discount is July 25 (10 days from July 15), and the last date for payment of the invoice is August 14 (30 days from July 15).

Table 32-1 will help you review and remember these dating terms.

Delivery terms are also important when a buyer is deciding on a source of supply for goods and services. As explained in Chapter 25, the terms for delivery include variations of FOB (free on board). From a buyer's standpoint, the best delivery terms are those in which the supplier pays all shipping charges. Therefore, as a buyer, you would negotiate FOB delivered or FOB store. The supplier would pay the shipping costs and be responsible for the goods until they

Table 32-1 Dating Terms			
Dating Terms	Example	Cash Discount	Final Payment
Ordinary	2/10, net 30	2 % if paid within 10 days of date of invoice	30 days from date of invoice
Advance	2/10, net 60 as of _____ date	2 % if paid within 10 days from advance date	60 days from advance date in dating terms
Extra	3/15, net 30 Extra 30	3 % if paid within 45 days of invoice date	60 days from invoice date
EOM	2/10, net 30 EOM	2 % if paid within 10 days after the last day of month of invoice date	30 days from the last day of the month
		except when first date is after the 25th day of the month—then it may be paid within ten days after the end of next month	30 days from last day of the next month
ROG	4/20, net 60 ROG	4 % if paid within 20 days of the date goods were received	60 days from date goods were received

Various discounts are used to encourage purchases by buyers and purchasing agents. If a bill is simply stated net 30, would a cash discount be permitted? When would the final payment be due if the invoice were dated June 10?

arrive at your store. The change in ownership occurs when you receive the goods. The supplier is responsible for any losses or damages that occurred to that point. In addition, the supplier must pay for insurance during the transport of the goods to your store.

A third variable that buyers should review before selecting a source is *special retail buying deals*. Two special types of buying procedures offered to retailers are *consignment buying* and *memorandum buying*.

In *consignment buying, goods are paid for only after they are purchased by the final consumer*. The supplier owns the goods until the retailer sells them. Many suppliers offer consignment buying when introducing a new line of goods to encourage retail buyers to carry the line. Since a buyer only pays for the goods when they are sold, no money is tied up in inventory. Thus, there is virtually no risk. The problem with consignment buying occurs when merchandise is stolen or damaged. Then there is often a question about who is responsible for and who must pay for the goods.

Memorandum buying occurs when the supplier agrees to take back any unsold goods by a certain date. The buyer pays for the total invoice (that is, for all the goods purchased) but is later reimbursed for goods returned in accordance with the agreement.

Step Three: Placing the Order

To place an order, most businesses prepare a *purchase order*, a legal contract between the buyer and the supplier that specifies the terms of the agreement. The purchase order includes information regarding the quantity, style, number, and unit price of each item purchased, as well as any special requests, such as shipping and delivery instructions.

Step Four: Obtaining Feedback and Evaluating Purchases

All buyers solicit feedback to determine whether the goods and services purchased meet the purposes for which they were bought. In an industrial setting, the goods and services are evaluated on the basis of how well they perform in the manufacturing process or in the general operation of the business. The costs of purchasing goods and services and their productivity are reviewed to see if they are in line with the buyer's expectations.

Retail and wholesale buyers are concerned with the sales movement of the merchandise they purchase. Therefore, buyers talk with customers to get firsthand knowledge of their reactions to the items purchased. They also study sales records to determine fast-selling and slow-selling items. Fast-selling goods may need to be ordered quickly to avoid running out of stock. Slow-selling goods must be analyzed to determine why they are not selling faster.

Many wholesale and retail buyers also compute stock turnover rates for individual items and for their department or store. Recall from Chapter 26 that stock turnover is the number of times the average stock has been sold and replaced in a given period of time.

Marketing Mathematics Related to Retail Buying

Marketing mathematics related to retail buying involves preparing a six-month merchandise plan similar to a budget. It includes projected sales, stock, reductions, and purchases. Planned sales, planned stock, planned reductions, and planned purchases must be computed. Buying figures must be converted into cost figures. The amount of money available for buying the product must be calculated. Figure 32-5 presents a six-month merchandise plan.

REAL WORLD MARKETING

The Fizz That Fizzled

Never mess with a good thing. That was the lesson the Coca–Cola Company learned when it came out with New Coke, only to have sales go flatter than a soda that's lost its fizz. Apparently, the problem was Coke drinkers' loyalties to the existing product. If Coca–Cola had done its homework, it might have discovered that its fans would rather fight than switch—which is exactly what they did. As a result, Coca–Cola reintroduced "Classic Coke."

Planned Sales

The first figure calculated on a merchandise plan is the planned sales figure. In most cases, this is determined by using the previous year's sales figure and adjusting it to reflect the firm's current-year sales goal. For example, suppose sales last year were $100,000 and this year's goal is to increase sales by 10 percent. Last year's sales figure is multiplied by 10 percent, and the resulting answer is added to the previous year's sales figure to indicate the planned sales figure for the current year.

A firm's goal for the current year is derived from a study of last year's sales, current market and economic conditions, and an analysis of competition. Projection of an accurate planned sales figure is important because all other figures on the merchandise plan are computed on the basis of this figure.

SIX-MONTH MERCHANDISE PLAN

Spring Season 19 —

Department _____

No. _____

		Feb.	March	April	May	June	July	Total
Sales	Last Year							
	Plan							
	Actual							
Retail Stock BOM	Last Year							
	Plan							
	Actual							
Retail Reductions	Last Year							
	Plan							
	Actual							
Retail Purchases	Last Year							
	Plan							
	Actual							

Figure 32-5 **Six-Month Merchandise Plan**
What is the purpose of a merchandise plan?

Beginning-of-the-Month (BOM) Stock

To arrive at the beginning-of-the-month inventory, apply a stock-to-sales ratio to the planned sales figures. Recall from Chapter 26 that a stock-to-sales ratio indicates how much stock is necessary to accommodate sales volume. For example, if the stock-to-sales ratio is 2:1 (which is usually reported as 2) and sales for the month are $5,000, the beginning-of-the-month inventory is $10,000 ($5,000 × 2).

To calculate the stock-to-sales ratio, you can analyze the previous year's records by dividing the beginning-of-the-month stock figures by the sale figures for each respective month. For example, suppose the stock figure for a given month was $15,000 and sales for that month were $3,000. The stock-to-sales ratio is 5 ($15,000 ÷ $3,000). If economic and market conditions remain the same this year, the same stock-to-sales ratio can be applied to the projected sales figures in the six-month plan.

Planned Reductions

Planned retail reductions include employee discounts, markdowns, and shortages. Shortages include clerical errors, employee pilferage, and shoplifting. These planned reductions are included in the merchandise plan because they affect the amount of money budgeted for purchases.

Planned retail reductions can be calculated in two different ways, depending on the firm's objectives or philosophy. One way is to calculate reductions as a percentage of planned sales. For example, let's say planned reductions have historically been 10 percent of planned sales. If planned sales for the month are $25,000, the planned reductions for that month would be $2,500 ($25,000 × .10 = $2,500).

Some firms set goals of reducing planned reductions from the previous year. Planned reductions are calculated as a percentage reduction from the previous year. For example, if a firm's goal is to reduce this year's planned reductions by 5 percent from last year's figure, and last year's reductions were $700, this year's planned reductions would be $665 ($700 × .05 = $35 reduction); ($700 – $35 = $665).

Planned Purchases

Planned purchases are the retail-dollar purchase figures a firm needs in order to achieve its sales and inventory projections. There is a formula for calculating the planned purchase figure:

PS + EOM stock + R – BOM stock = planned purchases

Planned sales (PS) plus planned stock at the end of the month (EOM stock—which is recorded as the beginning-of-the-month inventory for the following month) plus planned reductions (R), minus beginning-of-the-month stock (BOM stock) equals planned purchases.

The planned purchase figure is recorded as a retail figure on the merchandise plan because all figures on that plan are expressed in retail prices. To determine how much the planned purchase figure is in cost terms, apply the markup percentage applied to goods purchased and then subtract the planned markup.

For example, if planned purchases are $5,800 on the merchandise plan and the planned markup percentage on retail prices is 40 percent, the planned purchases are $3,480 ($5,800 × .40 = $2,320; $5,800 – $2,320 = $3,480). A faster way to calculate the same answer is to subtract the markup percentage from 100 percent to get the percentage of the retail price that cost represents. Then you apply that percentage to the planned purchase figure to get the value of planned purchases at cost. Using the above example, the calculations would be 100 – 40 = 60 percent; $5,800 × .60 = $3,480.

At any given time during the buying season, a buyer may want to know the *open-to-buy*. *Open-to-buy (OTB) is the amount of money left for buying goods.* The open-to-buy amount is the planned purchases figure less merchandise received and merchandise ordered.

For example, suppose that planned sales are $10,000, planned EOM stock is $25,000, markdowns are $500, and the BOM stock is $20,000. To calculate planned purchases, we compute as follows:

$10,000 (planned sales) + $25,000 (planned EOM stock) + $500 (reductions) – $20,000 (planned BOM stock) = $15,500 planned purchases.

Merchandise received against that planned purchase figure thus far is $6,500, and merchandise on order against it is $2,000. Thus, the present OTB is

$15,500 (planned purchases) – $6,500 (merchandise received) – $2,000 (merchandise ordered) = $7,000 OTB at the present time.

VOCABULARY REVIEW

Write two or three paragraphs incorporating these 11 vocabulary terms.

purchasing agent
wholesale buyer
retail buyer
resident buying office
advance dating
extra dating

end-of-month (EOM) dating
receipt-of-goods (ROG)
 dating
consignment buying
memorandum buying
open-to-buy (OTB)

FACT AND IDEA REVIEW

1. Depending on the purpose of the purchase, name the two different types of buyers that may perform the buying function.

2. Name and explain three kinds of buying situations in which all buyers may find themselves. Provide an example of each situation.

3. What are the four general steps in the buying process?

4. In resale buying, why do buyers put so much time and effort into determining customers' needs?

5. Name and explain two basic buying plans that retailers follow to help them make buying decisions about the actual goods and quantities of goods to purchase.

6. What sources of information do purchasing agents rely on to locate supply sources?

7. How do wholesale and retail buyers locate sources of supply?

8. Name at least five criteria that buyers can use to select sources.

9. What do the numbers in ordinary dating, such as 2/10, net 30, specify?

10. How are goods and services evaluated in an industrial setting?

11. Name three actions that many wholesale and retail buyers take to get feedback and evaluate purchases.

12. What computations are involved in preparing a merchandise plan?

CRITICAL THINKING

1. Compare and contrast the buying process for industrial buyers with the buying process for wholesale and retail buyers.

2. If your high school was considering the purchase of a new copier, what people in the school system might be thought of as influentials? Explain what power and influence each might have on the purchase decision.

3. A large retail store employs fashion coordinators to study fashion trends and upcoming colors for each season. What role might a fashion coordinator have in relation to the buyer for women's shoes?

4. Of what use and significance are want slips to retail buyers and resource files to all buyers?

5. Why do you think merchandise plans are prepared with retail figures instead of cost figures?

USING BASIC SKILLS

Math

1. If sales were $250,000 last year and this year's sales goal is a 10 percent increase, what should planned sales be?

2. Calculate the July stock-to-sales ratio for a business that had a July opening inventory of $70,000 and sales of $35,000.

3. Determine the BOM stock figure for the merchandise plan by applying a stock-to-sales ratio of 4 to planned sales of $22,000.

4. Compute planned purchases by using the following information:

Planned sales	$3,500
Planned EOM stock	9,000
Planned reductions	500
Planned BOM stock	8,500

5. Calculate the open-to-buy figure for a buyer, using the following information:

Planned sales	$10,000
Planned EOM stock	40,000
Planned reductions	1,000
Planned BOM stock	35,000
Merchandise on order	6,000
Merchandise received against planned purchases	4,000

6. Compute the actual amount that a buyer can spend by converting the planned purchase figure of $54,800 to cost. The customary markup used by the retailer is 60 percent.

7. Determine planned reductions for the merchandise plan by calculating the 10 percent reduction from last year's figure of $840.

8. If planned reductions are 5 percent of planned sales, what are the planned reductions for a merchandise plan that has $45,000 in planned sales for the month of February?

Communication

9. You work in a men's clothing store. A customer approaches you and asks for a sweater that the store does not carry. You have received similar requests for the same sweater from other customers. What would you say to the customer? How would you communicate this information to the store buyer?

Human Relations

10. If you were a retail buyer of dolls for a toy chain store such as Toys R Us that had more than 700 stores, what would you say to a supplier that has poorly designed packages? Let's say the packages break open easily and are difficult to stack on the shelves. How much power do you think you would have?

11. You observe a cashier making mistakes when putting SKU codes into the point-of-sale terminal. When you approach the cashier to tell her that she is making mistakes with the codes, she responds, "There are too many numbers to record for each item. When a customer buys a lot of items, I don't worry if I make a mistake with the SKU. Customers appreciate my fast service, so why should the store care if I make a few mistakes?" As this employee's supervisor, what would you say to make her understand the importance of the SKU codes?

APPLICATION PROJECTS

1. As a buyer, you have to select one of the following vendors from which to purchase 150 pairs of jeans. Here are the facts about each vendor.

Vendor A has a reputation for delivering goods two weeks later than promised. The price per pair of jeans is $20 each. There is a 1 percent quantity discount on all purchases over 100. Vendor A has dating terms of 2/10, net 30, and delivery terms of FOB shipping point. Shipping charges are approximately $19.

Vendor B has an excellent reputation for delivering on time. The price per pair of jeans is $22 with dating terms of 2/10, net 30, 30 extra, and delivery terms of FOB store.

Based on this information, determine the following:

a. The unit price per pair of jeans for Vendor A and for Vendor B, after all discounts and freight charges have been considered.

b. With which vendor would you place your order for 150 jeans: Vendor A or Vendor B? Why? Explain your reasons.

2. Determine the date until which the buyer may take advantage of the discount and the date by which the invoice must be paid for the following:

Invoice	Date Goods Were Received	Dating Terms
Jan. 22	Jan. 30	2/10, n30
Feb. 15	Feb. 25	3/10, n30, 60 extra
April 23	May 2	2/20, n60, as of Aug. 5
May 10	June 10	3/10, n30, EOM
Sept. 4	Sept. 30	2/10, n30, ROG
Oct. 29	Nov. 12	3/10, n60, EOM

MARKETING
INFORMATION
MANAGEMENT

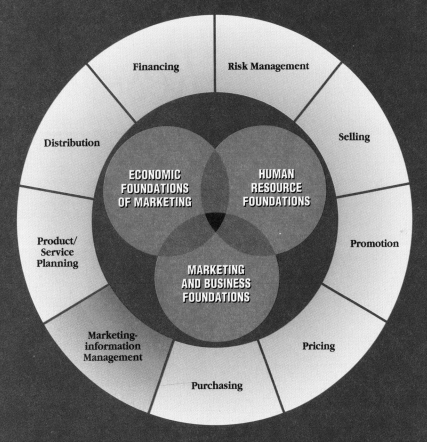

CHAPTERS

33 What Is Market Research?
34 Conducting Market Research

33

OBJECTIVES

After completing this chapter, you will be able to:

1. define marketing research,

2. tell how marketing research can lead to better business decisions, and

3. describe five important areas of marketing research.

WORDS TO KNOW

marketing research
advertising research
business research
operations research
corporate responsibility research
product research
sales and market research
test marketing

What Is Marketing Research?

Successful business planning requires information about potential target markets, the competition, individual customers, and their reaction to products. As a result, more and more decisions in our increasingly competitive marketplace are being based on the results of marketing research.

Marketing research takes much of the guesswork out of business operations by providing pertinent information for making sound business decisions. In this chapter, you will read about marketing research and understand its importance in our economy. You will also learn about the various types of marketing research and why they are so important to business success.

What Is Marketing Research?

Marketing research is the process of getting the marketing information needed to make sound business decisions. It involves the systematic gathering, recording, and analyzing of data about problems relating to the marketing of goods and services.

Marketing research can apply to any of the functions of marketing. For example, a food manufacturer introducing a new product line would investigate the financial aspects, the staff requirements, the distribution network, and the potential sales for the proposed product line.

The primary emphasis of most marketing research, however, is to obtain information about the preferences, opinions, habits, trends, and plans of potential customers. Information about customers and the size of a potential market, for example, helps businesses with product planning, advertising, and promotion.

Research can help a company's marketing operations in many ways. For example, it helps minimize losses or potential losses in the introduction of new or revised products. This is significant since only one out of every ten products introduced into the marketplace is accepted by consumers.

Who Uses Marketing Research?

Marketing research is valuable for organizations of any size. The size of the business, though, may affect how it conducts the research. Small businesses that do less than $4 million in annual sales usually do not have separate research departments. Here, marketing research is done informally by the owners, managers, or other employees.

Larger companies have formal research departments and specialists to plan and conduct marketing research. Some larger companies contract with marketing research companies (see Figure 33-1) to solve special marketing related problems.

The top 50 marketing research firms in the United States had combined worldwide revenues of $2.3 billion in 1978. About $1.6 billion was spent that year on marketing research in the U.S. alone.

Figure 33-1 **A Marketing Research Company**
Some larger companies contract with marketing research companies to help them solve marketing related problems. What special research services does this particular company advertise?

Businesses invest in marketing research to get positive results in the form of increased sales and profits. However, individual businesses are not the only organizations that find marketing research valuable.

Trade associations representing various manufacturers, wholesalers, and retailers, and various departments in both the state and federal governments conduct marketing research.

For example, industry trade associations, such as the National Retail Merchants Association, collect industry data to help their members understand the market for certain products and to help them with the operation of a business. The Consumer Product Safety Commission, a federal government agency, tests products to protect consumers from unsafe products.

Nature and Scope of Marketing Research

Marketing research can take place for any of the functions of marketing. The most significant areas of research are

- advertising research,
- business research,
- operations research,
- corporate responsibility research,
- product research, and
- sales and market research.

While marketing studies can be classified into one of these areas, data collected from one study can often be used to solve other business problems relating to the marketing of goods and services.

Advertising Research

Advertising research focuses on the advertising message and media. It is designed to measure two things. One is the effectiveness of the advertising message in producing the desired response in the people who receive it. The other is the effectiveness of the chosen media in delivering the message to consumers.

The effectiveness of an advertising message can be tested before the advertisement is run. For example, marketing researchers can study a consumer panel to get people's reactions to an advertisement. A consumer panel can be composed of a cross section of people. It can also be composed of people who share common characteristics—senior citizens, single parents, college-educated adults, or teenagers, for example. Oral, written, or observed behavioral responses are recorded to indicate panel members' reactions to the ad.

A common technique to study how effectively a message has been delivered is asking panel members if they recall having seen or read an advertisement. They can also be asked how they were influenced by the ad and whether they were motivated to buy the advertised product as a result.

Important data on broadcast advertising is assembled by the Arbitron Ratings Company, a subsidiary of the Control Data Corporation. Arbitron produces radio, television, and cable audience studies at the local market level, using mail diaries or meter-equipped households.

One way to test the effectiveness of an advertising message is to show it to a consumer panel. What kinds of questions would the interviewer ask panel members if testing their reaction to this ad before it is run? after it is run?

Mail diaries are records on which people report such viewer data as who is watching or listening to a station and what programs are tuned in. In meter-equipped households, devices attached to the television sets automatically monitor the type, time, and frequency of program viewing. By providing an estimate of the size and kind of audience that will be reached, Arbitron can help businesses decide on which television or radio program to advertise.

Business Research

Business research attempts to solve business problems related to long-range forecasting and future economic conditions. Business research usually looks at sales forecasting and economic forecasting.

Sales Forecasting. *Sales forecasting* is analyzing the market for a given product or line of products. A total estimate of the market in terms of sales is calculated. Then an individual share for a business is predicted.

The share assigned to an individual business is called the *sales penetration* of the market. Efforts are then directed by a business to increase the sales penetration of the market through changes in the product, pricing, promotion, or distribution.

Economic Forecasting. *Economic forecasting* is an attempt to predict the general economic conditions of a city, region, or the entire country. It is a highly specialized type of research requiring extensive knowledge of statistics and economics.

Several federal agencies are involved with determining key economic indicators, such as new construction of buildings, the rate of inflation, money supply, consumer indexes, and producer indexes. So, most businesses rely on government data to predict economic conditions. Depending on the economic outlook and general conditions for an area or for the country, a business will adjust its activities.

Research about general economic conditions can help a business plan for long-range expansion with new products or investments during good times. It can also help plan a careful downscaling of operations in less than favorable periods.

Operations Research

Operations research looks at methods and procedures that will make a business more effective and efficient in distributing its goods and services. It is concerned about day-to-day policies, procedures, rules, and regulations that might be improved upon, modified, or changed to better serve customers and employees.

Some examples of operations research include research activities regarding

- the effectiveness of computerized point-of-sale terminals,
- the impact of management policies on employees, and
- data on shoplifters to better control stock shortages and shrinkage.

Corporate Responsibility Research

Corporate responsibility research deals with consumer "right to know" concerns, environmental impact, social values, and policy studies. An example of corporate responsibility research is the work done by the Gallup Organization headquartered in Princeton, New Jersey. Gallup specializes in public opinion research and collects data through both face-to-face and telephone interviews.

For example, in a 1988 Gallup public opinion poll on the environment, 73 percent of those surveyed said they were seriously concerned about air pollution versus 46 percent in 1973. The most recent survey indicates that environmental concerns are of growing importance. Businesses will use the results of this research to design, manufacture, sell, and promote products that are environmentally safe.

This type of research provides businesses with the latest public opinions on corporate responsibilities and business ethics. Businesses use this information to direct future major business decisions and policies.

Product Research

Product research is concerned about product design and acceptance, competitive products, testing of existing products, package design, and product usage. Many products are designed, tested, changed, and introduced each year. Product research measures new product acceptance by the consumers and identifies opportunities to meet changing customer needs.

Product research also monitors major societal and population trends that can affect the development of new goods and services. To do this, researchers must note significant changes in population trends, life-styles, and demographics. One significant recent trend is the increase in the over-50 segment of the U.S. population. Many goods and services are changing in response to this. As people age, for example, they usually become increasingly health-conscious and aware of diet. Food manufacturers have responded to this by producing foods that are low in fat, low in sodium, high in fiber, and calcium- or vitamin-enriched.

Sales and Market Research

Sales and market research focuses on customer analysis, sales and market analysis, test marketing, and target market characteristics.

Customer analysis is the study of the behavior of the individual who makes buying decisions. Examples of those things used in customer analysis include questionnaires and interviews about customer attitudes, especially those relating to motivation to buy. Figure 33-2 shows a questionnaire used in market research.

Sales and market analysis is the study of the behavior of consumers as a group. The goal of sales and market analysis is to define the target market and investigate potential markets and sales for a product or service.

PLEASE MARK AS FOLLOWS: ⊟

The questionnaire should be completed by the principal driver of the vehicle indicated. Please answer only based on your experience with the dealership where you bought your vehicle (your selling dealer). Do not report experience with any other dealership. Thank you for taking the time to answer these questions.

	Completely satisfied	Very satisfied	Fairly well satisfied	Somewhat dissatisfied	Very dissatisfied
1. Now that you've had your vehicle for about nine months, please tell us how satisfied you are in the following areas					
a. Exterior quality of workmanship (fit and finish)?	☐	☐	☐	☐	☐
b. Interior quality of workmanship (fit and finish)?	☐	☐	☐	☐	☐
c. Engine power and pickup?	☐	☐	☐	☐	☐
d. Smoothness of transmission?	☐	☐	☐	☐	☐
e. Riding comfort?	☐	☐	☐	☐	☐
f. Ease of handling?	☐	☐	☐	☐	☐
g. Fuel economy?	☐	☐	☐	☐	☐
h. Quietness?	☐	☐	☐	☐	☐
i. Operation of the accessories (e.g., radio, air conditioner, heater, defroster, etc.)?	☐	☐	☐	☐	☐
j. Overall satisfaction with the vehicle?	☐	☐	☐	☐	☐

	Yes	No
2. Since the time of purchase, have you taken your Ford Motor Company vehicle to Nelson Ford, Inc., for any kind of service including warranty work or repairs you paid for?	☐	☐

3. Based on your visit(s) to Nelson Ford, Inc., for service, how satisfied would you say you are with each of the following? Mark one box across.	Completely satisfied	Very satisfied	Fairly well satisfied	Somewhat dissatisfied	Very dissatisfied
a. The attitude of service department personnel (their interest in you and your problems)	☐	☐	☐	☐	☐
b. Their overall treatment of you as a customer	☐	☐	☐	☐	☐
c. Their promptness in writing up your order	☐	☐	☐	☐	☐
d. Their politeness	☐	☐	☐	☐	☐
e. Their understanding of your problems	☐	☐	☐	☐	☐
f. Convenience of scheduling the work	☐	☐	☐	☐	☐
g. Convenience of service hours	☐	☐	☐	☐	☐
h. Length of time to complete the work	☐	☐	☐	☐	☐
i. Availability of needed parts	☐	☐	☐	☐	☐
j. Their completing all the work you requested	☐	☐	☐	☐	☐
k. The quality of work done (was it fixed right?)	☐	☐	☐	☐	☐
l. Explanation of work and charges (if any)	☐	☐	☐	☐	☐
m. Fairness of prices (if you were charged)	☐	☐	☐	☐	☐
n. Appearance of service department	☐	☐	☐	☐	☐

Figure 33-2 **Marketing Research Questionnaire**
Questionnaires such as this are frequently used in customer analysis. What kinds of information can be provided to the manufacturer and to the automotive dealer through the use of this questionnaire?

One type of customer motivation research is illustrated by the work of J.C. Penney Company which conducted a series of focus group sessions in the mid-1980s related to the life-styles of dual-income families. A *focus group* is composed of eight to ten people brought together to discuss a particular situation under the direction of a skilled interviewer.

The purpose of the J.C. Penney study was:

- to develop an increased understanding of dual-income family life-styles as they affect family, work, and leisure,
- to provide a greater insight into dual-income consumer attitudes and behavior, and

- to identify issues that have an impact on dual-income family life-styles and shopping behaviors so J.C. Penney could better meet the needs of these families.

As a result of these focus group sessions, J.C. Penney obtained vital information related to dual-income families, including effectiveness of sales promotion and advertising, level of quality desired in products, and attitudes toward private label merchandise and customer service.

One method of sales and market analysis is *test marketing*. **Test marketing** *occurs when a product is placed in one or more selected geographic areas and its sales performance under a proposed marketing plan is observed.*

In the new product development stage, products are test marketed in certain areas before they are distributed nationwide. (You will discover more about test marketing later in this chapter.)

For example, although the sales of cherry-flavored sodas had slowed early in 1988, Pepsi-Cola USA still introduced Cherry Pepsi in several test markets in the same year. Cherry-flavored soft drinks became popular in 1985 and enjoyed two years of steady market growth. This was due, in part, to the soft drink consumption by older consumers. They were bored with traditional cola and also looked back with nostalgia to the cherry-flavored fountain drinks they enjoyed as children.

Cherry-flavored soft drinks' share of the total soda market during the first five months of 1988 fell

CASE CHALLENGE

Coca-Cola Enters the Office

Coca-Cola Company has entered a new market by introducing a new compact soda dispenser for the business office. The dispenser unit, called "Breakmate," is manufactured by Bosch-Siemans, a West German appliance company.

Coca-Cola first began its office dispensing machine product development in 1971 when marketing research indicated that more than 1 million small offices of less than 45 employees did not have access to soft drinks. Since 1983, Coca-Cola and Siemans have jointly developed the compact machine to meet the company's carbonation, syrup, and water mixture requirements.

About 10,000 machines have been tested in the United States and another 40,000 in Europe. Since the fall of 1989, Coca-Cola has been selling and advertising the Breakmate machine in 30 target cities.

Coke charges employers only for the syrup, not for the machine or cups. Each syrup cartridge makes 31 drinks and costs about $8. The standard serving size is 6½ ounces.

1. How do you think Coca-Cola will advertise this product? What features and benefits will Coke promote to employers?
2. What is the target market for the Breakmate machines? Who will Coca-Cola use to distribute this product?
3. Why would a company prefer the Breakmate machine to a free-standing Coke vending machine?
4. What technical problems do you think the Coke product research team experienced that prevented it from introducing the product in the early 1970s?
5. Six other soft drink companies were approached by Siemans in the late 1970s to market a Siemans-developed fountain machine. None of the companies was interested. Why do you think Coca-Cola was interested? Do you think this new product innovation will be successful? Why or why not?

to about 2.5 percent of the total soft drink market compared to 3.5 percent the year before. Nevertheless, they were still expected to have retail sales of about $100 million, with a continual 2.5 percent market share over the years. So, Pepsi-Cola USA introduced Cherry Pepsi in test markets in Oregon and Wyoming.

Although early market test results were favorable, Pepsi-Cola USA announced that national distribution is not imminent. Because the related costs of introducing a product are high, Pepsi-Cola USA is continuing the test marketing before it distributes Cherry Pepsi nationally.

Various research services keep track of buying patterns of large groups. One such service, InfoScan, is a national and local market tracking system for the grocery industry. The system is based on 2,380 Universal Product Code scanner-equipped stores that are linked to a panel of 70,000 households. It provides information about product sales and records information about store features and couponing.

Advertising Research	focuses on	▪ advertising message ▪ media
Business Research	focuses on	▪ long-range forecasting ▪ future economic conditions
Operations Research	focuses on	▪ methods and procedures for better product distribution ▪ methods and procedures for improved business and employee performance
Corporate Responsibility	focuses on	▪ consumer "right to know" concerns ▪ environmental impact ▪ social values ▪ policy studies
Product Research	focuses on	▪ product design and acceptance ▪ competitive products ▪ testing existing products ▪ package design ▪ product usage
Sales and Market Research	focuses on	▪ consumer behavior ▪ sales and market analysis ▪ target market characteristics

Figure 33-3 **Six Areas of Marketing Research**
As a business owner, which type of research would you use if you wanted to investigate the potential market for a new product?

Limitations of Marketing Research

Figure 33-3 summarizes the six key areas of marketing research. Each plays a vital role in providing pertinent information to help businesses make sound business decisions. Few companies, though, can make use of as much marketing research as they would like. The amount of information that can be gathered is limited by the amount of money a company can afford to spend on the equipment and personnel needed to do the research. Often, there isn't time to do the research because decisions must sometimes be made before all possible data can be obtained.

There are other limitations, too. For example, customers in a test market situation may say they want a particular product. Nevertheless, there is no guarantee they will buy the product when it is actually produced for sale.

Also, there is usually a time lag between identifying the need for a product, collecting the marketing research, and presenting the findings so the business can decide whether to produce the product. Business conditions, customer buying habits, and customer preferences can all change over the time period of the study.

Despite those limitations, businesses still do a significant amount of marketing research to obtain the best possible information about customers and the market.

REAL WORLD MARKETING

Missing the Bull's Eye

When products are created and marketed, they are done so with particular target audiences in mind. Though marketers rely on research to determine these targets, sometimes even research misses the mark. Such has been the case with fruit juice–enriched sodas, such as Slice. The health–conscious consumer at whom they were targeted has largely ignored them in favor of sugary soft drinks.

VOCABULARY REVIEW

Write one or two paragraphs incorporating these eight vocabulary terms.

marketing research   product research
advertising research   sales and market research
business research   test marketing
operations research
corporate responsibility research

FACT AND IDEA REVIEW

1. What is marketing research?

2. What is involved in marketing research?

3. How does marketing research help a company's marketing operations?

4. What is advertising research? How can it help businesses?

5. What is business research? Give two examples of business research.

6. What is operations research?

7. What is corporate responsibility research?

8. What is product research?

9. What is sales and market research?

10. What are the limitations of marketing research?

CRITICAL THINKING

1. Should every type of business engage in marketing research? Why or why not? Explain what kind of marketing research should be done by a coin-operated car wash.

2. Explain why marketing researchers are so concerned about consumer attitudes and life-styles.

3. What are the advantages and disadvantages of test marketing?

4. What do you think marketing research would reveal about the differences between the life-styles of dual-income families with children and the life-styles of dual-income families without children? Consider time, income, product needs, shopping patterns, etc.

5. GM, Chevrolet, Pontiac, and Oldsmobile began production of all-plastic mini-vans in 1990. Do you think that plastic mini-vans and, in the future, plastic cars will be accepted by the American public? Why or why not?

USING BASIC SKILLS

Math

1. Demographic data indicates that more marketing efforts will be geared to older consumers as the baby boomers age. Compute the following using these U.S. Census Bureau data projections for persons over the age of 65.

Year	Population over the Age of 65
1980	26,000,000
1990	32,000,000
2000	35,000,000
2020	51,000,000

What is the percentage increase in the population group over the age of 65 from 1980 to 1990? 1980 to 2000? 1980 to 2020?

2. What is the increase in millions for the population over the age of 65 from the year 1980 to the year 2020?

Communication

3. Write a business letter requesting information from your local Chamber of Commerce on how it assists area businesses in conducting marketing surveys.

Human Relations

4. Which of the following jobs would you prefer? List the reasons for your decision. Consider life-styles, family obligations, and activities as part of your decision.

Job #1

A marketing research position in a large company that requires quotas to be met, paperwork to be completed, and some overtime. It includes travel opportunities. Dismissal is always possible if the work is not done satisfactorily.

Job #2

A marketing research position in a government agency that requires steady work and no overtime. Little travel is involved. Dismissal is unlikely unless you are extremely negligent. This job pays $50 a week less than Job #1.

APPLICATION PROJECTS

1. Consult your library for current business publications such as *Inc.*, the *Wall Street Journal*, *Business Week*, *Advertising Age*, and *Mass Market Retailers*. Find one current research activity being conducted by a company in the United States. Identify the activity and write a 200-word report on it that explains the scope and reasons for the research.

2. Prepare a 200-word report listing the information about long-term trends within a particular industry (automotive, electronics, communications, for example).

3. Prepare a 200-word report listing such market factors as population, income, education, trading area, and purchasing power that would make your city, area, region, or state an attractive place to locate a business. Consult city or county offices, regional planning authorities, the local chamber of commerce, or state offices for detailed market information.

4. Assume that you are a marketing manager. Identify ten questions that you would ask of a large research agency before you would contract for services related to advertising research.

5. Choose an existing consumer product in need of major changes or renovation (decay-fighting gum or voice-activated computers for the handicapped, for example). Research any published information about your product and any proposed changes for it. Present these changes and the rationale for them in a five-minute oral report to the class.

6. Identify at least ten consumer goods that will require adaptation because of a generally aging population.

7. Identify at least ten new consumer goods, services, or changes in goods or services that have occurred to serve the handicapped population in the United States.

8. Conduct a comparison shopping survey of three different stores on the price differences of five products. Summarize the results of your survey in a 200-word written report.

9. Design a marketing research survey (10–15 questions) for a good or service for your school store. Conduct the research and report your findings in an oral report to the class.

10. Visit the library and determine the demographics of your community (age, ethnic background, population, and income).

11. Select three businesses in the area. Locate them on a map and prepare a short oral report for the class on the geographical market each serves.

Conducting Marketing Research

OBJECTIVES

After completing this chapter, you will be able to:

1. describe the five steps in conducting marketing research, and

2. name two important characteristics of management information systems.

WORDS TO KNOW

problem definition
primary data
secondary data
survey method
observation method
experimental method
data analysis
management information system

As indicated in Chapter 33, marketing research is not a single act, but a series of activities. In this chapter you will review each step in the marketing research process. You will also understand the importance of an overall management information system to assist in the solution of problems faced by businesses today.

The Marketing Research Process

Five major steps are involved in the marketing research process:

1. problem definition,
2. obtaining data,
3. data analysis,
4. recommending solutions to the problem, and
5. implementing the findings.

Each step must be performed sequentially and systematically to arrive at a solution to a problem. Let's explore each step in depth.

Step 1: Problem Definition

The most difficult and yet the most important step in the marketing research process is defining the problem. *Problem definition occurs when a business clearly states what decisions need to be made and what information is required to make them.* For example, a new business needs to decide how to market its products. To that end, it will want to know who its potential customers are, where they live, how they buy, and who its competitors are.

Because money and time are limited, it is virtually impossible for marketing researchers to answer all the questions that confront a business. Therefore, each business has to prioritize its problems by determining which are the most important to solve at a given point in time. After all the problems have been prioritized and the most important ones selected for study, the next step of the marketing research process can begin.

Step 2: Obtaining Data

During this second step in the marketing research process, data are obtained and examined about the problem or problems being studied.

The word *data* means facts. There are two types of data used in marketing research: *primary* and *secondary*. **Primary data are data obtained for the first time and used specifically for the particular problem under study. Secondary data have already been collected and are used for some other purpose than the current study.** Businesses try to get secondary data before they get primary data. So, we'll explore secondary data first.

How Secondary Data Are Obtained

Secondary data are obtained from both *internal sources* (sources within the company) and *external sources* (sources outside the company). Good sources of internal secondary data are employees and the records or reports of the business. Such records could include budgets, sales figures, income and expense records, customer records, and inventory records.

External secondary data are obtained from five major sources.

1. *U.S. government agencies*. The Small Business Administration, the U.S. Department of Commerce, and the U.S. Bureau of the Census are good sources of secondary data. Publications such as the *Census of the Population* and the *Statistical Abstract of the United States* contain hundreds of tables, graphs, and charts useful in analyzing business situations. Federal government studies are relatively inexpensive data sources that can provide useful information and statistics about markets, people, and business activities.
2. *Business publications*. Good sources include such publications as *Inc.*, *Forbes*, *Business Week*, the *Wall Street Journal*, and *Sales and Marketing Management Magazine*.
3. *Commercial research agencies*. A.C. Neilsen, Gallup, and Arbitron are some of the major agencies.
4. *Trade publications, books, and monographs*. These can be obtained from trade associations such as the Food Marketing Institute and the National Retail Merchants Association.
5. *Local and state governments*. Information from local and state governments can include demographics and reports on specific markets, industries, and products.

Secondary Data

Internal	External
Employees	U.S. government agencies
Business records and reports	Business publications
	Commercial research agencies
	Trade publications, books, and monographs
	Local and state governments

Figure 34-1 **Sources of Secondary Data**

Secondary data have already been collected and used for some other purpose than the current marketing research study. Why do businesses try to use secondary data before they use primary data?

Advantages of Secondary Data.

Secondary data have several advantages over primary data. The former can be obtained more quickly because most secondary data sources can be found in public or college libraries. Obtaining secondary data is less expensive because the initial cost has already been paid by an agency or organization. In addition, some types of secondary data, such as nationwide population figures, are available through the U.S. Bureau of the Census. Any firm trying to collect such data as this would have to spend a great deal of time and money.

Disadvantages of Secondary Data.

There are two major disadvantages associated with secondary data.

First, the existing data may not be suitable for the problem under study. This is particularly likely for new and innovative products. For example, secondary data on contact lenses were largely unavailable from government agencies. Primary research had to be used to help manufacturers develop improved contact lenses.

Second, the data may be dated. For example, federal census data is collected only every ten years; projections about the current census may not always be accurate.

Despite these limitations, a business should always try to get secondary data first. It may be readily available at little or no cost. So, it could prove expensive to collect primary data without first evaluating all relevant secondary data.

How Primary Data Are Obtained

When marketing researchers cannot find the information they need from secondary data, they must use primary data. There are three basic methods used to collect primary data:

1. the survey method,
2. the observation method, and
3. the experimental method.

The Survey Method. *The survey method is a research technique in which information is gathered from people directly through the use of questionnaires.* It is the most frequently used method of collecting primary data.

The first step in this process is the creation of the *questionnaire* or *instrument*—a written list of questions pertinent to the identified problem. The questionnaire can be sent through the mail. The questions can be asked over the telephone or in personal interviews. A mailed questionnaire is an inexpensive way to reach a large audience. The return rate, however, is generally less than 15 percent.

Primary Data

Survey Method
Use of questionnaire

Observation Method
People's actions are observed and recorded

Experimental Method
One or more marketing variables observed under controlled conditions

Figure 34-2 **Sources of Primary Data**

Which method is frequently used to get information about employee performance or customer purchasing behavior?

Multiple Choice Question
What is your favorite fast-food restaurant?
_____ Kentucky Fried Chicken
_____ Burger King   _____ Taco Bell
_____ McDonald's   _____ Roy Rogers
_____ Wendy's
_____ Other (please specify _____)

Yes/No Question
Have you eaten at a McDonald's restaurant in the last month?
_____ Yes   _____ No

Scaled Response Questions
On a scale of 1–10, with 10 being the best, how would you rate the service you received in this restaurant today?

1   2   3   4   5   6   7   8   9   10

Please respond to the following statement by using the scale provided.
I think McDonald's should add a self-serve salad bar.

strongly agree   agree   no opinion   disagree
strongly disagree

Open-ended Question
In one word, how would you describe the work of the Ronald McDonald house?_____

Figure 34-3 **Sample Questions Used in a Written Questionnaire**

Questionnaires are used in the survey method to gather information from people directly. Read each question. What do you think is the identified problem for which McDonald's is trying to get information?

Researchers commonly pre-test written questionnaires with small groups in advance of a general mailing. This allows for correction of any misleading questions, directions, or problems before the instrument is mailed. Figure 34.3 gives you some of the various types of questions used in a written questionnaire.

The telephone interview is quick, efficient, and relatively inexpensive. However, the biggest problem with telephone interviews is some people's unwillingness to respond to the questions. People sometimes resent this approach to data collection because of uncertainty about the caller and how the information will be used, or resentment of the intrusion on personal time.

The personal interview, which involves face-to-face contact with people, is the most direct way to get

survey information. A major advantage to the personal interview is that most people prefer to talk rather than write. Therefore, it is often easier to get people to respond to personal interviews when they would not respond to a written questionnaire.

A disadvantage of the personal interview is that it is more costly than mail or telephone surveys. This is because personal interviewing requires hiring experienced interviewers who are skilled at asking nonbiased questions and in interpreting the answers correctly.

A form of personal interview that is increasing in popularity is the *focus group interview*. A focus group interview involves six to ten people who are brought together to informally discuss a particular situation under the direction of a skilled interviewer. The interaction in a focus group interview stimulates thinking and gets immediate reaction to an idea or concept.

The Observation Method. *The observation method is a research technique in which the actions of people are observed and recorded.* This method is frequently used to get information about employee performance or customer behavior when purchasing a good or service.

If the observation is properly performed and recorded, the results are often better than the survey technique. What people actually do is often a better indicator than what they say they will do.

One disadvantage of the observation technique is that it cannot measure attitude. Without additional information, the reasons for the person's behavior may not be clear.

The observation technique may use either *natural* or *contrived* observations.

With natural observation, customers or employees are viewed as they would normally act in a given situation. For example, a natural observation is one in which customers are observed by people or hidden cameras as they shop, enter, or leave a store.

Another form of natural observation is the *traffic count*—a count of people or cars as they pass by a store. For example, people can pass by without looking. They can stop, look, and walk on. They can stop, look, and enter the store.

Some observations are *contrived* (devised). For example, observers pose as customers to measure the effectiveness of the selling techniques used by salespeople. The salespeople are observed with respect to approach, sales presentation, product knowledge, and suggestion selling. This information can then be used to modify or improve employee training programs.

Whether a natural or contrived approach is used, the data from the observation must be recorded. For the observation technique to be successful, actions must be identified and behaviors noted.

The Experimental Method. *The experimental method is a research technique in which one or more marketing variables are observed under controlled conditions.*

For example, a business may want to compare the effectiveness of two different advertisements. To do so, the researcher will select two similar groups of consumers. Because the groups are supposed to be the same, they are the *controlled* condition. One group is shown one advertisement, and one group is shown the other. The advertisements are the *variables*. If one advertisement gets a better response, the business may choose it for its ad campaign.

The experimental method of marketing research is used least often. This is because of the high costs of setting up the research situation, the controlled setting, and such uncontrollable factors as people responding differently under controlled conditions than they normally would.

Step 3: Data Analysis

The third step in the marketing research process is *data analysis*. *Data analysis is the compiling, analyzing, and interpreting of the results of primary and secondary data collection.*

The accurate compiling of data allows marketing researchers to carefully analyze and interpret data in order to make recommendations to management regarding the problems being studied.

For example, XYZ Autos might want to survey customers about the quality of the dealership's repair service. Answers to questions on such things as the customer's opinion about the service would be organized so that the percentage of men and women responding to each question is clearly shown. Data will be cross-tabulated to determine such things as how men and women differ in their perceptions of the service. The results of the study might look like this:

Quality of Service	Men	Women
Excellent	30%	60%
Good	15%	10%
Average	20%	20%
Fair	20%	5%
Poor	15%	5%

As you can see, female customers of XYZ Autos generally have a more favorable impression of the quality of service than the male customers. Data from this marketing research study should become part of the dealership's total information system.

Step 4: Recommending Solutions to the Problem

Successful research usually results in the development of several alternatives or recommendations for solving a problem. Recommendations are usually presented in a report. They must be well-written and well-organized so the appropriate business managers will understand them. This means the recommendations must be clear and well supported by the research data.

A typical research report outline includes:

- title page;
- acknowledgments to people who assisted in the research effort;
- table of contents;
- lists of tables, figures, charts, and graphs;
- introduction (includes the problem under study, its importance, definitions, limitations of the study, and basic assumptions);

- review of the literature (including the results of any secondary data reviewed for purposes of the research effort);
- procedures used (research technique or techniques used to obtain primary data);
- findings;
- recommendations;
- summary and conclusions;
- appendices; and
- bibliography.

Step 5: Implementing the Findings

The research may indicate one of three things:

1. the research may have been nonconclusive,
2. the research may indicate that additional research is needed, or
3. the research may suggest specific courses of action.

After the research effort has been completed and recommendations implemented, a business should carefully monitor the results. A business needs to know not only whether the specific actions taken are successful, but also how successful the chosen research method was. If the implemented recommendations lead to increased profits through better sales, increased efficiency, reduced expenses, or better operations, then the research effort has been worthwhile.

Marketing research should be regarded as an ongoing process of problem solving. The results obtained through the marketing research effort should become a part of the total information available to a business for making future decisions.

Management Information Systems

Many larger businesses have implemented sophisticated *management information systems* to organize, collect, and store internal and external marketing research data for future decisions. *A management information system is a set of procedures and methods that regularly generates, stores, analyzes, and disseminates marketing decision information.*

Collecting useful marketing research data on a continuous basis provides key business decision-makers with information necessary to plan and implement marketing strategies. Data that should be a part of a management information system include:

- company records, such as sales results, expenses, and supplier data;
- competitors' records, such as their prices, location, and market share;

Steps in the Marketing Research Process

Step 1:	Problem Definition
Step 2:	Obtaining Data
Step 3:	Analyzing Data
Step 4:	Recommending Solutions to the Problem
Step 5:	Implementing the Findings

Figure 34-4 **Steps in the Marketing Research Process**
Marketing research is a series of steps that lead to the solution of a marketing problem. Do these steps have to be performed in this order? Why or why not?

CASE CHALLENGE

A Hamburger To Go . . . from the Frozen Food Department

Supermarkets currently rank second as suppliers of prepared take-out dinners. Fast-food restaurant chains have become increasingly concerned about losing sales to supermarkets as microwaveable foods, in-store delis, and take-out counters become increasingly popular. So, some restaurant chains have used marketing research to determine whether they could increase sales of their products in locations inside and outside their restaurants.

Wendy's, for example, conducted a six-month market test in conjunction with the Kroger food stores in Cincinnati and Columbus, Ohio, in 1988. The test tried to determine whether fresh ground beef with the Wendy's logo on it could be sold successfully in the Kroger stores' meat departments.

Both McDonald's and Burger King gathered data by exploring the sales of microwaveable foods in their restaurants and in grocery stores.

The next step in the research process for these companies was to analyze the sales results of their efforts to see if customers would accept recognized restaurant products in new forms and locations.

After the data were analyzed, recommendations were made on how to increase sales based on the marketing research activities each restaurant chain had undertaken.

The last step in the marketing research process will be to implement the recommendations of the research. Someday you might be able to purchase the Burger King Whopper, the Big Mac, Wendy's ground beef, or some other restaurant product in the frozen food department of your local grocery store or at a local deli or bakery.

1. What marketing problem did each of these companies define?
2. What types of data would these companies have used to get market information?
3. If customers can buy fast-food entrees from their supermarket or deli, are they likely to stop going to fast-food restaurants? Why or why not?

- customer profile data, such as the results of previous marketing studies regarding buying behavior, shopping patterns, and life-styles research; and
- government data, such as price trends and future projections for the economy.

Computers have made collection of data for marketing decision-making much easier. Computerized management information systems are able to store and retrieve large quantities of data easily and efficiently. For example, point-of-sale terminals provide information not only on the merchandise but on inventory levels.

There are some difficulties in implementing management information systems. A significant investment of time and money is required to set them up, and trained personnel are needed to maintain them. However, even small businesses today are recognizing the need for management information systems if they are to remain competitive.

CHAPTER 34 REVIEW

VOCABULARY REVIEW

Write two or three paragraphs on conducting marketing research, incorporating these eight vocabulary words.

problem definition
primary data
secondary data
survey method
observation method

experimental method
data analysis
management information system

FACT AND IDEA REVIEW

1. What is the first step in the research process?

2. What is the second step in the research process?

3. Explain the difference between primary and secondary data.

4. What are three sources of internal secondary data? What are five sources of external secondary data?

5. What are two advantages of using secondary data? What are two disadvantages of using secondary data?

6. Why should secondary data be used first when trying to solve marketing research problems?

7. What is the survey method of research? Tell three ways to conduct surveys.

8. What is the difference between a natural and contrived observation?

9. What is the experimental method of marketing research? Why is this method of research used less frequently than the survey and observation methods?

10. What is data analysis?

11. What is the fourth step in the marketing research process?

12. Identify the elements in a final marketing research report.

13. Does the implementation of research findings end the research process? Why or why not?

14. What is a management information system?

CRITICAL THINKING

1. Can business risks be eliminated by marketing research? Why or why not?

2. What sources of information would you use to identify the market for a new apparel and accessories store in your community?

3. Under natural observation, customers or employees do not know they are being observed. Do you think that this research technique is an invasion of privacy? Why or why not?

4. A store owner wants to know the effectiveness of window displays. Explain what variables the store owner would record during a natural observation.

5. Marketing research is growing in importance. What factors account for the increase in marketing research activities?

USING BASIC SKILLS

Math

1. A retailer conducts a traffic study to estimate yearly sales. Use the following data to estimate yearly sales for the retailer: 1,200 people pass the store each day, 5 percent enter the store and spend an average of $12, the store is open 315 days during the year.

2. Research indicates that 80 percent of the customers for a pizza store live within 1 mile of the store, another 15 percent live within 2 miles of the store, and the remaining 5 percent live within 5 miles of the store. Compute the number of customers who live within the various trading areas if the population of the area is 12,540.

Number of customers within 1 mile. _____

Number of customers between 1 and 2 miles of the store. _____

Number of customers between 2 and 5 miles from the store. _____

Number of customers within 2 miles of the store. _____

3. The manufacturer of Cheerios held a nationwide vote on important issues for kids across America. By election day November 8, 1988, 135,208 ballots were tabulated. From the results of the election, calculate the numbers that voted for their following favorite after-school activities:

playing outside (32%)   number of responses ____

watching TV (20%)   number of responses ____

playing sports (15%)   number of responses ____

reading (11%)   number of responses ____

doing homework (9%)   number of responses ____

other (13%)   number of responses ____

Communication

4. Write a 100-word memo to your instructor explaining the benefits of marketing research prior to the introduction of a new line of merchandise for your school store.

Human Relations

5. Your father would like to start a cottage security business for vacationers who close up their summer cottages for the winter. He feels that the absentee owners would like to have someone check on the buildings during the off-season to see if the furnaces are on and watch for signs of vandalism and storm damage. He is positive that he will be successful in this venture. You are not so sure. What kind of marketing research should your father perform before he starts this new business?

APPLICATION PROJECTS

1. Investigate a marketing research project for your community using the guidelines developed by National DECA for the Creative Marketing Project event. Topics could include downtown parking, community services, shoplifting, etc.

2. Investigate recent advertising research in the area of *hermeneutics* (the science of interpretation), *ethnography* (the study of cultures), or *semiotics* (the study of symbols). Give your results in a 200-word written report.

3. You are conducting research into the likes and dislikes of customers for a proposed frozen yogurt store in your community. Develop a list of ten survey questions to ask potential customers.

4. Identify a business to research. From the topics listed below, identify at least two secondary data sources for each of these items: size of market, characteristics of customers, income of customers, present sales volume of competitors, and information about trends in the industry.

5. You are the owner/operator of a local car wash. Design a ten-question survey to get information about the customers and their reaction to the service you provided.

6. Using the most recent *Survey of Buying Power* by Sales and Marketing Management and U.S. Census data, determine the following information about your community:
   a. population
   b. number of restaurants, retail stores, and gas stations, and the total sales for each
   c. number of households
   d. average family size
   e. average income
   f. estimated average age of the population
   g. average educational level

7. Based upon the research information you found in Application Project 6, develop a 200-word report on what new type of business might be successful in your community.

8. With direction from your instructor, interview customers in a mall or in your school store to determine how window displays affect their buying.

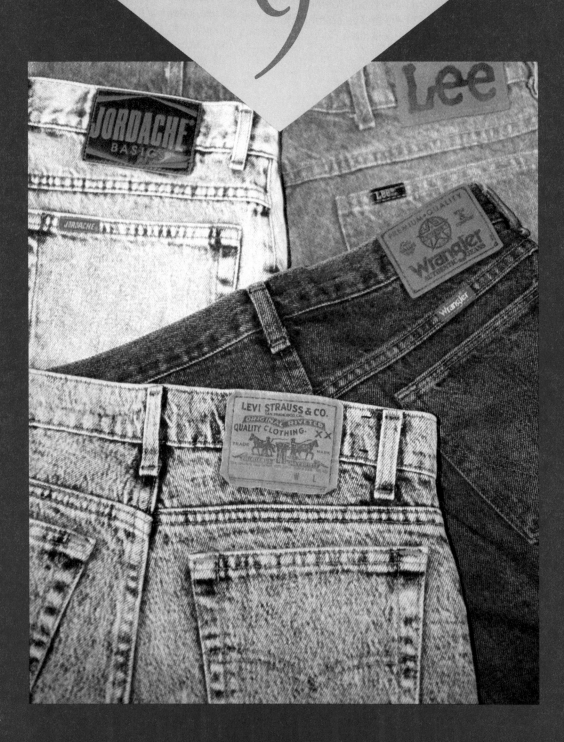

PRODUCT PLANNING

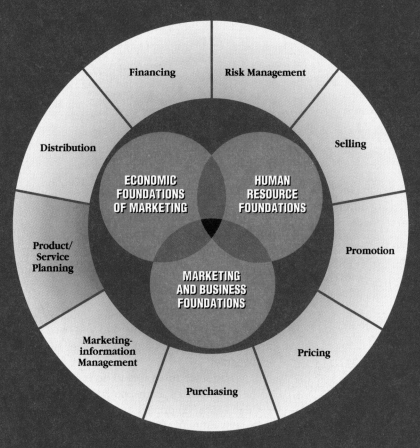

Financing

Risk Management

Distribution

Selling

ECONOMIC FOUNDATIONS OF MARKETING

HUMAN RESOURCE FOUNDATIONS

Product/ Service Planning

Promotion

MARKETING AND BUSINESS FOUNDATIONS

Marketing-information Management

Pricing

Purchasing

CHAPTERS
▼ ▼ ▼ ▼ ▼ ▼ ▼ ▼

After completing this chapter, you will be able to:

1. explain the nature and scope of product planning,

2. distinguish tangible, extended, and generic product features,

3. identify the various types of consumer and industrial products, and

4. list essential product plan elements for firms offering different types of goods and services.

WORDS TO KNOW

product planning
tangible product features
extended product features
generic product features
consumer goods
convenience goods
staples
impulse items
emergency goods
shopping goods
specialty goods
industrial goods

What Is Product Planning?

It's Saturday morning, and you have nothing for breakfast. No matter—there's a grocery store in the new mini-mall down the street.

The store turns out to be much smaller than you expected, the selection of items more limited. There's cereal, but only three kinds. There are milk and juice, but only in quarts. Your disappointment fades, however, with the aroma of freshly brewed coffee. You pour yourself a large cup on your way to the checkstand.

Walking home with your "breakfast," you make a mental note: this is not a place to do the weekly shopping. "That's handy information," you tell yourself. It's also good product planning.

Nature and Scope of Product Planning

Product planning encompasses all the decisions a business makes in the production and sale of its products, including those decisions relating to packaging, labeling, warranties, guarantees, branding, and product mix. A well-defined product plan allows a business to create sales opportunities, design appropriate marketing programs, develop effective advertising campaigns, coordinate the product mix offered to customers, add new products, and delete older products that no longer appeal to customers.

Product Features

Every product has features designed to satisfy the wants and needs of customers. Businesses usually divide these features into three categories—*tangible*, *extended*, and *generic*. It is a combination of all three that helps sell a product.

Tangible product features are those that can be seen or described with specifications, models, numbers, or names. Tangible features include the type of material used in the construction of an item, its size, color, taste, weight, and special qualities, such as performance efficiency.

Extended product features are the values, emotions, image, or special services that consumers expect with or from particular products. Values, emotions, and image include such things as sentimentality, love, convenience, prestige, status, and comfort. Service features range from familiar items, such as warranties, instructions for use, return policies, delivery, and repair, to such extras as cost-purchase training sessions and technical assistance.

Generic product features are those that relate to the customer's basic reasons for purchasing the product. Generic product features focus on what the product means to the customer in the broadest sense. For example, a car is purchased for transportation, a telephone for communication, a radio for entertainment, and a two-week cruise for recreation.

Steps in Product Planning

Developing a product plan involves four key steps. Each step centers on a particular set of decisions that must be made if a business is to differentiate its products from others and compete successfully. The steps are as follows:

1. Select the general type of product to manufacture or sell.
2. Specify the makeup of the product mix.
3. Develop any required packaging and labeling.
4. Choose the extended product features to be offered.

In this chapter, we will concern ourselves primarily with defining the various types of products that businesses can provide (Step 1). Product mix, packaging, and labeling (Steps 2 and 3) will be discussed in Chapter 36. Extended product features will be taken up in Chapter 37.

Product Selection

The first step in the product planning process, selecting the product type, is not as simple as it might initially seem. This is true whether the business doing the planning is a new one getting ready to market its first product or an established firm adding to its product line.

As you know, goods and services can be targeted to consumers or to industry. Within these categories, they can be manufactured for sale or rental, distributed directly or indirectly, and designed for impulse purchasing or careful comparison shopping. When a firm chooses any of these options, the choice affects multiple aspects of its product plan.

Consumer Goods

Consumer goods are products used by consumers for personal, family, or household purposes. Such goods are generally broken into three categories—*convenience goods, shopping goods,* and *specialty goods.* This classification is based on the time devoted to the purchase and the amount of knowledge required to make it.

Convenience Goods. *Convenience goods are inexpensive products that consumers purchase regularly, spending a minimum amount of time and effort on the purchase decision.* The most common convenience goods are grocery items.

The decision to purchase convenience goods can be made relatively quickly because it is based on past favorable experience with the product. Typically, however, the customer is not strongly committed to the product. If it is not available, he or she will accept a substitute. For example, if a customer usually buys Morton's salt but it is temporarily out of stock, he or she will readily switch to another brand. Neither product difference nor the purchase itself is deemed important enough to be worth a trip to another store.

Convenience goods can be further divided into *staples, impulse items,* and *emergency goods.* *Staples are basic food items that are used regularly and kept on hand at home in fairly large amounts.* They include such items as bread, milk, butter, eggs, flour, and sugar. *Impulse items are the kinds of goods that lend themselves to unplanned purchasing.* Such purchasing usually occurs because the items are placed in locations where they will get the customer's attention. Think of the eye-level displays surrounding checkstands in supermarkets. They are filled with such impulse items as candy, gum, magazines, and snacks. *Emergency goods are items purchased out of immediate need.* They might include allergy tablets during hay fever season, an ice scraper during a snowstorm, and a quart of oil during a regular fill-up at a service station.

Businesses that manufacture convenience goods must emphasize the time-saving features of their products. Product plans for convenience goods usually include several time-saving features. They are:

- easy to open,
- easy to use, and
- easy to dispose of after use.

Businesses that sell convenience goods should include the following elements in their product plans:

- convenient store locations with ample parking and easy accessibility to pedestrian and vehicular traffic;
- extended hours on weekdays and weekends so they can compete with convenience stores that are open 24 hours a day, 365 days a year;
- store layout that promotes self-service and quick purchase decision making;
- a wide assortment of product brands; and
- the heavy use of written and broadcast advertising, promotions, and in-store displays.

Shopping Goods. *Shopping goods are those purchased by consumers after a great deal of searching and comparing among similar products.* This process is much more time-consuming than shopping for convenience goods. Consumers must choose from a variety of sizes, colors, options, and prices. They must discern quality differences and decide which, if any, are important to them.

This process is further complicated by risk. Shopping goods are generally more expensive than convenience goods. They include at one end of the pricing scale such things as clothing, appliances, personal computers, and furniture, and at the other end of the scale vacations, automobiles, and houses. Because of their expense, such products are purchased less frequently. This means, in turn, that the customer may have had little or no personal experience with the brand or manufacturer. To reduce the risk of making an expensive mistake in these circumstances, the customer substitutes research for personal experience.

Businesses that manufacture shopping goods for sale to wholesalers and retailers must include the following features in their product plans:

- quality in the design, development, and manufacturing process;
- knowledgeable and well-trained sales representatives who are able to explain product features in detail and justify price differences;

REAL WORLD MARKETING

Dinner for the TV Generation

After World War II ended, an entrepreneur named Charles Swanson observed that 19 million women remained in the work force. He had the idea that they might need some help cooking meals—a notion that gave birth to Swanson's TV Dinners. The first 5,000 dinners hit supermarket frozen food sections in December, 1953—a time when a new invention called television was becoming popular. The verdict from a Swanson panel of experts—1,200 housewives and a few hotel chefs—was stomach-satisfying approval. The frozen TV dinner has become an American institution.

- extensive brand advertising to emphasize how their product is superior to their competitors' products;
- special promotional activities, such as point-of-purchase displays and manufacturer rebates; and
- warranties and special after-purchase features, including credit, technical assistance, and ease of shipping and delivery.

Businesses that sell shopping goods to the final consumer should include the following elements in their product plans:

- a wide assortment of prices, colors, sizes, and brands;

- a trained and experienced sales staff to explain the product features of several different brands;
- advertising that stresses store image and the different brands and products carried; and
- warranties, guarantees, and after-purchase services (such as credit, repair, and technical assistance) provided by the retailers and, in some cases, by the manufacturers.

Specialty Goods. *Specialty goods are those sought by customers who desire a particular product and/or brand.* The customers for specialty goods are so loyal to a particular brand that they will not accept a substitute. Indeed, they will even pay

C A S E   C H A L L E N G E

If You Liked the Theme Parks, You'll Love the Stores

The Walt Disney Company has been enormously successful in the entertainment field. The company owns movie production facilities and theme parks, such as Disneyland, Disneyworld, and Epcot Center. Recently, the firm announced its entrance into the retail field to market clothing, mugs, and other merchandise bearing the likenesses of Disney characters.

The Disney Company is not entirely new to the retail business. It has been operating similar stores in the Disney theme parks in California and Florida for years. Now, however, customers will be able to patronize such stores when they visit their local shopping malls.

The new stores are not just toy stores for kids. They cater to adults, too. For example, they offer ceramic figurines of Disney characters for the serious adult collector. During the Christmas season, they provide a line of holiday merchandise, such as tree ornaments, to lure adults into the store. They also stock an assortment of

T-shirts, knapsacks, videos, mugs, books, and other items that are as colorful as any Disney cartoon classic. Finally, each store has the look and wonderland atmosphere of Disneyland that children and adults both enjoy.

1. Speculate about the product plan formulated by the Disney Company for its new stores.
   a. What elements do you think were included to appeal to children? to appeal to adults?
   b. What extended services might have been included for shoppers?
2. What problems might the new stores create for existing Disney facilities? Why do you think the company proceeded anyway?
3. How does the target market for the mall stores differ from the target market for the theme park stores?
4. Do you think the new Disney stores will be successful? Why or why not?

There are three types of consumer service businesses—rented-goods, owned-goods, and non-goods. Into which category does each of the businesses shown here fit? Suggest two more examples of each type, excluding those given in your text.

more or go out of their way to purchase the product of their choice. For example, some customers will only buy Ford Mustangs, Levi's jeans, or Hunt's ketchup, though other firms make similar products that are arguably of the same quality.

Consumer goods are viewed differently by different customers. What are convenience goods to some are shopping goods to others and specialty goods to still others. Consider an example. Cold tablets are viewed by many customers as convenience goods.

These customers will purchase any brand of cold tablet or even a generic product. Some customers, however, treat cold tablets as shopping goods, carefully reading the ingredients and evaluating the features of different products. Finally, some customers demand a particular cold remedy, such as Contac cold capsules, and will buy no other.

Manufacturers strive to develop products that will be perceived as specialty goods by consumers. That is why they spend so much money on advertising and brand promotion.

Consumer Services

There are three kinds of consumer service—rented-goods services, owned-goods services, and non-goods services.

A *rented-goods service* provides a product that the customer rents and uses. Examples include firms that rent automobiles, trailers, office space, apartments, videotapes, and tuxedos.

The rented-goods customer signs an agreement and pays a fee to the business for the use of the rented item for a specified time. A deposit or prepayment is also frequently required of the customer to insure against damage to or loss of the leased goods. An example of such a prepayment is a security deposit on an apartment. Sometimes a credit card imprint or a blank check is accepted in place of a cash payment.

An *owned-goods service* is one that alters, improves, or repairs products already owned by a customer. Examples include a car wash, a landscaping service, a shoe repair shop, a dry cleaner, and a television repair business.

A *non-goods service* provides personal and professional services to customers for a fee. These services can include advice, assistance, or physical treatment. Examples include those services provided by doctors, lawyers, accountants, realtors, stockbrokers, insurance agents, teachers, and babysitters.

Businesses that provide consumer services should include the following elements in their product plans:

- maintenance and constant reevaluation of established standards,
- flexible rather than fixed pricing (prices are usually stated in ranges),
- personal selling,
- promotion through word-of-mouth and testimonials; and

- emphasis on professional skills and image to encourage repeat business.

Industrial Goods

Industrial goods are those purchased for the production of other goods or for resale to consumers. They include machinery, raw materials, and supplies. Such goods are purchased by manufacturers, wholesalers, retailers, government, and nonprofit organizations.

Consider these examples of industrial goods and the organizations that use them. An automobile manufacturer buys steel to build auto bodies. A department store buys television sets for resale to its customers. A construction firm buys a bulldozer for excavation work. An area vocational center buys floor wax, cleaners, and vacuum equipment for building maintenance.

Because the industrial market is so large, the goods produced for it are frequently divided into three groupings: *installations and accessory equipment; raw materials, components, and fabricated parts;* and *industrial supplies.* Each of these subcategories of products has its own peculiar planning needs. Producers in all three areas, however, share one common trait—they seek out their customers rather than having their customers seek them out. Therefore, influencing store shopping behavior does not figure in their product plans.

Installations and Accessory Equipment. Installations and accessory equipment are used to *make* products. In other words, they are part

---

REAL WORLD MARKETING

Tutzi

As the demand for his nameless chocolate chews grew, candymaker Leo Hirschfield was faced with a delicious problem: what to call the little moneymakers. His first thought was to name them after his childhood sweetheart in Austria, Tutzi. However, figuring Americans would find it hard to pronounce the word, Hirschfield changed the spelling to Tootsie Roll.

of the production process, not part of the product itself. Installations and accessory equipment are expensive items that have a long, useful life. Because of their relative permanence, they are considered a capital investment. An example would be an auto manufacturing plant with its lathes, drill presses, computers, and robotic equipment.

Businesses that build installations and sell equipment to manufacturers should consider the following factors in their product plans:

- careful hiring practices directed toward building a skilled work force;
- emphasis on the product features of durability, dependability, and long life; and
- provision of customer follow-up, technical assistance, and equipment and facility maintenance.

Raw Materials, Components, and Fabricated Parts.

Raw materials, components, and fabricated parts are items used in the production process, either by being consumed or by becoming part of the final product. For business purposes, they are treated as direct material expenses rather than capital investment.

Raw materials include unprocessed items from mines, forests, or farms. Examples include iron ore, limestone, oil, coal, wood, grain, cotton, and other agricultural products.

Component parts are items that have already undergone some kind of manufacturing process, changing them from their original form. Steel, cement, wood pulp, flour, textiles, and chemicals are examples of component parts. Typically, these items undergo further changes before reaching the consumer. Wood pulp, for example, is made into wood panels, flour into bread, and textiles into clothing.

Fabricated parts are items that are placed in products without further change. Examples include fans put into air conditioning equipment; glass windshields, radios, and batteries installed in cars; and electronic circuitry incorporated in television sets and computers.

Businesses that sell raw materials, components, and fabricated parts should include the following elements in their product plans:

- mechanisms for providing prompt and efficient shipping to customers,
- strict quality control measures,

- maintenance of an active and effective sales force to bring in business (especially repeat orders), and
- emphasis on securing long-term contracts to meet all of a customer's needs for a particular raw material or product.

Industrial Supplies.

Industrial supplies are items that support or facilitate the use of a business's installations, equipment, and materials. They are not part of the final product. Rather than contributing directly to its manufacture, they are treated as indirect expense items in the firm's budget.

Industrial supplies include such things as computer paper; stationery; pens and pencils; paint; cleaning products; and repair items such as nuts and bolts, tape, and caulking compound. Unlike installations, raw materials purchased in bulk, and components, industrial supplies are all relatively inexpensive. As such, they require little time-consuming decision making for their purchase. Still, there are other considerations that businesses selling such products should include in their product plans. They are:

- mechanisms to ensure the availability of sufficient product to meet customer demand,
- simplification of ordering procedures, and
- prompt delivery.

Industrial Services

There are two types of industrial services—maintenance and repair, and business advisory.

Maintenance and repair services include general cleaning, repair, painting, and decorating. Examples include a company that contracts to maintain the heating and air conditioning units of a manufacturing firm, a janitorial service that cleans government buildings, and a computer repair business that services local school districts.

Business advisory services include management consulting, engineering, legal, and accounting businesses. Consider these examples. An interior design firm is hired to perform "office landscaping." An engineering firm is hired by the state to assist in bridge design. An accounting service is hired to help prepare tax returns. Since the quality of industrial services varies with the provider, most firms have in-house personnel to monitor and evaluate the work done.

VOCABULARY REVIEW

Use each of these vocabulary terms in a sentence related to the chapter content.

product planning	staples
tangible product features	impulse items
extended product features	emergency goods
generic product features	shopping goods
consumer goods	specialty goods
convenience goods	industrial goods

FACT AND IDEA REVIEW

1. What is meant by product planning?

2. Name three types of product features and provide two examples of each.

3. List the four steps in the product planning process.

4. In what ways are convenience goods, shopping goods, and specialty goods alike? How do they differ from each other?

5. Name three product planning considerations for businesses that sell convenience goods and three for businesses that manufacture convenience goods.

6. Distinguish a non-goods service from an owned-goods service.

7. Name three product planning considerations for businesses that provide consumer services.

8. What are industrial goods?

9. How do industrial supplies differ from other forms of industrial goods?

10. What are the two types of industrial services?

CRITICAL THINKING

1. Why is information about how products are viewed by customers important to product planning?

2. How could a business that knew its products were viewed as specialty goods by its customers develop a product plan to serve them?

3. For each of the items below, list one generic and several tangible and extended product features. Explain how these features might affect product planning for the item.

   a. business suit

   b. mechanic's coveralls

   c. wristwatch

   d. a centralized air conditioning system

   e. microwave oven

   f. travel agency

4. Discuss how product planning might differ for a large retailer and a large manufacturer. For your analysis, choose firms that are familiar to you.

USING BASIC SKILLS

Math

1. An electrical appliance and repair business charges $12 an hour for labor.

   a. What would be the bill for 6¾ hours of work?

   b. Assume that in the above situation the business used $209 for equipment and supplies, $62 worth of wire, and employed an apprentice at a trainee rate of $5 an hour. What would be the total charges to the customer?

2. You work in a video store that sells Nintendo video games. Three of the most popular games include Mike Tyson's Punch-out, which retails for $70 each; W.W.F. Wrestle-mania, which retails for $45 each; and Double Dare, which retails for $40 each. If a customer buys three Punch-outs, two Wrestle-manias, and one Double Dare, how much is she spending for all of these video games? Your total should include a 6 percent sales tax.

Communication

3. Develop a written product plan of about three pages for a truck company that is planning to diversify into the building and selling of buses. Identify possible target markets, product features, and considerations relating to advertising, sales, promotion, and staffing. Explain your reasons for including each element in your plan.

Human Relations

4. You are a buyer of ready-to-wear for a large urban department store. Early one afternoon, you're confronted by an exasperated customer who's ready to walk out of your department because of the clutter of merchandise. She complains that too many sizes, colors, and styles are jammed together on too many racks with too little space between them. "I came here to shop for a few bargains, not to arm-wrestle with jogging suits," she fumes. How do you explain to her the dilemma retailers face in deciding just how much merchandise to stock? What's too much of an item? What's not enough? What are the costs and benefits for customers and retailers alike of carrying a large assortment of items?

APPLICATION PROJECTS

1. Select five items from your kitchen for a product analysis. Identify at least five tangible and two extended features for each.
2. Do some preliminary comparison shopping for an appliance you are interested in buying. Find the most recent review of the item in *Consumer Reports*. Using it, identify five product features that are important to you. Based on those features, select the brand and model you think would meet your needs. How would a manufacturer and a retailer use this information in product planning? Prepare a written or oral report explaining the reasons for your decision.
3. Do a survey of service businesses in your community, using the Yellow Pages as a guide.
   a. Identify five rented-goods service businesses in your area, and name the products they rent.
   b. Identify five owned-goods service businesses in your area. Name the products with which

they deal and the specific services they provide.
   c. Identify five non-goods service businesses in your area, and describe the types of services they provide.
   d. From your research, how many of the businesses cater to consumers and how many cater to industrial buyers? Explain.
4. Choose a retail business. Think about the mix of products you would choose to stock it. What kinds of shopping goods, convenience goods, and specialty goods would you carry, and how many of each would you put on your shelves? Write a 200-word report on your business explaining your choices in terms of the market you want to reach and the image you want to project.
5. Service businesses of all kinds are growing. With your classmates, brainstorm ideas for the types of services that will be in high demand in the next decade. Choose four of these businesses, tell what kinds of services they will provide, what market they will serve, and why the demand will grow.
6. Choose a manufacturing business, such as an electronic equipment manufacturer. Describe the types of products they produce (convenience, shopping, or specialty). Write a 200-word paper on the features of the products and the elements that should be included in a product plan.
7. Items that were once considered shopping goods sometimes become convenience goods over the course of time. In the early part of the twentieth century, for example, the telephone was a specialty item. Now, most people would not do without one. Working in groups of four to five, list at least three products that are specialty goods today but may become convenience goods in 50 years or less.

Branding, Packaging, and Labeling

OBJECTIVES

After completing this chapter, you will be able to:

1. identify the elements and characteristics of product mix,

2. explain the role of branding in product planning,

3. list the principal functions of product packages, and

4. summarize common product labeling requirements.

WORDS TO KNOW

product mix
product line
product item
product width
product depth
mixed-brand strategy
package
label

Did you ever notice that in certain sections of a supermarket one company's products seem to dominate? This happens because of the way the various items are packaged—the label is colorful; the brand name or logo stands out; the package sizes, shapes, and materials are what you expect and need for proper storage and convenient use.

What you have discovered is the importance of branding, packaging, and labeling to promotion and sales. In this chapter, you will explore these three areas, with an emphasis on incorporating them early in the product planning process.

Product Mix

The second step in product planning involves determining *product mix*. *The different products that a company makes or sells compose its **product mix***. A large manufacturer may have hundreds of products in its product mix. Procter and Gamble, for example, makes hand soaps, body lotions, dish detergents, laundry detergents, shampoos, cosmetics, powders, deodorants, and suntan products—just to name a few!

A retailer must carefully plan and evaluate its product mix. The types and number of products and brands to be carried must be based on the image the business wants to project and the market it is trying to serve. Customers want a good selection of merchandise. Nevertheless, additional products or brands may not increase sales. In fact, it may take away from existing sales.

Product Lines and Items

*A **product line** is a group of closely related products manufactured and/or sold by a business.* Examples include all the different car models produced by Ford, all the cereals produced by Kellogg's, and all the cake mixes produced by Pillsbury.

Retailers frequently sell more than one product line. A sporting goods store, for example, might carry both the Spalding and Wilson lines of tennis rackets. A supermarket might stock both the Libby and Del Monte canned fruit lines. A video store might sell the Kodak, Memorex, and Scotch videocassette product lines.

*A **product item** is a specific model, brand, or size of product within a product line.* Typically, retailers carry several product items for each product line they sell. For example, a department store that carries the Guess? jeans product line will have an assortment of sizes and styles for both men and women. A computer store handling the Apple computer product line would carry several Apple models, such as the Apple IIGS, the Macintosh Plus, and the Macintosh SE.

Product Width and Depth

A product mix is defined by the *width* and *depth* of its product offerings. ***Product width** refers to the number of different product lines a business manu-*factures or sells. **Product depth** refers to the number of product items offered within each product line.

For example, a retailer that stocks several different brands of jeans, such as Jordache, Levi's, Lee, and Wrangler, is demonstrating product width. The product depth is the number of sizes, price ranges, colors, or styles for each different brand of jeans.

Both manufacturers and retailers must decide on the width and depth of merchandise assortment to carry. Assortment strategies vary with the type of business. For example, Red Lobster restaurants specialize in seafood dinners. They have great depth within a narrow product line. Other restaurants offer broader menus that include steak, chicken, and pasta dinners as well as seafood. Their product assortment shows great width but probably has much less depth than Red Lobster's.

Determining the kind of product mix a business should manufacture or sell involves answering many questions. What kind of product offerings do the customers want? How have competitors reacted to existing products? How many product lines and product items should be carried? Should existing product lines be expanded, contracted, or even deleted? What kind of image does each product and each product line project? What kind of image does the business want to project?

The overall objectives of each type of business help to answer these questions. Some possible business objectives for manufacturers and retailers include:

- increasing sales by adding new product lines and items,
- maintaining market share by developing new product lines, and
- increasing sales for a product by creating or identifying new product uses.

Branding

Almost every product has a brand. Some brands are well known worldwide. For example, in a 1988 study of consumers in Western Europe, Japan, and the United States, the most recognized and respected brands were (in order) Coke, IBM, Sony, Porsche, McDonald's, Disney, Honda, Toyota, Seiko, BMW, Volkswagen, Mercedes, Pepsi, Kleenex, Nestle, and

Rolex. Top brands among U.S. consumers alone were Coke, Campbell's, Pepsi, AT&T, McDonald's, American Express, Kellogg's, IBM, Levi's, Sears, Disney, Hershey's, NBC, and MasterCard.

Role of Brands in Product Planning

When new products are developed or changes are made to existing products, a company must decide on the market that will be served by the product and create the product's image accordingly through its design, pricing, distribution, and promotion.

For example, Ford Motor Company manufactures several different product lines to serve different markets. The Lincoln is marketed as a luxury car for the affluent customer. The Ford product line is designed to appeal to the middle-class customer.

The Ford Division, of course, must also make brand decisions on the number of product offerings to have within each product line. The number of products within each brand (Escort, Fairlane, Taurus, Thunderbird, Probe) and styles (four-door, two-door, convertible, hard-top) are also planned to meet the needs of the specific target market.

The higher-priced Ford might be similar in cost and performance to a Lincoln. However, the manufacturer has created a perceived difference in the minds of customers through the use of branding and other marketing strategies. Retailers can also create this perceived difference through the combinations of brands they carry and the marketing strategies they use.

REAL WORLD MARKETING

The Great Green Hope

In developing an ad campaign for Minnesota Canning Company's line of canned vegetables, Chicago's Leo Burnett agency hit on the idea of using an American folk hero. A Paul Bunyan type, the agency felt, might help sell the product line. The friendly giant they created, with his green scales and resounding "ho-ho-ho," caught on with the American public. So, the Minnesota Canning Company changed its name to Green Giant.

Corporate Symbols. Recall from Chapter 19 that there are four categories of brands—brand names, brand marks, trade characters, and trademarks. These are often combined to form a firm's *corporate symbol*—a firm's name, logo, and/or trade characters.

Because corporate symbols help establish a company image (traditional or progressive, for example), they are important to product planning. If a company's corporate symbol is well-recognized and accurately represents the company's desired image, it becomes a permanent part of the company's product planning.

Nevertheless, corporate symbols are sometimes changed when a business adds new product lines; seeks new markets for its products; or seeks to modify, simplify, or improve its image. In 1984, for example, almost 900 U.S. corporations voluntarily adopted new names.

Corporate names are also changed as a result of such external forces as lawsuits and court decisions. For example, the divestiture of AT&T's Bell system led to corporate name changes for regional Bell companies.

National Brands. The four brand categories—brand names, brand marks, trade characters, and trademarks—can be used independently or in combination with each other to establish a distinct brand.

National brands (also called manufacturer brands) are nationally recognized as a result of national advertising. Some national brands are so popular that they help attract customers to a business that sells them.

National brands generate the majority of sales for most product categories. For example, 70 percent of all food products, 65 percent of all appliances, 80 percent of all gasoline, and 100 percent of all automobiles are sold under national brands.

National brands not only identify a given product but also indicate a standard quality and price. They appeal to customers who want consistent quality, dependable product performance, status—and who will not take risks with unknown goods and services.

Private Brands. As you learned in Chapter 19, *private brands* appeal to customers who want the quality and performance of national brands at a lower price. Many large department stores and retail chains now have private brands.

CASE CHALLENGE

Slacks by Any Other Name

Sometimes a company is forced to come up with a creative solution to a serious marketing problem. In 1981, this happened to Haggar, a well-known men's clothing manufacturer. Haggar had been receiving complaints from retail department and specialty stores that customers were buying Haggar products for less at discount stores.

The company dealt with the problem by creating another line of menswear. The new line had the Haggar quality look but a different name. The name selected, Reed St. James, had an upscale tone. The Reed St. James product sold at a wholesale price 11–12 percent below its higher-priced Haggar cousin.

The principal buyers of the new line were such mass marketers as Gemco, Venture, Target, and Gold Circle. They sold the new line for 20–25 percent less than the traditional department stores' retail price for merchandise bearing the Haggar label. The idea not only solved Haggar's immediate problem but also expanded and diversified the company's product mix.

1. Why was it important for Haggar to protect its national brand?
2. How could Haggar sell a product of equal quality for 11–12 percent less than its regular wholesale price?
3. How did Haggar benefit from the new marketing strategy? How did its wholesale customers benefit? its retail customers?

Private brands are popular because they usually carry higher gross margins (and are thus more profitable for the seller) than national brands. They are better controlled by retailers because they cannot be sold by competitors and thus can lead to retailer (rather than to manufacturer) loyalty.

Some private brands, such as Sears' Kenmore line of appliances and Craftsmen tools, have become so popular and respected that they rival national brands in sales and customer recognition.

Unbranded Merchandise. Some especially price-conscious customers are unwilling to pay the prices for either national or private label brands. These customers often purchase generic products. Recall from Chapter 19 that these are "no frills" products that carry no brand name and are generally sold in supermarkets and discount stores. Such products are often priced 30–50 percent lower than nationally advertised brands and 10–15 percent lower than the private label brands offered by some retailers. Generics cost less because they are not heavily advertised or promoted.

Generic products were first introduced by the Jewel supermarkets in Chicago. Beginning with only a few products, they have now expanded into more than 320 product categories, including vitamins, auto parts, toys, and T-shirts. They have captured more than 10 percent of the sales volume for canned fruit cocktail, garbage bags, nondairy creamers, paper towels, frozen apple juice, butter, and vitamins. Generics are now offered in more than 250 chains throughout the United States. More than 75 percent of all U.S. supermarkets carry at least some generic items in their stores.

You can see that product planners must know their markets and their customers well. The make-up of the brands they carry (national, private, or generic) is a direct result of customer likes and dislikes. By understanding buyer preferences for certain products, a business can provide a proper balance of products for its target market.

Branding Strategy

Some manufacturers and retailers use a *mixed-brand strategy* to sell products. *A **mixed-brand strategy** is one based on the simultaneous offering of national, private, and generic brands*. For example, Union Carbide produces generic garbage bags, while its Glad Division advertises that its Glad garbage bags "are superior to the thin, bargain bags." In this way, Union Carbide can maximize its profits by selling a generic product without damaging the reputation and hopefully the sales of its branded product. A mixed-brand strategy allows a business to reach several target markets, maintain brand loyalty, and increase the overall product mix offered by customers.

Packaging and Its Functions

A package is the physical container or wrapping for a product. Because a package represents the size, shape, and final appearance of a product at the time of sale, it is important to product planning. In fact, it is estimated that some 10 percent of a product's retail price is spent on package development, design, and the package itself.

A package does much more than hold a product. It has many functions, all of which will be explained below. Companies take great care in designing or re-designing the packages for their products. For example, Domino's, a pizza chain, changed from a square pizza delivery box to an eight-sided "octabox" container. It took two years of study and 50 prototypes to come up with a distinctive package that is cheaper to produce, keeps pizzas hotter longer, and prevents the pizza topping from sticking to the top of the box.

Promoting and Selling the Product

Customer reaction to a product's package and brand name largely determines the success or failure of a product in the marketplace. A well-designed package, for example, is a powerful point-of-purchase selling device because it can make a product stand out from its competition. With stores becoming ever more self-service oriented in their layout, this function is especially important.

Attractive, colorful, and artistic packages have promotional value, too. Because a package carries a brand name, it serves as a constant reminder to the customer of the product's manufacturer.

A better container can even create new sales or help to minimize possible lost sales to competitors for the same products. For example, pump toothpaste containers were designed to be neater, cleaner, easier to use, and less wasteful than toothpaste tubes. The new containers have not replaced the tubes. However, they now provide a choice for people who prefer this type of package, and they appear along with toothpaste tubes on display shelves. Thus, pump type dispensers create new sales for some individuals and also prevent lost sales due to competitors offering similar products.

Defining Product Identity

Packages are often used to invoke prestige, convenience, status, or other positive product attributes in the eyes of the customer. Such packages can be a crucial part of an overall marketing strategy for a product—particularly its advertising component. Examples of such packaging include the use of egg-shaped containers for L'Eggs stockings, Hunt's squeezable plastic ketchup bottle, checkered lids for Smucker's jellies and preserves, and the creation of artistic, distinctive containers for women's and men's fragrances.

Providing Information

The package also provides information for the customer. Many packages give directions for using the product and information about its contents, nutritional value (where applicable), and potential hazards.

For certain items, preprinted prices and inventory codes are placed on packages to assist with inventory control and management. An example of this is the Universal Product Code used in the food industry.

Meeting Customer Needs

Product packages often come in various sizes to meet the needs of different market segments. So-called family packs of food and grocery items are designed to meet the needs of larger families. Smaller packages are made for individuals. Specific examples include multi-packs of beverages such as soda and juice, single-serving cans of soup, and family meals at fast-food outlets.

Packages and package design must also keep up with changing life-styles. When designing packages,

A package does more than just hold the product. How do the containers shown here fulfill other key package functions?

product planners analyze customer life-styles. For example, two-income families and singles are two growing market segments, both of which place a premium on time and convenience. Knowing this has led product planners to design microwaveable dinners that can be prepared quickly in neatly designed packages that minimize or even eliminate the use of other pans, pots, or dinnerware to make and serve the meal.

Ensuring Safe Use

A package can improve product safety for the customer. Many products formerly packaged in glass, for example, now come in plastic containers. This eliminates potential injuries from breakage.

To avoid product tampering, many nonprescription drugs, cosmetics, and food items are now sold in tamper-resistant packages. These include jars and plastic containers with sealed lids and *blister-packs*— packages with preformed plastic bubbles surrounding individual items arranged on a cardboard backing.

Countless other products are packaged in child-proof containers. These have lids that make them more difficult to open and thus reduce the chances of accidental spills and poisonings.

Protecting the Product

A package must protect a product during shipping, storage, and display. It must also protect the product from breakage and (in the case of food items) from spoilage.

Product planners know that a poorly designed package that does not protect the product will cost a business money for goods that can't be sold. Also, a damaged or spoiled product creates a bad image and leads to a reduction in future sales.

Basic protective materials for packages include cardboard, glass, metal, plastic, and wood. Food products, for example, are typically sold in boxes, metal cans, glass bottles and jars, and plastic containers. Variations on these basic forms include aerosol cans and pump dispensers.

Airtight containers retard spoilage. These include lidded containers and sealed wraps of foil or plastic.

Products such as yogurt, cheese, lunch meat, and salad dressings are packaged this way.

Labeling

*A **label** is an information tag, wrapper, seal, or imprinted message that is attached to a product or its package*. Labeling plays a major role in product planning strategy. Its main functions are to inform customers about a product's contents and directions for use, and to protect businesses from legal liability for mishaps involving their products. Fear of litigation, consumer pressure, government regulations, and concern for consumer safety have all led manufacturers to place more information on their labels and packages.

Labels often contain a brand name, logo, ingredients, directions, and special promotional messages. Many package labels also must meet local, state, and federal standards. The federal Fair Packaging and Labeling Act (1966) was passed to protect consumers from deceptive labeling. This law states that product packages must tell customers exactly what the package contains. The act covers most products sold in supermarkets. It requires, for example, that food packages list all ingredients in descending order of weight or volume. Nutrition labeling must also appear on any product that makes a health or nutritional claim. Examples include low-fat or sugar-free foods.

Labels usually provide consumers with instructions for the proper use and care of products. They also give manufacturers a convenient place to communicate warranty information and product-use warnings. For example, notices of electrical hazard, flammability, and poisonous ingredients are required on the labels of certain categories of products.

The Food and Drug Administration (FDA) also requires the manufacturers of certain products to place health warnings on their packages. For example, beginning in 1989, all alcoholic beverages had to carry the following statement on their labels: "According to the Surgeon General, women should not drink alcoholic beverages during pregnancy because of the risk of birth defects. Consumption of alcoholic beverages impairs the ability to drive a car or operate machinery and may cause health problems." Similar warnings of health risks have been required for years on cigarettes.

VOCABULARY REVIEW

Write one or two paragraphs describing a line of products that your family uses. Incorporate these vocabulary terms.

product mix	product depth
product line	mixed-brand strategy
product item	package
product width	label

FACT AND IDEA REVIEW

1. What is meant by the term *product mix*?

2. Explain the difference between a product line and a product item.

3. Explain the difference between product width and product depth.

4. Name six brands that are known and respected worldwide.

5. Suggest three reasons why corporate symbols might be changed.

6. In what product areas and among what kinds of retailers have generics taken hold?

7. List six functions that a product's package serves.

8. Identify three kinds of information commonly found on product labels.

CRITICAL THINKING

1. Procter and Gamble, the nation's largest advertiser, introduced a new line of generic, lower-priced paper towels without advertising support. What was the company's strategy? What are the arguments in its favor? What are the arguments against it?

2. New product names must be chosen carefully. They should be aimed at a specific need and an existing market, rather than creating a market with a name. Explain this distinction by comparing the product name "Lean Cuisine" with the product name "Yuppie Yummies."

3. Child-proof packages have a problem: many of them tend to be adult-proof, too. Do some supplemental product planning for an over-the-counter drug that is packaged in this manner—aspirin, for example. Address the problems of older people in opening the packages. Suggest some ways product manufacturers can help.

4. The ultimate product package is the grocery bag. Today, many supermarkets are switching from paper bags to biodegradable plastic bags. Try to reconstruct the product planning behind this move. What are the economic and environmental reasons for the switch?

USING BASIC SKILLS

Math

1. Robinson & Perry Advertising Agency billed Sky High Air Cargo Service $3,500 for the development of Sky High's corporate symbol. Robinson & Perry's designer was paid $1,500 for her creative work on this project. Her salary was what percentage of the entire amount?

Communication

2. Food industry groups favor irradiation of certain foods to kill insects. They argue that the procedure is safe, that it does no harm to either the food or the consumer. Consumer groups, however, are not so sure. They argue that the irradiation destroys nutrients, kills beneficial microorganisms, and thus leaves the food susceptible to spoilage. Research the issue. Then prepare a statement of your own position on the issue, framed as a newspaper or television editorial.

Human Relations

3. You're working a check stand at the local supermarket. A customer politely but emphatically requests that you enter all product and price codes by hand and avoid passing any of his

purchases over the laser scanner, which he believes is harmful. What do you do? It's the 5 p.m. rush, there are other customers in line, and you're under great pressure to keep things moving as quickly as possible. How would you deal with the customer? How would you deal with any of the others in line who complain about your handling of the situation?

APPLICATION PROJECTS

1. Identify five companies that have changed their names within the last five years. Give the new name and the reason for the change. Then describe the new image that the company is trying to project.

2. Identify five household items commonly purchased in a grocery store or supermarket. Note the brand name, the elements of the product's corporate symbol, the packaging materials used, and any required labeling elements (health warnings, for example). Then write a one- or two-paragraph description of how each product's package performs the basic package functions listed in this chapter.

3. Make a survey of grocery and drug products, noting any warning labels that appear. Try to find at least a dozen different types of products that carry such labels. Then write a three-page report describing the nature of the warnings (and the products carrying them), their placement and prominence, and your evaluation of their effectiveness.

4. Visit a store that carries a variety of items, such as a grocery store or electronics store. Choose three products, such as laundry detergent or tape recorders, and evaluate the product width and depth of each. Explain how the selection increases or decreases the potential sales of those products.

5. Your store offers a wide but shallow product range. You think it will do better with more depth, but you only have so much capital to increase your inventory. Using what you have learned up to this point about advertising, display, marketing, and sales, write a short paper explaining how you will decide which products you will cut and which you will add.

6. Working in small groups, discuss the advantages and disadvantages of offering a narrow but deep product selection and a wide but shallow product selection. Present your findings to the class.

7. Research generic products—when they were introduced, how they affect sales of brand name products, and their quality. Write a 200-word report on the results of your research.

8. Some consumer groups say that generic prescription drugs are not as good as name brand prescription drugs. Research this issue and write a 200-word report describing your findings. Include your opinion on the subject and explain why you feel the way you do.

37

After completing this chapter, you will be able to:

1. distinguish different types of warranties,

2. explain the importance of warranties to product planning,

3. identify additional extended product features,

4. summarize the major provisions of consumer and product safety legislation, and

5. describe how businesses can reduce their risk of being sued for product liability.

WORDS TO KNOW

warranty
express warranty
full warranty
limited warranty
implied warranty
warranty of merchantability
warranty of fitness for a particular
  purpose
disclaimer
extended service contracts
lemon laws

Extended Product Features

LIMITED THREE YEAR WARRANTY

1 Please mail the attached Warranty Registration Card within ten (10) days after you purchase this garment. Gore warrants the GORE-TEX® fabric in this garment against delamination of fabric from the GORE-TEX® membrane and against leakage if the major cause of leakage is membrane failure for three (3) years from the date of purchase. Gore will repair or replace this garment free of charge if it does not meet this warranty. ALL OTHER EXPRESS WARRANTIES ARE DISCLAIMED AND NO IMPLIED WARRANTIES ARE INTENDED. Any implied warranties are limited to three (3) years from date of purchase. UNDER NO CIRCUMSTANCES WILL GORE BE RESPONSIBLE FOR INCIDENTAL OR CONSEQUENTIAL DAMAGES. This warranty gives you specific legal rights; you may also have other legal rights which vary from state to state. Some states do not allow limitations on how long an implied warranty will last or the exclusion of incidental or consequential damages, so these limitations may not apply to you.

2 This warranty covers defects arising in normal use only and does not cover fabric or membrane damage from misuse, negligence, accident, chemicals or fire. This warranty does not cover any part of the garment other than the GORE-TEX® fabric. Gore does not manufacture garments; the seams and other parts of the garments are the manufacturer's responsibility.

3 Gore will repair or replace this garment without charge to you if it fails to perform pursuant to this warranty. Call 1-800-638-9800 toll-free to obtain a return authorization number and return instructions, or if you have any questions. We cannot honor warranty claims without an authorization number.

4 This warranty is made by W.L. Gore & Associates, Inc., Fabrics Division, 3 Blue Ball Road, P.O. Box 1130, Elkton, Maryland 21921.

GORE-TEX® is a Registered Trademark of W.L. Gore & Associates, Inc.

GORE·TEX®
fabric

GORE·TEX® REGISTRATION

O ne of the most common extended features that customers expect manufacturers to provide is a warranty. This is a promise to stand behind the materials, construction, and performance of a product for a certain period of time.

In this chapter, you will learn about warranties and extended service contracts. You will study the principal federal and state statutes governing these and other product features. Finally, you will learn about product liability suits and what businesses can do to prevent them.

Warranties

A **warranty** is a promise, or guarantee, given to a customer that a product will meet certain standards. Typically, these standards apply to materials, workmanship, and/or performance.

A *guarantee* is another term for warranty. The major difference in the use of the two terms is in the promotion of goods and services. For example, the term guarantee (or guaranteed) is usually used for promotional phrases, such as "money-back guarantee," "guaranteed not to shrink more than three percent," "guaranteed for 1,000 average hours," or "satisfaction guaranteed."

Warranty text is usually framed as a series of specific promises, such as "Zenith warrants that it will repair, replace, or adjust any parts, excluding the picture tube, that are found to be defective." All warranties set time or use limits for coverage. (The most familiar language is that usually found in auto warranties—"Warranty ends at 36 months or 36,000 miles, whichever occurs first.") Finally, the typical warranty in some measure limits the seller's liability.

Businesses are not required by law to issue warranties. Most do, however, to convince their customers of the quality of their products. In fact, for some companies—notably automobile manufacturers—warranties are a key component of their product advertising.

Warranties come in two different forms—*express* and *implied*. These forms, in turn, can be divided into specific types.

Express Warranties

An **express warranty** is one that is explicitly stated, in either writing or spoken words, to induce a customer to buy. If the warranty is written, it can appear in a number of places—on the product packaging, in the product literature, in an advertisement, or as part of a point-of-purchase display. All that is required is that the location be convenient, or easily accessible to customers before purchase. Whether written or spoken, the warranty must be clearly worded so that customers can easily understand its terms. Spoken warranties, however, even if clearly worded, may not be enforceable unless they are reduced to writing.

Here is an example of how an express warranty works. A written ad states that a portable stereo headset will operate when the user jogs. You purchase one of the headsets and discover almost immediately that it shorts out during jogging. You are entitled to whatever relief is specified in the warranty. Assume further that the package in which the headset came features a runner using the product in the rain. You find that the product shorts out in the rain. Once again, you are entitled to warranty relief because the illustration constitutes a promise of performance, even though the promise is not a written one.

There are two types of written warranties—a *full warranty* and a *limited warranty*. Under a *full warranty, if a product is found to be defective within the warranty period, it will be repaired or replaced at no cost to the purchaser*. All parts and labor are covered. Today, full warranties are rarely offered on consumer goods.

A **limited warranty** is one that offers less coverage than a full warranty. It may exclude certain parts of the product from coverage. It may also require the customer to bear some of the expense for repairs resulting from defects. It is not uncommon, for example, for a limited warranty to specify that the manufacturer will pay for replacement parts but charge the customer for labor or shipping.

Implied Warranties

Most major purchases that customers make are covered by written warranties provided by manufacturers. Where there is no written warranty, implied-warranty laws apply.

An **implied warranty** is one that exists automatically by state law whenever a purchase takes place. There are two types of implied warranties—a *warranty of merchantability* and a *warranty of fitness for a particular purpose*.

A **warranty of merchantability** amounts to a promise from the seller that the product sold is fit for its intended purpose. For example, a can opener will open cans. A vacuum cleaner will clean carpets. A men's shaver will remove facial hair.

A **warranty of fitness for a particular purpose** arises when the seller advises a customer that a product is suitable for a particular use and the customer acts on that advice. For example, a customer buys a small truck based on a car salesman's assurances that it will pull a trailer of a certain weight. If it turns out that the truck cannot tow the anticipated load, then

Bugs Burger—Bug Killer

Alvin "Bugs" Burger started Bugs Burger Bug Killers in 1960 with $300. He built the company into a 44-state enterprise with 15,000 hotel and restaurant clients and $30 million a year in revenues. Burger recently sold the business to Johnson's Wax pesticide division.

Burger attributes his success to the service guarantees his company offered. He told his first customer, "If I don't eliminate your problem 100 percent, I don't get paid." This statement gradually evolved into a whole series of formal commitments, including the following:

1. No money will be paid until all pests are removed from the premises.
2. Any dissatisfied client will receive a refund for up to 12 months of service.
3. If a guest or customer sees a pest, Bugs Burger will pay for the guest's room or meal, send a letter of apology, and pay for a future meal or stay.

Such service does not come cheap. The company charges ten times more than its competitors. It also requires clients to increase the frequency of service calls, change trash removal procedures, and make needed repairs.

1. Would 100 percent service guarantee work in all business enterprises? Why or why not?
2. Would you be willing to pay ten times as much for a product with a 100 percent guarantee? If so, for which product(s)?
3. The promise of guaranteed results is not only a marketing tool but a part of the operational structure. How would you motivate employees to perform at 100 percent efficiency?
4. Do you think that making clients responsible for their actions is a good policy? Doesn't dictating a client's behavior infringe on the rights of that company's owners to operate their businesses as they see fit?

the dealership must take back the truck and refund the buyer's money.

Warranty Disclaimers

Sometimes warranties have disclaimers to protect the businesses issuing them. *A disclaimer is a statement that contains exceptions to and exclusions from a warranty*. Disclaimers are often used to limit damages that can be recovered by a customer. A common form of disclaimer, for example, limits recovery to a refund of the purchase price and specifically excludes any other costs that may have been incurred by the owner as a result of the product's failure to operate properly. Another common disclaimer waives the customer's rights under implied-warranty laws.

REAL WORLD MARKETING

Meet the Beetle

In the 1950s, Detroit, the nation's car capital, was thinking big. However, Volkswagen, the new dream machine, was anything but big or flashy. How to sell it became Doyle Dane Bernbach's big puzzle. The agency's solution was to think small. Ads celebrated VW's economy and unchanging design. VW, one copy tag read, "doesn't go in one year and out the other." Both agency and client came out big winners.

LIFETIME SERVICE GUARANTEE
(LIMITED WARRANTY)

The Dealer warrants to the original retail Purchaser any eligible Genuine Ford Part (any part or accessory made or sold by Ford Motor Company) installed by the Dealer in a Ford Motor Company car or light truck. If such part fails in normal use and service, the Dealer will repair or replace it with Ford Authorized Replacement Parts. In such cases, repair or replacement by the Dealer shall be done free of charge to the Purchaser—including labor. The Lifetime Service Guarantee does not apply to parts repaired or replaced under any applicable new or used vehicle warranty or to the initial installation of an accessory.

When a Ford Authorized Replacement Part is no longer serviced (or stocked) by Ford Motor Company, the Dealer reserves the right to refund the money originally paid by the Purchaser for the particular parts and related labor.

The Purchaser's only requirements are that:

• He must return the vehicle to the Dealer during normal business hours for warranty services.

• The Purchaser must give the Dealer his own copy of the original repair order. It indicates that the Dealer had performed an eligible repair at an earlier date.

THIS WARRANTY DOES NOT COVER:
• TO THE EXTENT ALLOWED BY LAW, THE PURCHASER'S LOSS OF TIME, INCONVENIENCE, LOSS OF USE OF THE VEHICLE, TOWING EXPENSE, COMMERCIAL LOSS, OR CONSEQUENTIAL DAMAGE;

• PART REPLACEMENT THAT RESULTS FROM ACCIDENT, ABUSE, MISUSE, NEGLECT, ALTERATION, OR IMPROPER MAINTENANCE;

• PART REPLACEMENT THAT RESULTS FROM NORMAL SCHEDULED MAINTENANCE SUCH AS POINTS, PLUGS, CONDENSERS, FILTERS, LUBRICANTS, PCV VALVES;

• THE NORMAL WEAR OUT OF BRAKE LININGS, CLUTCH FACINGS, AND WINDSHIELD WIPER BLADES;

• BATTERIES, BELTS, HOSES, FLUIDS, CHEMICALS, PAINTS, SHEET METAL, BRIGHT METAL AND TRIM ALSO ARE NOT COVERED;

• INCOMPLETE REPAIRS PERFORMED AT THE CUSTOMER'S REQUEST, LABOR-ONLY REPAIRS, OR REPAIRS MADE WITH NON-FORD OR NON-MOTORCRAFT PARTS.

THERE IS NO OTHER EXPRESS WARRANTY ON FORD MOTOR COMPANY SUPPLIED REPLACEMENT PARTS AND ACCESSORIES USED IN THIS DEALERSHIP'S REPAIRS.

THE WARRANTOR SHALL NOT BE LIABLE FOR LOSS OF TIME, INCONVENIENCE, COMMERCIAL LOSS, OR CONSEQUENTIAL DAMAGES.

SOME STATES DO NOT ALLOW THE EXCLUSION OR LIMITATION OF INCIDENTAL OR CONSEQUENTIAL DAMAGES, SO THE ABOVE LIMITATION OR EXCLUSION MAY NOT APPLY TO YOU.

THIS WARRANTY GIVES YOU SPECIFIC LEGAL RIGHTS, AND YOU MAY HAVE OTHER RIGHTS WHICH VARY FROM STATE TO STATE.

Exclusions or disclaimers must be made to stand out from the rest of a warranty's text. How was this accomplished in this warranty? Why do you think such devices are required?

Role of Warranties in Product Planning

Warranties are an important element of product planning. They are probably the major extended feature that customers expect when they make a purchase. From a business's viewpoint, however, warranties are significant because they

- force a company to focus on customer needs,
- set clear standards of performance,
- generate customer feedback,
- encourage quality control, and
- boost promotional efforts.

The importance of warranties is further demonstrated by widespread use among leading manufacturers and retailers of extended service contracts. *Extended service contracts provide parts and repair services for a specified length of time beyond a product's normal warranty period.* Customers usually pay extra for such a contract at the time they purchase the covered product. Such an arrangement has benefits for both businesses and customers. Businesses benefit by receiving post-purchase revenues. Customers benefit from the assurance of continued satisfactory product performance.

Other Extended Product Features

In addition to warranties and service contracts, product planners provide additional extended product features to help create customer satisfaction after the sale.

Other extended product features include delivery, installation, billing, service after the sale, directions for use, technical assistance, and training.

Product planners must constantly evaluate a product's extended features from a customer viewpoint. They should be able to answer yes to questions such as these.

1. Was the product delivered on time?
2. If installation was necessary, was it done properly?
3. Was the bill for the product or service accurate and timely?
4. If needed, was the service provided promptly, courteously, and correctly?
5. If needed, were technical assistance and training provided?
6. Were directions for use properly written?

Extended product features are so important because they are often remembered and used long after the price of the product has been forgotten.

Consumer Laws and Agencies

A working knowledge of relevant federal, state, and local laws is essential for businesspeople today. Manufacturers must be sure that their products meet all the requirements of the law—that they are safe, adequately labeled, and accurately advertised. If they are not, the manufacturer could face fines or costly recalls.

To keep abreast of statutory requirements, larger companies often employ consumer affairs or legislative specialists to advise management. Smaller companies often join industry trade associations to stay informed on existing and pending laws that affect their products. What follows is a brief survey of the kinds of laws that specialists concern themselves with.

Federal Statutes

Many of the warranty features already discussed in this chapter have their origins in a federal statute called the *Magnuson-Moss Consumer Product Warranty Act* of 1975. This statute governs written warranties for all consumer products costing $15 or more. It sets minimum standards for such warranties, rules for making them available before a product is sold, and provisions for lawsuits against manufacturers if they are not fulfilled.

Other federal statutes protect consumers by forcing companies to manufacture and sell safe products. The *Consumer Product Safety Act* of 1972, for example, established the Consumer Product Safety Commission (CPSC). This agency is responsible for monitoring the safety of more than 11,000 mostly nonfood items, such as toys, televisions, lamps, lawn mowers, appliances, and electrical wiring. The agency is empowered to issue standards for the construction, testing, packaging, and performance of these products.

If, in the course of its investigations, the CPSC finds any product that it believes to be defective or dangerous, it has three alternatives. It can

1. require that warning labels be attached to the product,
2. recall the product and order repairs, or
3. prohibit the product's sale.

In December 1988, for example, the commission banned the sale of lawn darts, an outdoor game advertised as a form of family recreation. As a result of its investigation, the commission found that during a ten-year period, lawn darts caused nearly 6,700 injuries and three deaths. Most of the victims (75 percent) were under 15 years of age.

The *Food, Drug, and Cosmetic Act* is another federal statute designated to assure consumers that the products they buy will be safe. "Safe" in this case means pure, wholesome, and effective (also informatively labeled and truthfully advertised). The act is enforced by the Food and Drug Administration, which certifies new drugs and inspects drug and food-processing plants. The agency also regulates the advertising and sale of such medical devices as hearing aids and pacemakers.

Other products are regulated by different federal agencies, and some are regulated by more than one agency. Automobiles, for example, have their emission standards set by the Environmental Protection Agency (EPA), their window (price) stickers regulated by the Federal Trade Commission, and any potentially dangerous design flaws investigated by the National Transportation Safety Board (NTSB). Making sure products meet this multiplicity of standards is an important function of product planning.

State Statutes

Many states have also passed consumer protection laws. Most are aimed at poorly made or poorly serviced products. For example, 45 states have now passed so-called lemon laws.

Lemon laws are statutes designed to protect consumers from poorly built cars. Under most lemon laws, a car is a "lemon" if it is out of service at least 30 days during the first year of ownership or if four attempts have been made to fix the same problem. Lemon owners are entitled to a refund or a comparable replacement car.

Many states have incorporated *arbitration programs* into their lemon laws. In an arbitration, an impartial third party (such as a representative of the Better Business Bureau) decides the crucial issues—for example, whether a vehicle has met the standard of a lemon and, if so, how much of a refund is due. In most cases, the arbitrator's ruling is not binding on the parties. If the owner is not satisfied with the outcome, he or she can sue the carmaker in a court of law. The principal benefit of arbitration, however, is that it saves all parties the long delays and excessive costs often associated with a lawsuit.

The most common form of state regulation mainly affects service businesses. Most states require certain individuals—auto mechanics, realtors, building contractors, and barbers, for example—to meet special training requirements. Before they can legally practice their professions, these people must apply to the state for licensing or certification. The process frequently involves testing and the payment of a substantial fee.

Consumer Remedies and Responsibilities

What happens when the extended features that a business has built into a product fail—when, for example, buyers do not feel that the product's warranty has protected them adequately? In such circumstances, customers always have the option of suing.

Product Liability Suits

Consumers can sue manufacturers or retailers on at least three grounds—breach of federal law (written warranty), breach of state law (implied warranty), and negligence. *Negligence* means failure to take proper or reasonable care. In the area of product safety (defects resulting in personal injury), courts have held manufacturers and retailers liable for defects in products.

As part of product planning, businesses can take steps to minimize liability suits. Manufacturers should produce safe products to begin with.

They should examine product design and look at what might go wrong. As part of this process, they should test their products thoroughly. They should give special attention to package design because courts assume that consumers view product and package as a single unit. Specifically, they should be sure that clear warnings are given on the package about any potential hazards involved in using the product.

Retailers can limit their liability by questioning manufacturers before accepting a product for sale. They should obtain the manufacturer's test data and determine the company's ability to stand behind the product before it is put on their shelves.

Consumer Responsibilities

As a final line of defense against liability, businesses should encourage their customers to be responsible consumers. They should take every opportunity to remind their customers of their duty to be informed—especially to read and follow the directions provided on products.

Customers should also be reminded of their responsibility to be honest in their purchases and use of products. Shoplifting, switching price tags, short-changing cashiers, and using coupons for products never purchased are all dishonest and illegal practices that raise prices for all consumers.

Finally, customers should be reminded that they have a responsibility to complain reasonably. Their first step should be to seek an adjustment from the retailer. If they do not receive satisfaction, they should next try the Better Business Bureau or the consumer affairs department of the manufacturer. Only when these options have been exhausted should they resort to government agencies or lawsuits.

VOCABULARY REVIEW

Use each of the following terms in a sentence.

warranty
express warranty
full warranty
limited warranty
implied warranty
warranty of merchantability

warranty of fitness for a
    particular purpose
disclaimer
extended service contracts
lemon laws

FACT AND IDEA REVIEW

1. How does an express warranty differ from an implied warranty?

2. How does a full warranty differ from a limited warranty?

3. Why are warranty disclaimers used by businesses?

4. Why are warranties significant to businesses?

5. What is an extended service contract? Who pays for it, and how long does it last?

6. Identify three extended product features that are frequently part of product planning.

7. What does the Consumer Product Safety Commission do?

8. What does the Food and Drug Administration do?

9. What is a lemon, as in the term *lemon laws*?

10. Suggest three legal grounds on which businesses can be sued for product liability.

11. List three consumer responsibilities that businesses should encourage their customers to assume.

CRITICAL THINKING

1. In 1966, Atlanta-based Orkin Exterminating Company began offering "lifetime" guarantees of continued protection for buildings it treated for termites. Annual inspections were conducted without raising customers' annual fees. The company abandoned this policy in 1975. In 1980, Orkin told 200,000 customers with the existing contracts that it was raising their annual renewal fees at least $25. Why do you think the company did this? Do you think the Federal Trade Commission, which regulates deceptive advertising practices, supported the company? Why or why not?

2. If in its advertising a company such as Ford stresses the quality of its products, why does it sell extended service contracts to its customers? Doesn't this imply that Ford products are subject to failure? Resolve this apparent contradiction.

3. The federal Environmental Protection Agency (EPA) has broad powers that can affect entire industries. For example, EPA rules issued in 1988 specify new requirements for underground storage tanks that could force the closure of 20 percent of all service stations. Among other things, the rules require stations to obtain pollution liability insurance or pay damages in the event that their tanks leak. Many station owners complain that the required insurance is either unavailable or that the premiums are prohibitively high. Do you think the EPA should have the power to issue such regulations? Why or why not? What alternate solutions to the problem can you suggest? What are the advantages and disadvantages of your approach(es)?

4. Lemon laws that incorporate arbitration are currently undergoing reevaluation and revision in several states (among them California). Decisions of the arbitrators seldom favor auto buyers, consumer advocates have noted, and they suggest that there is a need to "arbitrate the arbitrators." Support the theory that both the outcome and the criticism could have been anticipated. Then suggest some revisions to the state laws that might be acceptable to both sides.

USING BASIC SKILLS

Math

1. Your tire warranty reads as follows: "This limited warranty applies to all owners of the tire using it in noncommercial passenger service. If our examination shows that a passenger tire covered

by this warranty has become unserviceable due to workmanship or materials defect during its tread life (i.e., worn down to $\frac{3}{32}$ of an inch groove depth), it will be replaced on a "pro-rata tread wear basis." A "pro-rata" basis means that you will be given a discount proportional to the remaining tire life at the time of replacement. (In other words, if 70 percent of the tire's tread was gone when the tire failed, you would be given a 30 percent discount on a replacement.) Compute the remaining percentage of tire life and the cost of a replacement tire in the following circumstances:

Tread Depth	Tread Life Expired	Tread Life Remaining	New Tire Cost	Customer Cost
$\frac{5}{32}$	80%	_____	$ 79.40	_____
$\frac{6}{32}$	50	_____	57.25	_____
$\frac{7}{32}$	40	_____	113.79	_____
$\frac{3}{32}$	90	_____	65.00	_____
$\frac{2}{32}$	100	_____	45.99	_____

2. A service maintenance contract is offered to purchasers of contact lenses, entitling them to discounts on replacement lenses. The price for coverage is $20 for one year or $35 for two years.

   a. Over a two-year period, how much can lens purchasers save by purchasing one two-year contract rather than two one-year contracts?

   b. What is the percentage amount of savings over the two-year period?

Communication

3. Even though warranties are supposed to be written in clear, simple language, many consumers still find them difficult to understand. Find an example of a fairly long and detailed warranty—perhaps one for a major appliance or an automobile. Then rewrite it in your own words.

Human Relations

4. You are appearing as a business expert on "Consumer Issues and Answers," a local television talk show. The host asks you to answer the following viewer question: "Why is it that warranties always exclude the things most likely to happen or most expensive to repair? That just proves they're advertising gimmicks, right?" What would you say?

APPLICATION PROJECTS

1. Find a warranty for a small appliance and read the document carefully. Then answer the following questions.

   a. Is the warranty full or limited? How do you know?

   b. To what remedy is the purchaser entitled if a manufacturer's defect is found?

   c. Describe the required procedure for obtaining warranty repairs. Include the name and address of the nearest service center, and note what, if any, charges the customer must pay.

   d. List any disclaimers that the warranty contains.

2. From newspapers, magazines, catalogues, and circulars, clip ads that use the words *warranty*, *warrant*, *guarantee*, or *guaranteed*. Assemble these ads into a bulletin board display on firms that use warranties as a key promotional element. *Note*: Include hangtags and statements from product literature in the display, if these are available.

PART

10

ENTREPRENEURSHIP

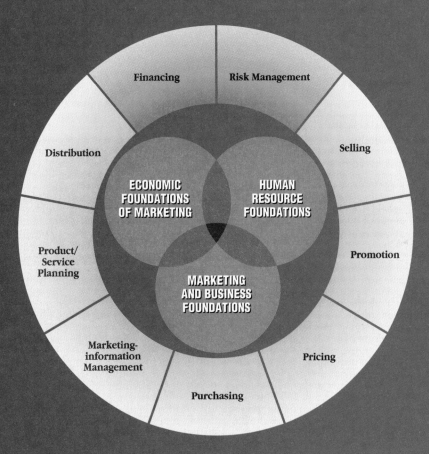

OBJECTIVES

After completing this chapter, you will be able to:

1. define entrepreneurship,

2. identify the risks involved in entrepreneurship,

3. discuss the advantages and disadvantages of entrepreneurship,

4. identify the personal characteristics and skills entrepreneurs need,

5. explain the scope of small business in the American economy,

6. identify forms of business ownership,

7. discuss the importance and purpose of a business plan, and

8. identify the major sections of a business plan.

WORDS TO KNOW

entrepreneurship
entrepreneurs
franchise
sole proprietorship
partnership
corporation
stockholders
business plan

What Is Entrepreneurship?

This chapter introduces you to the process of starting and managing your own business. You will look at the advantages and disadvantages of business ownership. You will discover what special personal qualities and skills are needed for success. In addition, you will learn the purpose and elements of a well-developed business plan.

What Is Entrepreneurship?

Have you ever wished you were the boss? Did you ever think you had a good idea for a good or service? Do you like to plan your own day and make your own decisions? Then you might consider *entrepreneurship*.

Entrepreneurship is the process of starting and managing your own business. As you know, everyone in the United States is free to start, own, and operate a business. *Entrepreneurs are people who attempt to earn money and make profits by taking the risk of owning and operating a business.* If you have ever provided babysitting services, cut someone's lawn, or had a lemonade stand, you have already been an entrepreneur.

Some entrepreneurs single-handedly make a major contribution to our economy. For example, Henry Ford introduced the mass-production of automobiles, thus making them affordable to the average person. Ray Kroc made McDonald's the largest fast-food restaurant chain in the world. Former secretary Bette Graham developed Liquid Paper to paint over typing errors; the product is now sold worldwide. Steven Jobs and Steven Wozniak began Apple Computer, Inc., working mostly from their homes, and soon turned it into an international business.

These entrepreneurs became famous and wealthy. However, there are many entrepreneurs who do not dream of fame and riches. They are simply people who want to be their own bosses and make their own business decisions. They were willing to put in the effort and dedication it takes to be successful at running their own businesses.

The Risk of Entrepreneurship

Starting a new business is a risk because it is a major commitment of time, money, and effort. So, new business owners must be risk-takers. Often, they quit their current jobs, work long hours, invest their savings, and borrow money—with no guarantee that the new business will succeed.

Some 60 percent of those who start a business are between the ages of 25 and 40. By then, people usually have the work experience, the personal drive, the financial resources, and the willingness to take business risks. People over the age of 40 are usually established in life. They may have the money and experience it takes to start a business. However, they

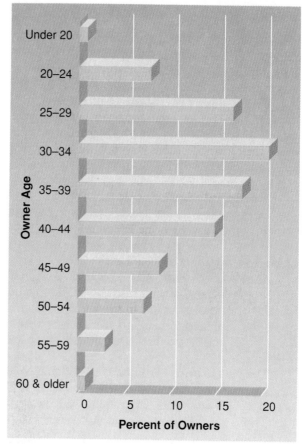

Figure 38-1 Owner Age When People Start Their Own Businesses

Most people start a new business between the ages of 25 and 40. Which age group has the highest percentage of people starting their own businesses?

may be reluctant to do so because of family commitments or fear of losing what they have achieved. Figure 38-1 shows percentages of owner age when new businesses formed for people ranging in age from under 20 to 60 years and older.

The fear of losing money with a new business venture (or, at least, the fear of not making *enough* money) is very real. Most new businesses that survive employ only a few people and provide a living only for the business owner and his or her family. Some 8,400 new businesses are started each week. Studies show that two out of three new firms close their doors within four years of opening.

You can see, then, that owning and operating your own business can be risky. There are no guarantees of success. Nevertheless, being an entrepreneur has its advantages.

Advantages of Entrepreneurship

If going into business for yourself is such a risky venture, why do so many people choose to do it? Here are some of the major reasons why people go into business for themselves.

Personal Freedom. Entrepreneurs are not controlled by any other managers in their organizations. They set their own work schedules. They make their own decisions, try out their own new ideas, and direct their energies into business activities as they see fit.

Personal Satisfaction. Personal freedom leads to the personal satisfaction of doing what you enjoy each day. By being in control of their businesses and their work settings, entrepreneurs are much more in control of their lives.

Increased Income. Personal satisfaction usually leads people to work hard at what they enjoy. Working hard usually results in making more money. Thus, the incentive to make money—coupled with the personal satisfaction that comes from doing so—is always present.

Self-esteem. Freedom, satisfaction, and increased income add up to a greater feeling of self-esteem. People who work hard and are well rewarded for it, both personally and financially, are truly successful people.

Disadvantages of Entrepreneurship

The advantages of being an entrepreneur are definitely exciting and motivating. Nevertheless, there are some disadvantages, too.

Risk and Potential Loss of Income. New businesses usually have a restricted cash flow because of start-up costs. This may mean that an entrepreneur's first year or more of operation does not meet his or her personal financial needs. Entrepreneurs enjoy improved earnings only if the business is successful. If they do not have the necessary personal or technical skills, their businesses will probably fail. With failures comes a loss of employment, status, and invested money.

Long, Irregular Hours. Entrepreneurs are not 40-hour-a-week people. It is quite possible that a new business will demand 12 to 16 hours a day in addition to weekends and holidays. Usually, new business owners do not even take vacations until the business proves successful.

Need for Daily Discipline. Running a business may be personally and financially rewarding. However, it also requires doing many tedious, time-consuming tasks.

For example, the business owner may have to do general cleaning and maintenance because there is not enough money to hire someone else to do it. Also, there is usually a lot of paperwork involved in any business operation. Accounts payable, accounts receivable, payroll, and forms to fill out for all levels of government regulations require precise record keeping.

It takes a great deal of self-discipline to keep up with all these things on a daily, weekly, and monthly basis. They are just as important as actually selling the good or service.

Despite these disadvantages, the lure of being one's own boss attracts countless people each year. Those who are successful at it have certain personal characteristics that enable them to succeed where others fail. What are these personal qualities? Are you a budding entrepreneur?

Characteristics of a Successful Entrepreneur

To be a successful entrepreneur, you must have strong organizational skills, tremendous drive, and leadership ability. You must have the special skills and knowledge necessary to operate the business you have chosen. In addition, you must be in good physical and mental condition to work the hours the business will require.

It also helps to have parents or relatives who are already in business for themselves. Studies have shown that the family is a major influence on who becomes an entrepreneur. Being around people who are successful entrepreneurs positively influences children to feel that they can be successful entrepreneurs, too.

People who become entrepreneurs tend to think they are in control. They think that their hard work and determination—not luck or fate—will make their business successful.

They also have a spirit of adventure. They get a great deal of satisfaction from taking risks and achieving goals.

Self-Evaluation

The first seven questions consider your personality characteristics.

		YES	NO
1.	Do you like to make your own decisions?	—	—
2.	Do you enjoy competition?	—	—
3.	Do you have willpower and self-determination?	—	—
4.	Do you plan ahead?	—	—
5.	Do you like to get things done on time?	—	—
6.	Can you take advice from others?	—	—
7.	Can you adapt to changing conditions?	—	—

The next series of questions considers your physical, emotional, and financial well-being.

		YES	NO
8.	Do you understand that owning your own business may entail working 12 to 16 hours a day, probably six days a week and maybe on holidays?	—	—
9.	Do you have the physical stamina to handle a business?	—	—
10.	Do you have the emotional strength to withstand the strain?	—	—
11.	Are you prepared to lower your living standard for several months or years?	—	—
12.	Are you prepared to lose your savings?	—	—
13.	Do you know which skills and areas of expertise are critical to the success of your business?	—	—
14.	Do you have these skills?	—	—
15.	Does your idea for a business use these skills?	—	—
16.	Can you find the people that have the expertise you lack?	—	—
17.	Do you know why you are considering this business?	—	—
18.	Will your business meet your career aspirations?	—	—

Figure 38-2 **Self-evaluation**

Answer each question honestly. As you do, ask yourself why each of these points could be important in running a small business.

Do You Have What It Takes?

Before you think about owning your own business, you have to honestly ask yourself, "Do I have what it takes to go into business for myself?"

You can answer this question by doing a *self-evaluation*—an assessment of your personal qualities, abilities, interests, and skills. The self-evaluation in Figure 38-2 was developed by the Small Business Administration. Take a few minutes right now to answer each question on a separate piece of paper. Think before you answer—and be honest with yourself.

As you can see from answering the questions in Figure 38-2, starting a business requires careful self-evaluation. Answering yes to most or all of these questions should be an indication that you have the right characteristics for success. You should also consider the experiences of family, friends, and other businesspeople already in the same or a similar business. Find out about their experiences. Also, do library research on the type of business you wish to start. All this information taken together should give you a good indication of whether you are ready and able to join the ranks of America's millions of small businesspeople.

The Importance of Entrepreneurship in Our Economy

As you learned in the introduction to this chapter, small businesses provide jobs for almost 50 percent of the labor force. (Eighty percent of the new jobs created came from businesses that were less than five years old.)

Small businesses also produce 38 percent of the Gross National Product (GNP) in the United States. (Recall from Chapter 3 that the GNP measures the total value of a nation's goods and services produced in a given period of time.) Figure 38-3 shows the GNP of small businesses in the U.S. compared to the world's largest national economies.

Small businesses benefit the economy and society in other ways, too. They offer consumers more choices of goods and services. They help improve products and processes. They challenge existing businesses to become more efficient and provide better goods and services. They also offer on-the-job training to many students who then use this valuable experience to open small businesses of their own.

Ways to Enter Business

Some 420,000 businesses are started each year. Obviously, some of them are new, without any prior existing business on which to build. In addition to developing a new business, there are three other ways to enter business: *purchase an existing franchise business, purchase an existing non-franchise business,* or *take over the family business.*

Purchasing an Existing Franchise Business

A franchise is a legal agreement to begin a new business in the name of a recognized company. Fast-food restaurants are the most well-known franchise businesses.

The *franchisee* (the person purchasing the franchise) buys a system of operation that has proven successful over the years. All business planning—called *prepackaging*—is done by the *franchisor,* the owner of the existing business. Prepackaging generally includes management training and assistance with advertising, merchandising, and day-to-day operations.

The biggest disadvantages of franchising are the large amount of capital needed to purchase most franchises and the high initial fees charged to begin operations. Also, the franchisor may limit the franchisee's choices as to how the business is run.

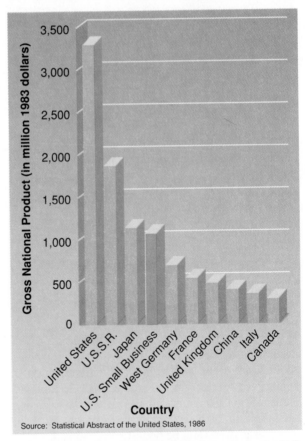

Source: Statistical Abstract of the United States, 1986

Figure 38-3 **Output of Small Businesses in the U.S. Compared to the World's Largest Economies**
The GNP of U.S. small businesses compares most closely to that of which country?

Purchasing an Existing Non-franchise Business

When you buy an existing non-franchise business, you usually receive little or no help from the previous owner. Therefore, you must investigate why the business is being sold. You must carefully examine the business records and the condition of the property, inventory, and fixtures. You must also determine the reputation of the business in the community. A bad business reputation may mean that you will have to work hard to restore customer goodwill.

Taking Over the Family Business

Some of the same considerations for purchasing an existing business also apply for a family business. You must review business records and the overall condition of the property and inventory. You must determine the reputation of the business in the community. In addition, you need to explore potential conflicts and concerns with family members.

Forms of Business Organization

Just as you can choose which good or service to provide, you can also choose the legal organization or structure your business will take. As an entrepreneur, your choices of business organization are *sole proprietorship*, the *partnership*, and the *corporation*. We will look at each briefly here. Chapter 40 will give you a more complete description of each when we talk about organizing a proposed business.

The Sole Proprietorship

A *sole proprietorship is a business owned and operated by one person.* This is the most common form of business ownership. People usually become sole proprietors when they have a special skill by which they can earn a living. Beauticians, plumbers, auto mechanics, and writers, for example, are sole proprietors.

In addition to having a special skill, the sole proprietor must provide the money and management skill to run the business. In return for all this responsibility, the sole proprietor is entitled to all the profits.

There are several other advantages to a sole proprietorship, too. It is relatively easy to start. All business decisions made are your own. It is generally taxed less than other forms of business. It allows more freedom from government regulation.

Problems can develop in a sole proprietorship when it becomes necessary to expand business operations but the only money available is the owner's personal assets. Also, making all the decisions yourself without the input and advice of others can be difficult. Bad business decisions result in business failure.

The Partnership

A *partnership is a legal agreement between two or more people to be jointly responsible for the success or failure of a business.* It is a more complicated form of business ownership than the sole proprietorship. The partners share the profits if the business is a success and share the losses if it fails.

There are several advantages to a partnership. It combines the skills of the owners. It may have access to more money and thus may operate and expand more easily. It allows each partner a voice in the management of the business. It is taxed and regulated less heavily than a corporation.

Despite these advantages, there are some disadvantages to partnerships, too. The owners may not always agree on business decisions. The actions of one partner are legally binding on the other partners. This means that all partners must assume their share of the business debt. They must also be responsible for the shares of the other partners if they cannot pay. Finally, the business is dissolved if one partner dies. It can be reorganized as a new partnership, but the process is time-consuming and costly.

The Corporation

A *corporation is a business that is chartered by a state and legally operates apart from the owner(s).* It is the most complicated form of business organization we have looked at in this chapter. Think of a corporation as a person. It can own property, borrow money, and make contracts.

Although a corporation can be any size, larger firms are usually organized as corporations. Those who work for a corporation are not necessarily the people who own it (although they may be).

Why Pay More?

When the Meijer family opened their first grocery store in the rural community of Greenville, Michigan, in 1934, the odds were against their success. The country was gripped by a devastating depression. Most people—the Meijers included—had little money.

Not to be discouraged, Henrik Meijer purchased $338.76 worth of merchandise on credit and opened his first "Thrift Market" store. His competitors were 22 other stores in the area.

Henrik appreciated his customers' financial condition. He wanted to help them find the best bargains they could. So, he looked for quality merchandise at low prices. He traveled great distances to buy out shelves of merchandise from chain stores in the state. He then offered it to his customers at exceptional savings—even with his subsequent markups.

Even though his business was successful, Henrik and his family worked long hours to keep it going. Henrik loved the competition.

He also respected and valued his customers and wanted to make shopping easy for them. To encourage self-service, Henrik's son, Fred, bought a dozen double-handled wicker baskets and put them at the front of the store. Above them he placed a sign that read, "Take a basket. . .Help yourself."

Customers quickly followed his instructions and learned a new approach to shopping. Self-service soon became the cornerstone to the business. Initially drawn to the store by good value and good service, customers were soon won over with this added element of convenience.

Today, the Meijer self-service discount chain has grown to 55 stores in Michigan and Ohio. It continues to offer customers the goods and services they want. Even after more than a half century in business, Meijer maintains a reputation for quality products at fair prices, and friendly, courteous service.

1. What entrepreneurial characteristics did Henrik Meijer have that made him successful?
2. What risks did the Meijer family face when they started their business?
3. How did the Meijer family meet their customers' needs?
4. What innovation did the Meijer family bring to retailing?

The value of a corporation is divided into equal units called shares of stock. These shares of stock are sold through the *stock market* to individual investors called *stockholders. Stockholders are the people who actually own the corporation.* Each stockholder is liable (responsible) for the losses of the corporation only to the extent of his or her individual investment. (This is commonly referred to as *limited liability.*) Corporations form governing bodies called *boards* to manage the affairs of the business and the interests of the stockholders.

There are four key advantages to this form of business organization. Each owner has limited liability. It is easy to raise money for expansion. People can easily enter and leave the business simply by buying or selling their shares of stock. Each operation area of the business can be professionally managed by an expert in that area.

Among the disadvantages to the corporation are the complexity of forming it, increased government regulation, and higher taxes on the profits of the corporation and on each stockholder. Also, accounting and record keeping are much more complex than for the other two major forms of business organization.

It is important to be flexible in approaching the legal form of ownership when establishing a new business. Often, a business starts out as a sole proprietorship, grows into a partnership, and ultimately ends up as a corporation. The entrepreneurs you read about at the beginning of this chapter—Henry Ford, Ray Kroc, Bette Graham, Steven Jobs, and Steven Wozniak—watched their businesses grow from sole proprietorships or partnerships to major corporations.

Developing the Business Plan

Once you have done your self-analysis, explored the types of business organization, and selected a method of entry into the business world, you need to develop your *business plan*. *A **business plan** is a proposal that describes every part of your new business to potential investors and financing agencies*. It maps out the course of your business and helps you do three things:

1. *Obtain financing*. It is expensive to open a business, and you will probably need financial assistance. Your business plan will help convince investors that your business idea will be profitable.
2. *Guide the opening of the business*. The plan identifies procedures necessary to legally establish the business.
3. *Manage the business successfully*. The plan is a management tool that helps you identify the month-to-month steps you must take to ensure that your business operates profitably.

A business plan must be well-organized and easy-to-read. It should contain a description and analysis of the business situation, an organizational and marketing plan, and a financial plan. We will look at each briefly here. Then we will explore each in more detail in the remaining chapters of this unit.

Description and Analysis of the Business Situation

The description and analysis section introduces the proposed business by explaining and describing it and the goods or services it will sell. It discusses the need for the product and tells about the existing competition. It also contains information about your business experience and training (and those of any other

people to be involved in the new venture). Essentially, it should show your willingness to take risks.

This section of your business plan includes a trading area analysis that deals with geographic, demographic, and economic data. It also includes a market segment analysis in which you explain your target market and discuss customer buying patterns and how you will accommodate them.

Finally, it discusses your chosen business location. It shows the location in relation to suppliers of the raw materials needed for your business, as well as its geographic relationship to your competitors. The availability, costs, traffic patterns, and nearness to competition of the potential location are explained.

Organization and Marketing Plan

This section of the business plan tells how you plan to organize, manage, and develop the new business. It contains an organizational chart, a description of your current and anticipated staffing needs, and a description of how you intend to pay, train, and supervise employees.

It also details how you plan to sell your product and how you intend to reach and satisfy customers with your goods or services. The details of your proposed goods and services are explained along with your potential suppliers, manufacturing or selling methods, and inventory policies. Pricing strategies and promotional plans are also included. Finally, it tells how you will bring your business to the attention of potential customers, how you plan to serve them, and how you will keep them coming back for more.

Financial Plan

Potential lenders and investors will want to look at the financial estimates for the new business. They want to know that their efforts will be as profitable for them as it will be for you. So, the financial plan section shows what monies are needed to start the business, as well as the projected income and cash flow expected for at least the first year of operation.

It also contains statements of projected income and expenses, as well as statements of personal and external sources of capital which will include money requested from the specific lender or investor. Each will want to know your other sources of money. They want the assurance that you are, in fact, getting *enough* money to operate until the business is profitable.

VOCABULARY REVIEW

Write two or three paragraphs on entrepreneurship, incorporating these eight vocabulary terms.

entrepreneurship	partnership
entrepreneurs	corporation
franchise	stockholders
sole proprietorship	business plan

FACT AND IDEA REVIEW

1. Define entrepreneurship.
2. Why is starting a new business such a risk?
3. Identify four advantages and three disadvantages of being an entrepreneur.
4. Give three characteristics of a successful entrepreneur.
5. Why should you do an honest self-evaluation if you are considering becoming an entrepreneur?
6. Identify three reasons why small businesses are important to the economy.
7. In addition to developing a new business, what are three other ways of getting into business?
8. List three advantages and three disadvantages of the sole proprietorship.
9. List three advantages and three disadvantages of a partnership.
10. List three advantages and three disadvantages of a corporation.
11. What is a business plan? Why is it so important?
12. What are the three sections of a business plan?

CRITICAL THINKING

1. Do you think money and material gain are the most important reasons for becoming an entrepreneur? If you answer no to this question, what do you consider the most important reasons for becoming an entrepreneur?

2. What are the disadvantages of working for others as opposed to being your own boss? Would these disadvantages be enough to make you consider starting your own business? Why?
3. If a franchisee has a new product idea, who should get credit for it—the franchisee or the franchisor?
4. How could a poorly written business plan hurt a new venture?

USING BASIC SKILLS

Math

1. If 8,400 businesses are started each week, how many businesses are started in a two-year period?
2. If an entrepreneur works 11 hours a day, five days a week, 52 weeks a year, how many hours is the person working annually?

Communication

3. Prepare a three-minute speech on the information that should be included in a partnership agreement. Use library resources for information.
4. Write a 250-word report on the functions and services provided by the U.S. Small Business Administration.
5. Using this book and other sources, write a 250-word paper on why the entrepreneur is so important to the economy of the United States.
6. Write your local Chamber of Commerce to arrange for a resource speaker to talk to your class on "Small Business Opportunities in Our Community."

Human Relations

7. A very good friend of yours has an idea to start a small video rental business. She is very excited about this new venture. However, you have heard that small video stores are being replaced by superstores with 8,000 or more tapes in stock. You have also heard that the cost of opening a store

has risen from $50,000 a few years ago to between $150,000 and $200,000 today. What would you tell your friend to do before she invests in this kind of business?

APPLICATION PROJECTS

1. Obtain a copy of National DECA's Entrepreneurship Event (Organizing a Business). Identify the three main sections of the event and outline topics covered in each section of the event. You will work more with this throughout this unit.

2. Complete a series of entrepreneurial aptitude tests provided by your teacher to find out about your interest in business ownership. In small groups of four to five students each, discuss with each other your personal qualities and aptitudes for business ownership.

3. Interview a small business owner-manager in your community to discover why that person started his or her own business. In a 200-word report, write about the job duties and tasks typically performed on a daily, weekly, and/or monthly basis by the business owner.

4. Research and identify factors you need to know when you buy a franchise.

5. Identify your hobbies and interests. Then list as many business ideas relating to your hobbies and interests as you can identify.

6. Choose an entrepreneur. He or she may be a well-known historical or modern figure, or someone in your community or family. Write a 200-word biography of the person and examine the characteristics that have made him or her successful.

7. Take a walk down the main business street in your community or through your favorite local shopping mall. Notice how many businesses are chain stores and how many are independently operated. Choose two independent businesses you know or find interesting. Explain why you feel they could not effectively be replaced by chain stores offering the same goods or services.

8. Research how people buy stock. Then give a five-minute oral report to your classmates on the kinds of stock there are, the way they are bought and sold, how much they cost, and the risks involved in buying stock.

9. Entrepreneurs often look into the future to see where new market needs will be. Describe the kinds of businesses that you think will boom in the next 25 years. Explain why you think they will do so, and how you would go about getting the knowledge or training to enter one of them.

10. Research the companies already in one of the fields you listed in Application Project #9. Describe how you would compete with them if you were to enter the field. Tell whether your business would be a sole proprietorship, a partnership, or a corporation, and why this would be the most effective way to run your particular business.

11. Today, many professional people, such as doctors, attorneys, and chiropractors, are incorporating themselves. Research the trend and give a five-minute oral report explaining why professionals are doing this.

39

After completing this chapter, you will be able to:

1. describe and analyze a proposed business situation,

2. analyze how your personal education, training, strengths, and weaknesses would affect your proposed business,

3. analyze a trading area for a proposed business with respect to geographic, demographic, and economic data,

4. perform a market segment analysis, including selecting a target market for a proposed business, and

5. analyze potential locations for a proposed business.

business philosophy
trading area
buying behavior

Describing and Analyzing a Proposed Business

As you learned in Chapter 38, a business plan gives an overall picture of a proposed business to potential investors and financing agencies. It gives a description of the business, an organization and marketing plan, and a financial plan. When properly prepared, a good business plan not only helps you develop your ideas but also provides a way for you to evaluate your results.

In this chapter, you will begin learning how to prepare a business plan. Specifically, you will look at how to describe and analyze a business situation. The remaining chapters in this unit will concentrate on developing an organization and marketing plan, and financing your business.

Before You Begin a Business

Before beginning any new business, you must ask yourself a number of questions. Your success depends on answering them honestly.

- Are you offering a good or service that will meet the needs and wants of customers?
- Do you have the necessary business experience, training, and financial backing it takes to be successful?
- Who are your competitors?
- Who will buy your good or service?
- Where will you locate your business?
- Will you buy or rent the property?

Let's take a look at a potential entrepreneur, a marketing student named Roger Rathburne. As you read his story, think of how Roger could be answering the above six questions about his potential business.

Roger worked in a videotape rental store near his college campus. He noted that increasing numbers of customers wanted to buy quality blank videotapes, but at reasonable prices.

Roger felt that he could sell quality blank tapes at much lower prices than his current employer was selling them for. So, he planned to begin a mail-order blank videotape business, contracting with overseas suppliers, and working out of his home to keep his expenses and prices low.

Roger believed his product had great sales potential because of the increasing popularity of VCRs and video camcorders. He was sure that he could provide a quality product at competitive prices.

Unfortunately, Roger did not have enough money to start his business. He needed to convince the local bank to loan him money to buy his initial inventory and begin promoting his product.

Before the bank would loan Roger any money, it wanted to know that Roger had thought out the details of his business operation and that he was prepared to manage it properly. Roger had to convince the bank he knew what he was doing and that his business had the potential for making a profit. He needed a business plan, organized according to the outline in Figure 39-1.

Description of the Proposed Business Situation

This section of your business plan begins with a description of the type of business you plan to open and a self-analysis of your skills and abilities. Present data or significant trends that will influence the success of your business. Explain how a current or changing situation has created an unfulfilled consumer want that your business will address.

Next, give your *business philosophy*. A *business philosophy tells how you think the business should be run and shows your understanding of your firm's role in the marketplace*. It reveals your attitude toward your customers, employees, and competitors.

Once you start a business, your business philosophy will help you create a customer following. For example, part of the business philosophy of The Limited, Inc., is that the customer should always be happy with the merchandise. Thus, its principal customer policy is that no sale is ever final. Customers can always return regularly priced merchandise and even sale merchandise if they are dissatisfied with it. This business philosophy has earned The Limited a loyal following of customers over the years.

Next, fully describe your product. Tell the advantages and benefits it will provide for consumers and why it will be successful. If you have sold your good or service before and thus know it well, tell about it here. Roger Rathburne, for example, could give statistics on the increasing use of VCRs and video camcorders. By doing this, he can show the need

Outline for a Business Plan

I. **Description and analysis of the proposed business situation**
  A. Type of business
  B. Business philosophy
  C. Description of good or service
  D. Self-analysis
    1. Education and training
    2. Strengths and weaknesses
    3. Plan for personal development
  E. Trading area analysis
    1. Geographic, demographic, and economic data
    2. Competition
  F. Market segment analysis
    1. Target market
    2. Customer buying behavior
  G. Analysis of potential location

II. **Organization and marketing plan**
  A. Proposed organization
    1. Type of ownership
    2. Steps in establishing business
    3. Personal needs
  B. Proposed good/service
    1. Manufacturing plans, inventory policies
    2. Suppliers
  C. Proposed marketing plan
    1. Pricing policies
    2. Promotional activities

III. **Financial plan**
  A. Sources of capital
    1. Personal sources
    2. External sources
  B. Projected income and expenses
    1. Personal financial statement
    2. Personal balance sheet
    3. Income statement(s)
    4. Projected start-up costs
    5. Projected personal needs
    6. Projected business income
    7. Projected business expenses
    8. Projected cash flow

Figure 39-1 **Outline for a Business Plan**

A business plan describes every part of a proposed business to potential investors and financing agencies. Why do those who might give a potential entrepreneur financial backing want to know that the proposed business will make a profit?

for people to buy quality, blank videotapes at reasonable prices.

Include as many facts as you can obtain. Speculation and statements of belief do not in themselves convince investors to lend you money. Consult recent issues of the *Wall Street Journal, Business Weekly, Fortune, Money,* and other business publications for regional and national business information.

Self-analysis

This section of your business plan includes a *self-analysis*—a description of your personal education, training, strengths, weaknesses, and a plan for personal development in your field.

For example, if you are interested in fashion and want to start a fashion boutique, you must be able to accurately predict fashion trends. You must also be able to buy, display, price, and advertise your merchandise correctly. In this part of the business plan, you would tell which skills you have in this area and

which you do not. (If you do not have some of the skills you need, tell how other people will be able to help you or special training that will help you acquire the skills.)

Indicate the education and training you have had so far to prepare you for operating your new business. For example, in addition to your primary educational experience, you may have taken an accounting course or worked part-time in the accounting department of a retail store. This shows you will be able to understand and interpret your business's financial statements.

Mention any future plans to continue your schooling—whether trade school or college—to improve your skills for operating your business.

If you have a special license needed to open the business, mention that here, too. If you do not have the required license, you should be able to say here that you have applied for one. Examples of businesses requiring special licenses are beauty and barber shops, construction companies, and mechanical and electrical repair businesses.

Finally, include the special personality traits and work habits you have that will help you to operate your proposed business. A statement about your motivation and willingness to work hard adds strength to your business plan.

Analysis of the Proposed Business Situation

The analysis section of your business plan contains three parts:

- Trading area analysis,
- Market segment analysis, and
- Analysis of potential location.

Trading Area Analysis

*A **trading area** is the geographical area from which a business draws its customers.* Before going into business, you must completely analyze the trading area with respect to geographic, demographic, and economic data, as well as competition. Information about the population in your trading area is available from your local Chamber of Commerce or your State Department of Commerce. You can also consult the most recent local census data in your local library.

Geographic, Demographic, and Economic Data. Geographic data includes population distribution. It tells how many people live in a certain area.

As you know, demographics are such easily identified and measurable population statistics as age, gender, and marital status. Knowing the demographics of your trading area will help you identify any trends happening now or in the future that will have a direct impact on your business. For example, if you plan to open a children's clothing store and your trading area is fast becoming a family neighborhood, you will definitely want to note this.

Prevailing economic conditions are among the major factors affecting a business. Economic factors include economic growth projections, trends in pricing, interest rates, and government regulations. For example, a tax increase levied by the local, state, or federal government will affect buying power.

It is important to include how much *disposable income* the potential customers in your trading area are likely to have. This means personal income from wages, salaries, interest, and profits, minus federal, state, and local taxes. Disposable income is also referred to as *buying income*.

A special measurement called a *buying power index* has been developed to help new business owners determine the buying power for a given area. The index combines disposable income, population size, and retail sales figures into an overall indicator of an area's sales potential. These factors are then expressed as a percentage of total sales. Buying power indexes can be helpful in deciding where to locate your business. You can find more information on buying power indexes in the *Survey of Buying Power*, which is published annually by *Sales and Marketing Management* magazine.

National and regional economic conditions will have an effect locally, too. For example, a new federal trade regulation might mean that a local factory will expand and bring more people (and thus, more potential customers with a demand for your product) into the area.

Will your business be affected by seasonal fluctuations? Are technological advancements happening now or in the future that could affect the demand or need for your product or service? You may not know the answers to these questions, but you should know how to find the information you need.

A good source of information on local economic conditions is your local bank. Bank officials often have business projections for major geographical areas and for most types of businesses located in their immediate area. In addition, many states have Departments of Commerce to assist new entrepreneurs in obtaining important information about economic trends within the state and within industries. Other good sources of information are related business publications available at schools, public libraries, colleges, and universities.

Competition. As a new business operator, you must analyze your competition. List all the competitors in your trading area, along with their types of products, prices, general quality of goods and services, and their strengths and weaknesses. Show how your business will be superior to the competition based on these factors. Figure 39-2 lists a series of questions to ask yourself when analyzing your competition.

A Cookie in the Spotlight

It's almost everyone's favorite cookie. Every year, thousands of them are baked in kitchens across the country. Nevertheless, it took Famous Amos to put the chocolate chip cookie in the celebrity spotlight.

Wally Amos first learned to eat chocolate chip cookies in his aunt's kitchen. He didn't plan to have a business selling them, however. Instead, he went into the music business as an agent.

Years later, he discovered the famous "Toll House" recipe on the back of the Nestle's chocolate chip package. He started making cookies himself and experimenting with the recipe.

When Amos visited producers to book his clients, he often took some of his cookies along to break the ice. Everybody raved about his cookies, but they didn't book his clients.

Amos became more and more disenchanted with the music business. He started thinking of other businesses he could go into that he would love and believe in. When a friend suggested he start selling his cookies, he thought it was a perfect idea.

Amos didn't have much money, but he had friends in the music industry who loved his cookies. So, he wrote a proposal detailing what he wanted to do, how he wanted to do it, and why. Then he enclosed samples of his cookies with the proposal. His friends thought it was such a sweet deal, they loaned Amos $25,000 to start the Famous Amos Chocolate Chip Cookie Company.

Amos planned to promote his cookies as he did his music clients. He wanted people to think Famous Amos chocolate chip cookies were a lot of fun. He put on a casual shirt and a Panama hat and gave the cookies a personality. He handed them out on the street from a big bag shaped like a cookie. He threw parties to promote his cookies. Throughout it all, he never forgot his emphasis on quality. Famous Amos's cookies led the way for other exclusive cookie stores.

1. What sorts of things would Wally Amos have included in the description and analysis section of his business plan about:
   - the type of business he was opening,
   - the trading area analysis,
   - the market segment analysis, and
   - the analysis of a potential location.
2. What were Famous Amos's strengths and skills for opening a cookie company?

Some good sources of information about your competitors are the Yellow Pages, annual reports, trade associations, your local Chamber of Commerce, and business publications such as *Dun and Bradstreet* reports.

Market Segment Analysis

A market segment analysis is a description of your target market and the buying behavior of your potential customers.

Analyzing Your Competition

1. How many similar competing businesses are in your trading area?

2. Where are they located?

3. What are their prices?

4. What is the quality of their goods or services?

5. What customer services do they provide?

6. What is their sales volume?

7. Are they expanding their operations?

8. How do they sell their goods or services?

9. How do they advertise or promote their goods or services?

10. What are their strengths?

11. What are their weaknesses?

Figure 39-2 **Analyzing Your Competition**
When analyzing your competition for a business plan, ask yourself these questions. Why is it so important to list your competitors' weaknesses as well as their strengths?

Target Market. As you know, your target market represents customers who have a common set of characteristics. Here are the characteristics commonly used to identify a target market.

Location of customers:
- region,
- county size,
- size of city,
- density of population, and
- climate of area.

Demographics of customers:
- age,
- gender,
- marital status,
- family size,
- income,
- occupation,
- education,
- religion, and
- culture or ethnic background.

You must carefully identify your target market because the needs and wants of different groups of potential buyers must be addressed differently in the marketing of goods and services.

For example, families can live in the same city and have similar educations, occupations, and incomes. However, their needs for entertainment, furniture, food, clothing, or personal services may vary greatly depending on their religious or ethnic background. The latter, in fact, may define entirely different target markets.

Your task as an entrepreneur is to decide which target market to serve and how best to do it. The best way to make this decision is to be guided by the way the members of the target market perceive themselves and their own needs.

Customers' Buying Behavior. After you have identified your target market, you will also need to explain how the potential customer *buying behavior* associated with it will be good for your business.

Buying behavior is the process individuals use to decide what they will buy and from where and whom they will buy it. For example, if you plan to open a children's toy store, you have used demographic information to determine how many families with children are in your target market. You also know the approximate average family income. From your earlier analysis of the competition (other toy stores serving the same target market), you have an idea of how much disposable income these families spent on children's toys and which toys they bought. You also know which stores in which locations did the most business. This is your target market's buying behavior.

You can then put this information together to make decisions about how your store might best serve these same customers, given their buying behavior. Do you want to try to take business away from other toy stores, or do you want to try to sell items not offered in the other stores? Do you want to get your customers to buy a lot of low-priced items or a few high-priced ones?

Analysis of Potential Locations

After you have analyzed your trading area and your market segment, including your target market and your competition, you are ready to select your location. Determining where to locate your business is one of your most important decisions because location has a direct effect on your sales.

Your analysis should include whether you will buy or rent the property, how you will control customer traffic, and the nearness to your competition. Your location will determine your hours of operation and the number of customers who will see and patronize your business.

For example, if you are located in a shopping mall or shopping center, your business hours will probably be set by the management association. In either place, you can also usually depend on fairly constant customer traffic generated by the other businesses in the same location.

Where you locate in a mall or shopping center depends upon available space and the nature of your business. If your business relies on impulse buying and thus needs many customers passing by, as do restaurants, it may be worthwhile to spend the extra money to rent the best available site. If customer count is not quite so crucial, site location is less important. The money you save on rent can be used to advertise or promote your business.

If you decide to locate in your home or in a separate building, consider these factors.

- Is parking available?
- How far are you from a residential area?
- Is the neighborhood safe?
- Will traffic congestion be a problem?
- On which side of the street will you locate?

In addition, you need to look at some personal issues about the location of your business. Do you want to be near family and friends? Do you want to locate in a neighborhood away from where you currently live?

After you have answered these questions, you are ready to find a specific site. Your first step should be to learn about any local ordinances or laws that may affect your business. For example, if you intend to build, you will need to get the necessary building permits. If you are planning to operate a regulated business, such as a children's day-care center or a restaurant, you will need to get the necessary approvals and permits required by your community to operate. If you are unsure about local regulations, meet with your local or county officials to find out what is required.

VOCABULARY REVIEW

Use each of the following terms in a sentence, based on your reading of chapter content.

business philosophy   buying behavior
trading area

FACT AND IDEA REVIEW

1. What is a business philosophy? Why is it important?

2. What seven major elements are included in the description of the business situation section of the business plan?

3. Why is self-analysis critical to developing a business plan? What aspects of your abilities should you discuss in the self-analysis section of your business plan?

4. What is a trading area? Why is it important to analyze the trading area in your business plan?

5. What is meant by disposable income? Why is it important to know how much disposable income your potential customers have?

6. What is the buying power index? How can an entrepreneur use the buying power index?

7. What sources can an entrepreneur use to find out about competition that already exists for a proposed good or service?

8. Why is the identification of your target market essential to your business plan?

9. Identify five characteristics commonly used to identify a target market.

10. What is buying behavior? Why is it so important to understand customer buying behavior in your target market?

11. Identify at least three factors to consider when planning a location for a business.

CRITICAL THINKING

1. React to this statement: "Employees are the most valued asset to a small business." Do you agree or disagree? Explain your answer.

2. Some people argue that government should only regulate business and never provide assistance for new business start-ups. What do you think should be the government's role in relation to new business ventures?

3. What are some of the factors that a new business can control? What are some uncontrollable factors?

4. How can you determine a need for a good or service?

USING BASIC SKILLS

Math

1. Total yearly sales for the "Personally Yours" apparel store were $287,255. Determine the average monthly sales for the store.

2. You have three salespeople working for you who receive both an hourly wage and a commission on sales. Each earns a different hourly rate and a different commission percentage on sales. Determine their total gross weekly wage given the following information:

	Worker 1	Worker 2	Worker 3
Hourly Wage	$3.55	$3.75	$4.25
Hours Worked	30	25	40
Sales	$235.00	$387.50	$756.00
Commission Percentage	3½%	4%	3%
Weekly Wage	_____	_____	_____

3. A student was paid $3.75 an hour and double time on Sunday. What was the total weekly wage if the student worked 4 hours on Sunday, 4 hours on Wednesday, 3½ hours on Thursday, and 6 hours on Saturday?

Communication

4. With the direction of your instructor, write a business letter inviting a local businessperson to speak on the importance of store location to a successful business.

5. Interview a local business owner about the skills and personal traits and abilities he or she needs to run his or her business well. Write a 100-word report on your findings.

6. Research and prepare a five-minute oral presentation on how economic conditions can influence the profits for a new business.

Human Relations

7. Your marketing teacher has just presented information on the importance of personal skills in owning and operating a business. After school, a friend of yours who is an excellent auto mechanic says to you, "Anyone can be successful in business as long as they have the right technical skills." What would you say to your friend?

APPLICATION PROJECTS

1. Develop a section of a business plan using instructor guidelines or those prepared by National DECA for the Entrepreneurship Event (Organizing a Business). Prepare a three-page section (Part I) entitled "Description and Analysis of the Business Situation." These activities will help you complete this project.

a. Select a proposed business operation selling consumer products (manufacturing, retail, wholesale, or service). Describe the type of business, the major good or service involved, appealing factors about the business, factors you think will make it more successful, and proposed hours of operation.

b. Describe your aspirations and career objectives, educational experiences, and related work experiences that will help you be successful in the business.

c. Make a chart of your competitors' strengths and weaknesses. Analyze their goods, services, facilities, prices, selection, advertising, personnel, and distribution or delivery methods.

d. Use the *Survey of Buying Power* by Sales and Marketing Management along with U.S. census data to identify the economic data for the location of the proposed business.

e. Identify the target market for the proposed business by looking at potential customers' geographic location, average age, gender, family size, income, occupation, nationality, race, and such things as educational level and religious background.

f. Visit the city or township clerk and write a report about zoning regulations for your proposed site.

g. List all important factors for the proposed business location, such as traffic patterns and costs of renting or owning.

h. Conduct a customer traffic study at several sites. Select your preferred site.

Organizing and Marketing a Proposed Business

40

After completing this chapter, you will be able to:

1. evaluate forms of business ownership,

2. identify the steps in forming a business,

3. plan personnel needs,

4. develop an organization chart,

5. provide details related to goods or services to be offered, including suppliers, manufacturing plans, and inventory policies,

6. develop pricing policies, and

7. develop a marketing and promotion plan.

WORDS TO KNOW

unlimited liability
general partnership
limited partnership
foreign corporation
Subchapter S corporation
DBA
Articles of Incorporation
job description
organization chart

I n this chapter you will learn how to prepare the organization and marketing section of your business plan. You will compare legal forms of business ownership and determine which is the best for your business. You will look at how to plan for your personnel needs to handle managerial, financial, legal, and production functions.

Suggestions for identifying potential suppliers, developing manufacturing plans, and determining inventory and pricing policies will be discussed. Finally, you will learn how to identify, plan, and develop promotional activities for your proposed business.

Your Proposed Organization Plan

The organization section of your business plan is essentially a blueprint. It lays the foundation for the structure of your proposed business.

Type of Ownership

Your first step is to decide which type of ownership best suits your proposed business. The legal form of business organization you select may make the difference between business success and business failure. It determines how fast you can get your business decisions implemented, how well you compete in the marketplace, and how quickly you can raise additional money for expansion.

As you learned in Chapter 38, there are three principal types of business organization: the proprietorship, the partnership, and the corporation. Each has its advantages and disadvantages. One is not better than the others. The one you select depends on such circumstances as your financial condition, the type of business you want to start, the number of employees you will hire, the business risk involved, and your tax situation.

Remember that you can change your initial decision about the type of business organization you feel is best. As your business grows and prospers, your financial and tax situations may require you to change the form of organization.

Sole Proprietorship. As you learned in Chapter 38, the sole proprietorship is owned and operated by one person. If you choose this form of ownership, you have complete control over the business. However, you are also responsible for all business debts or legal judgments against the business.

For example, if the debts of your business exceed its assets (that is, all of its resources), your creditors can claim all of your own personal assets, such as your car, home, and savings. This responsibility is called *unlimited liability*. *Unlimited liability means that your financial liability is not limited to your investment in the business, but extends to your total ability to make payments.*

However, any profits from your business are your personal income. They are taxed at your own personal rate, which is lower than most, if not all, business tax rates.

Partnership. In a partnership, two or more people are legally responsible for the success or failure of the business. Like a sole proprietorship, a partnership is subject to relatively little regulation and is fairly easy to establish. A partnership agreement, usually prepared by an attorney, specifies the responsibilities of each partner.

There are two types of partnerships: *general* and *limited*. *In a general partnership, each partner shares in the profits and losses.* As in the sole proprietorship, each partner has unlimited liability for the company's debts. Also, each partner's share of the profits is taxed as personal income.

Because of the unlimited liability you face as a member of a general partnership, you might want to establish a *limited partnership*. *In a limited partnership, each limited partner is liable for any debts only up to the amount of his or her investment in the company*.

Every limited partnership, however, must have at least one general partner who has unlimited liability. In exchange for their limited liability, limited partners have no voice in the management of the partnership. The withdrawal of a limited partner does not dissolve the partnership if you and your partners decide to continue doing business.

If you decide to establish a limited partnership, you must give public notice stating that one or more partners have limited liability. Otherwise, it is assumed that a general partnership exists and all partners have unlimited liability. You can get additional information regarding limited partnerships by contacting your state Department of Commerce.

REAL WORLD MARKETING

If You Can't Beat 'Em, Buy 'Em

At first, such popcorn classics as Jiffy Pop and Orville Redenbacher hoped the new kid on the block, with its claims of all-natural non-junk food popcorn, would simply go away. However, by 1988, sales at three-year-old Smartfoods had jumped from $35,000 to $10 million, and the new kid could no longer be ignored. In January of 1989, Frito–Lay, which seldom acquires companies, did what any big gun would do in this age of corporate takeovers. It bought Smartfoods for a tidy $15 million.

Corporation. The most complicated form of business ownership, the corporation is chartered by a state and legally operates apart from the owners. It is composed of shareholders (or stockholders, the owners of the corporation), directors, and officers.

A corporation can own assets, borrow money, and perform business functions without directly involving the shareholders. Therefore, it is subject to more government regulation than a sole proprietorship or a partnership. The profits are subject to double taxation, but the liability of the shareholders is limited. Owners of the corporation are not responsible for debts incurred by the corporation.

Corporations can be *incorporated* (established) in the state where they will do business or in another state. It is best for most small businesses to incorporate in the state where they are going to do business.

Otherwise, they may have to do business as a *foreign corporation*. *A **foreign corporation** is incorporated under the laws of a different state from the one in which it does business*. Foreign corporations must seek approval from and register with each state in which they intend to do business.

Some new businesses can also be established as *Subchapter S corporations*. *A **Subchapter S corporation** is a small business that is taxed like a partnership or proprietorship*.

There are strict provisions for Subchapter S corporations. The business, for example, can have no more than 35 shareholders. It must be incorporated in the United States. It can have no more than 20 percent of its gross revenues from investment-type income, and no more than 80 percent of its gross revenues from foreign sources. You can learn more information

C A S E   C H A L L E N G E

You Try Harder When It's Your Own

Imagine a company with several thousand employees, all of whom can say they own a piece of the firm. Does this sound impossible? Would you like to own a piece of the company that also employs you?

One company that has made employee ownership work is Avis, the "we try harder" car rental people. The employees bought the company in 1987 through an employee stock ownership plan.

As you can imagine, it takes a lot of money to buy a company such as Avis. The employees borrowed money to buy all the shares of stock. As the company pays off the debt, the trustee who holds the employees' shares distributes them to the employees according to their pay.

At the end of the first year, Avis's 12,500 employees each owned about 10 shares for every $1,000 of their pay. (At a salary of $20,000 a year, for example, an Avis employee would own 200 shares.) When the debt is paid off around the year 2004, the Avis employees will own all 24 million shares of stock.

Studies have shown that when employees actively take part in making company decisions, the company grows 11 percent faster than without employee participation. So, Avis keeps employees involved and keeps lines of communication open.

In a survey of 1,000 typical car renters, Avis found that 77 percent of them believed employee ownership would make Avis's service even better than it was. They were right. Customers almost immediately began to notice a difference. Complaints about service dropped 35 percent in the first year.

You can see, then, that it really does make a difference when the company is your own. Avis's new motto is: "We're trying harder than ever."

1. What do you think might be some of the most difficult problems to resolve in an employee-owned business?
2. What are some of the advantages to working for an employee-owned company?

about Subchapter S corporations by consulting IRS publication No. 589 or by calling your Internal Revenue Office.

Whether or not you choose to file as a Subchapter S corporation, you must still show your internal corporate organization in your business plan. This includes the development of corporate bylaws, the selection of a board of directors, and the election of officers who will actually run the corporate operations. In small corporations, the members of the board of directors frequently are elected as the officers of the corporation.

Steps in Establishing Your Business

Once you have detailed in your business plan what type of business ownership you have chosen, you need to show the steps you will take to establish your business.

DBA. If you establish a sole proprietorship or partnership, you must file for a *DBA* (Doing Business As) at your local county clerk's office. *A DBA is a registration process by which your county government officially recognizes that your business exists.*

There is usually a filing fee for registration, but the process protects the name of your business for a certain number of years. However, this name protection applies only to the county where your business is registered.

If you decide on a proprietorship or partnership, there is one thing you must do before you register. Check with all the county clerks in your trading area and with your state Department of Commerce to see if any other business is using your chosen business name. This reduces the chances that someone will later sue you to prevent your use of their business name.

Articles of Incorporation. If you want to form a corporation, you must file *Articles of Incorporation* with the Corporation and Securities Bureau in your state Department of Commerce. *Articles of Incorporation identify the name and address of your business, its purpose, the names of the initial directors, and the amount of stock that will be issued to each director.*

There is a filing fee, but your business becomes protected and no other business may register under your name. The necessary forms, applications, and information on filing fees are also obtained from your state Department of Commerce.

The type of business organization is important to the overall success of your business. The decision is somewhat complicated, so you must get the best advice possible before starting operations. Discuss the advantages and disadvantages of each business form with an accountant, an attorney, or some other business advisor. If you elect to form a corporation, the laws of your state may require you to hire an attorney. Check your state laws for specific requirements regarding incorporation.

Licenses. Depending on what business you enter and where you locate, you may have to obtain one or more licenses. Individual states license many businesses and occupations, such as doctors, accountants, cosmetologists, barbers, marriage counselors, and pharmacists. Licensing is done for these reasons:

- to protect the public from unscrupulous people,
- to establish minimum standards of education and training for people who practice a particular profession,
- to maintain the health and welfare of all citizens,
- to regulate where businesses can locate, and
- to protect neighborhoods and the environment.

In addition to state licenses, your community may require special local licenses or permits to comply with zoning ordinances, building codes, and safety standards. For example, most communities require you to obtain a license before you open a hotel, restaurant, or movie theater in the area. Be sure to check with your local government and your state Department of Licensing and Regulation prior to starting your business.

Personnel Needs

Whether you organize as a proprietorship, partnership, or a corporation, your business plan must show your personnel needs. Potential investors need to know that you can identify the essential jobs your business will need to run properly. They also will want you to identify, as much as you can, the people who will do those jobs.

Table 40-1 shows the typical functions in a business. Notice that some of the functions are repeated under more than one category. By identifying all the necessary functions, you will be able to begin planning an organizational structure for your business.

STATE OF CALIFORNIA

INQUIRIES MAY BE DIRECTED TO:
STATE BOARD OF COSMETOLOGY
1020 N STREET
SACRAMENTO, CALIFORNIA 95814

KM 096126   COSMETOLOGIST LICENSE

THE UNDERNOTED HAVING COMPLETED ALL   VALID UNTIL: 01/31/90
STATUTORY REQUIREMENTS IS HEREBY LICENSED
UNDER THE BUSINESS AND PROFESSIONS CODE.

SIGNATURE:

FLORES LUPE
11821 VISTA DE CERRAS DRIVE
MORENO VALLEY   CA 92360

OPERATOR LICENSE MUST BE DISPLAYED AT PRIMARY WORK STATION

_____ Post in Public View _____

Table 40-1
Business Functions

Administration	Production	Marketing
Operations	Operations	Advertising
Personnel	Purchasing	Sales
Financial	Manufacturing	Public Relations
Legal	Distribution	Service
Public Relations	Service	

Shown in this table are the typical functions performed in most businesses in three general categories: administration *(running the business),* production *(making the product), and* marketing *(selling the product). Choose any of the above functions, such as purchasing. Name two positions you would find in that area.*

Cosmetologists must display their operating licenses at all times during the business day. Why do you think it is particularly important to license people giving such personal care services as manicures?

Most new businesses are one-person operations. If this is your case, then you will do all the business functions. However, if you plan to divide responsibilities among partners or hire people, you must identify how everyone fits into the organizational structure.

You need to prepare *job descriptions* for your partners, employees, and yourself. *Job descriptions are written statements listing the requirements of a particular job.* Each job description includes the purpose of the job, qualifications needed, duties to be performed, equipment to be used, and expected working conditions.

After various job descriptions have been prepared, you are ready to develop an *organization chart. An organization chart is a diagram of the various jobs and functions that are found in a company.* It should be drawn with the jobs and major duties identified and clear lines of authority shown.

Sometimes outside professional help is needed to keep a business going and growing. Entrepreneurs are often afraid to spend money on such professional services as accounting. This can be a fatal mistake. These trained professionals will help you avoid making serious mistakes that can result in business failure. If you decide to use outside professionals, identify them and their responsibilities on your organization chart. A core group of professionals that can help you are shown on Table 40-2.

You can also use paid professional assistance to identify employment practices in your state or locality. For example, new business owners need to be familiar with laws regulating minimum wages, occupational health and safety, unemployment compensation, and worker's disability insurance. Another source of information about employment laws is your state Department of Labor. State agencies publish many inexpensive or free publications to help new entrepreneurs understand various employment laws, rules, and regulations.

Table 40-2
Professional Services

Professional	Service Provided
Accountant	bookkeeping, taxes, cash flow
Attorney	legal form of organization, contracts
Banker	loans, billing services, credit and collection systems
Insurance Agent	needs evaluation, insurance, risk management

Here are some of the professional services that new business owners are likely to need. Which of the above professionals would you call if you needed to resolve a legal dispute with one of your business partners?

Proposed Good or Service

This section of your business plan includes your manufacturing plans, inventory policies, and suppliers. Let's say you plan to introduce a new product, such as custom bumper stickers. Perhaps you are going to replicate and sell an existing product. In both cases, you would prepare a purchasing plan that gives the following information:

- name of your item,
- name and address of your supplier,
- discount offered,
- delivery time,
- freight cost, and
- fill-in policy (how quickly orders can be filled).

Closely related to your purchasing plan is your inventory policy. You need to show how you will manage the goods you purchase or manufacture. How much, for example, will you keep on hand? How will you keep track of what to order and what has been sold?

Your inventory system depends on the size and scope of your proposed business. You may not need an extensive system. Trade associations and many suppliers can give you suggestions for an inventory control system that is best for your business.

If you are planning a service business, you should come up with a plan that addresses how, when, and who will provide the service to your customers. State the services provided by your competitors, describe the additional services you will provide, and estimate

REAL WORLD MARKETING

Where There's Smoke, There Are Ribs

Fire fighters usually take turns cooking for the others at the station. One wonders, however, if Carl English Jr., of the San Francisco Fire Department, is asked to cook more often. At 28, English started the Firehouse Bar-B-Que Restaurant using an old family recipe to turn out tasty barbecued meats. He now has four restaurants and sells his Firehouse sauce throughout the country.

their costs. By analyzing your competitors' expenses and your own expenses for providing a service, you can show how you will price your service without pricing yourself out of the market.

Your Proposed Marketing Plan

At this point in your business plan, you have selected your business organization, identified your staffing needs, and detailed your goods/service policies. You are now ready to develop your marketing policies—that is, the way you will price, display, and market your good or service.

This part of the business plan discusses proposed pricing policies, such as costs and markups compared to your competition. It also discusses personal and nonpersonal promotional activities, as well as your promotional plan for the year.

Pricing Policies

As you know, pricing your goods or services is an important aspect of running a successful business. You must be able to set a price high enough to cover your costs and make a profit for your business but low enough to attract customers. Among the factors to consider in setting your prices are:

- your total cost for a product, including any delivery or service charges you must pay;
- your other expenses, such as rent, advertising and promotion costs, employee payroll, supplies, and any other recurring costs;
- the amount of profit you want to make on the good or service;
- the price being charged by your competitors (suppliers, competitors' catalogs and price lists, and advertising will keep you in touch with this); and
- your customers' wants and needs.

In a broader sense, your prices also need to reflect what is going on in the economy. During such poor economic times as a recession, customers tend to be more price-conscious. So, your prices will need to stress value. During more prosperous times, your customer will probably be less price-conscious and less resistant to higher prices. You will need to price your goods or services to match your customers'

expectations of quality and value, while at the same time remaining competitive in the market.

If you are planning a service business, your prices should be based on the value of the service to your customer. The price you charge may have little relationship to your costs. For example, if you provide secretarial services to clients who cannot type, they may feel your prices are a bargain. However, you must make sure that your prices are not too high and that the quality of your services are similar to or better than your competitors' to keep your customers coming back to your company.

Promotional Activities

Here you need to identify ways you will reach the greatest number of potential customers in your target market with the most economical use of your time and money.

The simplest method of promoting your business is through personal efforts aimed at providing quality goods and services to your customers. If your present customers are satisfied, their word-of-mouth advertising will attract additional customers.

Unfortunately, your personal efforts and word-of-mouth advertising will reach only so many people. Your promotional strategy should attract the greatest number of potential customers. So, you must advertise through other, nonpersonal promotional methods.

As you learned in Chapter 20, there are two categories of advertising: institutional and promotional. Institutional advertising creates a favorable impression and goodwill for your business. Promotional advertising is designed to increase sales.

In this part of your business plan, you will need to identify the category of advertising you will use (institutional, promotional, or both) as well as the advertising media you will use. State why they are right for your business. In addition, you should present a year-long budget for advertising. Answering these questions will help you develop promotional strategies:

- What is the best type of advertising to reach your target market—institutional advertising, promotional advertising, or both?
- What are the benefits of the various media in which you have chosen to advertise your business?
- What is your advertising budget?
- What other things do you need to include in your year-long plan?

VOCABULARY REVIEW

Write two or three paragraphs on developing an organization and marketing plan for your business plan, incorporating these nine vocabulary terms.

unlimited liability
general partnership
limited partnership
foreign corporation
Subchapter S corporation

DBA
Articles of Incorporation
job description
organization chart

FACT AND IDEA REVIEW

1. What three major elements are included in the organization of the business plan?

2. What three things does the legal form of your business determine?

3. What is unlimited liability? How does unlimited liability affect the type of business organization selected by an entrepreneur?

4. What are the two different kinds of partnerships? Explain the difference between them.

5. What three groups of people are involved with the corporate form of ownership?

6. What is a foreign corporation?

7. What is a Subchapter S corporation? Identify three criteria used to establish a Subchapter S corporation.

8. What does DBA mean?

9. What are Articles of Incorporation?

10. Identify five reasons for licensing certain occupations or businesses.

11. Why is planning personnel needs important for new businesses? How can job descriptions be used to assist in determining personnel needs?

12. What is an organization chart?

13. What information does a purchasing plan include?

14. Tell five things you should consider when setting your pricing policies.

CRITICAL THINKING

1. Why would a company want to incorporate its business in a state other than the one in which it is located?

2. Why do you think there should be government regulations on new business start-ups?

3. How would you determine which job positions you need to fill in your new business?

4. Under what conditions can a small business take the role of being a price-cutter?

5. Why would you have an accountant, attorney, or business advisor assist you in establishing your business?

USING BASIC SKILLS

Math

1. Some businesses calculate markup as a percentage of the cost of merchandise. This method of pricing is known as the *cost method*. The formula for this is:
   Retail price = (Cost x Markup %) + Cost

   Calculate the retail price using the above formula for the following situations:

Cost of Merchandise	Markup on Cost	Retail Price
$ 70.00	30%	_____
$ 115.00	45%	_____
$1,500.00	145%	_____
$ 23.40	15%	_____
$ 58.95	33⅓%	_____

2. Another more widely used method to compute retail price is called the *retail method*. This is used more frequently than the cost method because most business records use retail sales figures for their records. The formula for the retail method of pricing is:

$$\text{Retail Price} = \frac{\text{Cost of Merchandise}}{100\% - \text{Markup \%}}$$

Calculate the retail price using the above formula for the following situations:

Cost of Merchandise	Markup % on Retail	Retail Price
$ 250.00	45%	_____
$1,250.00	66⅓%	_____
$ 16.25	15%	_____
$ 5.35	33⅓%	_____
$ 9.50	50%	_____

Communication

3. Develop a written employee policy for personal appearance and grooming which you would institute in your business. Pay careful attention to hairstyles, personal hygiene, and dress in developing your policy.

4. Write a business letter under the direction of your instructor inviting an attorney to discuss the steps involved in establishing a corporation in your state.

Human Relations

5. Write a response to the following Dear Abby letter:

Dear Abby:
You won't believe how boring my job is. I have to answer the telephone all day. There is no change all day long from my saying, "Hello, this is the Sunshine Company." Sometimes we have only two phone calls an hour. It's the same job over and over. I want to work. However, I almost fall asleep on the job. What should I do?
Signed
I'm Bored

APPLICATION PROJECT

Develop a section of a business plan using instructor guidelines or guidelines and criteria prepared by National DECA for the Entrepreneurship Event (Organizing a Business). Prepare a three-page Part II entitled "Proposed Organization and Marketing Plan." These activities will help you complete this section of your project.

a. Develop a written list of the goods and services you would offer in a business of your choice. Explain the rationale for your decision.

b. Prepare a written report on the advantages of using a certified public accountant to maintain records. Detail what records the accountant should supply to the owner.

c. Research data processing systems to aid small business owners. Report on the costs, advantages, and disadvantages of each system.

d. Investigate which legal form you would select for a business. Write a report on the advantages and disadvantages that affected your decision.

e. Write your state Department of Commerce to get information about the steps required to establish a business in your state.

f. Develop a one-month promotional plan for your business. The plan should contain a budget, selection of media, and a plan to evaluate its effectiveness.

g. Develop a list of special promotional events that would be conducted for each month of the year for a selected business.

h. Prepare a written report on the pricing policies you will use in your selected business. Include information on price image, loss leaders, above-average markup, average markup, below average markup, special sales, and markdown policies.

i. Report on the noninsurable risks you would be willing to assume as a new business owner.

j. Collect several employee application forms from area stores. Design a new application form for your selected business.

k. Prepare an organization chart for a new business. Explain the need for the positions and the reporting relationships that exist.

l. Investigate wage and salary data for jobs identified in your business plan. Explain the salary plan and fringe benefit package that you would offer to new employees.

m. Develop a written plan for handling employee complaints and grievances in your selected business.

41

OBJECTIVES

After completing this chapter, you will be able to:

1. identify sources of capital,

2. understand financial statements,

3. determine start-up costs for a business,

4. determine your personal income needs,

5. project business income,

6. project business expenses, and

7. estimate needed cash flow.

WORDS TO KNOW

capital
debt capital
equity capital
collateral
credit union
personal financial statement
balance sheet
asset
liability
net worth
income statement
operating ratios

Financing a Proposed Business

As you now know, it is expensive to start and operate a business. Unless you are already wealthy, you will need to borrow money to begin business operations. So, every good business plan contains a financial plan—a section telling what it will cost to establish and maintain the business.

This chapter will show you how to prepare a financial plan to convince potential investors that you will wisely spend and repay the money you borrow to begin your enterprise. You will learn how to identify your capital needs and how to develop a plan that will meet those needs. You will read about several of the key sources of business capital. In addition, you will discover how to project your business income and expenses, and how to display that information in a way that will help persuade investors to loan you money.

Sources of Capital

Capital means the funds needed to finance the operation of a business. The term capital also includes all goods used to produce other goods. Nevertheless, when we refer to capital in this chapter, we are talking about money.

When entrepreneurs open their own businesses, they usually need a substantial amount of capital. There are several ways to raise the capital for a new business. You can use money from your personal savings. However, most ways to raise capital for a new business venture involve borrowing money from banks, credit unions, relatives, friends, suppliers, and/or previous business owners.

Borrowing money can work to your advantage. Borrowing money and repaying it builds your credit standing. This means it will be easier for you to borrow money in the future. Also, the interest you pay on a loan is a tax-deductible business expense.

The method you choose to raise money depends on the amount involved. Money needed for operating expenses is usually repaid within a year. A large amount of money borrowed to build a new facility, to purchase equipment, or to start an inventory will be repaid over a longer period of time. The method you use to raise money also determines your degree of ownership in your own business.

If you raise money by *borrowing* it, you have an obligation to repay the loan with interest, but no ownership passes to the lender. *Borrowing is also*

CASE CHALLENGE

Financing the American Dream

Many people come to the United States looking for the American Dream. Nevertheless, they may not speak English or have a credit history here. Thus, banks may deny them financial help to get their businesses started.

So, how do many of these people find the money to go into business within a few years of their arrival? The answer is loan clubs.

Loan clubs let resourceful newcomers help themselves. They are made up of 10 to 20 people who each agree to contribute the same amount of money each month to a kitty. Each month, the money collected goes to one of the club members. The first month's kitty may go to the neediest person in the group. Members may also bid for the kitty by offering rates of interest. The highest rate of interest gets the kitty. Everyone in the group continues to contribute money until every member has received the kitty. Then the group usually disbands.

Although members of a loan club may not know each other, they know the club organizer. He or she keeps the records and vouchers for the group members. If anyone fails to make payments, the club organizer makes up the difference. In return for this responsibility, the group organizer may get his or her turn at the kitty interest-free.

So far, these clubs have helped Vietnamese, Koreans, Mexicans, and West Indians raise anywhere from a few hundred dollars to thousands of dollars. People have gone to loan clubs to borrow money for such things as shrimp boats, restaurants, graphic equipment, and stores.

Loan clubs work because people in ethnic communities tend to be close and trusting. People in loan clubs rarely default because they don't want to jeopardize their standing in the community.

1. If you were a loan club organizer, what questions would you ask a potential member?
2. Why do you think loan clubs limit their membership to 10 to 20 people?

*called using **debt capital**.* There is a major disadvantage to this method of raising money. If you cannot pay back your debt capital, you could be forced into bankruptcy. Investors or co-owners may not force this, but they will want to tell you how to run your business.

If you *raise* money by selling part of the interest in the business to investors, you do not need to repay the money or pay interest. However, the investor becomes a co-owner in your business. *Raising money by selling part of the business itself is called using equity capital*. The larger the amount of equity capital you use in your business, the greater degree of control you will lose to your investors.

Personal Savings

The most common method of financing a business is using personal savings. Even though you might not want to do this, you probably cannot avoid investing all or part of your savings. As you know, starting any new business involves risk. Your prospective investors and creditors will expect you to share in that risk.

If you intend to use your personal savings, it may be better for you to use personal property as *collateral* for a loan. *Collateral is something of value that a borrower pledges to a lender to ensure repayment of a loan.* Some examples of collateral are jewelry, vehicles, bonds, stocks, machinery, the cash value of insurance policies, and real estate.

Banks

Commercial banks, the most numerous and widespread lending agencies in the United States, are the most common sources of business financing. They know their local area and local economy well and offer a number of different loans and services on competitive and government-regulated terms.

Banks evaluate potential lenders on criteria called the six *C*'s of credit: *capital, collateral, capability, character, coverage,* and *circumstances.*

Capital. How much of your own money or capital is to be invested in your new business? Banks, like other potential investors, will want to know how much of an investment of capital you are willing to put into your new venture.

Collateral. What assets (things of monetary value) can be used as collateral for a loan? (We will talk more about assets later in this chapter.) Lenders will usually require the value of the collateral to be greater than the amount of the loan. Some banks will require a guaranty of personal assets (in effect, a promise that you have the assets you claim to have) and a pledge that you will repay the loan. Banks want to know that your loan will be repaid, even if your business fails.

Capability and Character. A resume of your previous training and related work experience, including professional and personal references, will answer questions about your capability and character.

Coverage and Circumstances. The last two items that a banker will take into account when considering your loan application are the amount of insurance coverage that you will carry and the general circumstances of your business as described in the description and analysis section of your business plan.

Filling out loan application forms can be a lengthy and often tedious process. Contact a banker or the loan officer of your local bank. He or she will help you complete the necessary documentation.

Credit Unions

*A **credit union** is a cooperative association formed by labor unions or groups of employees for the benefit of its members.* Credit unions often charge lower interest rates on loans than banks do. To borrow money from a credit union, however, you must be a member. Check with your parents, guardians, and/or relatives to determine your eligibility, since credit unions often accept memberships for relatives. Credit unions also use the 6 *C*'s of credit to determine if they will accept your loan application.

If you have thoroughly analyzed yourself and your business and have developed a sound marketing and financial plan, the chances are good that either a bank or a credit union will approve your loan.

Relatives and Friends

Many people begin their businesses with funds borrowed from relatives and friends. You should be cautious about doing this, however. An old saying tells us that two of the quickest ways to lose friends are to lend them money or to borrow money from them. You must consider whether starting a new business is worth the risk of losing or alienating people close to you.

A Bird's-Eye View of Success

The winter of 1916 was typically cold in the northern reaches of Canada. It was so cold, in fact, that the food supplies that reached a 30-year-old student of wildlife on assignment from America arrived frozen solid. Most people would curse frozen food. This man saw an opportunity in it. He went to work on a technique for quick-freezing vegetables, which he later sold to General Foods for $1 million. His name, which still appears on their frozen food line, was Clarence Birdseye.

If you do choose to borrow money from your family or friends, avoid future problems and misunderstandings by putting all agreements in writing. Identify the period of the loan, any interest to be paid, and your payment schedule.

If relatives or friends become investors in your business, determine the amount of control you will retain, whether you can buy back their interest at a later time, and how you will share the profits with them. Be sure that each person investing in your business can afford and is willing to possibly lose the money invested. Remember, no business—even yours—is guaranteed to succeed.

Partners and Shareholders

As you learned in Chapters 38 and 40, having partners is another way to raise money. Partners may bring in their own money and have access to other sources unavailable to you. However, if you form a partnership, you lessen your degree of ownership. You may have to share control of the business with your partner.

If you form a corporation, you sell stock to shareholders as a way of raising capital. As you learned in the previous chapter, you need to incorporate and obtain a charter to operate as a corporation.

Because each shareholder in a corporation has limited liability (that is, limited responsibility for debt), a corporation can raise large amounts of money from its shareholders. Although shareholders influence general corporate policy decisions, you can still control the corporation's daily activities by holding a majority of the shares.

Suppliers and Previous Owners

Some suppliers may provide you with a low interest loan to purchase inventory, furniture, fixtures, and equipment on a delayed payment basis. This method of raising capital can improve your credit rating and allow you to stretch your available cash. Also, as mentioned earlier, the interest on loan payments is a tax-deductible business expense.

If you are purchasing an existing business, consider the previous owner as a potential source of capital. Many sole proprietors want to see their businesses continue after their own retirement. They may be willing to provide you with a loan and a favorable repayment plan to get you started.

As you can see, there are many potential sources of capital to explore when seeking financing for your business. To make sure you have carefully researched all the available sources of capital, answer these questions.

1. What amount of your own savings will you put into the business?
2. Do you know the pros and cons of debt capital versus equity capital?
3. Did you check all of these sources of capital?
    Personal savings
    Banks
    Credit unions
    Relatives and Friends
    Partners and Shareholders
    Suppliers and Previous Owners
4. Did you complete a personal financial statement?
5. Did you contact a banker or loan officer for a loan application?
6. Do you have a good rating on the 6 Cs of credit?
    Capital
    Collateral
    Capability
    Character
    Coverage
    Circumstances
7. Did you contact a professional advisor, such as a lawyer or accountant, about ways to finance your business?

Understanding Financial Statements

After you have identified your source or sources of capital, you must develop three important financial statements to submit with your business plan: the *personal financial statement*, the *balance sheet*, and the *income statement*.

The latter two provide the financial overview of your business. They are important for future planning, evaluating your business, and preparing your tax returns.

The Personal Financial Statement

The *personal financial statement* is a summary of your current personal financial condition. It essentially tells the investor about the money you have in personal savings and in other investments, such as real estate. It also tells what you owe for such things as rent or house payments, credit card payments, school loans, and automobile loans. It is a very important part of any loan application for a new business. Figure 41-1 shows a personal financial statement.

PERSONAL FINANCIAL STATEMENT
August, 19 —

Assets

Cash	$	500.00
Savings accounts		1,500.00
Stocks, bonds, other securities		750.00
Accounts/Notes receivable		0.00
Life insurance cash value		0.00
Rebates/Refunds		0.00
Auto ('88 van)		18,000.00
Real estate (residence)		75,000.00
Vested pension plan		25,000.00
Other assets (lakefront property)		15,000.00
TOTAL ASSETS	$	135,750.00

Liabilities

Accounts payable (bank cards)		1,875.00
Contracts payable		0.00
Notes payable (mortgage)		28,500.00
Taxes payable		2,500.00
Real estate loans		0.00
Other liabilities ('88 van)		15,500.00
TOTAL LIABILITIES	$	48,375.00

TOTAL ASSETS	$	135,750.00
LESS TOTAL LIABILITIES	$	48,375.00
NET WORTH	$	

Figure 41-1 **Estimating Personal Living Expenses**

A personal financial statement shows your financial condition to date. Based on the figures shown here, what is your total net worth?

The Balance Sheet

The **balance sheet** *is a summary of your business assets, liabilities, and capital.* Figure 41-2 shows a typical balance sheet.

Assets. *An asset is anything of monetary value that is owned by your business.* Assets are classified as current and fixed.

Current assets are expected to be converted into cash in the upcoming year. Examples of current assets include cash in the bank, accounts receivable (money owed to you by your customers), and inventory.

Fixed assets are used over a period of years to operate your business. Examples of fixed assets include land, buildings, equipment, furniture, and fixtures—all of which you own.

Liabilities. *A liability is a debt owed by you for your business.* Liabilities are classified as current or long-term.

Current liabilities are the debts that you pay off during each business year. Some examples of current liabilities are accounts payable (money owed to suppliers), notes payable (money owed to a bank), and accrued liabilities (wages, taxes, interest, and other bills due but not paid as of the balance sheet date).

Long-term liabilities are debts that are not due to be paid in the coming year. Some examples of long-term liabilities are mortgages and loans.

BALANCE SHEET
August, 19 —

	YEAR I	YEAR II
Current Assets		
Cash	$ 5,000	$ 6,000
Accounts receivable	12,000	14,000
Inventory	150,000	265,000
Fixed Assets		
Real estate	$ 100,000	$ 105,000
Fixtures and equipment	50,000	50,000
Vehicles	15,000	14,000
Other Assets		
License	$ 100	$ 100
Goodwill	10,000	10,000
TOTAL ASSETS	$ 342,100	$ 464,100
Current Liabilities		
Notes payable (due within one year)	$ 125,000	$ 250,000
Accounts payable	10,000	15,000
Accrued expenses	5,000	5,000
Taxes owed	7,000	7,500
Long-Term Liabilities		
Notes payable (due after one year)	$ 75,000	$ 80,000
Other	15,000	20,000
TOTAL LIABILITIES	$ 237,000	$ 377,500
NET WORTH (ASSETS minus LIABILITIES)	$	$

TOTAL LIABILITIES plus NET WORTH should equal ASSETS

Figure 41-2 **Balance Sheet**

A balance sheet is a dollars and cents description of your existing or projected business. Based on the figures shown here, what is the net worth of your business for year I and year II?

Capital. As we mentioned earlier, capital is the funds needed to finance the operation of a business. It is also *net worth*.

Net worth is the difference between the assets of a business and its liabilities. Net worth, also known as *owner's equity*, is the value of the business after subtracting any financial obligations. To put this into a simple formula:

$$\text{Assets} - \text{Liabilities} = \text{Net Worth}$$

The Income Statement

The income statement, also known as a profit and loss statement, is a summary of your business's income and expenses during a specific period, such as a month, a quarter, or a year.

The income statement for an existing business details the previous year's earnings. The income statement for a new or planned business states the earnings projected for the upcoming year. Figure 41-3 shows a sample projected quarterly income statement.

PROJECTED QUARTERLY INCOME STATEMENT

	Month 1	Month 2	Month 3	Month 4	Month 5	Month 6	Month 7	Month 8	Month 9	Month 10	Month 11	Month 12	TOTAL
Total Net Sales	30,000.00	40,000.00	35,000.00										105,000.00
Cost of Goods Sold	19,500.00	26,000.00	22,750.00										68,250.00
GROSS PROFIT	10,500.00	14,000.00	12,250.00										36,750.00
Controllable Expenses													
Salaries	4,800.00	6,400.00	5,600.00										16,800.00
Payroll taxes	60.00	80.00	70.00										210.00
Security	300.00	400.00	350.00										1,050.00
Advertising	300.00	400.00	350.00										1,050.00
Automobile	450.00	600.00	525.00										1,575.00
Dues and subscriptions	15.00	20.00	17.50										52.50
Legal and accounting	300.00	400.00	350.00										1,050.00
Office supplies	120.00	160.00	140.00										420.00
Telephone	90.00	120.00	105.00										315.00
Utilities	90.00	120.00	105.00										315.00
Miscellaneous	360.00	480.00	420.00										1,260.00
Total Controllable Expenses	6,885.00	9,180.00	8,032.50										24,097.50
Fixed Expenses													
Depreciation	180.00	240.00	210.00										630.00
Insurance	240.00	320.00	280.00										840.00
Rent	810.00	1,080.00	945.00										2,835.00
Taxes and licenses	330.00	440.00	385.00										1,155.00
Loan payments (interest)	150.00	200.00	175.00										525.00
Total Fixed Expenses	1,710.00	2,280.00	1,995.00										5,985.00
TOTAL EXPENSES	8,595.00	11,460.00	10,027.50										
NET PROFIT (LOSS) (before taxes)	1,905.00	2,540.00	2,222.50										

Figure 41-3 **Income Statement**

An income statement is a summary of your business's income and expenses during a specific period. Based on the figures shown here, what are your total expenses and your net profit for the quarter?

As you will see, it is divided into these five sections.

1. Net sales—total sales minus sales taxes and deductions for your discounts, returns, and allowances.
2. Cost of goods sold—the total amount spent to produce or purchase the materials you sold during a specific period of the year. Cost of goods sold represents your beginning inventory plus any materials or products purchased, minus your ending inventory at the end of a given time period. (You will look at this later in the chapter when you learn how to project your business expenses.)
3. Gross profit or gross margin—the difference between the net sales and the cost of goods sold.
4. Expenses—the costs of operating the business. These are divided into such variable expenses as salaries, taxes, office supplies, and utilities, and such fixed expenses as insurance, rent, licenses, and interest on loans.
5. Net profit or net loss before taxes. Net profit is the money left over after all the expenses have been deducted from the gross profit. If the total expenses exceed the gross profit, your business experienced a net loss.

You can get information on start-up costs from people who are already in a similar business, and from related trade associations. State and local government agencies such as your state Department of Commerce are valuable sources of cost information.

You can write to the following sources for start-up information by type of business:

1. Small Business Administration
   P.O. Box 15434
   Fort Worth, TX 76119

2. Dun and Bradstreet
   99 Church Street
   New York, NY 10007

3. Bank of America
   Small Business Reporter
   Department 3120
   P.O. Box 37000
   San Francisco, CA 94137

Other sources of information about start-up costs include college and university business libraries, local and state Chambers of Commerce, Better Business Bureaus, Credit Bureaus, the Small Business Administration, and your state Department of Commerce. You can also learn a lot about these costs by reading business publications available from your public library.

Projecting Start-up Costs

There are two categories of business start-up costs: *one-time costs* and *continuing costs*.

One-time costs will not be repeated after your business is started. Examples of one-time costs include licenses and permits; deposits for telephone installation; and charges for installation of equipment, fixtures, and machinery.

Continuing costs are the expenses you will pay throughout the life of the business. Examples of continuing costs are such items as salaries; rent; advertising; supplies; insurance; repairs; maintenance; and federal, state, and local taxes.

You must carefully study your financing needs before you start business. You must estimate your start-up costs and project how much money you will need for your first year of operation.

Projecting Personal Needs

Many small businesses fail because they initially cannot pull in enough profit to pay their owners enough for living expenses. New businesses rarely support their owners right from the start. Unfortunately, many people don't understand this.

Therefore, in addition to a sound business plan, you should project your living expenses and household cash needs month-by-month for at least your first year of business. You may have to lower your current living standards to do this.

You should plan to have enough cash on hand to pay your personal expenses for more than your first month of operation. In fact, some experts suggest that you have enough start-up capital for the first three months of business.

Set aside your money for living expenses in a savings account. Do not use the money for any other purpose. This fund will help you get through the start-up period. The chart in Figure 41-4 will help you estimate how much money you should have in this account.

Projecting Business Income

The income your business will produce depends on the total yearly volume of sales it generates. Potentially, the more you sell, the more money you will make. So, you need to project the sales volume for your business.

You do this by determining the amount of money you want to earn and the percentage of average annual net profit. This will give you the total yearly sales your business must bring in for you to earn your desired amount of personal income. You can use this formula:

Annual Income Desired ÷ Percentage of
Average Annual Net Profit =
Total Yearly Sales Volume

For example, let's say you want to earn $20,000 in profits for the first year. From your industry research, you know the average annual net profit for the business you plan to operate is 5 percent. To bring in an annual rate of $20,000, you must have sales of $400,000.

$$\frac{20,000}{.05} = \$400,000$$

Most new businesses grow slowly in the beginning, so you should carefully estimate your sales volume. Trade associations, your banker, other businesspeople, and industry business publications can help you in making your projected sales and income estimates.

Your estimated sales volume (in this case, $400,000) becomes the yardstick by which you measure all business-related expenses.

Projecting Business Expenses

Your first step in projecting business expenses is to determine a yearly figure for the cost of goods sold.

Cost of goods sold can be expressed as a percentage of sales. When this is done, the relationship between cost of goods sold and sales becomes an *operating ratio*.

Operating ratios represent a comparison of costs and expenses of one business to another. For example, the percentage expense of advertising can be used as an operating ratio and can be compared to the percentage of advertising expense for similar businesses.

Basic operating ratios indicate the ratio of any specific expense to the amount of sales. They are available for most businesses from such trade and industrial associations as the National Retail Merchants Association, government agencies such as the Small Business Administration, business publications such as *Dun and Bradstreet* reports, and from banks. You need to get the appropriate ratios for your kind of business in order to estimate income and expenses in your business plan.

By using the operating ratio for cost of goods sold and your estimated sales volume, you can identify expenses. You simply substitute the ratios with dollar amounts on your projected income statement.

Projecting Cash Flow

A cash flow projection is a budget forecast of the cash, checks, or money orders that you anticipate receiving and spending during a specific period (usually in a month). It shows your expected revenue and expenses as well as such liabilities as loan payments, and thus allows you to see if you will have enough money to pay your bills.

What can you do if you project that you will need additional money during the year? If your business has potential and your balance sheet shows it to be financially strong, you will probably be able to borrow additional money to keep the business going during the start-up period and during slow sales months. You can repay your loan when sales become greater than your expenses.

Even if your cash flow projections indicate that you will need to borrow money to meet monthly needs, you will want to include your balance sheet and projected income statement in your business plan. It is never too early to show potential lenders that you are a good manager who plans to succeed in your new business.

COST-OF-LIVING BUDGET
FOR AN AVERAGE MONTH
BASED ON AN AVERAGE INCOME OF $38,000

Regular Monthly Payments

Rent or mortgage (including taxes)	$ 450.00
Cars (including insurance)	250.00
Appliances/TV	0.00
Home improvement loan	300.00
Personal loan	55.00
Health plan	50.00
Life insurance premiums	15.00
Other insurance premiums	20.00
Miscellaneous (bank account service fees)	10.00
TOTAL	$ 1,150.00

Personal Expenses

Clothing, cleaning, laundry	$ 110.00
Drugs	10.00
Doctors and dentists	50.00
Education	0.00
Dues	10.00
Gifts and contributions	40.00
Travel	50.00
Newspapers, magazines, books	10.00
Auto upkeep, gas, and parking	50.00
Spending money, allowances	20.00
TOTAL	$ 350.00

Household Operating Expenses

Telephone	50.00
Gas and electricity	120.00
Water and garbage	30.00
Other household expenses, repairs, maintenance	20.00
TOTAL	$ 220.00

Tax Expenses

Federal and state income taxes	175.00
Personal property taxes	350.00
Other taxes	25.00
TOTAL	$ 550.00

BUDGET SUMMARY

Regular Monthly Payments	1,150.00
Household Operating Expenses	220.00
Food Expenses	560.00
Personal Expenses	350.00
Tax Expenses	$ 550.00
MONTHLY TOTAL	$

Food Expenses

Food—at home	500.00
Food—away from home	60.00
TOTAL	$ 560.00

Figure 41-4 **Estimating Personal Living Expenses**

Filling out this form will help you estimate how much money you should set aside for living expenses when you start your business. Based the figures shown here, what is your monthly total for cost-of-living expenses?

VOCABULARY REVIEW

Write one or two paragraphs about how you would finance a proposed business, incorporating these 12 vocabulary terms.

capital
debt capital
equity capital
collateral
credit union
personal financial
  statement

balance sheet
asset
liability
net worth
income statement
operating ratios

FACT AND IDEA REVIEW

1. What is capital?

2. What is the difference between debt capital and equity capital?

3. What is the most common method of financing a business?

4. What is collateral? Give three examples of things that are used as collateral.

5. What are the six C's on which banks evaluate potential lenders?

6. What is a credit union?

7. How can a corporation raise capital?

8. What is a personal financial statement?

9. What is a balance sheet? What three things does a balance sheet show?

10. What are assets? Tell the difference between current and fixed assets.

11. What is a liability? What is the difference between current liabilities and long-term liabilities?

12. What is net worth?

13. What is an income statement? What are the five sections of an income statement?

14. Explain the two categories of business start-up costs.

15. What are operating ratios?

CRITICAL THINKING

1. What financial considerations would be different when financing a manufacturing service, a franchise, or a retail business?

2. What sources could you use to determine the total cash needed to start a business?

3. What factors would you consider in selecting a lender for a business?

4. What do you think are some of the legal issues new businesses have to deal with?

5. How do you think computers can assist in the financial analysis of a new business.

USING BASIC SKILLS

Math

1. The income statement in Figure 41.3 shows the projected business income for the first quarter of the year. On a separate sheet of paper, write down figures for each of the categories shown. Net sales for month 4 totaled $45,000; for month 5, $50,000; and for month 6, $60,000. Then tell what would be your total expenses and your net profit for the second quarter.

Communication

2. Make a list of possible sources of employees for a new business in your community. Identify the agency, address, and the person(s) or department to contact.

Human Relations

3. Write a letter in response to the following situation.
Dear Abby,
I have been working very hard for a new business in our town. I have not missed a single day during the months of June and July. On August 3, a group of my friends asked me to go to the beach with them. I told them that I had to work. They said to me, "They won't miss you for one day." One friend

said, "My father takes two days off each month. He calls in and tells his boss that he is sick." Another friend told me, "This is a summer job. Don't worry about it so much. Have some fun. School is almost ready to start." Another friend said, "If you want to be part of our group next year, you better come to the beach with us." I want to keep my friends, yet I want a good work record. Should I go to the beach with my friends? If yes, why? If no, why not?
Signed,
Confused

APPLICATION PROJECTS

1. Develop a section for your business plan using instructor guidelines or guidelines and criteria prepared by National DECA for the Entrepreneurship Event (Organizing a Business). Prepare Part III entitled "Proposed Financing Plan." The following activities will help you complete this section of your project.

   a. Develop your own Personal Financial Statement.

   b. Based on an average month, project your personal living expenses.

   c. Project monthly sales for one year for your proposed business. Prepare a chart showing possible seasonal fluctuations in sales. Discuss how cash flow would be handled during the slower months.

   d. Identify the fixed and variable expenses of your proposed business.

   e. Determine the desired profit, profit as a percentage of sales, average markup, and average merchandise turnover for your proposed business by interviewing a businessperson in your selected business area.

   f. Use Dun and Bradstreet publications to get financial statistics for your business.

   g. Detail the assets to be used in your proposed business. Divide them into current and fixed assets.

   h. Detail the capital that will be required to start your business. Calculate the monthly and yearly payments (including interest) for any financing you may require.

   i. Identify start-up costs for your proposed business, including the cost of equipment, supplies, and inventory.

2. Write a 200-word report on sales trends for a selected business in your area. Identify the business, the sales five years ago, the current sales, and the projected sales for the next five years.

3. Invite a real estate agent to your class to discuss the advantages and disadvantages of owning or leasing a building. Have the person give you purchase estimates and lease estimates for various locations in your community.

4. Talk to a loan officer in your local bank about the reasons that borrowers default on loans. In a five-minute oral report, tell the class what you discovered and explain the steps you would take to avoid defaulting on a loan.

5. Write a 200-word paper on the development of credit unions. Tell how people usually join credit unions and the advantages of belonging to them.

PART
11

CAREER
PLANNING

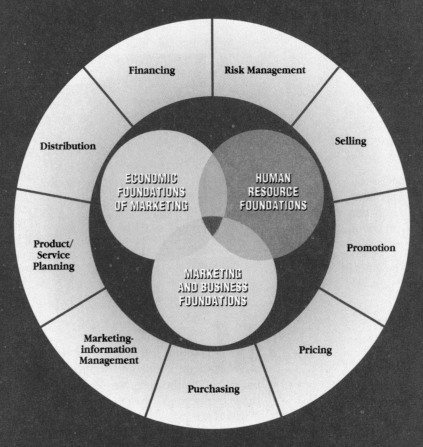

CHAPTERS

▼ ▼ ▼ ▼ ▼ ▼ ▼ ▼

42 Careers in Marketing
43 Self-Assessment and Career Research
44 Career Decision-Making
45 Employability Skills

42

After completing this chapter, you will be able to:

1. discuss the importance of marketing careers in a free enterprise economy,

2. explain why opportunities in marketing are increasing at a faster rate than opportunities in production,

3. list the principal specialties within the marketing career cluster and explain how they can be modified to reflect an individual's personal interests, and

4. describe the major benefits of working in marketing.

WORDS TO KNOW

management training programs
Associate of Arts (A.A.)
Bachelor of Arts (B.A.)
Bachelor of Science (B.S.)
Bachelor of Education (B.Ed.)
fringe benefits

Careers in Marketing

Marketing careers are important to society. Without them, goods and services could not be distributed to buyers, and producers would produce only enough to supply their own needs. If that were the case, the economy as we know it would not exist.

Fortunately, in the United States, Canada, and other countries with free-enterprise economies, a large group of people is engaged in marketing goods and services. In fact, the system of distribution is so effective that we usually take it for granted. In other economies, however, the distribution of goods and services is often shockingly inefficient.

Employment Trends

In 1990, about 25 million Americans earned a living in retailing and wholesaling. That number is expected to rise over the decade of the nineties even as opportunities in closely related areas fall.

Of the two basic functions of business, production and marketing, job opportunities in marketing are growing while those in production are shrinking. The reason for the change is obvious. Production jobs lend themselves to automation and mechanization. In recent years, this has reduced the number of production workers needed by many companies. Marketing, on the other hand, has not been mechanized nearly as much because it requires personal contact.

As an example, consider the use of computers. A single computer and a series of industrial robots can replace a whole production line of workers. A computer system installed in a marketing department, however, is far more likely to enhance the capabilities of its employees rather than replace them.

Indeed, changes in the marketplace have created the need for more rather than fewer marketing professionals. The blurring of gender roles, the rise in the number of single-person households, changing preferences in recreational activities, and the increase in foreign competition—all must be monitored through market research and marketing information systems. To track these and other quickly developing trends, companies are expanding their marketing programs and staffs.

An Overview of Marketing Careers

Marketing provides perhaps the greatest diversity of opportunities of any career field. The range of jobs in marketing is broader than just retailing and wholesaling. Careers in marketing include all the activities required to distribute goods and services to consumers and follow up on their purchase. When considered in this broad sense, marketing activities account for about one in every three American jobs.

Educational Requirements

Marketing offers opportunities to people with diverse educational backgrounds. There are many marketing jobs that require only a high school diploma. You can advance much faster and further, though, if you continue your education.

Most large companies, for example, have *management training programs*. *Management training programs provide usually six months to two years of closely supervised on-the-job management training.* To be selected for one of these programs, you usually must have at least an associate's degree or perhaps even a bachelor's degree. *An Associate of Arts (A.A.) is a degree from a two-year college (usually a junior or community college).* Graduates of such schools can either go directly into the work force or apply their two years of study toward a four-year degree. *A degree from a four-year college or university usually is called a Bachelor of Arts (B.A.), Bachelor of Science (B.S.), or Bachelor of Education (B.Ed.), depending on the course of study on which it is based.*

If you want to advance in marketing research or consulting or move into top management, you will probably need even more than a bachelor's degree. You might need to receive a graduate school degree in marketing. This usually means two or three more years of study beyond a four-year degree.

Career Specialties

The field of marketing is so diverse that you can choose a career from a number of different specialties. These include marketing research, product management, promotion, retailing, sales, and top management. You may also choose the type of business in which you want to work—that is, the kind of good or service that interests you. For example, you might choose marketing research as your specialty and automobile products as the business in which you want to work.

Within marketing, there is considerable freedom to move from one type of business to another. Many of the marketing skills you develop working, say, a retail sales job in home furnishings will readily transfer to selling other types of goods and services. Thus, more than most other workers, you can shape your career to your own interests and adjust your goals to the opportunities as they present themselves.

Just to give you an idea of the diversity of opportunities in marketing, a sample of job titles organized by type of work activity and range of earnings is shown in Figure 42-1. Note that most of the titles are career positions rather than entry-level jobs.

Sample Job Titles

Position	Estimated Salary Range (1990)
Marketing Research	
Market research interviewer	$12,000–$18,000+
Fieldwork director	$12,000–$38,000+
Junior research analyst	$16,000–$25,000+
Research analyst	$22,000–$40,000+
Senior research analyst	$45,000–$70,000+
Associate research director	$55,000–$75,000+
Director of research	$75,000–$110,000+
Product Management	
Marketing analyst	$16,000–$30,000+
Senior marketing analyst	$19,000–$40,000+
Assistant product manager	$30,000–$50,000+
Product manager	$40,000–$72,000+
Group product manager	$45,000–$100,000+
General manager (hotel)	$80,000–$100,000+
Promotion	
Media planner	$13,000–$33,000+
Assistant account executive	$15,000–$32,000+
Account executive	$27,000–$44,000+
Art director	$38,000–$72,000+
Vice president	$38,000–$72,000+
Retailing	
Department manager	$12,000–$24,000+
Executive trainee	$17,000–$28,000+
Assistant buyer	$17,000–$33,000+
Department store manager	$20,000–$55,000+
Supermarket store manager	$28,000–$44,000+
Buyer	$22,000–$75,000+
Sales	
Salesperson	$12,000–$22,000+
Travel agent	$12,000–$50,000+
Real estate agent	$12,000–$100,000+
Insurance agent	$17,000–$100,000+
Field sales trainee	$18,000–$28,000+
Field salesperson	$22,000–$50,000+
Sales manager	$38,000–$80,000+
Broker (stocks and bonds)	$40,000–$800,000+
Top Management	
Senior public relations executive	$45,000–$65,000+
Senior sales executive	$55,000–$100,000+
Director of marketing	$75,000–$120,000+
Vice president of marketing	$80,000–$800,000+

Figure 42-1 **Marketing Career Cluster Sample Job Titles**
Each specialty area in marketing offers a clear career path with increasing challenges, responsibilities, and salary. How would you describe the relative earnings potential of a department store manager and a supermarket manager?

CASE CHALLENGE

Let Your Interests Be Your Guide

You will spend much of your life working. So, it makes sense to work in a field that encompasses as many of your interests as possible. The question is, how can you merge your interests with a career in marketing?

Most kinds of work fall into one of 12 career interest areas. The jobs in each area are similar in the nature of the work or the environment in which they are done. Here are the 12 areas.

1. Artistic interest area—includes the visual arts, the performing arts, craft arts, amusement, and modeling.
2. Scientific interest area—includes the physical sciences, the life sciences, and laboratory technology.
3. Plants and animals interest area—including animal training and care, and general work usually done outdoors.
4. Protective interest area—includes safety and law enforcement, and security services.
5. Mechanical interest area—includes engineering technology, craft technology, land and water vehicle operation, materials control, and such general work as lifting and carrying materials, tools, and equipment.
6. Industrial interest area—includes hand and machine production work, quality control, and such general work as loading and unloading machinery.
7. Business detail interest area—includes oral communications, records keeping, and business routine functions.
8. Selling interest area—includes general sales and vending.
9. Accommodating interest area—includes hospitality services, barber and beauty services, passenger services, customer services, and attendant services.
10. Humanitarian interest area—includes nursing and therapy services, and child and adult care.
11. Leading–influencing interest area—includes educational and library services and rules enforcement.
12. Physical performing—includes sports and physical feats.

In every one of these areas, there is a need for the marketing skills reviewed earlier in this chapter: marketing research, product management, promotion, retailing, sales, and top management. In fact, you have many career possibilities in each area. If you are interested in selling, for example, you could sell goods and services to or from businesses in any of these fields. If you are interested in advertising, you could write copy, design graphics, or buy space for ads promoting products in any of these areas.

By looking at the opportunities in marketing as well as your own interests, you can put together your own personalized list of career options. For example, if you like the sciences but do not wish to become a doctor, nurse, medical technologist, veterinarian, or other type of caregiver, you can sell medical equipment or supplies, or work in community relations for a hospital.

Throughout this book, you have read about people who used their marketing skills along with their determination and effort to create their own unique place in the business world. You can do the same.

1. What is your favorite extracurricular activity? How could you turn this activity into a career in marketing?
2. Certain aspects of a job may appeal to some people but not interest others. What might be some of the pluses and minuses of selling farm equipment? computers? medical supplies? food products? airplane parts?

Benefits of a Marketing Career

Perhaps the most obvious benefit of a career in marketing is the opportunity to make an above-average income. Of course, you won't earn any more money in an entry-level marketing job than you would in many other entry-level positions. As a counter clerk in a fast-food restaurant, for example, you will probably earn the minimum wage. Even in an entry-level job, however, it's nice to know that potential earnings in marketing are excellent.

At the beginning of 1990, starting salaries for entry-level jobs in marketing ranged from $10,000 to $16,000 for high school graduates. New workers with an associate's degree earned between $12,000 and $24,000; beginners with a bachelor's degree in business administration earned between $25,000 and $54,000.

The high visibility afforded by many marketing jobs means that young people who excel get noticed early in their careers—and promoted frequently. What skills do you think are required to make a successful presentation in the circumstances shown here?

Besides earning you a good salary, a position in marketing may entitle you to some helpful and valuable extras. *Fringe benefits (also called perquisites or "perks") are benefits, privileges, or monetary payments beyond salary or wages that go with a job.* Examples include the use of a company car, an expense account, and bonuses for doing outstanding work.

In addition, most jobs in marketing, especially those beyond entry-level positions, are interesting and varied. Many involve a great deal of contact with people, and this in itself is often enjoyable and growth-producing.

Rapid Advancement

You will usually have more opportunities to advance in a marketing career than in almost any other area of business. This is because of the high visibility that many marketing positions have.

Consider a few examples. People who work in marketing frequently present and shape their ideas in meetings with company managers and executives. People who work in sales get constant feedback on their efforts in the form of sales figures that are regularly reviewed by upper-level management. People who work in advertising may develop ad campaigns that win critical acclaim from professional associations. What all these situations make clear is that people who work in marketing do the kinds of things that command attention, especially from management. If they do well, they are far more likely to be credited

Corporate CEOs with Marketing Backgrounds

Apple Computer	John Sculley (1983 —)
Avon Products	Hicks B. Waldron (1984 —)
Campbell Soup	R. Gordon McGovern (1981—)
Colgate-Palmolive	Reuben Mark (1984 —)
Dun & Bradstreet	Charles W. Moritz (1985 —)
Federated Department Stores	Howard Goldfeder (1981 —)
Firestone	John J. Nevin (1981 —)
General Mills	H. Brewster Atwater, Jr. (1981 —)
IBM	John F. Akers (1985 —)
Johnson & Johnson	James E. Burke (1977 —)
K Mart	Bernard M. Fauber (1980 —)
McDonald's	Fred L. Turner (1974 —)
Nordstrom	Bruce A. Nordstrom (1971 —)
J.C. Penney	William R. Howell (1984 —)
Quaker Oats	William D. Smithburg (1982 —)
Ralston-Purina	William P. Stiritz (1982 —)
Sears Roebuck	Edward A. Brennan (1986 —)
Whirlpool	Jack D. Sparks (1983 —)
Xerox	David T. Kearns (1982 —)

Figure 42-2 **Corporate CEOs with Marketing Backgrounds**
Corporate CEOs are frequently drawn from the ranks of marketing professionals. To judge from the list of companies presented here, in what kind of companies is this espcially true?

with their successes and rewarded for them. In terms of a job, this means winning promotions faster in marketing than in other careers.

In fact, because of their high visibility, marketing and sales careers offer the fastest route to middle and top management. A recent survey showed that more chief executive officers (CEOs) reach the top of their organizations through marketing and sales than through any other career area. Figure 42-2 lists just a few of the companies whose CEOs fit this descrip-

tion. All earn at least several hundred thousand dollars per year plus bonuses. Some earn millions.

Why does marketing provide such an abundance of opportunities? Business has learned that a marketing orientation is necessary for success. Sam Walton, the founder of Wal-Mart, said, "The key to success must be that we truly embrace the philosophy that our sole reason for being is to serve, even spoil, our wonderful customers." Of course, Walton might have added, " . . . for a profit."

VOCABULARY REVIEW

Write a paragraph using all of the following vocabulary terms.

management training programs

Associate of Arts (A.A.)

Bachelor of Arts (B.A.)

Bachelor of Science (B.S.)

Bachelor of Education (B.Ed.)

fringe benefits

FACT AND IDEA REVIEW

1. Why are marketing careers important in a free enterprise system?

2. How do the trends in marketing and production jobs compare? What accounts for the differences in the trends?

3. About what percentage of all jobs does marketing account for in the American economy?

4. What educational background do you need to enter the field of marketing?

5. What is a management training program?

6. List four career specialties within the field of marketing.

7. What are the main benefits of careers in marketing?

8. Why do jobs in marketing often lead to rapid career advancement?

CRITICAL THINKING

1. Why do you think experience in marketing seems to be a prerequisite for attaining a top-level position in a company?

2. Discuss how the marketing skills you would learn in a fast-food restaurant could be transferred to an industrial sales position.

USING BASIC SKILLS

Math

1. In your entry-level job as a salesclerk, you made $12,000 a year. After much hard work and a long series of promotions, you became director of marketing at $120,000 a year. This is what percentage of your original salary?

2. Your salary as art director of Sell-Win Toys is $53,000. If in addition you earn a bonus of 5 percent of your annual salary, what would be your total earnings for the year?

Communication

3. Many jobs in marketing involve a great deal of personal contact and require a high level of communication skills. Explain how and why such skills might be important in the following marketing careers.

   a. Personnel director for a large retail chain

   b. Advertising director

   c. Public Relations specialist

Human Relations

4. Suppose you have a sales position with a company. You enjoy the work and excel at it. In fact, you do so well that the company promotes you to sales manager. However, you soon find that supervising others does not suit you as well as sales did. What would you do?

5. How would you relate to a female supervisor? How would you relate to a male supervisor? If you feel that you would relate to each one differently because of his or her gender, tell why this would make a difference to you.

APPLICATION PROJECTS

1. List ten people you know who are employed. Do the work activities of these people involve marketing? How and to what extent? Compare your list with those of other students in your class.

2. Majoring in marketing in college could prepare you for a variety of careers, including work in television or radio. Find out what marketing opportunities exist in radio and television.

3. Ask your teacher or work-coordinator to assist you in contacting a local businesswomen's organization and a minority businessperson's organization. See if you can get a representative from each group to come and speak to your class about the opportunities for women and minorities in the marketing field.

4. Research the management training program of a local company that offers one. Report your findings to your classmates. Include the advantages and disadvantages of getting involved in such a program.

5. Read the classified section of your paper for one week. Bring to class five entry-level positions that could lead to marketing careers.

6. Shown below are two people in various marketing careers: warehouse management and visual merchandising. For each person shown, answer these questions:

   a. What are the employment trends in this area of marketing?

   b. What kind of eduction and training does this person need for this position?

   c. What would be the range of this person's job duties?

   d. What would be the advantages to having this job? the disadvantages?

   e. What would be the opportunities for advancement in this job?

   f. What would be the general salary range?

   g. Does this particular job in marketing appeal to you? Why or why not?

Self-Assessment and Career Research

OBJECTIVES

After completing this chapter, you will be able to:

1. list your interests, values, skills, and aptitudes,

2. describe your life-style goals,

3. define the amount and type of education and training you are willing to pursue to qualify for a career,

4. name, locate, and use three important sources of job and career information,

5. describe the duties, responsibilities, and working conditions of three jobs, and

6. describe the skills, aptitudes, education, and training needed for success in three careers.

WORDS TO KNOW

values
life-style goals
aptitude
Dictionary of Occupational Titles (DOT)
career outlook
Occupational Outlook Handbook (OOH)
Guide for Occupational Education (GOE)
career consultation

Your career choice will affect you in many ways throughout your life. So, you will want to give this decision careful consideration. The following seven-step procedure works well in making important career choices.

1. Define your needs or wants.
2. Analyze your resources.
3. Identify your choices.
4. Gather information on each choice.
5. Evaluate your choices.
6. Make your decision.
7. Plan how you will reach your goal.

In this chapter, you will learn how to assess your needs, wants, and personal resources (Steps 1 and 2). You will also learn how to research careers by identifying your choices and gathering information on each choice (Steps 3 and 4).

Self-Assessment

As you assess each of your needs, wants, or qualifications, record your findings. Use a special notebook or a section in a career planning notebook, and label it "Self-Assessment File." You can summarize your various assessments in paragraph form or, where appropriate, use a rating scale.

Your Values

Things that are important to you are your values. Defining your system of values provides guideposts for your life, and it is absolutely essential in choosing a career. When you have clear values, you know what you want out of life, and you can choose a career that is compatible with your values and aspirations.

How do you know what your values are? The things and activities on which you spend your time and money are good indicators of your values.

Your Life-style Goals

The word *life-style* refers to the way you live. Dr. Arnold Mitchell, author of *The Nine American Life-styles*, studied thousands of Americans over the age of 18. He learned a great deal about how people live and how satisfied they are with their lives. For example, he learned that the happiest, most satisfied people have the greatest control over how they spend their time. Most of these people are well educated, motivated to succeed, and have incomes well above the average. Dr. Mitchell's work showed the effect that a career has on total life-style.

Your life-style is made up of many things, including the following:

- where you live (city or rural area);
- the type of housing you live in;
- the school you attend;
- your favorite foods, clothing, and leisure activities;
- your relationships with your family and friends;
- your mode of transportation; and
- your part-time job.

These and all the other things that make up your life-style can be grouped into categories of related activities called life-style elements. Listings of such elements vary but usually include career, family, friends, leisure, spiritual well-being, and personal choices. These elements can be used to construct a simple diagram of a person's life-style (Figure 43-1).

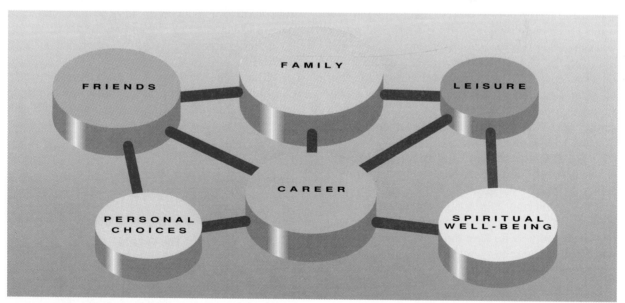

Figure 43-1 **Life-Style Patterns**
This diagram shows the life-style pattern of someone for whom family is the most important part of life. How might the diagram look for someone who values career most, has no immediate family but many friends, and whose principal non-work interest is participation in religious activities?

When diagrammed, a life-style pattern shows the more important elements as larger circles and the less important elements as smaller circles. Because everyone's life-style is different, no two life-style patterns are exactly the same. Notice, however, that as a matter of format, career is located at the center of the life-style diagram. This is because work is the central activity in most people's lives.

Goal Setting. The first step toward achieving the life-style you want is setting goals. The process of setting goals is essentially one of looking into the future, then working backwards. You start by setting your long-range goals, those furthest in the future. Next, you set the medium-range goals that will help move you toward it. Finally, you set your short-range goals, the most immediate ones that will start you on your way toward your medium-range objectives.

The first goals are long-range goals based on your dream life-style pattern for some time in the future. *These life-style goals reflect your vision of how you see yourself living in the future.* These long-range goals will determine all the others.

How do you set such important goals? You do some meaningful, directed daydreaming about your future. How do you want to be living, say, 20 years from now? Do you want to be married? Do you want children? If so, how many? What leisure activities will you pursue? Are they expensive? Will you want to do a lot of entertaining? What type of home will you want? Once you visualize all these needs and wants, you can make plans for attaining them.

Clearly, though, the key to your dream is the right career because your earnings will pay for your life-style. Remember, too, that your career not only supports your life-style but is a part of it. The right career will be compatible with all the other elements in your life-style pattern.

Goal Orientation. A goal-oriented person is intellectually and emotionally directed toward achieving goals. How goal-oriented are you? Can you focus on achieving your goals even when it means giving up something else you would like? You probably know people who have difficulty achieving long-range goals because they are constantly lured away by the pleasures of the moment.

Suppose that your dream life-style depends on a career that requires a four-year degree. To achieve this goal, your study time will have to take the place of many fun activities you could be doing. You will also have to give up many things you could buy if you were not spending money on tuition. However, if your goals are important to you, and if you are goal-oriented, you will make the necessary sacrifices.

If you do decide to pursue further education and training beyond high school, you will need to start thinking now about how you will pay the costs. Education is expensive, and the price is going up every year. Nevertheless, it is still the best investment you can make.

Your Interests

You will probably spend 30 to 40 years working, so you will want to choose work that interests you. Of course, many jobs can become routine after a few years. That's when people hope to get promoted to a more challenging job.

Throughout the 1970s and '80s, the average worker changed careers at the rate of three times during a lifetime. Some of these people initially made the wrong career decision. Others decided to choose a field that interested them more than their current one. Sometimes changing career fields is the right thing to do. Nevertheless, it is costly to retrain for a new career. If you can remain interested over the years in a general career area, then you are less likely to make a mid-career switch to something totally different.

Later, when you research a variety of careers, you will make judgments about how interesting each type of career would be. Your judgments will probably be more accurate if you first inventory your own interests.

There are several ways of evaluating your interests. You can write down all the things you like to do in your leisure time, especially those things that might

---

REAL WORLD MARKETING

The Vid Kid

I t's never too young to start developing your talents. At a young age, Rawson Stovall bought a computer and became an expert at using it. At 10 he began reviewing video games for the Abilene Reporter–News. Today his column, originally called "The Vid Kid," appears in about 20 newspapers.

turn into on-the-job activities. Be sure to list them all. It's surprising how often hobbies and recreational activities lead to successful and satisfying careers.

If you've taken part in school activities, sports, and social activities, you may have a long list of interests. If your list is short, perhaps you need to try out some new hobbies or other leisure activities to learn whether you want to pursue them.

Your favorite classes in school, too, may suggest careers you would find interesting. List them according to the ones you like best. Do you enjoy marketing classes, or do you find math more appealing? You may be able to narrow it down a bit here. For example, when studying marketing, which topics were most interesting to you?

Another way to find out about your interests is to take an interest survey. There are many interest surveys available, and they all help you identify careers that would interest you. One of these, the *World of Work Career Interest Survey*, is similar to a test, but there are no right or wrong answers. You are given a long list of activities, and you decide how much you would like doing each of them. Then you score your own survey to learn which career areas you would probably find most interesting. Your school counselor or marketing teacher can probably arrange for you to take one of these surveys.

Your Skills and Aptitudes

Values and interests are important in self-assessment because they help you picture what you want your life to become, and they may suggest certain careers. Beyond that, it takes certain skills to be successful in any career. Just having an interest in something doesn't make you qualified.

For a career goal to be realistic, you have to have an *aptitude* for the work. *An aptitude is a knack, or a potential, for learning a certain skill.* If you don't have much aptitude for skills required in a certain career, even a high level of interest won't help make you a success. For example, a person who doesn't enjoy

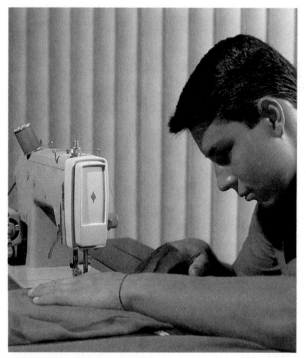

Activities you like and willingly pursue on your own are good indicators of possible career interests. What careers might these bobbies lead to?

writing will never succeed as an advertising copy-writer. The person who can't describe the benefits of products won't have much success selling.

You can see, then, that it is important to identify your aptitudes before you get serious about choosing a career. Begin a new page in your self-assessment file, and list all the things you have done well. Do you find it easy to sell cookies, candy bars, or whatever your DECA or marketing class sold to raise funds? Are you good at organizing committees and getting everyone to do their jobs? Is math easy for you? Have you won any prizes for your creative ability? Write down every-thing you can think of.

The grades you earn in school may indicate your aptitudes. If most of your written reports earned As and Bs, you probably have an aptitude for writing. Your grades in individual classes may indicate your best mental aptitudes. Of course, if you don't make a real effort to do well in a class, you may have more aptitude than your grades reflect. In that case, though, developing even a strong aptitude into a useful skill will be unlikely until you try harder.

There are a number of tests that can help indi-cate areas of strength. If you are interested in taking an aptitude test, ask your school counselor about it.

Perhaps you have already developed certain skills that will be useful in a career that interests you. If so, list them on a separate sheet of paper in your self-assessment file. Then add to your list as you develop new skills. Your skills list will be very helpful when you apply for a job.

Your Personality

Dr. John Holland identified six basic personality types and described how they relate to career choices. He also developed a personality test called *The Self-Directed Search* to help people learn what mix of per-sonality types they happen to be. Taking this test would provide another piece of information to help you make the right career choice. If you would like to take it, talk with your school counselor.

However, you may not need to take a test to learn about your own personality or how it will fit with certain careers. To see how well you can assess your own personality traits, use a new page in your self-assessment file to list all the words that describe you. Then, as you research careers, try to find one that fits well with your own traits.

Your Work Environment

Your work environment refers to where you work—the place and the conditions that prevail there. Working conditions include sights, sounds, and smells.

Many factors affect working conditions—geographic location, for example. If you work out-doors, it makes a big difference whether you live and work in St. Paul, Minnesota, or San Diego, California. Whether you work during the day or at night also affects your working conditions.

You don't have to know all your preferences about working conditions now, but you should start thinking about them. Then, when you read about the working conditions of a certain career, you will have a better idea of whether that career would be accept-able to you.

Your Relationship Preferences

All jobs require working with data, people, or things—alone or in some combination. For example, a salesperson who sells a product deals mainly with people and things; a travel agent, mainly with people and data (travel information); a computer program-mer, mainly with data.

Think about your own preferences. Do you like working with large groups, or do you prefer working with one or two people at a time? Do you get lonely when you work on a project for hours without seeing anyone else? A little reflection will probably indicate how much you like working with people.

Do you like writing short stories or doing in-volved math problems? Do the hours pass quickly when you're working on a computer? If your answers are yes, then you probably like working with data.

Do you enjoy spending Saturdays working on your car or fixing things around the house? If so, then you probably like working with things.

Take some time to assess your preferences for data, people, and things. Talk with a family member about it, or rank your preferences on a scale of 1 to 10 (10 being the highest). Then consult some references. *The **Dictionary of Occupational Titles (DOT)**, for ex-ample, describes more than 20,000 jobs in terms of their relationships with data, people, and things.* You can use the DOT to compare your preferences with the profiles of jobs you find interesting. We will fur-ther explore the DOT later in this chapter.

CASE CHALLENGE

For the Love of Art

Abraham Livingston Gump was only 11 when his eyesight began to fail. His hazy vision only allowed him to see things at close range. Yet, he became one of the best-known and most trusted art dealers in San Francisco.

Gump stopped studying at 13 due to the strain on his eyes, but he never stopped learning. He memorized the stories people told him about the art he was buying. Whenever he wanted to learn about a new field, his wife would read books on the subject to him.

When A.L. (as he came to be called) first started in his father's art business, he did only uncomplicated work because of his eyes. Nevertheless, he wanted to sell. By the time he and his brothers took over the business, his advice on art was sought by many of San Francisco's leading citizens.

Gump, however, was more than a merchant. He had a sure sense of what was good art and what was beautiful. He helped artists by bringing them together with patrons who could appreciate their work. He took time with his clients, teaching them about the pieces they were buying, trying to instill a little of his own appreciation for their beauty.

When Gump first began to learn about oriental art, he had a hard time convincing his family it would sell. They eventually agreed to dedicate a small part of the store to the speciality.

Gump learned everything he could about oriental art by talking to people and having his wife read to him. He inspected every piece that came his way. He became so knowledgeable about oriental pieces that he once astonished a European art dealer by telling the difference between an original antique vase and a copy. Although his vision was too dim to see the color, Gump knew the weight and texture of the vase was wrong.

Gump was one of the first in San Francisco to appreciate jade. He gambled that others would learn to appreciate it, too, and began to import it. When he went to China to buy jade, he earned the respect of the merchants there by being able to tell the quality of the stones simply by touch.

Gradually, Gump's gave more space in the store to oriental art. The name *Gump's* became—and still is—synonymous with fine oriental art.

1. How did A.L. Gump merge his interests and his values with his business?
2. Was A.L. Gump a short-range or a long-range goal setter?

Career Assessment

Now begin a new section in your career planning notebook. Label it "Career Assessment File." The information you write here will be compared with your self-assessment section to make a career decision.

Even if you have already chosen a career goal, select at least two or three other careers to research and assess. By learning about several careers now, you will save time later if your first choice turns out to be inappropriate.

If you have a career goal in mind, list it first. Then add any others you think might be possibilities. Try to leave some space at the bottom of your list. That way, if you eliminate some of your first choices as a result of what you learn, you can add others to take their place.

Work Values

Certain values are important to success on the job—any job. These include honesty, dependability, diligence, and team spirit.

In addition, however, each job and each career field have their own special work values. For example, most retail marketing careers would place a high value on working long hours, getting along with other people, coping with stress, and being willing to work for lower pay initially.

As you research the careers you have selected, try to look beyond the duties and responsibilities. Consider the values that are important for success and satisfaction in each field.

Life-style Fit

Some careers will fit your life-style goals better than others. As you research each career, try to determine how compatible it will be with the other elements of your life-style.

If spending time with your family is important to you, for example, then you probably wouldn't want a career that requires a great deal of travel. If leisure time is important, then you probably wouldn't be happy working weekends.

Look for a career that enhances the other elements of your life-style. At the very least, choose a career that doesn't conflict with them.

Salaries and Benefits

As you look at each career, ask whether it will provide the financial support for the life-style you want. Be sure to consider both salary and such fringe benefits as paid vacations, life insurance, health insurance, and a pension (or retirement) plan.

Everyone wants paid vacations, so you will no doubt be on the lookout for that one. Life insurance is especially important for young families. If your employer pays for this or if you can pay lower premiums through an employer-sponsored group plan, then you can save some money for other things. The high cost of health care today makes health insurance a necessity. Some employers pay the premiums for all their employees. Others have group plans that save you money. You may not think a retirement plan is important since retirement seems a long way off. Nevertheless, many older workers continue working into their seventies because they are not covered by such a plan.

Many others must rely on social security alone, which supports only the most basic life-style.

Some careers provide more fringe benefits than others. Some, for example, regularly pay bonuses or give discounts on merchandise. Some even make recreational facilities available to their employees.

Career Outlook

Suppose you find a career that seems interesting, one in which you could do well and one that will satisfy your life-style goals. You then need to see what the *career outlook* is in the field.

*The availability of jobs is called the **career outlook**.* Try to find a job in a field where the career outlook is good. This means one in an area that is growing and will therefore provide many job opportunities and many opportunities for advancement.

Education and Training

Every job requires a certain level of education and training. Some require only graduation from high school. Others require a year or two of post-high school education or training. Some require four or more years of college.

In your self-assessment, you considered how much time and money you are willing to devote to your education and training. Now look at the education and training requirements of various careers. For example, what if the career that fits your values, interests, aptitudes, and life-style goals requires more education and training than you are willing to pursue?

Duties and Responsibilities

More than anything else, jobs are distinguished by their duties and responsibilities. Job duties are the things you will be doing. Responsibilities are the things you must think about to make certain that your duties are completed satisfactorily. For example, one of your duties may be to type business reports. Your responsibilities include completing the work neatly, correctly, and on time.

While you are researching careers, then, you should learn all you can about the duties and responsibilities of each job you are considering. That way, you can be more sure of matching yourself with a career that you will find interesting and can excel in.

Career education need not take place in the classroom. What types of careers do you think lend themselves to on-the-job training?

Skills and Aptitudes Required

You know that it takes more than just an interest in a job or career to succeed. Every job requires different types and levels of skills.

Skill development takes time. The higher the level of skill, the longer it will take you to learn. You won't need fully developed, high-level skills when you begin your first full-time job. You can develop entry-level skills and refine more advanced skills on the job. Then, you can begin advancing to more responsible, higher-paying jobs.

As you research each career, note the skills needed to perform the required duties and exercise the required responsibilities. Then determine what aptitudes would be helpful in learning those skills. For example, suppose you are considering a career in advertising. When you look at the job description of advertising copywriter, you learn that the skill used most is writing. If you haven't done much writing, you probably haven't developed much writing skill. The next question is, then, do you have an aptitude for writing?

Consider another example. When you look at the job description of advertising layout artist, you learn that you would need good artistic skills. Perhaps you've done a lot of sketching and are developing your art skills further. If not, do you have an aptitude for sketching and design work?

Helpful Personality Traits

Personality is the total, complex mix of emotional and behavioral characteristics that makes each person unique. You have probably noticed that people in some careers seem to have similar personality traits. Does this mean that the type of work you do affects your personality, or do people with certain personality traits tend to choose specific careers? The answer to both questions, of course, is yes.

Your personality is affected, sometimes in minute ways, by all your life experiences. Since the work you do to earn a living will probably become the central activity in your life, it will certainly affect your personality. Your interpersonal relationships with other people at your workplace will have the greatest effect.

A popular belief about salespeople is that they must have outgoing personalities. That is not totally true, of course. In reading the sales unit in this book, you learned that many successful salespeople do not have outgoing personalities. However, they enjoy helping other people. A very quiet person who is uncomfortable with strangers will have a very difficult time on most sales jobs.

Work Environment

Working conditions vary greatly from one job to another. For example, there are big differences in the work environments of an office, a department store, and a factory.

If you work in an office, your work environment will probably be well-lighted and air-conditioned, with the temperature maintained somewhere between 68 and 72 degrees. Offices are fairly free of dust, odors, and loud noises. Most of the time, you will sit on a comfortable chair while carrying out your duties and responsibilities. Many people feel that an office provides the ideal work environment.

If you work on the floor of a large department store, you will tire a lot faster than if you work in an office simply because you are on your feet most of the time. As a salesperson on the floor, though, your work environment will usually still be free of dust, odors, and loud noises.

This may not be the case if you work in a factory. Some jobs in factories are dangerous, since many of the workers use tools and equipment that can cause injury. Because of this, many factory workers must wear safety glasses or goggles and other protective clothing. Some factory environments expose workers to hazardous chemicals as well. You may get to sit down at least part of the time if you work in a factory, but you're also likely to find yourself lifting and moving heavy objects.

If you work outdoors, your work environment will depend a great deal on the weather. Other working conditions can vary as much as on an indoor job.

As you study the working conditions of the careers you have selected, try to learn these things about each job:

- Is the work done indoors or outdoors?
- Is the work done sitting down or standing up?
- Is the work environment dusty, smelly, or especially noisy?
- Is the work environment dangerous? If so, what are the risks?

Working conditions should be a key element in assessing any career. Can you see any advantages that these two very different job environments share?

- Is the work physically tiring (perhaps involving a great deal of lifting, stretching, or walking)?
- Is the work done on a regular shift, such as 9–5, or must it be done at night or on weekends?

Work Relationships

As you research careers, note the data/people/things relationships in the specific jobs you have selected. Almost every job requires working with other people to some extent. Some jobs—those in retail sales, for example—require you to work with people (mostly complete strangers) almost constantly. Other jobs require you to work almost constantly with data or things.

Research Resources

To research careers, you will need to gather information from a variety of sources. The best ones are *libraries, career consultations,* and actual *work experience.*

Libraries

You can find many good career information resources in your school or public library. Many school libraries have a special section, usually called the Career Information Center, devoted to career information. Others may simply carry career materials. In either case, you will find *books, magazines, pamphlets, films, videos* and *special references* that will tell you more about your career choices.

Books. Look up "careers" in your library's card catalog to see a list of all the available books on choosing a career. If you want information on a particular career, such as advertising, sales, or management, look up that topic in the card catalog. (Note that many libraries now keep their card catalogs on microfilm.)

Magazines. Most magazines are published weekly or monthly, so magazine articles provide the most up-to-date career information. You can locate articles on careers you want to research in the *Reader's Guide to Periodical Literature.* The *Reader's Guide* is

an index of leading magazine and journal articles. It is available in book form or on microfilm. Articles are listed in alphabetical order by subject.

Pamphlets. Many libraries maintain files of career information pamphlets. These are often prepared by government agencies or large private corporations. They usually provide specific information, such as the outlook for new jobs in one career area. Educational opportunities are covered in pamphlets prepared by colleges, trade schools, and the military services. Ask your librarian where these pamphlets are located.

Films and Videos. Most libraries have a collection of films and video cassettes. Ask your librarian whether there are any available on careers that interest you. After you know where these materials are located and how to use the equipment, you can watch them whenever you want.

Special References. The U.S. Department of Labor publishes three reference books that are especially helpful in career research. They are the *Dictionary of Occupational Titles*, the *Occupational Outlook Handbook*, and the *Guide for Occupational Exploration.* Most school and public libraries have all these reference books.

The *Dictionary of Occupational Titles (DOT)* (discussed earlier) describes approximately 20,000 jobs. (Several hundred more jobs that have emerged since the publication of the dictionary are defined in the *DOT Supplement*.) The *DOT* is a big book—more than 1,300 pages—but it is well organized. Just use the alphabetical index to look up the job titles that interest you.

Following each title you will find a nine-digit code number. You use this number to locate the job description you want in the front section of the *DOT.* The *DOT* number provides a sophisticated way of classifying jobs into career clusters and worker functions. For example, recall that every job requires a worker to function to some degree in relation to data, people, and things. The middle three digits of the *DOT* number indicate the nature of this relationship for the given job title. This is explained fully in the *DOT* introduction.

You should write down the *DOT* numbers of the jobs you are researching. This will save you some time because other sources also use these numbers to organize their information.

The Occupational Outlook Handbook (OOH) provides detailed information on more than two hundred occupations and is updated every two years. It is especially helpful and easy to use in locating such information as:

- education and training requirements,
- usual hours of work,
- working conditions,
- salaries,
- job or career outlook, and
- sources of additional information.

Such things as salaries and job outlook can change quickly. To avoid being misled by outdated information, be sure you are using the latest edition of the *OOH*. For the latest information on recent changes, refer to the *Occupational Outlook Quarterly*. This is a supplement to the *OOH* that is published four times a year.

The Guide for Occupational Exploration (GOE) is a reference that organizes the world of work into 12 interest areas, which it then further subdivides into work groups and subgroups. For example, the interest area *Selling* is divided into the three work groups *Sales Technology, General Sales,* and *Vending.*

Each work group is then further divided into the subgroups *Wholesale, Retail, Demonstration and Sales,* and five others. The *GOE* includes the following types of career information:

- kind of work done,
- skills and abilities needed,
- interests and aptitudes, and
- required background or preparation.

The *GOE's* 12 interest areas are also used in the *Career Interest Survey* and the *General Aptitude Test Battery (GATB).* The *GATB* is an aptitude test developed by the U.S. Department of Labor. Using all these resources together provides a coordinated approach in your career planning process.

The Community

Your own business community is another excellent source of career information. There are two important ways you can use this resource in your research. First, you can call on those who work in your community to learn about their careers first-

Even if you don't have any personal contacts with people in your chosen career area, you can arrange for your own career consultations by making a few phone calls. What advantages might this procedure have over other methods of securing interviews?

hand. Second, you can research the careers that interest you most by getting some actual on-the-job experience.

Career Consultations. *A career consultation is an informational interview with someone who works in a career that interests you.* You can learn a great deal about the demands and opportunities of a career from someone with experience. Those who have met the challenges of a career are usually happy to talk about it.

Ask both your teacher and your counselor for suggestions about whom you should interview. They may have lists of people in the community who enjoy talking with young people about their work. Family members can also sometimes give you leads.

If you don't get some good suggestions from others, use the telephone directory to compile your own list of potential interviewees. For some careers, you will have to list companies and then call each to find out whom you should interview. For example, suppose you are interested in becoming a retail buyer. Buyers are not listed under their own category in the Yellow Pages, so you will have to call the store first to get the name of someone you can contact.

If possible, interview the person where he or she works. That's usually more convenient for the person, and it will give you a chance to see the workplace. You may even get to see others actively engaged in the work you want to learn about.

Before any career consultation, prepare a list of questions that you want to ask. Here are some suggestions.

- How do you spend most of your time on the job? Which work activities do you like most? Which do you like least?
- What skills will I need to do this type of work? What skills will I need to advance?
- What education and training will I need? Can I complete some of the training after I begin working?
- How much time do you spend working with data? with people? with things?
- What personal qualities are helpful in this type of work?
- What are your hours of work? Do people in this career often work overtime? evenings? weekends?
- Is the work done mostly indoors or outdoors? Do most work activities require sitting, standing, or being on the move? Is the work environment sometimes hot, cold, noisy, or dusty? Is the work dangerous in any way?
- Will there be an increase in job opportunities in this field over the next several years? What impact will automation and new technology have on job opportunities in the next few years?

On-the-job Experience. You can learn a great deal about a career by reading and by interviewing those who work in the field. There are many things, however, that you cannot learn about a job until you try it for yourself.

Many students work part-time after school, on weekends, or during the summer months. If you choose a job in a career field that interests you, you will benefit in the following ways.

- You can try out some of the work activities of your career and decide how much you like doing them.
- You can experience the work environment of the career.
- You can develop work habits that will help you succeed in your career.
- You can broaden your understanding of the world of work and smooth the transition from school to work.

Does your school have a work-experience program? (You may know it by another name, such as cooperative education, cooperative work experience, work study, diversified occupations, or something similar.) Many vocational work-experience programs include the word *cooperative* in their names because the programs represent a cooperative effort by school and employers. In these programs, the teacher-coordinator teaches a class related to the job and also supervises students on the job.

Another way to get some work experience is to do volunteer work. Many communities have a volunteer center that lists organizations needing volunteers. If your community doesn't have such a center, then check with such organizations as local hospitals, schools, humane societies, the YMCA/YWCA, and the American Red Cross.

Most volunteer jobs are in the areas of health, education, recreation, and office work. They may not provide many opportunities to try out work activities typical of marketing careers. However, you can develop skills that can be transferred to marketing.

VOCABULARY REVIEW

Use the following vocabulary terms in a paragraph on doing career research.

values
life-style goals
aptitude
Dictionary of Occupational
  Titles (DOT)
career outlook

Occupational Outlook
  Handbook (OOH)
Guide for Occupational
  Education (GOE)
career consultation

FACT AND IDEA REVIEW

1. List six elements of life-style.

2. How can daydreaming help you in planning for your future?

3. How can making a list of your hobbies help you in the career planning process?

4. For a career goal to be realistic, what must you have besides an interest in the field?

5. How does personality type relate to career search?

6. Why is it valuable to assess your preferences for working with data, people, or things? Give one example of a career that deals principally with each of these three areas.

7. Why should you research careers with your life-style goals in mind?

8. Name three common fringe benefits. How might the fringe benefits of a job or profession affect your career choice?

9. What is a career outlook, and why is it an important piece of information in your career research?

10. What distinguishes one job from another more than anything else?

11. Why is it valuable to consider your personality traits when researching careers?

12. List three examples of working conditions.

13. List three questions you might ask when researching the work environment of a job or profession.

14. What are the three best sources of information about careers?

15. List the career resources you might find in a school or public library.

CRITICAL THINKING

1. Who or what has influenced your values most in the past? How have these influences changed now that you are older? How do you think they will change in the future?

2. How can a hobby lead to a career? Think of your own hobbies and hobbies of people you know or have read about. Brainstorm ways that these hobbies could become professions.

3. Think of someone you know who seems happy on the job. Does his or her personality type match the requirements of the job? Is the job a good match for the person's interests, values, and skills? What do you think makes that person happy on that job?

4. Why is it important to set goals? What could happen if you don't set goals for the future? Do your life-style goals have to be the same as your parents' life-style goals or those your parents have for you?

5. Many more companies are offering child care programs to their employees. Why do you think child care has become such an important fringe benefit? What are the advantages for the companies who provide child care? How do the employees benefit?

6. Choose one of the career paths you are researching. Discuss ways you would get on-the-job experience related to that career.

USING BASIC SKILLS

Math

1. Suppose a company offers you a job paying $20,000 a year when you graduate from high school. This company pays college graduates 20 percent more than high school graduates. You estimate total costs of attending college at $8,000 a year. If you graduate from college after four years, how long will it take to pay for your college education using your extra earnings? (Disregard the earnings you would give up while attending college.)

2. Use the *Occupational Outlook Handbook* to find the current salaries for two marketing careers that interest you. What is the annual difference in those two salaries? Disregarding pay increases over the years, how much more would you make in the higher paying job over a ten-year period?

Communication

3. Choose two or three marketing-related job ads from your local newspaper for study and analysis. Describe how the ads refer to work values, life-style goals, salary, fringe benefits, career outlook, duties and responsibilities, required skills and aptitudes, required education and training, personality traits, work environment, and involvement with data/people/things. Which of these characteristics do the ads seem to emphasize? Do you think potential employees would be attracted to these ads? Why or why not?

4. Write down what you would say in a telephone call requesting a career consultation. What impression would you want to make? Describe the tone of voice and manner of speaking you would use to make that impression.

Human Relations

5. Imagine that your career research is complete, that you have made your choice of career and fulfilled the educational requirements. Upon graduation, you are offered a job in advertising.

The salary and fringe benefits are acceptable, the work is challenging and satisfying, and you seem to be doing well at it. A few weeks into the job, however, you discover that three of your closest co-workers routinely take 90-minute lunch breaks, even when they have been warned not to do so by your supervisor. You tell your co-workers that you will no longer take long lunches with them and that you will only take the allotted hour each day. Your co-workers, however, seem to resent the fact that you don't join them, and they become less and less friendly and helpful toward you in the office. How do you handle this?

6. As the personnel manager of a company that prides itself on exceptional customer service, what qualities would you look for in a potential employee? In the hiring decision, is it possible that those qualities could be more important than a person's credentials?

APPLICATION PROJECTS

1. List the areas to look for when researching careers: work values, life-style goals/salary, fringe benefits, career outlook, duties and responsibilities, required skills and aptitudes, required education and training, personality traits, work environment, involvement with data/people/things. Rank these items according to how important they are to you in making a career choice. Compare your list with a partner's, and discuss the reasons for any differences.

2. As in the previous question, list the important considerations in choosing a job. Interview two working people in the field of marketing. To what extent do each of the listed factors contribute to their liking or disliking their work? Did any of these factors affect their decisions to accept their present employment? What was most important to them when they were job hunting?

3. Conduct a career consultation in one of the career areas you are researching. Present your findings to the class.

44

After completing this chapter, you will be able to:

1. prepare a profile of your self-assessment and career needs and opportunities,

2. match your own needs, wants, and potential qualifications with a realistic and satisfying career,

3. list and describe your long-range, medium-range, and short-range goals, and

4. develop a plan to reach your goals.

personal career profile
planning goals
specific goal
realistic goal
area vocational schools
area vocational centers
technical institutes

Career Decision Making

Have you completed your own self-assessment by defining your needs and wants and then analyzing your resources? Have you identified some career choices and gathered information about them? If so, you are ready for the last three steps in the career planning process—evaluating your choices, making your decision, and planning to reach your goal.

In your self-assessment, you looked inward to gain a better understanding of your own needs, wants, and potential qualifications for work. You daydreamed about your future and set some life-style goals. Then you read about, discussed, and perhaps even tried out several careers that seemed likely possibilities.

Now you will evaluate the demands and opportunities of the marketing careers you have researched and decide which will make your life-style goals come true. Finally, you will develop a plan of action that will guide you as you prepare for your chosen career.

Evaluating Your Choices

In the next step of the career planning process, you will match what you learned in your self-assessment with the career information you gathered. The best match should be the most logical career choice.

Some people begin an informal career planning process while they are still in elementary school. This informal process is based primarily on observation, with little reality testing. They see their parents and adult acquaintances in their work roles. They also see people in work roles on television and in the movies. Magazine articles, too, provide even preteens with some informal information about careers.

If you've been engaged in an informal career planning process for months or years, then a more formal evaluation of your choices may not take very long. You may decide on your marketing career goal after just a few hours of concentration. However, if you had no career goals in mind when you began this class, it may take a while to reach your decision.

You will be more efficient in evaluating your choices if you organize your task before you begin. Plan a time when you can spend at least an hour in this matching process. Of course, an hour probably won't be enough time to reach one of the most important decisions in your life—but allow at least that much time to get started.

Get out all the notes you made on self-assessment and all the information you gathered on careers. You may be able to take it all in and reach a logical decision without more writing, but it will be easier if you do this matching process on paper. *Use a personal career profile, an evaluation format that allows you to compare your self-assessment side-by-side with a particular career assessment.* Figure 44-1 on page 486 provides an example.

On the left side of the profile, write the information about yourself just once. Then make several photocopies—one for each career that you researched. Using these copies, fill in the career information on the right by referring to your notes. After you complete each profile, reread all the information carefully. Then ask yourself the following questions.

- Does this career match my personal values? Do the work values important in this career match my personal values?
- Does this career fit my life-style goals? Will it provide adequate income? Is the job outlook good for this career?
- Am I willing to continue my education and training as required for this career? Will I have the money to do so?
- Will the duties and responsibilities of this career interest me? Will I be able to perform them well?
- Will I have the skills required for this career? Do I have the aptitudes to learn the skills needed to advance in this career?
- How will my personality fit this career?
- Will I find the work environment and work relationships in this career satisfactory?

Using a personal career profile has a major advantage—you can refer to it again and again in the months and years ahead. Many people have doubts about their decision after they have made their choice. The profile makes it easy for you to review your evaluation, either to convince yourself of its wisdom or to change your decision based on your review.

Making Your Decision

You are now ready for the next-to-last step in the career planning process. It's time to make your choice! What career do you want to pursue?

You may feel that you aren't ready to make such an important decision. Perhaps you want more time to make up your mind. After all, you don't want to make a mistake that could affect you for years—maybe even the rest of your life!

Your choice of a career *is* important. In fact, it may be the most important decision you will ever make. However, don't wait until you are absolutely certain about a career choice before you make your decision. If you do that, you may be waiting for years! Make the best choice you can now, even if you think you may change it later. Even a flexible goal will give you something to aim for.

Do you know any recent high school graduates who have not made career choices? Do they have life-style goals? If they do, are they making any progress toward achieving them, or are they waiting for something to happen that will provide their dream life-

Personal Career Profile

Name **Robert Woo**   Date **September 4, 19 —**

		Match (1–5, with 5 being the best match)
Personal Information	**Career Information**	

Your Values: *The value scales I took showed that I like to help other people (humanitarianism). I like to be a leader. Doing creative things is fun, too.*	**Values:** *As a teacher I would have a chance to help others—that's what it's all about. Teachers certainly have plenty of opportunities to be leaders, too. Teachers also need to be creative!*	
Your Interests: *My hobby interests have always been photography, reading, and theater. My career interest survey showed that I might like a career in leading/influencing, selling, the arts, or maybe a "humanitarian" career.*	**Career Duties and Responsibilities:** *As a teacher, I would present information, direct student discussions and activities in class. I would help each student individually, too. (Maybe I could teach marketing or general business.) A teacher's working conditions would be good in most schools. (Summers off!)*	
My Personality: *I like people, and I have a good attitude toward learning. I have an "open" mind. I'm enthusiastic, too. However, I don't have the energy and drive that some people have. I don't know if I could work night after night.*	**Type of Personality Needed:** *A teacher must like kids, even when they aren't very likeable. I would have to prepare my lesson every day—couldn't just forget about it. Teachers need to be organized, too.*	
Data–People–Things Preferences: *I think I like working with people most of all. I wouldn't want to be stuck in an office all day with only "data" to talk to. I also wouldn't like working only with things. Some data would be all right, though.*	**Data–People–Things Relationships:** *Teachers work mostly with people—their students, other teachers, the principal, parents. They work with data (information), too, though. I don't think they work much with things.*	
Skills and Aptitudes: *I may have some natural teaching skills—the kids at the YMCA always come to me for help. I helped several kids in Miss Moore's class. Business classes are easy for me.*	**Skills and Aptitudes Needed:** *Being able to present information so students can understand it is a very important skill. Of course, you must know your subject. An appetite for learning new approaches to teaching is important, too.*	
Education/Training Acceptable: *I sure never thought I would go to college—I never even liked doing the homework in high school! However, here I am a senior with no real prospects of a good job. Maybe college is the answer.*	**Education/Training Required:** *Four years of college (it sounds like forever, but I guess it does go fast) is required before you can begin teaching in most states. Some states require course work beyond that.*	

Figure 44-1 **Personal Career Profile**

A personal career profile helps you compare your self-assessment with a particular career assessment. Based on this personal career profile, how well does Robert Woo's personal information match the career information shown? Rank each category from 1–5 as shown on the profile.

style? Some 30-year-olds, for example, haven't made their first career decision; most of them will remain behind schedule in their careers all their lives. Make your first decision now, and you can get on with planning the rest of your life. You will only reach your goals by taking control of your life. Don't wait for something to happen that will put your life in order—do it yourself.

Your career decision, even one you may change later, will be a positive influence on your life. It will give you a sense of direction, providing a map that shows where you want to go and how you can get there.

In a few months or a year, you may feel your choice was not appropriate. You may have overlooked some important information about a career, or you may decide that you don't want to make the sacrifices necessary to reach your goal. Just remember that you can review your career planning process anytime. You will probably do this when circumstances change, and you have doubts about your career decision. If you decide that another career is more appropriate for you, then it is no disgrace to change your goal. In fact, it's the right thing to do.

Once again, however, don't spend too much time making up you mind. If a change is appropriate, make the decision and get on with your life. How many people do you know who have spent tens of thousands of dollars and years of their life pursuing the wrong goals? How many adults do you know who are unhappy in their careers? When you know it's not right, make a change.

So, don't be afraid of making the wrong decision. If you make a mistake, you can correct it. Even a choice you have doubts about is better than no choice at all.

Developing a Plan of Action

Have you decided which of the marketing careers you researched is the best match with your self-assessment? If so, you can begin planning how you will achieve your career goal. A plan doesn't guarantee success, but it will outline the steps that you will need to follow to reach your ultimate goal.

Formulating Planning Goals

The small steps you take to get from where you are now to where you want to be are **planning goals**.

They give your life a sense of direction and move you steadily toward your ultimate career goal. Every time you reach a planning goal, you gain confidence to move out boldly toward the next one.

Be Specific. How do you know whether you are making progress toward your ultimate goal? The answer is, by making your planning goals specific. *A* **specific goal** *is stated in exact terms and includes some details.* The goal statement *I want to become a success* is not specific. The goal statement *I want to earn a degree in marketing from Kansas University* is specific. This is the type of planning goal that moves you along toward your ultimate goal.

Specific goals make it easy to see what you need to do to succeed. Write out statements of all your planning goals. Then read each one to see whether you can make it more specific.

Be Realistic. Planning goals must also be realistic. *A* **realistic goal** *is one that you have a reasonable chance of achieving.* Few people can reasonably expect to become president of General Motors. If you have limited artistic talent, you can't reasonably expect to become a commercial artist. Think about your skills and aptitudes. They will guide you in both your ultimate career goal and your planning goals.

Work Backward. When you set your planning goals, you begin with your ultimate career goal. Then you decide what long-range goals you will need to reach to achieve your ultimate goal, what medium-range goals you will need to reach to achieve your long-range goals, and so on. You work backward, starting with your most distant objective and moving closer to your present position in time.

Suppose, for example, your ultimate career goal is to own your own advertising agency by age 40. One long-range goal might be to become an advertising executive by the time you are 30. After you have decided on your long-range goals, think about what medium-range and short-range goals will help you progress toward each long-range goal. One of your medium-range goals might be to earn a degree in marketing. A short-range goal would be to gain admission to the college of your choice.

Planning goals can help you test your ultimate career goal. For example, suppose one of your medium-range goals is to work part-time in an advertising agency. Your work experience may reinforce your career decision, and you will be confident that it was a good one. There is also a possibility, however, that it will have the opposite effect. It may convince you that advertising isn't nearly as satisfying as you thought it would be. In this case, testing your decision may lead to your changing your ultimate career goal.

Fulfilling Educational Requirements

Whatever your career choice, your plan of action to reach your goal will include some education and training. The amount will vary from a few days of on-the-job training to four or more years of college.

Graduation from high school is the minimum educational requirement for most marketing jobs. You may be able to get a job without a high school diploma, but there would be few opportunities for advancement. In addition, the jobs that are available to those without a diploma are usually jobs no one really wants.

There is a close correlation between amount of education and lifetime earnings. Various studies show that the average college graduate earns about 40 percent more in a lifetime than the average high school graduate. For those beginning work in 1995, this will amount to an estimated $700,000 in extra income over a lifetime.

On-the-job Training. You can learn many jobs through on-the-job training. The time required varies from a few days to several years. Starting pay is low, but your income will increase as you gain

C A S E   C H A L L E N G E

Young Independents

Not everyone wants to work for someone else—or should. Some people are cut out to work for themselves, and some ambitious entrepreneurs don't even wait until they're out of high school to begin their careers.

All over the country, elementary school, junior high school, and high school students have not only begun their career decision making but are also running successful businesses. They raise bees and sell the honey, perform magic tricks at parties, make fashion jewelry, or develop computer programs.

Joanne Marlowe liked to make stuffed toys. She started selling her patterns in magazines and packaging the scraps of fabric needed to make the toys. By age 14, she was designing clothes for herself, her friends, and her family. The demand for her clothes grew so much that at age 19 she opened her own dress designing business.

John Shorb was 12 when he began cutting lawns, but he took his work seriously. While his friends were out playing, John was building his business. He learned all he could about landscaping, trimming, weeding, and seeding. By the

time he was 19, his landscaping business had 120 regular customers and 5 full-time and 4 part-time summer employees. He was earning $125,000 a year.

Robert Lewis Dean was 15 when he borrowed $1,500 from his parents to buy an old Cadillac. He taught himself how to fix it up and sold it for a profit. Five years later he was the owner of several limousine services earning almost $2 million a year.

Surveys of young businesspeople show the one thing they have in common is their optimism. They know working for themselves will not be easy, but they are more attracted by the opportunities than deterred by the difficulties. They are determined to succeed.

1. What qualities do you think it takes to go into business for yourself?
2. What kinds of short-, medium-, and long-range goals would you set for yourself if you wanted to start your own business?
3. How could each of the businesses mentioned in this Case Challenge lead to a career in marketing?

Thanks for the (Better) Memory

Like many immigrants, An Wang came to the U.S. in the 1940s with little money and speaking little English. In six years, however, he had a Ph.D. from Harvard and had invented a magnetic core memory that expanded a computer's ability to store information. He sold his invention to IBM and started Wang Laboratories. In 1988, Wang joined Thomas Edison, Alexander Graham Bell, and the Wright Brothers in the National Inventors Hall of Fame.

experience. Some businesses have structured training programs, including classroom instruction. (You may have already gone through this type of training with your current cooperative education or work experience program—particularly if you are working in a retail environment.)

Other businesses combine on-the-job experience with classes at a local community college. Some businesses pay tuition for their employees enrolled in courses that will help them on the job.

If you are interested, ask your local state employment service about opportunities for on-the-job training. Of course, you may apply directly to businesses where you know there are on-the-job training programs.

Area Vocational Schools and Area Vocational Centers. *Area vocational schools are post-secondary institutions offering instruction in vocational education.* Since these schools are supported by taxes, you may attend them for free or for a very low cost. Programs are available for both high school students and adults.

Area vocational centers (also called skills centers) serve secondary students from a geographical area. The students may attend a half-day of high school and spend the other half-day at the vocational center.

Technical Institutes. *Technical institutes (also called trade schools) are two-year, post-secondary institutions offering instruction in vocational or technical education.* The costs usually range from a few hundred to several thousand dollars for a complete program. If you enroll in a technical institute, you will only take courses in your chosen field. So, you can complete most programs in two years or less.

Community Colleges. Community colleges are two-year colleges offering general and vocational education to colleges and universities. These tax-supported colleges are sometimes called junior colleges or city colleges. You can attend a community college for a lot less money than you would spend to attend a trade school. You can often transfer up to two years of community college credit to a four-year college or university.

Colleges and Universities. Some jobs in marketing do not require graduation from college. Many of these same jobs, though, will provide more opportunities for advancement if you have a college degree. Even as a beginner, you will earn a higher salary if you graduated from college.

Community colleges offer students whose career choices demand more education an alternative to trade schools and four-year colleges. Why is a community college a good choice for students who are not entirely sure how much more education they might want or need?

Choosing the Best Education for You

Choosing education is much like choosing a career. Follow the complete decision-making process to select the best program and the best school for you. Your school counselor is a good place to start when you want information on vocational schools and centers, technical institutes, community colleges, and colleges and universities. He or she will have a bookshelf full of catalogs from these institutions. Your school and public libraries are also likely to have information on them.

Choose the program and school that will best prepare you for your career. If you are not graduating this school year, there is still time to enroll in additional marketing classes and related courses that will help you toward your career goal. If you are planning education and training beyond high school, consider the following questions:

- What is my ultimate career goal?
- What courses can I still take that will help me reach my career goal?
- What education and training beyond high school is required to reach my career goal?
- How much of this education and training must I complete before I enter this career?
- Where can I get this education and training?
- How much will this education and training cost, and how will I get the money?
- How much education and training can I get on the job? What part-time jobs will help?

Outlining Your Plan

After you have answered these questions, begin writing your personal plan of action—and it *is* important for you to write it down. Figure 44-2 provides an example. Begin with your long-range goals, then write down your medium-range goals and finish with your short-range goals. Write down the date that you plan to begin working toward and the date you expect to reach each goal. This will help keep you on track toward your ultimate career goal—the one that turns your dream life-style into reality!

Goal	Date
Ultimate Career Goal:	
Vice President of Sales	2020
Long-Range Goals:	
2. Director of Sales	2015
1. Regional Sales Manager	2008
Medium-Range Goals:	
5. Begin job as District Sales Manager	2001
4. Complete university degree in marketing	2001
3. Begin job as Area Sales Representative	1998
2. Begin university courses in marketing (fall semester)	1997
1. Begin job as Sales Trainee	1997
Short-Range Goals:	
4. Complete two-year college program for A.A.	1997
3. Graduate from high school	1996
2. Take second year of marketing in high school	1996
1. Take part-time job in sales	1996

Figure 44-2 **Personal Plan of Action**
When written down, your personal plan of action for achieving your career goals should look something like this. Why are the entries numbered backwards?

VOCABULARY REVIEW

Write a definition for each of the following vocabulary terms.

personal career profile
planning goals
specific goal
realistic goal

area vocational schools
area vocational centers
technical institutes

FACT AND IDEA REVIEW

1. What are the final three steps in the career planning process as outlined in your text?

2. What is the purpose of a personal career profile?

3. Why is it important to make a career decision now, even if it is one you may change later?

4. Describe the usefulness of planning goals.

5. Give three examples of *specific* planning goals.

6. Suppose your long-range goal is to become a buyer for a chain of grocery stores. Identify the goals below as either short-range or medium-range:

   a. Getting a summer job bagging groceries in a supermarket

   b. Applying to a college to study retail business

   c. Getting your first job out of college as an assistant buyer

   d. Participating in a DECA chapter in high school

7. Match each person in the first group with a *realistic* career goal from the second group.

   People

   a. Interested in sports, skilled in math

   b. Interested in sports, skilled in art

   c. Skilled in football, received football scholarship to college

   d. Interested in sports, aptitude for business

   e. Interested in sports and the media

   Career goals

   (1) Television sports announcer

   (2) Professional football player

   (3) Accountant for professional football team

   (4) Professional football team manager

   (5) Sports magazine graphic designer

8. What are the differences between area vocational schools and technical institutes?

9. What are the advantages of attending a community college?

10. Do all careers require a college education? What difference can a college diploma make in a job?

CRITICAL THINKING

1. Describe the informal career planning process, and discuss the influences you have experienced as part of it.

2. Why is it difficult for some people to take control of their lives? Why is it advantageous to do so as soon as possible? What could happen if you don't?

3. What is the value of having career goals that are flexible?

4. If your long-range goal is to run your own video production company, what are some short-range goals that you could achieve while still in high school?

5. If your area of career interest is banking, what career-related activities could you pursue before college?

6. Suppose you are a junior in high school and have decided that your long-range goal is to become a hotel manager. List some possible short- and medium-range goals that would help you toward your ultimate goal.

7. Why do you think a person with a college degree tends to command a higher salary than a person without a degree?

8. Why do you think it is important to write down your plan of action for achieving your career goals?

USING BASIC SKILLS

Math

1. In an entry-level management position, the wage for a person with a college degree is $23.22 per hour. Without a degree, the wage for the same job is $17.44 per hour.

   a. By what percentage does the college-educated individual's hourly wage exceed his/her fellow employee's?

   b. How much more would the person with the college degree make in a month, working 40 hours per week?

Communication

2. In telling others about your career goals in the field of marketing, you use a great deal of jargon. Your listeners have little marketing experience and look at you with raised eyebrows. What does this response tell you? What can you do about it?

3. Select an area vocational school, technical institute, community college, college, or university in which you are interested. Write a letter requesting information about entrance requirements and courses of study. Conclude with a request for an application of admission.

Human Relations

4. Suppose your parents have spent thousands of dollars putting you through college to become a commercial artist. You have landed your first job and shortly find that you are uncomfortable with the realities of such work—the high pressure, long hours, and competitive nature do not suit you. You feel you may have even chosen the wrong career. What do you tell your parents?

5. You have always loved plants and flowers and have decided that your long-range goal is to own a retail garden shop. You have an opportunity to work in a local garden shop as soon as you graduate, get on-the-job training, work your way up, and eventually buy into the business. Your parents want you to go to college first. What should you do? How would you explain your decision to your parents?

APPLICATION PROJECTS

1. Go to the library and find a magazine article about someone who has made a mid-life career change. Summarize the article orally or in writing for your classmates. Be sure to answer the following questions:

   a. What was the career change?

   b. Why did the person make it?

   c. How did the person feel afterward about his or her new career? about the process of change he or she had gone through?

2. Write to the National Association of Trade and Technical Schools (2021 K Street NW, Washington, DC 20006). Ask for information about trade schools in your area. Use the materials you are sent as the basis for a bulletin board display.

3. Form a small group with some of your classmates and share each other's written goals/plans.

Employability
Skills

OBJECTIVES

After completing this chapter, you will be able to:

1. name the legal record that you must have before you can begin working,

2. locate job leads from a variety of sources,

3. write a letter of application and complete a standard application form,

4. write a resume and cover letter,

5. prepare for and conduct yourself properly during a job interview, and

6. follow up a job interview.

WORDS TO KNOW

job lead
public employment agencies
private employment agencies
direct calling
standard English
references
resume
cover letter

I f you have chosen your ultimate career goal and written a plan of action for achieving it, then you have some short-range goals. One of these is probably to get some work experience in your chosen career, whether it is in marketing or some other field. Even if your planning hasn't progressed this far, you may still be interested in a part-time job to earn money for clothes, a car, or educational expenses.

Whatever your reason for wanting to work, you will benefit from having some proven methods of conducting a job search. That is what you will learn in this chapter. Keep in mind that the same methods can be used to find a part-time job now and an entry-level job when you are ready for full-time work.

Getting a Work Permit

If you are a minor under the age of 18, most states require a work permit before you can legally begin working. However, in some states such as Michigan, a cooperative education training agreement can serve as a legal work permit.

State and federal labor laws designate certain jobs as too dangerous for young workers. Most of these jobs are performed in hazardous environments or involve the use of power-driven machinery. The laws also limit the number of hours that young people can work in one day or one week. For example, more hours of work are allowed during summer vacations than during the school year.

A work permit establishes for the employer that it is legal for the student to do the type of work offered. In some states, work permits must specify the *exact* job duties and hours of work. In these cases, both the employer and student fill out sections of an application for the permit. The employer, student, and the student's parent must sign the application before a work permit is issued.

Ask your marketing teacher or counselor whether you will need a work permit and, if so, where you can get one. Work permits are usually issued by a designated school official. Check on this now so you can avoid possible delays when you are ready to go to work.

Finding Job Openings

When you are ready for a full-time job in your chosen career, you will want one that matches your needs, wants, and qualifications. For now, though, your main interest in finding a job is probably to earn some money. Even so, you most likely won't be happy with just any job. You'll want one that you can enjoy and at which you can be successful.

How do you go about finding such a job? The most productive first step is to contact all of the sources available to you that might produce a job lead. *A job lead is information about a job opening.* Sometimes the information is incomplete. For example, you may hear that a nearby department store is looking for part-time salespeople. You don't know which department needs workers or to whom you should apply. Sometimes you have to follow up skimpy leads and fill in the rest of the information yourself, rather like a detective. Finding the right job requires getting as many job leads as possible and then promptly following up on each of them.

Exploring Sources of Job Leads

When there is low unemployment among adult workers, it is easy to find leads for both full-time and part-time jobs in marketing and most other career areas. When the unemployment rate rises, leads are harder to find; and it may take a little longer to find the right job. In either situation, the available sources of leads are the same.

Your Counselor. Retail stores and other businesses often call school counselors, asking them to refer qualified students for part-time or temporary jobs. Because school counselors usually have contacts in the business community, they sometimes hear about full-time jobs, too. Your counselor may know of a job that matches your interests and abilities.

Cooperative Education and Work-Experience Programs. Most high schools have a cooperative education program in which students work part-time on a job related to one of their classes. If the marketing class you are enrolled in is part of a cooperative program, you may already be working on a part-time job in marketing. Cooperative education teachers have contacts in the business community because they place and supervise students on part-time jobs. Therefore, if you have taken a cooperative education class or know the teacher of the class well, he or she may be a good source of job leads.

Many schools also offer a cooperative education program that is not limited to just one career area, such as marketing. This type of program is usually known as a work experience program, but it may go by a number of other names. In most schools, the work experience coordinator has hundreds of contacts in the business community. Therefore, he or she may be one of your best sources of job leads.

Schools have a good record of placing students in jobs that fit their interests and abilities. This is probably because teachers, counselors, and work experience coordinators know their students so well. Don't sit back and relax, however, thinking a teacher or someone else in your school will find the right job for you. There are almost always more students looking for jobs than there are jobs to be filled. That means several well-qualified students will probably be referred for every job opening. Thus, you might follow up several good leads and still not get a job because of the competition.

Family and Friends. One of your best sources of job leads often turns out to be members of your own family. Adult friends of your family and your own personal friends can be good sources, too.

Family members and friends often hear of job openings where they work. They may not immediately know of the perfect job for you, but they will ask their friends and co-workers about openings.

Do you have any friends who have started new jobs recently? If so, they may know of some job openings that weren't quite right for them but may be exactly what you are looking for. Ask them if they have any leads.

Make a list of family and personal friends who might help you find job leads. Do any of them own or manage their own business? They may need someone with your qualifications. If not, they probably have many business contacts, and one of them may be looking for a good worker like you.

Add to your list the names of friends who work for companies where you would like to work. Then add the names of school friends and neighbors who are somehow connected with a business that interests you. For example, perhaps a classmate's mother or father works for a company that has an opening that's just what you are looking for.

Most businesses welcome applications from friends of their employees. They know their employees would not recommend anyone who is not well qualified for the job.

Some young people are not comfortable asking influential friends for job leads. They want to get a job on their own. There is nothing wrong, however, with getting a job through a family member or friends if you are qualified. Many jobs are never advertised because they are filled by friends of present employees. So, don't overlook this important source of job leads.

Former Employers. Have you ever held a job? Even if it was just a temporary job, such as baby-sitting or mowing lawns, your former employers may be good sources of job leads. If they were satisfied with your work, they will probably want to help you find a job.

Professional People in Your Personal Life. You probably have periodic contact with professional people in your personal life—doctors, dentists, or lawyers. If you have established a good rapport with these people, they will be happy to help you in your job search. Ask them for names of people that you can contact.

Newspaper Ads. Read the help wanted ads in your local newspaper. Some papers separate jobs by type, such as sales jobs, accounting jobs, and so on. In most areas, the Sunday edition has the most ads.

The help wanted ads are not only a good source of job leads, but they will also teach you a great deal about the local job market. You will learn the salaries offered and the qualifications required for different types of jobs.

Promptly follow up every ad that looks as though it could lead to the job you want. If you wait a day or two, the job will probably be filled. Be aware,

The classified ads in your local newspaper can give you a quick overview of the job market in your area. Check your own newspaper. How would you characterize the situation in your community?

however, that not every ad represents a legitimate job offer. Ads that require you to make a deposit of money are not usually genuine job offers but thinly disguised attempts to sell you something. Ads that require you to enroll in a course (and pay a fee) before you can be hired fall into the same category. People who place ads like these will take your money, but they don't usually have any jobs to offer.

Employment Agencies. The main function of employment agencies is to match workers with jobs. Most larger cities have two types of employment agencies—public and private. *Public employment agencies are supported by state or federal taxes and offer their services free to both job applicants and employers. Private employment agencies, which are not supported by taxes, must earn a profit to stay in business.* They charge a fee for their services, which is paid by either the job applicant or the employer.

Public employment agencies are identified by the names of the states in which they are located. The Texas State Employment Service and the California State Employment Development Department are examples. In some cities, the state employment service is the only one available.

When you fill out an application form at the public employment agency near you, you will be interviewed to determine your interests and qualifications. Then, when a job is listed that matches your interests and qualifications, the agency will call you. You will be told about the company and the job duties, then referred for an interview if you are still interested.

Private employment agencies often have job leads that are not listed with public agencies. So, if you aren't getting all the leads you want, consider applying at a private agency. Remember, however, that private agencies charge a fee if they place you on a job. The fee for matching workers with higher-level jobs is often paid by the employer. The placement fee on entry-level jobs is usually paid by the employee. Thus, if you are a beginning worker, you will probably have to pay the fee yourself.

When you apply for placement through a private agency, you will have to sign a contract. Read it carefully. It will specify how much you will pay if you are referred to a job and hired. The amount is usually a percentage of your salary for the first several months or even the first full year of employment.

Company Personnel Offices. Large companies have personnel offices to handle employment matters, including the hiring of new workers. You may check on job openings by telephoning that office or by making a personal visit. Some personnel offices list openings on a bulletin board. You can stop by at your convenience and see if anything new has been posted.

If you know that you would like to work for a certain company, and it has a personnel office, stop by often. Get to know the people who work there, and you will have a better chance of being hired.

Direct Calling. The more job leads you have, the better your chances of finding a job that is right for you. If you don't have many leads, you may want to do some direct calling.

Direct calling is the process of contacting potential employers in person or on the telephone. Do this when you think you would like to work for certain companies but are unsure whether they have any openings. You can use the Yellow Pages to compile a list of company names, addresses, and telephone numbers.

With direct calling, you may get more consideration by calling in person than by inquiring about a job on the telephone. Either way, direct calling takes a lot of time. If you contact enough employers, though, you may find a job opening that interests you.

Letters of Inquiry. Writing a letter of inquiry is a variation of direct calling. You use the technique under the same circumstances and for the same reason—when you want to know whether a company has openings in the career area of your interest. Instead of making your inquiries by phone or in person, however, you write a letter.

REAL WORLD MARKETING

Removing Barriers

R on Mace was nine when polio put him in a wheelchair. He became an architect and designer with the goal of removing the everyday barriers that frustrate disabled people. His company, Barrier Free Environments, Inc., uses Mace's concept of "universal design" to design buildings and products that anyone can use, regardless of age or disability.

How do you know to whom you should address your correspondence? You find out by doing a little research. You look up the company's number in the telephone directory, then call and ask for the name of the individual who hires new employees. At that point you will learn whether the company has a personnel office or whether department heads do their own hiring. (In the latter case, ask for the name of the head of the department in which you would like to work—marketing, for example.) Confirm the spelling of any names you are given and the position of the person you will be contacting. Thank the person who gave them to you. Then verify the company's address, particularly asking for the correct ZIP Code or any postal box, floor, or suite numbers.

Now you are ready to write your letter of inquiry. See page 109 of Chapter 9 to review the elements of a business letter. Figure 45-1 provides an example.

735 North Fairfield
Dallas, Texas 75221
March 15, 19 – –

Mr. John Robinson
Sears Roebuck and Co.
5334 Ross Avenue
Dallas, TX 75206

Dear Mr. Robinson:

On May 17, I shall graduate from Sam Houston High School with a major emphasis in sales and marketing. While in high school, I have worked in sales part-time, but now I am most eager to begin my first full-time job in sales.

As I have always been impressed by the courteous, efficient salespeople in your store, I am very much interested in a job at Sears. If you anticipate a need for any full-time, permanent employees in the next several months, I would like to apply.

May I have an application form, or should I call for an interview at your convenience? My home telephone is 924-7884.

Sincerely,

Charlene J. Graham

Charlene J. Graham

Figure 45-1 **Letter of Inquiry**
You write a letter of inquiry when you want to know whether a company has openings in the career area of your interest. Why would you write a letter instead of making inquiries by phone or in person?

Expanding Your List of Job Leads

Getting new job leads and following up the ones you already have should be overlapping processes. That is, as you follow up on existing leads, you should at the same time be looking for new ones. Here's how you do it. First you get as many job leads from your firsthand sources as possible. Then you expand your list by getting referrals from the people you see. Each time you follow up a lead that doesn't result in a job, ask your interviewer to suggest others you might contact. Try to get at least one or preferably two new leads from each interview.

Why should you do this? Consider it psychological insurance. Remember, many other people are looking for work, too. You may not get the job you want, or you may have to turn down a job that doesn't meet your expectations. Having other possibilities will keep you from getting discouraged in these circumstances. If you have a long list of leads, you can simply follow up the next one.

Applying for a Job

Employers look for the most qualified person to fill a job. They will decide whether to hire you based in part on how you look and what you say during an interview. More than anything else, though, they will want to know whether you have the ability to do the work.

Employers have several ways of getting this information. Most ask job seekers to fill out an application form. Some request additional documents—a separate letter of application or (for more responsible, higher-paying jobs) a resume. Finally, some employers administer one or more employment tests to applicants.

If you are qualified for a job, the way you present your qualifications may be the determining factor in whether you are hired. If you follow the suggestions on the next few pages, you will increase your chances of success.

Using Standard English

Everything you write and say to a prospective employer should be in *standard English*. *Standard English* is the formal style of writing and speaking that you have learned in school. It is standard because it means the same thing to everyone.

Most people do not use standard English for all their communication. In some situations, it isn't necessary. For example, when you write a letter to a close relative, you simply write what's on your mind and you don't worry much about form. When you chat with a friend on the telephone, you may use slang or colloquialisms. These practices make for comfortable and easy personal conversation, but they have no place in business. Most communication in business is formal, and that means standard English.

Standard English employs correct grammar, spelling, pronunciation, and usage. For example, "Marilyn *has* a job interview" is standard English. "Marilyn *have* a job interview" is not. The repeated use in conversation of the interjection *you know* is non-standard English. Non-standard pronunciations are another common lapse. (An accent, either regional or foreign, does not indicate non-standard English.)

Employers will have several opportunities to evaluate your English. When they read your application form, they will notice whether you use and spell words correctly. If you write or type a letter of application or a resume, they will have another chance to evaluate your ability (or inability) to write. Finally, when you are interviewed, the employer will listen to you speak and will evaluate your grammar and pronunciation. If an employer sees or hears non-standard English in these situations, your paperwork will probably be "filed" in the wastebasket.

Filling Out Application Forms

Most employment application forms are short (from one to four pages), and most ask the same or similar questions. Because companies usually design their own forms, however, each one is a little different.

For the prospective employer, the application form provides information about your qualifications so company personnel can decide whether to interview you. For you as an applicant, the form offers an opportunity to present your qualifications in a way that will make the employer want to talk with you in person.

Follow the suggestions below, and you will have a good chance of being selected for an interview.

- Fill out the application form as neatly as possible. Spell all words correctly. (If you fill out the form at home, use a dictionary to look up the spellings of any words you are unsure of. If you fill out the form at the place of employment, use words you know how to spell.)
- If you can, take the application form home and fill it out on a typewriter. If you are not a good typist, make a photocopy of the form, fill out the copy, and get a friend who types well to complete the original. If you are requested to complete the form at the place of employment, use a pen.
- Answer every question that applies to you. If a question does not apply to you, write "NA" (meaning "Not Applicable") or draw a short line in the space. This will show that you did not overlook the item.
- Use your full name, not a nickname, on the form. On most applications, your first name, middle initial, and last name are requested. Provide your complete address, including your ZIP Code.
- If there is a question on job preference, list a specific job title. Do not write "Anything" as an answer. Employers expect you to know what type of work you can and want to do.
- Most application forms include a section on education. Write the names of all the schools you have attended and the dates of attendance. If there are several, make a list for your own reference before you apply for a job.
- There will be a section on previous work experience on the form. You may not have had much experience, but you can include even short-term or unpaid jobs. Fill out this section in *reverse chronological order*, beginning with your current or most recent job and ending with your first job.
- Be prepared to list several *references*. *References are people who know your work habits and personal traits so well that they will recommend you for the job.* Try to use professional references such as your teachers, friends established in business, or former employers. Do not list classmates, relatives, or personal friends.

- Sign your name using your first name, middle initial, and last name. Your signature should be written, never typed or printed.

An example of a completed application form is shown in Figure 45-2.

Writing Letters of Application

Most employers prefer application forms because they are specifically structured to provide just the information the employer needs to reach a decision on interviews. However, some employers request that an applicant write a letter of application instead.

When you write a letter of application, you are essentially writing a sales pitch. You are trying to convince an employer that you are the best person to fill a specific job opening. So, tell why you are interested in the position and what your special qualifications for it are. Don't write a sad story about needing the job because you are behind on your car payments.

The following suggestions will help you write an impressive letter of application.

- Write a first draft to get down most of the main points. Then rewrite your letter, making changes and additions until it says exactly what you want it to say. Ask a teacher or friend in business to read and critique your letter. Then put the final touches on it and type a perfect copy.
- In your first sentence, describe how you learned about the job opening. If a friend who knows the employer gave you the lead, you might say, "At the suggestion of Mr. Charles Williams, I am writing about the job as mail order clerk in your store." If you are writing in response to a newspaper ad, you might say, "I am responding to your ad for an advertising assistant in the *Daily News*."
- In your second sentence, state expressly that you are applying for the job. You might say, "I would like to be considered an applicant for this position."
- In the second paragraph, describe how your education and experience qualify you for the job. If you have a lot to say about both your education and your experience, use a separate paragraph for each. If you don't have much experience, just write about your education in more detail. Mention classes you have taken that are related to the job.

SEARS, ROEBUCK AND CO.
APPLICATION
FOR EMPLOYMENT

PLEASE PRINT INFORMATION REQUESTED IN INK

Date April 6, 19 – –

SEARS IS AN EQUAL OPPORTUNITY EMPLOYER and fully subscribes to the principles of Equal Opportunity unity. Sears has adopted an Affirmative Action Program to ensure that all applicants and employees are considered for hire, promotion and job status, without regard to race, color, religion, sex, national origin, age, handicap, or status as a disabled veteran or veteran of the Vietnam Era.

To protect the interests of all concerned, applicants for certain job assignments must pass a physical examination before they are hired.

NOTE: This application will be considered active for 90 days. If you have not been employed within this period and are still interested in employment at Sears, please contact the office where you applied and request that your application be reactivated.

Name Graham,   Charlene   Joan   **Social Security Number** 541-62-6351

Last   First   Middle   (Please present your Social Security Card for review.)

Address   735   North Fairfield Street   Dallas,   Texas   75221

Number   Street   City   State   Zip Code

County Dallas

Previous Address — —

Number   Street   City   State   Zip Code

Current phone or nearest phone (214) 924-7486

Best time of day to contact after 4 p.m.

(Answer only if position for which you are applying requires driving.)

If hired, can you furnish proof of age?   Yes ☒   No ☐   Licensed to drive car?   YES ☐   NO ☐

If hired, can you furnish proof that you are legally entitled to work in U.S.?   Yes ☒   No ☐   Is license valid in this state?   YES ☐   NO ☐

Have you ever been employed by Sears or a subsidiary of Sears?   YES ☐   NO ☒   If so when and where last employed?   Position

Former employees of Sears and certain Subsidiaries may be entitled to service credit under the Pension Plan based on prior employment with Sears, Roebuck and Co., Homart Development Co., Sears investment Management Co., Sears Roebuck Acceptance Corp., Sears, Roebuck de Puerto Rico, Inc., Sears Roebuck Overseas, Inc., Sears Securities Sales, Inc., Terminal Freight Handling Co., Allstate Insurance Company and their Subsidiaries, Lifetime Foam Products, Pacific Installers, and Sears, S.A. (Central America), Dean Witter Reynolds Organization, Inc. and their Subsidiaries, Coldwell Banker and their Subsidiaries and Sears World Trade.

Have you a relative in the employ of Sears in the store or unit to which you are applying?   No

A PHYSICAL OR MENTAL DISABILITY WILL NOT CAUSE REJECTION IF IN SEARS MEDICAL OPINION YOU ARE ABLE TO SATISFACTORILY PERFORM IN THE POSITION FOR WHICH YOU ARE BEING CONSIDERED. Alternative placement, if available, of an applicant who does not meet the physical standards of the job for which he/she was originally considered is permitted.

Do you have any physical or mental impairment which may limit your ability to perform the job for which you are applying?   No

If yes, what can reasonably be done to accommodate your limitation?

	School Attended	No. of Years	Name of School	City/State	Grad-uate?	Course or College Major	Average Grades
EDUCATION	Grammar	7	Esperanza Elementary	Dallas, TX	Yes		B+
	Jr. High	3	Andrews Junior High	Dallas, TX	Yes		B
	Sr. High	3	Sam Houston High School	Dallas, TX	Yes	Marketing/Bus.	A–
	Other						
	College					Degree	

	BRANCH OF SERVICE	DATE ENTERED SERVICE*	DATE OF DISCHARGE*	HIGHEST RANK	SERVICE-RELATED SKILLS AND EXPERIENCE APPLICABLE TO CIVILIAN EMPLOYMENT
MILITARY SERVICE					

*Do not complete if applying in the state of California.

What experience or training have you had other than your work experience, military service and education? (Community activities, hobbies, etc.)

I am interested in the type of work I have checked: ☒ Sales   ☐ Office   ☐ Mechanical   ☐ Warehouse   ☐ Other Specify

Or the following specific Job

I am seeking (*check only one*):
- ☐ Temporary employment (6 days or less)
- ☐ Seasonal employment (one season, e.g. Christmas)
- ☒ Regular employment (employment for indefinite period of time)

If temporary, indicate dates available

I am available for (*check only one*):
- ☐ Part Time
- ☒ Full-Time **Work**

If part-time, indicate maximum hours per week _____ and enter hours available in block to the right.

HOURS AVAILABLE FOR WORK	
Sun.	To
Mon.	8 a.m. To 6 p.m.
Tues.	8 a.m. To 6 p.m.
Wed.	8 a.m. To 6 p.m.
Thurs.	8 a.m. To 6 p.m.
Fri.	8 a.m. To 6 p.m.
Sat.	8 a.m. To 6 p.m.

Have you been convicted during the past seven years of a serious crime involving a person's life or property?
☒ NO   ☐ YES   If yes explain

10534 Rev. 9 / 83

(SEE REVERSE SIDE)

Figure 45-2   **Job Application**

A job application form provides information about your qualifications so company personnel can decide whether to interview you. How long did Charlene Graham work at Chicken Annie's? Why did she leave that company?

REFERENCES

LIST BELOW YOUR FOUR MOST RECENT EMPLOYERS. BEGINNING WITH THE CURRENT OR MOST RECENT ONE. IF YOU HAVE HAD LESS THAN FOUR EMPLOYERS, USE THE REMAINING SPACES FOR PERSONAL REFERENCES. IF YOU WERE EMPLOYED UNDER A MAIDEN OR OTHER NAME. PLEASE ENTER THAT NAME IN THE RIGHT HAND MARGIN. IF APPLICABLE, ENTER SERVICE IN THE ARMED FORCES ON THE REVERSE SIDE.

NAMES AND ADDRESSES OF FORMER EMPLOYERS BEGINNING WITH THE CURRENT OR MOST RECENT	Nature of Employer's Business	Name of your Supervisor	What kind of work did you do?	Starting Date	Starting Pay	Date of Leaving	Pay at Leaving	Why did you leave? Give details
1 NOTE—State reason for and length of inactivity between present application date and last employer. Name: Merchandise Mart Address: 2800 Tyler Avenue Tel No 925-9021 City: Dallas, State: Texas Zip Code: 75221	Department Store	Mr. Travis	Sales	Month Nov. / Year 90	/ Per Week	Month / Year	/ Per Week	Still employed part-time
2 NOTE—State reason for and length of inactivity between fast employer and second last employer. Name: Chicken Annie's Address: 1700 South Vernon Avenue Tel. No. 924-6318 City: Dallas, State: Texas Zip Code: 75221	Fast Food	Mrs. Riley	Sales	Month Jan. / Year 90	$80 / Per Week	Month Oct. / Year 90	$95 / Per Week	To accept a job with more hours and higher pay.
3 NOTE—State reason for and length of inactivity between second last employer and third last employer. Name: Mr. Paul Crawford (former teacher) Address: 3614 Rayburn Avenue Tel. No. 925-1163 City: Dallas, State: Texas Zip Code: 75221				Month / Year	/ Per Week	Month / Year	/ Per Week	
4 NOTE—State reason for and length of inactivity between third last employer and fourth last employer. Name: Miss Irene Jenkins Address: 1222 Oakwood Street Tel. No. 925-7611 City: Dallas, State: Texas Zip Code: 75221				Month / Year	/ Per Week	Month / Year	/ Per Week	

I certify that the Information contained In this application is correct to the best of my knowledge and understand that any misstatement or omission of information is grounds for dismissal in accordance with Sears, Roebuck and Co. policy. I authorize the references listed above to give you any and all information concerning my previous employment and any pertinent Information they may have, personal or otherwise, and release all parties from all liability for any damage that may result from furnishing same to you. In consideration of my employment, I agree to conform to the rules and regulations of Sears, Roebuck and Co., and my employment and compensation can be terminated with or without cause, and with or without notice, at any time, at the option of either the Company or myself. I understand that no unit manager or representative of Sears, Roebuck and Co. other than the President or Vice-President of the Company, has any authority to enter into any agreement for employment for any specified period of time, or to make any agreement contrary to the foregoing. in some states, the law requires that Sears have my written permission before obtaining consumer reports on me, and I hereby authorize Sears to obtain such reports.

Applicant's Signature _Charlene J. Graham_

NOT TO BE FILLED OUT BY APPLICANT

INTERVIEWER'S COMMENTS	Date of Emp.		Tested	(Store will enter dates as required.)		Mailed	Completed
	Dept. or Division	Regular ☐ Part-Time ☐	Physical examination scheduled for		References Requests		
	Job Title		Physical examination form completed		Consumer Report		
	Job Title Code	Job Grade			With. Tax (W–4)		
	Compensation Arrangement				State With. Tax		
	Manager Approving		Review Card prepared	Minor's Work Permit			
Prospect for			Time card prepared	Proof of Birth			
1. 2.	Employee No.	Rack No.		Training Material Given to Employee			

Unit Name and Number_____

- List your references in the next paragraph. (Be sure to ask the permission of these people before you list them in your letter.)
- In your last paragraph, ask for a personal interview at the employer's convenience. If you are available for an interview only during certain hours or on certain days, state when these are. Then provide a telephone number where you can be reached.

Many businesses receive dozens of application letters every week. (Indeed, if they advertised in the newspaper, they may receive hundreds of letters.) Businesses interview only a small portion of those who write, namely, only those people who have effectively presented their qualifications in a neatly written letter. If you can do this, you will have a big advantage over most applicants. Take the time to develop an effective letter of application, one you are really proud of. Then you can use it as a model for other letters for other jobs. Of course, you will have to change the first paragraph, but most of the letter will need only minor modifications.

As with any sales pitch, a good first impression counts, so type your letter. If you are not a good typist, ask a friend to type it for you. If you don't have a friend who's a good typist, hire someone.

The sample letter shown in Figure 45-3 will give you some idea of how your finished letter should look. Be sure to include all the elements of a business letter. In particular, duplicate the salutation and complimentary closing as shown, including punctuation.

Preparing Resumes

A good letter of application may convince an employer to grant you an interview. However, a resume and cover letter are even more impressive.

A *resume* (pronounced REZ-oo-MAY) is a brief summary of personal information, education, skills, work experience, activities, and interests. (See the sample in Figure 45-4 on page 504). It organizes all the facts about you that relate to the job you want. Thus, it saves the employer time before and during an interview.

Because your resume outlines all the important details about your qualifications for a particular job, you won't need a complete letter of application to accompany it. When you send an employer a resume, you enclose just a very brief cover letter. *A cover letter is a letter of application without the information on education and experience*. (Figure 45-5 on page 505 shows a sample cover letter.) It simply introduces you and allows you to say why you can do a good job for the company. You may want to emphasize one or two facts that make you especially well-qualified for this particular job.

There are many variations in the format of resumes, but most are in short outline form (usually one or two pages). Most resumes include the following types of information:

- Basic identification—provide name, address, and telephone number.
- The position for which you are applying—give a specific job title. (If you use the same basic resume for several jobs, change this item.)
- Education—list the schools you attended, the years of attendance, and any courses taken that qualify you for the job. (This item also may need to be tailored to fit different jobs.)
- Skills—outline those that qualify you for this type of work.
- Experience—list any experience related to the job for which you are applying. This includes volunteer work. If you haven't any related experience, list such jobs as baby sitting, lawn mowing, or delivering papers.
- Activities and awards—list school or other activities related to the job you want, along with any awards you have received.
- References—if your resume is short, list three; if your resume is a bit long, simply write "References available on request." (In both cases, ask for permission first.)

Although a resume is not required for many jobs, it is a polished and professional-looking document that can give you an edge over other applicants. It has a few other advantages as well. First, you can describe your qualifications using words that parallel a description of job duties. Of course, you have to be honest, but in a resume you have more latitude in describing your education and work experience than you have on an application form. Second, if you prepare your resume before you start applying for jobs, it will be much easier to fill out all those application forms. For this reason, some people prepare a resume as the first step in the job application process. Third, even if you are not hired, many employers will keep your resume on file for a certain period of time. If they have an opening for which you qualify in the next several months, they may call you.

1603 Loomis Street
Winfield, Kansas 67156
April 11, 19 – –

Ms. DeEtta Clark
North American Aircraft Co.
4000 Southwest Blvd.
Wichita, KS 67202

Dear Ms. Clark:

Mr. Richard Crandell, my marketing instructor at Arkansas City Community College, advised me this morning of the commercial artist position that you have open. I wish to apply for this position.

On May 17, I will graduate from Arkansas City Community College with a major in marketing and a special emphasis on advertising and commercial art. I have also taken commercial art courses during the past two summers at Southwestern College. My overall grade average in college is B+.

For the past three years, I have assisted the advertising manager at Rubbermaid, here in Winfield, by preparing more than 30 ads that have run nationally. One of these ads, which I prepared myself, won an award at the recent advertising convention in Chicago.

My father taught me to fly when I was in high school, so a job in advertising with an aircraft manufacturing company would combine my two greatest interests. It would be a dream come true! May I have an interview at your convenience? You can reach me most weekdays after 3 p.m. at (316) 221-5288.

Yours truly,

Karen Anderson

Karen Anderson

Figure 45-3 **Letter of Application**
A letter of application is a sales pitch telling an employer why you are the best person to fill a specific job opening. What things did Karen Anderson state in this letter that would qualify her for the commercial artist position at North American Aircraft Company?

Frank Johnson
1235 East Tenth Avenue
Ventura, CA 93003
(805) 964-6264

Objective:

Marketing Analyst

Experience:

9/89–4/91 ASSISTANT MARKETING ANALYST
Ventura Volvo
6580 Leland Street
Ventura, CA

Used computer to estimate sales by model and make recommendations for inventory. Accessed data bases using computer terminal to study inventory in relation to buying estimates. Studied historical applications, including media ads, price and color changes, and impact of season.

6/88–9/89 MARKETING ASSISTANT
KVEN Radio
Ventura, CA

Assisted Communications Manager in publishing articles and ads, sales presentations, vendor contracts, and trade shows. Contacted vendors for advertising needs (charts, overheads, banners).

Education:

1989–1991 Ventura College. AA in Marketing. Dean's Honor Roll four semesters.
Courses included:

Marketing I and II
Marketing Information Systems
Advertising
Economics I and II
Computer Science

1986–1989 Ventura High School. Graduated in upper 10 percent of class. Served as Vice President of DECA two years.

Personal:

Hobbies include writing computer programs, tennis, and photography.

References:

Available upon request.

Figure 45-4 **Resume**
A resume is a brief summary of personal information, education, skills, work experience, activities, and interests. How might Frank Johnson's hobby of writing computer programs help him in a job as marketing analyst?

1235 East Tenth Avenue
Ventura, CA 93003
April 6, 19 – –

Ms. Linda Morrison
Metromedia-West Television
3200 Beverly Drive
Beverly Hills, CA 90123

Dear Ms. Morrison:

Your ad for a marketing analyst in Sunday's Los Angeles *Times* described exactly the position that I am seeking. As you will see from the resume I have enclosed, my qualifications match up very well with the requirements listed in your ad.

My education, experience, and DECA participation (for which our school won a national award) have prepared me to fulfill your needs in marketing analysis.

After you have read my resume, I would appreciate an appointment for an interview. I will call back next week to arrange a time convenient to you.

Sincerely,

Frank Johnson

Frank Johnson

Figure 45-5 **Cover Letter Accompanying a Resume**
A cover letter is an introductory letter of application without the information on education and experience. Why do you think a cover letter should accompany a resume?

Interviewing for a Job

Application forms, letters of application, and resumes are all important parts of the job application process. Their purpose is to create enough interest on the part of an employer that he or she will want to interview you. It is what happens during the interview that causes most employers to choose one applicant over others.

You, of course, want the interviewer to choose you for the job, so you will need to plan for a successful interview. Your plan should include three steps—*preparing for an interview, conducting yourself properly during an interview,* and *following up an interview.*

Preparing for an Interview

In every interview you will ever have, the employer's first impression of you will greatly affect whether you are offered a job. Remember, you never have a second chance to make a first impression. Appropriate grooming and dress, body language that shows confidence, and use of standard English all combine to make a good first impression. With some preparation, you can control all of these.

Dress and Grooming. A few years ago, employees in sales and office jobs followed a strict dress code. Men always wore suits, white shirts, ties, and leather shoes with dark socks. Women wore business suits or very conservative dresses, medium high-heeled shoes, and nylons. Today, employees in many stores and offices dress much more casually. This does not mean, however, that you can dress casually for every interview and still make a good impression.

Appropriate dress for an interview will depend in part on the type of job you are seeking. If you are being interviewed for a sales job, for example, you will probably want to follow formal dress rules. As a salesperson, you will need to make a good impression on potential customers. In the interview, you will need to show that you can dress appropriately to make that impression. If you are being interviewed for a job as a stock clerk, then more casual wear may be acceptable.

Try to find out how the other employees dress on the job. The standard will vary a great deal from one company to another. To ensure that you make a good first impression, dress somewhat more formally than company employees do on the job. This is the safe approach. Many employers feel that if you don't care enough to dress up for the interview, then you don't care enough about the job.

Regardless of its style, your hair should be clean and neat. Male job applicants should be aware that many employers don't like beards or long hair on young men. It may be unfair, but that's the way it is. Employers pay the bills, and that includes your salary if you are hired. If you want a job, you will have to please the employer.

It's a good idea not to wear a great deal of jewelry to a job interview because it can be distracting. Young women should use makeup sparingly for much the same reason. In addition, many interviewers will notice your hands, so be sure they are clean and that your nails are neatly trimmed.

Things To Know. Before you schedule an interview, find out something about the company. You will make a better impression if you can talk intelligently about the company's goods or services. It will show that you are interested in the firm, not just in the money you will earn as an employee. Some companies print brochures that explain the business they are in. Other print catalogs that describe their goods or services. You can also learn about a company's business from looking in the Yellow Pages or talking with family members or your teachers.

If you call for an interview appointment, write down the date and time, and ask for the interviewer's name. Check the spelling after you write down the name, and make sure you can pronounce it correctly.

Before your interview, carefully read your resume several times. Be ready to answer any questions about your education, work experience, or other qualifications.

The following questions are often asked of job applicants during interviews. If you practice answering them beforehand, you will feel more confident. Get a family member or friend to help you by asking the questions and giving you feedback on how you answer.

- Why do you want to work for this company?
- Do you want permanent or temporary work?
- Why do you think you can do this job?
- What jobs have you had? Why did you leave?
- What classes did you like best in school?
- What school activities did you participate in?
- What do you want to be doing five years from now?
- Do you prefer working alone or with others?
- What is your main strength?
- How do you spend your spare time?
- What salary do you expect?
- What grades have you received in school?
- How do you feel about working overtime?
- How many days were you absent from school last year?
- Why should I hire you?
- When can you begin work?

Conducting Yourself Properly During an Interview

Always go alone for a job interview. Some young people take a friend along for moral support, but this

Listening alertly and well is a valuable interview technique. How can it help you make a good impression?

is a mistake. Employers seldom hire anyone who can't handle an interview alone.

Plan to arrive for your interview about five to fifteen minutes early. If you have to travel across town, allow some extra time in case you run into traffic. If you are even a little late or rush in at the last minute, you will appear careless and thus make a bad impression. Don't be too early, though. Waiting outside the interviewer's door for half an hour is not comfortable for you or the employer.

Before you meet the interviewer, you may see a receptionist or personnel assistant. If you do, be very courteous and polite to this person. The interviewer may ask his or her opinion of you after you are gone.

If you have not already filled out an application form, the receptionist or assistant may give you one and ask you to complete it. In this case, you may have to complete the form before you are interviewed. Be prepared for this by always having a good pen with you. (Some people take two pens, just in case one runs out of ink.) If you have prepared a resume, take two copies to the interview—one to leave with your interviewer if he or she wants it and one to help you fill out an application form.

You may be introduced to the interviewer by the receptionist or assistant, or you may have to introduce yourself. In the latter case, say something like, "Good afternoon, I'm Lois Anderson, and I'm here about the retail clerk job." Speak clearly and loudly enough to be heard, and smile.

If the interviewer offers to shake hands, grasp the person's hand firmly. Don't give a "limp fish" handshake (it makes some people think you have a weak personality), but don't grab the interviewer's hand and crush it, either! If the interviewer doesn't offer to shake hands, don't offer your hand.

Remain standing until you are asked to sit down. If you are not asked to sit down, then stand for the interview—it will probably be a short one. When you do sit down, lean forward slightly toward the interviewer. This shows that you are interested in the job and in what the interviewer is saying.

If you have a purse or briefcase with you, place it on the floor by your chair. Never put anything on the interviewer's desk, even if there is room. Don't let your eyes wander over papers on the interviewer's desk—it may look as though you are trying to read company correspondence.

It is normal to feel a little nervous at the beginning of an interview. Everyone does. You will relax as the interview progresses. Keep your hands in your lap, and try to keep them still. Of course, you would never chew gum during an interview.

Look the interviewer in the eye most of the time and listen to him or her carefully. This, too, shows your interest. (Some people don't trust a person who can't look them in the eye.)

What To Say During an Interview. Most interviewers begin by asking specific questions. Answer each question honestly. If you don't know the answer to a particular question, say so. (If you try to fake it, the interviewer will probably sense it.) Keep your answers short. No interviewer wants to listen to long stories, but don't be too brief, either. If many of the questions seem to call for a simple yes or no, then elaborate a little.

Two particular questions often cause problems for young job applicants. These questions are "What type of work would you like to do?" and "What wage (or salary) do you expect?" You will probably answer the first question all right by giving the name of the specific job you want. The question about expected wage or salary is a little more difficult. If you specify a sum that's too high, you probably won't be offered the job. If you mention a figure that's too low, you may be paid less than other employees for the same type of work. Perhaps the best answer is something like "I'm sure you know better than I do what a fair wage (or salary) would be. What do you usually pay for this type of work?" In other words, try to turn the question back to the interviewer. If you are pressed for an answer, mention a rate you know others get for the same type of work. So that you are prepared for this before the interview, find out what the going rate is for the type of work you want by checking with your marketing teacher.

In some cases, your interviewer will simply say something like, "Tell me about yourself." If that happens, you will have to do most of the talking. You will have to anticipate what the interviewer would like to know and present the information clearly. This type of interview is often difficult for the job applicant. If you have instant recall of everything on your application form or resume, you will probably handle the situation well. Just be sure to cover all your qualifications for the job and say why you would like to work for this particular company. (This is one of those instances in which knowing something about the company will help you move the interview along smoothly.)

Your interviewer may not mention pay at all. In that case, wait until the interview is almost over, then ask how much the job pays. (If you ask about pay too early, it may appear that you are only interested in the money.)

If you are applying for a full-time, permanent job, you will probably receive some fringe benefits. These may include a paid vacation and insurance coverage. If your interviewer doesn't mention this, it's all right to ask—but wait until near the end of the interview. (You don't want to sound too anxious to take a vacation from this job.)

In most cases, the interviewer will expect you to ask some questions. (If you don't, he or she will think you aren't interested in the job or the company.) While your interviewer may answer some of your questions when discussing the job and the company, you will probably still have others you want answered. If your interviewer asks whether you have any questions, that, of course, is your cue to ask them. If your interviewer does not ask, he or she will probably pause after telling you about the job and asking about your qualifications. That is the time for you to ask your own questions. The questions listed below are among those most often asked by young applicants.

- What are the hours of work?
- Do you prefer that employees wear a certain type of clothing on the job?
- What are the opportunities for advancement?
- What is the pay?
- When will I be notified if I am hired?

During the interview, be enthusiastic—especially when you are talking about school, your work experience, and the company. Shift your eyes occasionally so that you don't stare, but look your interviewer in the eye most of the time.

You may be asked to a second interview with someone else in the company, such as a department head. This usually means you made a good impression in your first interview, and your chances of being offered the job are good.

Closing the Interview. At the close of the interview, one of several things can happen. You may be offered the job and accept, you may be offered the job but decline, or you may be told that you will not be hired. More likely, however, you will be told that a decision will be made later.

You will be able to sense when the interview is almost over. The interviewer will say something like, "Well, Mario, thank you for coming in" or "We'll decide by the end of the week." This is your cue to ask any last-minute questions. Then you should stand, smile, and thank your interviewer for his or her time. Usually, the interviewer will extend a hand for a handshake. Shake hands and go. Be sure to thank the receptionist or personnel assistant on your way out.

Following Up an Interview

After every interview, take a few minutes to evaluate your performance. Do this whether you were offered the job or not. Which questions did you answer best? Which ones did you not answer very well? Were there any total disasters? Did you use standard English? Each interview is a learning experience that will help prepare you for the next one.

What Are You Telling the Interviewer?

You are interviewed for a job developing a new product. The team is working against a short deadline. There is no time for delays. You are calm, informed, polite, and interested during the interview, but you don't get the job. What happened?

You know the basics of body language—shake hands firmly, look the interviewer in the eyes—but there's more to it than that. Your posture, gestures, and other body movements also tell other things about you—about the way you make decisions and the way you work with others. For example, nodding your head occasionally indicates that you're paying attention.

Anita Brick and Alice Levy of Decision Dynamics use "movement theory" to analyze people's decision-making style and leadership abilities. They look at a sample of 250 to 300 movements a person makes during a two-hour interview. The movements the person uses most often give Brick and Levy clues to the person's character. Will this person jump to a decision without thinking much about it? Is she methodical, doing research before making a decision? Is she sensitive to others, or does she remain aloof from the people she works with?

Companies that have worked with Decision Dynamics have found their analyses surprisingly accurate. They have helped executives minimize their shortcomings and emphasize their strengths.

Understanding the meaning behind movements also helps companies decide who to hire. If your movements show you are too opinionated to work well in a group or too deliberate in your thinking to keep pace with a short deadline, that may be why you didn't get the job.

1. Why do you think interviewers need to analyze body movements and gestures? Why can't they get all the information they need simply by asking the applicant questions?
2. If an applicant says one thing but his or her body movements and gestures indicate the opposite, which do you think the interviewer will believe? Why?

If an employer is interviewing several people, it is unlikely you will be offered the job the same day as your interview. The employer will want some time to consider all the applicants before making a decision. Many employers will check your references and call the school for a recommendation. This may take several days to a week or more. In the meantime, you can follow up your interview with a telephone call, a short thank-you letter, or a visit.

Unless you were told not to call, it is all right to telephone the employer five or six days after the interview. Ask to speak with the person who interviewed you. Then give your name and ask if he or she has made a decision on the job. This will let the employer know that you are still interested.

A thank-you letter is an appropriate way to follow up many interviews. Because most people don't bother to do this, you will look good by comparison. Your letter should be brief and to the point. Simply thank the employer for the time given you and reaffirm your interest in the job. If you forgot to mention something during the interview that will help qualify you for the position, include it—but be brief. Your letter may be either handwritten or typed, but it must be neat.

If the company is nearby or if you know the employer personally, you may prefer to stop by rather than call or write. In that case, you can thank the employer in person for the time given you and ask when a decision is expected.

VOCABULARY REVIEW

Use the following vocabulary words in a paragraph describing an effective job search.

job lead
public employment
  agencies
private employment
  agencies

direct calling
standard English
references
resume
cover letter

FACT AND IDEA REVIEW

1. What is a job lead?

2. List seven sources of job leads.

3. How can family members and friends help you in a job search?

4. How do you use the job leads you already have to produce new ones?

5. What is standard English, and why is it advisable to use it when communicating with an employer?

6. Given the choice of dressing casually or dressing up a bit for a job interview, which would you do and why?

7. List five of the most common questions an interviewer might ask.

8. When should you plan to arrive for a job interview?

9. Describe how you would introduce yourself to an interviewer.

10. What should you say if an interviewer asks you what kind of work you would like to do?

11. How should you respond if an interviewer asks you what wage or salary you want?

12. Why is it important to have studied your resume before a job interview?

13. How can you tell when an interview is over?

14. What is the purpose of following up a job interview? How is this done?

CRITICAL THINKING

1. How would you feel about getting a job through a family or personal friend? Would you rather find a job on your own? Why or why not?

2. If you were interested in working for a particular company, would you prefer to visit the personnel office in person, call on the phone, or write a letter of inquiry? Why?

3. Who would make good references for you and why?

4. If you were an employer, what qualities do you think you would look for in a job seeker's application, application letter, or resume?

5. What do you think about a situation in which a potential employer denies an applicant a job because he has long hair or a beard?

USING BASIC SKILLS

Math

1. There are 207 applicants for 5 new positions at the Merchandise Outlet. What percentage of applicants will be hired?

2. Of the 30 members of your class, 20 have found jobs for the summer. Of those 20, 15 found their jobs through friends, family, or personal acquaintances. What percentage of the jobs acquired by your classmates were from personal contacts?

Communication

3. Assume you would like to work for a local mail order company that sells electronic gadgets, but you don't know if there are any job openings. Write a letter of inquiry regarding summer employment.

4. Write a script for a direct call to a sporting goods store, inquiring about the availability of a part-time job. Practice aloud and then make your "call" for your class.

Human Relations

5. Without your realizing it, your marketing teacher has sent both you and your best friend on interviews for the same job. Both of you really want the job. How can you prevent this from interfering with your friendship?

6. You are scheduled for a job interview. You arrive at the receptionist's desk terribly nervous and suddenly go completely blank. You can't remember the name of the person with whom you have the interview. What do you say to the receptionist? What might you have done to avoid this situation?

APPLICATION PROJECTS

1. Find out from a teacher or counselor where you go to get a work permit. Investigate any restrictions on the type of job that can be held by students in your state.

2. Share any of your own letters of application or resumes with other students in your class. Assist each other in improving language, correcting grammar, and simplifying formats.

3. Make a list of questions you would want answered before a job interview was over.

4. With a classmate, devise and present a series of skits designed to show how body language and verbal communication can contribute to or detract from the success of a job interview. Consider including the following characters:

   a. the know-it-all applicant;

   b. the shy, nervous applicant who is unwilling (or unable) to provide information; and

   c. the applicant whose English is non-standard.

5. For one week, go through your newspaper's classified section and find jobs in the marketing field.

   a. At the end of the week, choose one company and research it.

   b. Prepare for an imaginary interview at this firm by writing out the answers to the list of questions commonly asked by interviewers.

   c. Working in groups of four to five, with one student acting as the interviewer, interview for the job. Have the other members of the group give you suggestions on ways to improve your performance.

6. Make a list of your special interests. Talk to your counselor about jobs available in an area of marketing that is compatible with your interests and your qualifications for those jobs. Discuss any extra skills you need to acquire.

7. Research the cooperative education and work experience programs available through your school. Write a short paper on how they can help you achieve your goals in the field of marketing.

8. Make a list of all the professionals, friends, family members, and former employers who might be able to help you find work.

9. Get a sample application form from your counselor. Make a list of all the information that you need in order to fill out such a form. Keep it handy to refer to when you apply for a job. Check your spelling and see that all information is correct. If you list references, be sure you get the permission of each person.

10. Prepare a letter of application for a marketing job of your choice and a resume.

Glossary

A

ad layout. A rough draft that shows the general arrangement and appearance of a finished ad.

adjacent colors. Colors located next to each other on the color wheel that contrast only slightly, such as blue and green.

advance dating. Dating in which the manufacturer indicates a date other than the invoice date from which the dating terms take effect. It is sometimes offered to businesses that buy before the buying season.

advertising. The nonpersonal presentation and promotion of ideas, goods, and services by an identified sponsor.

advertising agencies. Companies that exist solely to help clients sell their products.

advertising proof. A proof that shows exactly how an ad will appear when printed.

advertising research. The process of getting the information needed to make sound decisions about the advertising message and media.

allowance. A partial return of the sale price for merchandise that the customer has kept.

apron. A form attached to the invoice before the merchandise moves through checking and marking.

aptitude. A knack or potential for learning a certain skill.

area vocational centers. Centers serving secondary students from a geographic area. Also called *skills centers*.

area vocational schools. Post-secondary institutions offering instruction in vocational education.

Articles of Incorporation. Identify the name and address of a business, its purpose, the names of the initial directors, and the amount of stock that will be issued to each director.

assertive. Standing up for your doubts, beliefs, and ideas.

asset. Anything of monetary value that is owned by a business.

Associate of Arts (A.A.). A degree from a two-year college, usually a junior or community college.

assumption close. A method of closing a sale by assuming that the customer is ready to buy.

B

Bachelor of Arts (B.A.). A degree from a four-year college or university for a course of study in the arts, humanities, or social sciences.

Bachelor of Education (B.Ed.). A degree from a four-year college or university for a course of study in education.

Bachelor of Science (B.S.). A degree from a four-year college or university for a course of study in the sciences.

balance of trade. The difference in value between exports and imports of a nation.

balance sheet. A summary of a person's business assets, liabilities, and capital.

basic stock list. A stock list that specifies the minimum amount of merchandise that should be on hand for specific products. It is usually used for staple items, such as groceries, cosmetics, housewares, china, and stationery.

blind check method. A method of checking merchandise using a list made from an invoice of only style numbers and descriptions.

blocks. Interference to understanding a message. The primary blocks to understanding are distractions, emotional blocks, and planning a response.

body language. The physical movements and positions of the body that communicate thoughts.

boomerang method. A method of handling objections by making the objection into a selling point.

brand. A name, design, or symbol that identifies the products of a company or group of companies.

break-even point. The point at which sales revenue equals the costs and expenses of making and distributing a product.

broadcast media. Radio and television.

business. An activity that satisfies economic needs by planning, organizing, and controlling resources to produce and market goods and services.

business cycle. A recurring change in the economy of a nation. A business cycle has four phases: prosperity, recession, depression, and recovery.

business philosophy. Tells how you think the business should be run and shows your understanding of your firm's role in the marketplace.

business plan. A proposal that describes every part of your new business to potential investors and financing agencies.

business research. Research that attempts to solve business problems related to long-range forecasting and future economic conditions.

business risk. The possibility of business loss or failure.

buying behavior. The process individuals use to decide what they will buy and from where and whom they will buy it.

buying signals. Things a customer says or does to indicate a readiness to buy.

capital. The funds needed to finance the operation of a business.

capitalism. An economy in which the means of production, distribution, and exchange of goods and services is done chiefly by private individuals or corporations.

career consultation. An informational interview with someone who works in a career that interests you.

career outlook. The availability of jobs in a particular field.

carload. The minimum number of pounds of freight needed to fill a boxcar.

cash sale. A transaction in which the customer pays for his or her purchases by cash or check.

channel of distribution. The path a product takes from the producer or manufacturer to the final user.

channels. The avenues by which a message is delivered, such as sound or sight.

clip art. Stock drawings, photographs, and headlines clipped from a printed sheet and pasted into an advertisement.

closing the sale. Obtaining the customer's positive agreement to buy.

COD. Cash on delivery, a sale that occurs when a customer pays for merchandise at the time of delivery.

cognitive dissonance. Doubt about a buying decision after the purchase has been made.

coinsurance policy. An insurance policy in which the insured business and the insurance company both share in the risk if there is a loss.

cold canvassing. A method of trying to locate potential customers with little or no direct help other than that, perhaps, from a telephone directory. Also called *blind prospecting*.

collateral. Something of value that a borrower pledges to a lender to ensure repayment of a loan.

command economy. An economy in which the government decides the basic economic questions of what should be produced, how it should be produced, and who should have goods and services. Also called a *planned economy*.

common carrier. A motor carrier that provides transportation services to any business in its operating area for a fee.

communication. The process of exchanging information, ideas, and feelings.

communism. A system of government in which all economic activity is conducted by the state, which is dominated by a single political party. Communism, according to socialist theory, is socialism in its perfect form.

community relations. The activities that a business uses to acquire or maintain the respect of the community.

competition. The struggle between companies for customers.

complementary colors. Colors that are found opposite each other on the color wheel and create the greatest contrast, such as red and green.

compound interest. Interest paid on both the principal and the accumulated interest.

consignment buying. Buying in which the goods are paid for only after they have been purchased by the final consumer.

consumer affairs specialists. People who handle customer complaints and serve as consumer advocates within a firm.

consumer goods. Products used by consumers for personal, family, or household purposes.

Consumer Price Index (CPI). A measurement of the change in price over a period of time of some 400 specific goods and services used by the average urban household, such as food, housing, and transportation.

consumerism. The societal effort to protect consumer rights by putting legal, moral, and economic pressure on business.

contests. Games or activities that require the participant to demonstrate a skill.

contract carrier. A motor carrier that provides transportation services on a selective basis, according to agreements between the carrier and the shipper.

controlling. A management function involving setting employee standards, evaluating performance, and solving problems.

convenience goods. Inexpensive products that consumers purchase regularly, spending a minimum of time and effort on the purchase decision.

cooperative advertising. Advertising of manufacturers' or suppliers' products that are placed by local merchants in local media with the merchant's name, and for which the manufacturer or supplier pays all or part of the cost.

copy. The selling message in a written advertisement.

corporate responsibility research. Research dealing with the consumer's "right to know" concerns, environmental impact, social values, and policy studies.

corporation. A business that is chartered by a state and legally operates apart from the owners.

cost-plus pricing. Pricing in which all costs and expenses are calculated and then the desired profit is added to arrive at a price.

cover letter. A letter of application without the information on education and experience.

credit union. A cooperative association formed by labor unions or groups of employees for the benefit of its members.

culture. The sum total of a people's learned behaviors as it relates to heritage.

customer advisory boards. Panels of consumers who make suggestions on new goods and services.

customer benefit. The advantage or personal satisfaction a customer will get from a good or service.

D

data analysis. The process of compiling, analyzing, and interpreting the results of primary and secondary data collection.

DBA. Doing Business As, a registration process by which your county government officially recognizes that your business exists.

debt capital. Money raised through borrowing.

decimal number. A fraction or mixed number whose denominator is a multiple of 10.

demand. The willingness and ability of consumers to buy products.

democracy. A form of government in which there is usually more than one political party from which to choose representatives to run the government.

democratic socialism. A combination of capitalism and socialism in economic theory and democracy in political theory.

demographics. Statistics about the personal characteristics of a population, such as age, gender, income, ethnic background, education, and occupation.

demonstration method. A method of handling objections by illustrating one or more features of a good or service.

derived demand. A demand for goods and services that is based on the demand for other goods and services. For example, the market for industrial goods and services is based on the demand for consumer goods and services.

Dictionary of Occupational Titles (DOT). Describes more than 20,000 jobs in terms of their relationship with data, people, and things.

digit. A symbol representing a number, such as 3. Digits can be combined to represent larger numbers, such as 14 and 2,647.

direct calling. The process of contacting potential employers in person or on the telephone.

direct check method. A method of checking merchandise by checking it directly against the actual invoice or purchase order.

direct close. A method of closing a sale by asking for the sale.

direct denial method. A method of handling objections by providing proof and accurate information in answer to the objections.

direct distribution. Distribution in which goods or services are sold from the producer directly to the final user; no intermediaries are involved.

disclaimer. A statement that contains exceptions to and exclusions from a warranty.

discount sale. A sale with a reduced price for customers who qualify.

discretionary income. The money left after paying for such basic living necessities as food, shelter, and clothing.

display. The visual and artistic aspects of presenting a product to a target group of customers.

disposable income. The money left after taking out taxes.

distractions. Blocks to effective listening, such as noises and other environmental factors, interruptions by other people, and competing thoughts that creep into your mind.

dock. The specific area where deliveries are made by carriers.

dollar control. In inventory management, the planning and monitoring of the total inventory investment that a business makes during a stated period of time.

dummy invoice check method. A method of checking merchandise by counting on a form similar to an invoice, but with descriptions, quantities, sizes, and styles omitted.

E

economic risks. Business risks that occur from changes in overall business conditions. These changes can include the amount or type of competition, changing consumer life-styles, population changes, limited usefulness or stylishness of some products, product obsolescence, government regulation, inflation, or recession.

economy. The way a nation makes decisions for using its resources to produce and distribute goods and services. Also called an *economic system*.

elastic demand. Situations when a slight change in price creates a large change in demand for a product.

emergency goods. Items purchased out of immediate need.

emotional blocks. Biases against the opinions expressed by a sender that block your understanding.

emotional motive. A feeling of satisfaction a customer desires in a product, such as social approval, recognition, power, or love.

empathize. To understand a person's situation or frame of mind.

end-of-month (EOM) dating. Dating in which the billing terms take effect at the end of the month.

endless chain method. A method of obtaining leads by asking previous customers for the names of potential customers.

entrepreneurs. People who attempt to earn money and make profits by taking the risk of owning and operating a business.

entrepreneurship. The process of starting and managing your own business.

equity capital. Money raised by selling part of the business itself.

ethics. Guidelines for good behavior.

exchange. Merchandise brought back to be replaced by other merchandise.

exclusive distribution. Distribution involving a limited number of intermediaries, so that only one intermediary is assigned to each geographic territory.

excuse. An insincere reason for not buying or not seeing the salesperson.

exempt carrier. A motor carrier that is free from direct regulation of rates and operating procedures.

experimental method. A research technique in which one or more marketing variables are observed under controlled conditions.

exports. Goods sold to other countries.

express carrier. A parcel carrier, such as Federal Express, that guarantees national next-day delivery for items weighing about ten pounds or less.

express warranty. A warranty that is explicitly stated, in either writing or spoken words, to induce a customer to buy.

extended coverage. Additional protection on a basic fire protection policy to cover such natural disasters as wind, earthquakes, explosions, or smoke damage.

extended product features. The values, emotions, image, or special services that consumers expect with or from particular products.

extended service contracts. Service contracts that provide parts and repair services for a specified length of time beyond a product's normal warranty period.

extensive decision making. Decision making used when a customer has little or no previous experience because the item is infrequently purchased.

extra dating. Dating in which the manufacturer grants additional days before the dating terms take effect. It is sometimes offered to encourage a buyer to purchase new merchandise.

F

family life cycle. The evolution of a family, from a young single adult to retirement.

feedback. The receiver's response to a message.

fidelity bonds. Bonds that protect a business from employee dishonesty.

finance. Money management as a supporting function for management.

fixtures. Store furnishings, such as display cases, counters, shelving, racks, and benches.

flexible-price policy. A pricing policy that permits customers to bargain for merchandise.

floor limit. The maximum amount a salesperson may allow a customer to charge without special authorization.

foreign corporation. A corporation that is incorporated under the laws of a different state from the one in which it does business.

formal balance. Placing large items with large items and small items with small items in a display.

fraction. A number used to describe a part of some standard amount.

franchise. A legal agreement to begin a new business in the name of a recognized company.

fringe benefits. Benefits, privileges, or monetary payments beyond salary or wages that go with a job. Also called *perquisites* or *perks*.

full warranty. A warranty stating that a product found to be defective within the warranty period will be repaired or replaced at no cost to the purchaser.

G

general partnership. A partnership in which each partner shares in the profits and losses of the business.

generic product features. The features of a product that relate to the customer's basic reasons for purchasing the product.

generic products. Products that do not carry a brand name.

geographics. Studies about the characteristics of where potential customers live.

goods. Merchandise that satisfies our needs and wants and has monetary value.

greeting approach method. A method of approaching the customer in which the salesperson welcomes the customer to the store.

Gross National Product (GNP). A measurement of the total value of a nation's goods and services produced in a given period of time, generally one year.

gross profit. The difference between sales revenue and the cost of goods sold.

gross sales. The total of all sales for any period of time.

Guide for Occupational Education (GOE). Organizes the world of work into 12 interest areas, which it then further subdivides into work groups and subgroups.

H

headline. The lettering, slogan, or saying that gets readers' attention, arouses their interest, and leads them to read the rest of the ad.

human risks. Business risks caused by human mistakes and the unpredictability of employees or customers.

I

illustration. The photograph or drawing used in a print advertisement.

image. The way a business or organization is defined in people's minds.

implied warranty. A warranty that exists automatically by state law whenever a purchase takes place.

imports. Goods purchased from other countries.

impulse items. Goods that lend themselves to unplanned purchasing.

income statement. A summary of the income and expenses of a business during a specific period, such as a month, quarter, or year. Also known as a *profit and loss statement*.

indirect distribution. Distribution in which intermediaries are involved in the sale of goods or services.

industrial goods. Goods purchased for the production of other goods or for resale to consumers.

industrial marketing. Marketing of goods and services to organizations or businesses for their operations or for resale to others.

inelastic demand. Situations when a change in price has very little effect on the demand for a product.

informal balance. Balancing a large item with several small items in a display.

inside sales. Selling efforts that take place at the salesperson's place of business, such as a retail store.

institutional advertising. Advertising that creates a favorable impression and goodwill for a business or an organization.

insurance policy. A contract between a business and an insurance company to cover a certain business risk.

intensive distribution. Distribution making use of all suitable outlets for a product.

interest. The money paid for the use of money borrowed or invested.

intermediary. A member of a channel of distribution that helps move products from the producer to the final user.

invoice. The supplier's statement that the order has been filled and the merchandise is being sent.

J

jargon. Words that have meaning only in a particular career field.

job description. A written statement listing the requirements of a particular job.

job lead. Information about a job opening.

L

label. An information tag, wrapper, seal, or imprinted message attached to a product or its package.

layaway. A sale in which merchandise is removed from stock and kept in a separate storage area until the customer pays for it. Also known as *will-call*.

layman's terms. Words the average customer can understand.

lemon laws. Statutes designed to protect consumers from poorly built cars.

liability. A debt owed by you for your business.

life-style goals. Your vision of how you see yourself living in the future.

life-style. The pattern of behavior followed in a person's life, including how time and money are spent.

limited decision making. Decision making used when a person buys goods and services that he or she has purchased before, but not on a regular basis.

limited partnership. A partnership in which each limited partner is liable for any debts only up to the amount of his or her investment in the company.

limited warranty. A warranty that offers less coverage than a full warranty.

local radio advertising. Radio advertising that is done by a local business for its target market and is limited to a specific geographical area.

loss leader. An item priced at cost to draw customers into a store.

M

maintained markup. The difference between an item's final sale price and its cost.

management. The process of achieving company goals by effective use of human resources, technology, and material resources.

management information system. A set of procedures and methods that regularly generates, stores, analyzes, and disseminates marketing decision information.

management training programs. Closely supervised on-the-job management training usually lasting six months to two years.

market. All the potential customers that share common needs and wants, and who have the ability and willingness to buy the product.

market economy. An economy in which the government lets the market decide the basic economic questions of what should be produced, how it should be produced, and who should have goods and services. Also called *capitalism* or a *modified free enterprise system*.

market position. A company's standing in the market compared to its competitors.

market segmentation. Identification of target markets and developing products that appeal to them.

market share. A company's share of the total sales volume generated by all competitors in a given market.

marketing. The process of determining and satisfying the needs and wants of consumers through the exchange process, in which customers exchange their money for goods and services.

marketing mix. A combination of decisions about product, place, price, and promotion used to reach a target market and make a profit.

marketing research. The process of getting the marketing information needed to make sound business decisions.

marketplace. Wherever a product is sold to a buyer.

markup. The difference between the price of an item and its cost.

marquee. A sign used to display the store's name.

mass marketing. Use of a single marketing plan for one product to reach all consumers.

media. The agencies, means, or instruments used to convey messages.

memorandum buying. Buying when the supplier agrees to take back any unsold goods by a certain date.

merchandise approach method. A method of approaching the customer in which the salesperson makes a comment or asks questions about a product that the customer is looking at.

merchandise assortment. The amount of merchandise to stock for customers.

middle management. The people who carry out the decisions of top management.

milline rate. A comparison of the cost of advertising per person reached in one newspaper to the cost per person reached in another newspaper.

mixed-brand strategy. The simultaneous offering of national, private, and generic brands of products.

model stock list. A stock list that tells the styles, colors, sizes, and numbers of a broad category of merchandise that should always be kept in inventory. This general list is used for usually fashionable items that are subject to changes in demand and style.

modified free enterprise system. A market economy in which the government has some involvement and intervention in our lives.

monopoly. Exclusive control over a product or the means of production.

N

national spot radio advertising. Radio advertising on a local station-by-station basis for selected target markets in the country.

natural risks. Business risks that occur because of natural causes, such as floods, tornadoes, or fires.

net sales. The total of all sales, after subtracting sales returns and allowances.

net worth. The difference between the assets of a business and its liabilities. Also known as *owner's equity*.

network radio advertising. Advertising that is broadcast from a studio to all affiliated radio stations throughout the country.

never-out list. A stock list in which items are added or removed from the list as their popularity increases or declines. It is used for best-selling products that make up a large percentage of sales volume.

news release. A prewritten story about a company that is sent to the various media.

nonprice competition. The struggle between companies for customers, on the basis of factors that are not related to price.

nonverbal communication. A method of expressing yourself through body language.

O

objection. A concern, hesitation, doubt, or other honest reason a customer has for not making a purchase.

objections analysis sheet. A list that enumerates common objections and possible responses to those objections.

observation method. A research technique in which the actions of people are observed and recorded.

Occupational Outlook Handbook (OOH). Provides detailed information on more than 200 occupations and is updated every two years.

on-approval sale. An agreement that permits a customer to take merchandise, usually clothing, home for further consideration.

one-price policy. A pricing policy in which all customers are charged the same price for the goods and services offered for sale.

open-ended question. A question requiring more than a yes or no answer.

open-to-buy (OTB). The amount of money left for buying goods.

opening change fund. The coins and currency designated for a cash register for a given day's business.

operating ratios. A comparison of costs and expenses of one business with another.

operations research. Research that looks at methods and procedures that will make a business more effective and efficient in distributing its goods and services.

organization chart. A diagram of the various jobs and functions found in a company.

organizing. A coordinated effort to reach a company's goals. It involves assigning responsibility, establishing working relationships, and directing the work of employees.

outside sales. Selling efforts that take place outside the salesperson's place of business, such as door-to-door sales.

P

package. The physical container or wrapping for a product.

paraphrase. To restate the meaning of a statement in different words.

parcel post. A package service operated by the U.S. Postal Service.

partnership. A legal agreement between two or more people to be jointly responsible for the success or failure of a business.

penetration pricing. A pricing policy that sets a very low price for a new product during its introductory period.

percent. Parts per hundred; a number expressed as a percent represents the number of parts per hundred.

performance bonds. Bonds which insure against losses that might occur when work or a contract is not finished on time or as agreed. Also called *surety bonds*.

perpetual inventory system. A method of keeping track of the number of items a business handles by adjusting for sales, returns, allowances, and transfers to other stores and departments.

personal career profile. An evaluation form that allows you to compare your self-assessment side-by-side with a particular career assessment.

personal financial statement. A summary of a person's current personal financial condition.

physical distribution. The process of transporting, storing, and handling goods on the way from seller to customer.

physical inventory system. A method of counting merchandise by visually inspecting or counting it periodically to determine the quantity on hand.

planning. Deciding what will be done and how it will be accomplished.

planning goals. The steps you take to get from where you are now to where you want to be.

premiums. Prizes or rewards offered to a customer as an added inducement to make a purchase.

preretailing marking method. A method of marking merchandise in which pricing information is marked in advance by the seller on the retailer's copy of the purchase order.

price. The value of money (or its equivalent) placed on a good or service.

price competition. The struggle between companies for customers, focusing on the price of a product.

price discrimination. Charging different prices to similar customers in similar situations.

price fixing. An agreement between competitors on certain price ranges within which they set their own prices.

price guarantee. A promise that all discounts given to competitors will be offered to original purchasers as well.

price lining. A special pricing technique that requires a store to offer all merchandise in a given category at certain prices.

primary data. Facts obtained for the first time and used specifically for the particular problem under study.

principal. The amount of money borrowed or invested.

print media. Print means or instruments used to convey messages, such as newspapers, magazines, direct mail, signs, and billboards.

private carrier. A motor carrier owned and operated by an individual business that is providing its own transportation services for its commodities.

private employment agencies. Employment agencies that are not supported by taxes but must earn a profit to stay in business.

private parcel carrier. A parcel carrier, such as United Parcel Service, specializing in transporting packages weighing up to 50 pounds.

problem definition. A clear statement of the decisions a business needs to make and the information required to make them.

product depth. The number of product items offered within each product line.

product feature. A physical characteristic or quality of a good or service that explains what it is.

product item. A specific model, brand, or size of product within a product line.

product line. A group of closely related products manufactured and/or sold by a business.

product mix. The different products that a company makes or sells.

product planning. All the decisions a business makes in the production and sale of its products, including those decisions relating to packaging, labeling, warranties, guarantees, branding, and product mix.

product research. Research concerned with product design and acceptance, competitive products, testing of existing products, package design, and product usage.

product sample. A free trial size of a product that is sent through the mail, or distributed door-to-door or through retail stores and trade shows.

product width. The number of different product lines a business manufactures or sells.

production. The process of creating, growing, manufacturing, or improving on something produced by someone else.

profit. The money a business has brought in (its income) after the costs and expenses of running the business are subtracted.

promotion. Any form of communication that a business or organization uses to inform, persuade, or remind people about its products and improve its public image.

promotional advertising. Advertising designed to increase sales.

promotional mix. The combination of different types of promotion a business uses to persuade customers to buy its products.

proportion. The relationship between and among objects in a display.

prospect. A potential customer. Also called a *lead*.

public employment agencies. Employment agencies supported by state or federal taxes and offering their services free to both job applicants and employers.

public relations. Any activity designed to create goodwill toward a business.

publicity. Creating a demand for a business or product by placing news about it in publications or on radio, television, or stage.

purchasing agent. A person who buys goods and services that meet certain specifications for the lowest possible price from reliable vendors. Also called an *organizational buyer* or an *industrial buyer*.

Q

question method. A method of handling objections by questioning the customer in an effort to learn more about the objections raised.

quota. A limit on the quantity or the value of a product that may be imported or exported.

rate of interest. Interest expressed as a percentage of the principal.

rational motive. A conscious, factual reason for a purchase.

realistic goal. A goal that you have a reasonable chance of achieving.

rebate. A discount offered by a manufacturer for purchasing an item during a given time period.

receipt-of-goods (ROG) dating. Dating in which the terms begin when the buyer's firm receives the goods.

receiving record. A form that describes the goods received by a business. Also called a *log*.

reference groups. The people who influence a person's values, morals, and decisions.

references. People who know your work habits and personal traits so well that they will recommend you for a job.

related merchandise. A good or service that a customer should have in order to increase the use or enjoyment of the original purchase.

resident buying office. A retailer's representative in a central market, a geographic area where many suppliers are located.

resources. All the things used in producing goods and services.

resume. A brief summary of personal information, education, skills, work experience, activities, and interests.

retail buyer. A buyer who selects goods for resale. Also called a *buyer*.

retailers. Merchant intermediaries who sell goods to the ultimate consumer.

return. Merchandise brought back for a cash refund or credit.

reverse-operation system. Used in some calculators, you must enter the first amount, then the second amount, then finally the operation (added to, subtracted from, multiplied by, or divided into the first amount).

routine decision making. Decision making used when a person needs little information because of a high degree of prior experience with the product or the low perceived risk of purchasing.

sales and market research. Research focusing on customer analysis, sales and market analysis, test marketing, and target market characteristics.

sales promotion. The use of marketing devices, such as displays, premiums, and contests, to stimulate purchases.

sales transaction. The process of recording the sale and presenting the customer with proof of payment.

scarcity. Insufficiency of supply of goods, services, or resources. The concept of scarcity recognizes that people have unlimited wants and needs but only limited resources.

secondary data. Facts that have already been collected and are used for some other purpose than the current study.

selective distribution. Distribution using a limited number of outlets in a given geographic area to sell a product.

selling. The process of helping customers make satisfying buying decisions by communicating how products and their features match customers' needs.

service approach method. A method of approaching the customer in which the salesperson asks the customer if he or she needs assistance.

service close. A method of closing a sale by explaining services that overcome obstacles or problems.

services. Activities that satisfy needs and wants and have monetary value.

setting. Where communication takes place.

shopping goods. Goods purchased after a great deal of searching and comparing among similar products.

shrinkage. The difference between the recorded sales and the sales based on the actual count of merchandise. Also called *stock shortage*.

signature. The distinctive identification symbol for a business. Also called a *logo* or *logotype*.

simple interest. Interest paid only on the amount borrowed or invested (the principal).

skimming pricing. A pricing policy that sets a very high price for a new product to capitalize on the high demand for it during its introductory period.

social class. A way of grouping consumers from upper to lower levels according to several significant factors that tend to coincide, such as income, education, and occupation.

sole proprietorship. A business owned and operated by one person.

source marking. A method of marking merchandise in which the seller or manufacturer marks the price on the merchandise before delivering it to the retailer.

specialty goods. Goods sought by customers who want a particular product and/or brand.

specialty media. Relatively inexpensive novelty items used for advertising with a firm's name printed on each piece.

specific goal. A goal stated in exact terms, including some details.

spot check method. A method of checking merchandise by randomly checking one product only in a carton.

standard English. The formal style of writing and speaking that you have learned in school.

standard of living. A measurement of the amount of goods and services that people have in a nation.

standing room only close. A method of closing a sale by stating that the product is in short supply or the price will soon be going up.

staples. Basic items that are used regularly and kept on hand in fairly large amounts.

stimulus. A cue that motivates a person to act.

stock shortage. The difference between the recorded sales and the sales based on the actual count of merchandise. Also called *shrinkage*.

stock turnover. The number of times the average inventory has been sold and replaced in a given period of time.

stockholders. The people who own the corporation.

storage function. The marketing function of holding goods.

store layout. The way floor space is allocated to facilitate sales and serve the customer.

storefront. The total exterior of a business.

Subchapter S corporation. A small business that is taxed like a partnership or proprietorship.

suggestion selling. Selling additional goods or services to the customer.

superior point method. A method of handling objections by acknowledging the validity of the objections, then offsetting these objections with other features and benefits.

supervisor. A person responsible for carrying out the decisions of middle management.

supervisory-level management. The people who directly assign work duties and supervise workers on the job.

supply. The amount of goods that producers are willing to make and sell.

survey method. A research technique in which information is gathered from people directly through the use of questionnaires.

sweepstakes. A game of chance requiring no skill.

T

tangible product features. Features of a product that can be seen or described with specifications, models, numbers, or names.

tariff. A tax on imports. Also called a *duty*.

technical institutes. Two-year, post-secondary institutions offering instruction in vocational or technical education. Also called *trade schools*.

telemarketing. The process of selling over the telephone.

test marketing. Placing a product in one or more selected geographic areas and observing its sales performance under a proposed marketing plan.

third party method. A method of handling objections by using a previous customer or another neutral person who can give a testimonial about the product.

till. The cash drawer of a cash register.

ton-mile. The movement of one ton of freight one mile.

top management. The people with the greatest responsibility to plan, organize, and control the use of a company's human, technical, and material resources.

trading area. The geographical area from which a business draws its customers.

transporting function. The marketing function of moving goods from sellers to buyers.

trial close. An initial effort to close a sale.

U

unit control. In inventory management, planning and monitoring the quantities of merchandise that a business handles during a stated period of time.

unit pricing. Pricing that allows consumers to compare prices in relation to a standard unit or measure, such as an ounce or pound.

unlimited liability. Your financial liability is not limited to your investment in the business but extends to your total ability to make payments.

UPC. Universal Product Code, a symbol that appears as a series of bars and a row of numerals on an item, and is read by an electronic wand.

utility. An economic term that means value added to make products have value and use.

UVM. Universal Vendor Marketing, a type of code that appears as numbers across the top of a price tag, and is read by an electronic wand.

V

values. Things that are important to you.

visual merchandising. The coordination of all physical elements in a place of business so that it projects the right image to its customers.

W

warranty. A promise, or guarantee, given to a customer that a product will meet certain standards.

warranty of fitness for a particular purpose. An implied warranty arising when the seller advises a customer that a product is suitable for a particular use and the customer acts on that advice.

warranty of merchantability. A promise from the seller that the product sold is fit for its intended purpose; a type of implied warranty.

which close. A method of closing a sale by encouraging a customer to make a decision between two items.

wholesale buyer. A buyer who selects goods for resale. Also called a *buyer*.

wholesalers. Merchant intermediaries who buy large quantities of goods from manufacturers, store the goods, and resell them. In the industrial market, wholesalers are called *distributors*.

Y

yes, but method. A method of handling objections by first acknowledging the customer's objections and then revealing another point of view.

Index

Businesses, 39. *See also* Entrepreneurs;
    Entrepreneurship
  effect on business cycles, 26
  functions, 40–42, *443*
  in market and command economies, 7, 8, 14, 39
  organization charts, *42*, 443
  professional services for, *444*
  starting up, 424–425, 442–444
  types of organization, 40, 425–427, 440, 442
Buyers
  calling on, 165
  feedback and, 365
  product selection by, 359–360
  sources used by, 360, 362–365
  types, 358
Buying, 357. *See also* Industrial buying; Resale
  buying
  mathematics for, 365–367
  situations, 358
  special retail procedures, 365
  steps in, 358–365
Buying behavior, of customers, 436
Buying income. *See* Disposable income
Buying offices, 360
Buying partnerships, 362
Buying plans, 360
Buying power indexes, 433
Buying signals, 182

C

Cabbage Patch Dolls, 18
Calculators, using, 95–97
California Dream Barbie doll, 144
Canada Dry ginger ale, 245
Capital, *6*, 449, 454
  debt, 450
  equity, 450
  sources of, 449–451
  working, 281
Capitalism. *See also* Free enterprise system; Market
  economies
  in China, 10
  compared with socialism and communism, 8–9
Career consultation, 481

Career Interest Survey, 480
Career outlook, 476
Careers. *See also* Job searches
  changing, 472
  education for, 488–490
  evaluating, 475–479, 485, *486*
  planning for, 487–488, *490*
  researching, 479–481
  selecting, 470–481, 484–490
Careers in marketing, 462
  benefits, 466–467
  educational requirements, 463
  employment trends, 463
  selecting, 465
  specialties, 463, *464*
Carloads (railroad), 262–263
Carnegie, Dale, 114, 116
Carriers, motor, 261–262
Cars, marketing, 53–54, 66, 236
Carson, Rachel, 47
Carter Hawley Hale Stores, 136
Cash, balancing, 196
Cash discounts, 301, 338
  calculating, 351
Cash drawers, 194
Cash flow projections, 456
Cash on delivery (COD), 199, 303
Cash registers, 192
  electronic, 192–193
  using, 194–196
Cash sales, 198
Ceiling prices, 334, 338
Celler-Kefauver Antimerger Act, 20
Central markets, 360
Chain discounts, 339
Change funds, verifying, 194
Change, making, 194–196
Channels of distribution, *74*
  companies not in, 76
  in consumer market, 76–77
  direct and indirect, 76
  in industrial market, 76, 78–79
  manufacturers and, 76–78, 79, 82–83
  members of, 75, 323–324
  multiple, 79–80

application forms, 498–499, *500–501*
letters of application, 499, 502, *503*
resumes, 502, *504, 505*
Job descriptions, 443
Job duties and responsibilities, 476
Job searches, 493. *See also* Careers
applying for jobs, 498–504
interviewing, 505–509
locating job openings, 494–498
work permits, 494
Jobs, Steven, 284, 421, 427
Jordan, Michael, 68
Joseph E. Seagram & Sons, 53

K

Kaffee Klatsch, 466
Kenmore appliances, 404
Kennedy, John F., 46
Kentucky Fried Chicken, in China, 10
Kids' Meals, promotion of, 208
Kool-Aid, 386
Kroc, Ray, 421
Kroger Co. supermarkets, 242, 387
Kushner, Malcolm, 107

L

Labels
price, 274–275
product, 245, 407
Labor, defined, 6
Labor force (work force), 26, *63*
Ladies' Home Journal, 145
Lady Foot Locker, 254
Lady Speed Stick deodorant, 53
Lag indicators, 28, 29
Lancôme cosmetics, 53
Land (natural resources), 6
Laurenzo, Ninfa, 423
Layaway sales, 199
Layman's terms, 168
Layouts
of advertisements, 234–235

of stores, 241
Lead indicators, 28–29
Leads (sales prospects), 155
Lean Cuisine, 54
Lee, Spike, 68
Legal services, for businesses, *444*
L'Eggs panty hose, 79
Lemon laws, 415
Leo Burnett agency, 403
"Let the cat out of the bag", 186
Letterhead stationery, 109
Letters, 109, *110*
of application, 499, 502, *503*
cover letters, 502, *505*
of inquiry, 496, *497*
thank-you, 118, 509
Lever Brothers, 15
Levy, Alice, 509
Liabilities, 453–454
Liability
limited, 426
preventing suits for, 415
unlimited, 440
Liability insurance, 293
Libraries, career information in, 479–480
Licenses, for entrepreneurs, 442, *443*
Life insurance, 293
Life Savers, 6
Lifebuoy soap, 15
Life-styles, 65, *471*, 472
of consumers, 54–55, 65–68
goals for, 471–472, 476
Lighting
in displays, 248
in stores, 241–242
Limited liability, 426
Limited partnerships, 440
Limited, The, 139, 289, 431
Limited warranties, 411
Line, in displays, 245
Lines of force, in ads, 232
Liquid Paper, 421
List prices, 339
Listening skills, 104–106, 165
blocks affecting, 103, 105–106

O

Q

Route salespeople, 137
Rubbermaid wastebaskets, 336
Rumania, Queen of, 178
Run-of-paper advertising rate, 222

S

Salaries, careers and, 476
Sales. *See also* Customers; Industrial sales;
    Marketing; Prospecting; Selling; Visual
    merchandising
  activities after, 155, 184–188
  aids to, 169
  on-approval, 199
  business orientation to, 51
  careers in, *464*
  closing, 155, 182–184
  gross, 307
  handling objections in, 172–178
  initial approach in, 155, 158–160
  involving customers in, 169
  manufacturer's control over, 82
  net, 307
  preapproach in, 157
  recording, 192–199
  training for, 145
  types, 197–199
Sales and market analysis, 375
Sales and market research, 375–378
Sales and Marketing Management magazine, 433
Sales checks, *299, 300*
Sales contracts, 192
Sales forecasting, 374
Sales invoices, 272, 298
Sales penetration, 374
Sales promotion
  pros and cons of, 209
  types, 207–208
Sales representatives, 360
Sales revenue, prices and, *321*
Sales slips 196-197. *See also* Credit card sales
Sales tally, 196
Sales taxes, calculating, 302, 353
Sales transactions, 192
Sales volume, calculating, 456

Salespeople. 209. *See also* Selling
  commission pay for, 136
    knowledge of, 142–143, 146
    traits and skills of, 138–139
Samples of products, 208–209
San Francisco Fire Department, 444
Sanka coffee, 210
Sapolio soap, 106
Scanners, optical, 193, 276
Scarcity, concept of, 5, 6
Schindler, Robert, 245
Scope mouthwash, 324
Sears, Roebuck and Co., 325
  private brands, 404
Seasonal discounts, 301, 339
  calculating, 353
Secondary data, in marketing research, 382, *383*
Securities and Exchange Commission, 20
Selective distribution, 82
Self-assessment, 471–474
  in business plans, 432–433
    career assessment and, 485, *486*
    questionnaire, *423*
Self-Directed Search, The (Holland), 474
Self-esteem, encouraging in others, 114–115
Self-service selling, 209, 426
"Sell like hotcakes", 137
Selling 134-136. *See also* Customers; Sales;
    Salespeople; Suggestion selling
  of ideas, 116–118, 144
  nonpersonal, 209
  personal, 209
  steps in, 155
  types of, 136–138
Selling space, 241
Semirealistic settings, for displays, 244
Senior citizens, marketing to, 63, 157
Series discounts, 339
Service approach, in sales, 159
Service close, in sales, 183–184
Service contracts, 413
Service guarantees, 412
Service organizations. *See* Nonprofit organizations
Services, defined, 5

Trademarks, 210
Trading areas, 433
  analysis of, 434–436
Trading stamps, 207
Traffic counts, 384
Training, of employees, 126, 145, 289, 290
Transit advertising, 218
Transportation service companies, 264–266
Transporting goods, 261–264, 271, 302–304
  air carriers in, 264
  charges for, *302–304*
  motor carriers in, 261–262, 264–266
  pipelines in, 264
  railroads in, 262–263, 264, 265
  waterways in, 264
Trial close, 182
Trial sizes of products, 208–209
Trident chewing gum, 52
Troup, Diana, 144
Trucks, in transporting goods, 261–262, 264–266
Tupperware, 76
Turnover of stock, 281–282
TV Guide magazine, 219
Tylenol, 45, 253
Typefaces, for print ads, 235

U

Unemployment rate, 28
  1983 to 1988, *29*
Unfair sales laws, 327
Union Carbide, 404–405
Unions, in communist countries, 8
Unit control of goods, systems for, 282–284
Unit prices, 328
  calculating, 350
United Parcel Service (UPS), 265, 303, 304
United States. *See also* Free enterprise system
  advertising expenditures in, 345
  age groups in, *62*
  balance of trade, 1986, *31*
  businesses in, 39–40, 420, *421*, *424*
  economic system of, 7, *9*, 10, 13–21
  education levels in, 65
  exports and imports (1986), *31*

GNP of, *424*
  inflation in, 27
  monopolies in, 15
  occupations in, 64–65
  social services in, 9
  standard of living in, 27
  trade with China, 32
  unemployment in, *29*
  waste in, 45, 47
United States Maritime Commission, 264
Universal Product Code (UPC), 81, 193, 274, 276, 378, 405
Universal Vendor Marketing (UVM) code, 193
Universities, education in, 489
Unlimited liability, 440
Unsafe at Any Speed (Nader), 47
UPC (Universal Product Code), 81, 193, 274, 276, 378, 405
UPS (United Parcel Service), 265, 303, 304
Urban areas, categories, 65
US Sprint (firm), *58*
USSR. *See* Soviet Union
Utilities, of businesses, 42–43, 74–76
Utility, diminishing marginal, 16–17
Utility companies, as monopolies, 15
UVM (Universal Vendor Marketing) code, 193

V

Value added. *See* Business utilities
Values
  personal, 471
  work, 476
Vanderbilt, *Mrs.* Reginald, 178
Vehicle insurance, 292
"Vid Kid" newspaper column, 472
Video games reviewed, 472
Video store, shoplifting in, 314
VideOcart, in supermarket, 74
Visual merchandising, 239, 240-244. *See also* Displays
Vivitar TL125 camera, *148*
Vocational centers, 489
Vocational schools, 489
Vocational work-experience programs, 481

Voice
  quality of, 108–109, 118
  robotic, 276
Volkswagen automobiles, 412

W

Wagner, Lindsay, 236
Wal-Mart Stores, 467
Walls, in stores, 242, 245
Walt Disney Co. stores, 395
Walton, Sam, 467
Wang, An, 489
Wang Laboratories, 489
Want slips, *359*, 359
Warehouses, 266–267, 271
  and channels of distribution, 76
  sending goods to, 276
Warranties, 293, 410, 411-412. *See also*
    Guarantees
  disclaimers on, 412
  in product planning, 413
Warranty of fitness for a particular purpose,
    411–412
Warranty of merchantability, 411
Wastebaskets, 336
Wastes, hazardous, 46
Water
  marketing of, 347
  transportation via, 264
Weight Watchers, 54
Wellman, Inc., 47
Wendy's International, 208, 387
Wherehouse Entertainment, 314
Which close, in sales, 183, *184*
Wholesale buyers. *See* Buyers
Wholesale prices. *See also* Trade discounts
  calculating, 334–335
Wholesalers, 69, 75
  advantages of using, 81–82
Wickman, Carl Eric, 261
Will-call (layaway) sales, 199
Window displays, 241
Women in work force, *63*
Women's Wear Daily, 360

Work. *See* Careers; Job search
Work environment, 474
  career selection and, 478–479
Work-experience programs, 481, 494
Work force, 26, *63*
Work permits, 494
Workers, government protection of, 20–21
Working capital, 281
Working Woman magazine, 55
World of Work Career Interest Survey, 473
Wozniak, Steven, 129, 284, 421, 427
Writing skills, 109-110. *See also* Business writing

X

Xerox Corp., 362

Y

Yellow Pages, advertising in, 217–218
Yes, but method, in sales, *177*
Yuppies (Young Urban Professionals), 55

Z

Zoning ordinances, 20